X

THE FIST OF GOD

Against the background of the Gulf war, Frederick Forsyth has compiled his most powerful novel to date. He portrays with vividness and authority the characters who dominated the headlines and the stunning war technology at their disposal. But was there one other weapon that Saddam controlled that could have rained hideous death on British and American forces? Acting on a fragment of radio intercept, a London academic determines to find out. With all Iraq's military technology known to the West, what was Qubth-ut-Allah—the Fist of God? SAS man Mike Martin is sent into Kuwait to report on Iraqi strength and help the resistance, and later parachutes into Iraq on the most dangerous assignment of his life: to find and destroy the Fist of God. Not until you read *The Fist of God* will you learn why the Allies did not go to Baghdad or eliminate Saddam; why the ground invasion was delayed; who really destroyed the Scud threat to Israel, and who the secret agent was inside Saddam's inner circle...

THE FIST OF GOD

Frederick Forsyth

CHIVERS PRESS
BATH

First published 1994
by Bantam Press
a division of Transworld Publishers Ltd
This Large Print edition published by
Chivers Press
by arrangement with
Transworld Publishers Ltd
1995

ISBN 0 7451 7809 X

British Library Cataloguing in Publication Data available

Photoset, printed and bound in Great Britain by
REDWOOD BOOKS, Trowbridge, Wiltshire

For the widows and orphans of the Special Air Service Regiment.

And for Sandy, without whose support this would have been so much harder.

To those who know what really happened in the Gulf, and who spoke to me about it; my sincere thanks. You know who you are; let it be.

CAST OF PRINCIPAL CHARACTERS

THE BRITISH

MARGARET THATCHER	Prime Minister
JOHN MAJOR	Thatcher's successor as Prime Minister
LIEUTENANT-GENERAL SIR PETER DE LA BILLIÈRE	Commander, British Forces, Gulf Theatre
SIR COLIN MCCOLL	Chief, SIS
SIR PAUL SPRUCE	Chairman, British Medusa Committee
BRIGADIER J. P. LOVAT	Director, Special Forces
COLONEL BRUCE CRAIG	Commanding Officer, 22nd SAS Regiment
MAJOR MIKE MARTIN	Major, SAS
MAJOR 'SPARKY' LOW	SAS Officer, Khafji
DR. TERRY MARTIN	Academic and Arabist
STEVE LAING	Director of Operations, Mid-East Division, SIS
SIMON PAXMAN	Head of Iraq Desk, SIS
STUART HARRIS	British businessman, Baghdad
JULIAN GRAY	Head of Station, SIS, Riyadh
DR BRYANT	Bacteriologist, Medusa Committee
DR REINHART	Poison gas expert, Medusa Committee
DR JOHN HIPWELL	Nuclear expert, Medusa Committee
SEAN PLUMMER	Head of Arab Services, GCHQ

WING COMMANDER PHILIP CURZON	Commanding Officer, 608th Squadron, RAF
SQUADRON LEADER LOFTY WILLIAMSON	Pilot, 608th Squadron, RAF
FLIGHT LIEUTENANT SID BLAIR	Williamson's navigator
FLIGHT LIEUTENANT PETER JOHNS	Pilot, 608th Squadron, RAF
FLIGHT LIEUTENANT NICKY TYNE	Johns's navigator
SERGEANT PETER STEPHENSON	SAS man
CORPORAL BEN EASTMAN	SAS man
CORPORAL KEVIN NORTH	SAS man

THE AMERICANS

GEORGE BUSH	President
JAMES BAKER	Secretary of State
COLIN POWELL	Chairman, Joint Chiefs of Staff
GENERAL NORMAN SCHWARZKOPF	IC Coalition Forces, Gulf Theatre
LEIUTENANT-GENERAL CHARLES (CHUCK) HORNER	IC Coalition Air Forces, Gulf Theatre
BRIGADIER-GENERAL BUSTER GLOSSON	Deputy to Chuck Horner
BILL STEWART	Deputy Director (Operations), CIA
CHIP BARBER	Head, Middle East Division, CIA
WILLIAM WEBSTER	Director of Central Intelligence, CIA
DON WALKER	USAF fighter pilot

STEVE TURNER	USAF fighter squadron commander
RANDY ROBERTS	Wingman to Don Walker
JIM HENRY	Wizzo to Randy Roberts
HARRY SINCLAIR	Head of London Station, CIA
SAUL NATHANSON	Banker and philanthropist
'DADDY' LOMAX	Retired nculear physicist

THE ISRAELIS

GENERAL YAACOV 'KOBI' DROR	Head of Mossad
SAMI GERSHON	Head, Combatants Division, Mossad
DAVID SHARON	Head of Iraq Desk, Mossad
BENYAMIN NETANYAHU	Deputy Foreign Minister
ITZHAK SHAMIR	Prime Minister
GIDEON 'GIDI' BARZILAI	Mission controller, Operation Joshua
MOSHE HADARI	Arabist, Tel Aviv University
AVI HERZOG, ALIAS KARIM AZIZ	Mossad agent in Vienna

THE VIENNESE

| WOLFGANG GEMÜTLICH | Vice-president, the Winkler Bank |
| EDITH HARDENBERG | Gemütlich's private secretary |

THE KUWAITIS

AHMED AL-KHALIFA	Merchant
COLONEL ABU FOUAD	Resistance movement
ASRAR QABANDI	Heroine of resistance

THE IRAQIS

SADDAM HUSSEIN	President
IZZAT IBRAHIM	Deputy President
HUSSEIN KAMIL	Saddam's son-in-law, Head of MIMI (Ministry of Industry & Military Industrialization)
TAHA RAMADAN	Prime Minister
SADOUN HAMMADI	Deputy Premier
TARIQ AZIZ	Foreign Minister
ALI HASSAN MAJID	Governor-General, occupied Kuwait
GENERAL SAADI TUMAH ABBAS	Commander, Republican Guard
GENERAL ALI MUSULI	Commander, Engineering Corps
GENERAL ABDULLAH KADIRI	Commander, Armoured Corps
DR AMER SAADI	Deputy to Hussein Kamil
BRIGADIER HASSAN RAHMANI	Chief, Counter-Intelligence
DR ISMAIL UBAIDI	Chief, Foreign Espionage
BRIGADIER OMAR KHATIB	Chief, Secret Police (Amn-al-Amm)
COLONEL OSMAN BADRI	Colonel, Army Engineers
COLONEL ABDELKARIM BADRI	Colonel, Iraqi Air Force (fighter pilot)
DR JAAFAR AL-JAAFAR	Head, nuclear programme
COLONEL SABAAWI	Secret Police Chief, occupied Kuwait
DR SALAH SIDDIQUI	Nuclear engineer

THE FIST OF GOD

CHAPTER ONE

The man with ten minutes to live was laughing.

The source of his amusement was a story just told him by his personal aide, Monique Jaminé, who was driving him home that chill, drizzling evening of 22 March 1990 from his office to his apartment.

It concerned a mutual colleague in the offices of the Space Research Corporation offices at rue de Stalle, a woman regarded as a real vamp, a man-eater, who had turned out to be gay. The deception appealed to the man's lavatorial sense of humour.

The pair had left the offices in the Brussels suburb of Uccle at ten to seven, Monique driving the Renault 21 estate. She had, some months earlier, sold her employer's own Volkswagen because he was such a rotten driver she feared he would end by killing himself.

It was only a ten-minute drive from the offices to his apartment in the centre block of the three-building Cheridreu complex off rue François Folie, but they stopped halfway at a baker's shop. Both went inside, he to buy a loaf of his favourite *pain de campagne*. There was rain in the wind; they bowed their heads, failing to notice the car that followed behind them.

Nothing strange in that. Neither was trained in tradecraft; the unmarked car with its two dark-jowled occupants had been following the scientist for weeks, never losing him, never approaching, just watching; and he had not seen it. Others had, but he did not know.

Emerging from the shop just in front of the

1

cemetery, he tossed his loaf into the back seat and climbed aboard to complete the journey to his home. At ten minutes after seven Monique drew up in front of the plate-glass doors of the apartment block, set 15 metres back off the street. She offered to come up with him, to see him home, but he declined. She knew he would be expecting his girl-friend Helene and he did not wish them to meet. It was one of his vanities, in which his adoring female staff indulged him, that Helene was just a good friend, keeping him company while he was in Brussels and his wife in Canada.

He climbed out of the car, the collar of his belted trenchcoat turned up as ever, and hefted onto his shoulder the big black canvas bag that hardly ever left him. It weighed over fifteen kilograms and contained a mass of papers, scientific papers, projects, calculations and data. The scientist distrusted safes and thought illogically that all the details of his latest projects were safer hanging from his shoulder.

The last Monique saw of her employer, he was standing in front of the glass doors, his bag over one shoulder, loaf under the other arm, fumbling for his keys. She watched him go through the doors, and the self-locking plate glass swing closed behind him. Then she drove off.

The academic lived on the sixth of the eight-floor block. The two elevators ran up the back wall of the building, encircled by the stairs with a fire-door on each landing. He took the lift and stepped out at the sixth floor. The dim, floor-level lights of the lobby came on automatically as he did so. Still jangling his keys, leaning against the weight of his bag and clutching his loaf, he turned left and left again across the russet-brown carpet and tried to get his key into

2

the lock of his apartment door.

The killer had been waiting on the other side of the lift-well which jutted into the dimly lit lobby. He came quietly round the lift-shaft holding his silenced 7.65-mm Beretta automatic, which was wrapped in a plastic bag to prevent the ejected cartridges spilling all over the carpet.

Five shots, fired from less than a metre range, all into the back of the head and neck, were more than enough. The big, burly man slumped forward against his door and slithered to the carpet. The gunman did not bother to check; there was no need. He had done this before, practising on prisoners, and knew his work was done. He ran lightly down the six levels of stairs, out of the back of the building, across the tree-studded gardens and into the waiting car. In an hour he was inside his country's embassy, in a day out of Belgium.

Helene arrived five minutes later. At first she thought her lover had had a heart attack. In a panic she let herself in and called the paramedics. Later she realized her friend's own doctor lived in the same block and summoned him as well. The paramedics arrived first.

One of them tried to shift the heavy body, still facing downwards. The man's hand came away covered in blood. Minutes later he and the doctor had pronounced the victim quite dead. The only other occupant of the four flats on that floor came to her door, an elderly lady who had been listening to a classical concert and heard nothing behind her solid timber door. Cheridreu was that kind of block, very discreet.

The man on the floor was Dr Gerald Vincent Bull, wayward genius, gun designer to the world and more

3

latterly armourer for Saddam Hussein of Iraq.

* * *

In the aftermath of the murder of Dr Gerry Bull some strange things began to happen all over Europe. In Brussels Belgian Counter-Intelligence admitted that for some months he had been followed on an almost daily basis by a series of unmarked cars containing two men of swarthy East Mediterranean appearance.

On 11 April British Customs officers seized on the docks of Middlesbrough eight sections of huge steel pipes, beautifully forged and milled and able to be assembled by giant flanges at each end, drilled to take powerful nuts and bolts. Triumphant officers announced that these tubes were not for a petrochemical plant as specified on the bills of lading and the export certificates but were parts of a great gun barrel designed by Gerry Bull and destined for Iraq. The farce of the Supergun was born, and it would run and run, revealing double-dealing, the stealthy paws of several Intelligence agencies, a mass of bureaucratic ineptitude and some political chicanery.

Within weeks bits of Supergun began popping up all over Europe. On 23 April Turkey announced it had stopped a Hungarian truck carrying a single ten-metre steel tube for Iraq, believed to be part of the gun. The same day Greek officials seized another truck with steel parts and held the hapless British driver for several weeks as an accomplice.

In May the Italians intercepted 75 tons of parts made by Società della Fucine, and a further 15 tons of parts were confiscated at the Fucine works near Rome. The latter were of a titanium steel alloy and

4

destined to be part of the breech of the gun, as were more bits and pieces yielded by a warehouse at Brescia in northern Italy.

The Germans came in, with discoveries at Frankfurt and Bremerhaven, manufactured by Mannesmann AG, also identified as parts of the by now world-famous Supergun.

In fact Gerry Bull had placed the orders for his brainchild skilfully and well. The tubes forming the barrels were indeed made in England by two firms, Walter Somers of Birmingham and Sheffield Forgemasters. But the eight intercepted in April 1990 were the last of fifty-two sections, enough to make two complete barrels 156 metres long and with an unbelievable 1-metre calibre, capable of firing a projectile the size of a cylindrical telephone booth.

The trunnions or supports came from Greece, the pipes, pumps and valves that formed the recoil mechanism from Switzerland and Italy, the breech block from Austria and Germany, the propellant from Belgium. In all, seven countries were involved as contractors and none knew quite what they were making.

The popular Press had a field-day as did the exultant Customs officers and the British legal system which began eagerly prosecuting any innocent party involved. What no-one pointed out was that the horse had bolted. The intercepted parts constituted Superguns Two, Three and Four.

As for the killing of Gerry Bull, it produced some weird theories in the media. Predictably, the CIA was nominated by the CIA-is-responsible-for-everything brigade. This was another nonsense. Although Langley has, in the past and under certain circumstances, countenanced the elimination of certain parties, they have almost always been in the same business—contract officers turned sour, renegades and double-agents. The notion that the lobby at Langley is rather choked with the corpses of former agents gunned down by their own colleagues at the behest of genocidal directors on the top floor is amusing but wholly unreal.

Moreover Gerry Bull was not from that back-alley world. He was a well-known scientist, designer and contractor of artillery, conventional and very unconventional, an American citizen who had once worked for America for years and talked copiously to his American army friends about what he was up to. If every designer and industrialist in the weapons industry working for a country not (at that time) seen to be an enemy of America was to be 'wasted', some five hundred gentlemen across North and South America and Europe would have to qualify.

Finally, Langley has for at least the past ten years become grid-locked by the new bureaucracy of controls and oversight committees. No professional Intelligence officer is going to order a 'hit' without a written and signed order. For a man like Gerry Bull that signature would have to come from the Director of Central Intelligence himself.

The DCI at that time was William Webster, a by-the-book former judge from Kansas. It would be about as easy to get a signed 'hit' authority out of William Webster as to burrow a way out of Marion Penitentiary with a blunt teaspoon.

But far and away the league leader in the who-killed-Gerry-Bull enigma was of course the Israeli Mossad. The entire Press and most of Bull's friends and family jumped to the same conclusion. Bull was working for Iraq; Iraq was the enemy of Israel. Two and two equal four. The trouble is, in that world of shadows and distorting mirrors what may or may not appear to be two, when multiplied by a factor that may or may not be two, could possibly come out at four but probably will not.

The Mossad is the world's smallest, most ruthless and most gung-ho of the leading Intelligence agencies. It has in the past undoubtedly undertaken many assassinations, using one of the three 'kidon' teams—the word is the Hebrew for bayonet. The kidonim come under the Combatants or Komemiute Division, the deep-cover men, the hard squad. But even the Mossad has its rules, albeit self-imposed.

Terminations fall into two categories. One is 'operational requirement', an unforeseen emergency in which an operation involving friendly lives is put at risk and the person in the way has to be eased out of the way, fast and permanently. In these cases the supervising katsa or case officer has the right to 'waste' the opponent jeopardizing the entire mission and will get retroactive support from his bosses back in Tel Aviv.

The other category is for those already on the execution list. This list exists in two places: the private safe of the Prime Minister and the safe of the Head of Mossad. Every incoming Prime Minister is required to see this list, which may contain between thirty and eighty names. He may either initial each name, giving the Mossad the go-ahead on an 'if-and-when' basis, or insist on being consulted before each new mission. In either event, he must sign the execution order.

Broadly speaking, those on the list fall into three classes. There are the few remaining top Nazis, though this class has almost ceased to exist. Years ago, although Israel mounted a major operation to kidnap and try Adolf Eichmann because it wanted to make an international example of him, other Nazis were simply liquidated quietly. Class two are almost all contemporary terrorists, mainly Arabs who have already shed Israeli or Jewish blood like Ahmed Jibril, Abu Nidal, or who would like to, with a few non-Arabs thrown in.

Category three, which might have contained the name of Gerry Bull, are those working for Israel's enemies and whose work carries great danger for Israel and her citizens if it progresses any further.

The common denominator is that those targeted must have blood on their hands, either in fact or in prospect.

If a hit is requested, the Prime Minister will pass the matter to a judicial investigator so secret few Israeli jurists and no citizens have ever heard of him. The investigator holds a 'court' with the charge read out, a prosecutor and a defender. If Mossad's request is confirmed, the matter goes back to the Prime Minister for his signature. The kidon team does the rest ... if it can.

The problem with the Mossad-killed-Bull theory is that it is flawed at almost every level. True, Bull *was* working for Saddam Hussein, designing new conventional artillery (which could not reach Israel), a rocket programme (which might one day) and a giant gun (which did not worry Israel at all). But so were hundreds of others. Half a dozen German firms were behind Iraq's hideous poison gas industry, with whose products Saddam had already threatened Israel. Germans and Brazilians were working flat out on the rockets of Saad 16. The French were the prime movers and suppliers of the Iraqi research for a

8

nuclear bomb.

That Bull, his ideas, his designs, his activities and his progress deeply interested Israel there is no doubt. In the aftermath of his death much was made of the fact that in preceding months he had been worried by repeated covert entries into his flat while he was away. Nothing was ever taken, but traces were left. Glasses were moved and replaced; windows left open; a video tape rewound and removed from the player. Was he being warned, he wondered, and was the Mossad behind it all? He was and they were, but for a less-than-obvious reason.

In the aftermath, the swarthy strangers with the guttural accents who tailed him all over Brussels were identified by the media as the Israeli assassins preparing their moment. Unfortunately for the theory, Mossad agents do not run around looking and acting like Pancho Villa. They were there, all right, but nobody saw them; not Bull, not his friends or family, not the Belgian police. They were there in Brussels with a team who could look like and pass for Europeans—Belgians, Americans, whatever they chose. It was they who tipped off the Belgians that Bull was being followed by *another* team.

Moreover, Gerry Bull was a man of extraordinary indiscretion. He simply could not resist a challenge. He had worked for Israel before, liked the country and the people, had many friends in the Israeli army and could not keep his mouth shut. Challenged with a phrase like: 'Gerry, I bet you'll never get those rockets at Saad 16 to work...' Bull would leap into a three-hour monologue describing exactly what he was doing, how far the project had got, what were the problems, how he hoped to solve them... the lot. For an Intelligence service he was a dream of indiscretion.

9

Even in the last week of his life he was entertaining two Israeli generals at his office, giving them a complete up-to-the-minute picture, all tape-recorded by the devices in their briefcases. Why destroy such a cornucopia of inside information?

Finally, the Mossad has one other habit when dealing with a scientist or industrialist, but never with a terrorist. A final warning is always given; not a weird burglary aimed at moving glasses or rewinding video tapes, but a real verbal warning. Even with Dr Yahia El Meshad, the Egyptian nuclear physicist working on the first Iraqi nuclear reactor who was assassinated in his hotel room at the Meridien, Paris on 13 June 1980, the procedure was observed. An Arabic-speaking katsa went to his room and told him bluntly what would happen to him if he did not desist. The Egyptian told the stranger at his door to get lost—not a wise move. Telling a Mossad kidon team to perform an impractical act upon themselves is not a tactic approved by the insurance industry. Two hours later Meshad was dead. But he had had his chance. A year later the whole French-supplied nuclear complex at Osirak One and Two was blown away by an Israeli air strike.

Bull was different—a Canadian-born American citizen, genial, approachable and a whisky drinker of awesome talent. The Israelis could talk to him as a friend, and did constantly. It would have been the easiest thing in the world to send a friend to tell him bluntly that he had got to stop or the hard squad would come after him—nothing personal, Gerry, just the way things are.

Bull was not in the business of winning a posthumous Congressional Medal. Moreover he had already told the Israelis and his close friend George

10

Wong that he wanted out of Iraq—physically and contractually. He had had enough. What happened to Dr Gerry Bull was something quite different.

*   *   *

Gerald Vincent Bull was born in 1928 at North Bay, Ontario. At school he was clever and driven by an urge to succeed and earn the world's approval. At sixteen he could graduate but because he was so young the only college that would accept such a youngster was the University of Toronto, Engineering Faculty. Here he showed he was not just clever, but brilliant. At twenty-two he became the youngest-ever PhD. It was aeronautical engineering that seized his imagination and specifically ballistics—the study of bodies, whether projectiles or rockets, in flight. It was this that led down the road to artillery.

After Toronto he joined the Canadian Armament and Research Development Establishment, CARDE, at Valcartier, a then quiet little township outside Quebec. In the early 1950s Man was turning his face not only towards the skies but beyond them to space itself. The buzzword was 'rockets'. It was then that Bull showed he was something else apart from technically brilliant. He was a maverick— inventive, unconventional, and imaginative. It was during his ten years at CARDE that he developed the idea which would become his living dream for the rest of his days.

Like all new ideas Bull's appeared quite simple. When he looked at the emerging range of American rockets in the late 1950s he realized that nine-tenths of these then impressive-looking rockets were only

11

the first stage. Sitting right on top, only a fraction of the size, were the second and third stages and, even smaller, the tiny nipple of the payload.

The giant first stage was to lift the rocket up through the first 150 kilometres of air, where the atmosphere was thickest and gravity strongest. After the 150-km mark it needed much less power to drive the satellite on into space itself and orbit at between 400 and 500 kilometres above the earth. Every time a rocket went up, the whole of that bulky and very expensive first stage was destroyed—burnt out, to fall for ever into the oceans.

Supposing, Bull mused, you could punch your second and third stages, plus the payload, up those first 150 kilometres from the barrel of a giant gun? In theory, he pleaded with the money men, it was possible, easier, cheaper and the gun could be used over and over again.

It was his first real brush with politicians and bureaucrats, and he failed, mainly because of his personality. He hated them and they hated him.

In 1961 he got lucky. McGill University came in because it foresaw some interesting publicity. The US army came in for reasons of its own; guardian of American artillery, the Army was in a power play with the Air Force which was battling for control over all rockets or projectiles going above 100 kilometres. With their combined funds Bull was able to set up a small research establishment on the island of Barbados. The US army let him have a package of one out-of-storage 16-inch navy gun (the biggest calibre in the world), one spare barrel, one small radar tracking unit, a crane and some trucks. McGill set up a metal workshop. It was like trying to take on the Grand Prix racing industry with the facilities of a backstreet garage. But he did it; his career of amazing inventions had begun and he was thirty-three years old; shy, diffident, untidy, inventive and still a maverick.

He called his research in Barbados the High Altitude Research Project, or HARP. The old navy gun was duly erected and Bull began work on projectiles. He called them Martlet after the heraldic bird that appears on the insignia of McGill University.

Bull wanted to put a payload of instruments into earth orbit cheaper and faster than anyone else. He knew perfectly well that no human could withstand the pressures of being fired from a gun, but reckoned rightly that in the future 90 per cent of scientific research and work in space would be done by machines, not men. America under Kennedy and goaded by the flight of the Russian Gagarin pursued from Cape Canaveral the more glamorous but ultimately rather pointless exercise of putting mice, dogs, monkeys and eventually men up there.

Down in Barbados Bull soldiered on with his single gun and his Martlet projectiles. In 1964 he blew a Martlet 92 kilometres high, then added an extra 16 metres of barrel to his gun (it cost just $41,000), making the new 36-metre barrel the longest in the world. With this he reached the magic 150 kilometres with a 180-kilogram payload.

He solved the problems as they arose. A major one was the propellant. In a small gun the charge gives the projectile a single hard smack as it expands from solid to gas in a microsecond. The gas tries to escape its compression and has nowhere to go but out of the barrel, pushing the shell ahead of it as it does so. But with a barrel as long as Bull's, a special, slower-

13

burning propellant was needed not to split the barrel wide open. He needed a powder that would send his projectile up this enormous barrel in a long, steadily accelerating 'whoosh'. So he designed it.

He also knew that no instruments could withstand the 10,000 gravity force caused by the explosion of even the slower-burning propellant charge; so he designed a shock-absorber system to reduce it to 200 gravities. A third problem was the recoil. This was no pop-gun and the recoil would be enormous as the barrels, charges and payloads got bigger. So he designed a system of springs and valves to reduce it to acceptable proportions.

In 1966 Bull's old adversaries among the Canadian Defence Ministry bureaucrats got him by urging their minister to pull the finance. Bull protested that he could put a payload of instruments into space for a fraction of what it cost Cape Canaveral. To no avail. To protect its interest the US army transferred Bull from Barbados to Yuma, Arizona.

Here in November of that year he put a payload 180 kilometres up, a record that stood for twenty-five years. But in 1967 Canada pulled out completely, both the Government and McGill University. The US army followed suit. The HARP project closed down. Bull set himself up in a purely consultative basis at Highwater, an estate he had bought straddling the border of North Vermont and his native Canada.

There were two postscripts to the HARP affair. By 1990 it was costing $10,000 to put every kilogram of instruments into space with the Space Shuttle programme out of Cape Canaveral. To his dying day Bull knew he could do it for $600 per kilo. And in 1988 work began on a new project at Lawrence

Livermore National Laboratory, California. The project involves a giant gun but so far with a barrel only 4 inches in calibre and a barrel only 50 metres long. Eventually, and at a cost of hundreds of millions of dollars, it is hoped to build a much, much bigger one with a view to firing payloads into space. The project's name is Super-High Altitude Research Project, or SHARP.

Gerry Bull lived in and ran his complex at Highwater on the border for ten years. In that time he dropped his unfulfilled dream of a gun that would fire payloads into space and concentrated on his second area of expertise—the more profitable one of conventional artillery.

He began with the major problem—almost all the world's armies based their artillery part on the universal 155-mm howitzer field gun. He knew that in an artillery exchange the man with the longer range is king. He can sit back and blow the enemy away while remaining inviolate. Bull determined to extend the range and increase the accuracy of the 155-mm field gun. He started with the ammunition. It had been tried before but no-one had succeeded. In four years Bull cracked it.

In control tests the Bull shell went one and a half times the distance from the same 155 standard gun, was more accurate and exploded with the same force into 4,700 fragments as opposed to 1,350 for a NATO shell. NATO was not interested. By the grace of God, neither was the Soviet Union.

Undeterred, Bull ploughed on, producing a new full-bore extended-range shell. Still NATO was not interested, preferring to stay with their traditional suppliers and the short-range shell.

But if the Powers would not look, the rest of the
15

world did. Military delegations swarmed to Highwater to consult Gerry Bull. They included Israel (which was when he cemented friendships begun with observers in Barbados), Egypt, Venezuela, Chile and Iran. He also gave consultancies on other artillery matters to Britain, Holland, Italy, Canada and America, whose military scientists (if not the Pentagon) continued to study with some awe what he was up to.

In 1972 Bull was quietly made a US citizen. The next year he began work on the actual 155-calibre field gun itself. Within two years he had made another breakthrough, discovering that the perfect length for a cannon barrel was neither more nor less than forty-five times its calibre. He perfected a new redesign of the standard 155 field gun and called it the GC (for Gun Calibre)-45. The new gun, with his extended-range shells, would outgun any artillery in the entire Communist arsenal. But if he expected contracts he was disappointed. Again the Pentagon stayed with the gun lobby and its new idea for rocket-assisted shells at eight times the price per shell. The performance of both shells was identical.

Bull's fall from grace, when it came, started innocently enough when he was invited with CIA connivance to help improve the artillery and shells of South Africa, then fighting the Moscow-backed Cubans in Angola.

Bull was nothing if not politically naïve to an amazing degree. He went, found he liked the South Africans and got on well with them. The fact that South Africa was an international outcast for its apartheid policies did not worry him. He helped them redesign their artillery park along the lines of his increasingly sought-after GC-45 long-barrelled,

16

long-range howitzer. Later the South Africans produced their own version and it was these cannon that smashed the Soviet artillery, rolling back the Russians and Cubans.

Returning to America, Bull continued to ship his shells. President Jimmy Carter had come to power and political correctness was the new order. Bull was arrested and charged with illegal exports to a forbidden regime. The CIA dropped him like a hot potato. He was persuaded to stay silent and plead guilty. It was a formality, he was told; he would get a slap on the wrist for a technical breach, they said.

On 16 June 1980 a US judge sentenced him to a year in prison, with six months suspended, and a fine of $105,000. He actually served four months and seventeen days at Allenwood Jail, Pennsylvania. But for Bull that was not the point.

It was the shame and the disgrace that got to him, plus the sense of betrayal. How could they do this to him? he reasoned. He had helped America wherever he could, taken her citizenship, gone along with the CIA appeal of 1976. While he was in Allenwood his company SRC went bankrupt and closed down. He was ruined.

On emerging from jail he quit America and Canada for ever, emigrating to Brussels, starting again in a one-room walk-up with a kitchenette. Friends said later he was changed after the trial and never the same man again. He never forgave the CIA and he never forgave America; and yet he struggled for years for a rehearing and a pardon.

He returned to consultancy and took up an offer made to him before his trial—to work for China on the improvement of their artillery. Through the early and mid-eighties Bull worked mainly for Beijing and

17

redesigned their artillery park along the lines of his GC-45 cannon, now being sold under world licence by Voest-Alpine of Austria, who had bought the patents from Bull for a one-off payment of two million dollars. Bull always was a terrible businessman, or he would have been a multimillionaire.

While Bull had been away, things had happened. The South Africans had taken Bull's designs and improved greatly upon them, creating a towed howitzer called the G-5 from his GC-45 and a self-propelled cannon, the G-6. Both had a range with extended shells of forty kilometres. South Africa was selling them round the world. Because of his poor deal with the South Africans, Bull got not a penny in royalties.

Among clients for these guns was a certain Saddam Hussein of Iraq. It was these cannon that broke the human waves of Iranian fanatics in the eight-year Iran–Iraq war, finally defeating them in the Fao marshes. But Saddam Hussein had added a new twist, especially at the battle of Fao. He had put poison gas in the shells.

Bull then worked for Spain and Yugoslavia, converting the old Yugoslav army's Soviet-made 130-mm artillery to the new 155-mm cannon with the extended-range shells. Though he would never live to see it, these were the guns inherited by the Serbs on the collapse of Yugoslavia to pulverize the cities of the Croats and Muslims in the civil war. In 1987 he learnt that America would, after all, research the payloads-into-space cannon but with Gerry Bull firmly cut out of the deal.

That winter he received a strange phone call from the Iraqi Embassy in Bonn. Would Dr Bull like to visit Baghdad as Iraq's guest?

What he did not know was that in the mid-Eighties Iraq had witnessed 'Operation Staunch', a concerted American effort to shut off all sources of weapons imports destined for Iran. This followed the carnage among American marines in Beirut in an Iranian-backed attack on their barracks by Hezbollah fanatics.

Iraq's reaction, although they benefited in their war with Iran from Operation Staunch, was if they can do that to Iran, they can do it to us. From then on Iraq determined to import not the arms, but wherever possible the technology to make their own. Bull was first and foremost a designer; he interested them.

The mission to recruit him went to Amer Saadi, Number Two at the Ministry of Industry and Military Industrialization, known as MIMI. When Bull arrived in Baghdad in January 1988, Amer Saadi, a smooth cosmopolitan diplomat/scientist speaking English, French and German besides Arabic, played him beautifully.

Iraq, he said, wanted Bull's help with their dream to put peaceful satellites into space. To do this they had to design a rocket that could put the payload up there. Their Egyptian and Brazilian scientists had suggested the first stage would be to tie together five of the Scud missiles of which Iraq had bought 900 from the Soviet Union. But there were technical problems, many problems. They needed access to a supercomputer. Could Bull help them?

Bull loved problems, they were his *raison d'être*. He did not have access to a supercomputer, but on two legs he was the nearest thing. Besides, if Iraq really wanted to be the first Arab nation to put satellites

19

into space, there was another way ... cheaper, simpler, faster than rockets starting from scratch. Tell me all, said the Iraqi. So Bull did.

For just three million dollars, he said, he could produce a giant gun that would do the job. It would be a five-year programme. He could beat the Americans at Livermore to the punch. It would be an Arab triumph. Dr Saadi glowed with admiration. He would put the idea to his government and recommend it strongly. In the meanwhile, would Dr Bull look at the Iraqi artillery?

By the end of his one-week visit Bull had agreed to crack the problems of tying five Scuds together to form the first stage of a rocket of intercontinental or space-reaching performance; to design two new artillery pieces for the Army; and to put a formal proposal for his payload-into-orbit supergun.

As with South Africa, he was able to block his mind to the nature of the regime he was about to serve. Friends had told him of Saddam Hussein's record as the man with the bloodiest hands in the Middle East. But in 1988 there were thousands of respectable companies and dozens of governments clamouring to do business with big-spending Iraq.

For Bull the bait was his gun, his beloved gun, his life's dream, at last with a backer prepared to help him bring it to fulfilment and join the pantheon of scientists.

In March 1988 Amer Saadi sent a diplomat to Brussels to talk to Bull. Yes, said the gun designer, he had made progress on the technical problems of the first stage of the Iraqi rocket. He would be glad to hand them over on signature of a contract with his company, once again the Space Research Corporation. The deal was done. Iraq realized his offer of a gun for three million dollars was silly; they raised it to ten million but asked for more speed.

When Bull worked fast he worked amazingly fast. In one month he put together a team of the best available freelancers he could find. Heading the supergun team in Iraq was a British projects engineer called Christopher Cowley. Bull himself christened the rocket programme based at Saad 16 in northern Iraq Project Bird. The supergun task was named Project Babylon.

By May the exact specifications of Babylon had been worked out. It would be an incredible machine. One metre of bore; a barrel 156 metres long and weighing 1,665 tons—that is more than twice the height of Nelson's Column in London, the height of the Washington Monument. Four recoil cyclinders weighing 60 tons each and two buffer cylinders at 7 tons. The breech would weigh 182 tons.

The steel had to be special, withstanding 70,000 pounds per square inch of internal pressure and with a tensile strength of 1,250 Mega Pascals.

Bull had already made plain to Baghdad that he would have to make a smaller prototype, a Mini-Babylon with 350-mm bore weighing only 113 tons, but in this he could test nose cones which would also be useful for the rocket project. The Iraqis liked this—they needed nose cone technology as well.

The full significance of the insatiable Iraqi appetite for nose cone technology seems to have escaped Gerry Bull at the time. Maybe, in his limitless enthusiasm to see his life's dream realized at last, he just suppressed it. Nose cones of very advanced design are needed to prevent a payload burning up from friction heat as it re-enters earth's atmosphere. But orbiting payloads in space do not return; they

21

stay up there.

By late May 1988 Christopher Cowley was placing his first orders with Walter Somers of Birmingham for the tube sections that would make up the barrel of Mini-Babylon. The sections for full-scale Babylons One, Two, Three and Four would come later. Other strange steel orders were placed all around Europe.

The pace at which Bull was working was awesome. In two months he had covered ground that would have taken a government enterprise two years. By the end of 1988 he had designed for Iraq two new guns—self-propelled guns as opposed to the towed machines supplied by South Africa. Both pieces would be so powerful they could crush the guns of the surrounding nations of Iran, Turkey, Jordan and Saudi Arabia, who purchased from NATO and America.

Bull also managed to crack the problems of tying the five Scuds together to form the first stage of the Bird rocket, to be called Al-Abeid, the Believer. He had discovered the Iraqis and Brazilians at Saad 16 were working on faulty data produced by a wind tunnel that was itself malfunctioning. After that he handed over his fresh calculations and left the Brazilians to get on with it.

In May 1989 most of the world's armaments industry and Press, along with government observers and Intelligence officers, attended a great weapons exhibition in Baghdad. Considerable interest was shown in the mock-up prototypes of the two great guns. In December the Al-Abeid was test-fired to great media hoop-la and seriously jolted Western analysts.

Heavily covered by Iraqi TV cameras the great three-stage rocket roared off from the Al-Anbar

Space Research Base, climbed away from the earth and disappeared. Three days later Washington admitted that the rocket did indeed appear capable of putting a satellite into space.

But the analysts worked out more. If Al-Abeid could do that, it could also be an intercontinental ballistic missile. Suddenly Western Intelligence agencies were jerked out of their assumption that Saddam Hussein was no real danger, years away from being a serious threat.

The three main agencies, CIA in America, SIS in Britain and Mossad in Israel, came to the view that of the two systems the Babylon gun was an amusing toy and the Bird rocket a real threat. All three got it wrong. It was the Al-Abeid that did not work.

Bull knew why and he told the Israelis what happened. The Al-Abeid soared to 12,000 metres and was lost to view. The second stage refused to separate from the first. The third stage did not exist. It was a dummy. He knew because he had been charged with trying to persuade China to provide a third stage and would be going to Beijing in February.

He did indeed go, and the Chinese turned him down flat. While he was there he met and talked lengthily with his old friend George Wong. Something had gone wrong with the Iraqi business, something that was worrying the hell out of Gerry Bull, and it was not the Israelis. Several times he insisted he wanted 'out' of Iraq, and in a hurry. Something had happened, inside his own head, and he wanted out of Iraq. In this decision he was entirely right, but too late.

*   *   *

On 15 February 1990 President Saddam Hussein called a full meeting of his group of inner advisers at his palace at Sarseng, high up in the Kurdish mountains.

He liked Sarseng. It stands on a hilltop and through its triple-glazed windows he could gaze out and down to the surrounding countryside where the Kurdish peasants huddled through the bitter winters in their shacks and hovels. It was not many miles from the terrified town of Halabja where, for the two days of 17 and 18 March in the year 1988, he had ordered the 70,000 citizens to be punished for alleged collaboration with the Iranians.

When his artillery had finished, 5,000 of the Kurdish dogs were dead and 7,000 maimed for life. Personally he had been quite impressed with the effects of the hydrogen cyanide sprayed out from the artillery shells. The German companies who had helped him with the technology to acquire and create the gas, along with the nerve agents Tabun and Sarin, had his gratitude. They had earned it with their gas, so similar to the Zyklon-B which had so properly been used on the Jews years before and might well be again.

He stood before the windows of his dressing room and gazed down that morning. He had been in power, undisputed power, for sixteen years and he had been forced to punish many people. But much also had been achieved.

A new Sennacharib had risen out of Nineveh and another Nebuchadnezzar out of Babylon. Some had learnt the easy way, by submission. Others had learnt the hard, the very hard, way and were mostly dead. Still others, many others, had yet to learn. But they would, they would.

24

He listened as the convoy of helicopters clattered in from the south, while his dresser fussed to adjust the green kerchief he liked to wear in the V above his combat jacket to hide his jowls. When all was to his satisfaction he took his personal side-arm, a gold-plated Beretta of Iraqi make, holstered and belted, and secured it round his waist. He had used it before on a cabinet minister and might wish to again. He always carried it.

A flunkey tapped on the door and informed the President that those he had summoned awaited him in the conference room. When he entered the long room with the plate-glass windows dominating the snowy landscape, everyone rose in unison. Only up here at Sarseng did his fear of assassination diminish. He knew that the palace was ringed by three lines of the best of his Presidential Security Detail, the Amn-al-Khass, commanded by his own son Kusay, and that no-one could approach those great windows. On the roof were French Crotale anti-aircraft missiles and his fighters ranged the skies above the mountains.

He sat himself down in the throne-like chair at the centre of the top table that formed the cross-bar of the T. Flanking him, two on each side, were four of his most trusted aides. For Saddam Hussein there was only one quality he demanded of a man in his favour. Loyalty. Absolute, total, slavish loyalty. Within this quality, experience had taught him there were grades. Top of the list came family; after that the clan; then the tribe. There is an Arabic saying: 'I and my brother against our cousin; I and my cousin against the world.' He believed in it. It worked.

He came from the gutters of a small town called Tikrit and of the tribe of the al-Tikriti. An extraordinary number of his family and the al-Tikriti were in high office in Iraq and they could be forgiven any brutality, any failure, any personal excesses, provided they were loyal to him. Had not his second son, the psychopathic Uday, beaten a servant to death and been forgiven?

To his right sat Izzat Ibrahim, his first deputy, and beyond was his son-in-law, Hussein Kamil, head of the MIMI, the man in charge of weapons procurement. To his left were Taha Ramadan, Prime Minister, and beyond him Sadoun Hammadi, deputy premier and devout Shi'a Muslim. Saddam Hussein was Sunni, but his one and only area of tolerance was in matters of religion. As a non-observer (except when it suited), he did not care. His Foreign Minister, Tariq Aziz, was a Christian. So what? He did what he was told.

The Army chiefs were near the top of the stem of the T, the generals commanding the Republican Guard, the Infantry, the Armour, the Artillery and the Engineers. Further down came the four experts due to whose reports and expertise he had called the meeting.

Two sat to the right of the table: Dr Amer Saadi, technologist and deputy to his son-in-law, and beside him Brigadier Hassan Rahmani, head of the Counter-Intelligence wing of the Mukhabarat. Facing them were Dr Ismail Ubaidi, controlling the foreign arm of the Mukhabarat or Intelligence Service, and Brigadier Omar Khatib, boss of the feared Secret Police, the Amn-al-Amm.

The three Secret Service men had clearly defined tasks. Dr Ubaidi conducted espionage abroad; Rahmani counter-attacked foreign-mounted espionage inside Iraq; Khatib kept the Iraqi population in order, crushing all possible internal opposition through a combination of his vast network of watchers and informers and of the sheer, stark terror generated by the rumours of what he did to opponents arrested and dragged to the Abu Ghraib jail west of Baghdad or to his personal interrogation centre known jokingly as the Gymnasium beneath the AMAM headquarters.

Many had been the complaints brought to Saddam Hussein about the brutality of his secret police chief, but he always chuckled and waved them away. It was rumoured he personally had given Khatib his nickname, Al Mu'azib, the Tormentor. Khatib, of course, was al-Tikriti and loyal to the end.

Some dictators, when delicate matters are to be discussed, like to keep the meeting small. Saddam thought the opposite; if there was dirty work to be done they should all be involved. No man could say: I have clean hands, I did not know. In this way all around him would get the message: if I fall, you fall.

When all had resumed their seats the President nodded to his son-in-law Hussein Kamil, who called on Dr Saadi to report. The technocrat read his report without raising his eyes. No wise man raised his eyes to stare Saddam in the face. The President claimed he could read into a man's soul through his eyes, and many believed it. Staring into his face might signify courage, defiance, disloyalty. If the President suspected disloyalty the offender usually died horribly.

When Dr Saadi had finished, Saddam thought for a while.

'This man, this Canadian, how much does he know?'

'Not all, but enough I believe to work it out,

27

sayidi.'

Saadi used the honorific Arabic address equivalent to the Western 'sir', but more respectful. An alternative and acceptable title is Sayid Rais, or Mr President.

'How soon?'

'Soon, if not already, sayidi.'

'And he has been talking to the Israelis?'

'Constantly, Sayid Rais,' replied Dr Ubaidi. 'He has been friends of theirs for years. Visited Tel Aviv and given lectures on ballistics to their artillery staff officers. He has many friends there, possibly among the Mossad, though he may not know that.'

'Could we finish the project without him?' asked Saddam Hussein. His son-in-law Hussein Kamil cut in.

'He is a strange man. He insists on carrying all his most intimate scientific paperwork around with him in a big canvas bag. I instructed our Counter-Intelligence people to have a look at this paperwork and copy it.'

'And this was done?' The President was staring at Hassan Rahmani, his Counter-Intelligence chief.

'Immediately, Sayid Rais. Last month during his visit here. He drinks much whisky. It was doped and he slept long and deep. We took his bag and photocopied every page in it. Also we have taped all his technical conversations. The papers and the transcripts have all been passed to our comrade, Dr Saadi.'

The presidential stare swivelled back to the scientist.

'So, once again, can you complete the project without him?'

'Yes, Sayid Rais, I believe we can. Some of his

calculations make sense only to himself, but I have had our best mathematicians studying them for a month. They can understand them. The engineers can do the rest.'

Hussein Kamil shot his deputy a warning look. You had better be right, my friend.

'Where is he now?' asked the President.

'He has left for China, sayidi,' replied the Foreign Intelligence man Ubaidi. 'He is trying to find us a third stage for the Al-Abeid rocket. Alas, he will fail. He is expected back in Brussels in mid-March.'

'You have men there, good men?'

'Yes, sayidi. I have had him under surveillance in Brussels for ten months. That is how we know he has been entertaining Israeli delegations at his offices there. We also have keys to his apartment block.'

'Then let it be done. On his return.'

'Without delay, Sayid Rais.' Ubaidi thought of the four men he had in Brussels on arm's length surveillance work. One of them had done this before. Abdelrahman Moyeddin. He would give the job to him.

The three Intelligence men and Dr Saadi were dismissed. The rest stayed. When they were alone Saddam Hussein turned to his son-in-law.

'And the other matter. When will I have it?'

'I am assured, by the end of the year, Abu Kusay.'

Being 'family', Kamil could now use the more intimate title of 'Father of Kusay'. It also reminded the others present who was family and who was not. The President grunted.

'We shall need a place, a new place, a fortress; not an existing place, however secret. A new, secret place that no-one will know about. No-one but a tiny handful, not even all of us here. Not a civil

29

engineering project, but military. Can you do it?'

General Ali Musuli of the Army Engineers straightened his back, staring at the President's mid-chest.

'With pride, Sayid Rais.'

'The man in charge, your best, your very best.'

'I know the man, sayidi. A colonel. Brilliant at construction and deception. The Russian Stepanov said he was the best pupil in maskirovka that he had ever taught.'

'Then bring him to me. Not here, in Baghdad in two days. I will commission him myself. Is he a good Ba'athist, this colonel? Loyal to the party and to me?'

'Utterly, sayidi. He would die for you.'

'So would you all, I hope.' There was a pause, then, quietly, 'Let us hope it does not come to that.'

As a conversation-stopper it worked. Fortunately that was the end of the meeting anyway.

*   *   *

Dr Gerry Bull arrived back in Brussels on 17 March, exhausted and depressed. His colleagues assumed his depression was caused by his rebuff in China. But it was more than that.

Ever since he had arrived in Baghdad more than two years earlier he had allowed himself to be persuaded, because it was what he wanted to believe, that the rocket programme and the Babylon gun were for the launch of small, instrument-bearing satellites into earth orbit. He at least could see the enormous benefits in self-esteem and pride for the whole Arab world if Iraq could do that. Moreover, it would be lucrative, pay its way, as Iraq launched communications and weather satellites for other

30

nations.

As he understood it, the plan was for Babylon to fire its satellite-bearing missile south-east over the length of Iraq and on over Saudi Arabia and the south Indian Ocean and into orbit. That is what he had designed it for.

He had been forced to agree with his colleagues that no Western nation would see it that way. They would assume it was a military gun. Hence the subterfuge in the ordering of the barrel parts, breech and recoil mechanism.

Only he, Gerald Vincent Bull, knew the truth, which was very simple—it could not be used as a weapon launching conventional explosive shells, however gigantic those shells might be.

For one thing, the Babylon gun with its 156-metre barrel could not stay rigid without supports. It needed one trunnion, or support, every second of its 26 barrel sections, even if, as he foresaw, its barrel ran up the 45-degree side of a mountain. Without these supports the barrel would droop like wet spaghetti and tear itself apart as the joins ripped open.

Therefore, it could not raise or depress its elevation, nor traverse from side to side. So it could not pick a variety of targets. To change angle, up or down or side to side, it would have to be dismantled, taking weeks. Even to clean out and reload between discharges would take a couple of days. Moreover, repeated firings would wear out that very expensive barrel.

Lastly, Babylon could not be hidden from counter-attack. Every time it fired a gobbet of flame 90 metres long would leap from its barrel, spotted by every satellite and airplane. Its map co-ordinates would be with the Americans in seconds. Also its reverberation shock waves would reached any good seismograph as far as California. That was why he told anyone who would listen: 'It cannot be used as a weapon.'

His problem was that after two years in Iraq he had realized that for Saddam Hussein science had one application and one only; it was to be applied to weapons of war and the power they brought him, *and to nothing else*. So why the hell was he financing Babylon? It could only fire once in anger before the retaliatory fighter-bombers blew it to bits, and it could only fire a satellite or a conventional shell.

It was in China, in the company of the sympathetic George Wong, that he cracked it. It was the last equation he would ever solve.

CHAPTER TWO

The big Ram Charger sped down the main highway from Qatar towards Abu Dhabi in the United Arab Emirates, making good time. The air-conditioning kept the interior cool and the driver had some of his favourite country-and-western tapes filling the interior with back-home sounds.

Beyond Ruweis they were out in open country, the sea to their left only intermittently visible between the dunes, to their right the great desert stretching away hundreds of bleak and sandy miles towards Dhofar and the Indian Ocean.

Beside her husband Mrs Maybelle Walker gazed excitedly at the ochre-brown desert shimmering under the midday sun. Her husband Ray kept his eyes on the road. An oil man all his life, he had seen deserts before. 'Seen one, seen 'em all,' he would grunt when his wife made one of her frequent exclamations of wonderment at the sights and sounds that were so new to her.

But for Maybelle Walker it was all new and although she had packed enough medications before leaving Oklahoma to open a new branch of Eckerd, she had loved every minute of her two-week tour of the Arabian Gulf.

They had started in the north in Kuwait, then driven the off-road loaned them by the company south into Saudi Arabia through Khafji and Al-Khobar, crossed the causeway into Bahrain, then back and down through Qatar and into the UAE. At each stop-over Ray Walker had made a perfunctory 'inspection' of his company office—the ostensible reason for the trip—while she had taken a guide from the company office and explored the local sights. She felt very brave going down all those narrow streets with only a single white man for escort, unaware that she would have been in more danger in any one of fifty American cities than among the Gulf Arabs.

The sights enthralled her on her first and perhaps last journey outside the USA. She admired the palaces and the minarets, wondered at the torrent of raw gold on display in the gold souks, and was awed by the tide of dark faces and multicoloured robes that swirled about her in the Old Quarters.

She had taken photographs of everything and everyone so she could show the Ladies Club back home where she had been and what she had seen, and had taken to heart the warning by the company representative in Qatar to be careful of taking a picture of a desert Arab without his permission, as some still believed the taking of a photograph captured part of the target's soul.

33

She was, she frequently reminded herself, a happy woman and had much to be happy about. Married almost straight out of High School to her steady 'date' of two years, she found herself wedded to a good, solid man with a job in a local oil company who had risen steadily through the ranks as the company expanded until he was now finishing as one of the vice-presidents.

They had a nice home outside Tulsa and a beach house for summer vacations at Hatteras, between the Atlantic and Pamlico Sound in North Carolina. It had been a good thirty-year marriage, rewarded with one fine son. And now this, a two-week tour at the company's expense of all the exotic sights and sounds, smells and experiences of another world, the Arabian Gulf.

'It's a good road,' she remarked as they crested a rise and the strip of bitumen shimmered and shivered away in front of them. If the temperature inside the vehicle was 70 degrees, it was 120 out there in the desert.

'Ought to be,' her husband grunted, 'we built it.'

'The company?'

'Nah. Uncle Sam, goddamit.'

Ray Walker had a habit of adding the single word 'goddamit' when he dispensed pieces of information. They sat for a while in companionable silence while Tammy Wynette urged her to stand by her man, which she always had done and intended to do through their retirement.

Nudging sixty, Ray Walker was taking retirement with a good pension and some healthy stock options, and a grateful company had offered him a two-week all-expenses-paid first-class tour of the Gulf to 'inspect' its various outstations along the coast.

Though he, too, had never been there before, he had to admit he was less enthralled by it all than his wife, but he was delighted for her sake.

Personally he was looking forward to finishing with Abu Dhabi and Dubai, then catching the first-class cabin of an airliner aimed directly at the USA via London. At least he could order a long, cold Bud without having to scuttle into the company office for it. Islam might be all right for some, he mused, but after staying in the best hotels in Kuwait, Saudi Arabia and Qatar and being told they were completely dry he wondered what kind of a religion would stop a guy having a cool beer on a hot day.

He was dressed in what he perceived to be the rig-out of an oil man in the desert—tall boots, jeans, belt, shirt and Stetson—which was not entirely necessary as he was really a chemist in quality control.

He checked the mile-counter; 80 miles to the Abu Dhabi turn-off.

'Gonna have to take a leak, honey,' he muttered.

'Well then, you be careful,' warned Maybelle. 'There are scorpions out there.'

'But they can't leap two feet,' he said and roared at his own joke. Being stung on the dick by a high-jumping scorpion—that was a good one for the boys back home.

'Ray, you are a terrible man,' replied Maybelle and laughed also. Walker swung the Ram Charger to the edge of the empty road, switched off and opened the door. The blast of heat came in as from the door of a furnace. He climbed out and slammed the door behind him to trap the remaining cool air.

Maybelle stayed in the passenger seat as her husband walked to the nearest dune and unzipped his fly. Then she stared out through the windscreen and muttered: 'Oh my God, would you just look at that.'

She reached for her Pentax, opened her door and slithered to the ground.

'Ray, do you think he'd mind if I took his picture?'

Ray was facing the other way, absorbed in one of a middle-aged man's greater satisfactions.

'Be right with you, honey. Who?'

The Bedouin was standing across the road from her husband, having apparently walked out from between two dunes. One minute he was not there, the next he was. Maybelle Walker stood by the front fender of the off-road, her camera in her hand, irresolute. Her husband turned round and zipped himself up. He stared at the man across the road.

'Dunno,' he said. 'Guess not. But don't get too close. Probably got fleas. I'll get the engine started. You take a quick picture and if he gets nasty jump right in. Fast.'

He climbed back into the driver's seat and started the engine. That brought on the air-conditioner, which was a relief.

Maybelle Walker took several steps forward and held up her camera.

'May I take your picture?' she asked. 'Camera? Picture? Click-click? For my album back home?'

The man just stood and stared at her. His once-white djellaba, stained and dusty, dropped from his shoulders to the sand at his feet. The red-and-white flecked keffiyeh was secured on his head by a two-strand black cord and one of the trailing corners was tucked up under the opposite temple so that the cloth covered his face from the bridge of the nose downwards. Above the flecked cloth the dark eyes stared back at her. What little skin of forehead and

36

eye sockets she could see was burned brown by the desert. She had many pictures ready for the album she intended to make back home, but none of a tribesman of the Bedouin with the expanse of the Saudi desert behind him.

She raised her camera. The man did not move. She squinted through the aperture, framing the figure in the centre of the oblong, wondering if she could make the car in the time should the Arab come running at her. Click.

'Thank you very much,' she said. Still he did not move. She backed towards the car, smiling brightly. Always smile, she recalled the Reader's Digest once advising Americans confronted by someone who cannot understand English.

'Honey, get in the car,' her husband shouted.

'It's all right, I think he's OK,' she said, opening the door.

The tape had run out while she was taking the picture. That cut the radio station in. Ray Walker's hand reached out and hauled her into the car, which screeched away from the roadside.

The Arab watched them go, shrugged and walked behind the sand dune where he had parked his own sand-camouflaged Land-Rover. In a few seconds he, too, drove off in the direction of Abu Dhabi.

'What's the hurry?' complained Maybelle Walker. 'He wasn't going to attack me.'

'That's not the point, honey.' Ray Walker was tight-lipped, the man in control, able to cope with any international emergency. 'We're getting into Abu Dhabi and taking the next flight home. It seems this morning Iraq invaded Kuwait, goddamit. They could be here any hour.'

It was ten o'clock, Gulf Time, on the morning of 2

August 1990.

*   *   *

Twelve hours earlier Colonel Osman Badri waited, tense and excited, by the tracks of a stationary T-72 main battle tank near a small airfield called Safwan. Although he could not know it then, the war for Kuwait would begin there and it would end there, at Safwan.

Just outside the airfield, which had runways but no buildings on it, the main highway ran north and south. On the northward road, down which he had travelled three days earlier, was the junction where travellers could turn east for Basra or north-west for Baghdad.

South, the road ran straight through the Kuwaiti border post 5 miles away. From where he stood, looking south, he could see the dim glow of Jahra and beyond it, further east across the bay, the glow of the lights of Kuwait City itself.

He was excited because his country's time had come. Time to punish the Kuwaiti scum for what they had done to his country, for the undeclared economic warfare, for the financial damage and their haughty arrogance.

Had not Iraq for eight bloody years held off the hordes of Persia from sweeping into the northern Gulf and ending all their luxury lifestyles? And was her reward now to sit silent while the Kuwaitis stole more than their fair portion of the oil from the shared Rumailah field? Were they now to be beggared as Kuwait over-produced and drove the oil price downward? Should they now meekly succumb as the Al Sabah dogs insisted on repayment of the miserable

38

fifteen-billion-dollar loan made to Iraq during the war?

No, the Rais had got it right as usual. Kuwait was historically the nineteenth province of Iraq; always had been until the British drew their damned line in the sand in 1913, and created the richest emirate in the world. Now Kuwait would be reclaimed, this night, this very night, and Osman Badri would be a part of it.

As an army engineer he would not be in the first line, but he would come close behind with his bridging units, earth-movers, bulldozers and sappers to cut open the path should the Kuwaitis try to block it. Not that aerial surveillance had shown any obstructions. No earthworks, no sand berms, no anti-tank trenches, no concrete traps. But just in case, the engineers would be there under the command of Osman Badri to cut open the road for the tanks and mechanized infantry of the Republican Guard.

A few yards from where he stood, the field command tent was full of the senior officers poring over their maps and making last-minute adjustments to their plan of attack as the hours and minutes ticked by while they waited for the final 'Go' order from the Rais in Baghdad.

He had already seen and conversed with his own commanding general Ali Musuli who was in charge of the entire Engineer Corps of the Iraqi army and to whom he owed utter devotion for recommending him for the 'special duty' last February. He had been able to assure his chief that his, Badri's, men were fully equipped and ready to go.

As he stood talking with Musuli another general had strolled up and he had been introduced to Abdullah Kadiri, commander of the tanks. In the

39

distance he had seen General Saadi Tumah Abbas, commanding the élite Republican Guard, enter the tent. As a loyal Party member and worshipper of Saddam Hussein he had been perplexed to hear the tank general Kadiri mutter 'political creep' under his breath. How could this be? Was not Tumah Abbas an intimate of Saddam Hussein and had he not been rewarded for winning the crucial battle of Fao that finally beat the Iranians? Colonel Badri had dismissed from his mind rumours that Fao had actually been won by the now-vanished General Maher Rashid.

All around him men and officers of the Tawakkulna and Medina divisions of the Guard swarmed in the darkness. His thoughts strayed back to that memorable night in February when General Musuli had ordered him from his duties putting the finishing touches to the facility at Al-Qubai to report to headquarters in Baghdad. He assumed he would be re-assigned.

'The President wants to see you,' Musuli had said abruptly. 'He will send for you. Move into the officers' quarters here and keep yourself available night and day.'

Badri bit his lip. What had he done? What had he said? Nothing disloyal, that would have been impossible. Had he been falsely denounced? No, the President would not send for such a man. The wrongdoer would simply be picked up by one of the goon squads of Brig. Khatib's Amn-al-Amm and taken away to be taught a lesson. Seeing his face, Musuli burst out laughing, his teeth flashing beneath the heavy black moustache that so many senior officers wore in imitation of Saddam Hussein.

'Don't worry, he has a task for you, a special task.'

And he had. Within twenty-four hours Badri had been summoned to the lobby of the officers' quarters where a long black staff car was waiting for him, with two men from the Amn-al-Khass, the Presidential Security Detail. He was whisked straight to the presidential palace for the most thrilling and momentous meeting of his life.

The palace was then situated in the angle of Kindi Street and July 14th Street, near the bridge of the same name, both celebrating the date of the first of the two *coups* of July 1968 that brought the Ba'ath Party to power and broke the rule of the generals. Badri was shown into a waiting room and kept there for two hours. He was frisked thoroughly, twice, before being shown into the Presence.

As soon as the guards beside him stopped, he stopped, then threw up a quivering salute and held it for three seconds, before whipping off his beret and swinging it under his left arm. After that he remained at attention.

'So, you are the genius of maskirovka?'

He had been told not to look the Rais straight in the eyes, but when he was spoken to he could not help it. Saddam Hussein was in a good mood. The eyes of the young officer in front of him shone with love and admiration. Good, nothing to fear. In measured tones he told the engineer what he wanted. Badri's chest swelled with pride and gratitude.

For five months he had worked against the impossible deadline and succeeded with days to spare. He had had all the facilities the Rais had promised him. Everything and everyone was at his disposal. If he needed more concrete or steel he had but to ring Kamil on his personal number and the President's son-in-law provided it at once from

Ministry of Industry sources. If he needed more manpower hundreds of labourers would arrive, and always indentured Koreans or Vietnamese. They cut and they dug, they lived in miserable cantonments down in the valley during that summer, and then they were taken away, he did not know where.

Apart from the coolies, no-one came in by road, for the single rough track, eventually to be obliterated itself, was only for the trucks bringing steel and cargo, and the cement-mixers. Every other human being except the truck drivers came in by one of the Russian MIL helicopters and only when they arrived were the blindfolds removed, to be replaced when they left. This applied to the most senior as to the humblest Iraqi.

Badri had chosen the site himself, after days of scouting by helicopter over the mountains. He had finally picked his spot high in the Jebal Hamreen, north and further into the mountains from Kifri, where the hills of the Hamreen Range become mountains on the road to Sulaymaniyam.

He had worked twenty hours a day, slept rough on the site, bullied, threatened, cajoled and bribed amazing work performances from his men and finally it had been done before the end of July. The area had been cleared of every trace of work, every brick and lump of concrete, every piece of steel that might glint in the sun, every scrape and scratch on the rocks.

The three guardian villages had been completed and inhabited with their goats and sheep. Finally the single track had been obliterated, tumbled in rough rubble and scree into the valley beneath by an earth-mover trundling backwards, and the three valleys and the raped mountain had been restored to what they once were. Almost.

42

For he, Osman Badri, colonel of engineers, inheritor of the building skills that had erected Nineveh and Tyre, student of the great Stepanov of Russia, master of maskirovka, the art of disguising something to look like nothing or something else, had built for Saddam Hussein the Qa'ala, the Fortress. No-one could see it and no-one knew where it was.

Before it was closed over Badri had watched the others, the gun assemblers and the scientists, build that awesome cannon whose barrel seemed to reach up to the very stars. When all was complete they left, and only the garrison remained behind. They would stay and live there. None would walk out. Those who had to arrive or leave would do so by helicopter. None of these would land; they would hover over a small patch of grass away from the mountain. The few arriving or leaving would always be blindfolded. The pilots and crew would be sealed inside one single air base with neither visitors nor phones. The last wild grass seeds were scattered, the last shrubs planted and the Fortress was left alone to its isolation.

Though Badri did not know it, the workers who had arrived by truck were finally driven away, then transferred to buses with blackened windows. Far away in a gulch the buses containing the 3,000 Asian workers were stopped and the guards ran away. When the detonations brought down the mountainside all the buses were buried for ever. Then the guards were shot by others. They had all seen the Qa'ala.

Badri's reverie was interrupted by an eruption of shouting from the command tent and word ran quickly through the crowds of waiting soldiers that

43

the attack was 'Go'.

The engineer ran to his truck and hauled himself into the passenger seat as his driver gunned the engine. They held position as the tank crews of the two Guard divisions that would spearhead the invasion filled the air with ear-shattering noise and the Russian T-72s rumbled off the airfield and onto the road to Kuwait.

It was, he would later tell his brother Abdelkarim, a fighter pilot and colonel in the Air Force, like a turkey shoot. The miserable police post on the border was brushed aside and crushed. By 2 a.m. the column was over the border and rolling south. If the Kuwaitis were kidding themselves that this army, the fourth-largest standing army in the world, was going to advance to the Mutla Ridge and rattle its sabres until Kuwait acceded to the demands of the Rais, they were out of luck. If the West thought they would just capture the desired islands of Warbah and Bubiyan, giving Iraq its long-lusted-for access to the Gulf, they, too, were up the wrong tree. The orders from Baghdad were: take it all.

Just before dawn there was a tank engagement at the small Kuwaiti oil town of Jahra, north of Kuwait City. The only Kuwaiti armoured brigade had been rushed northwards, having been held back in the week before the invasion in order not to provoke the Iraqis.

It was one-sided. The Kuwaitis, supposed to be no more than merchants and oil-profiteers, fought hard and well. They held up the cream of the Republican Guard for an hour, allowing some of their Skyhawk and Mirage fighters further south at the Ahmadi base to get airborne, but they did not stand a chance. The huge Soviet T-72s cut to pieces the smaller Chinese

44

T-55s used by the Kuwaitis. The defenders lost twenty tanks in as many minutes, and finally the survivors pulled out and back.

Osman Badri, watching from a mile away as the mastodons swerved and fired in the belching clouds of dust and smoke while a pink line touched the sky over Iran, could not know that one day these same T-72s of the Medina and Tawakkulna divisions would themselves be blown apart by the Challengers and Abrams of the British and Americans.

By dawn the first point units were rumbling into the northwestern outskirts of Kuwait City, dividing their forces to cover the four highways giving access to the city from that quarter: the Abu Dhabi road along the seashore, the Jahra Road between Granada and Andalus suburbs, and the Fifth and Sixth Ring Motorways further south. After the split, the four prongs headed into central Kuwait.

Colonel Badri was hardly needed. There were no ditches for his sappers to fill in, nor obstructions to be blown away with dynamite, nor concrete bollards to be bulldozed. Only once did he have to dive for his life.

Rolling along through Sulaibikhat, quite close (though he did not know it) to the Christian cemetery, a single Skyhawk wheeled out of the sun and targeted the tank ahead of him with four air-to-ground rockets. The tank jolted, lost a track and began to burn. The panicking crew poured from the turret. Then the Skyhawk was back, going for the following trucks, flames flickering from its nose. Badri saw the tarmac erupting in front of him and hurled himself from the door just as his screaming driver hauled the lorry off the road, into a ditch and turned it over.

No-one was hurt but Badri was furious. The impudent dog. He finished the journey in another truck.

There was sporadic gunfire all through the day as the two divisions, with their armour, artillery and mechanized infantry, rolled through the sprawl of Kuwait City. At the Defence Ministry a group of Kuwaiti officers shut themselves in and tried to take on the invaders with some small arms they found inside.

One of the Iraqi officers, in a spirit of sweet reason, pointed out that they were dead men if he opened up with his tank gun. While a few Kuwaiti resisters argued with him before surrendering, the rest changed out of their uniforms into dish-dash and ghutra, and slipped away out the back. One of these would later become the leader of the Kuwaiti resistance.

The principal opposition occurred at the residence of the Emir Al Sabah, even though he and his family had long fled south to seek sanctuary in Saudi Arabia. It was crushed.

At sundown Colonel Osman Badri stood with his back to the sea at the northernmost point of Kuwait City on Arabian Gulf Street and stared at the façade of that residence, the Dasman Palace. Already a few Iraqi soldiers were inside the palace and now and then one would emerge carrying a priceless artefact torn from the walls, stepping over the bodies on the steps and the lawn to place the booty in a truck.

He was tempted to take something himself, a gift fine and worthy for his father at the old man's home in Qadisiyah, but something held him back. The heritage of that damned English school he had attended all those years ago in Baghdad, and all

46

because of his father's friendship with the Englishman Martin and his admiration of all things British.

'Looting is stealing, boys, and stealing is wrong. The Bible and the Koran forbid it. So do not do it.'

Even to this day he could recall Mr Hartley the headmaster of the Foundation Preparatory School, run under the British Council, lecturing his pupils, English and Iraqi, at their desks.

How often had he reasoned with his father since joining the Ba'ath Party that the English had always been imperialist aggressors, holding the Arabs in chains for centuries to reap their own profits?

And his father, who was now seventy and so much older because Osman and his brother had been born to the second marriage, had always smiled and said: 'Maybe they are foreigners, and infidel, but they are courteous and they have standards, my son. And what standards does your Mr Saddam Hussein have, pray?'

It had been impossible to get through the old man's thick skull how important the Party was to Iraq and how its leader would bring Iraq to glory and triumph. Eventually he ceased these conversations lest his father say something about the Rais that would be overheard by a neighbour and get them all into trouble. He disagreed with his father on this alone, for he loved him very much.

So, because of a headmaster twenty-five years before, he stood back and did not join in the looting of the Dasman Palace, even though it was in the tradition of all his ancestors and the English were fools.

At least his years at the Tasisiya (Foundation) Prep School had taught him fluent English, which

47

had turned out to be useful because it was the language in which he could best communicate with Colonel Stepanov, who had for a long time been the senior engineering officer with the Soviet Military Advisory Group before the Cold War came to its end and he went back to Moscow.

Osman Badri was thirty-five and the year 1990 was proving to be the greatest of his whole life. As he told his elder brother later: 'I just stood there with my back to the Gulf and the Dasman Palace in front of me and thought, "By the Prophet, we've done it. We've taken Kuwait at last. And in just one day." And that was the end of it.'

He was wrong, as it happened. That was just the beginning.

*   *   *

While Ray Walker was, to quote his own phrase, 'hauling ass' through Abu Dhabi airport, hammering the sales counter to insist on the American's constitutional right to an instant airline ticket, a number of his fellow countrymen were ending a sleepless night.

Seven time zones away in Washington the National Security Council had been up all night. In earlier days they used to have to meet personally in the Situation Room in the basement of the White House; newer technology meant they could confer by secure video link from their various locations.

The previous evening, still 1 August in Washington, early reports had indicated some firing along Kuwait's northern border. It was not unexpected. For days sweeps by the great KH-11 satellites over the northern Gulf had shown the

48

build-up of the Iraqi forces, telling Washington more than the US ambassador in Kuwait actually knew. The problem was: what were Saddam Hussein's intentions? To threaten or to invade?

Frantic requests had been sent the previous day to the CIA headquarters at Langley but the Agency had been less than helpful, turning in 'maybe' analyses on the basis of the satellite pictures garnered by the National Reconnaissance Office and political savvy already known to the State Department's Mid-East Division.

'Any half-ass can do that,' growled Brent Scowcroft, chairman of the NSC. 'Don't we have anyone right inside the Iraqi regime?'

The answer to that was a regretful 'no'. It was a problem that would recur for months.

The answer to the conundrum came before 10 p.m. when President George Bush went to bed and took no further calls from Scowcroft. That was after dawn Gulf Time, and the Iraqi tanks were beyond Jahra, entering the north-western suburbs of Kuwait City.

It was, the participants would recall later, quite a night. There were eight on the video link, representing the NSC, the Treasury, State Department, CIA, Joint Chiefs of Staff and Defence. A flurry of orders went out and were implemented. A similar series was coming out of a hastily convened COBRA (Cabinet Office Briefing Room Annex) committee meeting in London which was five hours away from Washington but only two from the Gulf.

Both governments froze all Iraqi financial assets lodged abroad, as well as (with the agreement of the Kuwaiti ambassadors in both cities) all Kuwaiti assets so that any new puppet government working for Baghdad could not get their hands on the funds.

These decisions froze billions and billions of petro-dollars.

President Bush was woken at 4.45 a.m. on 2 August to sign the documents. In London Mrs Margaret Thatcher, long up and about and raising seven levels of Cain, had already done the same before going to catch her plane for the States.

Another major step was to hustle together the United Nations Security Council in New York to condemn the invasion and call for an immediate withdrawal by Iraq. This was achieved with Resolution 660, signed at 4.30 a.m. that same morning.

Around dawn the video-link conference ended, the participants had two hours to get home, wash, change, shave and be back at the White House for the 8 a.m. full meeting of the NSC, chaired by President Bush in person.

Newcomers at the full meeting included Richard Cheney of Defence, Nicholas Brady of Treasury, and Attorney-General Richard Thornburgh. Bob Kimmitt continued to stand in for the State Department because Secretary James Baker and Deputy-Secretary Lawrence Eagleburger were both out of town.

Chairman of Joint Chiefs of Staff Colin Powell had arrived back from Florida bringing with him the general in charge of Central Command, a big burly man of whom more would be heard later. Norman Schwarzkopf was at Gen. Powell's side when they walked in.

George Bush left the meeting at 9.15 a.m. when Ray and Maybelle Walker were thankfully airborne and somewhere over Saudi Arabia heading north-west for home and safety. The President took a helicopter from the south lawn to Andrews Air Force base where he transferred to Air Force One and flew to Aspen, Colorado. He was scheduled to give an address on US defence needs. As it turned out it was an appropriate topic, but the day would be much busier than foreseen.

In mid-air he took a long call from King Hussein of Jordan, monarch of Iraq's smaller and much-overshadowed neighbour. The Hashemite King was in Cairo, conferring with Egyptian President Hosni Mubarak.

King Hussein was desperate that America give the Arab States a few days to try to sort things out without a war. He himself proposed a four-state conference including President Mubarak, himself, Saddam Hussein and under the chairmanship of His Majesty King Fahd of Saudi Arabi. He was confident such a conference would persuade the Iraqi dictator to withdraw from Kuwait peaceably. But he needed three, maybe four, days and no public condemnation of Iraq by any of the nations participant to the conference.

President Bush told him: 'You got it. I defer to you.' The unfortunate George had not yet met the lady from London who was waiting for him in Aspen. They met that evening.

The Iron Lady soon got the impression that her good friend was about to start wavering again. Within two hours she put a broom handle so far up the President's left trouser leg that it came out near the collar line.

'He cannot, he simply cannot, be allowed to get away with it, George.'

Faced with those flashing blue eyes and the cut-crystal tones slicing through the hum of the air-

51

conditioner, George Bush admitted that this was not America's intention either. His intimates later felt he was less worried by Saddam Hussein with his artillery and tanks than by that daunting handbag.

On 3 August America had a quiet word with Egypt. President Mubarak was reminded just how much his armed forces were dependent on American weaponry, just how much Egypt owed to the World Bank and the International Monetary Fund and just how much US aid came his way. On 4 August the Egyptian government issued a public statement roundly condemning Saddam Hussein's invasion.

To the Jordanian King's dismay but not to his surprise, the Iraqi despot at once refused to go to the Jeddah conference and sit beside Hosni Mubarak under the chairmanship of King Fahd.

For the King of Saudi Arabia it was a brutal snub delivered within a culture that prides itself on elaborate courtesy. King Fahd, who conceals a shrewd political brain behind an unfailingly gracious persona, was not pleased.

This was one of the two factors that blew away the Jeddah conference. The other was the fact that the Saudi monarch had been shown American photographs taken from space which proved the Iraqi army, far from halting its advance, was still in full battle order and moving south towards the Saudi border on the southern fringes of Kuwait.

Would they really dare to sweep on and invade Saudi Arabia itself? The arithmetic added up. Saudi Arabia has the biggest oil reserves in the world. Second comes Kuwait with over a hundred years of reserves at present production levels. Third is Iraq. By taking Kuwait, Saddam Hussein had reversed the balance. Moreover, 90 per cent of Saudi oil wells and reserves are locked into the far north-eastern corner of the kingdom, around Dharran, Al-Khobar, Dammam and Jubail and inland from these ports. The triangle lay right in the path of the advancing Republican Guard divisions, and the photos proved more divisions were pouring into Kuwait.

Fortunately His Majesty never discovered that the photographs were doctored. The divisions close to the border were digging in, but the bulldozers had been air-brushed out.

On 6 August the Kingdom of Saudi Arabia formally asked United States forces to enter the kingdom for its defence.

The first squadrons of fighter-bombers left for the Middle East the same day. Desert Shield had begun.

*   *   *

Brigadier Hassan Rahmani jumped out of his staff car and ran up the steps of the Hilton Hotel which had quickly been taken over as the headquarters of the Iraqi security forces in occupied Kuwait. It amused him as he swung through the glass doors into the lobby that morning of 4 August that the Hilton was right next to the American Embassy, both on the seashore with lovely views over the glittering blue waters of the Arabian Gulf.

The view was all the staff of the embassy were going to get for a while—at his suggestion the building had been immediately ringed with Republican Guards and would stay that way. He could not prevent foreign diplomats transmitting messages from inside their sovereign territory to their governments back home and he knew he did not have the supercomputers needed to break the more sophisticated codes such as the British and Americans would be using.

But as head of Counter-Intelligence for the Mukhabarat he could ensure they had little of interest to send home by confining their observations to the views from their windows.

That left, of course, the possibility of their obtaining information from fellow-nationals still at large in Kuwait by telephone. Another top priority; ensure that all outside telephone lines were cut or tapped—tapped would be better, but most of his best men were fully engaged back in Baghdad.

He swung into the suite of rooms that had been set aside for the Counter-Intelligence team, took off his army jacket, tossed it to the sweating aide who had brought up his two suitcases of documents and walked to the window to gaze down into the pool of the Hilton Marina. A nice idea to have a swim later, he thought, then noticed that two soldiers were filling their water bottles from it and two more were peeing into it. He sighed.

At thirty-seven Rahmani was a trim, handsome, clean-shaven man—he could not be bothered with the affectation of a Saddam Hussein-like moustache. He was where he was, and he knew it, because he was good at his job, not because of political clout, a technocrat in a world of politically elevated cretins.

Why, he had been asked by foreign friends, do you serve this regime? The question was usually asked when he had got them partly drunk at the bar of the Rashid Hotel or in a more private place. He was allowed to mix with them because it was part of his job. But every time he remained quite sober. He had no objection to liquor on religious grounds—he just ordered a gin and tonic but made sure the barman

54

knew to give him only tonic.

So he smiled at the question, shrugged and replied: 'I am an Iraqi and proud of it; which government would you have me serve?'

Privately, he knew perfectly well why he served a regime most of whose luminaries he privately despised. If he had any emotion in him, which he frequently claimed he did not, then it came out in a genuine affection for his country and its people; the ordinary people whom the Ba'ath Party had long ceased to represent.

But the principal reason was that he wanted to get on in life. For an Iraqi of his generation there were few options. He could oppose the regime and quit, to earn a hand-to-mouth living abroad dodging the hit-squads and making pennies translating from Arabic into English and back, or stay inside Iraq.

That left three options. Oppose the regime again, and end up in one of the torture chambers of that animal Omar Khatib, a creature he personally loathed in the full knowledge that the feeling was mutual; or try to survive as a freelance businessman in an economy being systematically run into the ground; or keep smiling at the idiots and rise within their rank through brains and talent.

He could see nothing wrong with the latter. Like Reinhard Gehlen serving first Hitler, then the Americans and then the West Germans; like Marcus Wolf serving the East German communists without believing a word they said, he was a chess player. He lived for the game, the intricate moves of spy and counter-spy. Iraq was his personal chessboard. He knew other professionals the world over could understand that.

Hassan Rahmani returned from the window, sat in

the chair behind the desk and began to make notes. There was one hell of a lot to do if Kuwait was ever to be even reasonably secure as the nineteenth colony of Iraq.

His first problem was that he did not know how long Saddam Hussein intended to stay in Kuwait. He doubted the man knew himself. There was no point in mounting a huge Counter-Intelligence operation, sealing all the leaks and security holes that he could, if Iraq was going to pull out.

Privately he believed Saddam could get away with it. But it would mean boxing clever, making the right moves, saying the right things. The first ploy had to be to attend that conference tomorrow in Jeddah, to flatter King Fahd until he could take no more, to claim Iraq wanted no more than a just treaty over oil, Gulf access and the outstanding loan, and he would go home to Baghdad. That way, keeping the whole thing in Arab hands and at all costs keeping the Americans and the Brits out, Saddam could rely on the Arab preference to keeping talking until hell freezes over.

The West, with its attention span of a few weeks, would get fed up and leave it to the four Arabs, two kings and two presidents, and so long as the oil kept flowing to create the smog that was choking them, the Anglo-Saxons would stay happy. Unless Kuwait was savagely brutalized the media would drop the subject, the Al Sabah regime would be forgotten in exile somewhere in Saudi Arabia, the Kuwaitis would get on with their lives under a new government and the quit-Kuwait conference could chew words for a decade until it didn't matter any more.

It could be done, but it would need the right touch. Hitler's touch—I only seek a peaceful settlement to my just demands, this is absolutely my last territorial ambition. King Fahd would fall for it—no-one had any love for the Kuwaitis anyway, let alone the Al Sabah lotus-eaters. King Fahd and King Hussein would drop them, as Chamberlain had dropped the Czechs in 1938.

The trouble was, Saddam was street-smart as hell or he wouldn't still be alive, but strategically and diplomatically he was a buffoon. Somehow, Hassan Rahmani reasoned, the Rais would get it wrong; neither pull out nor roll on, seize the Saudi oilfield and present the Western world with a *fait accompli* they could do nothing about except detroy the oil and their own prosperity for a generation.

The West meant America, with the Brits at their side, and they were all Anglo-Saxons. He knew about Anglo-Saxons. Five years at Mr Hartley's Tasisiya Prep School had taught him his perfect English, an understanding of the British and to be wary of that Anglo-Saxon habit of giving you a very hard punch on the jaw without warning.

He rubbed his chin where he had collected such a punch long ago, and laughed out loud. His aide across the room jumped a foot. Mike bloody Martin, where are you now?

Hassan Rahmani, clever, cultured, cosmopolitan, educated and refined, an upper-class scion who served a regime of thugs, bent to his task. It was quite a task. Of 1.8 million people in Kuwait that August only 600,000 were Kuwaitis. To them you could add 600,000 Palestinians, some of whom would stay loyal to Kuwait, some of whom would side with Iraq because the PLO had done so, and most of whom would keep their heads down and try to survive. Then 300,000 Egyptians, some of them no doubt working

57

for Cairo which nowadays was the same as working for Washington or London, and 250,000 Pakistanis, Indians, Bangladeshis and Filipinos, mainly blue-collar labourers or domestic servants—as an Iraqi he believed the Kuwaitis could not scratch a flea-bite on their arse without summoning a foreign servant.

And then 50,000 First World citizens—Brits, Americans, French, German, Spanish, Swedish, Danish—name it. And he was supposed to suppress foreign espionage ... He sighed for the days when messages meant messengers or telephones. As head of Counter-Intelligence he could seal the borders and cut the phone lines. Now any fool with a satellite could punch numbers into a cellular phone or a computer modem and talk to California. Hard to intercept or track the source, except with the best equipment, which he did not have.

He knew he could not control the out-flow of information or the steady dribble of refugees escaping over the border. Nor could he affect the over-flights of the American satellites, all of which he suspected had now been reprogrammed to swing their orbits over Kuwait and Iraq every few minutes. (He was right.)

There was no point in attempting the impossible, even though he would have to pretend he had, and had succeeded. The main target would have to be to prevent active sabotage, actual killing of Iraqis and destruction of their equipment, the formation of a real resistance movement. And he would have to prevent help reaching any resistance from outside in the form of men, know-how or equipment.

In this he would come up against his rivals of the AMAM, the secret police, who were installed two floors below him. Khatib, he had learnt that morning, was installing that thug Sabaawi, an oaf as brutal as himself, as head of AMAM in Kuwait. If resisting Kuwaitis fell into *their* hands they would learn to scream as loudly as dissidents back home. So he, Rahmani, would just stick to the foreigners. That was his brief.

*   *   *

That morning Dr Terry Martin finished his lecture at the School of Oriental and African Studies (SOAS), a faculty of London University off Gower Street, shortly before noon and retired to the senior staff common room. Just outside the door he ran into Mabel, the secretary he shared with two other senior lecturers in Arabic studies.

'Oh, Dr Martin, there's been a message for you.'

She fumbled in her attaché case, propping it up on one tweed-skirted knee, and produced a slip of paper.

'This gentleman rang for you. He said it was rather urgent if you could call him back.'

Inside the common room he dumped his lecture notes on the Abassid Caliphate and used a pay phone on the wall. The number answered at the second tone and a bright female voice just repeated the number back. No company name, just the number.

'Is Mr Stephen Laing there?' asked Martin.

'May I say who is calling?'

'Er, Dr Martin. Terry Martin. He called me.'

'Ah, yes, Dr Martin, would you hold on?'

Martin frowned. She knew about the call, knew his name. For the life of him, he could not recall any Stephen Laing. A man came on the phone.

'Steve Laing here. Look, it's *awfully* good of you to call back so promptly. I know it's incredibly short

59

notice, but we met some time ago at the Institute for Strategic Studies. Just after you gave that brilliant paper on the Iraqi arms procurement machine. I was wondering what you're doing for lunch.'

Laing, whoever he was, had adopted that mode of self-expression that is at once diffident and persuasive, hard to turn down.

'Today? Now?'

'Unless you have anything fixed. What had you in mind?'

'Sandwiches in the canteen,' said Martin.

'Couldn't possibly offer you a decent sole *meunière* at Scott's, could I? You know it, of course. Mount Street.'

Martin knew of it, one of the best and most expensive fish restaurants in London. Twenty minutes away by cab. It was half-past twelve. And he loved fish. And Scott's was way beyond his academic salary. Did Laing by any chance know these things?

'Are you actually with the ISS?' he asked.

'Explain over lunch, Doctor. Say one o'clock. Looking forward to it.' The phone went down.

When Martin entered the restaurant the head waiter came forward to greet him personally.

'Dr Martin? Mr Laing is at his table. Please follow me.'

It was a quiet table in a corner, very discreet. One could talk unoverheard. Laing, who by now he was sure he had never met, rose to greet him, a thin bony man in dark suit and sober tie with thinning grey hair. He ushered his guest to a seat and gestured with a raised eyebrow to a bottle of fine chilled Meursault that sat in the ice bucket. Martin nodded.

'You're not with the Institute, are you, Mr Laing?'

Laing was not in the least fazed. He watched the

60

crisp cool liquid poured and the waiter move away, leaving them a menu each. He raised his glass to his guest.

'Century House, actually. Does that bother you?'

The British Secret Intelligence Service works out of Century House, a rather shabby building south of the Thames between the Elephant and Castle and the Old Kent Road. It is not a new building and not really up to the job it is supposed to do and so labyrinthine inside that visitors really do not need their security passes; within seconds they get lost and end up screaming for mercy.

'No, just interested,' said Martin.

'Actually, it's we who are interested. I'm quite a fan of yours. I try to keep abreast but I'm not as clued-up as you.'

'I find that hard to believe,' said Martin, but he was flattered. When an academic is told he is admired, it is pleasing.

'Quite true,' insisted Laing. 'Sole for two? Excellent. I hope I have read all your papers delivered to the Institute, and the United Services people and Chatham. Plus, of course, those two articles in *Survival.*'

Over the previous five years, despite his youth at only thirty-five, Dr Martin had become more and more in demand as a speaker presenting erudite papers to such establishments as the Institute for Strategic Studies, the United Services Institute and that other body for the intensive study of foreign affairs, Chatham House. *Survival* is the magazine of the ISS and of each issue twenty-five copies go automatically to the Foreign and Commonwealth Office in King Charles Street, of which five filter down to Century House.

Terry Martin's interest for these people was not because of his scholastic excellence in medieval Mesopotamia, but for the second hat he wore. Quite as a private interest, he had begun years earlier to study the armed forces of the Middle East, attending defence exhibitions, cultivating friendships among manufacturers and their Arab clients, where his fluent Arabic had made him many contacts. After ten years he was a walking encyclopedia in his chosen pastime subject, and listened to with respect by the top professionals, much as the American novelist Tom Clancy is regarded as a world expert on defence equipment of NATO and the former Warsaw Pact.

The two soles *meunière* arrived and they began to eat with appreciation.

Eight weeks earlier Laing, who was at that time Director of Operations, Mid-East Division, at Century House, called up a pen portrait of Terry Martin from the Research people. He was impressed with what he saw.

Born in Baghdad, raised in Iraq and then schooled in England, Martin had left Haileybury with three Advanced Levels, all with distinction, in English, History and French. Haileybury had him down as a brilliant scholar and destined for a scholarship to Oxford or Cambridge.

But the boy, already a fluent Arab speaker, wanted to go on to Arabic studies so he had applied as a undergraduate to the SOAS in London, attending the spring interview of 1973. Accepted at once, he had joined in the autumn term of 1973, studying History of the Middle East.

He walked through a First Class degree in three years and then put in a further three years to his doctorate, specializing in Iraq of the eighth to the fifteenth centuries with particular reference to the Abassid Caliphate from AD 750 to 1258. He took his PhD in 1979, then one year off for a sabbatical—he was in Iraq in 1980 when Iraq invaded Iran, triggering the eight-year war, and this experience began his interest in Mid-East military forces.

On his return he was offered a lectureship at the age of only twenty-six, a signal honour at the SOAS which happens to be one of the best and therefore one of the toughest schools of Arabic learning in the world. He was promoted to a Readership in recognition of excellence in original research and became a Reader in Middle-East History at the age of thirty-four, clearly earmarked for a professorship by the age of forty.

So much had Laing read in the written biography. What interested him even more was the second string, the compendium of knowledge about Mid-East arms arsenals. For years it had been a peripheral subject, dwarfed by the Cold War, but now ...

'It's about this Kuwait business,' he said at last. The remains of the fish had been cleared away. Both men had declined a dessert. The Meursault had gone down very nicely and Laing had deftly ensured that Martin had most of it. Now two vintage ports had appeared as if unbidden.

'As you may imagine, there's been a hell of a flap-doodle going on these past few days.'

Laing was understating the case. The Lady had returned from Colorado in what the mandarins referred to as her Boadicea mode, a reference to that Ancient British queen who used to chop Romans off at the knees with the swords sticking out of her chariot wheels if they got in the way. Foreign Secretary Douglas Hurd was reputed to be thinking

63

of taking to wearing a steel helmet, and the demands for instant enlightenment had rained down on the spooks of Century House.

'The fact is, we would like to slip someone into Kuwait to find out exactly what is going on.'

'Under Iraqi occupation?' asked Martin.

'I'm afraid so, since they seem to be in charge.'

'So why me?'

'Let me be frank,' said Laing who intended to be anything but. 'We really do need to know what is going on inside. The Iraqi occupation army—how many, how good, what equipment. Our own nationals—how are they coping, are they in danger, can they realistically be got out in safety. We need a man in on the ground. This information is vital. So ... someone who speaks Arabic like an Arab, a Kuwaiti or Iraqi. Now, you, spend your life among Arabic-speakers, far more than I do...'

'But surely, there must be hundreds of Kuwaitis right here in Britain who could slip back in,' Martin suggested.

Laing sucked leisurely at a piece of sole that had stuck between two teeth.

'Actually,' he murmured, 'one would prefer one of one's own people.'

'A Brit? Who can pass for an Arab, right in the middle of them?'

'That's what we need. I'm afraid we doubt if there is one.'

It must have been the wine, or the port. Terry Martin was not used to Meursault and port with his lunch. Later he would willingly have bitten off his own tongue if he could have turned the clock back a few seconds. But he spoke and then it was too late.

'I know one. My brother Mike. He's a major in the

64

SAS. He can pass for an Arab.'

Laing hid the stab of excitement that jumped inside him as he removed the toothpick and the offending morsel of sole.

'Can he now?' he murmured. 'Can he now?'

CHAPTER THREE

Steve Laing returned to Century House by cab in a spirit of some surprise and elation. He had arranged the lunch with the academic Arabist in the hopes of recruiting him for another task, which he still had in mind, and had only raised the matter of Kuwait as a conversational ploy.

Years of practice had taught him to start with a question or a request that the target could not fulfil, then move on to the real matter at hand. The theory was that the expert, stumped by the first request, would be more amenable for his own self-respect to agreeing to the second.

Dr Martin's surprise revelation happened to answer a query that had already been raised during a high-level conference at Century the previous day. At the time it had been generally regarded as a no-hope wish. But if young Dr Martin was right ... A brother who spoke Arabic even better than he ... And who was already in the Special Air Service Regiment and therefore accustomed to the covert life ... Interesting, very interesting.

On arrival at Century, Laing marched straight in on his immediate superior, the Controller Middle East. After an hour together they both went upstairs to see one of the two Deputy Chiefs.

The Secret Intelligence Service, or SIS, also popularly if inaccurately known as M.I.6, remains even in the days of supposed 'open' government a shadowy organization that guards its secrecy. Only in recent years has a British government formally admitted that it exists at all. And it was as late as 1991 that the same government publicly named its boss, a move regarded by most insiders as a foolish and short-sighted one that served no purpose other than to force that unfortunate gentleman to the unwelcome novelty of needing bodyguards, paid for at public expense. Such are the futilities of political correctness.

The staff of the SIS are listed in no manual, but appear if at all as civil servants on the lists of a variety of ministries, mainly the Foreign Office under whose auspices the Service comes. The Budget appears in no accounts, being squirrelled away in the budgets of a dozen different ministries.

Even its shabby headquarters was for years supposed to be a state secret, until it became plain that any London cab driver, asked to take a passenger to Century House, would reply, 'Oh, you mean the Spook House, guv?' At this point it was admitted that if London's cabbies knew where it was, the KGB might have worked it out.

Although much less famous than the CIA, infinitely smaller and more meanly funded, the 'Firm' has earned a solid reputation among friend and foe for the quality of its 'product' (secretly gathered Intelligence). Among the world's major Intelligence agencies, only the Israeli Mossad is smaller and even more shadowy.

The man heading the SIS is known quite officially as the Chief and *never*, despite endless misnomers in the Press, as the Director-General. It is the sister organization, M.I.5 or the Security Service, responsible for Counter-Intelligence within the United Kingdom's borders, that has a Director-General.

In-house, the Chief is known as 'C' which ought to stand for Chief but does not. The first-ever chief was Admiral Sir Mansfield Cummings, and the 'C' comes from that long-dead gentleman's last name.

Under the Chief come two Deputy Chiefs and under them five Assistant Chiefs. These men rule the five main departments: Operations (who gather the covert information); Intelligence (who analyse it into a hopefully meaningful picture); Technical (responsible for false papers, mini-cameras, secret writing, ultra-compact communications and all the other bits of metal needed to do something illegal and get away with it in an unfriendly world); Admin. (covering salaries, pensions, staff lists, budget accountancy, Legal Office, Central Registry, etc.); and Counter-Intelligence (which tries to keep the Service clean of hostile penetration by vetting and checking).

Under Ops. come the Controllers, who handle the globe's various divisions—Western Hemisphere, Soviet Bloc, Africa, Europe, Mid-East and Australasia—with a side-office for Liaison, which has the ticklish task of trying to co-operate with 'friendly' agencies.

To be frank, it is not quite that tidy (nothing British is ever *quite* that tidy), but they seem to muddle through.

That August of 1990 the focus of attention was Mid-East, and particularly Iraq Desk, upon whom the entire political and bureaucratic world of

Westminster and Whitehall seemed to have descended like a noisy and unwelcome fan club.

The Deputy Chief listened carefully to what the Controller Mid-East and the Director Ops. for that region had to say and nodded several times. It was, he thought, or might be, an interesting option.

It was not that no information was coming out of Kuwait. In the first forty-eight hours, before the Iraqis closed down the international telephone lines, every British company with an office in Kuwait had been on the phone, the telex or the fax machines to their local man. The Kuwaiti Embassy had been bending the ear of the Foreign Office with the first horror stories and demanding instant liberation.

The problem was, virtually none of the information was of the sort the Chief could present to the Cabinet as utterly reliable. In the aftermath of the invasion Kuwait was one giant 'bugger's muddle' as the Foreign Secretary had so mordantly phrased it six hours earlier.

Even the British Embassy staff were now firmly locked in their compound on the edge of the Gulf, almost in the shadow of the needle-pointed Kuwait Towers, trying to contact by telephone those British citizens on a grossly inadequate list to see if they were all right. The received wisdom from these frightened businessmen and engineers was that they could occasionally hear gunfire—'Tell me something I *don't* know' was the reaction at Century to such gems of Intelligence.

Now a man in on the ground, and a trained deep-penetration, covert-ops. man who could pass for an Arab ... that could be very interesting. Apart from some rock-hard real information as to what the hell was going on in there, a chance existed to show the

68

politicians that something was actually being done and to cause William Webster over at the CIA to choke on his after-dinner mints.

The Deputy Chief had no illusions about Margaret Thatcher's almost kittenish esteem (mutual) for the SAS since that afternoon in May 1980 when they had blown away those terrorists at the Iranian Embassy in London, and she had spent the evening with the team at the Albany Street barracks drinking whisky and listening to their tales of derring-do.

'I think,' the Deputy Chief said at last, 'I'd better have a chat with the DSF.'

Officially the Special Air Service Regiment has nothing to do with the SIS. The chains of command are quite different. The active-service 22nd SAS (as opposed to the part-time 23rd SAS) is based at a barracks called simply 'Stirling Lines' outside the county town of Hereford in the west of England. Its commanding officer reports to the Director Special Forces, whose office is in a sprawl of buildings in west London. The actual office is at the top of a once-elegant pillared building covered in a seemingly perpetual skin of scaffolding, and part of a rabbit warren of small rooms whose lack of splendour belies the importance of the operations planned there.

The DSF comes under the Director of Military Operations (a general) who reports to the Chief of General Staff (an even higher general) and the General Staff comes under the Ministry of Defence.

But the 'Special' in the title of the SAS is there for a reason. Ever since it was founded in the Western Desert in 1941 by David Stirling the SAS has operated covertly. Its tasks have always included deep penetration, with a view to lying up and observing enemy movements; deep penetration with

69

a view to sabotage, assassination and general mayhem; terrorist elimination; hostage recovery; close protection, a euphemism for bodyguarding the high and mighty; and foreign training missions.

Like members of any élite unit, the officers and men of the SAS tend to live quietly within their own society, unable to discuss their work with outsiders, refusing to be photographed and rarely emerging from the shadows.

So because the lifestyles of the members of the two secret societies had much in common, the SIS and the SAS knew each other at least by sight and had frequently co-operated in the past, either on joint operations or with the Intelligence people 'borrowing' a specialist soldier from the Regiment for a particular task. It was something of this kidney that the Deputy Chief of the SIS (who had cleared his visit with Sir Colin, the Chief) had in mind when he took a glass of single-malt whisky from Brigadier J. P. Lovat in the covert London HQ that evening as the sun went down.

The unwitting object of such discussion and private musing in London and Kuwait was at that moment poring over a map in another barracks many miles away. For the past eight weeks he and his team of twelve instructors had been living in a section of the quarters assigned to the private bodyguard unit of Sheikh Zayed bin Sultan of Abu Dhabi.

It was a task the Regiment had undertaken many times before. All up and down the western shore of the Gulf, from the Sultanate of Oman in the south to Bahrain in the north, lies a chain of sultanates, emirates and sheikhdoms in and out of which the British have been pottering for centuries. The Trucial States, now the United Arab Emirates, were so called

70

because Britain once signed a truce with their rulers to protect them with the Royal Navy against marauding pirates in exchange for trading privileges. The relationship continues and many of these rulers have princely guard units trained in the finer points of close protection by visiting SAS instructor teams. A fee is paid, of course, but to the Ministry of Defence in London.

Major Mike Martin had a large map of the Gulf and most of the Middle East spread out over the mess hall table and was studying it, surrounded by several of his men. At thirty-seven he was not the oldest man in the room; two of his sergeants topped forty, tough, wiry and very fit soldiers whom a man twenty years their junior would have been extremely foolish to take on.

'Anything in it for us, Boss?' asked one of the sergeants.

As in all small, tight units, first names are widely used in the Regiment, but officers are normally called Boss by Other Ranks.

'I don't know,' said Martin. 'Saddam Hussein has got himself into Kuwait. Question is: will he get out of his own accord? If not, will the UN authorize a force to go in and throw him out? If yes, I would think there ought to be something in there for us to do.'

'Good,' said the sergeant with satisfaction and there were nods from the other six round the table. It had been too long, so far as they were concerned, since they had been on a real, high-adrenalin combat operation.

There are four basic disciplines in the Regiment and each recruit must master one of them. There are the Free-fallers, specializing in high-altitude parachute drops, the Mountainmen whose preferred

71

terrain is rock faces and the high peaks, the Armoured Scout Car men who drive and operate stripped-down, heavily armoured long-base Land-Rovers over open terrain, and the Amphibians, skilled in canoes, silent-running inflatables and sub-aqua work.

In his team of twelve, Martin had four Free-fallers including himself, four Scout Car men teaching the Abu Dhabis the principles of fast attack and counter-attack over desert ground, and, because Abu Dhabi lies by the Gulf, four sub-aqua instructors.

Apart from their own speciality, SAS men must have a good working knowledge of the other disciplines, so that interchangeability is common. They have to master more besides—radio, first aid, languages.

The basic combat unit consists of only four men. If one is ever out of action, his tasks will be quickly shared among the surviving three, whether they be operating the radio or as unit medic.

They pride themselves on a far higher educational level than any other unit in the Army, and because they travel the world languages are a 'must'. Every soldier must learn one, apart from English. For years Russian was a favourite, now going out of fashion since the end of the Cold War. Malay is very useful in the Far East where the Regiment for years fought in Borneo. Spanish is on the increase since the covert operations in Colombia against the cocaine lords of Medellín and Cali. French is learnt—just in case.

And because the Regiment had spent years assisting Sultan Qaboos of Oman in his war with Communist infiltrators from South Yemen into the interior of Dhofar, plus other training missions up and down the Gulf and in Saudi Arabia, many SAS men speak passable Arabic. The sergeant who had asked for some action was one of them, but he had to admit: 'The Boss is bloody amazing. I've never heard anyone like him. He even looks the part.'

Mike Martin straightened and ran a nut-brown hand through jet-black hair.

'Time to turn in.'

It was just after ten. They would be up before dawn for the usual ten-mile run with their charges before the sun became too hot. It was a chore the Abu Dhabis loathed but their sheikh insisted. If these strange soldiers from England said it was good for them, it was good for them. Besides, he was paying for it and he wanted value for his money.

Major Martin retired to his own quarters and slept quickly and deeply. The sergeant was right; he *did* look the part. His men often wondered if he got his olive skin, dark eyes and deep black hair from some Mediterranean forebears. He never told them, but they were wrong.

The maternal grandfather of both Martin boys had been a British tea-planter at Darjeeling in India. As kids they had seen pictures of him, tall, pink-faced, blond-moustached, pipe in mouth, gun in hand, standing over a shot tiger. Very much the pukka sahib, the Englishman of the Indian Raj.

Then in 1928 Terence Granger had done the unthinkable; he had fallen in love with and insisted on marrying an Indian girl. That she was gentle and beautiful was not the point. It was simply not done. The tea company did not fire him—that would have brought it out in the open. They sent him into internal exile (that was what they actually called it) to an isolated plantation in faraway Assam.

If it was supposed to be a punishment, it did not

73

work. Granger and his new bride, the former Miss Indira Bohse, loved it there—the wild, ravined countryside teeming with game and tigers, the deep green tea slopes, the climate, the people. And there Susan was born in 1930. They raised her there, an Anglo-Indian girl with Indian playmates.

By 1943 war had rolled towards India, with the Japanese advancing through Burma to the border. Granger was old enough not to have to volunteer but he insisted, and after basic training at Delhi was posted as a major to the Assam Rifles. All British cadets were promoted straight to major; they were not supposed to serve *under* an Indian officer, but Indians could make lieutenant or captain.

In 1945 he died in the crossing of the Irrawaddy. His body was never brought back; it vanished in those drenched Burmese jungles, one of tens of thousands who had seen some of the most vicious hand-to-hand fighting of the war.

With a small company pension his widow retreated back into her own culture. Two years later more trouble came. India was being partitioned in 1947. The British were leaving. Ali Jinnah insisted on his Muslim Pakistan in the north, Pandit Nehru settled for mainly Hindu India in the south. As waves of refugees of the two religions rolled north and south violent fighting broke out. Over a million died. Mrs Granger, fearful for her daughter's safety, sent her to complete her education with her late father's younger brother, a very proper architect of Haslemere, Surrey. Six months later the mother died in the rioting.

At seventeen Susan Granger came to England, the land of her fathers, that she had never seen. She spent one year at a girl's school near Haslemere and then two years as a trainee nurse at Farnham General Hospital, followed by one more as a secretary to a Farnham solicitor.

At twenty-one, the youngest permitted age, she applied to be a stewardess with the British Overseas Airways Corporation. She trained with the other girls at the BOAC school, the old converted St Mary's Convent at Heston, just outside London. Her nursing training was the clincher, and her looks and manner an added plus.

At twenty-one she was beautiful, with tumbling chestnut hair, hazel eyes and skin like a European with a permanent golden suntan. On graduation she was assigned to Number One Line, London to India, an obvious choice for a girl speaking fluent Hindi.

It was a long, long trip in those days aboard the four-propeller Argonaut. The route was London–Rome–Cairo–Basra–Bahrain–Karachi and Bombay. Then on to Delhi, Calcutta, Colombo, Rangoon, Bangkok and finally Singapore, Hong Kong and Tokyo. Of course, one crew could not do it all and the first crew stop-over was Basra in the south of Iraq, where the crew 'slipped' while another took over.

It was there in 1951, over a drink at the Port Club, that she met a rather shy young accountant with the Iraq Petroleum Company, then owned and run by the British. His name was Nigel Martin and he asked her to dinner. She had been warned about wolves—among the passengers, the crew and during the stop-overs. But he seemed nice, so she accepted. When he took her back to the BOAC station house where the stewardesses were quartered, he held out his hand. She was so surprised, she shook it.

Then she lay awake in the awful heat wondering

what it would be like to kiss Nigel Martin.

On her next stage through Basra he was there again. Only after they were married did he admit he was so smitten that he found out through the BOAC Station Officer Alex Reid when she was due again. That autumn of 1951 they played tennis, swam at the Port Club and walked through the bazaars of Basra. At his suggestion she took leave and came with him to Baghdad where he was based.

She soon realized it was a place she could settle down. The swarming throngs of brightly-coloured robes, the sights and smells of the street, the cooking meats by the edge of the Tigris, the myriad little shops selling herbs and spices, gold and jewels—all reminded her of her native India. When he proposed to her she accepted at once.

They married in 1952 at St George's Cathedral, the Anglican church off Haifa Street, and although she had no-one on her side of the church, many people came from the IPC and the embassy to fill both rows of pews.

It was a good time to live in Baghdad. Life was slow and easy, the boy-king Faisal was on the throne with Nuri-as-Said running the country and the overwhelming foreign influence was British. This was partly because of the powerful contribution of the IPC to the economy, partly because most of the army officers were British-taught, but mainly because the entire upper class had been potty-trained by starched English nannies, which always leaves a lasting impression.

In time the Martins had two sons, born in 1953 and 1955. Christened Michael and Terry they were as unalike as chalk and cheese. In Michael the genes of Miss Indira Bohse came through; he was black-haired, dark-eyed and olive-skinned; wags from the British community said he looked more like an Arab. Terry, two years later, took after his father, short, stocky, pink-skinned and ginger-haired.

At three in the morning Major Martin was shaken awake by an orderly.

'There is a message, sayidi.'

It was quite a simple message but the urgency coding was 'blitz' and the sign-off meant it came personally from the Director of Special Forces. It required no answer. It just ordered him back to London on the first available plane.

He handed over his duties to the SAS captain who was on his first tour with the Regiment and was his second-in-command for the training assignment and raced to the airport in civilian clothes.

The 2.55 a.m. for London should have left. Over a hundred passengers snored or grumbled on board as the stewardess brightly announced that the 'operational reason' for the ninety-minute delay would soon be sorted out.

When the doors opened again to admit a single, lean man in jeans, desert boots, shirt and bomber jacket with a tote bag over one shoulder, a number of those still awake glared at him. The man was shown to an empty seat in Club Class, made himself comfortable and within minutes of take-off tilted back his seat and fell fast asleep.

A businessman next to him who had dined copiously and with much illicit liquid refreshment, then waited two hours in the airport and two more on the plane, fed himself another antacid tablet and glowered at the relaxed, sleeping figure beside him.

'Bloody Arab,' he muttered and tried in vain to sleep.

Dawn came over the Gulf two hours later but the British Airways jet was racing towards the north-west, landing at Heathrow just before 10 a.m. local time. Mike Martin came out of the Customs Hall among the first because he had no baggage in the aircraft hold. There was no-one to meet him; he knew there would not be. He also knew where to go. He took a taxi.

*   *   *

It was not even dawn in Washington but the first indications of the coming sun pinked the distant hills of Prince Georges County where the Patuxent River flows down to join the Chesapeake. On the sixth and top floor of the big, oblong building among the cluster that forms the headquarters of the CIA and is known simply as Langley, the lights still burned.

Judge William Webster, the Director of Central Intelligence, rubbed fingertips over tired eyes, rose and walked to the picture windows. The swathe of silver birches that masked his view of the Potomac when they were in full leaf as they were now still lay shrouded in darkness. Within an hour the rising sun would bring them back to pale green. It had been another sleepless night. Since the invasion of Kuwait he had been catnapping between calls from the President, the National Security Council, the State Department and, so it seemed, just about anyone else who had his number.

Behind him, as tired as he, sat Bill Stewart, his Deputy Director (Operations), and Chip Barber, Head of Mid-East Division.

'So that's about it?' asked the DCI as if asking the question again might produce a better answer.

But there was no change. The position was that the President, the NSC and State were all clamouring for deep-mined hyper-secret Intelligence from inside the heart of Baghdad, from the innermost councils of Saddam Hussein himself. Was he going to stay in Kuwait? Would he pull out under threat of the United Nations Resolutions that were rolling out of the Security Council? Would he buckle in front of the oil embargo and the trade blockade? What was he thinking? What was he planning? Damn it, where was he at all?

And the Agency did not know. They had a head of station in Baghdad of course. But the man had been frozen out for weeks past. The Agency man was known to that bastard Rahmani who headed Iraqi Counter-Intelligence and it was now plain that what had been fed to the Head of Station for weeks had been all bullcrap. His best 'sources' were apparently working for Rahmani and had been telling him trash.

Of course, they had the pictures, enough pictures to drown in. The satellites, KH-11 and KH-12, were rolling over Iraq every few minutes taking happy snaps of everything in the entire country. Analysts were working round the clock identifying what *might* be a poison gas factory, what might be a nuclear facility—or might be what it claimed to be, a bicycle workshop.

Fine. The analysts of the National Reconnaissance Office, a part-CIA and part-Air Force enterprise, along with the boffins at ENPIC, the National Photographic Interpretation Centre, were putting together a picture that one day would be complete. This here is a major command post, this is a SAM missile site, this is a fighter base. Good, because the pictures tell us so. And one day, maybe, they would all have to be bombed back to the stone age. But what *else* had he got? Hidden away, stashed deep underground?

Now years of neglect of Iraq were bearing fruit. The men slumped in their chairs behind him were old-time spooks who had made their bones on the Berlin Wall when the concrete was not even dry. They went back a long way, before electronic gizmos took over the business of Intelligence-gathering.

And they had told him that the cameras of the NRO and the listening ears of the National Security Agency over at Fort Meade could not reveal plans, they could not spy out intentions, they could not go inside a dictator's head.

So the NRO was taking pictures and the ears of Fort Meade were listening and taping every word on every telephone call and radio message into, out of and inside Iraq. And still he had no answers.

The same Administration, the same Capitol Hill that had been so mesmerized with electronic gadgetry that they had spent billions of dollars developing and sending up every last gizmo that the ingenious mind of Man could devise, were now clamouring that they wanted answers the gizmos did not seem to be giving them.

And the men behind him were saying that elint, the name for electronic Intelligence, was a back-up and a supplement to humint, or human Intelligence-gathering, but not a substitute for it. Which was nice to know, but no solution to his problem.

Which was that the White House was demanding answers that could only be given with authority by a source, an asset, a spook, a spy, a traitor, whatever, placed high inside the Iraqi hierarchy. *Which he did not have.*

'You've asked Century House?'

'Yes, Director. Same as us.'

'I'm going to Tel Aviv in two days,' said Chip Barber. 'I'll be seeing Yaacov Dror. Shall I ask him?'

The DCI nodded. General Yaacov 'Kobi' Dror was the Head of the Mossad, most uncooperative of all the 'friendly' agencies. The DCI was still smarting over the case of Jonathan Pollard, run by the Mossad right inside America against the United States. Some friends. He hated to ask Mossad for favours.

'Lean on him, Chip. We are not messing around here. If he has a source inside Baghdad, we want it. We need that product. Meanwhile I'd better go back to the White House and face Scowcroft again.'

On that unhelpful note the meeting ended.

* * *

The four men who waited at the SAS London HQ that morning of 5 August had been busy most of the night.

The Director of Special Forces, Brigadier Lovat, had been on the phone for most of it, allowing himself a two-hour catnap in his chair between 2 and 4 a.m. Like so many combat soldiers he had long developed the knack of grabbing a few hours' 'kip' whenever and wherever the situation permitted. One never knew how long it might be until the next chance to recharge the batteries occurred. Before dawn he had washed and shaved and was ready to go on for another day running on all cylinders.

It was his call to a contact high in British Airways at midnight (London Time) that had held the airliner on the ground at Abu Dhabi. When the British establishment wants to move fast and cut the paperwork, knowing a 'chap' in the right place can prove extremely useful. The British Airways executive, roused at his home, did not ask why he should hold an airliner 3,000 miles away until an extra passenger could board it. He knew Lovat because they were members of the Special Forces Club in Herbert Crescent, knew roughly what he did and fulfilled the favour without asking why.

At the breakfast hour the orderly sergeant had checked with Heathrow that the Abu Dhabi flight had caught up a third of its ninety-minute delay and would land about ten. The major should be at the barracks close to 11 a.m.

A motor-cycle despatch rider had rushed up a certain personal career file from Browning Barracks, headquarters of the Parachute Regiment at Aldershot. The regimental adjutant had pulled it out of Records just after midnight. It was the file that covered Mike Martin's career in the Paras from the day he presented himself as an eighteen-year-old schoolboy and covered all the nineteen years he had been a professional soldier, except the two long periods he had spent on transfer to the SAS Regiment.

The commanding officer of 22nd SAS, Colonel Bruce Craig, another Scot, had driven through the night from Hereford, bringing with him the file that covered those two periods. He strode in just before dawn.

'Morning, JP. What's the flap?'

They knew each other well. Lovat, always known as JP or Jaypee, had been the man in command of the squad that had retaken the Iranian Embassy from the terrorists ten years earlier, and Craig had been a troop commander under him at the time. They went

82

back a long way.

'Century wants to put a man into Kuwait,' he said. That seemed to be enough. Long speeches were not his passion.

'One of ours? Martin?' The colonel tossed down the file he had brought.

'Looks like it. I've called him back from Abu Dhabi.'

'Well, fuck them. You going to go along with it?'

Mike Martin was one of Craig's officers and they, too, went back a long way. He did not like his men being 'pinched' from under his nose by Century House. The DSF shrugged.

'May have to. If he fits. If they feel like it, they'll probably go very high.'

Craig grunted and took a strong black coffee from the orderly sergeant, whom he greeted as Sid—they had fought in Dhofar together. When it came to politics, the colonel knew the score. The SIS might act diffident, but when they wanted to pull strings they could go as high as they liked. Both soldiers knew Mrs Margaret Thatcher quite well and were keen admirers; they also knew that like Churchill she had a penchant for 'action this day'. Century House would probably win on this one, if they wanted to. The Regiment would have to co-operate, even though Century would have the overall control under the guise of a 'joint mission'.

The two men from Century arrived just after the colonel and they were all introduced. The senior man was Steve Laing. He had brought with him Simon Paxman, Head of Iraq Desk. They were seated in a waiting room, given coffee and offered the two c.v. files to read. Both men buried themselves in the background of Mike Martin from the age of eighteen onwards. The previous evening Paxman had spent four hours with the younger brother learning about the family background and upbringing in Baghdad and Haileybury.

Martin had written a personal letter to the Paras during his last term at school in the summer of 1971 and been offered an interview that September at the Depot in Aldershot, close to the old parked Dakota out of which men of the British Paras had once dropped to try and take the bridge at Arnhem.

He was regarded by his school (the Paras always checked) as a moderate scholar but a superb athlete. That suited the Paras just fine. The boy was accepted and began training the same month, a gruelling twenty-two weeks that brought the survivors of the course to April 1972.

There were four weeks of square-bashing, basic weapons handling, basic fieldcraft and physical fitness; then two more of the same plus First Aid, signals and study of precautions against NBC (nuclear, bacteriological and chemical warfare).

The seventh week was for more fitness training, getting harder all the time, but not as bad as weeks eight and nine—endurance marches through the Brecon Range in Wales where strong and fit men have died of exposure, hypothermia and exhaustion.

Week ten saw the course at Hythe, Kent, for shooting on the range, where Martin, just turned nineteen, rated as a marksman. Weeks eleven and twelve were 'test' weeks carried out in open country near Aldershot—just running up and down sandy hills carrying tree trunks in the mud, rain and freezing hail of midwinter.

'Test week?' muttered Paxman, turning the page. 'What the hell has the rest been?'

After test week the young men got their coveted red beret and paratrooper smocks before three more weeks in the Brecons for defence exercise, patrolling and 'live firing' exercise. By then (late January 1972) the Brecons were utterly bleak and freezing. The men slept rough and wet without fires.

Weeks sixteen to nineteen were for the basic parachute course at RAF Abingdon, where a few more dropped out, and not just from the aircraft. At the end came 'wings parade' when the paratroopers' wings were pinned on. Though the report did not say so, many beers were sunk that night in the old 101 Club.

After two more weeks devoted to a field exercise called 'last fence' and some polishing-up of parade-ground drill skills, week twenty-two saw Pass-out Parade with proud parents at last allowed to see the spotty youths who had left them six months earlier.

Private Mike Martin had long been earmarked as a POM, potential officer material, and in May 1972 went to the Royal Military Academy, Sandhurst, joining the first of the new one-year Standard Military Courses which were then replacing the old-style two-year stints.

The result was that the Pass-out Parade in the spring of 1973 was the biggest ever held at Sandhurst with 490 officer cadets on parade as the remnants of the older Courses 51 and 52 joined the one-year men of the first SMC. The salute was taken by General Sir Michael Carver, later to become Field Marshal Lord Carver, Chief of Defence Staff.

The new Lieutenant Martin went straight to Hythe to take over a platoon in preparatory training for Northern Ireland, and commanded the platoon during twelve miserable weeks crouching in an observation post called Flax Mill which covered the ultra-Republican enclave of Ardoyne, Belfast. That summer, however, life was quiet at Flax because since Bloody Sunday of January 1972 the IRA tended to avoid the Paras like the plague.

Martin had been assigned to the Third Battalion, known as Three Para, and after Belfast returned to the Depot at Aldershot to command Recruit Platoon, putting newcomers through the same purgatory he had himself endured. In the summer of 1977 he returned to Three Para, by then based since the previous February at Osnabrück as part of the British Army of the Rhine.

It was another miserable time. Three Para was at Quebec Barracks, a tacky old former DP camp. The Paras were assigned to 'penguin mode' meaning that for three years out of every nine, or one tour out of three, they were off parachuting and used as ordinary lorry-borne infantry. All Paras hate penguin mode. Morale was low, fights broke out between the Paras and the Infantry, Martin had to punish men with whom he thoroughly sympathized. He stuck it for nearly a year, then in November 1977 he volunteered for transfer to the SAS.

Quite a proportion of the SAS come from the Paras, perhaps because the training has similarities, though the SAS claim theirs is harder. Martin's papers went through the Regiment's records office at Hereford where his fluent Arabic was noted, and he was invited to the selection course of the summer of 1978.

The SAS claims they take very fit men and then start work on them. Martin did the standard 'initial' selection course of six weeks, among other Paras, Marines and volunteers from infantry, armour,

86

artillery and even engineers. It is a simple course based on a simple precept.

On the first day a smiling instructor told them all: 'On this course, we don't try and train you. We try and kill you.'

They did too. Only 10 per cent pass the initial course into the SAS. It saves time later. Martin passed. Then came continuation training, jungle training in Belize and one extra month back in England devoted to resistance to interrogation. 'Resistance' means trying to stay silent while some extremely unpleasant practices are inflicted. The good news is that both the Regiment and the volunteer have the right every hour to insist on an RTU—return to unit.

'They're mad,' said Paxman, throwing down the file and helping himself to another coffee. 'They're all bloody mad.'

Laing grunted. He was engrossed in the second file; it was the man's experience in Arabia that he needed for the mission he had in mind.

Martin had spent three years with the SAS on his first tour, with the rank of captain and role of troop commander. He had opted for 'A' Squadron, the free-fallers—the Squadrons are A, B, C and G— which was a natural choice for a man who had jumped while in the Paras with their high-altitude free-fall display team, the Red Devils.

If the Paras had no cause to use his Arabic, the Regiment did. In the three years 1979–81 inclusive he had served alongside the Sultan of Oman's forces in Western Dhofar, taught VIP protection in two Gulf emirates, taught the Saudi National Guard in Riyadh and lectured the private bodyguards of Sheikh Isa of Bahrain. There were notations after

87

these listings in his SAS file: that he had redeveloped a strong boyhood bond with Arab culture, that he spoke the language like no other officer in the Regiment, and that he had a habit of going for long walks in the desert when he wanted to think a problem through, impervious to the heat and the flies.

The record showed he returned to the Paras after his three-year secondment to the SAS in the winter of 1981 and found to his joy that the Paras were taking part in Operation Rocky Lance during January and February 1982 in, of all places, Oman. So he came back to the Jebel Akdar for that period, before taking leave in March. In April he was hastily recalled— Argentina had invaded the Falklands.

Although One Para remained behind in the UK, Two and Three went to the South Atlantic. They sailed on the liner *Canberra*, hastily converted for military troopship use, and went ashore at San Carlos Water. While Two Para shifted the Argentines out of Goose Green, the CO, Col. H. Jones, winning a posthumous Victoria Cross in the process, Three Para tabbed right across East Falkland in the sleet and rain towards Port Stanley.

'I thought they called it yomping,' remarked Laing to Sergeant Sid who was refilling his coffee cup. The sergeant pursed his lips. Bloody civilians.

'The Marines call it yomping, sir. The Paras and the Regiment call it tabbing.'

Either way, the words mean force-marching in foul conditions while carrying 120 pounds of gear.

Three Para headquartered themselves at a lonely farm called Estancia House and prepared for the last assault on Port Stanley, which meant first taking the heavily defended Mount Longdon. It was in that vicious night of 11–12 June that Captain Mike Martin collected his bullet.

It started as a silent night attack on the Argentine positions which turned very noisy when Corporal Milne stepped on a mine which blew his foot off. The Argentine machine-guns opened up, the flares lit the mountain like day and Three Para could either run back to cover or into the fire and take Longdon. They took Longdon, with twenty-three dead and over forty injured. One of these was Mike Martin, nursing a slug through one leg and giving vent to a hissed stream of foul invective, fortunately in Arabic.

After most of the day on the mountainside, keeping eight shivering Argentine prisoners covered and trying not to faint, he was brought out to the advanced dressing station at Ajax Bay, patched up and helicoptered to the hospital ship *Uganda*. There he found himself in a bunk next to an Argentine lieutenant. During the cruise to Montevideo they became firm friends and still corresponded.

The *Uganda* stopped at the Uruguayan capital to let off her Argentines and Martin was among those fit enough to fly home by civilian airliner to Brize Norton. The Paras then gave him three weeks at Headley Court, Leatherhead, for convalescence.

That was where he met the nurse, Lucinda, who was to become his wife after a brief courtship. Perhaps she liked the glamour, but she was mistaken. They set up home in a cottage near Chobham, convenient for her job at Leatherhead and his at Aldershot. But after three years, having actually seen him for four and a half months, Lucinda quite properly put to him a choice: you can have the Paras and your bloody desert, or you can have me. He thought it over and chose the desert.

She was quite right to go. In the autumn of 1982 he had studied for Staff College, gateway to senior rank and a nice desk, perhaps in the Ministry. In February 1983 he fluffed the exam.

'He did it deliberately,' said Paxman, 'his CO's note here says he could have swanned through if he'd wanted.'

'I know,' said Laing. 'I've read it. The man's ... unusual.'

In the summer of 1983 Martin was posted to the job of British Staff Officer assigned to the Sultan of Oman's Land Forces HQ at Muscat and went straight into two more years secondment, keeping his Para badge but commanding the Northern Frontier Regiment, Muscat. He was promoted major in Oman in the summer of 1986.

Officers who have served one tour in the SAS can come back for a second, but only on invitation. Hardly had he landed back in England in the winter of 1987 when his uncontested divorce went through than the invitation came from Hereford. He went back as a squadron commander in January 1988, serving with Northern Flank (Norway), then with the Sultan of Brunei and six months with the internal security team at the Lines at Hereford. In June 1990 he was sent with his team of instructors to Abu Dhabi.

Sergeant Sid knocked and poked his head round the door.

'The brigadier asks if you'd care to rejoin him. Major Martin is on his way up.'

When Martin walked in Laing noted the sun-darkened face, hair and eyes, and shot a glance at Paxman. One down, two to go. He looks the part. Now, will he do it and can he speak Arabic like they say?

JP walked forward and took Martin's hand in his bone-crushing grip.

'Good to see you back, Mike.'

'Thank you, sir.' He shook hands with Colonel Craig.

'Let me introduce these two gentlemen,' said the DSF. 'Mr Laing and Mr Paxman, both from Century. They have a ... er ... proposition they would like to put. Gentlemen, fire ahead. Would you prefer to have Major Martin in private?'

'Oh, no, please,' said Laing hastily. 'The Chief is hoping that if anything results from this meeting it will definitely be a joint operation.'

Nice touch, thought JP, mentioning Sir Colin. Just to show how much clout these bastards intend to exercise if they have to.

All five sat down. Laing talked, explaining the political background, the uncertainty as to whether Saddam Hussein would get out of Kuwait quickly, slowly or not at all unless thrown out. But the political analysis was that Iraq would first strip Kuwait of every valuable, then stick around demanding concessions the United Nations was simply not in a mood to concede. One might be looking at months and months.

Britain needed to know what was going on inside Kuwait—not gossip and rumour, nor the lurid stories flying about the media, but rock-hard information. About the British citizens still stuck there, about the occupation forces and, if force had eventually to be used, whether a Kuwaiti resistance could be useful in pinning down more and more of Saddam's otherwise frontline troops.

Martin nodded and listened, asked a few pertinent

questions, but otherwise stayed silent. The two senior officers gazed out of the window. Laing concluded just after twelve.

'That's about it, Major. I don't expect an answer immediately, right now, but time is of the essence.'

'Do you mind if we have a few words with our colleague in private?' asked JP.

'Of course not. Look, Simon and I will trot back to the office. You have my desk number. Perhaps you'd let me know this afternoon?'

Sergeant Sid showed the two civilians out and escorted them down to the street where he watched them hail a taxi. Then he climbed back to his eyrie under the roof beams behind the scaffolding.

JP went to a small fridge and extracted three cold beers. When the tabs were off all three men took a swig.

'Look, Mike, you know what's what. That's what they want. If you think it's crazy we'll go along with that.'

'Absolutely,' said Craig. 'In the Regiment you get no black marks for saying no. This is their idea, not ours.'

'But if you want to go with them,' said JP, 'walk through the door, so to speak, then you're with them till you come back. We'll be involved, of course, they probably can't run it without us, but you'll be under them. They'll be in charge. When it's over, you come back to us as if you'd been on leave.'

Martin knew how it worked. He'd heard of others who had worked for Century. You just ceased to exist for the Regiment until you came back. Then they all said, 'Good to see you again,' and never mentioned or asked where you had been.

'I'll take it,' he said. Colonel Craig rose. He had to

get back to Hereford. He held out his hand.

'Good luck, Mike.'

'By the way,' said the brigadier, 'you have a lunch date. Just down the street. Century set it up.'

He handed Martin a slip of paper, bade him farewell and Mike Martin went back down the stairs to the street. The paper said his lunch was at a small restaurant four hundred yards away and his host was Mr Wafic Al-Khouri.

Apart from M.I.5 and M.I.6 the third major arm of British Intelligence is the Government Communications Headquarters, or GCHQ, a complex of buildings in a guarded compound outside the staid town of Cheltenham in Gloucestershire.

GCHQ is the British version of America's National Security Agency with which it co-operates very closely—the listeners whose antennae eavesdrop on almost every radio broadcast and telephone conversation in the world if they so wish.

Through its co-operation with GCHQ the American NSA has a number of outstations inside Britain, apart from its other listening posts all over the world, and GCHQ has its own overseas stations, notably a very large one on British sovereign territory at Akrotiri in Cyprus.

The Akrotiri station, being closer to the scene, monitors the Middle East, but passes all its product back to Cheltenham for analysis. Among the analysts are a number of experts who, although Arabs by birth, are cleared to a very high level. Such a one was Mr Al-Khouri who had long before elected to settle in Britain, naturalize and marry an English wife.

This genial former Jordanian diplomat now worked as a senior analyst in the Arabic Service of

GCHQ where, even though there are many British scholars of Arabic, he could often read a meaning behind the meaning of a taped speech by a leader in the Arab world. It was he who, at the request of Century, was waiting for Mike Martin at the restaurant.

They had a convivial lunch which lasted two hours, and spoke nothing but Arabic. When they parted, Martin left and strolled back towards the SAS building. There would be hours of briefings before he was ready to leave for Riyadh with a passport he knew Century would by then have ready, complete with visas in a false name.

Before he left the restaurant Mr Al-Khouri called a number from the wall phone by the men's room.

'No problem, Steve. He's perfect. In fact I don't think I've ever heard anyone like him. It's not scholar's Arabic, you know; it's even better, from your point of view. Street Arabic, every swear word, slang, piece of jargon ... no, not a trace of an accent ... yes, he can pass all right ... on just about any street in the Middle East. No, no, not at all, old chap. Glad to be of assistance.'

Thirty minutes later he had retrieved his car and was on the M4 heading back to Cheltenham. Before he entered the headquarters Mike Martin also made a call, to a number just off Gower Street. The man he was calling picked up the phone since it was in his office in SOAS where he was working over papers on an afternoon that called for no lectures.

'Hallo, Bro, it's me.'

The soldier had no need to introduce himself. Since they were at prep school together in Baghdad he had always called his younger brother Bro. There was a gasp at the other end of the line.

94

'Mike? Where the hell are you?'

'In London, in a phone booth.'

'I thought you were somewhere in the Gulf.'

'Got back this morning. Probably leave again tonight.'

'Look, Mike, don't go. It's all my fault . . . I should have kept my bloody mouth shut—'

His elder brother's deep laugh came down the line.

'I wondered why the buggers suddenly got interested in me. Take you to lunch, did they?'

'Yes, we were talking about something else. It just cropped up, sort of slipped out. Look, you don't have to go. Tell them I was mistaken—'

'Too late. Anyway, I've accepted.'

'Oh God—' In his office, surrounded by erudite tomes on medieval Mesopotamia, the younger man was almost in tears.

'Mike, look after yourself. I'll pray for you.'

Mike thought for a moment. Yes, Terry had always had a touch of religion. He probably would.

'You do that, Bro. See you when I get back.'

He hung up. Alone in his office the ginger-haired academic who hero-worshipped his soldier brother put his head in his hands.

When the British Airways 8.45 p.m. flight for Saudi Arabia lifted off from Heathrow that night, right on time, Mike Martin was on it with a fully visa-ed passport in another name, to be met just before dawn by Century's Head of Station at the Riyadh Embassy.

CHAPTER FOUR

Don Walker eased down on the brake pedal and the 1963 vintage Corvette Stingray paused for a moment at the main entrance to Seymour Johnson Air Force Base to let a couple of campers pass before emerging on to the highway.

It was hot. The August sun blasted down on the small North Carolina town of Goldsboro so that the tarmac seemed to shimmer like moving water up ahead. It was good to have the top down and feel the wind, warm though it was, running through his short blond hair.

He manoeuvred the classic sports car over which he lavished so much attention up through the slumbering town to Highway 70 then pulled on to Highway 13 for the north-east.

Don Walker, that hot summer of 1990, was twenty-nine years old, single, a fighter jockey and had just learnt that he was going to war. Well, maybe. Apparently it would depend on some weird Arab called Saddam Hussein.

That same morning the Wing Commander, Colonel (later General) Hal Hornburg, had laid it out; in three days, on 9 August, his squadron, the 336th 'Rocketeers' of the 9th Air Force of Tactical Air Command, was shipping out to the Arabian Gulf. The orders had come through from TAC command at Langley Air Force Base, Hampton, Virginia. So, it was on. The elation among the pilots had been ecstatic. What was the point of all those years of training if you never got to fire the goodies?

With three days to go there was a mass of work to

get through, and for him as Squadron Weapons Officer more than most. But he had begged for just twenty-four hours furlough to go and say goodbye to his folks and Lt.-Col. Steve Turner, Chief of Weapons, had told him if there was one tiny detail missing on 9 August when the F-15E Eagles rolled he, Turner, would personally kick ass. Then he had grinned and told Walker if he wanted to get back by sun-up he had better get moving.

So Walker was hammering up through Snow Hill and Greenville by nine that morning heading for the chain of islands east of Pamlico Sound. He was lucky his parents were not back in Tulsa, Oklahoma, or he could never have made it. Being August they were taking their annual vacation at the family beach house near Hatteras, a five-hour drive away from the base.

Don Walker knew he was a hot-shot pilot and he revelled in it. To be twenty-nine and to do the thing you love best in the world and to do it supremely well is a good feeling. He liked the base, he liked the guys and he adored the exhilaration and power of the McDonnell Douglas F-15 Strike Eagle that he flew, the ground-attack version of the 15C air superiority fighter. It was, he reckoned, the best piece of airplane in the whole US Air Force and the hell with what the men on the Fighting Falcons said. Only the Navy's F-18 Hornet might compare, or so they said, but he had never flown the Hornet and the Eagle was just fine by him.

At Bethel he turned due east for Columbia and Whalebone, which was where the highway turned into the island chain; with Kitty Hawk behind him to his left, he turned south towards Hatteras, where the road finally ran out and the sea was on all sides. He had had good vacations at Hatteras as a boy, going out to sea in the early dawn with his grandpa to take the bluefish, until the old man got sick and could not go any more.

Now his dad was retiring from the oil job in Tulsa maybe he and Mom would spend more time at the beach house and he could get down there more often. He was young enough not even to let the thought cross his mind that he might not come back from the Gulf, if there was a war.

Walker had graduated well out of high school in Tulsa at the age of eighteen with only one burning ambition—he wanted to fly. So far as he could recall, he had always wanted to fly. He spent four years at Oklahoma State, majoring in Aero-Engineering, graduating in June 1983. He had done his time with the Reserve Officer Training Corps and that fall he was inducted into the Air Force.

He underwent pilot training at Williams AFB, near Phoenix, Arizona, flying the T-33 and the T-38 and after eleven months, at wings parade, learnt he had passed as a distinguished graduate, fourth out of forty pupils. To his abiding joy the top five went to Fighter Lead-In School at Holloman AFB near Alamagordo, New Mexico. The rest of the course, he thought with the supreme arrogance of a young man destined to fly fighters, would be sent to become bomb-droppers or trash-carriers.

At Replacement Training Unit at Homestead, Florida, he finally quit the T-38 and converted to the F-4 Phantom, a big, powerful brute of a plane, but a real fighter at last.

Nine months at Homestead terminated with his first squadron posting, to Osan in South Korea, flying the Phantoms for a year. He was good, and he

98

knew it, and so apparently did the 'brass'. After Osan they sent him to USAF Fighter Weapon School at McConnell AFB, Wichita, Kansas.

Fighter Weapons run arguably what is the toughest course in the USAF. It marks out the high-fliers, career-wise. The technology of the new weapons is awe-inspiring. Graduates of McConnell have to understand every nut and bolt, every silicon chip and micro-circuit of the bewildering array of ordnance that a modern fighter plane can launch at its opponents, in the air or on the ground. Walker emerged again as a distinguished graduate, which meant every fighter squadron in the Air Force would be happy to have him.

The 336th at Goldsboro got him, in the summer of 1987, flying Phantoms for a year, followed by four months at Luke AFB, Phoenix, Arizona, converting to the Strike Eagle with which the Rocketeers were being re-equipped. He had been flying the Eagle for more than a year when Saddam Hussein invaded Kuwait.

The Stingray turned just before midday into the island chain; a few miles to his north stood the monument at Kitty Hawk where Orville and Wilbur Wright hauled their string-and-wire contraption into the air for a few yards to prove that Man really could fly in a powered airplane. If only they knew ...

Through Nags Head he followed the crawl of camper vans and trailers until they finally petered out and the road emptied past Cape Hatteras and on to the tip of the island. He ran the Stingray onto the driveway of his parents' timber-clad frame house just before one. He found them on the porch facing out over the calm blue sea.

Ray Walker caught sight of his son first and let out

a shout of pleasure. Maybelle came out from the kitchen where she had been preparing lunch and rushed into his embrace. His grandfather was sitting in his rocking-chair, looking at the sea. Don walked over and said: 'Hi, Grandpa, it's me, Don.'

The old man looked up and nodded and smiled; then he looked back at the ocean.

'He's not so good,' said Ray. 'Sometimes he knows you, sometimes he doesn't. Well, sit down and tell us the news. Hey, Maybelle, how's about a couple of beers for some thirsty guys?'

Over the beers Don told his parents he was off to the Gulf in five days. Maybelle's hand flew to her mouth; his father looked solemn.

'Well, I guess that's what it's for, the training and all,' he said at length.

Don swigged his beer and wondered not for the first time why parents always had to worry so much. His grandpa was staring at him, some kind of recognition in his rheumy eyes.

'Don's going off to war, Grandpa,' Ray Walker shouted at him. The old man's eyes flickered with life.

All his career he had been a marine, joining the corps straight out of school many, many years before. In 1941 he had kissed his wife goodbye and left her with her folks in Tulsa, along with their new-born baby Maybelle, to go to the Pacific. He had been with MacArthur on Corregidor and heard him say, 'I shall return,' and he had been twenty yards away from the general when MacArthur did return.

In between he had fought his way through a dozen miserable atolls in the Marianas and survived the hell of Iwo Jima. He carried seventeen scars on his body, all from combat, and was entitled to wear the ribbons of a Silver Star, two Bronze Stars and seven Purple

100

Hearts on his chest.

He had always refused to take a commission, happy to stay a master sergeant, for he knew where the real power lay. He had waded ashore at Inchon, Korea, and when they finally sent him to finish his corps days as an instructor at Parris Island his dress uniform carried more decorations than any other piece of cloth on the base. When they finally retired him after two deferments four generals showed up at his last parade, which was more than normally show up for another general.

The old man beckoned his grandson towards him. Don rose from the table and leant over.

'Watch out for them Japanese, boy,' the old man whispered, 'or they'll gitcha.'

Don put an arm round the old man's thin, rheumaticky shoulders.

'Don't you worry, Grandpa, they won't get anywhere near me.'

The old man nodded and seemed satisfied. He was eighty. It was not, finally, the Japanese or the Koreans who had got the immortal sergeant. It was old Mr Alzheimer. These days he spent most of his time in a pleasant dream with his daughter and son-in-law to look after him because he had nowhere else to go.

After lunch Don's parents told him about their tour of the Arabian Gulf, from which they had returned four days earlier. Maybelle went and fetched her pictures, which had just arrived back from the developer.

Don sat by his mother's side while she went through the pile, identifying the palaces and mosques, sea-fronts and markets of the chain of emirates and sheikhdoms she had visited.

'Now you be careful when you get down there,' she admonished her son. 'These are the kind of people you'll be up against. Dangerous people, just look at those eyes.'

Don Walker looked at the picture in her hand. The Bedouin stood between two sand dunes with the desert behind him, one trailing end of his keffiyeh tucked up and across his face. Only the dark eyes stared suspiciously out towards the camera.

'I'll be sure and keep a look-out for him,' he promised her. At that she seemed satisfied.

At five o'clock he reckoned he should head back to the base. His parents escorted him to the front of the house where his car was parked. Maybelle hugged her son and told him yet again to take care, and Ray embraced him and said they were proud of him. Don got into the car and reversed to swing into the road. He looked back.

From the house his grandfather, supported by two sticks, emerged onto the veranda. Slowly he placed the two sticks to one side and straightened up, forcing the rheumatism out of his old back and shoulders until they were square. Then he raised his hand, palm down, to the peak of his baseball cap and held it there, an old warrior saluting his grandson who was leaving for yet another war.

Don, from the car, brought up his hand in reply. Then he touched the accelerator and sped away. He never saw his grandfather again. The old man died in his sleep in late October.

*   *   *

It was already dark by then in London. Terry Martin had worked late, for although the undergraduates were away for the long summer vacation, he had lectures to prepare and because of the specialized vacation courses the school also ran he was kept quite busy, even through the summer months. But that evening he was forcing himself to find something to do, to keep his mind off his worry.

He knew where his brother had gone and in his mind's eye imagined the perils of trying to penetrate Iraqi-occupied Kuwait under deep cover.

At ten, while Don Walker was driving north from Hatteras, he left the school, bidding a courteous good night to the old janitor who locked up after him, and walked down Gower Street and St Martin's Lane towards Trafalgar Square. Perhaps, he thought, the bright lights would cheer him up. It was a warm and balmy evening.

At St Martin-in-the-Fields he noticed that the doors were open and the sound of hymns came from inside. He entered, found a pew near the rear and listened to the choir practice. But the choristers' clear voices only made his depression deeper. He thought back to the childhood he and Mike had shared thirty years earlier in Baghdad.

Nigel and Susan Martin had lived in a fine, roomy old house on two floors in Saadun, that smart district in the half of the city called Risafa. Mike had been born in 1953 and he two years later in 1955. His first recollection, when he was two, was of his dark-haired brother being dressed up to start his first day at Miss Saywell's kindergarten school. It had meant shirt and short trousers, with shoes and socks, the uniform of an English boy, and Mike had yelled in protest at being separated from his usual dish-dash, the white cotton robe that gave freedom of movement and kept the body cool.

Life had been easy and elegant for the British community in Baghdad in the Fifties. There was membership of the Mansour Club and of the Alwiya Club with its swimming-pool, tennis courts and squash court where officers of the Iraq Petroleum Company and the embassy would meet to play, swim, lounge or take cool drinks at the bar.

He could remember Fatima, their dada or nanny, a plump gentle girl from an up-country village whose wages were hoarded to make her a dowry so that she could marry a well set-up young man when she went back to her tribe. He used to play on the lawn with Fatima until they went to collect Mike from Miss Saywell's school.

Before each boy was three they were bilingual in English and Arabic, learning the latter from Fatima, or the gardener and the cook. Mike was especially quick at the language and as their father was a keen admirer of Arab culture the house was often full of his Iraqi friends.

Arabs tend to love small children anyway, showing far more patience with them than Europeans, and when Mike would dart about the lawn with his black hair and dark eyes, running free in the white dish-dash and chattering in Arabic, his father's friends would laugh with pleasure and shout: 'But, Nigel, he's more like one of us.'

There were outings at the weekends to watch the Royal Harithiya Hunt, a sort of English foxhunt transported to the Middle East, which hunted jackals under the mastership of the municipal architect Philip Hirst, with a 'mutton grab' of kuzi and vegetables for all afterwards. And there were wonderful picnics down the river on Pig Island set in the middle of the slow-moving Tigris which bisected the city.

After two years he had followed Mike to Miss Saywell's Kindergarten, but because he was so clever they went on together to the Foundation Prep School, run by Mr Hartley, at the same time.

He had been six and his brother eight when they turned up for their first day at Tasisiya, which contained some English boys but also Iraqi lads of upper-class parents.

By then there had already been one *coup d'état*. The boy-king and Nuri as-Said had been slaughtered and the neo-Communist General Kassem had taken absolute power. Though the two young English boys were unaware of it all, their parents and the English community were becoming worried. Favouring the Iraq Communist Party, Kassem was carrying out a vicious pogrom among the nationalist Ba'ath Party members, who in turn tried to assassinate the general. One of those in the group that tried and failed to machine-gun the dictator was a young firebrand called Saddam Hussein.

On his first day at prep school Terry had found himself surrounded by a group of Iraqi boys.

'He's a grub,' said one. Terry began to cry.

'I'm not a grub,' he sniffled.

'Yes, you are,' said the tallest boy. 'You're fat and white, with funny hair. You look like a grub. Grub, grub, grub.'

Then they all took up the chant. Mike appeared from behind him. Of course, they were all talking Arabic.

'Do not call my brother a grub,' he warned.

'Your brother? He doesn't look like your brother. But he does look like a grub.'

The use of the clenched fist is not part of Arab

105

culture. In fact it is alien to most cultures except in certain parts of the Far East. Even south of the Sahara the closed fist is not a traditional weapon. Black men from Africa and their descendants had to be taught to bunch the fist and throw a punch; then they became the best in the world at it. The closed-fist punch is very much a West Mediterranean and particularly Anglo-Saxon tradition.

Mike Martin's right-hand punch landed full on the jaw of the chief Terry-baiter and knocked him flat. The boy was not so much hurt as surprised. But no-one ever called Terry a grub again.

Surprisingly Mike and the Iraqi boy then became the best of friends. Throughout the prep-school years they were inseparable. The tall boy's name was Hassan Rahmani. The third member of Mike's gang was Abdelkarim Badri who had a younger brother, Osman, the same age as Terry. So Terry and Osman became friends as well, which was useful because Badri Senior was often to be found at their parents' house. He was a doctor and the Martins were happy to have him as their family physician.

It was he who helped Mike and Terry Martin through the usual childhood ailments of measles, mumps and chickenpox.

The older Badri boy, Terry recalled, was fascinated by poetry, his head always buried in a book of the English poets, and he won prizes for poetry reading even when up against the English boys. Osman, the younger one, was good at mathematics and said he wanted to be an engineer or an architect one day and build beautiful things. Terry sat in his pew that warm evening of 1990 and wondered what had happened to them all.

While they studied at Tasisiya things around them

in Iraq were changing. Four years after he came to power by murdering the King, Kassem himself was toppled and butchered by an army that had become worried by his flirtation with Communism. There followed eleven months of rule shared between the Army and the Ba'ath Party, during which the Ba'athists took savage revenge on their former persecutors, the Communists.

Then the Army ousted the Ba'ath, pushing them once again into exile, and ruled alone until 1968.

But in 1966 at the age of thirteen Mike had been sent to complete his education at an English public school called Haileybury. Terry duly followed in 1968. That summer his parents took him over to England in late June so they could all spend the long holiday together there before Terry joined Mike at Haileybury. That way they missed by chance the two coups, on 14 and 30 July, that toppled the Army and swept the Ba'ath Party to power under President Bakr, with a vice-president called Saddam Hussein.

Nigel Martin had suspected something was coming and had made his plans. He left the IPC and joined a British-based oil company called Burmah Oil, and after packing up the family's affairs in Baghdad, settled the family outside Hertford from where he could commute daily to London and his new job.

Martin senior became a keen golfer and at weekends his sons would often act as caddies when he played with a fellow executive from Burmah Oil, a certain Mr Denis Thatcher, whose wife was quite interested in politics.

Terry loved Haileybury, then under the headmastership of Mr William Stewart; both boys were in Melvill House whose housemaster then was

Richard Rhodes-James. Predictably Terry turned out to be the scholar and Mike the athlete. If Mike's protective attitude towards his shorter and chubbier brother had begun at Mr Hartley's school in Baghdad, it was confirmed at Haileybury, as was the younger boy's adoration of his sibling.

Scorning having a go at a place in university, Mike announced early that he wanted to make a career in the Army. It was a decision with which Mr Rhodes-James was happy to agree.

Terry Martin left the darkened church when the choir practice ended, walked across Trafalgar Square and caught a bus to Bayswater where he and Hilary shared a flat. As he passed up Park Lane he thought back to that final rugby match against Tonbridge with which Mike had ended his five years at Haileybury.

Tonbridge was always the toughest match, and that year it was a home game on the Terrace pitch. Mike was full-back, there were five minutes left to play and Haileybury was two points down. Terry was on the sidelines, like a faithful spaniel, watching his brother.

The oval ball came out of a scrum into the hands of the Haileybury fly-half who swerved round one opposition player and then passed to his nearest centre three-quarter. From behind them Mike began to run. Only Terry saw him start. He accelerated to full speed, then went straight through his own three-quarter line, intercepting on the burst a pass intended for the winger, punched a hole clean through the Tonbridge defence and went for the line. Terry was jumping up and down screaming madly. He would have given all his exam passes and all his scholarship papers to be out on that pitch running beside his brother, even though he knew his short white legs, with the ginger whiskers sticking out like hairs on a gooseberry, would not carry him ten yards on that field before the Tonbridge pack would hammer him.

There was a pause in the screaming as the Tonbridge full-back went in for the tackle. The two eighteen-year-old schoolboys met with a bone-jarring crunch, the Tonbridgian bounced off, winded, and Mike Martin went over to score the needed three points.

When the two teams came off the field Terry was standing by the roped passageway, grinning. Mike reached out and ruffled his hair.

'Well, we did it, Bro.'

And now by being stupid when he should have kept his mouth shut he had caused his brother to be sent into occupied Kuwait. He felt close to tears of worry and frustration.

He left the bus and scurried down Chepstow Gardens. Hilary, away for three days on business, should be back. He hoped so, he needed to be comforted. When he let himself in he called out and heard with joy the answering voice from the sitting room.

He entered the room and blurted out the stupid thing he had done. Then he felt himself enfolded in the warm, comforting embrace of the kind, gentle stockbroker with whom he shared his life.

*   *   *

Mike Martin had spent two days with the Head of Station in Riyadh, a station which had now been beefed up with the addition of two more men from Century.

109

The Riyadh Station normally works out of the embassy and since Saudi Arabia is regarded as a most friendly country to British interests it has never been regarded as a 'hard' posting requiring a large staff and complex facilities. But the ten-day-old crisis in the Gulf had changed things.

The newly created Coalition of Western and Arab nations adamantly opposed to Iraq's continued occupation of Kuwait already had two appointed co-Commanders-in-Chief, General Norman Schwarzkopf of the United States and Prince Khaled bin Sultan bin Abdulaziz, a forty-four-year-old professional soldier, trained at Sandhurst in England and in the States, a nephew of the King and son of the Defence Minister Prince Sultan.

Prince Khaled, in response to the British request, had been as gracious as usual and with remarkable speed a large detached villa had been acquired on the outskirts of the city for the British Embassy to rent.

Technicians from London were installing receivers and transmitters with their inevitable encryption machines for secure usage, and the place was about to become the headquarters of the British Secret Service for the duration of the emergency. Somewhere across town the Americans were doing much the same for the CIA, which clearly intended to have a very major presence. The animus that would later develop between the senior brass of the US armed forces and the civilians of the Agency had not yet begun.

In the interim, Mike Martin had stayed at the private house of the Station Head, Julian Gray. Both men agreed there would be no advantage in Martin being seen by anyone in the embassy. The charming Mrs Gray, a career wife, had been his hostess and never dreamt of asking who he was or what he was

110

doing in Saudi Arabia. Martin spoke no Arabic to the Saudi staff, just accepting the offered coffee with a smile and a 'Thank you' in English.

On the evening of the second day Gray was giving his final briefing. They seemed to have covered everything they could, at least from Riyadh.

'You'll be flying to Dharran tomorrow morning. Civilian flight of Saudia. They've stopped running direct into Khafji. You'll be met. The Firm has set up a despatcher in Khafji; he'll meet you and run you north. Actually, I think he's ex-Regiment. Sparky Low—do you know him?'

'I know him,' said Martin.

'He's got all the things you said you needed. And he's found a young Kuwaiti pilot you might like to talk to. He'll be getting from us all the latest pictures from the American satellites showing the border area and the main concentrations of Iraqi troops to avoid, plus anything else we get. Now, lastly, these pictures have just come in from London.'

He spread a row of large, glossy pictures out on the dining table.

'Saddam doesn't seem to have appointed an Iraqi Governor General yet; he's still trying to put together an administration of Kuwaiti quislings and getting nowhere. Even the Kuwaiti opposition won't play ball. But it seems there's already quite a Secret Police presence there. This one here seems to be the local AMAM chief, name of Sabaawi, quite a bastard. His boss in Baghdad, who may visit, is the Head of the Amn-al-Amm, Omar Khatib. Here.'

Martin stared at the face in the photograph, surly, sullen, a mix of cruelty and peasant cunning in the eyes and mouth.

'His reputation is pretty bloody. Same as his
111

sidekick in Kuwait, Sabaawi. Khatib is about forty-five, comes from Tikrit, a clansman of Saddam himself and a long-time henchman. We don't know much about Sabaawi, but he'll be more in evidence.'

Gray pulled over another photograph.

'Apart from the AMAM, Baghdad has sent in a team from the Mukhabarat's Counter-Intelligence bureau, probably to cope with the foreigners and any attempt at espionage or sabotage directed from outside their new conquest. The CI boss is this one here—got a reputation as cunning and nobody's fool. He may be the one to be careful of.'

It was 8 August. Another C-5 Galaxy rumbled overhead to land at the nearby military airport, part of the vast American logistic machine that was already in gear and pouring its endless material into a nervous, uncomprehending and extremely traditional Muslim kingdom.

Mike Martin looked down and stared at the face of Hassan Rahmani.

*   *   *

It was Steve Laing on the phone again.

'I don't want to talk,' said Terry Martin.

'I think we should, Doctor Martin. Look, you're worried about your brother, are you not?'

'Very much.'

'There's no need to be, you know. He's a very tough character, well able to look after himself. He wanted to go, no question of it. We gave him absolute right to turn us down.'

'I should have kept my mouth shut.'

'Try and look at it this way, Doctor. If the worst comes to the worst we may have to send a lot of other

112

brothers, husbands, sons, uncles, loved-ones out to the Gulf. If there's anything any of us can do to limit their casualties, shouldn't we try?'

'All right. What do you want?'

'Oh, another lunch, I think. Easier to talk man to man. Do you know the Montcalm Hotel? Say, one o'clock?'

'Despite the brains, he's quite an emotional little blighter,' Laing had remarked to Simon Paxman earlier that morning.

'Good Lord,' said Paxman, as an entomologist who has just been told of an amusing new species discovered under a rock.

The spymaster and the academic had a quiet booth to themselves—Mr Costa had seen to it. When the smoked salmon cornets had been served Laing broached his subject.

'The fact of the matter is, we may actually be facing a war in the Gulf. Not yet, of course; it will take time to build up the necessary forces. But the Americans have the bit between their teeth. They are absolutely determined, with the complete support of our good lady in Downing Street, to get Saddam Hussein and his thugs out of Kuwait.'

'Supposing he gets out of his own accord,' suggested Martin.

'Well fine, no war needed,' replied Laing, though privately he thought this option might not be so fine after all. There were rumours in the wind that were deeply disturbing, and had in fact given rise to his lunch with the Arabist.

'But if not, we shall just have to go in, under the auspices of the United Nations, and kick him out.'

'We?'

'Well, the Americans mainly. We'll send forces to

join them; land, sea, air. We've got ships in the Gulf right now, fighters and fighter-bomber squadrons heading south. That sort of thing. Mrs T is determined we'll not be seen to be slacking. At the moment it's just Desert Shield, stopping the bastard from getting any thoughts of moving south and invading Saudi Arabia. But it may come to more than that. You've heard of WMD of course?'

'Weapons of mass destruction. Of course.'

'That's the problem. NBC. Nuclear, bacteriological and chemical. Privately, our people at Century have been trying to warn the political masters for a couple of years about this sort of thing. Last year the Chief presented a paper "Intelligence in the Nineties". Warned that the great threat now, since the end of the Cold War, is and will be Proliferation. Jumped-up dictators of highly unstable aspect getting hold of seriously high-tech weaponry and then possibly using it. Top marks, they all said, jolly good; then did bugger all about it. Now of course they're all worried shitless.'

'He's got a lot of it, you know; Saddam Hussein,' remarked Dr Martin.

'That's the point, my dear fellow. We estimate Saddam has spent fifty billion dollars over the past decade on weapons procurement. That's why he's bankrupt—owes fifteen billions to the Kuwaitis, another fifteen to the Saudis, and that's just for loans made to him during the Iran-Iraq war. He invaded because they refused to write it all off and bung him another thirty billions to get his economy out of trouble.

'Now, the meat of the problem is that one-third of that fifty billion, an incredible seventeen billion greenbacks, has been spent acquiring WMD or the

114

means to make them.'

'And the West has woken up at last?'

'With a vengeance. There's a hell of an operation going on. Langley's been told to race around the world trying to trace every government that's ever sold anything to Iraq and check out the export permits. We're doing the same.'

'Shouldn't take that long if they all co-operate and they probably will,' said Martin as his wing of skate arrived.

'It's not that easy,' said Laing. 'Although it's early days it's already clear Saddam's son-in-law Kamil has set up a damnably clever procurement machine. Hundreds of small dummy companies all over Europe, North, Central and South America. Buying bits and bobs that didn't seem to mean much. Forging export applications, fudging the details of the product, lying about its end-use, diverting purchases through countries that were on the export certificate and the final destination. But put all the innocent-seeming bits and bobs together and you can get something really nasty.'

'We know he's got gas,' said Martin. 'He's used it on the Kurds and the Iranians at Fao. Phosgene, mustard gas. But I've heard there are nerve agents as well. No odour, no visible sign. Lethal and very short-lived.'

'My dear chap, I knew it. You're a mine of information.'

Laing knew all about the gas, but he knew more about flattery.

'Then there's anthrax. He's been experimenting with that, and maybe pneumonic plague. But you know, you can't just run up these things with a pair of kitchen gloves. You need some very specialized

115

chemical equipment. It should show up on the export licences,' Martin remarked.

Laing nodded and sighed with frustration.

'Should, yes. But the investigators are already running into two problems. A wall of obfuscation from some companies, mainly in Germany, and the question of dual-use. Someone ships out a cargo of pesticide—what could be more innocent in a country trying to boost its agricultural production, or so it says. Another company in another country ships a different chemical—same apparent reason, pesticide. Then some smart chemist puts them together and bingo—poison gas. Both the suppliers whine, "We didn't know".'

'The key will lie in the chemical blending equipment,' said Martin. 'This is high-tech chemistry. You can't mix these things up in a bath-tub. Find the people who supplied the turn-key factories and the men who assembled them. They may huff and puff, but they'll know exactly what they were doing when they did it. And what it was for.'

'Turn-key factories?' asked Laing.

'Whole plants, built from scratch by foreign contracted companies. The new owner just turns the key and walks in. But none of this explains our lunch. You must have access to chemists and physicists. I've only heard of these things because of a personal interest. Why me?'

Laing stirred his coffee thoughtfully. He had to play this one carefully.

'Yes, we have chemists and physicists. Boffins of all kinds. And no doubt they'll come up with some answers. Then we'll translate the answers into plain English. We're working in total co-operation with Washington on this. The Americans will do the same

116

and we'll compare our analyses.

'We'll get some answers, but we won't get them all. We believe you have something different to offer. Hence this lunch. You know most of our top brass still take the view that the Arabs couldn't assemble a kid's bicycle, let alone invent one.'

He had touched on a nerve and he knew it. The psycho-portrait he had ordered on Dr Terry Martin was about to prove its worth. The academic flushed deep pink, then controlled himself.

'I really do get pissed off,' he said, 'when my own fellow countrymen insist the Arab peoples are just a bunch of camel-herders who choose to wear tea-towels on their heads. Yes, I have actually heard it expressed that way. The fact is, they were building extremely complex palaces, mosques, ports, highways and irrigation systems when our ancestors were running around in bearskins. They had rulers and law-givers of amazing wisdom when we were in the Dark Ages.'

He leant forward and jabbed at the man from Century with his coffee spoon.

'I tell you, the Iraqis have among them some brilliant scientists and as builders they are beyond compare. Their construction engineers are better than anything for a thousand-mile radius round Baghdad, and I include Israel. Many may have been Soviet or Western trained, but they have absorbed our knowledge like sponges and then made an enormous input themselves...'

He paused and Laing pounced.

'Dr Martin, I couldn't agree with you more. I've only been with Century's Mid-East Division for a year, but I've come to the same view as you. That the Iraqis are a very talented people. But they happen to

117

be ruled by a man who has already committed genocide. Is all this money and all this talent really going to be put to the purpose of killing tens, maybe hundreds, of thousands of people? Is Saddam going to bring glory to the people of Iraq or is he going to bring them slaughter?'

Martin sighed.

'You're right. He's an aberration. He wasn't once, long ago, but he's become one. He's perverted the nationalism of the old Ba'ath Party into National Socialism, drawing his inspiration from Adolf Hitler. What do you want of me?'

Laing thought for a while. He was close, too close to lose his man now.

'George Bush and Mrs T have agreed that our two countries put together a body to investigate and analyse the whole area of Saddam's WMD. The investigators will bring in the facts as they discover them, the boffins will tell us what they mean. What has he got? How developed? How much of it? What do we need to protect ourselves from it, if it comes to war? Gas masks? Space suits? Antidote syringes? We don't know yet just what he has got or just what we'll need—'

'But I know nothing of these things,' Martin interrupted him.

'No, but you know something we don't. The Arab mind, Saddam's mind. Will he use what he's got, will he tough it out in Kuwait or quit, what inducements will make him quit, will he go to the end of the line? Our people just don't understand this Arab concept of martyrdom.'

Martin laughed.

'President Bush,' he said, 'and all the people around him, will act according to their upbringing.

118

Which is based on the Judeo-Christian moral philosophy supported by the Graeco-Roman concept of logic. And Saddam will react on the basis of his own vision of himself.'

'As an Arab and a Muslim?'

'Uhuh. Islam has nothing to do with it. Saddam doesn't give a stuff for the hadith, the codified teachings of the Prophet. He prays on camera when it suits him. No, you have to go back to Nineveh and Assyria. He doesn't mind how many have to die, so long as he thinks he can win.'

'He can't win, not against America. Nobody can.'

'Wrong. You use the word "win" as a Britisher or an American would use it. The way Bush and Scowcroft and the rest are using it even now. He will see it differently. If he quits Kuwait because he is paid to by King Fahd, which might have happened if the Jeddah conference had taken place, he can win with honour. To be paid to quit is acceptable. He wins. But America will not allow that.'

'No way.'

'But if he quits under threat, he loses. All Arabia will see that. He will lose, and probably die. So he will not quit.'

'And if the American war machine is launched against him? He'll be smashed to bits,' said Laing.

'It doesn't matter. He has his bunker. His people will die. Not important. But if he can hurt America, he will win. If he can hurt America badly, really badly, he will be covered in glory. Dead or alive. He will win.'

'Bloody hell, it's complicated,' sighed Laing.

'Not really. There's a quantum leap in moral philosophy when you cross the Jordan. Let me ask again, what do you want of me?'

119

'The committee is forming. To try and advise our masters on the question of these weapons of mass destruction. The guns, tanks, airplanes—the Ministries of Defence will deal with those. They're not the problem. Just ironmongery—we can destroy it from the air.

'Actually, there are two committees, one in Washington and one here in London. British observers on theirs, American observers on ours. There'll be people from the Foreign Office, Aldermaston, Porton Down. Century has two places. I'm sending a colleague, head of the Iraq Desk, Simon Paxman. I'd like you to sit with him, see if there's an aspect of interpretation that we might miss because it's a peculiarly Arab aspect. That's your forte—that's what you can contribute.'

'All right, for what I can contribute, which may be nothing. What's it called, the committee? When does it meet?'

'Ah yes, Simon will call you with the when and where. Actually, it's got an appropriate name. Medusa.'

* * *

A soft and warm Carolina dusk was moving towards Seymour Johnson Air Force Base that late afternoon of 10 August, beckoning the sort of evening for a pitcher of rum punch in the ice bucket and a corn-fed steak on the grill.

The men of 334th Tactical Fighter Squadron who were still not operational on the F-15E, and those of 335 TFS, The Chiefs, who would fly out to the Gulf in December stood by and watched. With 336th Squadron they made up 4th Tactical Fighter Wing of

120

the 9th Air Force. It was 336th who were on the move.

Two days of frenzied activity were at last coming to an end; two days of preparing the airplanes, planning the route, deciding on the gear, stashing the secret manuals and the squadron computer with all its battle tactics locked in its data bank into containers to be brought by the transports. Moving a squadron of warplanes is not like moving house, which can be bad enough. It is like moving a small city.

Out on the tarmac the twenty-four Eagles crouched in silence, fearsome beasts waiting for the spidery little creatures of the same species who had designed and built them to climb aboard and unleash with insignificant fingertips their awful power.

They were rigged for the long flight across the world to the Arabian peninsula in one single journey. Each Eagle had internal fuel tanks containing 13,000 pounds of aviation gasoline. Along their flanks, as if seam-welded, were two 'conformal' tanks, like shallow blisters designed to add minimum extra drag to the airflow round the hull once airborne. These conformals contained 5,000 pounds each. Hung beneath each hull were three long, torpedo-shaped external fuel tanks containing 4,000 pounds each. The fuel weight alone, 13.5 tons, was the payload of five Second World War bombers. And the Eagle is a fighter.

The crews' personal gear was packed in travel pods, formerly napalm pods now put to more humane use, canisters below the wings containing shirts, socks, shorts, soap, shaving tackle, uniforms, mascots and girlie magazines. For all they knew, it might be a long way to the nearest singles bar.

121

The great KC-10 tankers that would mother-hen the fighters all the way across the Atlantic, and on to the Saudi peninsula, all four of them feeding six Eagles each, were already aloft, waiting out over the ocean.

Later, an air caravan of Starlifters and Galaxies would bring the rest, the small army of riggers and fitters, electronics men and support staff, the ordnance and the spares, the power-jacks and workshops, the machine-tools and the benches. They could count on finding nothing at the other end; everything to keep two dozen of the world's most sophisticated fighter-bombers in the world up and combat-ready would have to be transported on that same odyssey halfway round the world.

Each Strike Eagle that evening represented forty-four million dollars worth of black boxes, aluminium, carbon-fibre composites, computers and hydraulics, along with some rather inspired design-work. Although that design had originated thirty years earlier, the Eagle was a new fighter plane, so long does research and development take.

Heading up the civic delegation from Goldsboro town was the community's mayor, Hal K. Plonk. This very fine public servant rejoices in the nickname awarded him by his grateful 20,000 fellow citizens of 'Kerplunk'—a soubriquet earned for his ability to amuse po-faced delegations from politically correct Washington with his southern drawl and fund of jokes. Some visitors from the capital have been known, after an hour of the mayor's rib-ticklers, to leave for Washington in search of trauma therapy. Naturally Mayor Plonk is returned to office after each term with an increased majority.

Standing beside the wing commander, Hal

122

Hornburg, the civic delegation gazed with pride as the Eagles, towed by their tractors, emerged from the hangars and the aircrew climbed aboard, the pilot in the forward seat of the dual cockpit and his weapons systems officer or 'wizzo' in the rear. Round each airplane a cluster of ground crew worked on the pre-start-up checks.

'Did I ever tell you,' asked the mayor pleasantly to the very senior Air Force officer beside him, 'the story of the general and the hooker?'

At this point Don Walker mercifully started his engines and the howl of two Pratt and Whitney F100-PW-220 turbojets drowned out the details of that lady's unfortunate experiences at the hands of the general. The F100 can convert fossil fuel to a lot of noise and heat and 24,000 pounds of thrust and was about to do so.

One by one the twenty-four Eagles of the 336th started up and began to roll the mile to the end of the runway. Small red flags fluttered under the wings, showing where pins secured the under-wing Sparrow and Sidewinder missiles to their pylons. These pins would only come out just before take-off. Their journey to Arabia might be a peaceful one, but to send an Eagle aloft with no means of self-defence at all would be unthinkable.

Along the taxiway to take-off point were groups of armed guards and Air Force police. Some waved, some saluted. Just before the runway the Eagles stopped again and were subjected to the final attentions of a swarm of ordnance men and ground crew. They chocked the wheels, then checked over each jet in turn, looking for leaks, loose fittings or panels—anything that might have gone wrong during the taxi-ing. Finally the pins on the missiles were pulled out.

Patiently, the Eagles waited, 63 foot long, 18 high and 40 across, weighing 40,000 pounds bone dry and 81,000 at maximum take-off weight, which they were close to now. It would be a long take-off run.

Finally the Eagles rolled to the runway, turned into the light breeze and accelerated down the tarmac. Afterburners kicked in as the pilots rammed the throttles through the 'gate' and 30-foot flames leapt from the tail pipes. Beside the runway the crew chiefs, heads protected by helmets from the fearsome noise, saluted their babies away on foreign assignment. They would not see them again until Saudi Arabia.

A mile down the runway, at 185 knots, the wheels left the tarmac and the Eagles were airborne. Wheels up, flaps up, throttles pulled back out of afterburn and into military power setting. The twenty-four Eagles turned their noses to the sky, established a climb rate of 5,000 feet per minute and disappeared into the dusk.

They levelled at 25,000 feet and an hour later saw the position lights and navigation strobe of the first KC-10 tanker. Time to top up. The two F100 engines have a fearsome thirst. With afterburner running they each get through 40,000 pounds of fuel per hour, which is why the afterburn or 'reheat' is only used for take-off, combat or emergency let's-get-out-of-here manoeuvres. Even at normal power settings, the engines need a top-up every one and a half hours. To get to Saudi Arabia they needed their KC-10s, their 'gas stations in the sky', desperately.

The squadron was by now in wide formation, each wingman formating on his element leader in line abreast, about a mile between wingtips. Don Walker, with his wizzo Tim behind him, glanced out to see his wingman holding station where he should be. Flying east, they were now in darkness over the Atlantic but the radar showed the position of every aircraft, and their nav. lights picked them out.

In the tail of the KC-10 above and ahead of him the boom operator opened the panel that protected his window on the world and gazed out at the sea of lights behind him. The fuel boom extended, waiting for the first customer.

Each group of six Eagles had already identified its designated tanker and Walker moved in for his turn. A touch on the throttle and the Eagle swam up under the tanker, in range of the boom. In the tanker the operator 'flew' his boom on to the nozzle protruding from the forward edge of the fighter's left wing. When he had 'lock on' the fuel began to flow, 2,000 pounds of JP4 per minute. The Eagle drank and drank.

When he was full, Walker pulled away and his wingman slid up to suckle. Across the sky three other tankers were doing the same for each of their six charges.

They flew through the night, which was short because they were flying towards the sun at 350 calibrated knots, about 500 miles per hour over the ground. After six hours the sun rose again and they crossed the coast of Spain, flying north off the African coast to avoid Libya. Approaching Egypt, part of the Coalition forces, the 336th turned south-east, drifted over the Red Sea and caught their first sight of that huge ochre-brown slab of sand and gravel called the Arabian desert.

After fifteen hours airborne, tired and stiff, the forty-eight young Americans landed at Dhahran in Saudi Arabia. Within hours they were diverted to their ultimate destination, the Omani airbase of Thumrait in the Sultanate of Oman.

Here they would live in conditions on which they would later look back with nostalgia, 700 miles from the Iraqi border and the danger zone, for four months until mid-December. They would fly training missions over the Omani interior when their support gear arrived, swim in the blue waters of the Indian Ocean and wait for whatever the good Lord and Norman Schwarzkopf had in store for them.

In December they would relocate into Saudi Arabia and one of them, though he would never know it, would alter the course of the war.

CHAPTER FIVE

Dhahran airport was choked. It seemed to Mike Martin as he arrived from Riyadh that most of the eastern seaboard wanted to be on the move. Situated at the heart of the great chain of oilfields that brought Saudi Arabia her fabulous wealth, it had long been accustomed to Americans and Europeans, unlike Taif, Riyadh, Yenbo and the other cities of the kingdom.

Even the bustling port of Jeddah was not accustomed to so many Anglo-Saxon faces on the street, but by the second week of August Dhahran was reeling from the invasion.

Some were trying to get out; many had driven across the causeway into Bahrain to fly out from there. Others were at Dhahran airport, wives and families of oil men mainly, heading for Riyadh and a connector flight home.

Others were coming in, a torrent of Americans with their weaponry and stores. Martin's own civilian flight just squeezed in between two lumbering C-5 Galaxies, two of an almost nose-to-tail air convoy from Britain, Germany and USA engaged in the steady build-up that would transform north-eastern Saudi Arabia into one great armed camp.

This was not Desert Storm, the campaign to liberate Kuwait, still five months away; this was just Desert Shield, designed to deter the Iraqi army, now increased to fourteen divisions deployed along the border and throughout Kuwait, from rolling south.

To a watcher at Dhahran airport it might seem impressive but a more intensive study would have revealed the protective skin was paper-thin. The American armour and artillery had not yet arrived—the earliest sea departures were just clearing the American coastline—and the stores carried by the Galaxies, Starlifters and Hercules were a fraction of the sort of cargo a ship could carry.

The Eagles based at Dhahran and the Hornets of the Marines on Bahrain, plus the British Tornados who had just arrived at Dhahran and hardly cooled down from their journey from Germany, had enough ordnance between them to mount half a dozen missions before running out.

It takes more than that to stop a determined onslaught of massed armour. Despite the impressive show of military hardware at a few airfields, north-eastern Saudi Arabia still lay naked under the sun.

Martin shouldered his way out of the milling throng of the arrivals hall, his tote bag over one shoulder, and caught sight of a familiar face among the crowd at the barrier.

On his first selection course for the SAS, when they

told him they were not going to try and train him but instead try and kill him, they had almost succeeded. One day he had marched 30 miles over the Brecons, some of the cruellest terrain in Britain, in freezing rain with 100 pounds of gear in his Bergen rucksack. Like the others he was beyond exhaustion, locked into a private world where all existence was a miasma of pain and only the will survived.

Then he saw the truck, that beautiful waiting truck. The end of the march and, in terms of human endurance, the end of the line. A hundred yards, 80, 50; and end to the all-consuming agony of his body crept nearer and nearer as his numbed legs drove him and the Bergen those last few yards.

There was a man sitting in the back of the truck, watching the rain-streaked pain-wracked face staggering towards him. When the tailboard was 10 inches from the outstretched fingers, the man rapped on the rear of the cab and the truck rolled away. It did not roll an extra 100 yards; it rolled for another 10 miles. Sparky Low had been the man in the truck.

'Hi, Mike, good to see you.'

That sort of thing takes an awful lot of forgiving.

'Hi, Sparky, how are things?'

'Bloody hairy, since you ask.'

Sparky hauled his nondescript four-wheel-drive Jeep out of the car-park and in thirty minutes they were clear of Dhahran and heading north. It was 200 miles up to Khafji, a three-hour run, but after the port of Jubail slipped by to their right they had at least some privacy. The road was empty, no-one had any appetite for a visit to Khafji, a small oil community on the border of Kuwait, now reduced to a ghost town.

'Refugees still coming over?' asked Martin.

128

'Some,' nodded Sparky, 'down to a trickle though. The main rush has come and gone. Those coming down the main road are mainly women and kids with passes—the Iraqis let them through to get rid of them. Smart enough. If I was running Kuwait I'd want to get rid of the expatriates too.

'Some Indians get through—the Iraqis seem to ignore them. Not so smart. The Indians have good information and I've persuaded a couple to turn round and go back with messages for our people.'

'Have you got the stuff I asked for?'

'Yep. Gray must have pulled some strings. It arrived in a truck with Saudi markings yesterday. I put it in the spare bedroom. We'll have dinner tonight with this young Kuwaiti Air Force pilot I told you about. He claims he has contacts inside, reliable people who might be useful.'

Martin grunted.

'He doesn't see my face. Might get shot down.'

Sparky thought it over.

'Right.'

Sparky Low's commandeered villa was not half bad, thought Martin. It belonged to an American oil executive from Aramco who had pulled their man out of there and back to Dhahran.

Martin knew better than to ask just what Sparky Low was doing in that neck of the woods. It was obvious that he, too, had been 'borrowed' by Century House and his task seemed to be intercepting the refugees filtering south and, if they would talk, debriefing them on what they had seen and heard.

Khafji was virtually deserted, apart from the Saudi National Guard who were dug in defensive positions in and around the town. But there were still a few

129

disconsolate Saudis wandering about and from one stallholder in the market, who could not believe that he had actually got a customer, Martin bought the clothes he needed.

Electric power was still running in Khafji in mid-August, which meant the air-conditioning functioned, as did the water-pump from the well and the water heater. There was a bath available, but he knew better than to take one.

He had not washed, shaved or brushed his teeth for three days. If Mrs Gray, his hostess back in Riyadh, had noticed the increasing odour, which she certainly had, she was too well bred to make mention of it. For dental hygiene Martin just picked his teeth with a splint of wood after a meal. Sparky Low did not mention it either, but then he knew the reason.

The Kuwaiti officer turned out to be a handsome young man of twenty-six who was consumed with rage at what had been done to his country and was clearly a supporter of the ousted Al Sabah royal dynasty, now lodged in a luxury hotel in Taif as guests of King Fahd of Saudi Arabia.

He was also bewildered to find that though his host was what he expected, a British officer in civilian casual dress, the third person at the meal appeared to be a fellow Arab but dressed in a soiled off-white 'thob' with a speckled keffiyeh on his head, one trailing corner tucked across the lower half of his face. Low introduced them.

'You are really British?' asked the young man in surprise. It was explained to him why Martin was dressed the way he was and why he kept his face covered. Captain Al-Khalifa nodded.

'My apologies, Major. Of course I understand.'

His story was clear and straightforward. He had

been called at his home on the evening of 1 August and told to report to Ahmadi Air Base where he was stationed. Through the night he and his fellow officers listened to radio reports of the invasion of their country from the north. By dawn his squadron of Skyhawk fighters was fuelled, armed and ready for take-off. The American Skyhawk, though by no means a modern fighter, could still prove quite useful in a ground attack role. It would never be any match for the Iraqi MiG 23, 25 or 29, or their French-built Mirage, but fortunately, on his one combat mission to date, he never met any.

He had found his targets in the northern suburbs of Kuwait City just after dawn.

'I got one of their tanks with my rockets,' he explained excitedly. 'I know, because I saw it brew. Then I'd only the cannon left, so I went for the lorries behind. Got the first one—it swerved into a ditch and rolled over. Then I was out of ammo so I flew back. But over Ahmadi the control tower told us to head south for the border and save the planes. I had just enough fuel to make Dhahran.

'We got over sixty of our aircraft out, you know. Skyhawks, Mirage and the British Hawk trainers. Plus Gazelles, Puma and Super-Puma helicopters. Now I'll fight from here and go back when we are liberated. When do you think the attack will start?'

Sparky Low smiled cautiously. The boy was so blissfully certain.

'Not yet, I'm afraid. You must be patient. There is preparatory work to be done. Tell us about your father.'

The pilot's father, it seemed, was an extremely wealthy merchant, a friend of the royal family and a power in the land.

131

'Will he favour the invasion forces?' asked Low.

The young Al-Khalifa was incensed.

'Never, never. He will do anything he can to assist the liberation.' He turned to the dark eyes above the chequered cloth. 'Will you see my father? You can rely on him.'

'Possibly,' said Martin.

'Will you give him a message from me?'

He wrote for several minutes on a sheet of paper and gave it to Martin. When he had driven back to Dhahran Martin burned the sheet in an ashtray. He could carry nothing incriminating into Kuwait City.

On the following morning he and Low packed the 'gear' he had asked for into the rear of the jeep and they drove south again as far as Manifah, then turned west along the Tapline Road which shadows the Iraqi border right the way across Saudi Arabia. It was called Tapline because TAP stands for Trans-Arabian Pipeline and the road serviced the pipeline carrying so much Saudi crude to the west.

Later the Tapline Road would become the main transport artery for the biggest military land armada ever seen as 400,000 American, 70,000 British, 10,000 French and 200,000 Saudi and other Arab soldiers massed for the invasion of Iraq and Kuwait from the south. But that day it was empty.

A few miles along it the jeep turned north again, back to the Saudi-Kuwaiti border but at a different place, well inland. Near the fly-blown desert village of Hamatiyyat on the Saudi side, the border is at its nearest point to Kuwait City itself.

Moreover, American photo-reconnaissance pictures obtained by Gray in Riyadh showed that the mass of Iraqi forces were grouped just above the border but near the coast. The further inland one

132

went, the thinner the scattering of Iraqi outposts. They were concentrating their forces between the Nuwaisib crossing-point on the coast and the Al-Wafra border post 40 miles inland.

The village of Hamatiyyat was 100 miles into the desert, tucked up into a kink in the line of the border that shortens the distance to Kuwait City.

The camels Martin had asked for were waiting for them at a small farm outside the village, a rangy female in her prime and her offspring, a cream-coloured calf with a velvet muzzle and gentle eyes, still at the suck. She would grow up to become as foul-tempered as the rest of her genus, but not yet.

'Why the calf?' asked Low as they sat in the jeep and watched the animals in the corral.

'Cover story. If anyone asks, I'm taking her to the camel farms outside Sulaibiya for sale. The prices are better there.'

He slid out of the jeep and shuffled on sandalled feet to rouse the camel-drover who dozed in the shade of his shack. For thirty minutes the two men squatted in the dust and haggled the price of the two beasts. It never occurred to the drover, glancing at the dark face, the stained teeth and the stubble, squatting in the dust in his dirty shift and his odour, that he was not talking to a trader of the Bedouin with money to spend on two good camels.

When the deal was settled Martin paid up from a roll of Saudi dinars that he had taken from Low and held under one armpit for a while until they were soiled. Then he led the two camels a mile away and stopped when they were shielded from prying eyes by the sand dunes. Low caught up in the jeep.

He had sat a few hundred yards from the drover's corral and watched. Though he knew the Arabian

133

peninsula well, he had never worked with Martin, and he was impressed. The man did not just pretend to be an Arab; when he slipped from the jeep he simply became a Bedou in every line and gesture.

Though Low did not know it, the previous day in Kuwait two British engineers, seeking to escape, left their apartment dressed in the white neck-to-floor Kuwaiti 'thob' with the ghutra head-dress on their heads. They got halfway to their car 50 feet away when a child called up from the gutter: 'You may dress like an Arab, but you still walk like English.' The engineers went back to their flat and stayed there.

Sweating in the sun but out of sight of any who might be surprised at such labour being carried out in the heat of the day, the two SAS men transferred the 'gear' into the baggage panniers that hung on either side of the she-camel. She was hunkered down on all fours, but still protested at the extra weight, spitting and snarling at the men who worked on her.

The 200 pounds of Semtex-H explosive went into one, each 5-pound block wrapped in cloth, with some hessian bags of coffee beans on top in case any curious Iraqi soldier insisted on looking. The other pannier took the sub-machine-guns, ammunition, detonators, time-pencils and grenades, along with Martin's small but powerful transceiver with its fold-away satellite dish and cadmium-nickel spare batteries. These, too, were topped with coffee bags.

When they were finished, Low asked: 'Anything more I can do?'

'No, that's it, thanks. I'll stay here till sundown. No need for you to wait.'

Low held out his hand.

'Sorry about the Brecons.'

134

Martin shook it.

'No sweat. I survived.'

Low laughed, a short bark.

'Yeah, that's what we do. We fucking survive. Stay lucky, Mike.'

He drove away. The camel rolled an eye, belched, regurgitated some cud and began to chew. The calf tried to get at her teats, failed and lay down by her side.

Martin propped himself against the camel saddle, drew his keffiyeh round his face and thought about the days to come. The desert would not be a problem, the bustle of occupied Kuwait City might be. How tight were the controls, how tough the road-blocks, how astute the soldiers that manned them? Century had offered to try and get him forged papers but he had turned them down. The Iraqis might change the ID cards.

He was confident the cover he had chosen was one of the best in the Arab world. The Bedouin come and go as they please. They offer no resistance to invading armies for they have seen too many—Saracen and Turk, Crusader and Knight Templar, German and French, British and Egyptian, Israeli and Iraqi. They have survived them all because they stay out of all matters political and military.

Many regimes have tried to tame them, all without success. King Fahd of Saudi Arabia, decreeing that all his citizens should have a house, built a handsome village called Escan, equipped with all modern facilities—a swimming-pool, lavatories, baths, running water. Some Bedouin were rounded up and moved in.

They drank the pool (it looked like an oasis), crapped on the patio, played with the taps and then

135

moved out, explaining politely to their monarch that they preferred to sleep under the stars. Escan was cleaned up and used by the Americans during the Gulf crisis.

Martin also knew that his real problem was his height. He was an inch under 6 foot and most Bedouin are far shorter than that. Centuries of sickness and malnourishment have left most disease-ridden and stunted. Water in the desert is only for drinking, by man, goat or camel; hence Martin's avoiding the bath. The glamour of desert living, he knew, is strictly for Westerners.

He had no identification papers, but that was not a problem. Several governments have tried to issue the Bedouin with ID papers. The tribesmen are usually delighted, because they make such good lavatory paper; better than a handful of gravel. For a policeman or soldier to insist on seeing a Bedou's ID papers is a waste of time, and both parties know it. From the authorities' point of view the main thing is that the Bedouin cause no trouble. They would never dream of getting involved in any Kuwaiti resistance movement. Martin knew that; he hoped the Iraqis did too.

He dozed until sundown, then mounted up. At his 'hut, hut, hut,' the camel rose to her feet, her baby suckled for a while, tethered behind her, and they set off at that ambling, rolling pace that seems to be very slow but covers an amazing amount of ground. The she-camel had been well fed and watered at the corral and would not tire for days.

He was well to the north-west of the Ruqaifah police post where a track road passes from Kuwait into Saudi when he crossed the border shortly before eight. The night was black, save for a low gleam from

136

the stars. The glow of Kuwait's Manageesh oilfield lay to his right, and would probably have an Iraqi patrol in it, but the desert ahead of him was empty.

On the map it was 50 kilometres or 35 miles to the camel farms just south of Sulaibiya, the outlying district of Kuwait City, where he intended to leave his beasts at livery until he needed them again. But before that he would bury the 'gear' in the desert and mark the spot.

Unless he was stopped and delayed, he would bury his cargo in darkness before sunrise, nine hours away. The tenth hour would bring him to the camel farms.

When the Manageesh oilfields dropped behind him he steered by his hand compass in a straight line for his destination. The Iraqis, as he had surmised, might patrol the roads, even the tracks, but never the empty desert. No refugee would try to escape that way, nor enemy to enter.

From the camel farms, after sunrise, he knew he could scramble on board a truck heading into the heart of town 20 miles further on.

Far above him, silent in the night sky, a KH-11 satellite of the National Reconnaissance Office slid across the sky. Years earlier, previous generations of American spy satellites had had to take their pictures and spit out the capsules at intervals in re-entry vehicles, to be laboriously recovered and the film processed.

The KH-11s, 64 foot long and weighing 30,000 pounds each, are smarter. As they take their images of the ground below them, they automatically encrypt the images into a series of electronic pulses which are beamed *upwards* to another satellite above them.

The receiver satellite is one of a network positioned in geo-synchronous orbit, meaning they drift through space at a speed and on a course that keeps them always above the same spot on the earth. In effect, they hover.

Having received the images from the KH-11, the hovering satellite can either beam them straight down to America or, if the curve of the earth gets in the way, bounce them across space to another hovering 'bird' which sends the pictures down to its American masters. Thus the NRO can collect its photographic information in 'real time', just seconds after the pictures were taken.

The bonus in war is huge. It means the KH-11 can see, for example, an enemy convoy on the move well in time to call up an air strike to blast the trucks into oblivion. The unfortunate soldiers in the lorries would never know how the fighter-bombers found them. For the KH-11s can work through night and day, cloud or fog.

The phrase has been used about them: 'all seeing'. Alas, it is a self-delusion. The KH-11 that night swept out of Saudi Arabia and over Kuwait. But it did not see the lone Bedou tribesman entering forbidden territory nor would it have cared if it had. It moved over Kuwait and into Iraq. It saw many buildings, great sprawls of industrial mini-cities, round Al-Hillah and Tarmiya, Al-Atheer and Tuwaitha, but it did not see what was in those buildings. It did not see the vats of poison gas in preparation, nor the uranium hexafluoride destined for the gas-diffusion centrifuges of the isotope separation plant.

It moved north, picking out the airfields, the highways and the bridges. It even saw the car-wreckers' yard at Al-Qubai, but took no notice. It

138

saw the industrial centres of Al-Quaim, Jazira and Al-Shirqat west and north of Baghdad, but not the devices of mass-death that were being prepared inside them. It passed over the Jebel Al Hamreen but it did not see the Fortress that had been built by the engineer Osman Badri. It saw only a mountain among other mountains, hill villages among other hill villages. Then it passed on over Kurdistan and into Turkey.

Mike Martin plodded on through the night towards Kuwait City, invisible in robes he had not worn for almost two weeks. He smiled on recalling the moment when, returning to his Land-Rover from a hike in the desert outside Abu Dhabi, he had been surprised to be intercepted by a plump American lady pointing a camera and shouting, 'Click, click' at him.

*   *   *

It had been agreed that the Medusa Committee should meet for its preliminary conference in a room beneath the Cabinet Office in Whitehall. The main reason was that the building was secure, being regularly swept against listening devices although it did seem that with Russians being so terribly *nice* these days they might have stopped at last attempting such tiresome practices.

The room to which the eight guests were led was two floors below ground level—Terry Martin had heard of the warren of shock-proof, bug-proof chambers where the most delicate matters of state could be discussed in complete discretion below the innocent-looking block opposite the Cenotaph.

Sir Paul Spruce took the chair, an urbane and

experienced bureaucrat with the rank of Assistant Permanent Secretary to the Cabinet. He introduced himself and then everyone to everyone. The American Embassy and thus the USA was represented by the Assistant Defence Attaché and Harry Sinclair, an astute and experienced officer from Langley, who had headed the CIA's London Station for the past three years.

Sinclair was a tall, angular man who favoured tweed jackets, frequented the opera, and got on extremely well with his British counterparts.

The CIA man nodded and winked at Simon Paxman whom he had met once at a Joint Intelligence Committee meeting, on which the CIA has a permanent seat in London.

Sinclair's job would be to note anything of interest that the British scientists might come up with, and convey that information back to Washington where the considerably larger American end of the Medusa Committee was also in session. All the findings would then be collated and compared in the continuing search to analyse Iraq's potential to cause appalling casualties.

There were two boffins from Aldermaston, the Atomic Weapons Research Establishment in Berkshire—they like to drop the word Atomic in front of WRE, but that is what Aldermaston is all about. Their job would be to try and elucidate from information out of the USA, Europe and anywhere else it could be gleaned, plus air photographs of possible Iraqi nuclear research facilities, just how far, if at all, Iraq had proceeded in its quest to crack the technology of making an atomic bomb of her own.

There were two other scientists, from Porton Down. One was a chemist, the other a biologist

140

specializing in bacteriology.

Porton Down has often been accused in the left-wing Press of researching chemical and bacteriological weapons for British use. In fact its research has for years been concentrated on seeking antidotes to any and all forms of gas and germ warfare that might be levelled at British and Allied troops. Unfortunately, it is impossible to develop antidotes to anything without first studying the properties of the toxin. The two boffins from Porton therefore had under their aegis, and in conditions of massive security, some pretty nasty substances. But then so, that 13 August, had Mr Saddam Hussein. The difference was, Britain had no intention of using them on Iraqis, but it was felt Mr Hussein might not be so forbearing.

The Porton men's job would be to see if, from lists of chemicals purchased by Iraq over a period of years, they could deduce what he had got, how much, how nasty and if usable. They would also study air photographs of a range of factories and plants in Iraq to see if any tell-tale signs in the form of structures of certain size and shape—decontamination units, emission-scrubbers—might identify the poison gas factories.

'Now, gentlemen,' Sir Paul began, addressing the four scientists, 'the principal burden rests upon you. The rest of us will assist and support where we can.

'I have here two volumes of Intelligence so far received from our people abroad, embassy staff, trade missions and the—ah—covert gentlemen. Early days yet. These are the first results from the cull of export licences to Iraq over the past decade, and needless to say they come from governments that are being most promptly helpful.

'We have thrown the net as wide as possible. Reference is made to exports of chemicals, building materials, laboratory equipment, specialized engineering products—just about everything but umbrellas, knitting wool and cuddly toys.

'Some of these exports, indeed probably the majority, will turn out to be quite normal purchases by a developing Arab country for peaceful purposes, and I apologize for what may turn out to be wasted time studying them. But please concentrate not only on specialized purchases for manufacture of weapons of mass destruction, but also on dual-use purchases—items which could be adapted or cannibalized for a purpose other than that stated.

'Now, I believe our American colleagues have also been at work.'

Sir Paul handed one of his files to the men from Porton Down and one to those from Aldermaston. The man from the CIA produced two files and did the same. The bewildered boffins sat facing a block of paperwork.

'We have tried,' explained Sir Paul, 'not to duplicate, the Americans and ourselves, but, alas, there may be some element of duplication. I apologize again. And now, Mr Sinclair.'

The CIA Head of Station, unlike the Whitehall civil servant who had almost sent the scientists to sleep with his verbosity, was direct and to the point.

'The thing is, gentlemen, we may have to fight these bastards.'

This was more like it. Sinclair spoke as the British like to think of Americans—direct, and unafraid to mince words. The four boffins gave him their rapt attention.

'If that day ever comes, we will go in first with air

142

power. Like the British, we will want to lose the absolute minimum possible in casualties. So, we'll go for their infantry, their guns, tanks and planes. We'll target their SAM missile sites, communications links, command centres. But, if Saddam uses weapons of mass destruction we would take awful casualties, both of us. So we need to know two things.

'One, what has he got? Then we can plan for gas masks, zip-up capes, chemical antidotes. Two, where the hell has he put it? Then we can target the factories and the storage depots—destroy it all before he can use it. So study the photographs, use magnifier glasses, look for the tell-tale signs. We'll keep tracing and interviewing the contractors who built him these factories and the scientists who equipped the interiors. That should tell us a lot. But the Iraqis may have moved it around a bit. So it comes back to you gentlemen, the analysts.

'You could get to save a lot of lives here, so give it your best shot. Identify the WMD for us and we'll go in and bomb seven shits out of it.'

The four scientists were smitten. They had a job to do and they knew what it was. Sir Paul was looking slightly shell-shocked.

'Yes, well, I'm sure we're all deeply grateful to Mr Sinclair for his ... er ... explanation. May I suggest we reconvene when either Aldermaston or Porton Down has something for us?'

When they left the building Simon Paxman and Terry Martin strolled in the warm August sunshine out of Whitehall and into Parliament Square. It was thronged with the usual columns of tourist coaches. They found an empty bench close to the marble block of Winston Churchill, glowering down on the impudent mortals who clustered beneath him.

143

'You've seen the latest from Baghdad?' asked Paxman

'Of course.'

Saddam Hussein had just offered to pull out of Kuwait if Israel pulled out of the West Bank and Syria out of Lebanon. An attempt at linkage. The United Nations had rejected it out of hand. The resolutions continued to roll out of the Security Council, cutting off Iraq's trade, oil exports, currency movements, air travel, resources. And the systematic destruction of Kuwait by the occupying army went on.

'Any significance?'

'No, just the usual huff and puff. Predictable. Playing to the audience. The PLO liked it, of course, but that's all. It's not a game plan.'

'Has he got a game plan?' asked Paxman. 'If so, no-one can work it out. The Americans think he's crazy.'

'I know. I saw Bush last night on TV.'

'Is he crazy, Saddam?'

'Like a fox.'

'Then why not move south into the Saudi oilfields while he has the chance. The American build-up is only starting, ours too. A few squadrons, carriers in the Gulf. But nothing on the ground. Air power alone can't stop him. That American general they've just appointed—'

'Schwarzkopf,' said Martin, 'Norman Schwarzkopf.'

'That's the chap. He reckons he'll need two full months before he has the forces to stop and roll back a full-scale invasion. So why not attack now?'

'Because that would be attacking a fellow Arab state with which he has no quarrel. It would bring

144

shame. It would alienate every Arab. It is against the culture. He wants to rule the Arab world, be acclaimed by it, not reviled by it.'

'He invaded Kuwait,' Paxman pointed out.

'That was different. He could claim that was correcting an imperialist injustice because Kuwait was always historically part of Iraq. Like Nehru invading Portuguese Goa.'

'Oh, come on, Terry. Saddam invaded Kuwait because he's bankrupt. We all know it.'

'Yes, that's the real reason. But the up-front reason is that he was reclaiming rightful Iraqi territory. Look, it happens all over the world. India took Goa, China took Tibet, Indonesia has taken East Timor. Argentina tried for the Falklands. Each time the claim is retaking a chunk of rightful territory. It's terribly popular with the home crowd, you know.'

'Then why are his fellow Arabs turning against him?'

'Because they think he won't get away with it,' said Martin.

'And he *won't* get away with it. They're right.'

'Only because of America, not because of the Arab world. If he is to gain the acclamation of the Arab world he must humiliate America, not his Arabian neighbour. Have you been to Baghdad?'

'Not recently,' said Paxman.

'It's full of pictures of Saddam portrayed as the desert warrior on a white charger with raised sword. All bunkum of course; the man's a back-street shooter. But that's how he sees himself.'

Paxman rose.

'It's all very theoretical, Terry. But thanks for your thoughts anyway. Trouble is, I have to deal with hard

145

facts. In any case, no-one can see how he can humiliate America. The Yanks have all the power, all the technology. When they're ready they can go in there and blow his Army and Air Force away.'

Terry Martin squinted up against the sun.

'Casualties, Simon. America can take many things, but she cannot take massive casualties. Saddam can. They don't matter to him.'

'But there aren't enough Americans there yet.'

'Precisely.'

*   *   *

The Rolls-Royce bearing Ahmed Al-Khalifa swept up to the front of the office block that announced itself in English and Arabic as the headquarters of Al-Khalifa Trading Corporation Ltd and hissed to a stop.

The driver, a big manservant, half-chauffeur half-bodyguard, stepped out of the driver's seat and went to the rear to open the door for his master.

Perhaps it was foolish to bring the Rolls, but the Kuwaiti millionaire had brushed aside all pleas to use the Volvo for fear of offending the Iraqi soldiers on the road-blocks.

'Let them rot in hell,' he had growled over breakfast. In fact the drive had been uneventful from his sumptuous home in its walled garden in the luxurious suburb of Andalus to the office block in Shamiya.

Within ten days of the invasion the disciplined and professional soldiers of the Iraqi Republican Guard had been withdrawn from Kuwait City to be replaced by the conscript rabble of the Popular Army. If he had hated the first, he had nothing but contempt for

146

the latter.

In their first few days the Guards had looted his city, but systematically and deliberately. He had seen them enter the National Bank and remove the five-billion-dollars worth of gold bullion that constituted the national reserve. But this was not looting for personal gain. The bullion bars had been placed in containers, sealed in trucks and driven to Baghdad.

The Gold Souk had yielded another billion dollars in solid gold artefacts and that had gone the same way.

The road-blocks of the Guards, distinguishable by their black berets and general bearing, had been strict and professional. Then, quite suddenly, they had been needed further south to take up position on the southern border facing Saudi Arabia.

In their place had come the Popular Army, ragged, unshaven and undisciplined and, for that reason, more unpredictable and dangerous. The occasional killing of a Kuwaiti for refusing to hand over his watch or his car gave testimony to that.

By the middle of August the heat came down like a hammer on an anvil. The Iraqi soldiers, seeking shelter, ripped up paving slabs and built themselves small stone huts down the streets they were supposed to be checking, and crawled inside. In the cool of the dawn and the evening they emerged to pretend to be soldiers. Then they harassed civilians, looting food and valuables under pretence of checking cars for contraband.

Mr Al-Khalifa normally liked to be at work by seven in the morning but, by delaying until ten when the sun was hot, he had swept past the stone bivouacs with the Popular Army inside them and no-one had stopped him. Two soldiers, scruffy and hatless, had

147

actually thrown up a shambolic salute at the Rolls-Royce, assuming it must contain some notability of their own side.

It could not last, of course. Some thug would steal the Rolls at gunpoint sooner or later. So what? When they had been driven back home—he was convinced they would be but did not know how—he would buy another.

He stepped out onto the pavement in gleaming white thob, the light cotton material of the ghutra, secured round his head with two black cords, falling about his face. The driver closed the door and returned to the other side of the car to take it away to the company car park.

'Alms, sayidi, alms. For one who has not eaten for three days.'

He had only half seen the man squatted on the sidewalk close to the door, apparently asleep in the sun, a sight common in any Middle Eastern city. Now the man was beside him, a Bedou in stained robes, hand outstretched.

His driver was striding back round the Rolls to send the mendicant away with a stream of curses. Ahmed Al-Khalifa held up his hand. He was a practising Moslem who tried to abide by the teachings of the Holy Koran, one of which is that a man should give alms as generously as he can.

'Park the car,' he ordered. From the side pocket of his robe he withdrew his wallet and extracted a 10 dinar note. The Bedou took the bill in both hands, the gesture indicating that the gift of the benefactor is so weighty that it needs two hands to support it.

'Shukran, sayidi, shukran.' Then without changing his tone of voice the man added, 'When you are in your office send for me. I have news from your

148

son in the south.'

The merchant thought he must have misheard. The man was shuffling away down the pavement, pocketing the banknote. Al-Khalifa entered the office block, nodded in greeting to the commissionaire, and went up to his top-floor office in something of a daze. When he was seated at his desk he thought for a moment, then pressed the intercom.

'There is a Bedouin tribesman on the pavement outside. I wish to speak to him. Please send him up.'

If his private secretary thought her employer had gone mad, she gave no sign of it. Only her wrinkled nose as she showed the Bedou into the cool of the office five minutes later indicated what she thought of the personal odour of her boss's unlikely guest.

When she left, the merchant gestured to a chair.

'You said you had seen my son?' he asked shortly. He half thought the man might be here for an even bigger banknote.

'Yes, Mr Al-Khalifa. I was with him two days ago in Khafji.'

The Kuwaiti's heart leapt. It had been two weeks and no news. He had learnt only indirectly that his only son had taken off that morning from Ahmadi Air Base and after that ... nothing. None of his contacts seemed to know what had happened. There had been much confusion that day, 2 August.

'You have a message from him?'

'Yes, sayidi.'

Al-Khalifa held out his hand.

'Please give it to me. I will reward you well.'

'It is in my head. I could bring no paper with me. So I memorized it.'

'Very well. Please tell me what he said.'

Mike Martin recited the one-page letter the

149

Skyhawk pilot had written, word for word.

'My dear Father, despite his appearance the man in front of you is a British officer...'

Al-Khalifa jerked in his chair and stared at Martin, having some difficulty believing his eyes or ears.

'He has come into Kuwait under cover. Now that you know this, you hold his life in your hands. I beg you to trust him, as he must now trust you, for he will seek your help.

'I am safe and well and based with the Saudi Air Force at Dhahran. I was able to fly one mission against the Iraqis, destroying one tank and a truck. I will fly with the Royal Saudi Air Force until the liberation of our country.

'Each day I pray to Allah that the hours will speed by until I can return and embrace you again. Your dutiful son, Khaled.'

Martin stopped. Ahmed Al-Khalifa rose, walked to the window and stared out. He took several long, deep breaths. When he had composed himself he returned to his chair.

'Thank you. Thank you. What is it you wish?'

'The occupation of Kuwait will not last a few hours or a few days. It will take some months, unless Saddam Hussein can be persuaded to pull out—'

'The Americans will not come quickly?'

'The Americans and the British and the French and the rest of the Coalition will need time to build up their forces. Saddam has the fourth-largest standing army in the world, over a million men. Some are rubbish, but many are not. This occupation force will not be dislodged by a handful of soldiers.'

'Very well. I understand.'

'In the meantime, it is felt that every Iraqi soldier and tank and gun that can be pinned down in the occupation of Kuwait cannot be used on the frontier—'

'You are talking of resistance, armed resistance, fighting back,' said Al-Khalifa. 'Some wild boys have tried. They have shot at Iraqi patrols. They were gunned down like dogs.'

'Yes, so I believe. They were brave but foolish. There are ways of doing these things. The point is not to kill hundreds, or be killed. The point is to make the Iraqi occupation army constantly nervous, always afraid, needing to escort every officer whenever he travels, never able to sleep in peace.'

'Look, Mr English, I know you mean well, but I suspect you are a man accustomed to these things and skilled at them. I am not. These Iraqis are a cruel and savage people. We know them of old. If we do what you say, there will be reprisals.'

'It is like rape, Mr Al-Khalifa.'

'Rape?'

'When a woman is to be raped, she can fight back or succumb. If she is docile she will be violated, probably beaten, maybe killed. If she fights she will be violated, certainly beaten, maybe killed.'

'Kuwait is the woman, Iraq the rapist. This I already know. So why fight back?'

'Because there is tomorrow. Tomorrow Kuwait will look in the mirror. Your son will see the face of a warrior.'

Ahmed Al-Kalifa stared at the dark-faced, bearded Englishman for a long time, then he said: 'So will his father. Let Allah have mercy on my people. What is it you want? Money?'

'Thank you, no. I have money.'

He had in fact 10,000 Kuwaiti dinars, abstracted from the ambassador in London, who had drawn it

151

from the Bank of Kuwait on the corner of Baker Street and George Street.

'I need houses to stay in. Six of them—'

'No problem. There are already thousands of abandoned apartments—'

'Not apartments, detached villas. Apartments have neighbours. No-one will investigate a poor man engaged to caretake an abandoned villa.'

'I will find them.'

'Also identity papers. Real Kuwaiti ones. Three in all. One for a Kuwaiti doctor, one for an Indian accountant and one for a market gardener from out of town.'

'All right. I have friends in the Interior Ministry. I think they still control the presses which produce the ID cards. What about the picture on them?'

'For the market gardener, find an old man on the street. Pay him. For the doctor and the accountant, choose men among your staff who look roughly like me but clean-shaven. These photographs are notoriously bad.

'Lastly, cars. Three. One white estate car, one four-wheel-drive jeep, one old and battered pick-up truck. All in lock-up garages, all with new plates.'

'Very well, it will be done. The ID cards and the keys to the garages and houses, where will you collect them?'

'Do you know the Christian cemetery?'

Al-Khalifa frowned.

'I've heard of it, I've never been there. Why?'

'It's on the Jahra Road in Sulaibikhat, next to the main Muslim cemetery. A very obscure gate with a tiny notice saying: FOR CHRISTIANS. Most of the tombstones are for Lebanese and Syriacs, with some Filipinos and Chinese. In the far right-hand corner is

152

one for a merchant seaman, Shepton. The marble slab is loose. Under it I have scraped a cavity in the gravel. Leave them there. If you have a message for me, same thing. Check the grave once a week for messages from me.'

Al-Khalifa shook his head in bewilderment.

'I'm not cut out for this sort of thing.'

Mike Martin disappeared into the maelstrom of people who teemed through the narrow streets and alleys of the Bneid-al-Qar district. Five days later, under Able Seaman Shepton's tombstone he found three identity cards, three sets of garage keys with locations, three sets of ignition keys and six sets of house keys with addresses on their tags.

Two days later an Iraqi truck coming back into town from the Umm Gudayr oilfield was blown to fragments by something it ran over.

* * *

The CIA's Head of Mid-East Division, Chip Barber, had been in Tel Aviv for two days when the phone in the office they had given him at the US Embassy rang. It was America's Head of Station on the line.

'Chip, it's OK. He's back in town. I fixed a meeting for four o'clock. That gives you time to grab the last flight out of Ben Gurion for Stateside. The guys say they'll come by the office and pick us up.'

The Head of Station was outside the embassy, so he spoke in generalities in case the line was tapped. It was, of course, but only by the Israelis, who knew anyway.

The 'he' was General Yaacov 'Kobi' Dror, Head of the Mossad; the office was the embassy itself and the guys were the two men from Dror's personal staff

153

who arrived in an anonymous car at ten minutes after three.

Barber thought fifty minutes was a lot to get from the embassy compound to the headquarters of the Mossad, which is situated in a tower block of offices called the Hadar Dafna Building on King Saul Boulevard.

But that was not where the meeting was to be. The car sped northwards out of town, past Sde Dov military airfield, until it picked up the coastal highway to Haifa.

Just outside Herzlia there is situated a large apartment-and-hotel resort called simply The Country Club. It is a place where some Israelis but mainly elderly Jews from abroad come to relax and enjoy the numerous health and spa facilities the place boasts. These happy folk seldom glance up the hill above the resort.

If they did, they would see, perched on the top, a rather splendid building commanding fine views over the surrounding countryside and the sea. If they asked what it was, they would be told it is the Prime Minister's summer residence.

The Prime Minister of Israel is indeed permitted to come there, one of very few who are, for this is the Mossad training school, known inside the Mossad as the Midrasha.

Yaacov Dror received the two Americans in his top-floor office, a light, airy room with the air-conditioning turned up high. A short, chunky man, he wore the regulation Israeli short-sleeved, open-necked shirt and smoked the regulation sixty cigarettes a day.

Barber was glad for the air-conditioning; smoke played merry hell with his sinuses.

154

The Israeli spy chief rose from his desk and came lumbering forward.

'Chip, my old friend, how are you these days?'

He embraced the taller American in a hug. It pleased him to rumble like a bad Jewish character-actor and play the friendly, genial bear. All an act. In previous missions as a senior operative, or katsa, he had proved he was very clever and extremely dangerous.

Chip Barber greeted him back. The smiles were as fixed as the memories were long. And it had not been *that* long since an American court had sentenced Jonathan Pollard of Navy Intelligence to a very long term for spying for Israel, an operation that had certainly been run against America by the genial Kobi Dror.

After ten minutes they were at the grist. Iraq.

'Let me tell you, Chip, I think you are playing it exactly right,' said Dror, helping his guest to another cup of coffee that would keep him awake for days. He stubbed his third cigarette into a big glass ashtray. Barber tried not to breathe, but had to give up.

'If we have to go in,' said Barber, 'if he won't quit Kuwait and we have to go in, we'll start with air power.'

'Of course.'

'And we'll be going for his weapons of mass destruction. That's in your interest too, Kobi. We need some co-operation here.'

'Chip, we've been watching those WMDs for years. Dammit, we've been warning about them. Who do you think all that poison gas, those germ and plague bombs, are destined for? Us. We were warning and warning and no-one took any notice. Nine years ago we blew apart his nuclear generators at Osirak, set him back ten years in his quest for a bomb, the world condemned us. America too—'

'That was cosmetic, we all know that.'

'OK, Chip, so now it's American lives on the line, it's not cosmetic any more. Real Americans might die.'

'Kobi, your paranoia is showing.'

'Bullshit. Look, it suits us for you to blow away all his poison gas plants, his plague laboratories and his atom-bomb research. It suits us fine. And we even get to stay out of it because now Uncle Sam has Arab allies. So who's complaining? Not Israel. We have passed you everything we have on his secret weapons programmes. Everything we have. No hanging back.'

'We need more, Kobi. OK, maybe we neglected Iraq a bit these past years. We had the Cold War to deal with. Now it's Iraq and we're short of product. We need information, not street-level garbage; real, high-level paydirt. So I'm asking you straight: do you have any asset, working for you, high in the Iraqi regime? We have questions to put, and we need answers. And we'll pay, we know the rules.'

There was silence for a while. Kobi Dror contemplated the tip of his cigarette. The other two senior officers looked at the table in front of them.

'Chip,' said Dror slowly, 'I give you my word. If we were running any agent right up inside the councils of Baghdad, I'd tell you. I'd pass it all over. Trust me, I don't.'

General Dror would later explain to his Prime Minister, a very angry Itzhak Shamir, that at the time he spoke he was not lying. But he really ought to have mentioned Jericho.

CHAPTER SIX

Mike Martin saw the youth first, or the boy would have died that day. He was driving his battered, stained and rusty pick-up truck, its rear laden with water melons he had bought at one of the outlying farms near Jahra, when he saw the white linen-dressed head pop up and down from behind a pile of rubble by the roadside. He also caught the tip of the rifle the boy was carrying before it disappeared behind the rubble.

The truck was serving its purpose well. He had asked for it in its present condition because he guessed, rightly, that sooner or later and probably sooner the Iraqi soldiers would start confiscating smart-looking cars for their own use.

He glanced in his rear-view mirror, braked and swerved off the Jahra Road. Coming up behind him was a lorry full of soldiers of the Popular Army.

The Kuwaiti youth was sighting up on the lorry, trying to hold the speeding vehicle in the sights of the rifle when a hard hand closed over his mouth and another pulled the rifle away from his grip.

'I don't think you really want to die today, do you?' a voice growled in his ear. The truck rolled past and the moment to take a pot-shot at it vanished as well. The boy had been frightened enough by his own actions; now he was terrified.

When the lorry disappeared the grip on his face and head relaxed. He twisted free and rolled onto his back. Crouching over him was a tall, bearded, hard-looking Bedou.

'Who are you?' he muttered.

157

'Someone who knows better than to kill one Iraqi when there are twenty others in the same truck. Where's your getaway vehicle?'

'Over there,' said the boy, who appeared to be about twenty, trying hard to grow his first beard. It was a motor-scooter, on its stand 20 yards away near some trees. The Bedou sighed. He laid down the rifle, an old Lee Enfield .303 the boy must have got from an antique store, and walked the youth firmly to his van.

He drove the short distance back to the rock pile; the rifle went under the water melons. Then he drove to the motor-scooter and hefted it on top of the cargo of fruit. Several melons burst.

'Get in,' he said.

They drove to a quiet spot near Shuwaikh Port and stopped.

'Just what do you think you were doing?' asked the Bedou.

The boy stared out through the fly-spotted windscreen. His eyes were moist and his lip trembled.

'They raped my sister. A nurse ... at the Al Adan Hospital. Four of them. She is destroyed.'

The Bedou nodded.

'There will be much of that,' he said. 'So, you want to kill Iraqis?'

'Yes, as many as I can. Before I die.'

'The trick is, not to die. If that is what you want, I think I had better train you. Or you won't last a day.'

The boy snorted.

'The Bedouin do not fight.'

'Ever heard of the Arab Legion?' The youth was silent. 'And before them Prince Faisal and the Arab Revolt? All Bedouin. Are there any more like you?'

The youth turned out to be a law student, studying

at Kuwait University before the invasion.

'There are five of us. We all want the same. I chose to be the first to try.'

'Memorize this address,' said the Bedou. He gave it, a villa in a back street in Yarmuk. The boy got it wrong twice, then right. Martin made him repeat it twenty times.

'Seven o'clock tonight. It will be dark. But curfew is not till ten. Arrive separately. Park at least 200 yards away and walk the rest. Enter at two-minute intervals. The gate and door will be open.'

He watched the boy ride away on his scooter and sighed. Pretty basic material, he thought, but for the moment it's all I've got.

The young people turned up on time. He lay on a flat roof across the street and watched them. They were nervous and unsure, glancing over their shoulders, darting into gateways, then out again. Too many Bogart movies. When they were all inside he gave them ten more minutes. No Iraqi security men appeared. He slipped down from his roof, crossed the road and entered the house from the back. They were sitting in the main room with the lights on and the curtains undrawn. Four young men and a girl, dark and very intense.

They were looking towards the door to the hall when he entered from the kitchen. One minute he was not there and the next he was. The youngsters had one glimpse of him before he reached out and switched off the light.

'Draw the curtains,' he said quietly. The girl did it. Woman's work. Then he put the light back on.

'Never sit in a lighted room with the curtains open,' he said. 'You do not want to be seen together.'

He had divided his six residences into two groups.

159

In four he lived, flitting from one to another in no particular sequence. Each time, he left tiny signs for himself—a leaf wedged in the door jamb, a tin can on the step. If ever they were missing he would know the house had been visited. In the other two he had stored half the 'gear' he had brought in from its grave in the desert. The place he had chosen to meet the students was the least important of his dwelling places, and now one he would never use again to sleep in.

They were all students except one who worked in a bank. He made them introduce themselves.

'Now you need new names.' He gave them five new names. 'You tell no-one else—not friends, parents, brothers, *anyone* those names. Whenever they are used, you know the message comes from one of us.'

'What do we call you?' asked the girl who had just become 'Rana'.

'The Bedou,' he said. 'It will do. You, what is this address again?'

The young man he pointed at thought, then produced a slip of paper. Martin took it from him.

'No pieces of paper. Memorize everything. The Popular Army may be stupid, but the Secret Police are not. If you are frisked, how do you explain this?'

He made the three who had noted the address burn their slips of paper.

'How well do you know your city?'

'Pretty well,' said the oldest of them, the twenty-five-year-old bank clerk.

'Not good enough. Buy maps tomorrow, street maps. Study as for your final exams. Learn every street and alley, every square and garden, every boulevard and lane, every major public building, every mosque and courtyard. You know the street signs are coming down?'

They nodded. Within fifteen days of the invasion, after recovering from their shock, the Kuwaitis were beginning a form of passive resistance, of civil disobedience. It was spontaneous and uncoordinated. One of the moves was the ripping down of street names. Kuwait is a complicated city to start with; deprived of street names it became a maze.

Iraqi patrols were already becoming comprehensively lost. For the Secret Police, finding a suspect's address was a nightmare. At main intersections, signposts were being ripped up in the night, or turned around.

That first night he gave them two hours on basic security. Always have a cover story that checks out, for any journey and any rendezvous. Never carry incriminating paper. Always treat Iraqi soldiers with respect verging on deference. Confide in no-one.

'From now on you are two people. One is the original you, the one everyone knows, the student, the clerk. He is polite, attentive, law-abiding, innocent, harmless. The Iraqis will leave him alone because he does not threaten them. He never insults their country, their flag or their leader. He never comes to the attention of the AMAM. He stays alive and free. Only on a special occasion, on a mission, does the other person appear. He will become skilled and dangerous, and still stay alive.'

He taught them about security; attending a meeting at a rendezvous. Turn up early, park well away. Go into the shadows. Watch for twenty minutes. Look at the surrounding houses. Check for heads on the roof, the waiting ambush party. Listen for the scuff of a soldier's boot on gravel, the glow of a cigarette, the clink of metal on metal. When they still had time to get home before the curfew he

161

dismissed them. They were disappointed.

'What about the invaders? When do we start killing them?'

'When you know how.'

'Is there nothing we can do?'

'When the Iraqis move about, how do they do it? Do they march?'

'No, trucks, vans, jeeps, stolen cars,' said the law student.

'Which have petrol caps,' said the Bedou, 'which come off with a quick twist. Sugar lumps, twenty lumps per petrol tank. It dissolves in the petrol, passes through the carburettor and turns to hard caramel in the heat of the engine. It destroys the engine. Be careful not to be caught. Work in pairs and after dark. One keeps watch, the other slips in the sugar. Replace the petrol cap. It takes ten seconds.

'A piece of plywood, four inches by four, with four sharpened steel nails through it. Drop it down under your thob till it slips out by your feet. Nudge it with your toe under the leading edge of the tyre of a stationary vehicle.

'There are rats in Kuwait, so there are shops that sell rat poison. Buy the white, strychnine-based kind. Buy dough from a baker. Mix in the poison, using rubber gloves, then destroy the gloves. Bake up the bread in the kitchen oven, but only when you are alone in the house.'

The students stared, open-mouthed.

'We have to give it to the Iraqis?'

'No, you carry the loaves in open baskets on scooters, or in the trunks of cars. They will stop you at road-blocks and steal it. We meet here again in six days.'

Four days later Iraqi trucks began to break down.

162

Some were towed away and others abandoned, six lorries and four jeeps. The mechanics found out why, but could not discover when or by whom. Tyres began to blow out and the plywood squares were handed over to the Security Police who fumed and beat up several Kuwaitis siezed at random on the streets.

Hospital wards began to fill with sick soldiers, all with vomiting and stomach pain. As they were hardly ever given food rations by their own army and lived hand-to-mouth at their road-blocks and in their stone-slab cantonments up and down the streets, it was assumed they had been drinking polluted water.

Then at the Amiri Hospital in Dasman a Kuwaiti lab technician ran an analysis of a sample of vomit from one of the Iraqis. He approached his departmental chief in great perplexity.

'He's been eating rat poison, Professor, but he says he only had bread for three days, and some fruit.'

The professor was puzzled.

'Iraq army bread?'

'No, they didn't deliver any for some days. He took it from a passing Kuwaiti baker's boy.'

'Where are your samples?'

'On the bench, in the lab. I thought best to see you first.'

'Quite right. You have done well. Destroy them. You have seen nothing, you understand?'

The professor walked back into his office shaking his head. Rat poison, who the hell had thought of that?

*　　　*　　　*

The Medusa Committee met again on 30 August,

163

because the doctor of bacteriology from Porton Down felt he had discovered all he could at that point about Iraq's germ warfare programme, such as it was, or appeared to be.

'I'm afraid we are looking at somewhat slim pickings,' Dr Bryant told his listeners. 'The main reason is that the study of bacteriology can quite properly be carried out at any forensic or veterinary laboratory using the same laboratory equipment that you would find in any chemical lab, and which won't show up on export permits.

'You see, the overwhelming majority of the product is for the benefit of Mankind, for the curing of diseases, not the spreading of them. So nothing could be more natural than for a developing country to want to study bilharzia, beri-beri, yellow fever, malaria, cholera, typhoid or hepatitis. These are human diseases. There is another range of animal diseases the veterinary colleges might quite properly want to study.'

'So there's virtually no way of establishing whether Iraq today has a germ-bomb facility or not?' asked Sinclair of the CIA.

'Virtually not,' said Bryant. 'There's a record to show that way back in 1974, when Saddam Hussein was not on the throne, so to speak—'

'He was vice-president then, and the power behind the throne,' said Terry Martin. Bryant was flustered.

'Well, whatever ... Iraq signed a contract with the Institut Merieux in Paris to build them a bacteriological research project. It was supposed to be for veterinary research into animal diseases, and it may have been.'

'What about the stories of anthrax cultures for use against humans?' the American asked.

'Well, it's possible. Anthrax is a particularly virulent disease. It mainly affects cattle and other livestock, but can infect humans if they handle or ingest products from infected sources. You may recall the British government experimented with anthrax on the Hebridean island of Grinard during the Second World War. It's still out of bounds.'

'That bad, eh? Where would Hussein get this stuff?'

'That's the point, Mr Sinclair. You'd hardly go to a reputable European or American laboratory and say, "Can I have some nice anthrax cultures because I want to throw them at people." Anyway, he wouldn't need to. There are diseased cattle all over the Third World. One would only have to note an outbreak and buy a couple of diseased carcases. But it wouldn't show up on government paperwork.'

'So, he could have cultures of this disease for use in bombs or shells, but we don't know. Is that the position?' asked Sir Paul Spruce. His rolled-gold pen was poised above his notepad.

'That's about it,' said Bryant. 'But that's the bad news. The better news is, I doubt if it would work against an advancing army. I suppose that if you have an army advancing against you, and you are ruthless enough, you'd want to stop them in their tracks.'

'That's about the shape of it,' said Sinclair.

'Well, anthrax wouldn't do that. It would impregnate the soil if dropped from a series of air bursts above and ahead of the Army. Anything growing from that soil—grass, fruit, vegetables— would be infected. Any beast feeding off the grass would succumb. Anyone eating the meat, drinking the milk or handling the hide of any such beast would

165

catch it. But the desert is not a good vehicle for such spore cultures. Presumably our soldiers will be eating pre-packed meals and drinking bottled water?'

'Yep, they are already,' said Sinclair.

'Then it wouldn't have much effect unless they breathed the spores in. The disease has to enter humans by ingestion into the lungs or the food passages. Bearing in mind the gas hazard, I suspect they will be wearing gas masks anyway?'

'We plan on it, yes sir.'

'So do we,' added Sir Paul.

'Then, I don't really see why anthrax,' said Bryant. 'It wouldn't stop the soldiers in their tracks like a variety of gases, and those who did catch it could be cured with powerful antibiotics. There is an incubation period, you see. The soldiers could win the war and then fall sick. Frankly, it's a terrorist weapon rather than a military one. Now, if you dropped a vial of anthrax concentrate in the water supply on which a city depended, you might start a catastrophic epidemic which would overwhelm the medical services. But if you're going to spray fighting men in a desert, I'd choose one of the various nerve gases. Invisible and fast.'

'So, no indication, if Saddam has a germ warfare lab, where it might be?' asked Sir Paul Spruce.

'Frankly, I'd check with all the West's veterinary institutes and colleges. See if there have been any visiting professorships or delegations to Iraq over the past ten years. Ask those who went whether there was any facility that was absolutely off-limits to them and surrounded by quarantine precautions. If there was, that will be it,' said Bryant.

Sinclair and Palfrey wrote furiously. Another job for the checkers.

'Failing that,' concluded Bryant, 'you could try human Intelligence. An Iraqi scientist in this field who has quit and settled in the West. Researchers in bacteriology tend to be thin on the ground, quite a tight group, like a village really. We usually know what is going on in our own countries, even in a dictatorship like Iraq. Such a man might have heard, if Saddam has got this facility, where he put it.'

'Well, I'm sure we are deeply grateful, Dr Bryant,' said Sir Paul as they rose. 'More work for our governments' detectives, eh, Mr Sinclair? I have heard that our other colleague at Porton Down, Dr Reinhart, will be able to give us his deductions on the matter of poison gases in about two weeks. I shall, of course, stay in touch, gentlemen. Thank you for your attendance.'

*   *   *

The group in the desert lay quietly watching the dawn steal across the sand dunes. The youngsters had not realized when they came to the house of the Bedou the previous evening that they would be away all night. They thought they would get another lecture.

They had brought no warm clothing and nights in the desert are bitter, even at the end of August. They shivered and wondered how they would explain to their distraught parents. Caught by the curfew? Then why not telephone? Out of order ... it would have to do.

Three of the five wondered if they had made the right choice after all, but it was too late to go back now. The Bedou had simply told them it was time they saw some action, and led them from the house to a rugged off-road four-wheel-drive vehicle parked

167

two streets away. They had been out of town and off the road into the flat, hard desert, before the curfew. Since entering the desert they had seen no-one.

They had driven south for 20 miles across the sand until they had intercepted a narrow road which they suspected ran from the Manageesh oilfield to their west towards the Outer Motorway in the east. All the oilfields, they knew, were garrisoned by Iraqis and the main highways were infested with patrols. Somewhere to their south sixteen divisions of Army and Republican Guards were dug in, facing Saudi Arabia and the growing tide of Americans pouring in. They felt nervous.

Three of the group lay in the sand beside the Bedou, watching the road in the growing light. It was quite narrow. Approaching vehicles would have to swerve to the gravelled verge to pass each other.

Covering one half of the road was a plank studded with nails. The Bedou had taken it from his truck and laid it there, covering it with a blanket made from old hessian sacks. He had made them scoop sand over the blanket until it looked just like a small drift of sand blown from the desert by the wind.

The other two, the bank clerk and the law student, were spotters. Each lay on a sand dune 100 yards up and down the road looking for approaching vehicles. They had been told if the vehicles were a large Iraqi truck, or several in number, they should wave in a certain way.

Just after 6 a.m. the law student waved. His signal meant 'Too much to handle'. The Bedou pulled at the fishing-line he held in his hand. The plank slithered off the road. Thirty seconds later two lorries crammed with Iraqi soldiers went by unharmed. The Bedou ran to the road and replaced the plank, the hessian and the sand.

Then minutes later the bank clerk waved. It was the right signal. From the direction of the motorway a staff car came bowling down the road towards the oilfield.

The driver never thought to swerve to avoid the bar of sand, but only caught the nails with one front wheel. It was enough. The tyre blew out, the blanket wrapped round the wheel and the car swerved violently. The driver caught the swerve in time, steadied the car and it rolled to a stop half on and half off the road. The side that was off the road bogged down.

The driver sprang out of the front and two officers emerged from the back, a major and a junior lieutenant. They shouted at the driver who shrugged and whined, pointing at the wheel. The jack would never get under it—the car was at a crazy angle.

To his stunned pupils the Bedou muttered, 'Stay here', rose and walked down the sand to the road. He had a Bedouin camel blanket over his right shoulder, covering his right arm. He smiled broadly and hailed the major.

'Salaam aleikhem, sayidi Major. I see you have a problem. Perhaps I can help. My people are just a short distance away.'

The major reached for his pistol, then relaxed. He glowered and nodded.

'Aleikheni salaam, Bedou. This spawn of a camel has driven my car off the road.'

'It will have to be pulled back, sayidi. I have many brothers.'

The distance had closed to 8 feet when the Bedou's arm came up. When he had asked for machine-pistols or submachine-guns, he had wanted the Heckler and

169

Koch MP5 or the Mini-Uzi. The latter, being Israeli, was out of the question in Saudi Arabia, and there were no HKs either. So he settled for the Kalashnikov AK-47, the MS version with the folding stock, this one made by Omnipol of Czechoslovakia. Then he had taken the stock right off and filed the noses of the 7.62 ammunition blunt. No need to put a bullet right through a man and out the other side.

He fired in the SAS fashion, two round bursts, pause, two rounds, pause ... The major was hit in the heart at a range of 8 feet. A slight move of the AK to the right caught the lieutenant in the breast-bone causing him to fall on the driver who was rising from his tattered front wheel. When the man straightened he was just in time to die from the third pair of bullets in the chest.

The noise of the firing seemed to echo in the dunes, but the desert and the road were empty. He summoned the three terrified students from their hiding-places.

'Put the bodies back in the car, the driver behind the wheel, the officers in the back,' he told the two males. To the girl he gave a short screwdriver, its blade honed to a needle point.

'Stab the petrol tank three times.'

He looked to his watchers. They signalled nothing was coming. He told the girl to take her handkerchief, wrap it round a stone, knot it and soak it in petrol. When the three bodies were back in the car he lit the soaking handkerchief and tossed it into the pool of petrol spurting from the tank.

'Now, move.'

They needed no further bidding, running through the sand dunes to where he had parked the truck off-road. Only the Bedou thought to pick up the plank and bring it with him. As he turned into the dunes the main body of petrol in the burning car caught and fire-balled. The staff car disappeared in flames.

They drove back towards Kuwait in awed silence. Two of the five were with him in the front, the other three behind.

'Did you see?' asked Martin at last. 'Did you watch?'

'Yes, Bedou.'

'What did you think?'

'It was ... so quick,' said the girl Rana at last.

'I thought it was a long time,' said the banker.

'It was quick and it was brutal,' said Martin. 'How long do you think we were on the road?'

'Half an hour?'

'Six minutes. Were you shocked?'

'Yes, Bedou.'

'Good. Only psychopaths are not shocked the first time. There was an American general once, Patton. Ever heard of him?'

'No, Bedou.'

'He said it was not his job to ensure his soldiers died for their country, it was his job to make sure the other poor bastards died for theirs. Understand?'

George Patton's philosophy does not translate well into Arabic, but they worked it out.

'When you go to war, there is a point up to which you can hide. After that point there is a choice. You die or he dies. Make your choice now, all of you. You can go back to your studies, or go to war.'

They thought for several minutes. It was Rana who spoke first.

'I will go to war, if you will show me how, Bedou.'

After that the young men had to agree.

171

'Very well. But first I will teach you how to destroy, kill and stay alive. My house, two days' time, at dawn when curfew is lifted. Bring school textbooks, all of you, including you, Banker. If you are stopped, be natural; you are just students going to study. True, in a way, but different studies. You have to get off here. Find your way into town by different trucks.'

They had rejoined the tarred roads and reached the Fifth Ring motorway. He pointed out a garage where trucks would stop and the drivers would give them lifts. When they had gone he went back to the desert, uncovered his buried radio, drove three miles from the burial site, opened the satellite dish and began to talk on his encrypted Motorola to the designated house in Riyadh.

An hour after the ambush the burnt-out staff car was found by the next patrol. The bodies were taken to the nearest hospital, Al Adan near Fintas on the coast.

The forensic pathologist who did the autopsy under the eyes of a glowering colonel of the AMAM secret police spotted the bullet holes, tiny pinpricks in the sealed-over charred flesh. He was a family man with daughters of his own. He knew the girl nurse who had been raped.

He drew the sheet back over the third body and began to peel off his gloves.

'I'm afraid they died of asphyxia when the car caught fire after the crash,' he said. 'May Allah have mercy.'

The colonel grunted and left.

At his third meeting with his band of volunteers the Bedou drove them far out into the desert, to a spot west of Kuwait City and south of Jahra where they could be alone. Seated in the sand like a picnic party,

172

the five youngsters watched as their teacher took a haversack and poured out on to his camel blanket an array of strange devices. One by one he identified them.

'Plastic explosive. Easy to handle, very stable.'

They went several shades paler when he squeezed the substance in his hands like modelling clay. One of the young men, whose father owned a tobacco shop, had brought on request a number of old cigar boxes.

'This,' said the Bedou, 'is a detonator with time pencil combined. When you twist this butterfly screw at the top, a phial of acid is crushed. The acid begins to burn its way through a copper diaphragm. It will do so in sixty seconds. After that the mercury fulminate will detonate the explosive. Watch.'

He had their undivided attention. Taking a piece of Semtex the size of a cigarette packet, he placed it in the small cigar box and inserted the detonator into the heart of the mass.

'Now when you twist the butterfly like this, all you have to do is close the box and wrap an elastic band round the box ... so ... to hold it closed. You only do this at the last moment.'

He placed the box on the sand in the centre of the circle.

'However, sixty seconds is a lot longer than you think. You have time to walk to the Iraqi truck, or bunker or half-track, toss in the box and walk away. Walk, never run. A running man is at once the start of an alarm. Leave enough time to walk round one corner. Continue walking, not running, even after you hear the explosion.'

He had half an eye on the watch on his wrist. Thirty seconds.

'Bedou...' said the banker.

173

'Yes?'

'That's not a real one, is it?'

'What?'

'The bomb you just made. It's a dummy, right?'

Forty-five seconds. He reached forward and picked it up.

'Oh no. It's a real one. I just wanted to show you how long sixty seconds really is. Never panic with these things. Panic will kill you, get you shot. Just stay calm at all times.'

With a deft flick of the wrist he sent the cigar box spinning away over the dunes. It dropped behind one and exploded. The bang rocked the sitting group and fine sand drifted back on the wind.

High over the northern Gulf an American AWACS plane noted the explosion on one of its heat sensors. The operator drew it to the attention of the mission controller who peered at the screen. The glow from the heat source was dying away.

'Intensity?'

'Size of a tank shell I guess, sir.'

'OK. Log it. No further action.'

'You will be able to make these yourselves by the end of today. The detonators and time pencils you will carry and store in these,' the Bedou said.

He took an aluminium cigar tube, wrapped the detonator in cotton wool and inserted it into the tube, screwing the top back on.

'The plastic you will carry like this.'

He took the wrapper of a bar of soap, rolled 4 ounces of explosive into the shape of a soap bar and wrapped it, sealing it with an inch of sticky tape.

'The cigar boxes you acquire for yourselves. Not the big kind for Havanas, the small kind for cheroots. Always keep two cheroots in the box in case you are

174

stopped and frisked. If an Iraqi ever wants to take the cigar tube, or the box, or the soap off you, let him.'

He made them practise under the sun until they could unwrap the 'soap', empty out the cheroots, prepare the bomb and wind the elastic band round the box in thirty seconds.

'You can do it in the back of a car, the men's room of a café, in a doorway or at night behind a tree,' he told them. 'Pick your target first, make sure there are no other soldiers standing well to one side who will survive, then twist the butterfly, close the box, elastic-band it, walk up, toss the bomb and walk away. From the moment you twist the butterfly, count slowly to fifty. If at fifty seconds you have not parted company with it, throw it as far as you can. Now, mostly you will be doing this in darkness, so that's what we'll do now.'

He made the group blindfold each member one by one, then watch as the student fumbled and dropped things. By late afternoon they could do it by touch. In the early evening he gave them the rest of the contents of the haversack, enough for each student to make six bars of soap, and six time-pencils. The tobacconist's son agreed to provide all the small boxes and aluminium tubes. They could acquire cotton wool, soap wrappers and elastic bands for themselves. Then he drove them back to town.

*　　　*　　　*

Through September the AMAM headquarters in the Hilton Hotel began to receive a stream of reports of a steadily escalating level of attacks on Iraqi soldiers and military equipment. Colonel Sabaawi became more and more enraged as he became more and more frustrated.

This was not the way it was supposed to be. The Kuwaitis, he had been told, were a cowardly people who would cause no trouble. A touch of the Baghdad methods and they would do as they were told. It was not working out quite like that.

There were in fact several resistance movements in being, most of them random and uncoordinated. In the Shia district of Rumaithiya Iraqi soldiers simply disappeared. The Shia Muslims had especial reason to loathe the Iraqis for their co-religionists, the Shia of Iran, had been slaughtered in hundreds of thousands during the Iran–Iraq war. Iraqi soldiers who wandered into the rabbit warren of alleys that make up Rumaithiya district had their throats cut and the bodies were dumped in the sewers. They were never recovered.

Among the Sunnis the resistance was centred on the mosques where the Iraqis seldom ventured. Here messages were passed, weapons swapped and attacks planned.

The most organized resistance came from the leadership of Kuwaiti notables, men of education and wealth. Mr Al-Khalifa became the banker, using his funds to provide food so that the Kuwaitis could eat, and other cargoes hidden beneath the food that came in from outside.

The organization aimed at six goals, five of them a form of passive resistance. One was for documentation: every resister was supplied with perfect documentation forged by resisters within the Interior Ministry. A second was for Intelligence— keeping a stream of information about Iraqi movements heading in the direction of the Coalition headquarters in Riyadh, particularly about Iraqi manpower and weapons strengths, coastal fortifications and missile deployments. A third branch kept the services functioning—water, electricity, fire brigades and health. When finally, in defeat, Iraq turned on the oil taps and began to destroy the sea itself, Kuwaiti oil engineers told the American fighter-bombers exactly which valves to rocket in order to turn off the flow.

Community Solidarity Committees circulated through all the districts, often contacting the Europeans and other First World residents still holed up in their flats and keeping them out of the way of the Iraqi trawl nets.

A satellite phone system was smuggled in from Saudi Arabia in the dummy fuel tank of a jeep. It was not encrypted like Martin's but, by keeping it constantly on the move, the Kuwaiti resistance could avoid Iraqi detection and contact Riyadh whenever there was something to pass on. An elderly radio ham worked throughout the occupation, sending 7,000 messages to another ham in Colorado, which were passed on to the State Department.

And there was the offensive resistance, mainly in the charge of a Kuwaiti lieutenant-colonel, one of those who had escaped the Ministry of Defence building on the first day. Because he had a son called Fouad, his code name was Abu Fouad, father of Fouad.

Saddam Hussein had finally given up trying to form a puppet government, and appointed his half-brother Ali Hassan Majid as Governor-General.

The resistance was not just a game. A small but extremely dirty war developed underground. The AMAM responded by setting up two interrogation centres, at the Kathma Sports Centre and the

Qadisiyah Stadium. Here the methods of AMAM chief Omar Khatib were imported from the Abu Ghraib prison outside Baghdad and used extensively. Before the liberation 500 Kuwaitis were dead, of whom 250 were executed, many after prolonged torture.

Counter-Intelligence chief Hassan Rahmani sat at his desk in the Hilton Hotel and read the reports prepared by his on-the-spot staff. He was making a brief visit from his Baghdad duties on 15 September. The reports he read made gloomy reading.

There was a steady increase of attacks on Iraqi outposts on lonely roads, guard huts, vehicles and road-blocks. This was mainly the AMAM's problem—local resistance came under them and, predictably in Rahmani's view, that brutal oaf Khatib was making a camel's breakfast out of it.

Rahmani had little time for the torture to which his rival in the Iraqi Intelligence structure was so devoted. He preferred to rely on patient detective work, deduction and cunning, even though he had to concede that in Iraq it was terror and nothing else that had kept the Rais in power all these years. He had to admit, with all his education, that the street-wise, devious psychopath from the alleys of Tikrit frightened him.

He had tried to persuade his president to let him have charge of internal Intelligence in Kuwait, but the answer had been a firm 'no'. It was a question of principle, the Foreign Minister Tariq Aziz had explained to him. He, Rahmani, was charged to protect the state from espionage and sabotage from foreign sources. The Rais would not concede that Kuwait was a foreign country. It was the nineteenth province of Iraq. So, it was Omar Khatib's job to

178

ensure compliance.

As he contemplated his sheaf of reports that morning in the Hilton Hotel, Rahmani was rather relieved he did not have the task. It was a nightmare, and as he had predicted Saddam Hussein had played his cards consistently wrongly.

The taking of Western hostages as human shields against attack was proving a disaster, totally counter-productive. He had missed his chance to roll south and take the Saudi oilfields, forcing King Fahd to the conference table, and now the Americans were pouring into the theatre.

All attempts to assimilate Kuwait were failing, and within a month, probably less, Saudi Arabia would be impregnable with its American shield along the northern border.

Saddam Hussein, he believed, could neither get out of Kuwait without humiliation, nor stay in there if attacked without a bigger one. Yet the mood around the Rais was still one of confidence as if he were convinced something would turn up. What on earth did the man expect? That Allah himself would lean down from heaven and smash his enemies in the face?

Rahmani rose from his desk and walked to the window. He liked to stroll as he thought; it marshalled his brain. He looked down from the window. The once-sparkling marina was now a garbage tip.

There was something about the reports on his desk that disturbed him. He went back and scanned them again. Yes, something odd. Some of the attacks on Iraqis were with handguns and rifles, others with bombs made from industrial TNT. But here were others, a constant niggling stream, that clearly indicated a plastic explosive had been used. Kuwait

179

had never had plastic explosives, least of all Semtex-H. So who was using it and where did they get it?

Then there were the radio reports, of an encrypted transmitter somewhere out in the desert that moved all the time, coming on air at different times, talking scrambled nonsense for ten or fifteen minutes and then going silent, and always on different bearings.

Then there were these reports of a strange Bedou who seemed to wander about at will, appearing, disappearing and reappearing, and always a trail of destruction in his wake. Two badly injured soldiers had reported, before they died of wounds, having seen the man, tall and confident in a red-and-white chequered keffiyeh, one trailing end drawn across his face.

Two Kuwaitis under torture had mentioned the legend of the invisible Bedou but claimed they had never actually seen him. Sabaawi's men were trying to persuade the prisoners with even more pain to admit they had. Fools. Of course they would invent anything to stop the agony.

The more Hassan Rahmani thought about it, the more he became convinced he had a foreign infiltrator on his hands, definitely part of his authority. He found it hard to believe there was any Bedou who knew about plastic explosives and encrypted transceivers—if they were from the same man. He might have trained up a few bomb planters, but he also seemed to be carrying out a lot of the attacks himself.

It would just not be possible to pick up every Bedou wandering around the city and the desert—that would be the AMAM way, but they would be pulling out fingernails for years and getting nowhere.

180

For Rahmani the problem resolved itself into three choices. Capture the man during one of his attacks, but that would be haphazard and possibly never happen. Capture one of his Kuwaiti associates and trace the man to his lair. Or take him crouched over his transmitter in the desert.

Rahmani decided on the last. He would bring in from Iraq two or three of his best radio-detector teams, post them at different points and try to triangulate on the source of the broadcast. He would also need an army helicopter on stand-by with a team of Special Forces ready to move. As soon as he got back to Baghdad he would set it in motion.

*   *   *

Hassan Rahmani was not the only man that day in Kuwait who was interested in the Bedou. In a suburban villa miles away from the Hilton a handsome, moustached young Kuwaiti in a white cotton thob sat in an armchair and listened to a friend who had come to him with an interesting snippet.

'I was just sitting in my car at the traffic lights, watching nothing in particular when I noticed this Iraqi army truck on the opposite side of the intersection. It was parked there, with a group of soldiers round the bonnet, eating and smoking. Then a young man, one of our own, walked out of a café clutching what looked like a tiny box. It was really small. I thought nothing of it until I saw him flick it under the lorry. Then he turned the corner and disappeared. The lights changed, but I stayed where I was.

'In five seconds the truck disintegrated. I mean, it just blew apart. The soldiers were all on the ground
181

with their legs off. I've never seen such a small package do so much damage. I tell you, I hung a U and got out of there before the AMAM came along.'

'Plastic,' mused the army officer. 'What would I not give for some of that. It must have been one of the Bedou's men. Who is that bastard, anyway? I'd love to meet him.'

'The point is, I recognized the boy.'

'What?' The young colonel leant forward, his face alight with interest.

'I wouldn't have come all this way just to tell you what you will have heard already. I tell you, I recognized the bomb-thrower. Abu Fouad, I've been buying cigarettes from his father for years.'

*   *   *

Dr Reinhart, when he addressed the Medusa Committee in London three days later, looked tired. Even though he had relinquished all his other duties at Porton Down, the documentation he had taken away with him from the first meeting and the supplementary information that had come pouring in ever since had given him a monstrous task.

'The study is probably not yet complete,' he said, 'but a fairly comprehensive picture emerges.

'Firstly, of course, we know that Saddam Hussein has a large poison gas production capacity, I estimate at over a thousand tons a year.

'During the Iran–Iraq war some Iranian soldiers who had been gassed were treated here in Britain and I was able to examine them. We could recognize phosgene and mustard gas even then.

'The worse news is that I have no doubt that Iraq now has substantial supplies of two far more lethal
182

gases, nerve agents of German invention called sarin and tabun. If these were used in the Iran–Iraq war, and I think they were, there would have been no question of treating the victims in British hospitals. They would be dead.'

'How bad are these ... er ... agents, Dr Reinhart?' asked Sir Paul Spruce.

'Sir Paul, do you have a wife?'

The urbane mandarin was startled.

'Well, yes, as a matter of fact I do.'

'Does Lady Spruce ever use perfume from a spray atomizer?'

'Yes, I do believe I have seen her do that.'

'Have you ever noticed how fine the spray from an atomizer is? How small the droplets?'

'Yes, indeed, and bearing in mind the price of perfume, I'm very glad of it.'

It was a good joke. Anyway Sir Paul liked it.

'Two of those droplets of sarin or tabun on your skin and you're dead,' said the chemist from Porton.

No-one smiled.

'The Iraqi search for nerve gases goes back to 1976. In that year they approached the British company ICI explaining they wanted to build a pesticides plant to produce four bug-killers—but the materials they asked for caused ICI to turn them down flat. The specifications the Iraqis showed were for corrosion-resistant reactor vessels, pipes and pumps that convinced ICI the real end-goal was not chemical pesticides but nerve gas. The deal was refused.'

'Thank God for that,' said Sir Paul and made a note.

'But not everyone refused them,' said the former Viennese refugee. 'Always the excuse was that Iraq needed to produce herbicides and pesticides, which of course need poisons.'

'They could not have really wanted to produce these agricultural products?' asked Paxman.

'No chance,' said Reinhart. 'To a professional chemist the key lies in the quantities and the types. In 1981 they got a German firm to build them a laboratory with a very special and unusual lay-out. It was to produce phosphorus pentachloride, the starter chemical for organic phosphorus which is one of the ingredients of nerve gas. No normal university research laboratory would need to handle such hideously toxic substances. The chemical engineers involved must have known that.

'Further export licences show orders for thiodiglycol. Mustard gas is made from it when mixed with hydrochloric acid. Thiodiglycol, in small quantities, may be used also used for making the ink for ball-point pens.'

'How much did they buy?' asked Sinclair.

'Five hundred tons.'

'That's a lot of ball-points,' muttered Paxman.

'That was in early 1983,' said Reinhart. 'In the summer their big Samarra poison gas plant went into operation, producing yperite, which is mustard gas. They began using it on the Iranians in December.

'During the first attacks by the Iranian human waves, the Iraqis used a mixture of yellow rain, yperite and tabun. By 1985 they had improved the mixture to one of hydrogen cyanide, mustard gas, tabun and sarin, achieving a 60 per cent mortality rate among the Iranian infantry.'

'Could we just look at the nerve gases, Doctor?' asked Sinclair. 'That would seem to be the really deadly stuff.'

'It is,' said Dr Reinhart. 'From 1984 the chemicals

184

for which they were shopping were phosphorus oxychloride, which is an important precursor chemical for tabun, and two sarin precursors, trimethyl phosphite and potassium fluoride. Of the first of those three they tried to order 250 tons from a Dutch company. That's enough pesticide to kill every tree, shrub and blade of grass in the Middle East. The Dutch turned them down like ICI, but they still bought two uncontrolled chemicals at that time: dimethylamine for making tabun and isopropanol for sarin.'

'If they were uncontrolled in Europe, why could they not be used for pesticides?' asked Sir Paul.

'Because of the quantities,' Reinhart replied, 'and the chemical manufacturing and handling equipment, and the factory lay-outs. To a skilled chemist or chemical engineer none of these purchases could be other than for poison gas.'

'Do you know who the main supplier over the years has been, Doctor?' asked Sir Paul.

'Oh yes. There has been some input of a scientific nature from the Soviet Union and East Germany in the early days, and some exports from about eight countries, in most cases of small quantities of uncontrolled chemicals. But 80 per cent of the plants, lay-outs, machinery, special handling equipment, chemicals, technology and know-how came from West Germany.'

'Actually,' drawled Sinclair, 'we've been protesting to Bonn for years. They always trashed the protests. Doctor, can you identify the chemical gas plants on those photos we gave you?'

'Yes, of course. Some factories are identified in the paperwork, others you can see with a magnifying glass.'

The chemist spread five large air-photos on the table.

'I do not know the Arab names, but these numbers identify the photographs for you, do they not?'

'Yep, you just point out the buildings,' said Sinclair.

'Here, the whole complex of seventeen buildings ... here, this big single plant ... you see the air scrubber unit? And here, this one ... and this whole complex of eight buildings ... and this one.'

Sinclair studied a list brought from his attaché case. He nodded grimly.

'As we thought. Al-Qaim, Fallujah, Al-Hillah, Salman Pak and Samarra. Doctor, I'm very very grateful to you. Our guys in the States figured out exactly the same. They'll all be targeted for the first wave of attacks.'

When the meeting broke up Sinclair, with Simon Paxman and Terry Martin, strolled up to Piccadilly and had a coffee at Richoux.

'I don't know about you guys,' said Sinclair as he stirred his cappuccino, 'but for us the bottom line is the gas threat. General Schwarzkopf is convinced already that's what he calls the nightmare scenario. Mass gas attacks, a rain of air bursts over all our troops. If they go, they'll go in masks and gas capes, head to foot. The good news is, this gas doesn't live long once exposed to air. It touches the desert, it's dead. Terry, you don't look convinced.'

'This rain of air bursts,' said Martin. 'How's Saddam supposed to launch them?'

Sinclair shrugged.

'Artillery barrage, I guess. That's what he did against the Iranians.'

'You're not going to pulp his artillery? It's only got

186

a range of 30 kilometres. Must be out there in the desert somewhere.'

'Sure,' said the American, 'we have the technology to locate every gun and tank out there, despite the digging-in and the camouflage.'

'So, if his guns are broken, how else does Saddam launch the gas rain?'

'Fighter-bombers, I guess.'

'But you'll have destroyed them, too, by the time the ground forces move,' Martin pointed out. 'Saddam will have nothing left flying.'

'OK, so Scud missiles, whatever. That's what he'll try. And we'll waste them one by one. Sorry guys, gotta go.'

'What are you getting at, Terry?' asked Paxman when the CIA man had gone. Terry Martin sighed.

'Oh, I don't know. It's just that Saddam and his planners will know all that. They won't underestimate American air power. Simon, can you get me all Saddam's speeches over the past six months? In Arabic, must be in Arabic.'

'Yes, I suppose so. GCHQ in Cheltenham will have them, or the BBC Arabic Service. On tape or transcript?'

'Tape, if possible.'

For three days Terry Martin listened to the guttural, haranguing voice out of Baghdad. He played and replayed the tapes and could not get rid of the nagging worry that the Iraqi despot was making the wrong noises for a man in such deep trouble. Either he did not know or recognize the depth of his trouble, or he knew something his enemies did not.

On 21 September Saddam Hussein made a new speech, or rather a statement, from the Revolutionary Command Council that used his own particular vocabulary. In the statement he declared there was not the slightest chance of any Iraqi retreat from Kuwait, and that any attempt to eject Iraq would lead to 'the mother of all battles'.

That was how it was translated. The media loved it and the words became quite a catchphrase.

Dr Martin studied the text and then rang Simon Paxman.

'I've been looking at the vernacular of the Upper Tigris valley,' he said.

'Good God, what a hobby,' replied Paxman.

'The point is, the phrase he used, "the mother of all battles".'

'Yes, what about it?'

'The word translated as battle. Where he comes from, it also means casualty or bloodbath.'

There was silence down the line for a while.

'Don't worry about it.'

But despite that, Terry Martin did.

CHAPTER SEVEN

The tobacconist's son was frightened and so was his father.

'For pity's sake, tell them what you know, my son,' he begged the boy.

The two-man delegation from the Kuwait Resistance Committee had been perfectly polite when they introduced themselves to the tobacconist, but quite insistent that they wished his son to be frank and truthful with them.

The shopkeeper, though he knew he had been given two pseudonyms instead of real names, had enough wit to realize he was talking to powerful and influential members of his own people. Worse, it had come as a total surprise to him to learn that his son was involved in active resistance at all.

Worst of all, he had just learnt that his offspring was not even with the official Kuwaiti resistance, but had been seen tossing a bomb under an Iraqi truck at the behest of some strange bandit of whom he had never heard. It was enough to give any father a heart attack.

The four of them sat in the drawing room of the tobacconist's comfortable house in Keifan while one of the visitors explained that they had nothing against the Bedou, but simply wished to contact him so that they could collaborate.

So the boy explained what had happened from the moment his friend had been pulled down behind a pile of rubble at the moment he was about to fire at a speeding Iraqi truck. The men listened in silence, only the questioner occasionally interjecting with another query. It was the one who said nothing, the one in dark glasses, who was Abu Fouad.

The questioner was particularly interested in the house where the group met with the Bedou. The boy gave the address, then added: 'I do not think there is much point in going there. He is extremely watchful. One of us went there once to try and talk to him, but the place was locked. We do not think he lives there, but he knew we had been. He told us never to do that again. If it ever happened, he said, he would break contact and we would never see him again.'

Sitting in his corner, Abu Fouad nodded in approval. Unlike the others, he was a trained soldier and he thought he recognized the hand of another trained man.

189

'When will you meet him next?' he asked quietly.

There was a possibility the boy could pass a message, an invitation to a parley.

'Nowadays, he contacts one of us. The contacted one brings the rest. It may take some time.'

The two Kuwaitis left. They had descriptions of two vehicles, a battered pick-up apparently the disguise of a market gardener bringing his fruit into town from the countryside, and a powerful off-road for journeys into the desert.

Abu Fouad ran the numbers of both vehicles past a friend in the Ministry of Transport, but the trace ran out. Both numbers were fictional. The only other lead was through the identity cards the man would have to carry to pass those ubiquitous Iraqi road-blocks and checkpoints.

Through his committee he contacted a civil servant in the Interior Ministry. He was lucky. The man recalled running off a phoney identity card for a market gardener from Jahra. It was a favour he had done for the millionaire Ahmed Al-Khalifa six weeks earlier.

Abu Fouad was elated and intrigued. The merchant was an influential and respected figure in the Movement. But it was always thought he was strictly confined to the financial, non-combatant side of things. What on earth was he doing as the patron of the mysterious and lethal Bedou?

*   *   *

South of the Kuwaiti border the incoming tide of American weaponry rolled on. As the last week of September slid by, General Norman Schwarzkopf, buried in the rabbit warren of secret chambers two

190

floors below the Saudi Air Force Ministry on Old Airport Road, Riyadh, finally realized that he had enough strength at last to declare Saudi Arabia safe from Iraqi attack.

In the air General Charles 'Chuck' Horner had built an umbrella of constantly patrolling steel, a fast-moving and amply provisioned armada of air-superiority fighters, ground-attack fighter-bombers, air-to-air refuelling tankers, heavy bombers and tank-busting Thunderbolts, enough to destroy the incoming Iraqis on the ground and in the air.

He had airborne technology that could and did cover by radar every square inch of Iraq, that could sense every movement of heavy metal rolling on the roads, moving through the desert or trying to take to the air, that could listen to every Iraqi conversation on the air waves and pin-point any source of heat.

On the ground Norman Schwarzkopf knew he now had enough mechanized units, light and heavy armour, artillery and infantry to receive any Iraqi column, hold it, surround it and liquidate it.

In the last week of September, in conditions of such total secrecy that not even America's Allies were told, the plans were made to move from defensive role to offensive. The assault on Iraq was planned, even though the United Nations mandate was still limited to securing the safety of Saudi Arabia and the Gulf States, and only that.

But he also had problems. One was that the number of Iraqi troops, guns and tanks deployed against him was double the number when he arrived in Riyadh six weeks earlier. Another was that he would need double the amount of Coalition forces to liberate Kuwait than that needed to secure Saudi Arabia.

191

Norman Schwarzkopf was a man who took George Patton's dictum very seriously; one dead American or Brit or Frenchie or any other Coalition soldier or airman was one too many. Before he would go in he would want two things: double the amount of force he presently had; and an air assault guaranteed to 'degrade' by 50 per cent the strength of the Iraqi forces arrayed north of the border.

That meant more time, more equipment, more stores, more guns, more tanks, more troops, more airplanes, more fuel, more food, more stores and a lot more money. Then he told the stunned armchair Napoleons on Capitol Hill that if they wanted a victory they had better let him have it all.

Actually, it was the more urbane Chairman of Joint Chiefs of Staff General Colin Powell who passed the message on, but he softened the language down a bit. Politicians love to play the games of soldiers but they hate to be addressed in the language of soldiers.

So the planning in that last week of September was utterly secret. As it turned out, it was as well it was done. The United Nations, leaking peace plans at every seam, would wait until 29 November before giving the go-ahead to use all necessary force to evict Iraq from Kuwait unless she quit by 16 January. Had planning started at the end of November it could never have been completed in time.

*   *   *

Ahmed Al-Khalifa was deeply embarrassed. He knew Abu Fouad of course, who and what he was. Further, he sympathized with his request. But he had given his word, he explained, and he could not go

192

back on it.

Even to his fellow-Kuwaiti and fellow-resister, he did not reveal that the Bedou was in fact a British officer. But he did agree to leave a message for the Bedou in a place he knew the man would find it sooner or later.

The following morning he left a letter, with his personal recommendation urging the Bedou to agree to meet Abu Fouad, under the marble tombstone of Able Seaman Shepton in the Christian cemetery.

*　　*　　*

There were six soldiers in the group, headed by a sergeant, and when the Bedou came round the corner they were as surprised as he.

Mike Martin had garaged his small truck in the lock-up and was making his way across the city on foot towards the villa he had chosen for that night. He was tired and, unusually, his alertness was blunted. When he saw the Iraqis and knew they had seen him, he cursed himself. In his job, men can die for a moment's lack of alertness.

It was well after curfew and though he was quite used to moving through the city when it was deserted of law-abiding citizens and only the Iraqi patrols were on the prowl, he made a point of moving through the ill-lit side-streets, across the darkened patches of waste ground and down the black alleys, just as the Iraqis made a point of sticking to the main highways and intersections. That way, they never troubled each other.

But following Hassan Rahmani's return to Baghdad and his vitriolic report on the uselessness of the Popular Army, some changes were taking place.

The green berets of the Special Forces had begun to appear.

Though not classed with the élite Republican Guard, the Green Berets were at least more disciplined than the rabble of conscripts called the Popular Army. It was six of these who stood quietly by their truck at a road junction where normally there would have been no Iraqis.

Martin just had time to lean heavily on the stick he carried with him and adopt the posture of an old man. It was a good posture, for in the Arab culture the old are given respect or at least compassion.

'Hey, you,' shouted the sergeant, 'come over here.'

There were four assault rifles trained on the lone figure in the chequered keffiyeh. The old man paused, then hobbled forward.

'What are you doing out at this hour, Bedou?'

'Just an old man trying to get to his home before the curfew, sayidi,' the man whined.

'It's past the hour of curfew, fool. Two hours past.'

The old man shook his head in bewilderment.

'I didn't know, sayidi, I have no watch.'

In the Middle East watches are not indispensable, just highly prized, a sign of prosperity. Iraqi soldiers arriving in Kuwait soon acquired one; they just took them. But the word 'Bedouin' comes from 'bidun' meaning 'without'.

The sergeant grunted. The excuse was possible.

'Papers,' he said.

The old man used his spare hand to pat his soiled robe.

'I seem to have lost them,' he pleaded.

'Frisk him,' said the sergeant. One of the soldiers moved forward. The hand grenade strapped to the inside of Martin's left thigh felt like one of the water

194

melons from his truck.

'Don't you touch my balls,' said the old Bedou sharply. The soldier stopped. One in the back let out a giggle. The sergeant tried to keep a straight face.

'Well, go on, Zuhair, frisk him.'

The young soldier Zuhair hesitated, embarrassed. He knew the joke was on him.

'Only my wife is allowed to touch my balls,' said the Bedou. Two of the soldiers let out a guffaw and lowered their rifles. The rest did the same. Zuhair still held back.

'Mind you, it doesn't do her any good. I'm long past that sort of thing,' said the old man.

It was too much. The patrol roared with laughter. Even the sergeant grinned.

'All right, old man. On your way. And don't stay out again after dark.'

The Bedou limped off to the corner of the street, scratching under his clothes. At the corner he turned. The grenade, priming arm sticking clumsily out to one side, skittered across the cobbles and came to rest against the toe-cap of Zuhair. All six stared at it. Then it went off. It was the end of the six soldiers. It was also the end of September.

*   *   *

That night, far away in Tel Aviv, General Yaacov Kobi Dror of the Mossad sat in his office in the Hadar Dafna building, taking a late-night drink after work with an old friend and colleague, Shlomo Gershon, always known as Sami.

Sami Gershon was Head of the Combatants or Komeniute Division, the section responsible for running the 'illegal' agents, the dangerous cutting

195

edge of espionage. He had been one of the other two present when his chief had lied to Chip Barber.

'You don't think we should have told them?' he asked, because the subject had come up again. Dror swirled his beer in the bottle and took a swig.

'Screw them,' he growled, 'let them recruit their own bloody assets.'

As a teenage soldier he had once crouched under his Patton tank in the desert in the spring of 1967 and waited while four Arab States prepared to settle accounts with Israel once and for all. He still recalled how the outside world had confined itself to muttering, 'Tut, tut'.

With the rest of his crew, commanded by a twenty year old, he had been one of those under Israel Tal who had punched a hole straight through the Mitla Pass and driven the Egyptian army back to the Suez Canal.

And he recalled how, when Israel had destroyed four armies and four air forces in six days, the same Western media that had wrung its hands at his country's impending obliteration in May had accused Israel of bully-boy tactics by winning.

From then on Kobi Dror's philosophy was made. Screw them all. He was a sabra, born and raised in Israel, and had none of the breadth of vision nor forbearance of people like David Ben Gurion.

His political loyalty lay with the far-right Likud Party, with Menachem Begin who had been in the Irgun and Itzhak Shamir, formerly of the Stern Gang.

Once, sitting at the back of the class, listening to one of his staff lecture the new recruits, he had heard the man use the phrase 'friendly Intelligence Agencies'. He had risen and taken over the class.

196

'There is no such thing as a friend of Israel, except maybe a diaspora Jew,' he told them. 'The world is divided into two: our enemies and neutrals. Our enemies we know how to deal with. As for neutrals, take everything, give nothing. Smile at them, slap them on the back, drink with them, flatter them, thank them for their tip-offs, and tell them nothing.'

'Well, Kobi, let's hope they never find out,' said Gershon.

'How can they? There's only eight of us who know. And we're all in the Office.'

It must have been the beer. He was overlooking someone.

*   *   *

In the spring of 1988 a British businessman called Stuart Harris was attending an industrial fair in Baghdad. He was sales director of a company in Nottingham that made and sold road-grading equipment. The fair was under the auspices of the Iraqi Ministry of Transport. Like almost all Westerners, he had been billeted at the Rashid Hotel on Yafa Street, which had been built mainly for foreigners and was always under surveillance.

On the third day of the exhibition Harris had returned to his room to find a plain envelope pushed under his door. It had no name on it, just his room number, and the number was right.

Inside was a single sheet of paper and another completely plain envelope of the airmail type. The slip of paper said in English and in block capitals: ON YOUR RETURN TO LONDON PASS THIS ENVELOPE TO NORMAN AT THE ISRAELI EMBASSY.

That was all. Stuart Harris was panic-stricken,

terrified. He knew the reputation of Iraq, of its dreaded Secret Police. Whatever was in the plain envelope could get him arrested, tortured, even killed.

To his credit, he kept cool, sat down and tried to work things out. Why him, for example? There were scores of British businessmen in Baghdad. Why pick Stuart Harris? They could not know he was Jewish, that his father had arrived in England in 1935 from Germany as Samuel Horowitz, could they?

Though he would never find out, there had been a conversation two days earlier in the fairground canteen between two functionaries of the Iraqi Transport Ministry. One had told the other of his visit to the Nottingham works the previous autumn; how Harris had been his host on the first and second day, then disappeared for a day, then come back. He, the Iraqi, had asked if Harris had been ill. It was a colleague who had laughed and told him Harris had been off for Yom Kippur.

The two Iraqi civil servants thought nothing more of it, but someone at the next booth did. He reported the conversation to his superior. The senior man appeared to take no notice, but later became quite thoughtful and ran a check on Mr Stuart Harris of Nottingham, establishing his room number at the Rashid.

Harris sat and wondered what on earth to do. Even if, he reasoned, the anonymous sender of the letter had discovered he was Jewish, there was one thing they could not have known. No way. By an extraordinary coincidence, Stuart Harris was a sayan.

The Israeli Institute for Intelligence and Special Operations, founded in 1951 on the order of Ben

198

Gurion himself, is known outside its own walls as the Mossad, Hebrew for Institute. Inside its walls it is never, ever called that, but always 'the Office'. Among the leading Intelligence Agencies of the world it is by far the smallest. In terms of on-the-payroll staff, it is tiny. The CIA headquarters at Langley, Virginia, has about 25,000 employees on its staff and that excludes all the outstations. At its peak the KGB's First Chief Directorate, responsible like the CIA and Mossad for foreign Intelligence-gathering, had 15,000 case officers around the world, some 3,000 based at the Yazenevo headquarters.

Mossad has only between 1,200 and 1,500 employees at any time and less than forty case officers, called katsas.

That it can operate on such a slim budget and tiny staff, and secure the 'product' that it does, depends on two factors. One is the ability to tap into the Israeli population at will—a population still amazingly cosmopolitan and containing a bewildering variety of talents, languages and geographical origins.

The other factor is an international network of helpers or assistants, in Hebrew, sayanim. These are diaspora Jews (they must be wholly Jewish on both sides) who, although probably loyal to the country in which they reside, will also have a sympathy with the state of Israel.

There are 2,000 in London alone, 5,000 in the rest of Britain and ten times that number in the USA. They are never brought into operations, just asked for favours. And they must be convinced the help they are asked to give is not for an operation against their country of birth or adoption. Conflicting loyalties are not allowed. But they enable operational costs to be cut by a factor of up to ten.

For example: a Mossad team arrives in London to mount an operation against a Palestinian undercover squad. They need a car. A motor-trade sayan is asked to leave a legitimate second-hand car at a certain place with the keys under the mat. It is returned later, after the operation. The sayan never knows what it was used for; his books say it was out to a possible customer on approval.

The same team needs a 'front'. A property-owning sayan lends an empty shop, and a confectionery sayan stocks it with sweets and chocolates. They need a mailing 'drop'; a real-estate sayan lends the keys to a vacant office on his books.

Stuart Harris had been on holiday at the Israeli resort of Eilat when, at the bar of the Red Rock, he fell into conversation with a pleasant young Israeli who spoke excellent English. At a further conversation the Israeli brought a friend, an older man who quietly elicited from Harris where his feelings towards Israel lay. By the end of the holiday Harris had agreed that, if there was ever anything he could do...

At the end of the holiday he went home as advised and got on with his life. For two years he waited for the call, but no call ever came. However, a friendly visitor kept periodically in touch—one of the more tiresome jobs of katsas on foreign assignment is to keep tabs on the sayanim on their list.

So Stuart Harris sat in a wave of rising panic in a hotel room in Baghdad and wondered what to do. The letter could well be a provocation—he would be intercepted at the airport trying to smuggle it out. Slip it into someone else's bag? He did not feel he could do that. And how would he recover it in London?

Finally, he calmed down, worked out a plan and did it exactly right. He burned the outer envelope and the note in an ashtray, crushed the embers and flushed them down the pan. Then he hid the plain envelope under the spare blanket on the shelf above the wardrobe, having first wiped it clean.

If his room was raided he would simply swear he had never needed the blanket, never climbed to the top shelf, and the letter must have been left by a previous occupant.

In a stationery shop he bought a stout manila envelope, sticky label and sealing tape; from a post office enough stamps to send a magazine from Baghdad to London. He abstracted a promotional magazine extolling the virtues of Iraq from the trade fair and even had the empty envelope stamped with the exhibition logo.

On the last day, just before leaving for the airport with his two colleagues, he retired to his room. He slipped the letter into the magazine and sealed them in the envelope. He addressed it to an uncle in Long Eaton and stuck on the label and the stamps. In the lobby, he knew, was a post box, and the next collection was in four hours. Even if the envelope was steamed open by the goons, he reasoned, he would be over the Alps in a British airliner.

It is said that luck favours the brave or the foolish or both. The lobby *was* under surveillance by men from the AMAM, watching to see if any departing foreigner was approached by an Iraqi trying to slip him something. Harris carried his envelope under his jacket and beneath his left armpit. A man behind a newspaper in the corner was watching, but a trolley of baggage rolled between them as Harris dropped the envelope in the mail box. When the watcher saw

201

him again, he was at the desk handing in his key.

The brochure arrived at his uncle's house a week later. Harris had known his uncle was away on holiday and, as he had a key in case of fire or burglary, he used it to slip in and retrieve his package. Then he took it down to the Israeli Embassy in London and asked to see his contact. He was shown into a room and told to wait.

A middle-aged man entered, enquired his name, and why he wanted to see 'Norman'. He explained, took the airmail envelope from his pocket and laid it on the table. The Israeli diplomat went pale, asked him to wait again, and left.

The embassy building at 2 Palace Green is a handsome structure, but its classical lines give no indication of the wealth of fortifications and technology that conceal the Mossad London Station in the basement. It was from this underground fortress that a younger man was summoned urgently. Harris waited and waited.

Though he did not know it, he was being studied through a one-way mirror as he sat there with the envelope on the table in front of him. He was also being photographed while records were checked to ensure he really was a sayan and not a Palestinian terrorist. When the photograph of Stuart Harris of Nottingham from the files checked with the man behind the one-way mirror, the young katsa finally entered the room.

He smiled, introduced himself as Rafi and invited Harris to start his story at the very beginning, right back in Eilat. So Harris told him. Rafi knew all about Eilat (he had just read the entire file), but he needed to check. When the narrative reached Baghdad he became interested. He had few queries at first,

202

allowing Harris to narrate in his own time. Then the questions came, many of them, until Harris had relived all he had done in Baghdad several times. Rafi took no notes, the whole thing was being recorded. Finally he used a wall phone to have a muttered conversation in Hebrew with a senior colleague next door.

His last act was to thank Stuart Harris profusely, congratulate him on his courage and cool head, exhort him never to mention the entire incident to *anyone*, and wished him safe journey back home. Then Harris was shown out.

A man with anti-blast helmet, flak-jacket and gloves took the letter away. It was photographed and X-rayed. The Israeli Embassy had already lost one man to a letter bomb, and did not intend to lose another.

Finally the letter was opened. It contained two sheets of onion-skin airmail paper covered in script. In Arabic. Rafi did not speak Arabic, let alone read it. Neither did anyone else on London Station, at least not well enough to read spidery Arabic handscript. Rafi sent a copious and heavily encrypted radio report to Tel Aviv, then wrote an even fuller account in the formal and uniform style called NAKA in the Mossad. The letter and the report went into the diplomatic bag and caught the evening flight by El Al from Heathrow to Ben Gurion.

A despatch rider with an armed escort met the courier right off the plane and took the canvas bag destined for the big building on King Saul Boulevard where, just after the breakfast hour, it found itself in front of the head of the Iraq Desk, a very able young katsa called David Sharon.

He *did* both speak and read Arabic, and what he read in those two onion-skin pages of letter left him with the same sensation he felt the first time he threw himself out of an airplane over the Negev desert while training with the Paras.

Using his own typewriter, avoiding secretary and word-processor, he typed out a literal translation of the letter in Hebrew. Then he took them both, plus Rafi's report as to how Mossad had come by the letter, to his immediate chief, Director of Mid-East Division.

What the letter said, in effect, was that the writer was a high-ranking functionary in the topmost councils of the Iraqi regime and that he was prepared to work for Israel for money, but only for money.

There was a bit more, and a post-box address at Baghdad's principal post office for a reply, but that was the gist of it.

*   *   *

That evening there was a high-level meeting in Kobi Dror's private office. Present were he and Sami Gershon, Head of the Combatants. Also Eitan Hadar, Sharon's immediate superior as Director for Mid-East, to whom he had taken the Baghdad letter that morning. David Sharon himself was summoned.

From the outset Gershon was dismissive.

'It's a phoney,' he said. 'I've never seen such a blatant, clumsy, obvious attempt at entrapment. Kobi, I'm not sending any of my men in there to check it out. It would be sending the man to his death. I wouldn't even send an oter to Baghdad to try to make contact.'

An oter is an Arab used by the Mossad to establish
204

preliminary contact with a fellow-Arab, a low-level go-between and a lot more dispensable than a full-fledged Israeli katsa.

Gershon's view seemed to prevail. The letter was a madness, apparently an attempt to lure a senior katsa to Baghdad for arrest, torture, public trial and public execution. Finally Dror turned to David Sharon.

'Well, David, you have a tongue. What do you think?'

Sharon nodded regretfully.

'I think Sami almost certainly has to be right. Sending a good man in there would be crazy.'

Eitan Hadar shot him a warning look. Between Divisions there was the usual rivalry. No need to hand victory to Gershon on a plate.

'Ninety-nine per cent of the chances say it has to be a trap.'

'Only ninety-nine?' asked Dror teasingly. 'And the one per cent, my young friend?'

'Oh, just a foolish idea. It just occurred to me, the one per cent might say that out of the blue we have a new Penkovsky.'

There was dead silence. The word hung in the air like an open challenge. Gershon expelled his breath in a long hiss. Kobi Dror stared at his Iraq Desk Chief. Sharon looked at his fingertips.

In espionage there are only four ways of recruiting an agent for infiltration into the high councils of a target country.

The first is far and away the most difficult: to use one of your own nationals, but trained to an extraordinary degree to pass for a national of the target country right in the heart of that target. It is almost impossible, unless the infiltrator was born and raised in the target country and can be eased back in,

205

with a cover story to explain his absence. Even then, he will have to wait years to rise to useful office with access to secrets, a sleeper for up to ten years.

Yet once, Israel had been the past masters of this technique. This was because, when Israel was young, Jews poured in who had been raised all over the world. There were Jews who could pass as Moroccans, Algerians, Libyans, Egyptians, Syrians, Iraqis and Yemenis. This was apart from all those coming from Russia, Poland, Western Europe and North and South America.

The most successful of these was Elie Cohen, born and raised in Syria. He was slipped back into Damascus as a Syrian who had been away for years and had now returned. With his Syrian name, Cohen became an intimate of high-ranking politicians, civil servants and generals, who spoke freely to their endlessly generous host at his sumptuous parties. Everything they said, including the entire Syrian battle plan, went back to Tel Aviv just in time for the Six Day War. Cohen was exposed, tortured, and publicly hanged in Revolution Square, Damascus. Such infiltrations are extremely dangerous and very rare.

But the years passed, the original immigrant Israelis became old; their sabra children did not study Arabic and could not attempt what Elie Cohen had done. This was why, by 1990, the Mossad had far less brilliant Arabists than one might imagine.

But there was a second reason. Penetration of Arab secrets is more easily accomplished in Europe or America. If an Arab State is buying an American fighter, the details can more easily be stolen and at a lot less risk in America. If an Arab high-up seems susceptible to an approach, why not make it while he is visiting the fleshpots of Europe? That is why by 1990 the vast bulk of Mossad operations were conducted in low-risk Europe and America rather than the high-risk Arab States.

The king of all the infiltrators, however, was Marcus Wolf who for years ran the East German Intelligence net. He had one great advantage—an East German could pass for a West German.

During his time 'Mischa' Wolf infiltrated scores and scores of his agents into West Germany, one of them becoming the personal private secretary of Chancellor Willi Brandt himself. Wolf's speciality was the prim, dowdy little spinster secretary who rose to become indispensable to her West German minister-employer, and who could copy every document that crossed her desk for transmission back to East Berlin.

The second method of infiltration is to use a national of the aggressor Agency, but posing as someone coming from a third nation. The target country knows the infiltrator is a foreigner, but is persuaded he is a friendly, sympathetic foreigner.

Mossad again did this brilliantly with a man called Ze'ev Gur Arieh. He was born Wolfgang Lotz of Mannheim, Germany, in 1921. Wolfgang was six foot tall, blond, blue-eyed, uncircumcized and yet Jewish. He came to Israel as a boy, was raised there, took his Hebrew name, fought with the underground Haganah and went on to become a major in the Israeli army. Then the Mossad took him in hand.

He was sent back to Germany for two years to perfect his native German and 'prosper' with Mossad money. Then, with a new gentile German wife, he emigrated to Cairo and set up a riding school.

It was a great success. Egyptian staff officers loved

to relax with their horses, attended by the champagne-serving Wolfgang, a good right-wing, anti-semitic German in whom they could confide. And confide they did. Everything they said went back to Tel Aviv. Lotz was eventually caught, was lucky not to be hanged, and after the Six Day War was exchanged for Egyptian prisoners.

But an even more successful impostor was another German of an earlier generation. Before the Second World War Richard Sorge was a foreign correspondent in Tokyo, speaking Japanese and with high contacts in Hideki Tojo's government. That government approved of Hitler and assumed Sorge was a loyal Nazi—he certainly said he was.

It never occurred to Tokyo that Sorge was not a German Nazi—he was a German Communist in the service of Moscow. For years he laid the war plans of the Tojo regime open for Moscow to study. His great *coup* was his last. In 1941 Hitler's armies stood before Moscow. Stalin needed to know urgently: would Japan mount an invasion of the USSR from her Manchurian bases? Sorge found out; the answer was no. Stalin could transfer 40,000 Mongol troops from the East to Moscow. The Asiatic cannon fodder held the Germans at bay for a few more weeks until winter came and Moscow was saved.

Not so Sorge; he was unmasked and hanged. But before he died, his information had probably changed history.

The most common method of securing an agent in the target country is the third: simply to recruit such a man when he is already 'in place'. Recruitment can be tediously slow or surprisingly fast. To this end 'talent spotters' patrol the diplomatic community looking for a senior functionary of 'the other side' who may appear disenchanted, resentful, dissatisfied, bitter or in any way susceptible to recruitment.

Delegations visiting foreign parts are studied to see if one can be taken aside, given a fine old time and approached for a change of loyalty. When the talent spotter has tabbed a 'possible', the recruiters move in, usually starting with a casual friendship which becomes deeper and warmer. Eventually the 'friend' suggests his pal might do him a small favour, a minor and inconsequential piece of information is needed.

When the trap is sprung, there is no going back, and the more ruthless the regime the new recruit is serving, the less likely he will be to confess all and throw himself on that regime's non-existent mercy.

The motives for being so recruited to serve another country vary. The recruit may be in debt, in a bitter marriage, passed over for promotion, revolted by his own regime, or simply lust for a new life and plenty of money. He may be recruited through his own weaknesses, sexual or homosexual, or simply by sweet talk and flattery.

Quite a few Soviets, like Penkovsky and Gordievsky, changed sides for genuine 'conscience' reasons, but most spies who turn on their own country do so because they share a quite monstrous vanity, a conviction that they are truly important in the scheme of things.

But the weirdest of all the recruitments is called simply the 'walk-in'. As the phrase implies, the recruit simply walks in, unexpected and unannounced, and offers his services.

The reaction of the agency so approached is always one of extreme scepticism—surely this must be a 'plant' by the other side? Thus when, in 1960, a tall Russian approached the Americans in Moscow, declared he was a full colonel of the Soviet Military Intelligence arm, the GRU, and offered to spy for the West, he was rejected.

Bewildered, the man approached the British, who gave him a try. Oleg Penkovsky turned out to be one of the most amazing agents ever. In his brief, thirty-month career he turned over 5,500 documents to the Anglo-American operation that 'ran' him, and every one of them was in the 'secret' or 'top secret' category. During the Cuba missile crisis the world never realized that President Kennedy knew the full hand of cards that Nikita Khruschev had to play, as a poker player with a mirror behind his opponent's back. The mirror was Penkovsky.

The Russian took crazy risks, refusing to come out to the West while he had the chance. After the missile crisis he was unmasked by Soviet Counter-Intelligence, tried and shot.

None of the other three Israelis in Kobi Dror's room that night in Tel Aviv needed to be told anything about Oleg Penkovsky. In their world, he was part of legend. The dream hovered in all their minds after Sharon had dropped the name. A real, live, gold-plated, twenty-four-carat traitor in Baghdad? Could it be true, could it possibly be true?

Kobi Dror gave Sharon a long, hard look.

'What have you in mind, young man?'

'I was just thinking,' said Sharon with feigned diffidence, 'a letter ... no risks to anyone ... just a letter ... asking a few questions, difficult questions, things we would like to know ... he comes up or he doesn't.'

Dror glanced at Gershon. The man who ran the 'illegal' agents shrugged. I put men in on the ground, the gesture seemed to say, what do I care about

210

letters?

'All right, young David. We write him a letter back. We ask him some questions. Then we see. Eitan, you work with David on this. Let me see the letter before it goes.'

Eitan Hadar and David Sharon left together.

'I hope you know what the hell you're doing,' the head of Mid-East muttered to his protégé.

The letter was crafted with extreme care. Several in-house experts worked on it, the Hebrew version at least. Translation would come later.

David Sharon introduced himself by his first name only, and right at the start. He thanked the writer for his trouble and assured him the letter had arrived safely at the destination the writer must have intended.

The reply went on to say that the writer could not fail to understand that his letter had aroused great surprise and suspicion, both by its source and its method of transmission.

David knew, he said, that the writer was clearly no fool and that therefore the writer would realize that 'my people' would need to establish some bona fides.

David went on to assure the writer that if this bona fides could be established, the writer's requirement for payment would present no problem, but clearly the product would have to justify the financial rewards that 'my people' were prepared to pay. Would the writer therefore be kind enough to seek to answer the questions on the attached sheet?

The full letter was longer and more complicated, but that was the burden of it. Sharon ended by giving the writer a mailing address in Rome for his reply.

The address was actually a discontinued safe house that the Rome Station had volunteered at Tel Aviv's urgent request. From then on, Rome Station would keep an eye on the abandoned address after all. If Iraqi security showed up at it, they would be spotted and the affair aborted.

The list of twenty questions was also carefully chosen and after much head-scratching. To eight of the questions Mossad already knew the answers, but could not be expected to know. So an attempt to fool Tel Aviv would not work.

Eight more questions concerned developments that could be checked for veracity after they had happened. Four questions were things that Tel Aviv really wanted to know, particularly about the intentions of Saddam Hussein himself.

'Let's see how high this bastard really goes,' said Kobi Dror when he read the list.

Finally a professor of Tel Aviv University's Arabic Faculty was called in to phrase the letter in that ornate and flowery style of the written language. Sharon signed it in Arabic with the Arab version of his own name, Daoud.

The text also contained one other point. David would like to give his writer a name, and if the writer in Baghdad did not object, would he mind being known simply as Jericho?

The letter was mailed from the only Arab country where Israel had an embassy—Cairo.

After it had gone, David Sharon got on with his work and waited. The more he thought it over, the more crazy the affair seemed to be. A post-office box, in a country where the Counter-Intelligence net was run by someone as smart as Hassan Rahmani, was horrendously dangerous. So was writing top-secret information 'in clear' and there was no indication that Jericho knew anything about secret writing.

212

Using the ordinary mails was also out of the question, if this thing developed. However, he reasoned, it probably would not.

But it did. Four weeks later Jericho's reply reached Rome and was brought unopened in a blast-proof box to Tel Aviv. Extreme precautions were taken. The envelope might be wired to explosives or smeared with deadly toxin. When the scientists finally declared it 'clean' it was opened.

To their stunned amazement, Jericho had come up with paydirt. All the eight questions to which Mossad already knew the answers were completely accurate. Eight more, troop movements, promotions, dismissals, foreign trips by identifiable luminaries of the regime, would have to wait for check-out as and when they occurred, if they ever did. The last four questions Tel Aviv could neither know nor check, but all were utterly feasible.

David Sharon wrote a fast letter back, in a text that would cause no security problems if intercepted. Dear Uncle, many thanks for your letter which has now arrived. It is wonderful to hear that you are well and in good health. Some among the points you raise will take time, but all being well I will write again soon. Your loving nephew, Daoud.

The mood was growing in the Hadar Dafna building that this man Jericho might be serious after all. If that was so, urgent action was needed. An exchange of two letters was one thing; running a deep-cover agent inside a brutal dictatorship was another. There was no way communication could continue on the basis of 'in clear' script, public mails and post-office boxes. They were a recipe for an early disaster.

A case officer would be needed to get into
213

Baghdad, live there and 'run' Jericho using all the usual tradecraft—secret writing, codes, dead-letter-boxes and a no-intercept means of getting the product out of Baghdad and back to Israel.

'I'm not having it,' Gershon repeated. 'I will not put a senior Israeli katsa into Baghdad on a "black" mission for an extended stay. It's diplomatic cover or he don't go.'

'All right, Sami,' said Dror, 'diplomatic cover it is. Let's see what we've got.'

The point of diplomatic cover is that a 'black' agent can be arrested, tortured, hanged—whatever. An accredited diplomat, even in Baghdad, can avoid such unpleasantness; if caught spying he will be declared *persona non grata* and expelled. It is done all the time.

Several major divisions of the Mossad went into overdrive that summer, especially Research. Gershon could already tell them he had no agent on the staff of any embassy accredited to Baghdad, and his nose was already well out of joint because of it. So the search began to find a diplomat who would suit.

Every foreign embassy in Baghdad was identified. From the capital cities of every country a list was acquired of all their staff in Baghdad. No-one checked out; no-one had ever worked for the Mossad before, who could be reactivated. There was not even a sayan on those lists.

Then a clerk came up with an idea: United Nations. The world body had one agency based in Baghdad in 1988, the UN Economic Commission for West Asia.

Mossad has a big penetration of the United Nations in New York and a staff list was acquired. One name checked out; a young Jewish Chilean

214

diplomat called Alfonso Benz Moncada. He was not a trained agent, but he *was* a sayan and, therefore, presumably prepared to be helpful.

One by one Jericho's tips came true. The checking process revealed the army divisions he said would be moved were moved; the promotions he foretold duly happened, the dismissals took place.

'Either Saddam himself is behind this farago, or Jericho is betraying his country from arsehole to elbow,' was Kobi Dror's judgement.

David Sharon sent a third letter, also innocently couched. For his second and third missive the professor had not been needed. The third letter referred to an order by the Baghdad-based client for some very delicate glassware and porcelain. Clearly, said David, a little more patience was needed so that a means of transshipment could be devised that would guarantee the cargoes from accidental disaster.

A Spanish-speaking katsa already based in South America was sent hotfoot to Santiago, and persuaded the parents of Señor Benz to urge their son home immediately on compassionate leave because his mother was seriously ill. It was the father who telephoned his son in Baghdad. The worried son applied for and at once got three weeks' compassionate leave and flew back to Chile.

He was met not by a sick mother but by an entire team of Mossad training officers who begged him to accede to their request. He discussed the matter with his parents and agreed. The emotional pull of the needs of the Land of Israel, which none of them had ever seen, was strong.

Another sayan in Santiago, without knowing why, lent his summer villa, detached in a walled garden,

215

out of the city near the sea, and the training team went to work.

It takes two years to train a katsa to run a deep-cover agent in hostile terrain, and that is the minimum. The team had three weeks. They worked sixteen-hour days. They taught the thirty-year-old Chilean secret writing and basic codes, miniature photography and reduction of photographs to microdots. They took him out on the streets and taught him how to spot a tail. They warned him never to shake a tail, except in absolute emergency if carrying deeply incriminating material. They told him if he even thought he was being followed to abort the rendezvous or the pick-up and try again later.

They showed him how to use combustible chemicals stored in a false fountain-pen to destroy incriminating evidence in seconds while sheltering in any men's lavatory, or just round a corner.

They took him out in cars to show him how to spot a car tail, one acting as instructor and the rest of the team as the 'hostiles'. They taught him until his ears rang and his eyes ached and he begged for sleep.

Then they taught him about dead-letter-boxes or 'drops'—secret compartments where a message may be left or another collected. They showed him how to create one from a recess behind a loose brick in a wall, or under a tombstone, in a crevice in an old tree or beneath a flagstone.

After three weeks Alfonso Benz Moncada bade goodbye to his tearful parents and flew back to Baghdad via London. The senior instructor leant back in his chair at the villa, passed an exhausted hand-over his forehead and told the team: 'If that bugger stays alive and free, I'll make the pilgrimage to Mecca.'

216

The team laughed; their leader was a deeply Orthodox Jew. All the time they had taught Moncada, none of them knew what he was going to do back in Baghdad. It was not their job to know. Neither did the Chilean.

It was during the stop-over in London that he was taken to the Heathrow Penta Hotel. There he met Sami Gershon and David Sharon, and they told him.

'Don't try and identify him,' Gershon warned the young man. 'Leave that to us. Just establish the "drops" and service them. We'll send you the lists of things we want answered—you won't understand them, they'll be in Arabic. We don't think Jericho speaks much English, if at all. Don't ever try to translate what we send you. Just put it in one of the you-to-him "drops" and make the appropriate chalk mark so he knows to go and service the drop.

'When you see his chalk mark, go and service the him-to-you box and get his answer back.'

In a separate bedroom Alfonso Benz Moncada was given his new luggage. There was a camera that looked like a tourist's Pentax but took a snap-on cartridge with over a hundred exposures in it, plus an innocent-looking aluminium strut frame for holding the camera at exactly the right distance above a sheet of paper. The camera was pre-set for that range.

His wash-kit included combustible chemicals disguised as after-shave and various invisible inks. The letter-writing wallet held all the treated paper for secret writing. Lastly, they told him the means for communicating with them, a method they had been setting up while he was training in Chile.

He would write letters concerning his love of chess—he already was a chess fan—to his pen pal Justin Bokomo of Uganda, working in the General

Secretariat of the UN building in New York. His letters would *always* go out of Baghdad in the UN diplomatic mail pouch for New York. The replies would also come from Bokomo in New York.

Though Benz Moncada did not know it, there was a Ugandan called Bokomo in New York. There was also a Mossad katsa in the mail room to effect the intercepts.

Bokomo's letters would have a reverse side which, when treated, would reveal Mossad's question list. This was to be photocopied when no-one was looking and passed to Jericho in one of the agreed 'drops'. Jericho's reply would probably be in spidery Arabic script. Each page was to be photographed ten times (in case of smudging) and the film despatched to Bokomo.

Back in Baghdad the young Chilean, with his heart in his mouth, established six 'drops', mainly behind loose bricks in old walls or ruined houses, under flagstones in back alleys and one under a stone window-sill of a derelict shop.

Each time he thought he would be surrounded by the dreaded AMAM, but the citizens of Baghdad seemed as courteous as ever and no-one took any notice of him as he prowled, apparently a curious foreign tourist, up and down the alleys and side-streets of the Old Quarter, the Armenian Quarter, the fruit and vegetable market at Kasra and the old cemeteries; anywhere he could find crumbling old walls and loose flagstones where no-one would ever think of looking.

He wrote down the locations of the six 'drops', three to contain messages from him to Jericho and three for replies from Jericho to him. He also devised six places—walls, gates, shutters, where an innocent chalk mark would alert Jericho that there was a message for him, or him that Jericho had a reply ready and sitting in a dead-letter-box awaiting collection.

Each chalk mark responded to a different 'drop'. He wrote down the locations of these 'drops' and chalk-mark sites so precisely that Jericho could find them on written description only.

All the time he watched for a tail, either driving or on foot. Just once he was under surveillance, but it was clumsy and routine, for the AMAM seemed to pick occasional days to follow occasional diplomats. The following day there was no tail, so he resumed again.

When he had it all ready, he wrote it down with typewriter having memorized every detail, destroyed the ribbon, photographed the sheets, destroyed the paperwork and sent the film to Mr Bokomo. Via the mail room of the UN building on the East River, New York, the small package came back to David Sharon in Tel Aviv.

The risky part was getting all this information to Jericho. It meant one last letter to that damnable post-office box in Baghdad. Sharon wrote to 'his friend' that the papers he needed would be deposited at exactly noon in fourteen days, 18 August 1988, and should be picked up no more than one hour later.

The precise instructions, in Arabic, were with Moncada by the 16th. At five to noon on the 18th he entered the post office, was directed to the post box and dropped the bulky package in. No-one stopped or arrested him. An hour later Jericho unlocked the box and withdrew the package. He, too, was not stopped or arrested.

With secure contact now established, traffic began

to flow. Jericho insisted he would 'price' each consignment of information that Tel Aviv wanted, and if the money was deposited the information would be sent. He named a very discreet bank in Vienna, the Bank Winkler in the Ballgasse, just off Franziskanerplatz, and gave an account number.

Tel Aviv agreed, and immediately checked out the bank. It was small, ultra-discreet and virtually impregnable. It clearly contained a numbered account that matched, because the first transfer of 20,000 dollars by Tel Aviv into it was not returned to the transferring bank with a query.

The Mossad suggested Jericho might care to identify himself 'for his own protection, in case anything went wrong and his friends to the West could help'. Jericho refused point blank; he went further. If any attempt were made to survey the 'drops' or close in on him in any way, or if ever the money was not forthcoming, he would shut off immediately.

Mossad agreed, but tried other ways. Psycho-portraits were drawn, his handwriting studied, lists of Iraqi notables drawn up and studied. All the back-room boys could guess was that Jericho was middle-aged, of medium education, probably spoke little or hesitant English and had a military or quasi-military background.

'That gives me half the bloody Iraqi High Command, the top fifty in the Ba'ath Party and John Doe's cousin Fred,' growled Kobi Dror.

Alfonso Benz Moncada 'ran' Jericho for two years and the product was twenty-four-carat gold. It concerned politics, conventional weapons, military progress, changes of command, armaments procurement, rockets, gas, germ warfare and two attempted *coups* against Saddam Hussein. Only on Iraq's nuclear progress was Jericho hesitant. He was asked, of course. It was under deep secrecy and known only to the Iraqi equivalent of Robert Oppenheimer, the physicist Dr Jaafar Al-Jaafar. To press too hard would be to invite exposure, he reported.

In the autumn of 1989 he told Tel Aviv that Gerry Bull was under suspicion and under surveillance in Brussels by a team from the Iraqi Mukhabarat. The Mossad, who were by then using Bull as another source for progress on Iraq's rockets programme, tried to warn him as subtly as they could. There was no way they would tell him to his face what they knew—it was tantamount to telling him they had an asset high in Baghdad, and no Agency will ever blow away an asset like that.

So the katsa controlling the substantial Brussels Station had his men penetrate Bull's apartment on several occasions through the autumn and winter, leaving oblique messages by rewinding a video tape, changing wine glasses about, leaving a patio window open, even a long strand of female hair on his pillow.

The gun scientist became worried all right, but not enough. When Jericho's message concerning the intent to liquidate Bull came through, it was too late. The 'hit' had been carried out.

Jericho's information gave the Mossad an almost-complete picture of Iraq in the build-up to the invasion of Kuwait in 1990. What he told them about Saddam's weapons of mass destruction confirmed and amplified the pictorial evidence that had been passed over to them by Jonathan Pollard, by then sentenced to life in prison.

Bearing in mind what Mossad knew, and what

221

they assumed America must also know, they waited for America to react. But as the chemical, nuclear and bacteriological preparations in Iraq progressed, the torpor in the West continued, so Tel Aviv stayed silent.

Two million dollars had passed from the Mossad to the numbered account of Jericho in Vienna by August 1990. He was expensive, but he was good and Tel Aviv reckoned he was worth it. Then the invasion of Kuwait took place and the unforeseen happened. The United Nations, having passed the Resolution of 2 August calling on Iraq to withdraw at once, felt it could not continue to support Saddam by maintaining a presence in Baghdad. Abruptly on 7 August the Economic Commission for West Asia was closed down and its diplomats recalled.

Benz Moncada was able to do one last thing. He left a message in a 'drop' telling Jericho that he was being expelled and contact was now broken. However, he might return and Jericho should continue to scan the places where the chalk marks were put. Then he left. The young Chilean was extensively debriefed in London until there was nothing left he could tell David Sharon.

Thus Kobi Dror was able to lie to Chip Barber with a straight face. At the time, he was *not* running an asset in Baghdad. It would be too embarrassing to admit that he had never discovered the traitor's name and now he had even lost contact. Still, as Sami Gershon had made plain, if the Americans ever found out ... With hindsight, perhaps he really should have mentioned Jericho.

CHAPTER EIGHT

Mike Martin visited the tomb of Able Seaman Shepton in the cemetery of Sulaibikhat on 1 October and discovered the plea from Ahmed Al-Khalifa.

He was not particularly surprised. If Abu Fouad had heard of him, he also had heard of the steadily growing and spreading Kuwaiti resistance movement and of its shadowy leading light. That they should eventually have to meet was probably inevitable.

In six weeks the position of the Iraqi occupation forces had changed dramatically. In their invasion they had had a walk-over, and had begun their occupation with a sloppy confidence, assured that their stay in Kuwait would be as effortless as the conquest.

The looting had been easy and profitable, the destruction amusing and the using of the womenfolk pleasurable. It had been the way of conquerors that went back to the days of Babylon.

Kuwait, after all, was a fat pigeon, ready for the plucking. But in six weeks the pigeon had begun to peck and scratch. Over a hundred soldiers and eight officers had either disappeared or been found dead. The disappearances could not all be explained by desertions. For the first time the occupation forces were experiencing fear.

Officers no longer travelled in a single staff car, but insisted on a truck-load of escorting troops. Headquarters buildings had to be guarded night and day, to the point where Iraqi officers had taken to firing over the heads of their sleeping sentries to wake them up.

The nights had become periods of no-go for anything less than a substantial troop movement. The road-block teams huddled inside their redoubts when darkness fell. And still the mines went off, the vehicles burst into flame or seized up with ruined engines, the grenades were thrown and the soldiers disappeared with cut throats into sewers or garbage skips.

The escalating resistance had forced the High Command to replace the Popular Army with the Special Forces, good fighting troops who ought to be at the front line in case the Americans came. Early October for Kuwait was not, to echo Churchill's phrase, the beginning of the end, but it was the end of the beginning.

Martin had no means of replying to Al-Khalifa's message when he read it in the graveyard, so it was not until the following day that he deposited his answer.

He agreed to meet, he said, but on his own terms. To have the advantage of darkness but to avoid the curfew at 10 p.m. he called for a meeting at half-past seven. He gave exact directions as to where Abu Fouad should park his car and the small grove of trees where he would meet. The place he indicated was in the district of Abrak Kheitan, close to the main highway from the city to the now shattered and unused airport.

Martin knew it to be an area of traditional, stone-built houses with flat roofs. On one of those roofs he would be waiting for two hours before the rendezvous to see if the Kuwaiti officer was being followed and if so by whom; his own bodyguards or the Iraqis. In a hostile environment the SAS officer

224

was still at large and in combat because he took no chances, none at all.

He knew nothing of Abu Fouad's concept of security and was not prepared to assume it was brilliant. He established the meeting for the evening of the 7th, and left his reply beneath the marble slab. Ahmed Al-Khalifa retrieved it on the 4th.

* * *

Dr John Hipwell, when he reappeared before the Medusa Committee, would never have been taken during a casual meeting for a nuclear physicist, let alone one of those scientists who spent his working days behind the massive security of the Atomic Weapons Establishment at Aldermaston designing plutonium warheads for the soon-to-be-fitted Trident missiles.

A passing observer would have assumed a bluff, Home Counties farmer, more at home leaning wisely over a pen of fat lambs at the local market than supervising the cladding of lethal discs of plutonium in pure gold.

Although the weather was still mild he wore, as in August, his square-patterned shirt, wool tie and tweed jacket. Without waiting to be asked, he used his big red hands to fill and tamp a briar pipe with shag tobacco before starting into his report. Sir Paul Spruce twitched his pointed nose in distaste and gestured for the air-conditioning to be raised a notch.

'Well, gentlemen, the good news is that our friend Mr Saddam Hussein does not have an atomic bomb at his disposal. Not yet, not by a long chalk,' said Hipwell as he disappeared into a cloud of pale blue smoke.

There was a pause while the boffin attended to his personal bonfire. Perhaps, Terry Martin mused, if you risk every day collecting a lethal dose of plutonium rays the occasional pipe of tobacco does not really matter. Dr Hipwell glanced at his notes.

'Iraq has been on the trail of her own nuclear bomb since the mid-1970s, when Saddam Hussein really came to power. It seems to be the man's obsession.

'In those years Iraq bought a complete nuclear reactor system from France, which was not bound by the Nuclear Non-Proliferation Treaty of 1968 for that very purpose.'

He sucked contentedly and tamped the glowing brush-fire at the top of his briar once again. Drifting embers settled on his notes.

'Forgive me,' said Sir Paul, 'was this reactor for the purposes of generating electricity?'

'Supposed to be,' agreed Hipwell. 'Absolute rubbish of course, and the French knew it. Iraq has the third largest oil deposits in the world. They could have had an oil-fired power station for a fraction of the price. No, the point was to fuel the reactor with low-grade uranium, called yellowcake or caramel, which they could persuade people to sell them. After use in a reactor, the end-product is plutonium.'

There were nods round the table. Everyone knew that the British reactor at Sellafield created electricity for the power grid and spewed out the plutonium that went to Dr Hipwell for his warheads.

'So, the Israelis went to work,' said Hipwell. 'First, one of their commando teams blew up the huge turbine at Toulon before it was shipped, setting the project back two years. Then in 1981, when Saddam's precious Osirak One and Two plants were about to start up, Israeli fighter-bombers swept in

226

and blew the lot to Kingdom come. Since then, Saddam has never succeeded in buying another reactor. After a short while, he stopped trying.'

'Why the hell did he do that?' asked Harry Sinclair from his end of the table.

'Because he changed direction,' said Hipwell with a broad smile, as of one who has solved *The Times* crossword in half an hour. 'Up till then he was pursuing the plutonium road to an atomic bomb. Ever since, he has been pursuing the uranium road. With some success by the way. But not enough. Yet...'

'I don't understand,' said Sir Paul Spruce. 'What is the difference between a plutonium-based and a uranium-based atomic bomb?'

'Uranium is simpler,' said the physicist. 'Look ... there are various radio-active substances that can be used for a chain reaction, but for your simple, basic, effective atom bomb, uranium's the ticket. That's what Saddam has been after since 1982—a basic uranium-based atomic bomb. He hasn't got there yet, but he's still trying and he'll get there one day.'

Dr Hipwell sat back with a broad beam as if he had settled the enigma of the Creation. Like most of those round the table, Sir Paul Spruce was still perplexed.

'If he can buy this uranium for his destroyed reactor, why can't he make a bomb with it?' he asked.

Dr Hipwell pounced upon the question like a farmer on a bargain.

'Different kinds of uranium, my dear. Funny stuff, uranium. Very rare. From 1,000 tons of uranium ore, all you get is a block the size of a cigar box. Yellowcake. It's called Natural Uranium, with an isotope number of 238.

'You can power an industrial reactor with it, but

not make a bomb. Not pure enough. For a bomb you need the lighter isotope, Uranium 235.'

'Where does that come from?' asked Paxman.

'It's inside the yellowcake. In that one cigar-box-sized block there is enough Uranium 235 to stick under one fingernail without discomfort. The devil is, getting the two separated. It's called isotope separation. Very difficult, very technical, very expensive and very slow.'

'But you said Iraq is getting there,' pointed out Sinclair from the end of the table.

'He is, but he's not there yet,' said Hipwell. 'There's only one viable way of purifying and refining the yellowcake to the required ninety-three per cent pure.

'Years ago, in the Manhattan Project, your chaps tried several methods. They were experimenting, see? Ernest Lawrence tried one way, Robert Oppenheimer tried another. In those days they used both methods in complementary fashion and created enough Uranium 235 to make Little Boy.

'After the war the centrifuge method was invented and slowly perfected. Nowadays only this method is used. Basically, you put the feedstock into a thing called a centrifuge, which spins so fast the whole process has to be done in a vacuum or the bearings would turn to jelly.

'Slowly the heavier isotopes, the ones you don't want, are drawn to the outer wall of the centrifuge and bled off. What's left is a little bit purer than when you started. Just a little bit. You have to do it over and over again, thousands of hours, just to get a wafer of bomb-grade uranium the size of a postage stamp.'

'But he *is* doing it?' pressed Sir Paul.

'Yep. Been doing it for about a year. These centrifuges ... to save time we link them in series, called cascades. But you need thousands of centrifuges to make up a cascade.'

'If they've been going down that road since 1982, why has it taken so long?' asked Terry Martin.

'You don't go into the hardware store and buy a uranium gas diffusion centrifuge off the shelf,' Hipwell pointed out. 'They tried at first, but were turned down—the documents show that. Since 1985 they have been buying the component parts to build their own on-site. They got about 500 tons of basic uranium yellowcake, half of it from Portugal. They bought much of the centrifuge technology from West Germany...'

'I thought Germany had signed a whole range of international agreements limiting the spread of nuclear bomb technology,' protested Paxman.

'Maybe they have, I wouldn't know about the politics,' said the scientist. 'But they got the bits and pieces from all over the place—you need designer lathes, special ultra-strong maraging steel, anti-corrosion vessels, special valves, high-temperature furnaces called "skull" furnaces because that's what they look like; plus vacuum pumps and bellows—this is serious technology we are talking about. Quite a bit, plus the know-how, came from Germany.'

'Let me get this straight,' said Harry Sinclair, 'has Saddam got any isotope separation centrifuges working yet?'

'Yes, one cascade. It's been functioning for about a year. And another one coming on stream soon.'

'Do you know where all this stuff is?'

'The centrifuge assembly plant is at a place called Taji—here.' The scientist passed a large aerial photo

229

over to the American and ringed a series of industrial buildings.

'The working cascade seems to be underground somewhere not far from the old wrecked French reactor at Tuwaitha, the reactor they called Osirak. I don't know whether you'll ever find it with a bomber—it's certainly underground and camouflaged.'

'And the new cascade?'

'No idea,' said Hipwell, 'could be anywhere.'

'Probably somewhere else,' suggested Terry Martin. 'The Iraqis have been practising duplication and dispersal, ever since they put all their eggs in one basket and the Israelis blew the basket away.'

Sinclair grunted.

'How sure are you,' asked Sir Paul, 'that Saddam Hussein cannot have his bomb yet?'

'Easy,' said the physicist. 'It's a question of time. He hasn't had long enough. For a basic but usable atomic bomb, he will need 30 to 35 kilograms of pure Uranium 235. Starting cold a year ago, even assuming the working cascade can function twenty-four hours a day—which it can't—a spinning programme needs at least twelve hours per centrifuge.

'You need a thousand spins to get from 0 per cent pure to the required 93 per cent. That's five hundred days of spinning. But then there's cleaning, servicing, maintenance, break-downs. Even with a thousand centrifuges operating in a cascade now and for the past year, you'd need five years. Bring in another cascade next year—shorten it to three years.'

'So he won't have his 35 kilograms until 1993 at the earliest?' interjected Sinclair.

'No, he can't.'

'One final question. If he gets the uranium, how much longer to an atomic bomb?'

'Not long. A few weeks. You see, a country undertaking to make its own bomb will have the nuclear engineering side running in parallel. Bomb-engineering is not all that complicated, so long as you know what you are doing. And Jaafar does—he will know how to build one and trigger it. Dammit, we trained him at Harwell.

'But the point is, on a time-scale alone Saddam Hussein cannot have enough pure uranium ready yet. Ten kilograms, tops. He's three years short—minimum.'

Dr Hipwell was thanked for his weeks of analysis and the meeting ended.

Sinclair would return to his embassy and write up his copious notes which would go to America in heavy code. There they would be compared with the analyses of the American counterparts, physicists drawn from the laboratories of Sandia, Los Alamos and principally Lawrence Livermore in California, where for years a secret section called simply Department Z had been monitoring the steady spread of nuclear technology around the world on behalf of the State Department and the Pentagon.

Though Sinclair could not know it, the findings of the British and American teams confirmed each other to a remarkable degree.

Terry Martin and Simon Paxman left the same meeting and wandered across Whitehall in the benign October sunshine.

'Quite a relief,' said Paxman. 'Old Hipwell was quite adamant. Apparently the Americans agree entirely. That bastard is nowhere near his atom bomb yet. One less nightmare to worry about.'

231

They parted at the corner, Paxman to cross the Thames towards Century House, Martin to cross Trafalgar Square and head up St Martin's Lane towards Gower Street.

*   *   *

Establishing what Iraq had, or even probably had, was one thing. Finding out precisely where it was situated was another. The photography went on and on. The KH-11s and KH-12s drifted across the heavens in endless sequence, photographing what they saw on the Iraqi land beneath them.

By October another device had entered the skies, a new American reconnaissance plane so secret that Capitol Hill did not know about it. Code-named Aurora, it flew on the fringes of inner space, reaching speeds of Mach 8, almost 5,000 miles per hour, riding its own fireball—the ramjet effect—far beyond Iraqi radar or interceptor missiles. Not even the technology of the dying USSR could spot Aurora, which had replaced the legendary SR-71 Blackbird.

Ironically, while the Blackbird was eased out of commission another even more aged 'old faithful' was plying its trade above Iraq that autumn. Almost forty years old, nicknamed the Dragon Lady, the U-2 was still flying and still taking pictures. It was back in 1960 that Gary Powers was shot down in a U-2 over Sverdlovsk, Siberia, and it was the U-2 that spotted the first Soviet missiles being deployed in Cuba in the summer of 1962, even though it was Oleg Penkovsky who identified them as offensive and not defensive weapons, thus blowing away Khruschev's phoney protests and sowing the seeds of his own eventual destruction.

The U-2 of 1990 had been re-equipped as a 'listener' rather than a 'watcher', and redesignated TR-1, though it still did photography.

All this information, from the professors and scientists, analysts and interpreters, the trackers and the watchers, the interviewers and researchers, built up a picture of Iraq through the autumn of 1990, and a frightening picture it became.

From a thousand sources the information finally channelled into a single and very secret room two floors below the Saudi Air Force Ministry on Old Airport Road. The room, along the street from where the military brass sat in conference and discussed their unauthorized (by the United Nations) plans for the invasion of Iraq, was called simply 'The Black Hole'.

It was in the Black Hole that British and American targeters, drawn from all three services and of all ranks from private to general, pin-pointed the sites that would have to be destroyed. Finally, they would have made up General Chuck Horner's air-war map. It contained eventually 700 targets. Six hundred were military—in the sense of being command centres, bridges, airfields, arsenals, ammunition dumps, missile sites and troop concentrations. The other hundred were concerned with weapons of mass destruction—research facilities, assembly plants, chemical labs, storage depots.

The gas centrifuge manufacturing line at Taji was listed, as was the approximate, assumed position of the centrifuge cascade underground somewhere in the Tuwaitha complex.

But the water-bottling plant at Tarmiya was not there, nor was Al-Qubai. No-one knew about them.

A copy of the comprehensive report by Harry

Sinclair in London joined other reports emanating from various parts of the United States and abroad. Finally a synthesis of all these in-depth analyses found its way to a very small and very discreet State Department think-tank, known only to a restricted group in Washington as the Political Intelligence and Analysis Group. The PIAG is a sort of analytical hothouse for foreign affairs and produces reports that are absolutely not for public consumption. Indeed, the unit answers only to the Secretary of State, at that time Mr James Baker.

*   *   *

Two days later Mike Martin lay flat on a roof that gave him a commanding view of the section of Abrak Kheitan where he had set up his rendezvous with Abu Fouad.

At almost exactly the appointed hour he watched a single car leave the King Faisal Motorway leading to the airport and pull into a side-street. The car cruised slowly down the street, away from the bright lights of the highway and the occasional traffic, and into darkness.

He saw the outline stop at the place he had described in his message to Al-Khalifa. Two people got out, a man and a woman. They looked around, checked that no other car had followed them off the highway and slowly walked on, towards the place where a grove of trees covered a vacant lot.

Abu Fouad and the woman had been told to wait up to half an hour. If the Bedou had not shown up, they were to abort and go home. They actually waited forty minutes before returning to the car. Both were frustrated.

'He must have been detained,' said Abu Fouad to his companion. 'An Iraqi patrol perhaps. Who knows? Anyway, damn. I'll have to start again.'

'I think you're crazy to trust him,' said the woman. 'You have no idea who he is.'

They spoke softly, the Kuwaiti resistance leader looking up and down the street to ensure no Iraqi soldiers had appeared while he was away.

'He's successful and cunning, and he works like a professional. That's all I need to know. I would like to collaborate with him, if he's willing.'

'Then I have nothing against that.'

The woman uttered a short scream. Abu Fouad jerked in his seat.

'Don't turn round. Let's just talk,' said the voice from the back seat. In his rear-view mirror the Kuwaiti saw the dim outline of a Bedouin keffiyeh and caught the odour of one who lives rough. He let out his breath in a long exhalation.

'You move quietly, Bedou.'

'No need to make a noise, Abu Fouad. It attracts Iraqis. I don't like that, except when I am ready.'

Abu Fouad's teeth flashed under his black moustache.

'Very well, now we have found each other. Let us talk. By the way, why hide in the car?'

'If this meeting had been a trap for me, your first words when you got back into the car would have been different.'

'Self-incriminating...'

'Of course.'

'And then ...?'

'You would be dead.'

'Understood.'

'Who is your companion? I made no mention of

companions.'

'You set up the rendezvous, it was I who had to trust you also. She is a trusted colleague. Asrar Qabandi.'

'Very well. Greetings, Miss Qabandi. What do you want to talk about?'

'Guns, Bedou. Kalashnikov machine-pistols, modern hand-grenades, Semtex-H. My people could do so much more with that sort of thing.'

'Your people are being caught, Abu Fouad. Ten surrounded in the same house by an entire company of Iraqi infantry under AMAM leadership. All shot. All youngsters.'

Abu Fouad was silent. It had been a major disaster.

'Nine,' he said at last. 'The tenth played dead and crept away later. He is injured and we are taking care of him. It was he who told us.'

'What?'

'That they were betrayed. If he had died we would not have known.'

'Ah, betrayal. Always the danger in any resistance movement. And the traitor?'

'We know him, of course. We thought we could trust him.'

'But he is guilty?'

'It seems so.'

'Only seems?'

Abu Fouad sighed.

'The survivor swears only the eleventh man knew of the meeting, and the address. But it could be there was a leak somewhere else; or one of them was tailed—'

'Then he must be tested, this suspect. And if guilty, punished. Miss Qabandi, would you leave us for a

236

while, please.'

The young woman glanced at Abu Fouad, who nodded. She left the car and walked back to the grove of trees. The Bedou told Abu Fouad carefully and in detail what he wanted him to do.

'I will not be leaving the house until seven o'clock,' he finished, 'so under no circumstances must you make the phone call until half-past seven. Understood?'

The Bedou slipped out of the car and disappeared among the dark alleys running between the detached houses. Abu Fouad drove up the street and picked up Miss Qabandi. Together they drove home.

The Bedou never saw the woman again. Before the liberation of Kuwait Asrar Qabandi was caught by the AMAM, rigorously tortured, gang raped, shot and decapitated. Before she died, she never said a thing.

*   *   *

Terry Martin was on the phone to Simon Paxman, who was still inundated with work and could have done without the interruption. It was only because he had taken a liking to the fussy professor of Arabic studies that he took the call.

'I know I'm being a bother, but do you have any contacts at GCHQ?'

'Yes, of course,' said Paxman. 'In the Arabic Service, mainly. Know the Director of it, come to that.'

'Could you possibly give him a call and ask if he'd see me?'

'Well, yes, I suppose so. What have you in mind?'

'It's the stuff coming out of Iraq these days. I've

237

studied all Saddam's speeches, of course, and watched the announcements about hostages, human shields, and seen their ghastly attempts at PR on the television. But I'd like to see if there's anything else being picked up, stuff that hasn't been cleared by their Propaganda Ministry.'

'Well, that's what GCHQ does,' admitted Paxman. 'I don't see why not. If you've been sitting in with the Medusa people, you've got the clearance. I'll give him a call.'

That afternoon, by appointment, Terry Martin motored west to Gloucestershire and presented himself at the well-guarded gate of the sprawl of buildings and antennae that comprise the third main arm of British Intelligence alongside M.I.6 and M.I.5, the Government Communications Headquarters.

The Director of the Arabic Service was Sean Plummer, under whom worked that same Mr Al-Khouri who had tested Mike Martin's Arabic in the Chelsea restaurant eleven weeks earlier, though neither Terry Martin nor Plummer knew that.

The Director had agreed to see Martin in the midst of a busy day because, as a fellow Arabist, he had heard of the young scholar of the SOAS and admired his original research on the Abassid Caliphate.

'Now, what can I do for you?' he asked when they were both seated with a glass of mint tea, a luxury Plummer permitted himself to escape the miseries of institution coffee. Martin explained that he was surprised at the paucity of the intercepts he had been shown coming out of Iraq. Plummer's eyes lit up.

'You're right, of course. As you know, our Arab friends tend to chatter like magpies on open circuits. The last couple of years, the interceptible traffic has

238

slumped. Now, either the whole national character has changed or—'

'Buried cables,' said Martin.

'Precisely. Apparently Saddam and his boys have buried over 45,000 miles of fibre-optic communication cables. That's what they're talking on. For me it's an absolute bastard. How can I keep giving the spooks in London another round of Baghdad weather reports and Mother Hussein's bloody laundry lists?'

It was his manner of speaking, Martin realized. Plummer's service delivered a lot more than that.

'They still talk of course—ministers, civil servants, generals—right down to chit-chat between tank commanders on the Saudi border. But the serious, top-secret phone calls are off the air. Never used to be. What do you want to see?'

For the next four hours Terry Martin ran his eye over a range of intercepts. Radio broadcasts were too obvious; he was looking for something in an inadvertent phone call, a slip of the tongue, a mistake. Finally he closed the files of digests.

'Would you,' he asked, 'just keep an eye open for anything really odd, anything that just doesn't make sense?'

*   *   *

Mike Martin was beginning to think he should one day write a tourist's guide to the flat roofs of Kuwait City. He seemed to have spent an impressive amount of time lying on one of them surveying the area beneath him. On the other hand, they did make superb positions for an LUP or lying-up position.

He had been on this particular one for almost two

239

days, surveying the house whose address he had given to Abu Fouad. It was one of the six he had been lent by Ahmed Al-Khalifa, and one he would now never use again.

Although it was two days since he had given the address to Abu Fouad, and nothing was supposed to happen until tonight, 9 October, he had still watched, night and day, living off a handful of bread and fruit.

If Iraqi soldiers arrived before 7.30 on the evening of the 9th, he would know who had betrayed him—Abu Fouad himself. He glanced at his watch. Seven-thirty. The Kuwaiti colonel should be making his call about now, as instructed.

Across the city, Abu Fouad was indeed lifting the phone. He dialled a number, which was answered at the third ring.

'Salah?'

'Yes, who is this?'

'We have never met but I have heard many good things about you—that you are loyal and brave, one of us. People know me as Abu Fouad.'

There was a gasp at the end of the phone.

'I need your help, Salah. Can we, the movement, count on you?'

'Oh yes, Abu Fouad. Please tell me what it is you want.'

'Not I personally, but a friend. He is wounded and sick. I know you are a chemist. You must at once take medications to him—bandages, antibiotics, pain-killers. Have you heard of the one they call the Bedou?'

'Yes, of course. But do you mean to say you know him?'

'Never mind, but we have been working together for weeks. He is hugely important to us.'

240

'I will go downstairs to the shop right now and select the things he needs, and take them to him. Where do I find him?'

'He is holed up in a house in Shuwaikh and cannot move. Take pencil and paper.'

Abu Fouad dictated the address he had been given. At the other end of the phone it was noted.

'I will drive over at once, Abu Fouad. You can trust me,' said Salah the chemist.

'You are a good man. You will be rewarded.'

Abu Fouad hung up. The Bedou had said he would phone at dawn if nothing happened and the chemist would be in the clear.

Mike Martin saw, rather than heard, the first truck just before half-past eight. It was rolling on its own momentum, the engine off to make no sound; and it trundled past the intersection of the street before coming to a halt a few yards further on and just out of sight. Martin nodded in approval.

The second truck did the same a few moments later. From each vehicle twenty men descended quietly. Green Berets who knew what they were doing. The men moved in column up the street, headed by an officer who grasped a civilian. The man's white dish-dash glimmered in the half-darkness. With all the street names ripped down, the soldiers would need a civilian guide to find this road. But the house numbers were still up.

The civilian stopped at a house, studied the number plate and pointed. The captain in charge had a hurried and whispered conversation with his sergeant, who took fifteen men down a side-alley to cover the back.

Followed by the remaining soldiers, the captain tried the steel door to the small garden. It opened.

241

The men surged through.

Inside the garden the captain could see that a low light burned in an upstairs room. Much of the ground floor was taken by the garage, which was empty. At the front door all pretence of stealth vanished. The captain tried the handle, found it was locked and gestured to a soldier behind him. The man fired a brief burst from his automatic rifle at the lock in the timber setting and the door swung open.

With the captain leading, the Green Berets rushed in. Some went for the darkened ground-floor rooms, the captain and the rest went straight up for the master bedroom.

From the landing the captain could see the interior of the low-lit bedroom, the armchair with its back to the door, and the chequered keffiyeh peeping out over the top. He did not fire. Colonel Sabaawi of the AMAM had been specific; this one he wanted alive for questioning. As he rushed forward the young officer did not feel the snag of the nylon fishing-line against his shins.

He heard his own men bursting in through the back, and others pounding up the stairs. He saw the slumped form in the soiled white robe, filled out by the cushions, and the big water melon wrapped in the keffiyeh. His face contorted with anger and he had the time to snarl an insult at the trembling chemist who stood in the doorway.

Five pounds of Semtex-H may not sound much and it does not look very large. The houses of that neighbourhood are built of stone and concrete, which was what saved the surrounding residences, some of which were occupied by Kuwaitis, from more than superficial damage. But the house in which the soldiers stood virtually disappeared. Tiles from

242

its roof were later found several hundred yards away.

The Bedou had not waited around to watch his handiwork. He was already two streets away, shuffling along, minding his own business, when he heard the muffled boom, like a door being slammed, then the one-second hollow silence, then the crash of masonry.

Three things happened the following day, and all after dark. In Kuwait the Bedou had his second meeting with Abu Fouad. This time, the Kuwaiti came alone to the rendezvous, in the shadow of a deep arched doorway only 200 yards from the Sheraton which had been taken over by dozens of senior Iraqi officers.

'You heard, Abu Fouad?'

'Of course. The whole city is buzzing. They lost over twenty men and the rest injured.' He sighed. 'There will be more random reprisals.'

'You wish to stop now?'

'No. We cannot. But how much longer must we suffer?'

'The Americans and the British will come. One day.'

'Allah make it soon. Was Salah with them?'

'He brought them. There was only one civilian. You told no-one else?'

'No, just him. It must have been him. He has the lives of nine young men on his head. He will not see Paradise.'

'So. What more do you want of me?'

'I do not ask who you are or where you come from. As a trained army officer I know you cannot be just a simple Bedou camel-drover from the desert. You have supplies of explosive, guns, ammunition, grenades. My people could also do much with these

243

things.'

'And your offer?'

'Join with us and bring your supplies. Or stay on your own but share your supplies. I am not here to threaten, only to ask. But if you want to help our resistance, this is the way to do it.'

Mike Martin thought for a while. After eight weeks he had half his supplies left, still buried in the desert, or scattered through the two villas he used not for living but for storage. Of his other four houses, one was destroyed and the other, where he had met with his pupils, compromised. He could hand over his stores and ask for more by night-drop—risky but feasible, so long as his messages to Riyadh were not being intercepted, which he could not know. Or another camel trip across the border and a return with two more panniers. Even that would not be easy—there were now sixteen divisions of Iraqis ranged along that border, three times the number when he had entered.

It was time to contact Riyadh again and ask for instructions. In the meanwhile, he would give Abu Fouad almost all he had. There was more south of the border; he would just have to get it through somehow.

'Where do you want it delivered?' he asked.

'We have a warehouse in Shuwaikh Port. It is quite secure. It stores fish. The owner is one of us.'

'In six days,' said Martin.

They agreed the time and the place where a trusted aide of Abu Fouad would meet the Bedou and guide him the rest of the journey to the warehouse. Martin described the vehicle he would be driving and the way he would look.

That same night, but two hours later because of the time difference, Terry Martin sat in a quiet restaurant not far from his apartment, and twirled a glass of wine in one hand. The guest he awaited entered a few minutes later, an elderly man with grey hair, glasses and a spotted bow-tie. He looked round enquiringly.

'Moshe, over here.'

The Israeli bustled over to where Terry Martin had risen, and greeted him effusively.

'Terry, my dear boy, how are you?'

'Better for seeing you, Moshe. Couldn't let you pass through London without at least a dinner and a chance to chat.'

The Israeli was old enough to be Dr Martin's father, but their friendship was based on common interest. Both were academics and keen students of ancient Mid-Eastern Arab civilizations, their cultures, art and languages.

Professor Moshe Hadari went back a long way. As a young man he had excavated much of the Holy Land with Yigael Yadin, himself both a professor and an army general. His great regret was that, as an Israeli, much of the Middle East was forbidden to him, even for scholarship. Still, in his field he was one of the best and, that field being a small one, it was inevitable that the two scholars should meet at some seminar, as they had done ten years earlier.

It was a good dinner, and the talk flowed over the latest research, the newest tiny fresh perceptions of the way life had been in the kingdoms of the Middle East ten centuries earlier.

Terry Martin knew he was bound by the Official Secrets Act so his recent activities on secondment to

245

Century House were not for discussion. But over coffee their conversation came quite naturally round to the crisis in the Gulf and the chances of a war.

'Do you think he will pull out of Kuwait, Terry?' the professor asked. Martin shook his head.

'No, he can't unless he is given a clearly marked road, concessions he can use to justify withdrawal. To go naked, he falls.'

Hadari sighed.

'So much waste,' he said, 'all my life, so much waste. All that money, enough to make the Middle East a paradise on earth; all that talent, all those young lives. And for what? Terry, if war comes, will the British fight with the Americans?'

'Of course. We've already sent the 7th Armoured Brigade and I believe the 4th Armoured will follow. That makes a division, apart from the fighters and the warships. Don't worry about it. This is one Mid-East war in which Israel not only may, but must, sit on her thumbs.'

'Yes, I know,' said the Israeli gloomily. 'But many more young men will have to die.'

Martin leant forward and patted his friend on the arm.

'Look, Moshe, the man has got to be stopped. Sooner or later. Israel, of all countries, must know how far he has got with his weapons of mass destruction. In a sense, we have just been finding out the true scale of what he has.'

'But our people have been helping, of course. We are probably his principal target.'

'Yes, in target analysis,' said Martin. 'Our principal problem is in hard, on-the-spot Intelligence. We simply don't have top-level Intelligence coming to us out of Baghdad. Not the

246

British, not the Americans and not even your people either.'

Twenty minutes later the dinner ended and Terry Martin saw Professor Hadari into a taxi to take him back to his hotel.

*   *   *

About the hour of midnight three triangulation stations were implanted in Kuwait on the orders of Hassan Rahmani in Baghdad.

They were radio dishes designed to track the source of a radio-wave emission and take a compass bearing on it. One was a fixed station, mounted on the roof of a tall building in the district of Ardiya, on the extreme southern outskirts of Kuwait City. Its dish faced towards the desert.

The other two were mobile stations, large vans with the dishes on the roof, an in-built generator for the electrical power and a darkened interior where the scanners could sit at their consoles and trawl the air waves for the transmitter they sought, which they had been told would probably 'send' from somewhere out in the desert between the city and the Saudi border.

One of these vans was outside Jahra, well to the west of its colleague in Ardiya, and the third was down the coast, in the grounds of the Al Adan Hospital where the law student's sister had been raped in the first days of the invasions. The Al Adan tracker could get a full cross-bearing on those reported by the scanners further north, pinning the source of the transmission down to a square a few hundred yards across.

At Ahmadi air base, where once Khaled Al-

Khalifa had flown his Skyhawk, a Soviet-built Hind helicopter gunship waited on twenty-four-hour stand-by. The crew of the Hind were from the Air Force, a concession Rahmani had had to squeeze out of the general commanding the IAF. The radio-tracking crews were from Rahmani's own Counter-Intelligence Service, drafted in from Baghdad and the best he had.

*   *   *

Professor Hadari spent a sleepless night. Something his friend had told him worried him deeply. He regarded himself as a completely loyal Israeli, born of an old Sephardic family who had emigrated just after the turn of the century along with men like Ben Yehuda and David Ben Gurion. He himself had been born outside Yaffa when it was still a bustling port of Palestinian Arabs and he had learnt Arabic as a small boy.

He had raised two sons, and seen one of them die in a miserable ambush in South Lebanon. He was grandfather to five small children. Who should tell him that he did not love his country?

But there was something wrong. If war came, many young men might die, as his Ze'ev had died, even if they were British and Americans and French. Was this the time for Kobi Dror to show vindictive, small-power chauvinism?

He rose early, settled his bill, packed and ordered a taxi for the airport. Before he left the hotel, he hovered for a while by the bank of phones in the lobby, then changed his mind.

Halfway to the airport he ordered his cab driver to divert off the M4 and find a phone booth. Grumbling

248

at the time and trouble this would take, the driver did so, eventually finding one on a corner in Chiswick. Hadari was in luck. It was Hilary who answered the phone at the Bayswater flat.

'Hold on,' he said, 'he's halfway out the door.'

Terry Martin came on the line.

'It's Moshe. Terry, I don't have much time. Tell your people the Institute *does* have a high source inside Baghdad. Tell them to ask what happened to Jericho. Goodbye, my friend.'

'Moshe, one moment, are you sure? How do you know?'

'It doesn't matter. You never heard this from me. Goodbye.'

The phone went dead. In Chiswick the elderly academic climbed back into his taxi and proceeded to Heathrow. He was trembling at the enormity of what he had done. And how could he tell Terry Martin that it was he, the professor of Arabic from the university, who had crafted that first reply to Jericho in Baghdad?

Terry Martin's call found Simon Paxman at his desk at Century House just after ten.

'Lunch? Sorry, I can't. Hell of a day. Tomorrow perhaps,' said Paxman.

'Too late, it's urgent, Simon.'

Paxman sighed. No doubt his tame academic had come up with some fresh interpretation of a phrase in an Iraqi broadcast that was supposed to change the meaning of life.

'Still can't make lunch. Major conference here, in-house. Look, a quick drink. The Hole-in-the-Wall, it's a pub underneath Waterloo Bridge, quite close to here. Say twelve o'clock? I can give you half an hour, Terry.'

'More than enough. See you,' said Martin.

Just after noon they sat over beers in the alehouse above which the trains of the Southern Region rumbled to Kent, Sussex and Hampshire. Martin, without revealing his source, narrated what he had been told that morning.

'Bloody hell,' whispered Paxman; there were people in the booth next boor. 'Who told you?'

'Can't say.'

'Well, you must.'

'Look, he went out on a limb. I gave my word. He's an academic and senior. That's all.'

Paxman thought. Academic and mixing with Terry Martin. Certainly another Arabist. Could have been on secondment to the Mossad. Whatever, the information had to go back to Century and without delay. He thanked Martin, left his beer and scuttled back down the road to the shabby block called Century.

Because of the lunchtime conference, Steve Laing had not left the building. Paxman drew him on one side and told him. Laing took it straight to the Chief himself.

Sir Colin, who was never given to overstatement, pronounced General Kobi Dror to be 'a most tiresome fellow', forsook his lunch, ordered something to be brought to his desk and retired to the top floor. There he put in a personal call on an extremely secure line to Judge William Webster, Director of the CIA.

It was only half-past eight in Washington, but the judge was a man who liked to start with the lark and he was at his desk to take the call. He asked his British colleague a couple of questions about the source of the information, grunted at the lack of one, but

250

agreed it was something that could not be let slide.

Mr Webster told his Deputy Director (Operations) Bill Stewart, who exploded with rage, and then had a half-hour conference with Chip Barber, Head of Ops. for the Middle East. Barber was even angrier, for he was the man who had sat facing General Dror in the bright room on the top of a hill outside Herzlia and had, apparently, been told a lie.

Between them, they worked out what they wanted done, and took the idea back to the Director.

In the mid-afternoon William Webster had a conference with Brent Scowcroft, Chairman of the National Security Council, and he took the matter to President Bush. Webster asked for what he wanted and was given full authority to go ahead.

The co-operation of Secretary of State James Baker was sought, and he gave it immediately. That night the State Department sent an urgent request to Tel Aviv, which was presented to its recipient the following morning, only three hours away due to the time gap.

The Deputy Foreign Minister of Israel at that time was Benyamin Netanyahu, a handsome, elegant, grey-haired diplomat, and the brother of that Jonathan Netanyahu who was the only Israeli killed during the raid on Idi Amin's Entebbe Airport in which Israeli commandos rescued the passengers of a French airliner hijacked by Palestinian and German terrorists.

Benyamin Netanyahu had been born a third-generation sabra and partly educated in America. Because of his fluency and articulateness, and his passionate nationalism, he was a member of Itzhak Shamir's Likud government and often Israel's persuasive spokesman in interviews with the Western media.

He arrived at Washington Dulles two days later on 14 October, somewhat perplexed by the urgency of the State Department's invitation that he fly to America for discussions of considerable importance.

He was even more perplexed when two hours of private talks with Deputy Secretary Lawrence Eagleburger revealed no more than a comprehensive over-view of developments in the Middle East since 2 August. He finished the talks thoroughly frustrated, and then faced a late-night plane back to Israel.

It was as he was leaving the State Department that an aide slipped an expensive pasteboard card into his hand. The card was headed with a personal crest and the writer, in elegant cursive script, asked him not to leave Washington without coming to the writer's house for a short visit, to discuss a matter of some urgency 'to both our countries and all our people'.

He knew the signature, knew the man, and knew the power and the wealth of the hand that wrote it. The writer's limousine was at the door. The Israeli minister took a decision, ordered his secretary to return to the embassy for both sets of luggage, and to rendezvous with him at a house in Georgetown two hours later. From there they would proceed to Dulles. Then he boarded the limo.

He had never been to the house before, but it was as he would have expected, a sumptuous building at the better end of M Street, not 300 yards from the campus of Georgetown University. He was shown into an expensively panelled library with pictures and books of superlative rarity and taste, and a few moments later his host entered, advancing over the Kashan rug with hand outstretched.

'My dear Bibi, how kind of you to spare the time.'

Saul Nathanson was both banker and financier, professions that had made him extremely wealthy but without any of the skulduggery that had marred Wall Street during the reigns of Boesky and Milken. His true fortune was hinted at rather than declared and the man himself was far too cultured to dwell upon it. But the Vandykes and Brueghels on his walls were not copies and his donations to charity, including some ensconced in the State of Israel, were legendary.

Like the Israeli politician, he was elegant and grey-haired, but unlike the slightly younger man he was tailored by Savile Row, London, and his silk shirts were from Sulka.

He showed his guest to one of a pair of leather club chairs before a genuine log fire, and an English butler entered with a bottle and two glasses on a silver tray.

'Something I thought you might enjoy, my friend, while we chat.'

The butler poured two Lalique glasses of the red wine and the Israeli sipped. Nathanson raised an enquiring eyebrow.

'Superb, of course,' said Netanyahu. Château Mouton Rothschild '61 is not easy to come by and not to be gulped. The butler left the bottle within reach and withdrew.

Saul Nathanson was far too subtle to barge into the meat of what he wanted to say. Conversational hors-d'oeuvres were served first. Then the Middle East.

'There's going to be a war, you know,' he said sadly.

'I have no doubt about it,' agreed Netanyahu.

'Before it is over many young Americans may well be dead, fine young men who do not deserve to die.

We must all do what we can to keep that number as low as humanly possible, wouldn't you say? More wine?'

'I could not agree more.'

What on earth was the man driving at? Israel's Deputy Foreign Minister genuinely had no idea.

'Saddam,' said Nathanson, staring at the fire, 'is a menace. He must be stopped. He is probably more of a menace to Israel than to any other neighbouring state.'

'We have been saying that for years. But when we bombed his nuclear reactor, America condemned us.'

Nathanson made a dismissive gesture with one hand.

'The Carter people. Nonsense, of course, all cosmetic nonsense for the face of things. We both know that, and we both know better. I have a son serving in the Gulf.'

'I didn't know. May he return safely.'

Nathanson was genuinely touched.

'Thank you, Bibi, thank you. I pray so every day. My first-born, my only son. I just feel that ... at this point in time ... co-operation between us all must be without stint.'

'Unarguable.' The Israeli had the uncomfortable feeling that bad news was coming.

'To keep the casualties down, you see. That's why I ask for your help, Benyamin, to keep the casualties down. We are on the same side, are we not? I am an American and a Jew.'

The order of precedence in which he had used the words hung in the air.

'And I am an Israeli and a Jew,' murmured Netanyahu. He, too, had his order of precedence.

254

The financier was in no way fazed.

'Precisely. But because of your education here you will understand how . . . well, how shall I phrase it? . . . emotional Americans can sometimes be. May I be blunt?'

A welcome relief, thought the Israeli.

'If anything were done that could in some small way keep the number of casualties down, even by a handful, both I and my fellow-countrymen would be eternally grateful to whoever had contributed that anything.'

The other half of the sentiment remained unsaid, but Netanyahu was far too experienced a diplomat to miss it. And if anything was done or not done that might increase those casualties, America's memory would be long and her revenge unpleasant.

'What is it you want from me?' he asked.

Saul Nathanson sipped his wine and gazed at the flickering logs.

'Apparently, there is a man in Baghdad. Code-name—Jericho . . .'

When he had finished, it was a thoughtful Deputy Foreign Minister who sped out to Dulles to catch the flight home.

CHAPTER NINE

The road-block that got him was at the corner of Mohammed ibn Kassem Street and the Fourth Ring Road. When he saw it in the distance Mike Martin was tempted to hang a U-turn and head back the way he had come.

But there were Iraqi soldiers stationed down the

road on each side at the approaches to the checkpoint, apparently just for that purpose, and it would have been crazy to try and out-run their rifle fire at the slow speed necessary for a U-turn. He had no choice but to drive on, joining the tail of the queue of vehicles waiting for check-through.

As usual, driving through Kuwait City, he had tried to avoid the major roads where road-blocks were likely to be set up, but crossing any of the six Ring Roads which envelop Kuwait City in a series of concentric bands could only be done at a major junction.

He had also hoped, by driving in the middle of the morning, to be lost in the jumble of traffic, or to find the Iraqis sheltering from the heat.

But mid-October had cooled the weather and the green-bereted Special Forces were proving a far cry from the useless Popular Army. So he sat at the wheel of the white Volvo estate car and waited.

It had still been black and deepest night when he had driven the off-road far out into the desert to the south and dug up the remainder of his explosives, guns and ammunition, the equipment he had promised to Abu Fouad. It had been before dawn when he made the transfer at the lock-up garage in the back streets of Firdous from the jeep to the estate car.

Between the transfer from vehicle to vehicle, and the moment when he judged the sun to be high enough and hot enough to send the Iraqis to seek shelter in the shade, he had even managed a two-hour nap at the wheel of the estate car inside the lock-up. Then he had driven the estate car out and put the off-road inside the garage, aware that such a prized vehicle would soon be confiscated.

256

Finally he had changed his clothes, swapping the stained and desert-soiled robes of the Bedou tribes man for the clean white dish-dash of a Kuwaiti doctor.

The cars in front of him inched forward towards the group of Iraqi infantry grouped round the concrete-filled barrels up ahead. In some cases the soldiers simply glanced at the driver's identity cards and waved them on; in other cases the cars were pulled to one side for a search. Usually, it was those vehicles that carried some kind of cargo that were ordered to the kerb.

He was uncomfortably aware of the two big wooden trunks behind him on the floor of the cargo area, containing enough 'goodies' to ensure his instant arrest and hand-over to the tender mercies of the AMAM.

Finally the last car ahead of him surged away and he rolled up to the barrels. The sergeant in charge did not bother to ask for identity papers. Seeing the big boxes in the rear of the Volvo, the soldier waved the estate car urgently in to the side of the road, and shouted an order to his colleagues who waited there.

An olive-drab uniform appeared at the driver's side window, which Martin had already rolled down. The uniform bent and a stubbled face appeared in the opera window.

'Out,' said the soldier. Martin descended and straightened up. He smiled politely. A sergeant with a hard, pock-marked face walked up. The private soldier wandered round to the rear door and peered in at the boxes.

'Papers,' said the sergeant. He studied the ID card that Martin offered, and his glance flickered from the blurred face behind the sylthane to the one standing

257

in front of him. If he saw any difference between the British officer facing him and the store clerk of the Al-Khalifa Trading Company whose portrait had been used for the card, he gave no sign.

The identity card had been dated as issued a year earlier, and in a year a man can grow a short black beard.

'You are a doctor?'

'Yes, Sergeant. I work at the hospital.'

'Where?'

'On the Jahra Road.'

'Where are you going?'

'To the Amiri Hospital in Dasman.'

The sergeant was clearly not of great education and within his culture a doctor rated as a man of considerable learning and stature. He grunted and walked to the back to the car.

'Open,' he said.

Martin unlocked the rear door and it swung up above their heads. The sergeant stared at the two trunks.

'What are these?'

'Samples, Sergeant. They are needed by the research laboratory at the Amiri.'

'Open.'

Martin withdrew several small brass keys from the pocket of his dish-dash. The boxes were of the cabin-trunk or portmanteau type, purchased from a luggage store, and each had two brass locks.

'You know these trunks are refrigerated?' said Martin conversationally, as he fiddled with the keys.

'Refrigerated?' The sergeant was mystified by the word. 'Yes, Sergeant. The interiors are cold. They keep the cultures at a constant low temperature. That guarantees they remain inert. I'm afraid if I open up,

258

the cold air will escape and they will become very active. Better stand back.'

At the phrase 'stand back' the sergeant scowled and unslung his carbine, pointing it at Martin, suspecting the boxes must contain some kind of weapon.

'What do you mean?' he snarled. Martin shrugged apologetically.

'I'm sorry, but I can't prevent it. The germs will just escape into the air around us.'

'Germs, what germs?' The sergeant was confused and angry, as much with his own ignorance as with the doctor's manner.

'Didn't I say where I worked?' he asked mildly.

'Yes, at the hospital.'

'True. The Isolation Hospital. These are full of smallpox and cholera samples for analysis.'

This time the sergeant did jump back, a clear two feet. The marks on his face were no accident; as a child he had nearly died of smallpox.

'Get that stuff out of here, damn you.'

Martin apologized again, closed the rear door, slid behind the wheel and drove away. An hour later he was guided into the fish warehouse in Shuwaikh Port and handed over his cargo to Abu Fouad.

*   *   *

United States Department of State
Washington, DC 20520
MEMORANDUM FOR: *James Baker, Secretary of State*
FROM: *Political Intelligence and Analysis Group*
SUBJECT: *Destruction of Iraqi War Machine*
DATE: *16 October 1990*

CLASSIFICATION: *Eyes only*

In the ten weeks since the invasion by Iraq of the Emirate of Kuwait, the most rigorous investigation has been undertaken, both by ourselves and our British Allies, of the precise size, nature and state of preparation of the war machine presently at the disposal of President Saddam Hussein.

Critics will doubtless say, with the usual benefit of hindsight, that such an analysis should have been accomplished prior to this date. Be that as it may, the findings of the various analyses are now before us, and present a very disturbing picture.

The conventional forces of Iraq alone, with its standing army of a million and a quarter men, its guns, tanks, rocket batteries and modern air force, combine to make Iraq far and away the most powerful military force in the Middle East.

Two years ago it was estimated that if the effect of the war with Iran had been to reduce the Iranian war machine to the point where it could no longer realistically threaten its neighbours, the damage inflicted by Iran on the Iraqi war machine was of similar importance.

It is now clear that, in the case of Iran, the severe purchasing embargo deliberately created by ourselves and the British has caused their situation to remain much the same. In the case of Iraq, however, the two intervening years have been filled by a rearmament programme of appalling vigour.

You will recall, Mr Secretary, that Western policy in the Gulf area and indeed the entire Middle East has long been based upon the concept of balance; the notion that stability and therefore the status quo can only be maintained if no nation in the area is permitted to acquire such power as to threaten into submission all its neighbours and thus establish dominance.

On the conventional warfare front alone, it is now clear that Iraq has acquired such a power and now bids to create such dominance.

But this report is even more concerned with another aspect of Iraqi preparations: the establishment of an awesome stock of Weapons of Mass Destruction, coupled with continuing plans for even more, and their appropriate international, and possibly inter-continental, delivery systems.

In short, unless the utter destruction of these weapons, those still in development, and their delivery systems is accomplished, the immediate future demonstrates a catastrophic prospect.

Within three years Iraq will, according to studies presented to the Medusa Committee and with which the British completely concur, possess its own atomic bomb and the ability to launch it anywhere within a 2,000-kilometre radius of Baghdad.

To this prospect must be added that of thousands of tons of deadly poison gas and a bacteriological war potential involving anthrax, tularemia and, possibly, bubonic and pneumonic plague.

Were Iraq ruled by a benign and reasonable regime, the prospect would still be daunting. The reality is that Iraq is ruled solely by President Saddam Hussein, who is clearly in the grip of two identifiable psychiatric conditions: megalomania and paranoia.

Within three years, failing preventative action, Iraq will be able to dominate by threat alone all the territory from the north coast of Turkey to the Gulf of Aden, from the seas off Haifa to the mountains of

261

Kandahar.

The effect of these revelations must be to change Western policy radically. The destruction of the Iraqi war machine and particularly the Weapons of Mass Destruction must now become the over-riding aim of Western policy. The liberation of Kuwait has now become irrelevant serving only as a justification.

The desired aim can now only be frustrated by a unilateral withdrawal of Iraq from Kuwait, and every effort must be made to ensure that this does not happen.

US policy, in alliance with our British Allies, must therefore be dedicated to four goals:

(a) Insofar as it is possible, covertly to present provocations and arguments to Saddam Hussein aimed at causing him to refuse to pull out of Kuwait.

(b) To reject any compromise he may offer as a bargaining counter for leaving Kuwait, thus removing the justification for our planned invasion and the destruction of his war machine.

(c) To urge the United Nations to pass without further procrastination the long-delayed Security Council Resolution 678, authorizing the Coalition Allies to begin the Air War as soon as they are ready.

(d) To appear to welcome but in fact to frustrate any peace plan which might enable Iraq to escape unscathed from her present dilemma. Clearly the UN Secretary-General, Paris and Moscow are the principal dangers here, likely to propose at any time some naïve scheme capable of preventing what must be done. The

262

*public, of course, will continue to be assured of
the opposite.*

*Respectfully submitted,
PIAG*

                *   *   *

'Itzhak, we really have to go along with them on this
one.'

The Prime Minister of Israel seemed as always
dwarfed by the big swivel chair and the desk in front
of it, when his Deputy Foreign Minister confronted
him in the Premier's fortified private office beneath
the Knesset in Jerusalem. The two Uzi-toting
paratroopers outside the heavy, steel-lined timber
door could hear nothing of what went on inside.

Itzhak Shamir glowered across the desk, his short
legs swinging free above the carpet, although there
was a specially-fitted footrest if he needed it. His
lined, pugnacious face beneath the grizzled grey hair
made him seem even more like some northern troll.

His Deputy Foreign Minister was different from
the Premier in every way; tall where the national
leader was short, elegant where Shamir was rumpled,
urbane where the Premier was choleric. Yet they got
on extremely well, sharing the same uncompromising
vision of their country and of Palestinians, so that the
Russian-born Prime Minister had had no hesitation
in picking and promoting the cosmopolitan
diplomat.

Benyamin Netanyahu had made his case well.
Israel needed America; her goodwill, which had once
been automatically guaranteed by the power of the
Jewish lobby but was now under siege on Capitol Hill

and in the American media, her donations, her weaponry, her veto in the Security Council. That was an awful lot to jeopardize for one alleged Iraqi agent being run by Kobi Dror down there in Tel Aviv.

'Let them have this Jericho, whoever he is,' urged Netanyahu. 'If he helps them destroy Saddam Hussein, the better for us.'

The Prime Minister grunted, nodded and reached for his intercom.

'Get on to General Dror and tell him I need to see him here in my office,' he told his private secretary. 'No, not when he's free. Now.'

Four hours later Kobi Dror left his Prime Minister's office. He was seething. Indeed, he told himself as his car swung down the hill out of Jerusalem and onto the broad highway back to Tel Aviv, he did not recall when he had been so angry.

To be told by your own Prime Minister that you had been wrong was bad enough. To be told you were a stupid arsehole was something he could have done without.

Normally he took pleasure in looking at the pine forests where, during the siege of Jerusalem when the highway of today was a rutted track, his father and others had battled to punch a hole through the Palestinian lines and relieve the city. But not today.

Back in his office he summoned Sami Gershon and told him the news.

'How the hell did the Yanks know?' he shouted. 'Who leaked?'

'No-one inside the Office,' Gershon said with finality. 'What about that professor? I see he's just got back from London.'

'Bloody traitor,' snarled Dror. 'I'll break him.'

'The Brits probably got him drunk,' suggested

264

Gershon. 'Boasting in his cups. Leave it, Kobi. The damage is done. What have we got to do?'

'Tell them everything about Jericho,' snapped Dror. 'I won't do it. Send Sharon. Let him do it. The meeting's in London, where the leak took place.'

Gershon thought it over and grinned.

'What's so funny?' asked Dror.

'Just this. We can't contact Jericho any more. Just let them try. We still don't know who the bastard is. Let them find out. With any luck they'll make a camel's arse out of it.'

Dror thought it over and eventually a sly smile spread across his face.

'Send Sharon tonight,' he said. 'Then we launch another project. I've had it in my mind for some time. We'll call it Operation Joshua.'

'Why?' asked Gershon, perplexed.

'Don't you remember exactly what Joshua did to Jericho?'

*   *   *

The London meeting was deemed important enough for Bill Stewart, Langley's Deputy Director (Operations), to cross the Atlantic personally, accompanied by Chip Barber of the Mid-East Division. They stayed at one of the Agency's safe houses, an apartment not far from the embassy in Grosvenor Square, and had dinner with a Deputy Director SIS and Steve Laing. The Deputy Director was for protocol, given Stewart's rank; he would be replaced at the debriefing of David Sharon by Simon Paxman who was in charge of Iraq.

David Sharon flew in from Tel Aviv under another name and was met by a katsa from the Israeli

265

Embassy in Palace Green. The British Counter-Intelligence Service M.I.5, which does not like foreign agents, even friendly ones, playing games at the port of entry, had been alerted by SIS and spotted the waiting katsa from the embassy. As soon as he greeted the new arrival 'Mr Eliyahu' off the Tel Aviv flight, the M.I.5 group moved in, warmly welcoming Mr Sharon to London and offering every facility to make his stay pleasant.

The two angry Israelis were escorted to their car, waved away from the concourse entrance and then followed sedately into central London. The massed bands of the Brigade of Guards could not have done a better job.

The debriefing of David Sharon began the following morning and it took the whole day and half the night. The SIS elected to use one of their own safe houses, a well-protected and efficiently 'wired' apartment in South Kensington.

It was (and still is) a large and spacious place, of which the dining room served as the site for the conference. One of the bedrooms housed the banks of tape-recorders and two technicians who recorded every word spoken. A trim young lady brought over from Century commandeered the kitchen and masterminded a convoy of trays of coffee and sandwiches to the six men grouped round the dining table.

Two fit-looking men in the lobby downstairs spent the day pretending to mend the perfectly functioning lift, while in fact ensuring that none but the known other inhabitants of the block got above the ground-floor level.

At the dining table were David Sharon and the katsa from the London embassy who was a 'declared'

266

agent anyway, the two Americans, Stewart and Barber from Langley, and the two SIS men, Laing and Paxman.

At the Americans' bidding, Sharon started at the beginning of the tale and told it the way it had happened.

'A mercenary? A walk-in mercenary?' queried Stewart at one point. 'You're not putting me on?'

'My instructions are to be absolutely frank,' said Sharon. 'That was the way it happened.'

The Americans had nothing against a mercenary. Indeed, it was an advantage. Among all the motives for betraying one's country, money is the simplest and easiest for the recruiter agency. With a mercenary one knows where one is. No tortured feelings of regret, no angst of self-disgust, no fragile ego to be massaged and flattered, no ruffled feathers to be smoothed. A mercenary in the Intelligence world is like a whore. No tiresome candle-lit dinners and sweet nothings are necessary. A fistful of dollars on the dressing table will do nicely.

Sharon described the frantic search for someone who could live inside Baghdad under diplomatic cover on extended stay, and the 'Hobson's choice' eventual selection of Alfonso Benz Moncada, his intensive training in Santiago and his re-infiltration to 'run' Jericho for two years.

'Hang on,' said Stewart, 'this *amateur* ran Jericho for two years? Made seventy collections from the drops and got away with it?'

'Yep. On my life,' said Sharon.

'What do you figure, Steve?'

Laing shrugged.

'Beginner's luck. Wouldn't have liked to try it in East Berlin or Moscow.'

'Right,' said Stewart, 'and he never got tailed to a drop? Never compromised?'

'No,' said Sharon. 'He was tailed a few times, but always in a sporadic and clumsy way. Going from his home to the Economic Commission building, or back; and once when he was heading for a drop. But he saw them and aborted.'

'Just supposing,' said Laing, 'he actually *was* tailed to a drop by a real team of watchers. Rahmani's Counter-Intelligence boys stake out the drop and roll up Jericho himself. Under persuasion, Jericho has to co-operate...'

'Then the product would have gone down in value,' said Sharon. 'Jericho really was doing a lot of damage. Rahmani wouldn't have allowed that to go on. We'd have seen a public trial and hanging of Jericho and Moncada would have been expelled, if lucky.

'It seems the trackers were AMAM people, even though foreigners are supposed to be Rahmani's turf. Whatever, they were as clumsy as usual. Moncada spotted them without trouble. You know how AMAM is always trying to move into Counter-Intelligence work...'

The listeners nodded. Inter-departmental rivalry was nothing new. It happened in their own countries.

When Sharon reached the point where Moncada was abruptly withdrawn from Iraq Bill Stewart let out an expletive.

'You mean he's switched off, out of contact ...? Are you telling us Jericho is out on the loose with no controller?'

'That's the point,' said Sharon patiently. He turned to Chip Barber. 'When General Dror said he was running no agent in Baghdad, he meant it.

268

Mossad was convinced Jericho, as an on-going operation, was belly-up.'

Barber shot the young katsa a look that said: pull the other leg, son, it's got bells on.

'We want to re-establish contact,' said Laing smoothly. 'How?'

Sharon laid out all six of the locations of the dead-letter-boxes. During his two years Moncada had changed two of them; in one case because a location was bulldozed for redevelopment, in another because a derelict shop was refurbished and reoccupied. But the six functioning drops and the six places where the alerting chalk marks had to be placed were the up-to-date ones that had come from his final briefing after his expulsion.

The exact location of these drops and of the sites for the chalk marks were noted to the inch.

'Maybe we could get a friendly diplomat to approach him at a function, tell him he's back on stream and the money's better,' suggested Barber, 'get round all this crap under bricks and flagstones.'

'No,' said Sharon, 'it's the drops, or you can't contact him.'

'Why?' asked Stewart.

'You're going to find this hard to believe, but I swear it's true. We never found out who he is.'

The four Western agents stared at Sharon for several minutes.

'You never identified him?' asked Stewart slowly.

'No. We tried, we asked him to identify himself for his own protection. He refused, threatened to shut off if we persisted. We did handwriting analyses, psycho-portraits. We cross-indexed the information he could produce and the stuff he couldn't get at. We ended up with a list of thirty, maybe forty men, all around

269

Saddam Hussein, all within the Revolutionary Command Council, the Army High Command or the senior ranks of the Ba'ath Party.

'Never could get closer than that. Twice we slipped a technical term in English into our demands. Each time they came back with a query. It seems he only speaks no, or very limited, English. But that could be a blind. He could be fluent, but if we knew that it would narrow the field to two or three. So he always writes in handscript, in Arabic.'

Stewart grunted, convinced.

'Sounds like Deep Throat.'

They recalled the secret source in the Watergate affair, leaking inside information to the *Washington Post*.

'Surely Woodward and Bernstein identified Deep Throat?' suggested Paxman.

'They claim so, but I doubt it,' said Stewart. 'I figure the guy stayed in deep shadow, like Jericho.'

Darkness had long fallen when the four of them finally let an exhausted David Sharon go back to his embassy. If there was anything more he could have told them, they were not going to get it out of him. But Steve Laing was certain that this time the Mossad had come clean. Bill Stewart had told him of the level of the pressure that had been exercised in Washington.

The two British and two American Intelligence officers, tired of sandwiches and coffee, adjourned to a restaurant half a mile away. Bill Stewart, who had an ulcer which twelve hours of sandwiches and high stress had not improved, toyed with a plate of smoked salmon.

'It's a bastard, Steve. It's a real four-eyed bastard. Like Mossad, we'll have to try and find an accredited diplomat already trained in all the tradecraft and get him to work for us. Pay him if we have to. Langley's prepared to spend a lot of money on this. Jericho's information could save us a lot of lives when the fighting starts.'

'So who does that leave us?' said Barber. 'Half the embassies in Baghdad are closed down already. The rest must be under heavy surveillance. The Irish, Swiss, Swedes, Finns?'

'The neutrals won't play ball,' said Laing. 'And I doubt they've got a trained agent posted to Baghdad on their own account. Forget Third World embassies—it means starting a whole recruiting and training programme.'

'We don't have the time, Steve. This is urgent. We can't go down the same road the Israelis went. Three weeks is crazy. It might have worked then, but Baghdad is on a war footing now. Things have to be much tighter in there. Starting cold, I'd want a minimum three months to give a diplomat the tradecraft.'

Stewart nodded agreement.

'Failing that, someone with legitimate access. Some businessmen are still going in and out, especially the Germans. We could produce a convincing German, or a Japanese.'

'The trouble is, they're short-stay chappies. Ideally, one wants someone to mother-hen this Jericho for the next ... what ... four months. What about a journalist?' suggested Laing.

Paxman shook his head.

'I've been talking with them all when they come out; being journalists, they get total surveillance. Snooping round back alleys won't work for a foreign correspondent—they all have a minder from the

271

AMAM with them, all the time. Besides, don't forget that outside of an accredited diplomat we're talking a black operation. Anyone want to dwell on what happens to an agent falling into Omar Khatib's hands?'

The four men at the table had heard of the brutal reputation of Khatib, Head of the AMAM, nicknamed al-Mu'azib, the Tormentor.

'Risks just may have to be taken,' observed Barber.

'I was referring more to acceptance,' Paxman pointed out. 'What businessman or reporter would ever agree, knowing what would be in store if he were caught? I'd prefer the KGB to the AMAM.'

Bill Stewart put down his fork in frustration and called for another glass of milk.

'Well, that's it then. Short of finding a trained agent who can pass for an Iraqi.'

Paxman shot a glance at Steve Laing, who thought for a moment and slowly nodded.

'We've got a guy who can,' said Paxman.

'A tame Arab? So has Mossad, so have we,' said Stewart, 'but not to this level. Message-carriers, gofers. This is high-risk, high-value.'

'No, a Brit, a major in the SAS.'

Stewart paused, his milk glass halfway to his mouth. Barber put down his knife and fork and ceased munching his steak.

'Speaking Arabic is one thing, passing for an Iraqi inside Iraq is a whole different ball game,' said Stewart.

'He's dark-skinned, black-haired, brown-eyed, but he's 100 per cent British. He was born and raised there. He can pass for one.'

'And he's fully trained in covert operations?' asked Barber. 'Shit, where the hell is he?'

'Actually, he's in Kuwait at the moment,' said Laing.

'Damn. You mean he's stuck in there, holed-up?'

'No. He seems to be moving about quite freely.'

'So if he can get out, what the hell's he doing?'

'Killing Iraqis actually.'

Stewart thought it over and nodded slowly.

'Big gonads,' he murmured. 'Can you get him out of there? We'd like to borrow him.'

'I suppose so, next time he comes on the radio. We would have to run him, though. And share the product.'

Stewart nodded again.

'I guess so. You guys brought us Jericho. It's a deal. I'll clear it with the judge.'

Paxman rose and wiped his mouth.

'I'd better go tell Riyadh,' he said.

*   *   *

Mike Martin was a man accustomed to making his own luck, but his life was saved that October by a fluke.

He was due to make a radio call to the designated SIS house in the outskirts of Riyadh during the night of the 19th, the same night the four senior Intelligence officers from the CIA and Century House were dining in South Kensington.

Had he done so, he would have been off the air, due to the two-hour time difference, before Simon Paxman could return to Century House and alert Riyadh that he was wanted.

Worse, he would have been on the air for five to ten minutes, discussing with Riyadh ways of securing a resupply of arms and explosives.

In fact he was in the lock-up garage where he kept his jeep just before midnight, only to discover that the vehicle had a flat tyre.

Cursing, he spent an hour with the jeep jacked-up, struggling to remove the wheel nuts which had been almost cemented into place by a mixture of grease and desert sand. At a quarter to one he rolled out of the garage and within half a mile noticed that even his spare tyre had developed a slow leak.

There was nothing for it but to return to the garage, and abandon the radio call to Riyadh.

It took two days to have both tyres repaired, and it was not until the night of the 21st that he found himself deep in the desert, far to the south of the city, turning his small satellite dish in the direction of the Saudi capital many hundreds of miles away, using the 'send' button to transmit a series of quick blips to indicate it was he who was calling and that he was about to come 'on air'.

His radio was basic, a ten-channel fixed-crystal set, with one channel designated for each day of the month in rotation. On the 21st, he was using Channel One. Having identified himself, he switched to 'receive' and waited. Within seconds a low voice replied: 'Rocky Mountain, Black Bear, read you five.'

The codes identifying both Riyadh and Martin corresponded with the date and the channel, just in case someone hostile tried to muscle in on the waveband.

Martin went to 'send' and spoke several sentences.

On the outskirts of Kuwait City to the north, a young Iraqi technician was alerted by a pulsing light on the console he monitored in the commandeered apartment on top of a residential block. One of his

274

sweepers had caught the transmission and locked on.

'Captain,' he called urgently. An officer from Hassan Rahmani's Counter-Intelligence signals section strode over to the console. The light still pulsed, the technician was easing a dial to secure a bearing.

'Someone has just come on the air.'

'Where?'

'Out in the desert, sir.'

The technician listened through his earphones as his direction-finders stabilized on the source of the transmission.

'Electronically scrambled transmission, sir.'

'That has to be him. The boss was right. What's the bearing?'

The officer was reaching for the telephone to alert his other two monitoring units, the trailer-trucks parked at Jahra and the Al Adan Hospital down near the coast.

'Two-oh-two degrees compass.'

Two-oh-two degrees was 22 degrees west of due south and there was absolutely nothing out in that direction but the Kuwaiti desert that ran all the way to join the Saudi desert at the border.

'Frequency?' barked the officer as the Jahra trailer came on the line.

The tracker gave it to him, a rare channel down in the Very Low Frequency range.

'Lieutenant,' he called over his shoulder, 'get on to Ahmadi Air Base. Tell them to get that helicopter airborne, we've got a fix.'

Far away in the desert, Martin finished what he had to say and switched to 'receive' to get the answer from Riyadh. It was not what he had expected. He himself had spoken for only fifteen seconds.

'Rocky Mountain, Black Bear, return to the cave. I say again, return to the cave. Top urgent. Over and out.'

The Iraqi captain gave the frequency to both his other monitoring stations. In Jahra and the hospital grounds other technicians rolled their source-tracers to the indicated frequency and above their heads 4-foot-diameter dishes swung from side to side. The one on the coast covered the area from Kuwait's northern border with Iraq down to the border with Saudi. The Jahra scanners swept east to west, from the sea in the east to the Iraqi desert in the west.

Between the three of them, they could triangulate a 'fix' to within 100 yards and give a heading and distance to the Hind helicopter and its ten armed soldiers.

'Still there?' asked the captain.

The technician scanned the circular screen in front of him, calibrated round its edge with the points of the compass. The centre of the dish represented the point where he sat. Seconds earlier there had been a glittering line across the screen, running from the centre to compass heading two-oh-two. Now the screen was blank. It would only light up when the man out there transmitted again.

'No sir, he's gone off the air. Probably listening to the reply.'

'He'll come back,' said the captain.

But he was wrong. Black Bear had frowned over his sudden instructions from Riyadh, switched off his power, closed down his transmitter and folded up his antenna.

The Iraqis monitored the frequency for the rest of the night until dawn, when the Hind at Al Ahmadi shut off its rotors and the stiff, tired soldiers climbed back out.

*   *   *

Simon Paxman was asleep in a cot in his office when the phone rang. It was a cipher clerk from Communications in the basement. 'I'll come down,' said Paxman. It was a very short message, just decrypted, from Riyadh. Martin had been in touch and had been given his orders.

From his office Paxman phoned Chip Barber in his CIA flat off Grosvenor Square.

'He's on his way back,' he said. 'We don't know when he'll cross the border. Steve says he wants me to go down there. You coming?'

'Right,' said Barber. 'The DDO's going back to Langley on the morning flight. But I'm coming with you. This guy I have to see.'

During the 22nd the American Embassy and the British Foreign Office each approached the Saudi Embassy for a short-notice accreditation of a new junior diplomat to Riyadh. There was no problem. Two passports, neither in the name of Barber or Paxman, were visa-ed without delay and the men caught the 8.45 p.m. flight out of Heathrow, arriving at King Abdulaziz International Airport, Riyadh, just before dawn.

An American Embassy car met Chip Barber and took him straight to the US mission, where the hugely expanded CIA operation was based, while a smaller and unmarked saloon took Paxman away to the villa where the British SIS operation had quartered itself. The first news Paxman got was that Martin had apparently not crossed the border and checked in.

Riyadh's order to return to base was, from Martin's point of view, easier said than done. He had returned from the desert well before dawn on 22 October, and spent the day closing his operation down.

A message was left under the tombstone of Able Seaman Shepton in the Christian cemetery to explain to Mr Al-Khalifa that he had regretfully had to leave Kuwait. A further note for Abu Fouad explained where and how to collect the remaining items of arms and explosives that were still stashed in the two of his once-six villas.

By afternoon he had finished, and drove his battered pick-up truck out to the camel farm beyond Sulaibiya, where the last outposts of Kuwait City ran out and the desert began.

His camels were still there, and in good condition. The calf had weaned and was on its way to becoming a valuable animal, so he used it to settle the debt he owed the owner of the farm who had taken care of it.

Shortly before dusk he mounted up and headed south-south-west, so that when night fell and the chill darkness of the desert enfolded him, Martin was well clear of the last signs of habitation.

It took him four hours instead of the usual one to arrive at the place where he had buried his radio, a site marked by the gutted and rusted wreck of a car that had once, long ago, broken down and been abandoned there.

He hid the radio beneath the consignment of dates he had stored in the panniers. Even with these, the camel was far less laden than she had been when hauling her load of explosives and weapons into Kuwait nine weeks earlier.

If she was grateful, she gave no sign of it, rumbling

278

and spitting with disgust at having been evicted from her comfortable corral at the farm. But she never slackened her swaying gait as the miles slipped by in the darkness.

It was a different journey, however, from that of mid-August. As he moved south, Martin saw more and more signs of the huge Iraqi army that now infested the area south of the city, spreading itself further and further west towards the Iraqi border.

Usually he could see the glow of the lights of the various oil wells that stud the desert here and, knowing the Iraqis would be likely to occupy them, moved away into the sands to avoid them.

On other occasions he smelt the woodsmoke from their fires and was able to skirt the encampment in time. Once he almost stumbled on a battalion of tanks, hull-down behind horsehoe-shaped walls of sand facing the Americans and the Saudis across the border to the south. He heard the clink of metal on metal just in time, pulled the bridle sharply to the right and slipped away back into the sand dunes.

There had only been two divisions of the Iraqi Republican Guard south of Kuwait when he had entered, and they had been further to the east, due south of Kuwait City.

Now the Hammurabi Division had joined the other two, and eleven further divisions, mainly of the regular army, had been ordered by Saddam Hussein into south Kuwait to match the American and Coalition build-up on the other side.

Fourteen divisions is a lot of manpower, even spread over a desert. Fortunately for Martin they seemed to post no sentinels and slept soundly beneath their vehicles, but the sheer numbers of them pushed him further and further west.

279

The short, 50-kilometre hike from the Saudi village of Hamatiyyat to the Kuwaiti camel farm was out of the question; he was being pushed west towards the Iraqi border, marked by the deep cleft of the Wadi-al-Batin which he did not really want to have to cross.

Dawn found him well to the west of the Manageesh oilfield and still north of the Al Mufrad police post which marks the border at one of the pre-emergency crossing-points.

The ground had become more hilly and he found a cluster of rocks in which to spend the day. As the sun rose he hobbled the camel, who sniffed the bare sand and rock in disgust, finding not even a tasty thorn bush for breakfast, rolled himself in the camel blanket and went to sleep.

Shortly after noon he was awakened by the clank of tanks quite close by, and realized he was too near to the main road that runs from Jahra in Kuwait due south-west to cross into Saudi Arabia at the Al Salmi customs post. After sundown he waited until almost midnight before setting out. He knew the border could not be more than twelve miles to his south.

His late start enabled him to move between the last Iraqi patrols about 3 a.m., that hour when human spirits are lowest and the sentries tend to doze.

By the light of the moon he saw the Qaimat Subah police post slip by to one side, and two miles further on he knew he had crossed the border. To be on the safe side he kept going until he cut into the lateral road that runs east-west between Hamatiyyat and Ar-Rugi. There he stopped and assembled his radio dish.

Because the Iraqis to the north had dug in several miles on the Kuwait side of the border, and because General Schwarzkopf's plan called for the Desert

Shield forces also to lie back to ensure that, if attacked, they would know the Iraqis had truly invaded Saudi Arabia, Martin found himself in an empty no man's land. One day, that empty land would become a seething torrent of Saudi and American forces streaming north into Kuwait. But in the pre-dawn darkness of 24 October he had it to himself.

*　　　*　　　*

Simon Paxman was woken by a junior member of the Century House team who inhabited the villa.

'Black Bear has come on the air, Simon. He's crossed the border.'

Paxman was out of bed and running into the radio room in his pyjamas. A radio operator was on a swivel chair facing a console that ran along one complete wall of what had once been quite an elegant bedroom. Because it was now the 24th the codes had changed.

'Corpus Christi to Texas Ranger, where are you? Say again, state your position please.'

The voice sounded tinny when it came out of the console speaker, but it was perfectly clear.

'South of Qaimat Subah, on the Hamatiyyat to Ar-Rugi road.'

The operator turned to glance at Paxman. The SIS man pressed the send button and said: 'Ranger, stay there. There's a taxi coming for you. Acknowledge.'

'Understood,' said the voice. 'I'll wait for the black cab.'

It was not actually a black cab, it was an American Blackhawk helicopter that swept down the road two hours later, a loadmaster strapped in the open door

281

beside the pilot, masked with a pair of binoculars, scanning the dusty track that purported to be a road. From 200 feet the loadmaster spotted the man beside the camel and was about to fly on when the man waved.

The Blackhawk slowed to a hover and watched the Bedou warily. So far as the pilot was concerned, this was uncomfortably close to the border. Still, the map position he had been given by his squadron Intelligence officer was accurate and there was no-one else in sight.

It was Chip Barber who had fixed with the US army detail at Riyadh Military Air Base to lend a Blackhawk to pick up a Britisher who was due to come over the border out of Kuwait. The Blackhawk had the range. But no-one had told the army pilot about a Bedouin tribesman with a camel.

As the American army aviators watched from 200 feet, the man on the ground arranged a series of stones. When he had finished he stood back. The loadmaster focused his glasses on the display of stones. They said simply: HI THERE.

The loadmaster spoke into his mask.

'Must be the guy. Let's go get him.'

The pilot nodded, the Blackhawk curved round and down until it hovered a foot off the ground 20 yards from the man and his beast.

Martin had already taken the panniers and the heavy camel saddle off his animal and dumped them by the roadside. The radio set and his personal side-arm, the Browning 9mm thirteen-shot automatic favoured by the SAS, were in the tote bag slung over his shoulder.

As the helicopter came down the camel panicked and cantered off. Martin watched her go. She had served him well, despite her foul temper. She would come to no harm, alone in that desert. So far as she was concerned, she was home. She would roam freely, finding her own fodder and water, until some Bedou found her, saw no brandmark and gleefully took her for his own.

Martin ducked under the whirling blades and ran to the open door. Over the whine of the rotors, the loadmaster shouted: 'Your name please, sir.'

'Major Martin.'

A hand came out of the aperture to pull Martin into the hull.

'Welcome aboard, Major.'

At that point the engine noise drowned out further talk, the loadmaster handed Martin a pair of ear-defenders to muffle the roar, and they settled back for the run to Riyadh.

Approaching the city, the pilot was diverted to a detached villa on the outskirts of the city. Next to it was a patch of waste ground where someone had laid out three rows of bright orange seat cushions in the form of an H. As the Blackhawk hovered, the man in Arab robes jumped the 3 feet to the ground, turned to wave his thanks to the crew, and strode towards the house as the helicopter lifted away. Two house servants began to gather up the cushions.

Martin walked through the arched doorway in the wall and found himself in a flagged courtyard. Two men were emerging from the door of the house. One he recognized from the SAS Headquarters in west London, all those weeks ago.

'Simon Paxman,' said the younger man, holding out his hand. 'Bloody good to have you back. Oh, this is Chip Barber, one of our cousins from Langley.'

Barber shook hands and took in the figure before

him: stained, off-white robe from chin to floor, striped blanket folded and hung over one shoulder, a red-and-white checked keffiyeh with two black cords to hold it in place, a lean, hard, dark-eyed, black-stubbled face.

'Good to know you, Major. Heard a lot about you.' His nose twitched. 'Guess you could use a hot tub, eh?'

'Oh, yes, I'll get that sorted out at once,' said Paxman.

Martin nodded, said, 'Thanks,' and walked into the cool of the villa. Paxman and Barber came in behind. Barber was privately elated.

Damn, he thought to himself, I do believe this bastard could even do it.

It took three consecutive baths in the marble tub of the house obtained for the British by Prince Khaled bin Sultan for Martin to scrape off the dirt and sweat of weeks. He sat with a towel round his waist while a barber summoned for the purpose gave his matted hair a cut, then he shaved with Simon Paxman's wash-kit.

His keffiyeh, blanket, robes and sandals had been taken away to the garden where a Saudi servant had turned them into a satisfactory bonfire. Two hours later, in a pair of Paxman's light cotton trousers and a short-sleeved shirt, Mike Martin sat at the dining table and contemplated a five-course lunch.

'Would you mind telling me,' he asked, 'why you pulled me out?'

It was Chip Barber who answered.

'Good question, Major. Damn good question. Deserves a damn good answer. Right? Fact is, we'd like you to go into Baghdad. Next week. Salad or fish?'

284

CHAPTER TEN

Both the CIA and the SIS were in a hurry. Although little mention was made of it then or since, by late October there had been established in Riyadh a very large CIA presence and operation.

Before too long, the CIA presence was at loggerheads with the military chieftaincy a mile away in the warren of planning rooms beneath the Saudi Air Force Ministry. The mood, certainly of the air generals, was one of conviction that with the skilful use of the amazing array of technical wizardry at their disposal they could ascertain all they needed to know about Iraq's defences and preparations.

And an amazing array it was. Apart from the satellites in space supplying their constant stream of pictures of the land of Saddam Hussein; apart from the Aurora and the U-2 doing the same but at closer range, there were other machines of daunting complexity dedicated to providing airborne information.

Another breed of satellite, in geo-synchronous position, hovering over the Middle East, was dedicated to listening to what the Iraqis said, and these satellites caught every word uttered on an 'open' line. They could *not* catch the planning conferences held on those 45,000 miles of buried fibre-optic cables.

Among the airplanes, chief was the Airborne Warning and Control System, known as AWACS. These were Boeing 707 airliners, carrying a huge radar dome mounted on their backs. Turning in slow circles over the Northern Gulf, on twenty-four-hour per day rotating shifts, the AWACS could inform Riyadh within seconds of any air movement over Iraq. Hardly an Iraqi plane could move, nor mission take off but Riyadh knew its number, heading, course, speed and altitude.

Backing up the AWACS was another Boeing 707 conversion, the E8-A, known as J-STARS, which did for movements on the ground what AWACS did for movements in the air. With its big Norden radar scanning downwards and sideways, so that it could cover Iraq without ever entering Iraqi airspace, the J-STAR could pick up almost any piece of metal that began to move.

The combination of these and many more technical miracles on which Washington had spent billions and billions of dollars convinced the generals that if it was said, they could hear it, if it moved they could see it, and if they knew about it they could destroy it. They could do it, moreover, come rain or fog, night or day. Never again would the enemy be able to shelter under a canopy of jungle trees and escape detection. The eyes-in-the-sky would see it all.

The Intelligence officers from Langley were sceptical and it showed. Doubts were for civilians. In the face of this the military became irritable. They had a tough job to do, they were going to do it, and cold water they did not need.

On the British side the situation was different. The SIS operation in the Gulf theatre was nothing like that of the CIA, but it was still a large operation by the standards of Century House, and in the manner of Century of lower profile and more secretive.

Moreover the British had appointed as commander of all UK forces in the Gulf, and second-in-command to General Schwarzkopf, an unusual soldier of uncommon background.

Norman Schwarzkopf was a big, burly man of considerable military prowess and very much a soldier's soldier. Known either as Stormin' Norman or 'The Bear', his mood could vary from genial *bonhomie* to explosions of temper, always short-lived, which his staff referred to as the general 'going ballistic'. His British counterpart could not have been more different.

Lt.-Gen. Sir Peter de la Billière, who had arrived in early October to take command of the Brits, was a deceptively slight, lean, wiry man of diffident manner and reluctant speech. The big American extrovert and the slim British introvert made an odd partnership, which only succeeded because each knew enough of the other to recognize what lay behind the up-front presentation.

Sir Peter, known to the troops as PB, was the most decorated soldier in the British army, a matter of which he would never speak under any circumstances. Only those who had been with him in his various campaigns would occasionally mutter into their beer glasses of the icy cool under fire that had caused all those 'gongs' to be pinned to his tunic. He had also once been Commanding Officer of the SAS, a background that gave him a most useful knowledge of the Gulf, of Arabic and of covert operations.

Because the British commander had worked before with the SIS, the Century House team found a more accustomed ear to listen to their reservations than the CIA group.

The SAS already had a good presence in the Saudi theatre, holed up in their own secluded camp in the corner of a larger military base outside Riyadh. As a former commander of these men, General PB was concerned that their remarkable talents should not be wasted on workaday tasks that infantry or paratroopers could do. These men were specialists in deep penetration and hostage-recovery.

It had been mooted they might be used for extricating the British 'human shield' hostages in Saddam's hands, but the plan was dropped when the hostages were scattered throughout Iraq.

Sitting in that villa outside Riyadh during the last week of October, the CIA and SIS team came up with an operation that was very much within the scope of the unusual talents of the SAS. The operation was put to the local SAS commander and he went to work on his planning.

The afternoon of Mike Martin's first day at the villa was spent entirely in explaining to him the background to the discovery by the Anglo-American Allies of the existence of the renegade in Baghdad who had been code-named Jericho. He still had the right to refuse and rejoin the Regiment. During the evening he thought it over. Then he told the CIA–SIS briefing officers: 'I'll go in. But I have my conditions and I want them met.'

The main problem, they all acknowledged, was his cover story. This was not a quick in-and-out mission, depending on speed and daring outwitting the Counter-Intelligence net. Nor could he count on covert support and assistance such as he had met in Kuwait. Nor could he wander the desert outside Baghdad City as an errant Bedou tribesman.

All Iraq was by then a great armed camp. Even areas which on the map seemed desolate and empty were criss-crossed with army patrols. Inside Baghdad army and AMAM check-squads were everywhere, the military police looking for deserters and the AMAM for anyone at all who might be suspicious.

The fear in which the AMAM was held was well known to everyone at the villa; reports from businessmen and journalists, and British and American diplomats before their expulsion, amply testified to the omnipresence of the secret police which kept Iraq's citizens in dread and trembling.

If he went in at all, he would have to stay in. Running an agent like Jericho would not be easy. First, the man would have to be traced, through the dead-letter-boxes, and re-alerted that he was back in operation. The boxes might already be compromised and under surveillance. Jericho might have been caught and forced to confess all.

More, Martin would have to establish a place to live, a base where he could send and receive messages. He would have to prowl the city, servicing the 'drops' if Jericho's stream of inside information resumed, although now destined for new masters.

Finally, and worst of all, there could be no diplomatic cover, no protective shield to spare him the horrors that would follow capture and exposure. For such a man the interrogation cells of Abu Ghraib would be ready.

'What, er, exactly did you have in mind?' asked Paxman when Martin had made his demand.

'If I can't be a diplomat, I want to be attached to a diplomatic household.'

'That's not easy, old boy. Embassies are watched.'

'I didn't say embassy, I said diplomatic household.'

'A kind of a chauffeur?' asked Barber.

'No. Too obvious. The driver has to stay at the wheel of the car. He drives the diplomat around and is watched like the diplomat.'

'What then?'

'Unless things have changed radically, many of the senior diplomats live outside the embassy building, and if the rank is senior enough will have a detached villa in its own walled garden. In the old days such houses always rated a gardener-handyman.'

'A gardener?' queried Barber. 'For Chrissake, that's a manual labourer. You'd be picked up and recruited into the Army.'

'No. The gardener-handyman does everything outside the house. He keeps the garden, goes shopping on his bicycle for fish at the fish-market, fruit and vegetables, bread and oil. He lives in a shack at the bottom of the garden.'

'So, what's the point, Mike?' asked Paxman.

'The point is, he's invisible. He's so ordinary, no-one notices. If he's stopped, his ID card is in order and he carries a letter on embassy paper, in Arabic, explaining that he works for the diplomat, is exempt from service, and would the authorities please let him go about his business. Unless he is doing something wrong, any policeman who makes trouble for him is up against a formal complaint from the embassy.'

The Intelligence officers thought it over.

'It might work,' admitted Barber. 'Ordinary, invisible. What do you think, Simon?'

'Well,' said Paxman, 'the diplomat would have to be in on it.'

'Only partly,' said Martin, 'he would simply have to have a flat order from his government to receive and employ the man who will present himself, and then face the other way and get on with his job. What he suspects is his own affair. He'll keep his mouth shut if he wants to keep his job and his career. That's if the order comes from high enough.'

'The British Embassy's out,' said Paxman. 'The Iraqis would go out of their way to offend our people.'

'Same with us,' said Barber. 'Who had you in mind, Mike?'

When Martin told them, they stared at him in disbelief.

'You cannot be serious,' said the American.

'But I am,' said Martin calmly.

'Hell, Mike, a request like that would have to go up to ... well, the Prime Minister.'

'And the President,' said Barber.

'Well, we're all supposed to be such pals nowadays, why not? I mean, if Jericho's product ends up by saving Allied lives, is a phone call too much to ask?'

Chip Barber glanced at his watch. The hour in Washington was still seven hours earlier than that in the Gulf. Langley would be finishing its lunch. In London it was only two hours earlier, but senior officers might still be at their desks.

Barber went hotfoot back to the US Embassy and sent a 'blitz' message in code to the Deputy Director Operations, Bill Stewart, who, when he had read it, took it to the Director, William Webster. He, in turn, rang the White House and asked for a meeting with his President.

Simon Paxman was lucky. His encrypted phone call caught Steve Laing at his desk at Century House, and after listening the Head of Ops. for Mid-East rang the Chief at his home.

Sir Colin thought it over and placed a call to the Cabinet Secretary, Sir Robin Butler.

It is accepted that the Chief of the Secret

291

Intelligence Service has a right, in cases he deems to be an emergency, to ask for and secure a personal meeting with his Prime Minister, and Margaret Thatcher had always been notable for her accessibility to the men who ran the Intelligence services and the Special Forces. She agreed to meet the Chief in her private office in 10 Downing Street the following morning at eight.

She was, as always, at work before dawn and had almost cleared her desk when the Chief of the SIS was shown in. She listened to his bizarre request with a rather puzzled frown, demanded several explanations, thought it over and then, in her usual way, made her mind up without delay.

'I'll confer with President Bush as soon as he rises and we'll see what we can do. This, um, man ... is he really going to do that?'

'That is his intention, Prime Minister.'

'One of your people, Sir Colin?'

'No, he's a major in the SAS.'

She brightened perceptibly.

'Remarkable fellow.'

'So I believe, ma'am.'

'When this is over, I would rather like to meet him.'

'I'm sure that can be arranged, Prime Minister.'

When the Chief was gone the Downing Street staff placed the call to the White House, even though it was still the middle of the night, and set up the hotline connection for 8 a.m. Washington, 1 p.m. London. The Prime Minister's lunch was rescheduled by thirty minutes.

President George Bush, like his predecessor Ronald Reagan, had always found it hard to refuse the British Prime Minister something she wanted when she was firing on all cylinders.

'All right, Margaret,' said the President after five minutes, 'I'll make the call.'

'He can only say no,' Mrs Thatcher pointed out, 'and he shouldn't. After all, we've jolly well done a lot for him.'

'Yes, we jolly well have,' said the President.

The two heads of government made their calls within an hour of each other and the reply from the puzzled man at the other end of the line was affirmative. He would see their representatives, in privacy, as soon as they arrived.

That evening Bill Stewart headed out of Washington and Steve Laing caught the last connection of the day from Heathrow.

*   *   *

If Mike Martin had any idea of the flurry of activity his demand had started, he gave no sign of it. He spent 26 and 27 October resting, eating and sleeping. But he stopped shaving, allowing the dark stubble to come through again. Work on his behalf, however, was being carried out in a number of different places.

The SIS station head in Tel Aviv had visited General Kobi Dror with a final request. The Mossad chief had stared at the Englishman in amazement.

'You really are going to go ahead with this, aren't you?' he asked.

'I only know what I've been told to ask you, Kobi.'

'Bloody hell, on the black? You know he'll be caught, don't you?'

'Can you do it, Kobi?'

'Of course we can do it.'

'Twenty-four hours?'

Kobi Dror was playing his Fiddler on the Roof

293

role again.

'For you, Boy-chick, my right arm. But look, this is crazy, what you are proposing.'

He rose and came from behind his desk, draping an arm round the Englishman's shoulders.

'You know, we broke half our own rules, and we were lucky. Normally, we never have our people visit a dead-letter-box. It could be a trap. For us a dead-letter-box is one-way; from the katsa to the spy. For Jericho we broke that rule. Moncada picked up the product that way because there was no other way. And he was lucky, for two years he was lucky. But he had diplomatic cover. Now you want ... *this*?'

He held up the small photograph, of a sad-looking Arab-featured man with tufted black hair and stubble, the photo the Englishman had just received from Riyadh, brought in (since there are no commercial routes between the two capitals) by General de la Billière's personal HS-125 twin-jet communications plane. The 125 was standing at Sde Dov military airfield, where its livery markings had been extensively photographed.

Dror shrugged.

'All right. By tomorrow morning. My life.'

Mossad has, beyond any room for quarrel, some of the best technical services in the world. Apart from a central computer with almost two million names and their appropriate data; apart from one of the best lock-picking services on Earth, there exists in the basement and sub-basement of Mossad headquarters a series of rooms where the temperature is carefully controlled.

These rooms contain 'paper'. Not just any old paper; very special paper. Originals of just about every kind of passport in the world lie there, along with myriad other identity cards, driving licences, social security cards and suchlike.

Then there are the 'blanks', the unfilled identity cards on which the penmen can work at will, using the originals as a guide to produce forgeries of superb quality.

Identity cards are not the only speciality. Banknotes of virtually fool-proof likeness can, and are, produced in great quantities, either to help ruin the currencies of neighbouring but hostile nations, or fund Mossad's 'black' operations, the ones neither Prime Minister nor Knesset know about or wish to.

It had only been after some soul-searching that the CIA and SIS had agreed to go to Mossad for the favour, but they simply could not produce the identity card of a forty-five-year-old Iraqi labourer with the certainty of knowing it would pass any inspection in Iraq. No-one had bothered to find and abstract an original one to copy.

Fortunately the Sayeret Matkal, a cross-border reconnaissance group so secret that their name cannot even be printed in Israel, had made an incursion into Iraq two years earlier to drop an Arab oter who had some low-level contact to make there. While on Iraqi soil they had surprised two working men in the fields, tied them up and relieved them of their identity cards.

As promised, Dror's forgers worked through the night and by dawn had produced an Iraqi identity card, convincingly dirty and smudged as from long use, in the name of Mahmoud Al-Khouri, aged forty-five, from a village in the hills north of Baghdad, working in the capital as a labourer.

The forgers did not know that Martin had taken the name of the same Mr Al-Khouri who had tested

295

his Arabic in a Chelsea restaurant in early August; nor could they know that he had chosen the village from which his father's gardener had come, the old man who, long ago beneath a tree in Baghdad, had told the little English boy of the place where he was born, of its mosque and coffee shop and the fields of alfalfa and melons that surrounded it. There was another thing the forgers did not know.

In the morning Kobi Dror handed the identity card to the Tel Aviv-based SIS man.

'This will *not* let him down. But I tell you, this...' he tapped the photo with a stubby forefinger, 'this, your tame Arab, will betray you or be caught within a week.'

The SIS man could only shrug. Not even he knew that the man in the smudged photo was not an Arab at all. He had no need to know, so he had not been told. He just did what he was told—put the card on the HS-125, by which it was flown back to Riyadh.

Clothes had also been prepared, the simple dish-dash of an Iraqi working man, a dull brown keffiyeh and tough, rope-soled canvas shoes.

A basket weaver, without knowing what he was doing or why, was creating a wicker crate of osier strands to a most unusual design. He was a poor Saudi craftsman and the money the strange infidel was prepared to pay was very good, so he worked with a will.

Outside the city of Riyadh, at a secret army base, two rather special vehicles were being prepared. They had been brought by a Hercules of the RAF from the main SAS base further down the Saudi peninsula in Oman and were being stripped down and re-equipped for a long and rough ride.

The essence of the conversion of the two long-base

296

Land-Rovers was not armour and firepower but speed and range. Each vehicle would have to carry its normal complement of four SAS men, and one would carry a passenger. The other would carry a big-tyred cross-country motor-cycle, itself fitted with extra-long-range fuel tanks.

The American army again loaned its power on request, this time in the form of two of their big twin-rotor Chinook workhorse helicopters. They were just told to stand by.

*　　　*　　　*

Mikhail Sergevich Gorbachov was sitting as usual at his desk in his personal office on the seventh and top floor of the Central Committee Building on Novaya Plosehad, attended by two male secretaries, when the intercom buzzed to announce the arrival of the two emissaries from London and Washington.

For twenty-four hours he had been intrigued by the requests of both the American President and the British Prime Minister that he receive a personal emissary from each of them. Not a politician, not a diplomat. Just a messenger. In this day and age, he wondered, what message cannot be passed through the normal diplomatic channels? They could even use a hotline that was utterly secure from interception, although interpreters and technicians had to have access.

He was intrigued and curious, and as curiosity was one of his most notable features he was eager to solve the enigma.

Ten minutes later the two visitors were shown into the private office of the General Secretary of the CPSU and President of the Soviet Union. It was a long, narrow room with a row of windows along one side only, facing out on to New Square. There were no windows behind the President, who sat with his back to the wall at the end of a long conference table.

In contrast to the gloomy, heavy style preferred by his two predecessors Andropov and Chernenko, the younger Gorbachov preferred a light, airy décor. Desk and table were of light beech, flanked by upright but comfortable chairs. The windows were masked by net curtains.

When the two men entered he gestured his secretaries to leave. He rose from his desk and came forward.

'Greetings, gentlemen,' he said in Russian. 'Do either of you speak my language?'

One, whom he judged to be English, replied in halting Russian.

'An interpreter would be advisable, Mr President.'

'Vitali,' Gorbachov called one of the departing secretaries, 'send Yevgeny in here.'

In the absence of language, he smiled and gestured to his visitors to take a seat. His personal interpreter joined them in seconds and sat to one side of the presidential desk.

'My name, sir, is William Stewart. I am Deputy Director (Operations) for the Central Intelligence Agency in Washington,' said the American.

Gorbachov's mouth tightened and his brow furrowed.

'And I, sir, am Stephen Laing, Director for Operations, Mid-East Division, of British Intelligence.'

Gorbachov's perplexity deepened. Spies, chekisti, what on earth was this all about?

'Each of our agencies,' said Stewart, 'made a

request to its respective government to ask you if you would receive us. The fact is, sir, the Middle East is moving towards war. We all know this. If it is to be avoided, we need to know the inner counsels of the Iraqi regime. What they say in public and what they discuss in private, we believe to be radically different.'

'Nothing new about that,' observed Gorbachov drily.

'Nothing at all, sir. But this is a highly unstable regime. Dangerous—to us all. If we could only know what the real thinking inside the Cabinet of President Saddam Hussein is today, we might better be able to plan a strategy to head off the coming war,' said Laing.

'Surely that is what diplomats are for,' Gorbachov pointed out.

'Normally, yes, Mr President. But there are times when even diplomacy is too open, too public a channel for innermost thoughts to be expressed. You recall the case of Richard Sorge?'

Gorbachov nodded. Every Russian knew of Sorge. His face had appeared on stamps. He was a posthumous Hero of the Soviet Union.

'At the time,' pursued Laing, 'Sorge's information that Japan would not attack in Siberia was utterly crucial to your country. But it could not have come to you via the embassy.

'The fact is, Mr President, we have reason to believe there exists in Baghdad a source, quite exceptionally highly placed, who is prepared to reveal to us all the innermost councils of Saddam Hussein. Such knowledge could mean the difference between war and a voluntary Iraqi withdrawal from Kuwait.'

Mikhail Gorbachov nodded. He was no friend of Saddam Hussein either. Once a docile client of the USSR, Iraq had become increasingly independent and of late its erratic leader had been gratuitously offensive to the USSR.

Moreover the Soviet leader was well aware that if he wanted to carry through his Soviet reforms he would need financial and industrial support. That meant the goodwill of the West. The Cold War was over. It was a reality. That was why he had joined the USSR in the Security Council condemnation of Iraq's invasion of Kuwait.

'So, gentlemen, make contact with this source. Produce us information that the Powers can use to defuse this situation, and we will all be grateful. The USSR does not wish to see a war in the Middle East either.'

'We would like to make contact, sir,' said Stewart. 'But we cannot. The source declines to disclose himself, and one can understand why. For him the risks must be very great. To make contact we have to avoid the diplomatic route. He has made plain he will only use covert communications with us.'

'So, what do you ask of me?'

The two Westerners took a deep breath.

'We wish to slip a man into Baghdad to act as conduit between the source and ourselves,' said Barber.

'An agent?'

'Yes, Mr President, an agent. Posing as an Iraqi.'

Gorbachov stared at them hard.

'You have such a man?'

'Yes, sir. But he must be able to live somewhere. Quietly, discreetly, innocently—while he picks up the messages and delivers our own enquiries. We ask that he be allowed to pose as an Iraqi on the staff of a senior member of the Soviet Embassy.'

Gorbachov steepled his chin on the tops of his fingers. He was anything but a stranger to covert operations. His own KGB had mounted more than a few. Now he was being asked to assist the KGB's old antagonists to mount one, and to lend the Soviet Embassy as their man's umbrella. It was so outrageous he almost laughed.

'If this man of yours is caught, my embassy will be compromised.'

'No, sir, your embassy will have been cynically duped by Russia's traditional Western enemies. Saddam will believe that,' said Laing.

Gorbachov thought it over. He recalled the personal entreaty of one president and one prime minister in this matter. They evidently held it to be important, and he had no choice but to regard their goodwill to him as important. Finally he nodded.

'Very well. I will instruct General Vladimir Kryuchkov to give you his full co-operation.'

Kryuchkov was, at that time, Chairman of the KGB. Ten months later, while Gorbachov was on holiday on the Black Sea, Kryuchkov with Defence Minister Dmitri Yazov and others would launch a *coup d'état* against their own President.

The two Westerners shifted uncomfortably.

'With the greatest respect, Mr President,' asked Laing, 'could we ask that it be your Foreign Minister and him only in whom you confide?'

Eduard Shevardnadze was then Foreign Minister and trusted friend of Mikhail Gorbachov.

'Shevardnadze and him alone?' asked the President.

'Yes, sir, if you please.'

'Very well. The arrangements will be made only through the Foreign Ministry.'

When the Western Intelligence officers had gone, Mikhail Gorbachov sat lost in thought. They had wanted only him and Eduard to know about this. Not Kryuchkov. Did they, he wondered, know something the President of the USSR did not?

*   *   *

There were eleven Mossad agents in all, two teams of five and the operational controller whom Kobi Dror had picked personally, pulling him off a boring stint as lecturer to the recruits at the Training School outside Herzlia.

One of the teams was from the Yarid branch, a section of Mossad concerned with operational security and surveillance. The other was from Neviot whose speciality is bugging, breaking and entering—in short, anything where inanimate or mechanical objects are concerned.

Eight of the ten had good or reasonable German, and the mission controller was fluent. The other two were technicians anyway. The advance group for Operation Joshua slipped into Vienna over three days, arriving from different European points of departure, each with perfect passports and cover stories.

As with Operation Jericho, Kobi Dror was bending a few rules, but none of his subordinates was going to argue. Joshua had been designated 'ain efes', meaning a 'no-miss' affair, which, coming from the Boss himself, meant top priority.

Yarid and Neviot teams normally have seven to nine members, but because the target was deemed to

302

be civilian, neutral, amateur and unsuspecting, the numbers had been slimmed down.

Mossad's Head of Station in Vienna had allocated three of his safe houses, and three bodlim to keep them clean, tidy and provisioned at all times.

A bodel, plural bodlim, is usually a young Israeli, often a student, engaged as a gofer after a thorough check of his parentage and background. His job is to run errands, perform chores and ask no questions. In return he is allowed to live rent-free in a Mossad safe house, a major benefit for a short-of-money student in a foreign capital. When visiting 'firemen' move in, the bodel has to move out, but can be retained to do the cleaning, laundry and shopping.

Though Vienna may not seem a major capital, for the world of espionage it has always been very important. The reason goes back to 1945, when Vienna, as the Third Reich's second capital, was occupied by the victorious Allies and divided into four sectors—French, British, American and Russian.

Unlike Berlin, Vienna regained her freedom, even the Russians agreeing to move out, but the price was complete neutrality for Vienna and all Austria. With the Cold War getting under way during the Berlin Blockade of 1948, Vienna soon became a hotbed of espionage. Nicely neutral, with virtually no Counter-Intelligence net of its own, close to the Hungarian and Czech frontiers, open to the West but seething with East Europeans, Vienna was a perfect base for a variety of agencies.

Shortly after its formation in 1951 Mossad also saw the advantages of Vienna and moved in with such a presence that the Head of Station outranks the ambassador.

The decision was more than justified when the elegant and world-weary capital of the former Austro-Hungarian empire became a centre for ultra-discreet banking, the home of three separate United Nations agencies and a favoured entry point into Europe for Palestinian and other terrorists.

Dedicated to its neutrality, Austria has long had a Counter-Intelligence and internal security apparatus so simple to evade that Mossad agents refer to these well-intentioned officers as 'fertsalach', a not-terribly-complimentary word meaning a fart.

Kobi Dror's chosen mission controller was a tough katsa with years of European experience behind him in Berlin, Paris and Brussels.

Gideon Barzilai had also served time in one of the kidon execution units who had pursued the Arab terrorists responsible for the massacre of Israeli athletes at the 1972 Munich Olympic games. Fortunately for his own career, he had not been involved in one of the biggest fiascos in Mossad history, when a kidon unit shot down a harmless Moroccan waiter at Lillehammer, Norway, after wrongly identifying the man as Ali Hassan Salameh, the brains behind the massacre.

Gideon 'Gidi' Barzilai was now Ewald Strauss, representing a sanitary-ware manufacturer in Frankfurt. Not only were his papers in perfect order, but the contents of his briefcase would have revealed the appropriate brochures, order books and correspondence on headed company notepaper.

Even a phone call to his head office in Frankfurt would have confirmed his cover story, for the telephone number on the notepaper gave an office in Frankfurt manned by the Mossad.

Gidi's paperwork, along with that of the other ten

in his team, was the product of another division of Mossad's comprehensive back-up services. In the same sub-basement in Tel Aviv that housed the forgery department is another series of rooms dedicated to storing details of a truly amazing number of companies, real and fictional. Company records, audits, registrations and headed notepaper are stored in such abundance that any katsa on foreign operation can be equipped with a corporate identity virtually impossible to penetrate.

After establishing himself in his own apartment, Barzilai had an extended conference with the local Head of Station and began his mission with a relatively simple task: that of finding out everything he could about a discreet and ultra-traditional private bank called Winkler Bank, just off the Franziskanerplatz.

*   *   *

That same weekend two American Chinook helicopters lifted into the air from a military base outside Riyadh and headed north to cut into the Tapline Road running along the Saudi-Iraq border from Khafji all the way to Jordan.

Squeezed inside the hull of each skyhook was a single long-base Land-Rover, stripped down to basic essentials but equipped with extra-long-range fuel tanks. There were four SAS men travelling with each vehicle, and they squeezed into the area behind the flight crews.

The point of their final destination was beyond their normal range, but waiting for them on the Tapline Road were two large tankers, driven up from Dammam on the Gulf coast.

When the thirsty Chinooks set down on the road, the tanker crews went to work, until the helicopters were again brimming with fuel. Taking off, they headed up the road in the direction of Jordan, keeping low to avoid Iraqi radar situated across the border.

Just beyond the Saudi town of Badanah, approaching the spot where the borders of Saudi Arabia, Iraq and Jordan converge, the Chinooks set down again. There were two more tankers waiting to refuel them, but it was at this point they unloaded their cargoes and their passengers.

If the American aircrew knew where the silent Englishmen were going, they gave no sign, and if they did not, they did not enquire. The loadmasters eased the sand-camouflaged trucks down the ramps and onto the road, shook hands and said: 'Hey, good luck you guys.' Then they refuelled and set off back the way they had come. The tankers followed them.

The eight SAS men watched them go, then headed in the other direction, further up the road towards Jordan. Fifty miles north-west of Badanah they stopped and waited.

The captain commanding the two-vehicle mission checked his position. Back in the days of Colonel David Stirling in the Western Desert of Libya this had been done by bearings of sun, moon and stars. The technology of 1990 made it much easier and more precise.

In his hand the captain held a device no larger than a paperback book. It was called a Global Positioning System, or SATNAV or Magellan. Despite its size the GPS can position its holder to a square no bigger than 10 yards by 10 yards anywhere on the earth's surface.

The captain's hand-held GPS could be switched to either Q-Code or P-Code. The P-Code was accurate to the 10-by-10 yard square, but it needed four of the American satellites called NAVSTAR to be above the horizon at the same time. Q-Code needed only two NAVSTARS above the horizon but was accurate only to 100 yards by 100.

That day there were only two satellites to track by, but it was enough. No-one was going to miss anyone else 100 yards away in that howling wilderness of sand and shale, miles from anywhere between Badanah and the Jordanian border. Satisfied that he was on the rendezvous site, the captain switched off the GPS and crawled under the camouflage nets spread by his men between the two vehicles to shield them from the sun. The temperature gauge said it was 130° Fahrenheit.

An hour later the British Gazelle helicopter came in from the south. Major Mike Martin had flown from Riyadh in an RAF Hercules transport to the Saudi town of Al Jawf, the place nearest to the border at that point which had a municipal airport. The Hercules had carried the Gazelle with its rotors folded, its pilot, its ground crew and the extra fuel tanks needed to get the Gazelle from Al Jawf to the Tapline Road and back.

In case of watching Iraqi radar, even in this abandoned place, the Gazelle was skimming the desert, but the pilot quickly saw the Very starshell fired by the SAS captain when he heard the approaching engine.

The Gazelle settled on the road 50 yards from the Land-Rovers and Martin climbed out. He carried a kitbag over his shoulder and a wicker basket in his left hand, the contents of which had caused the

307

Gazelle pilot to wonder if he had joined the Royal Army Air Corps or some branch of the Farmers' Union. The basket contained two live hens.

Otherwise, Martin was dressed like the eight SAS men waiting for him; desert boots, loose trousers of tough canvas, shirts, sweater and desert-camouflage combat jacket. Round his neck was a chequered keffiyeh which could be pulled up to shield the face from the swirling dust, and on his head a round woollen Balaclava surmounted by a pair of heavy-duty goggles.

The pilot wondered why the men did not die of heat in all that gear, but then he had never experienced the chill of the desert night.

The SAS men hauled from the rear of the Gazelle the plastic jerrycans that had given the little reconnaissance chopper its maximum all-up weight, and refilled the tanks. When he was full up again, the pilot waved goodbye and took off, heading south for Al Jawf, the ride back to Riyadh and a return to sanity from these madmen in the desert.

Only when he was gone did the SAS men feel at ease. Though the eight with the Land-Rovers were D Squadron men, light-vehicle experts, and Martin was an A Squadron free-faller, he knew all but two. With greetings exchanged they did what British soldiers do when they have the time; they brewed up a strong pot of tea.

The point the captain had chosen to cross the border into Iraq was wild and bleak for two reasons. The rougher the country they were running over, the less chance there would be of running into an Iraqi patrol, and his job was not to outpace the Iraqis over open ground but to escape detection completely.

The second reason was that he had to deposit his

charge as near as possible to the long Iraqi highway that snakes its way from Baghdad westwards across the great plains of desert to the Jordanian border crossing at Ruweishid.

That miserable outpost in the desert had long become familiar to television viewers since the conquest of Kuwait because it was where the hapless tide of refugees—Filipinos, Bengalis, Palestinians and others—were wont to cross after fleeing the chaos the conquest had caused.

In this far north-western corner of Saudi Arabia the distance from the border to the Baghdad road was at its shortest. The captain knew that to his east, from Baghdad down to the Saudi border, the land tended to be flat desert, smooth as a billiard table for the most part, lending itself to a fast run from the border to the nearest road heading for Baghdad. But it was also likely to be occupied by army patrols and watching eyes. Here in the west of Iraq's deserts, the land was hillier, cut by ravines which would carry flash floods during the rains and which still had to be carefully negotiated in the dry season, but were virtually empty of Iraqi patrols.

The chosen crossing point was 50 kilometres north of where they stood, and beyond the unmarked border only another 100 to the Baghdad-Ruweishid road. But the captain reckoned he would need a full night, a lay-up under camouflage nets during the next day, and the night after, in order to deliver his charge to a point within walking distance of the road.

They set off at four in the afternoon. The sun still blazed and the heat made driving seem like moving past the door of a blast furnace. At six the dusk approached and the air temperature began to drop—fast. At seven it was completely black and the chill set

309

in. The sweat dried on them and they were grateful for the thick sweaters the Gazelle pilot had mocked.

In the lead vehicle the navigator sat beside the driver and ran a constant series of checks on their position and course. Back in their base, he and the captain had spent hours poring over a series of large-scale, high-definition photographs, kindly provided by an American U-2 mission out of their Taif base, which formed a picture better than a mere map.

They were driving without lights, but with a pen-torch the navigator kept track of their swerving passage, correcting every time a gully or defile forced them to divert several kilometres east or west.

Every hour they stopped to confirm position with the Magellan. The navigator had already calibrated the sides of his photographs with minutes and seconds of longitude and latitude, so that the figures produced by Magellan's digital display told them exactly where they were on the photos.

Progress was slow because at each ridge one of the men had to run forward and peer over, to ensure there was no unpleasant surprise on the other side.

An hour before dawn they found a steep-sided wadi, drove in and covered themselves with netting. One of the men withdrew to a nearby prominence to look down on the camp and order a few adjustments until he was satisfied a spotter plane would practically have to crash into the wadi to see them.

During the day they ate, drank and slept, two always on guard in case of a wandering shepherd or another lonely traveller. Several times they heard Iraqi jets high overhead and once the bleating of goats ranging a nearby hill. But the goats, who seemed to have no herdsman with them, wandered off in the opposite direction. After sundown they moved on.

There is a small Iraqi town called Ar-Rutba which straddles the highway and shortly before 4 a.m. they saw its lights dimly in the distance. Magellan confirmed they were where they wanted to be, just south of the town, a 5-mile hike to the road.

Four of the men scouted round until one found a wadi with a soft, sandy bottom. Here they dug their hole, silently, using the trenching tools slung on the sides of the Land-Rovers for digging them out of drifts. They buried the cross-country motor-cycle with its reinforced tyres, and the jerrycans of spare fuel to get it to the border, should the need arise. All were wrapped in tough polythene bags to protect against sand and water, for the rains had still to come.

To protect the cache from being washed away, they erected a cairn of rocks to prevent water-erosion.

The navigator climbed to the hill above the wadi and took an exact bearing from the spot to the radio mast above Ar-Rutba, whose red warning light could be seen in the distance.

While they worked Mike Martin stripped to the buff and from his kitbag took the robe, head-dress and sandals of Mahmoud Al-Khouri, the Iraqi labourer and gardener/handyman. With a cloth tote bag containing bread, oil, cheese and olives for breakfast, a tattered wallet with identity card and pictures of Mahmoud's elderly parents and a battered tin box with some money and a pen-knife, he was ready to go. The Land-Rovers needed an hour to get clear of the site before lying up for the day.

'Break a leg,' said the captain.

'Good hunting, Boss,' said the navigator.

311

'At least you'll have a fresh egg for breakfast,' said another and there was a subdued rumble of laughter. SAS men never wish each other 'good luck'—ever. Mike Martin waved a hand and began to hike across the desert to the road. Minutes later the Land-Rovers had gone and the wadi was empty again.

*   *   *

The Head of Station in Vienna had on his books a sayan who was himself in banking, a senior executive with one of the nation's leading clearing banks. It was he who was asked to prepare a report, as full as he could make it, upon the Winkler Bank. The sayan was told only that certain Israeli enterprises had entered into a relationship with Winkler, and wished to be reassured as to its solidity, antecedents and banking practices. There was, he was told regretfully, so much fraud going on these days.

The sayan accepted the reason for the enquiry and did his best, which was pretty good considering that the first thing he discovered was that Winkler operated along lines of almost obsessive secrecy.

The bank had been founded almost a hundred years earlier by the father of the present sole owner and president. The Winkler of 1990 was himself ninety-one and known in Viennese banking circles as Der Alte, the Old Man. Despite his age he refused to relinquish the presidency or sole controlling interest. Being widowed but childless, there was no natural family successor, so the eventual disposal of the controlling interest would have to await the one-day reading of his will.

Nevertheless, day-to-day running of the bank rested with three vice-presidents. Meetings with Old

312

Man Winkler took place about once a month at his private house, during which his principal concern seemed to be to ensure that his own stringent standards were being maintained.

Executive decisions were with the vice-presidents, Kessler, Gemütlich and Blei. It was not a clearing bank, of course, had no current-account holders and issued no cheque books. Its business was as a depository for clients' funds, which would be placed in rock-solid, safe investments, mainly on the European market.

If interest yields from such investments were never going to enter the 'top ten' performers league, that was not the point. Winkler's clients did not seek rapid growth or sky-high interest earnings. They sought safety and absolute anonymity. This Winkler guaranteed them, and it delivered.

The standards on which Old Man Winkler placed such stress included utter discretion as to the identity of the owners of its numbered accounts, coupled with a complete avoidance of what the Old Man termed 'new-fangled nonsense'.

It was this distaste for modern gimmickry that banned computers for the storage of sensitive information or account-control, fax machines and, where possible, telephones. Winkler Bank would accept instructions and information by telephone, but never divulge it over a phone line. Where possible, Winkler Bank liked to use old-fashioned letter-writing on its expensive cream linenfold headed paper, or personal meetings within the bank itself.

Within Vienna the bank messenger would deliver all letters and statements, in wax-sealed envelopes, and only for national and international letters would

313

the bank trust the public mailing system.

As for numbered accounts owned by foreign clients—the sayan had been asked to touch upon these—no-one knew quite how many there were, but rumour hinted at deposits of hundreds of millions of dollars. Clearly, if this was so, and given that a percentage of the secretive clients would occasionally die without telling anyone else how to operate the account, Winkler Bank was doing quite nicely, thank you.

Gidi Barzilai, when he read the report, swore long and loud. Old Man Winkler might know nothing of the latest techniques of phone-tapping and computer-hacking, but his gut instincts were right on target.

During the years of Iraq's build-up of her poison-gas-technology purchases, every one of those from Germany had been cleared through one of three Swiss banks. Mossad knew that the CIA had hacked into the computers of all three banks—originally the search had been for laundered drug money—and it was this inside information that had enabled Washington to file its endless succession of protests to the German government about the exports. It was hardly the CIA's fault that Chancellor Kohl had contemptuously rejected every one of the protests; the information had been perfectly accurate.

If Gidi Barzilai thought he was going to hack into the Winkler Bank central computer, he was mistaken; there wasn't one. That left room-bugging, mail-interception and phone-tapping. The chances were, none of these would solve his problem.

Many bank accounts need a 'losungswort', a coded 'release word', to operate them, to effect withdrawals and transfers. But account holders can usually use such a word to identify themselves in a phone call or a fax, let alone a letter. The way Winkler Bank seemed to operate, a high-value numbered account owned by a foreign client such as Jericho would have a much more complicated system for its operation; either a formal appearance with ample identification by the account-holder, or a written mandate prepared in a precise form and manner, with precise coded words and symbols appearing at precisely the pre-agreed places.

Clearly, Winkler Bank would accept an in-payment from anyone, any time, anywhere. Mossad knew that because they had been paying Jericho his blood money by transfers to an account inside Winkler identified to them by a single number. Persuading Winkler Bank to make a transfer *out* would be a whole different affair.

Somehow, from inside the dressing gown where he spent most of his life listening to church music, Old Man Winkler seemed to have guessed that illegal information-interception technology would outpace normal information-transfer techniques. Damn and blast the man.

The only other thing the sayan could vouchsafe was that such high-value numbered accounts would certainly be handled personally by one of the three vice-presidents and no-one else. The Old Man had chosen his subordinates well; the reputation of all three was that they were humourless, tough and well paid. In a word, impregnable. Israel, the sayan had added, need have no worries about Winkler Bank. He had, of course, missed the point. Gidi Barzilai, that first week of November, was already getting extremely fed up with the Winkler Bank.

*   *   *

There was a bus an hour after dawn, and it slowed for the single passenger sitting on a rock by the road 3 miles short of Ar-Rutba when he got up and waved. He handed over two grubby dinar notes, took a seat at the back, balanced his basket of chickens on his lap, and fell asleep.

There was a police patrol in the centre of the town, where the bus jolted to a halt on its old springs and a number of passengers got off to go to work or to the market, while others got on. But while the police checked the ID cards of those getting on, they contented themselves with glancing through the dusty windows at the few who remained inside and ignored the peasant with his chickens at the back. They were looking for subversives, suspicious characters.

After a further hour, the bus rumbled on to the east, rocking and swaying, occasionally pulling to the hard shoulder as a column of army vehicles roared past, their stubbled conscripts sitting morosely in the back, staring at the swirling dust clouds they raised.

With his eyes closed, Mike Martin listened to the chatter around him, latching on to an unaccustomed word or a hint of accent that he might have forgotten. The Arabic of this part of Iraq was markedly different to that of Kuwait. If he was to pass for an ill-educated and harmless fellagha in Baghdad, these out-of-town provincial accents and phrases would prove useful. Few things disarm a city cop more quickly than a hayseed accent.

The hens in their cage on his lap had had a rough ride, even though he had scattered corn from his pocket and shared the water from his flask, now inside a Land-Rover baking under netting in the desert behind him. With each lurch the birds clucked in protest, or squatted and crapped into the litter beneath them.

It would have taken a keen eye to observe that the base of the cage on its external measurement was 4 inches more than on the inside. The deep litter round the hens' feet hid the difference. The litter was only an inch deep. Inside the 4-inch deep cavity beneath the 20-by-20-inch cage were a number of items those police at Ar-Rutba would have found puzzling but interesting.

One was a foldaway satellite dish, turned into a stumpy rod like a collapsible umbrella. Another was a transceiver, but more powerful than that Martin had used in Kuwait. Baghdad would not offer the facility of being able to broadcast while wandering around the desert. Lengthy transmissions were 'out', which accounted, apart from the rechargeable cadmium-silver battery, for the last item in the cavity. It was a tape-recorder, but a rather special one.

New technology tends to start large, cumbersome and difficult to use. As it develops, two things happen. The 'innards' become more and more complicated, although smaller and smaller; the operation becomes simpler.

The radio sets hauled into France by the agents for the British Special Operations Executive during the Second World War were a nightmare by modern standards. Occupying a suitcase, they needed an aerial strung for yards up a drainpipe, had cumbersome valves the size of light bulbs and could only transmit messages on a Morse sender. This kept the operator tapping for ages, while German detector units could triangulate on the source and close in.

317

Martin's tape-recorder was simple to operate but carried some useful features inside. A ten-minute message could be read slowly and clearly into the mouthpiece. Before it was recorded on the spool, a silicon chip would have encrypted it into a garble that, even if intercepted, the Iraqis could probably not decode.

At the push of a button the tape would rewind. Another button would cause it to rerecord, but at one two-hundredth of the speed, reducing the message to a three-second 'burst', just about impossible to trace.

It was this 'burst' that the transmitter would send out when linked to the satellite dish, the battery and the tape-recorder. In Riyadh the message would be caught, slowed down, decrypted and replayed 'in clear'.

Martin left the bus at Ramadi where it stopped, and took another one onwards past Lake Habbaniyah and the old Royal Air Force base now converted to a modern Iraqi fighter station. The bus was stopped at the outskirts of Baghdad and all identity cards checked.

Martin stood humbly in the line, clutching his chickens, as the passengers approached the table where the police sergeant sat. When it was his turn, he set the wicker basket on the floor and produced his ID card. The sergeant glanced at it. He was hot and thirsty. It had been a long day. He gestured to the place of origin of the card-bearer.

'Where is this?'

'It is a small village north of Baji. Well known for its melons, bey.'

The sergeant's mouth twitched. 'Bey' was a respectful form of address that dated back to the Turkish empire, only occasionally heard and then only from people out of the real backwoods. He flicked a dismissive hand; Martin picked up his chickens and went back to the bus.

Shortly before seven the bus rolled to a stop and Major Martin stepped out into the main bus station in Kadhimiya, Baghdad.

CHAPTER ELEVEN

It was a long walk through the early evening from the bus station in the north of the city to the house of the Soviet First Secretary in the district of Mansour, but Martin welcomed it.

For one reason, he had been cooped in two separate buses for twelve hours, covering the 240 miles from Ar-Rutba to the capital, and they had not been luxury coaches. For a second, the walk gave him the chance to inhale once again the 'feel' of the city he had not seen since leaving on an airliner for London as a very nervous schoolboy of thirteen, and that had been twenty-four years earlier.

Much had changed. The city he remembered had been very much an Arab city, much smaller, grouped round the central districts of Shaikh Omar and Saadun on the north-western bank of the Tigris in Risafa, and the district of Aalam across the river in Karch. Within this inner city most of life had been; narrow streets, alleys, markets, mosques and their minarets dominating the skyline to remind the people of their subservience to Allah.

Twenty years of oil revenue had brought long, dual-carriageway highroads plunging through the once-open spaces, with roundabouts, flyovers and four-leaf-clover intersections. Cars had proliferated and skyscrapers pushed upwards into the night sky, Mammon nudging his old adversary.

Mansour, when he reached it down the long stretch of Rabia Street, was hardly recognizable. He recalled wide open spaces around the Mansour Club where his father had taken the family on weekend afternoons. Mansour was still clearly an up-market suburb, but the open spaces had been filled with streets and residences for those who could afford to live in style.

He passed within a few hundred yards of Mr Hartley's old preparatory school, where he had learnt his lessons and played in the breaks with his friends Hassan Rahmani and Abdelkarim Badri, but in the darkness did not recognize the street.

He knew just what job Hassan was doing now, but of Dr Badri's two sons he had heard no word in almost a quarter of a century. Had the little one, Osman, with his taste for maths, ever become an engineer, after all? he wondered. And Abdelkarim, who won prizes for reciting English poetry, had he in turn become a poet or a writer?

If he had marched in the manner of the SAS, heel-and-toe, shoulders swinging to assist the moving legs, he could have covered the distance in half the time. He could also have been reminded, like those two engineers in Kuwait, that 'you may dress like an Arab, but you still walk like an Englishman'.

But his shoes were not laced marching boots but canvas slippers with rope soles, the footwear of a poor Iraqi fellagha, so he shuffled along with bowed shoulders and head down.

In Riyadh they had shown him an up-to-date map of the city of Baghdad, and many photographs taken

320

from high altitude but magnified until, with a scanning glass, one could look into the gardens behind the walls, picking out the swimming-pools and cars of the wealthy and powerful.

All these he had memorized. He turned left into Jordan Street and just past Yarmuk Square took a right into the tree-lined avenue where the Soviet diplomat lived.

In the Sixties, under Kassem and the generals who followed him, the USSR had occupied a favoured and prestigious position in Baghdad, pretending to espouse Arab nationalism because it was seen to be anti-Western, while trying to convert the Arab world to Communism. In those years the Soviet Mission had purchased several large residences outside the embassy compound which could not accommodate the swelling staff, and as a concession these residences and their grounds had been accorded the status of Soviet territory. It was a privilege even Saddam Hussein had never got round to rescinding, the more so as until the mid-Eighties his principal arms supplier had been Moscow and 6,000 Soviet military advisers had trained his Air Force and Tank Corps with their Russian equipment.

Martin found the villa and identified it from the small brass plaque that announced this was a residence belonging to the Embassy of the USSR. He pulled on the chain beside the gate and waited.

After several minutes the gate opened to reveal a burly, crop-haired Russian in the white tunic of a steward.

'Da?' he said.

Martin replied in Arabic, the wheedling whine of a supplicant who speaks to a superior. The Russian scowled. Martin fumbled inside his robe and

321

produced his identity card. This made sense to the steward; in his country they knew about internal passports. He took the card, said, 'Wait', in Arabic and closed the gate.

He was back in five minutes, beckoning the Iraqi in the soiled dish-dash through the aperture into the forecourt. He led Martin towards the steps leading to the main door of the villa. As they reached the bottom of the steps a man appeared at the top.

'That will do, I will handle this,' he said in Russian to the manservant, who glowered at the Arab one last time and went back into the house.

Yuri Kulikov, First Secretary to the Soviet Embassy, was a wholly professional diplomat who had found the order he had received from Moscow outrageous but unavoidable. He had evidently been caught at dinner, for he clutched a napkin with which he dabbed his lips as he descended the steps.

'So, here you are,' he said in Russian. 'Now listen, if we have to go through with this charade, so be it. But I personally will have nothing to do with it. Panimayesh?'

Martin, who did not speak Russian, shrugged helplessly and said in Arabic: 'Please, bey?'

Kulikov took the change of language as dumb insolence. Martin realized with a delicious irony that the Soviet diplomat really thought his unwelcome new staff member was a fellow-Russian, sicked on to him by those wretched spooks up at the Lubyanka in Moscow.

'Oh, very well then, Arabic if you wish,' he said testily. He, too, had trained in Arabic, which he spoke well with a harsh Russian accent, and he was damned if he was going to be shown up by this agent of the KGB.

So he continued in Arabic.

'Here is your card. Here is the letter I was ordered to prepare for you. Now, you will live in the shack at the far end of the garden, keep the grounds in order, and do the shopping as the chef instructs. Apart from that, I do not want to know. If you are caught, I know nothing except that I took you on in good faith. Now, get about your business and get rid of those damned hens. I will not have chickens ruining the garden.'

Some chance, he thought bitterly, as he turned back to resume his interrupted dinner. If the oaf is caught up to some mischief the AMAM will soon know he is a Russian, and the idea that he is on the First Secretary's personal staff by accident will be as likely as a skating party on the Tigris. Yuri Kulikov was privately furious with Moscow.

Mike Martin found his quarters up against the rear wall of the quarter-acre garden, a one-room bungalow with a cot bed, a table, two chairs, a row of hooks on one wall and a wash handbasin set in a shelf in one corner.

Further discovery revealed an earth-closet close by and a cold-water tap in the garden wall. Toiletry would clearly be pretty basic and food presumably served from the kitchen door at the rear of the villa. He sighed. The house outside Riyadh seemed a long way away.

He found a number of candles and some matches. By their dim light he slung blankets across the windows and went to work on the rough tiles of the floor with his pen-knife.

An hour of scratching at the mouldy mortar brought four of them up, and a further hour of digging with a trowel from the nearby potting shed produced a hole to take his radio-transmitter, batteries, tape-recorder and satellite dish. A mixture of mud and spittle rubbed into the cracks between the tiles hid the last traces of his excavation.

Just before midnight he used his knife to cut away the false bottom of the hen-cage, tipping the litter into the real base, so that no trace remained of the four-inch cavity. While he worked the chickens scratched around the floor, looking hopefully for a non-existent grain of wheat but finding and consuming several bugs.

Martin finished off the last of his olives and cheese, and shared the remaining fragments of pitta bread with his travelling companions, along with a bowl of water drawn from the outside tap.

The hens went back into their cage and, if they found their home now 4 inches deeper than it used to be, they made no complaint. It had been a long day and they went to sleep.

In a last gesture, Martin pee-ed all over Kulikov's roses in the darkness before blowing out the candles, wrapping himself in his blanket and doing the same.

His body clock caused him to wake at 4 a.m. Extracting the transmitting gear in its plastic bags, he recorded a brief message for Riyadh, speeded it by two hundred times, connected the tape-recorder to the transmitter and erected the satellite dish, which occupied much of the centre of the shack but pointed out of the open door.

At 4.45 a.m. he sent a single-burst transmission on the channel of the day, dismantled it all and put it back under the floor.

The sky was still pitch black over Riyadh when a similar dish on the roof of the SIS residence caught the one-second signal and fed it down to the communications room. The transmitting time 'window' was from 4.30 a.m. until 5.00 a.m. and the listening watch was awake.

Two spinning tapes caught the burst from Baghdad and a warning light flashed to alert the technicians. They slowed the message down two hundred times until it came over the headphones 'in clear'. One noted it down in shorthand, typed it up, and left the room.

Julian Gray, the Head of Station, was shaken awake at 5.15.

'It's Black Bear, sir. He's in.'

Gray read the transcript with mounting excitement and went to wake Simon Paxman. The Head of Iraq Desk was now on extended secondment to Riyadh, his duties in London being taken over by his subordinate. He, too, sat up, wide awake, and read the sheet of flimsy.

'Bloody hell, so far so good.'

'The problem could start,' said Gray, 'when he tries to raise Jericho.'

It was a sobering thought. The former Mossad asset in Baghdad had been switched off for three full months. He might have been compromised, caught, or simply changed his mind. He could have been posted far away, the more so if he turned out to be a general now commanding troops in Kuwait. Anything could have happened. Paxman stood up.

'Better tell London. Any chance of coffee?'

'I'll tell Mohammed to get it together,' said Gray.

*   *   *

Mike Martin was watering the flower-beds by five-thirty when the house began to stir. The cook, a bosomy Russian woman, saw him from her window and, when the water was hot, called him over to the kitchen window.

'Kak nazyvaetes?' she asked, then thought for a moment and used the Arabic word: 'Name?'

'Mahmoud,' said Martin.

'Well, here's a cup of coffee, Mahmoud.'

Martin bobbed his head several times in delighted acceptance, muttering 'shukran' and taking the hot mug in two hands. He was not joking; it was delicious real coffee and his first hot drink since the tea on the Saudi side of the border.

Breakfast was at seven, a bowl of lentils and pitta bread, which he devoured. It appeared the houseman of the previous evening and his wife the cook looked after First Secretary Kulikov, who seemed to be single. By eight Martin had met the chauffeur, an Iraqi who spoke a smattering of Russian and was useful interpreting simple messages.

Martin decided not to get too close to the chauffeur who might be a plant by the AMAM secret police or even Rahmani's Counter-Intelligence people. That turned out to be no problem; agent or not, the chauffeur was a snob and treated the new gardener with contempt. He agreed, however, to explain to the cook that Martin had to leave for a while because their employer had ordered him to get rid of his chickens.

Back on the street, Martin headed for the bus station, liberating his hens on to a patch of waste ground on the way.

As in so many Arab cities, the bus station in Baghdad is not simply a place for boarding vehicles leaving for the provinces. It is a seething maelstrom of working-class humanity where people have things to buy and sell. Running along the south wall is a useful flea-market. It was here that Martin, after the appropriate haggle, bought a rickety bicycle that squeaked piteously when ridden but was soon grateful for a shot of oil.

He had known he could not circulate in a car, and even a motor-cycle would be too grand for a humble gardener. He recalled his father's houseman pedalling through the city from market to market, buying the daily provisions, and from what he could see a bicycle was still a perfectly normal way for working people to get about.

A little work with the pen-knife sawed off the top of the chicken cage, converting it into an open-topped square basket, which he secured to the rear pillion of the bicycle with two stout rubber cords, former car fan-belts, bought from a back-street garage.

He bicycled back into the city centre and bought four different coloured sticks of chalk from a stationer in Shurja Street, just across from St Joseph's Catholic Church where the Chaldean Christians meet to worship.

He recalled the area from his boyhood, the Agid al Nasara, or Area of the Christians, and Shurja and Bank streets were still full of illegally parked cars and foreigners prowling through the shops selling herbs and spices.

When he was a boy there had only been three bridges across the Tigris, the Railway Bridge in the north, the New Bridge in the middle and the King Feisal bridge in the south. Now there were nine. Four days after the start of the Air War still to come, there were none, for all had been targeted inside the Black Hole in Riyadh, and destroyed they duly were. But that first week of November the life of the city flowed across them ceaselessly.

The other thing he noticed was the presence everywhere of the AMAM secret police, though most of them made no attempt to be secret. They watched on street corners and from parked cars. Twice he saw foreigners stopped and required to produce their identity cards, and twice saw the same thing happen to Iraqis. The demeanour of the foreigners was of resigned irritation, but that of the Iraqis was of visible fear.

On the surface the city life went on and the people of Baghdad were good-humoured as he recalled them; but his antennae told him that beneath the surface the river of fear imposed by the tyrant in the great palace down by the river near the Tamuz Bridge ran strong and deep.

Only once that morning did he come across a hint of what many Iraqis felt every day of their lives. He was in the fruit and vegetable market at Kasra, still across the river from his new home, haggling the price of some fresh fruit with an old stallholder. If the Russians were going to feed him pulses and bread, he could at least back up this diet with some fruit.

Near by four AMAM men frisked a youth roughly before sending him on his way. The old fruitseller hawked and spat in the dust, narrowly missing a bunch of his own aubergines.

'One day the Beni Naji will come back and chase this filth away,' he muttered.

'Careful, old man, these are foolish words,' whispered Martin, testing some peaches for ripeness. The old man stared at him.

'Where are you from, brother?'

'Far away. A village in the north, beyond Baji.'

'Go back there, if you take an old man's advice. I

328

have seen much. The Beni Naji will come from the sky, aye, and the Beni el Kalb.'

He spat again and this time the aubergines were not so fortunate. Martin made his purchase of peaches and lemons and pedalled away. He was back at the house of the Soviet First Secretary by noon. Kulikov was long gone to the embassy and his driver with him, so though Martin was rebuked by the cook it was in Russian so he shrugged and got on with the garden.

But he was intrigued by the old man. Some, it seemed, could foresee their own invasion and did not oppose it. The phrase 'chase this filth away' could only refer to the secret police and, by inference, to Saddam Hussein.

On the streets of Baghdad the British are referred to as the Beni Naji. Exactly who Naji was remains lost in the mists of time, but it is believed he was a wise and holy man. Young British officers posted in those parts under the Empire used to come to see him, to sit at his feet and listen to his wisdom. He treated them like his sons, even though they were Christians and therefore infidel, so people called them the 'sons of Naji'.

The Americans are referred to as the Beni el Kalb. Kalb in Arabic is a dog, and the dog, alas, is not a highly regarded creature in Arab culture.

*   *   *

Gideon Barzilai could at least take one comfort from the report on the Winkler Bank provided by the embassy's banking sayan. It pointed for him the direction he had to take.

His first priority had to be to identify which of the

three vice-presidents, Kessler, Gemütlich and Blei, was the one who controlled the account owned by the Iraqi renegade Jericho.

The fastest route would be by phone call, but from the report Barzilai was sure none of them would admit anything over an open line.

He made his request by heavily encoded signal from the fortified underground Mossad Station beneath the Vienna Embassy and received his reply from Tel Aviv as fast as it could be prepared.

It was a letter, forged on genuine headed notepaper extracted from one of Britain's oldest and most reputable banks, Coutts of The Strand, London, bankers to Her Majesty the Queen.

The signature was even a perfect facsimile of the autograph of a genuine senior officer of Coutts in the Overseas section. There was no addressee by name, either on the envelope or the letter, which began simply, 'Dear Sir....'

The text of the letter was simple and to the point. An important client of Coutts would soon be making a substantial transfer into the numbered account of a client of the Winkler Bank, to wit Account Number So-and-So. Coutts' client had now alerted them that due to unavoidable technical reasons there would be a delay of several days in the effecting of the transfer. Should Winkler's client enquire as to its non-arrival on time, Coutts would be eternally grateful if Messrs Winkler could inform their client the transfer was indeed on its way and would arrive without a moment's unnecessary delay. Finally, Coutts would much appreciate an acknowledgement of the safe arrival of their missive.

Barzilai calculated that as banks love the prospect of incoming money, and few more than Winkler, the

330

staid old bank in the Ballgasse would give the bankers to the Royal House of Windsor the courtesy of a reply—by letter. He was right.

The envelope from Tel Aviv matched the paper, and was stamped with British stamps, apparently franked at the Trafalgar Square post office two days earlier. It was addressed simply to DIRECTOR, OVERSEAS CLIENT ACCOUNTS, WINKLER BANK, etc. There was, of course, no such position within the Winkler Bank, since the job was divided between three men.

The envelope was slipped, in the dead of night, through the letter-box of the bank.

The yarid surveillance team had been watching the bank for a week by that time, noting and photographing its daily routine, its hours of opening and closing, the arrival of the mail, the departure of the messenger on his rounds, the positioning of the receptionist behind her desk in the ground-floor lobby and the positioning of the security guard at a smaller desk opposite her.

Winkler did not occupy a new building. Ballgasse, and indeed the whole of the Franziskanerplatz area, lies in the old district, just off Singerstrasse. The bank building must once have been the substantial Vienna dwelling of a rich merchant family, solid and substantial, secluded behind a heavy timber door adorned with a discreet brass plaque. To judge from the lay-out of a similar house on the square which the yarid team had examined while posing as clients of the accountancy practice that dwelt there, it had only five floors with about six offices per floor.

Among their observations, the yarid team had noted that the outgoing mail was taken each evening just before the hour of closing to a mail box on the square. This was a chore performed by the commissionaire/guard, who then returned to the building to hold the door open while the staff trooped out. Finally he let in the night-watchman before going home himself. It was the night-watchman who shut himself in, slamming enough bolts across the timber door to keep out an armoured car.

Before the envelope for Coutts of London was dropped through the bank's door, the head of the neviot technical team had examined the mailing box on Franziskanerplatz and snorted with disgust. It was hardly a challenge. One of his team was a crack lockpick, and had it open and reclosed inside three minutes. From what he learnt the first time he did it, he could make up a key to fit, which he did. After a couple of minor adjustments, it worked as well as the postman's key.

Further surveillance revealed that the bank guard always dropped off the bank's outgoing mail between twenty and thirty minutes ahead of the regular 6 p.m. pick-up from the mail box by the official post-office van.

The day the Coutts letter went into the mail slot in the door, the yarid team and the neviot lockpick worked together. As the bank guard returned down the alley to the bank after making the drop-off that evening, the lockpick had the door of the mail-box open. The twenty-two letters going out from the Winkler Bank lay on top. It took thirty seconds to abstract the one addressed to Messrs Coutts of London, replace the rest and relock the box.

All five of the yarid team had been posted in the square in case anyone tried to interfere with the 'postman' whose uniform, hurriedly purchased in a second-hand shop, bore a marked resemblance to the

332

real uniforms of Viennese mailmen.

But the good citizens of Vienna are not accustomed to agents from the Middle East breaking the sanctity of a mail-box; there were only two people in the square at the time and neither took any notice of what appeared to be a post-office employee going about his lawful business. Twenty minutes later the real mail-clearer did his job, but the passers-by were gone and replaced by fresh ones.

Barzilai opened Winkler's reply to Coutts and noted that it was a brief but courteous reply of acknowledgement, written in passable English, and signed by Wolfgang Gemütlich. The Mossad team leader now knew exactly who handled the Jericho account. All that remained was to break him or penetrate him. What Barzilai did not know was that his problems were just beginning.

*　　*　　*

It was well after dark when Mike Martin left the Russian compound in Mansour. He saw no reason to disturb the Russians by going out through the main gate; there was a much smaller wicket-gate in the rear wall with a rusty lock to which he had been given the key. He wheeled his bicycle out into the alley, relocked the door and began to pedal.

It would be, he knew, a long night. The Chilean diplomat Moncada had described perfectly well to the Mossad officers who debriefed him when he came out just where he had sited the three dead-letter-boxes destined for messages from him to Jericho and where to put the chalk marks to alert the invisible Jericho that a message awaited him. Martin felt he had no choice but to use all three at once, with an

333

identical message in each.

He had written out those messages in Arabic on flimsy airmail paper and folded each one into a square sylthane bag. The three bags were taped to his inner thigh. The chalk sticks resided in a side pocket.

His first stop was the Alwazia cemetery across the river in Risafa. He knew it already, remembered from long ago, and studied at length on photographs in Riyadh. Finding a loose brick in darkness was another matter.

It took ten minutes, scrabbling with fingertips in the darkness of the walled compound, before he found the right one. But it was just where Moncada had said. He eased the brick from its niche, slipped one sylthane envelope behind it and replaced the brick.

His second drop was another old and crumbling wall, this time near the ruined citadel in Aadhamiya, where a stagnant pond is all that remains of the ancient moat. Not far from the citadel is the Imam Aladham Shrine, and between them a wall, as old and crumbled as the citadel itself. Martin found the wall and the single tree growing against it. He reached behind the tree and counted ten courses of bricks down from the top. The tenth brick down rocked like an old tooth. The second envelope went behind it and the brick went back. Martin checked to see if anyone was watching, but he was completely alone; no-one would want to come to this deserted place after dark.

The third and last drop was another cemetery, but this time the British one, long abandoned in Waziraya near the Turkish Embassy. As in Kuwait, a grave, but not a scrape beneath the marble of the tomb but the inside of a small stone jar cemented where the headstone would be, at one end of a long-abandoned plot.

'Never mind,' murmured Martin to whatever long-dead warrior of the Empire lay beneath, 'just carry on, you're doing fine.'

Because Moncada had been based at the United Nations building miles down the Matar Sadam Airport Road, he had wisely made his chalk-mark sites closer to the wider-spaced roads of Mansour, where they could be seen from a passing car. The rule was that whoever, Moncada or Jericho, saw a chalk mark, he should note which drop it referred to then erase it with a damp cloth. The placer of the mark, passing a day or so later, would see that it had gone and know his message had been received and (presumably) the drop visited and the package retrieved.

In this way both agents had communicated with each other for two years and never met.

Martin, unlike Moncada, had no car, so he cycled the whole distance. His first mark, a St Andrew's cross in the figure of X, was made with blue chalk on the stone post of the gate of an abandoned mansion.

The second was in white chalk on the rusty-red sheet-iron door of a garage at the back of a house in Yarmuk. It took the form of a cross of Lorraine. The third was in red chalk—a crescent of Islam with a horizontal bar through the middle, placed on the wall of the compound building of the Union of Arab Journalists on the edge of Mutanabi district. Iraqi journalists are not encouraged to be a very investigative crowd, and a chalk mark on their wall would hardly make headlines.

Martin could not know whether Jericho, despite Moncada's warning that he could return, was still patrolling the city, peering from his car window to see if marks had been placed on walls. All he could now do was check daily, and wait.

It was 7 November when he noticed that the white chalk mark was gone. Had the garage-door owner decided to clean up his sheet of rusty metal of his own accord?

Martin cycled on. The blue chalk on the gate post was missing; so was the red mark on the journalists' wall.

That night he serviced the three dead-letter-boxes dedicated to messages from Jericho to his controller.

One was behind a loose brick in the rear of the wall enclosing the Kasra vegetable market off Saadun Street. There was a folded sheet of onion-skin paper for him. The second drop, under the loose stone window-sill of a derelict house up an alley in that maze of tacky streets that make up the souk on the north bank of the river near Shuhada Bridge, yielded the same offering. The third and last, under the loose flagstone of an abandoned courtyard off Abu Nawas, gave up a third square of thin paper.

Martin hid them under sticky tape around his left thigh and pedalled home to Mansour.

By the light of a flickering candle he read them all. The message was the same. Jericho was alive and well. He was prepared to work again for the West, and understood that the British and Americans were now the recipients of his information. But the risks had now increased immeasurably, and so would his fees. He awaited agreement to this and an indication of what was wanted.

Martin burnt all three messages and crushed the ashes to powder. He already knew the answer to both queries. Langley was prepared to be generous, really generous, if the product was good. As for the information needed, Martin had memorized a list of questions concerning Saddam's mood, his concept of strategy, and locations of major command centres and sites of manufacture for weapons of mass destruction.

Just before dawn he let Riyadh know: JERICHO IS BACK IN THE GAME.

*   *   *

It was on 10 November that Dr Terry Martin returned to his small and cluttered office in the School of Oriental and African Studies to find a scrap of paper from his secretary placed four-square on his blotter.

A Mr Plummer called; said you had his number and would know what it was about.

The abruptness of the text indicated Miss Wordsworth was miffed. She was a lady who liked to protect her academic charges with the possessive wrap-around security of a mother hen. Clearly, this meant knowing what was going on at all times. Callers who declined to tell her why they were phoning or what the matter concerned did not meet with her approval.

With the autumn term in full swing and a whole cast of new students to cope with, Terry Martin had almost forgotten his request to the Director of Arabic Services at the Government Communications Headquarters.

When he rang, Plummer was out at lunch; afternoon lectures kept Martin busy until four. His connection with Gloucestershire found its target just before he went home at five.

'Ah, yes,' said Plummer. 'You recall you asked for

337

anything odd, anything that did not make sense? We picked up something yesterday at our outstation in Cyprus that seems to be a bit of a stinker. You can listen to it, if you like.'

'Here in London?' asked Martin.

'Ah, no, afraid not. It's on tape here of course, but frankly you'd need to hear it on the big machine with all the enhancement we can get. A simple tape-player wouldn't have the quality. It's rather muffled; that's why even my Arab staff can't work it out.'

The rest of the week was fully booked for both of them. Martin agreed to motor over on Sunday and Plummer offered to stand him lunch at a 'quite decent little pub about a mile from the office'.

The two men in tweed jackets caused no raised eyebrows in the beamed hostelry and each ordered the Sunday-roast dish of the day, beef and Yorkshire pudding.

'We don't know who is talking to whom,' said Plummer, 'but clearly they are pretty senior men. For some reason the caller is using an open telephone line and appears to have returned from a visit to forward headquarters in Kuwait. Perhaps he was using his car phone; we know it wasn't on a military net, so probably the person being spoken to was not a military man. Senior bureaucrat, perhaps.'

The beef arrived and they ceased talking while it was served with roast potatoes and parsnips. When the waitress left their corner booth Plummer went on.

'The caller seems to be commenting on Iraqi Air Force reports that the Americans and Brits are flying an increasing number of aggressive fighter patrols right up to the Iraqi border, then veering away at the last minute.'

Martin nodded. He had heard of the tactic. It was

338

designed to monitor the Iraqi air-defence reactions to such seeming attacks on their air space, forcing them to 'illuminate' their radar screens and SAM missile sights, thus revealing their exact positions to the watching AWACS circling out over the Gulf.

'The speaker refers to the Beni el Kalb, the sons of dogs, meaning the Americans, and the listener laughs and suggests Iraq is wrong to respond to these tactics, which are evidently meant to trap them into revealing their defensive positions.

'Then the speaker says something which we can't work out. There's some garbling at this point, static or something. We can enhance most of the message to clear the interference, but the speaker muffles his words at this point.

'Anyway, the listener gets very annoyed and tells him to shut up and get off the line. Indeed, the listener, the one we believe to be in Baghdad, slams the phone down. It's the last two sentences I'd like you to hear.'

After lunch Plummer drove Martin over to the monitoring complex, which was still functioning precisely as on a weekday. GCHQ operates a seven-day-per-week schedule. In a sound-proofed room rather like a recording studio Plummer asked one of the technicians to play the mystery tape. He and Martin sat in silence as the guttural voices from Iraq filled the room.

The conversation began as Plummer had described. Towards the end, the Iraqi who had initiated the call appeared to become excited. The voice pitch rose.

'Not for long, Rafeek. Soon we shall—'

Then the clutter began and the words were garbled. But their effect on the man in Baghdad was electric. He cut in.

'Be silent, ibn-al-gahba.'

Then he slammed the phone down, as if suddenly and horribly aware that the line was not secure.

The technician played the tape three times at slightly different speeds.

'What do you reckon?' asked Plummer.

'Well, they're both members of the Party,' said Martin. 'Only Party hierarchs use the address Rafeek, Comrade.'

'Right, so we have two bigwigs chatting about the American arms build-up and the US Air Force provocations against the border.'

'Then the speaker gets excited, probably angry, with a hint of exultation. Uses the phrase "not for long—".'

'Indicating some changes are going to be made?' asked Plummer.

'Sounds like it,' said Martin.

'Then the garbled bit. But look at the listener's reaction, Terry. He not only slams the phone down, he calls his colleague "son of a whore". That's pretty strong stuff, eh?'

'Very strong. Only the senior man of the two could use that phrase and get away with it,' said Martin. 'What the hell provoked it?'

'It's the garbled phrase. Listen again.'

The technician played the single phrase again.

'Something about Allah?' suggested Plummer. 'Soon we shall be with Allah? Be in the hands of Allah?'

'It sounds to me like: "Soon we shall have ... something ... something ... Allah."'

'All right, Terry. I'll go along with that. Have the help of Allah perhaps ...?'

340

'Then why would the other man explode in rage?' asked Martin. 'Attributing the goodwill of the Almighty to one's own cause is nothing new. Nor particularly offensive. I don't know. Can you let me have a run-off tape to go home with me?'

'Sure.'

'Have you asked our American cousins about it?'

Even in a few weeks exposed to this bizarre world, Terry Martin was picking up the lingo. To the British Intelligence community, their own colleagues are the 'friends' and the American counterparts the 'cousins'.

'Of course. Fort Meade caught the same conversation, off a satellite. They can't work it out either. In fact, they don't rate it highly. For them it's on the back-burner.'

Terry Martin motored home with the small cassette tape in his pocket. To Hilary's considerable annoyance he insisted on playing and replaying the brief conversation over and over again on their bedside cassette-player. When he protested Terry pointed out that Hilary sometimes worried and worried over a single missing answer in *The Times* crossword puzzle. Hilary was outraged at the comparison.

'At least I get the answer the following morning,' he snapped, and rolled over and went to sleep.

Terry Martin did not get the answer the following morning, or the next. He played his tape during breaks between lectures, and at other times when he had a few spare moments, jotting down possible alternatives for the jumbled words. But always the sense eluded him. Why had the other man in that conversation been so angry about a harmless reference to Allah?

341

It was not until five days later that the two gutturals and the sibilant contained in the garbled phrase made sense.

When they did, he tried to get hold of Simon Paxman at Century House, but was told his contact was away until further notice. He asked to be put through to Steve Laing, but the Head of Ops. for the Mid-East was also not available.

Though he could not know it, Paxman was on extended stay in the SIS headquarters in Riyadh, and Laing was visiting the same city for a major conference with Chip Barber of the CIA.

*　　*　　*

The man they called the 'spotter' flew into Vienna from Tel Aviv via London and Frankfurt, was met by no-one, and took a taxi from Schwechat Airport to the Sheraton Hotel where he had a reservation.

The spotter was rubicund and jovial, an all-American lawyer from New York with documents to prove it. His American-accented English was flawless, not surprising as he had spent years in the States, and his German passable.

Within hours of arriving in Vienna he had employed the secretarial services of the Sheraton to compose and draft a courteous letter on his law firm's headed notepaper to a certain Wolfgang Gemütlich, Vice-President of the Winkler Bank.

The notepaper was perfectly genuine and, should a phone check be made, the signatory really was a senior partner at that most prestigious New York law firm, although he was away on vacation (something Mossad had checked out in New York) and was certainly not the same man as the visitor to Vienna.

The letter was both apologetic and intriguing, as it was meant to be. The writer represented a client of great wealth and standing who now wished to make substantial lodgements of his fortune in Europe.

It was the client who had personally insisted, apparently after hearing from a friend, that the Winkler Bank be approached in the matter, and specifically in the person of the good Herr Gemütlich.

The writer would have made a prior appointment, but both his client and the law firm placed immense importance upon utter discretion, avoiding open phone lines and faxes to discuss client business, so the writer had taken advantage of a European visit to divert to Vienna personally.

His schedule, alas, only permitted him three days in Vienna, but if Herr Gemütlich would be gracious enough to spare him an interview, he, the American, would be delighted to come to the bank.

The letter was dropped by the American personally through the bank's letter-box during the night, and by noon of the next day the bank's messenger had deposited the reply with the Sheraton. Herr Gemütlich would be delighted to see the American lawyer at ten the following morning.

From the moment the Spotter was shown in, his eyes missed nothing. He took no notes, but no detail escaped and none were forgotten. The receptionist checked his credentials, phoned upstairs to confirm he was expected, and the commissionaire took him up—all the way to the austere timber door upon which he knocked. Never was the Spotter out of sight.

Upon the command 'Herein' the commissionaire opened the door and ushered the American visitor in,

343

withdrawing and closing it behind him before returning to his desk in the lobby.

Herr Wolfgang Gemütlich rose from his desk, shook hands, gestured his guest to a chair opposite him, and resumed his place behind his desk.

The word 'gemütlich' in German means 'comfortable' with a hint of geniality. Never was a man less aptly named. This Gemütlich was thin to the point of cadaverous, in his early sixties, grey-suited, grey-tied with thinning hair and face to match. He exuded greyness. There was not a hint of humour in the pale eyes and the welcoming smile of the papery lips was less of a grin than the rictus of something on a slab.

The office conveyed the same austerity as its occupier; dark-panelled walls, framed degrees in banking in place of pictures and a large ornate desk whose surface was bare of any hint of clutter.

Wolfgang Gemütlich was not a banker for fun; clearly all forms of fun were something of which he disapproved. Banking was serious; more, it was life itself. If there was one thing which Herr Gemütlich seriously deplored, it was the spending of money. Money was for saving, preferably under the aegis of Winkler Bank. A withdrawal could cause him serious acidic pain, and a major transfer from a Winkler account to somewhere else would ruin his entire week.

The Spotter knew he was there to note and report back. His primary task, now accomplished, was to identify the person of Gemütlich for the yarid team out in the street. He was also looking for any safe that might contain the operational details of the Jericho account, and security locks, door bolts, alarm systems—in short, he was there to case the joint for an eventual burglary.

Avoiding specifics of the amounts his client wished to transfer to Europe, but hinting at their immense size, the Spotter kept the conversation to enquiring as to the level of security and discretion maintained by the Winkler Bank. Herr Gemütlich was happy to explain that numbered accounts with Winkler were impregnable and discretion was obsessive.

Only once during the conversation were they interrupted. A side door opened to admit a mouse of a woman, bearing three letters for signature. Gemütlich frowned at the nuisance.

'You did say they were important, Herr Gemütlich. Otherwise...' said the woman. At second glance she was not as old as her appearance would have indicated, perhaps forty. The scraped-back hair, the bun, the tweed suit, lisle stockings and flat shoes suggested more.

'Ja, ja, ja...' said Gemütlich and held out his hand for the letters. 'Entschuldigung...' he asked his guest.

He and the Spotter had been using German, after establishing that Gemütlich spoke only halting English. The Spotter, however, got to his feet and bobbed a small bow at the newcomer.

'Grüss Gott, Fräulein,' he said. She looked flustered. Gemütlich's guests did not usually rise for a secretary. However the gesture forced Gemütlich to clear his throat and mutter: 'Ah, yes, er... my private secretary, Miss Hardenberg.'

The Spotter noted that too as he sat down.

When he was shown out, with assurances that he would offer his client in New York a most favourable account of the Winkler Bank, the regime was the same as for entry. The commissionaire was

345

summoned from the front hall and appeared at the door. The Spotter made his farewells, and followed the man out.

Together they went to the small, grille-fronted lift, which clanked its way downwards. The Spotter asked if he might use the men's room before he left. The commissionaire frowned as if such bodily functions were not really expected within Winkler Bank, but stopped the lift at the mezzanine floor. Close to the elevator doors he indicated to the Spotter an unmarked wooden door and the Spotter went in.

It was clearly for the bank's male employees; a single stall, a single booth, wash handbasin and towel roll and a wall cupboard. The Spotter ran the taps to create noise, and did a quick check of the room. A barred, sealed window, run through with the wires of an alarm system—possible but not easy. Ventilation by automatic fan. The closet contained brooms, pans, cleaning fluids and a vacuum cleaner. So they *did* have cleaning staff. But when did they work? Nights or weekends? If his own experience was anything to go by, even the cleaner would work inside the private offices only under supervision. Clearly, the commissionaire or the night-watch could easily be 'taken care of', but that was not the point. Kobi Dror's orders were specific; no clues to be left behind.

When he emerged from the men's room, the commissionaire was still outside. Seeing that the broad marble steps to the lobby half a floor down were further along the corridor, the Spotter smiled, gestured to it and strode along the corridor rather than take the lift for such a short ride.

The commissionaire trotted after him, escorted him down to the lobby and ushered him out of the door. He heard the big brass tongue of the self-locking mechanism close behind him. If the commissionaire were upstairs, he wondered, how would the female receptionist admit a client or messenger boy?

He spent two hours briefing Gidi Barzilai on the internal workings of the bank, so far as he had been able to observe them, and the report was gloomy. The head of the neviot team sat in, shaking his head.

They could break in, he said. No problem. Find the alarm system and neutralize it. But as for leaving no trace, that would be a bastard. There was a night-watchman who probably prowled at intervals. And then, what would they be looking for? A safe? Where? What type? How old? Key or combination or both? It would take hours. And they would have to silence the night-watch. That would leave a trace. Dror had forbidden it.

The Spotter flew out of Vienna and back to Tel Aviv the next day. That afternoon, from a series of photographs he identified Wolfgang Gemütlich and, for good measure, Fräulein Hardenberg. When he had gone, Barzilai and the neviot team leader conferred again.

'Frankly, I need more inside information, Gidi. There's too much I don't know still. The papers you need, he must keep in a safe. Where? Behind the panelling? A floor safe? In the secretary's office? In a special vault in the basement? We need inside information here.'

Barzilai grunted. Long ago, in training, one of the instructors had told them all: there is no such thing as a man with no weak point. Find that point, press the nerve, he'll co-operate. The following morning the whole yarid and neviot teams began an intensive

347

surveillance of Wolfgang Gemütlich.

But the acidulous Viennese was about to prove the instructor wrong.

*   *   *

Steve Laing and Chip Barber had a major problem. By mid-November Jericho had come up with his first response to the questions put to him via a dead-letter-box in Baghdad. His price had been high but the American government had made the transfer into the Viennese account without a murmur.

If Jericho's information was accurate, and there was no reason to suspect not, then it was extremely useful. He had not answered all the questions, but he had answered some and confirmed others already half-answered.

Principally, he had named quite specifically seventeen locations linked to the production of weapons of mass destruction. Eight of these were locations already suspected by the Allies; of these he had corrected the locations of two. The other nine were new information, chief among them the exact spot of the buried laboratory in which operated the functioning gas diffusion centrifuge cascade for the preparation of bomb-grade Uranium 235.

The problem was: how to tell the military without blowing away the fact that Langley and Century had a high-ranking asset betraying Baghdad from the inside?

Not that the spymasters distrusted the military. Far from it, they were senior officers for a reason. But in the covert world there is an old and well-tested rule called 'need to know'. A man who does not know something cannot let it slip, however inadvertently. If

348

the men in civilian clothes simply produced a list of fresh targets out of nowhere, how many generals, brigadiers and colonels would work out where it must have come from?

In the third week of the month Barber and Laing had a private meeting in the basement of the Saudi Air Force Ministry with General Buster Glosson, deputy to General Chuck Horner who commanded the air war in the Gulf theatre.

Though he must have had a first name, no-one ever referred to Brig.-Gen. Glosson as other than 'Buster' and it was he who had planned and continued to plan the eventual comprehensive air attack on Iraq that everyone knew would have to precede any ground invasion.

Both London and Washington had long since concurred in the view that, regardless of Kuwait, Saddam Hussein's war machine had simply got to be destroyed, and that very much included the manufacturing capabilities for gas, germs and atom bombs.

Before Desert Shield had finally destroyed any chance of a successful Iraqi attack on Saudi Arabia, the plans for the eventual air war were well advanced, under the secret code name of Instant Thunder. The true architect of that air war was Buster Glosson.

By 16 November the United Nations and various diplomatic chancelleries round the world were still scratching around for a 'peace plan' to end the crisis without a shot being fired, a bomb dropped or a rocket launched. The three men in the subterranean room that day all new that such a call-it-all-off plan was just not going to happen.

Barber was concise and to the point. As you know, Buster, we and the Brits have been trying to get hard identification of Saddam's WMD facilities for months now. The USAF general nodded warily. He had a map along the corridor with more pins than a porcupine, and each one a separate bombing target. What now?

So we started with the export licences and traced the exporting countries, then the companies in whose countries who had fulfilled the contracts. Then the scientists who fitted out the interiors of these facilities, but many of them were taken to the sites in black-windowed buses, lived on base and never really knew where they had been.

Finally, Buster, we checked with the construction people, the ones who actually built most of Saddam's poison gas palaces. And some of them have come up roses. Real paydirt.

Barber passed the new list of targets across to the general. Glosson studied them with interest. They were not identified with map-grid references such as a bomb-campaign plotter would need, but the descriptions were enough to identify from the air-photos already available.

Glosson grunted. He knew some of the listings were already targets; others had question marks so far, now being confirmed; others were new. He raised his eyes.

'This is for real?'

'Absolutely,' said the Englishman. 'We are convinced the construction people are a good source, maybe the best yet, because they are hard-hats who knew what they were doing when they built these places and they talk freely, more so than the bureaucrats.'

Glosson rose.

'OK. You gonna have any more for me?'

'We'll just keep digging up there in Europe, Buster,' said Barber. 'We get any more hard-fact targets, we'll pass them on. They've buried a hell of a lot of stuff, you know. Deep under the desert. We're talking major construction projects.'

'You tell me where they've put 'em, and we'll blow the roof down on them,' said the general.

Later, Glosson took the list to Chuck Horner. The USAF chief was shorter than Glosson, a gloomy-looking, crumpled man with a bloodhound face and all the diplomatic subtlety of a rhino with piles. But he adored his air and ground crews, and they responded in kind.

It was known he would fight their corner against the contractors, the bureaucrats and the politicians right up to the White House if he thought he had to, and never once moderate his language. What you saw was what you got.

Visiting the Gulf States of Bahrain, Abu Dhabi and Dubai where some of his crews were posted, he avoided the fleshpots of the Sheratons and Hiltons where the good life flowed (literally), in order to chow with the flight crews down at the base and sleep in a cot in the bunkhouse.

Serving men and women have no appetite for dissembling; they know quickly what they like and what they despise. The USAF pilots would have flown string-and-wire biplanes against Iraq for Chuck Horner. He studied the list from the covert Intelligence people and grunted. Two of the sites showed up on the maps as bare desert.

'Where they get this from?' he asked Glosson.

'Interviewing the construction teams who built them, so they say,' said Glosson.

'Bullcrap,' said the general, 'those cocksuckers

351

have got themselves someone in Baghdad. Buster, we don't say anything about this. To anyone. Just take their goodies and rack 'em up on the hit-list.' He paused and thought, then added, 'Wonder who the bastard is.'

*　　　*　　　*

Steve Laing made it home to London on the 18th, to a London in frenzied turmoil over the crisis gripping the Conservative government as a back-bench Member of Parliament sought to use the party rules to topple Mrs Margaret Thatcher from the premiership.

Despite his tiredness, Laing took the message on his desk from Terry Martin and rang him at the school. Because of the academic's excitement Laing agreed to see him for a brief drink after work, delaying Laing's return to his home in the outer suburbs by as little as possible.

When they were settled at a corner table in a quiet bar in the West End, Martin produced from his attaché case a cassette-player and a tape. Showing them to Laing he explained his request weeks ago to Sean Plummer, and their meeting the previous week.

'Shall I play it for you?' he asked.

'Well, if the chaps at GCHQ can't understand it, I know damn well I can't,' said Laing. 'Look, Sean Plummer's got Arabs like Al-Khouri on his staff. If they can't work it out . . .'

Still, he listened politely.

'Hear it?' asked Martin excitedly, 'the "k" sound after "have"? The man's not invoking the help of Allah in Iraq's cause. He's using a title. That's what got the other man so angry. Clearly, no-one is

352

supposed to use that title openly. It must be confined to a very tiny circle of people.'

'But what does he actually say?' asked Laing in complete bewilderment. Martin looked at him blankly. Didn't Laing understand anything?

'He is saying that the vast American build-up doesn't matter, because "soon we shall have Qubth-ut-Allah".'

Laing still looked perplexed.

'A weapon,' urged Martin, 'it must be. Something to be available soon that will hold the Americans.'

'Forgive my poor Arabic,' said Laing, 'but what *is* Qubth-ut-Allah?'

'Oh,' said Martin, 'it means the Fist of God.'

CHAPTER TWELVE

After eleven years in power and having won three general elections, the British premier actually fell on 20 November, although she did not announce her decision to resign until two days later.

The chattering classes of the London cocktail circuit put her political demise down to her isolation in the community of the politicians of the European Community. It was, of course, complete nonsense; the British people will never dump a leader for upsetting foreigners.

Within thirty months the Italian government which had engineered her recent isolation at the Rome conference had itself been swept from power and some of its members into jail on charges of such corruption as to make that otherwise fine country virtually ungovernable.

The French government had been swept from power in a massacre not seen since the Feast of Saint Bartholomew. The German chancellor was facing recession, unemployment, neo-Nazism and public-opinion polls showing him the German people had not the slightest intention of abandoning their beloved and all-powerful Deutschmark in favour of some pot-metal token issued to them by Monsieur Delors in Brussels.

The real reasons for her fall were four, all linked. The first was that, when a back-bench MP used an obscure Party rule to challenge her and make her formal re-election by the Conservative MPs at Westminster unavoidable, she chose an election management team of ineffable incompetence.

Secondly, she allowed herself to be persuaded to choose that moment, 18 November, to go to Paris for a conference. If ever there was a time to be seen out and about in the corridors of Westminster, urging, exhorting, cajoling, reassuring the waverers, hinting at preferment for the loyal and outer darkness for the untrustworthy, that was the time.

The key voting element was a group of about fifty MPs with marginal constituencies—a majority of under 5,000—who feared they might lose their seats at the next election if she stayed. Half of them lost their nerve—and later their seats anyway.

The key to these fifty Members was the Poll Tax, a recently introduced measure for raising local government revenue, which was widely seen across the nation as unworkable and grossly unfair. One hint in those days that the worst inequities of the tax would be addressed and reformed, and Mrs Thatcher would have swept back on the first ballot.

There would have been no second ballot, and the

challenger would have disappeared into obscurity. In the ballot of 20 November she needed a two-thirds majority; she was just four votes short, forcing a run-off second ballot.

Within hours what had started as a few dislodged stones tumbling down a hill had become a landslide. After consulting her Cabinet, who told her she would now lose, she resigned.

To head off the challenger, the Chancellor of the Exchequer, John Major, stood for the top job and won.

The news hit the soldiers in the Gulf like a body-blow, Americans and British alike. Down in Oman, American fighter pilots, who were now consorting daily with SAS men from the nearby base, asked the British what was going on and received helpless shrugs in return.

Strung out along the Saudi-Iraqi border, sleeping beneath their Challenger tanks in a desert becoming colder and colder as the winter set in, men of the 7th Armoured Brigade, the Desert Rats, listened to their transistors and swore noisily.

Mike Martin heard the news when the Iraqi chauffeur swaggered over and told him. Martin contemplated the news, shrugged and asked: 'Who is she?'

'Fool,' snapped the chauffeur, 'the leader of the Beni Naji. Now, we will win.'

He went back to his car to resume listening to Baghdad radio. In a few moments First Secretary Kulikov hurried from the house and was driven straight back to his embassy.

That night Martin sent a long 'burst' transmission to Riyadh, containing the latest batch of answers from Jericho and an added request from himself for further instructions. Crouched by the doorway of his shack to ward off any intruders, for the satellite dish was positioned in the doorway facing south, Martin waited for his reply. A low, pulsing light on the console of the small transceiver told him at half-past one in the morning that he had his reply.

He dismantled the dish, stored it back beneath the floor with the batteries and transceiver, slowed down the message and listened to it play back.

There was a fresh list of demands for information from Jericho and an agreement to the agent's last demand for money, which had now been transferred into his account. In under a month the renegade on the Revolutionary Command Council had earned over a million dollars.

Added to the list were two further instructions for Martin. The first was to send Jericho a message which, not in the form of a question, it was hoped he could somehow filtrate into the thinking of the planners of Baghdad.

It was to the effect that the news from London probably meant that the Coalition action to recover Kuwait would be called off if the Rais stood firm.

Whether this disinformation reached the highest councils of Baghdad will never be known, but within a week Saddam Hussein had claimed the toppling of Mrs Thatcher was due to the revulsion of the British people at her opposition to him.

The final instruction on Mike Martin's tape that night was to ask Jericho if he had ever heard of a weapon or weapon system referred to as the Fist of God.

By the light of a candle Martin spent most of the rest of the night writing the questions in Arabic onto two sheets of thin airmail paper. Within twenty hours the papers had been secreted behind the loose brick in the wall close to the Imam Aladham shrine in Aadhamiya.

It took a week for the answers to come back. Martin read the spidery Arabic script of Jericho's handwriting and translated everything into English. From a soldier's point of view, it was interesting.

The three Republican Guard divisions facing the British and Americans along the border, the Tawakkulna and Medina, now joined by the Hammurabi, were equipped with a mix of T54/55, T62 and T72 main battle tanks, all three Russian.

But on a recent tour, General Abdullah Kadiri of the Armoured Corps had discovered to his horror that most of the crews had removed their batteries and used them to power fans, cookers, radios and casette-players. It was doubtful if, in combat conditions, any of them would now start. There had been several executions on the spot and two senior commanders had been relieved and sent home.

Saddam's half-brother, Ali Hassan Majid, now Governor-General of Kuwait, had reported that the occupation was becoming a nightmare, with attacks on Iraqi soldiers still unquenchable and desertions rising. The resistance showed no signs of abating despite vigorous interrogations and numerous executions by Colonel Sabaawi of the AMAM and two personal visits by his boss, Omar Khatib.

Worse, the resistance had now somehow acquired plastic explosive called Semtex-H, which was much more powerful than industrial dynamite.

Jericho had identified two more major military command posts, both constructed in subterranean caverns and invisible from the air.

The thinking in the immediate circle around

357

Saddam Hussein was definitely now that a seminal contribution on the fall of Margaret Thatcher had been his own influence. He had twice reiterated his absolute refusal even to consider pulling out of Kuwait.

Finally, Jericho had never heard of anything code-named the Fist of God, but would listen for such a phrase. Personally, he doubted there existed any weapon or weapon system unknown to the Allies.

Martin read the entire despatch onto tape, speeded it up and transmitted it. In Riyadh it was seized upon avidly and the radio technicians logged its time of arrival: 23.55 hours, 30 November 1990.

*   *   *

Leila Al-Hilla came out of the bathroom slowly, pausing in the doorway with the light behind her to raise her arms to the doorposts on each side and pose for a moment.

The bathroom light, shining through the négligée, showed off her ripe and voluptuous silhouette to full advantage. It should do; it was black, of the sheerest lace and had cost a small fortune, a Paris import acquired from a boutique in Beirut.

The big man on the bed stared hungrily, ran a furred tongue along a thick lower lip and grinned.

Leila liked to dawdle in the bathroom before a session of sex. There were things to be washed and anointed, eyes to be accentuated with mascara, lips to be etched in red and perfumes to be applied, different aromas for different parts of her body.

It was a good body at thirty summers, the sort clients liked; not fat but well-curved where it ought to be, full hipped and breasted, with muscle beneath the

358

curves.

She lowered her arms and advanced towards the dim-lit bed, swinging her hips, the high-heeled shoes adding four inches to her height and exaggerating the hip-swing.

But the man on the bed, on his back and naked, covered like a bear in black fur from chin to ankles, had closed his eyes.

Don't go to sleep on me now, you oaf, she thought, not tonight when I need you. Leila sat on the side of the bed and ran sharp red fingernails up through the hair of the belly to the chest, tweaked each nipple hard, then ran her hand back again, beyond the stomach to the groin.

She leant forward and kissed the man on the lips, her tongue prising an opening. But the man's lips responded half-heartedly and she caught the strong odour of arak.

Drunk again, she thought; why can't the fool stay off the stuff? Still, it had its advantages, that bottle of arak every evening. Oh well, to work.

Leila Al-Hilla was a good courtesan and she knew it. The best in the Middle East, some said, and certainly among the most expensive.

She had trained years ago, as a child, in a very private academy in Lebanon where the sexual wiles and tricks of the ouled-nails of Morocco, of the nautsh girls of India and the subtle technocrats of Fukutomi-cho were practised by the older girls while the children watched and learnt.

After fifteen years as a professional on her own, she knew that 90 per cent of the skill of a good whore had nothing to do with the problem of coping with insatiable virility. That was for porn magazines and films.

359

Her talent was to flatter, compliment, praise and indulge, but mainly to elicit a real male erection out of an endless succession of jaded appetites and faded powers.

She ran her probing hand out of the groin and felt the man's penis. Sighed inwardly. Soft as marshmallow. General Abdullah Kadiri, Commander of the Armoured Corps of the Army of the Republic of Iraq, was going to need a little encouraging this evening.

From beneath the bed where she had secreted it earlier she took a soft cloth bag and tipped its contents on to the sheet beside her.

Smearing her fingers with a thick, creamy jelly, she lubricated a medium-sized dildo-vibrator, lifted one of the general's thighs and slipped it expertly into his anus.

General Kadiri grunted, opened his eyes, glanced down at the naked woman crouching beside his genitals and grinned again, the teeth flashing beneath the thick black moustache.

Leila pressed the disc on the base of the vibrator and the insistent pulsing throb began to fill the general's lower body. Beneath her hand the woman felt the limp organ begin to swell.

From a flask with a tube sticking through the seal she half-filled her mouth with a swig of tasteless, odourless petroleum jelly, then leant forward and took the man's stirring penis into her mouth.

The combination of the oily smoothness of the jelly and rapid probing of her skilful pointed tongue began to have an effect. For ten minutes, until her jaw ached, she caressed and sucked until the general's erection was as good as it was ever going to be.

Before he could lose it she had lifted her head,

swung an ample thigh across him, inserted him into her and settled across his hips. She had felt bigger and better, but it was working—just.

Leila leant forward and swung her breasts over his face.

'Ah, my big, strong, black bear,' she cooed, 'you are superb, as ever.'

He smiled up at her. She began to rise and settle, not too fast, rising until the helmet was just still between the labia, settling slowly until she had enveloped everything he had. As she moved, she used developed and practised vaginal muscles to grip and squeeze, relax, grip and squeeze.

She knew the effect of the double-incitement. General Kadiri began to grunt and then shout, short harsh cries forced out of him by the sensation of the deep pulsing throb in his sphincter area and the woman rising and falling on his shaft with steadily increasing rhythm.

'Yes, yes, oh yes, this is so good, keep going, darling,' she panted into his face until finally he had his orgasm. While he climaxed into her hips, Leila straightened her torso, towering over him, jerking in spasm, screaming with pleasure, faking her own tremendous climax.

When he was spent he deflated at once and in seconds she had removed herself and his dildo, tossing it to one side lest he fall asleep too soon. That was the last thing she wanted after all her hard work. There was yet more work to do.

So she lay beside him and drew the sheet over them both, propping herself on one elbow, letting her bosom press against the side of his face, smoothing his hair and stroking his cheek with her free right hand.

'Poor bear,' she murmured, 'are you very tired? You work too hard, my magnificent lover. They work you too hard. What was it today, eh? More problems on the council, and always you who has to solve them? Mmmmmm? Tell Leila, you know you can tell little Leila.'

So, before he slept, he did.

Later, when General Kadiri snored away the effects of arak and sex, Leila retired to the bathroom where, with door locked and seated on the lavatory with a tray across her lap, she noted everything down in a neat, crabbed Arabic script.

Later still, in the morning, the sheets of flimsy paper rolled into a hollowed-out tampon to avoid the security checks, she would hand it over to the man who paid her.

It was dangerous, she knew, but it was lucrative, double earnings for the same job, and one day she intended to be rich; rich enough to leave Iraq for ever and set up her own academy, perhaps in Tangier, with a string of nice girls to sleep with and Moroccan houseboys to whip whenever she felt the need.

*   *   *

If Gidi Barzilai had been frustrated by the security procedures of the Winkler Bank, two weeks of trailing Wolfgang Gemütlich was driving him to distraction. The man was impossible.

After the Spotter's identification, Gemütlich had quickly been followed to his house out beyond the Prater Park. The next day, while he was at work, the yarid team had watched the house until Frau Gemütlich left to go shopping. The girl member of the yarid team had gone after her, in touch with her

362

colleagues by personal radio, so that she could warn them of the lady's return. In fact the banker's wife was away for two hours, more than ample time.

The break-in by the neviot experts was no problem, and bugs were quickly planted in sitting room, bedroom and telephone. The search, quick, skilled and leaving no trace, yielded nothing. There were the usual papers: deeds to the house, passports, birth certificates, marriage lines, even a series of bank statements. Everything was photographed, but a glance at the private bank account revealed no evidence of embezzlement from Winkler Bank—there was even a horrible chance the man would turn out to be completely honest.

The wardrobe and bedroom drawers revealed no sign of bizarre personal habits—always a good blackmail lever among the respectable middle classes—and indeed the neviot team leader, having watched Frau Gemütlich leave the house, was not surprised.

If the man's personal secretary was a mousy little thing, his wife was like a scrap of discarded paper. The Israeli thought he had seldom seen such a downcast little shrimp.

By the time the yarid girl came on the radio with a muttered advice that the banker's wife was heading home, the neviot experts were finished and out. The front door was relocked by the man in the telephone company uniform after the rest had scuttled out the back and through the garden.

From then on, the neviot team would man the tape-recorders in the van down the street to listen to the goings-on inside the house.

Two weeks later a despairing neviot leader told Barzilai they had hardly filled one tape. On the first evening they had recorded eighteen words. She had said: 'Here's your dinner, Wolfgang'—no reply. She had asked for new curtains—refused. He had said: 'Early day tomorrow, I'm off to bed.'

'He says it every bloody night, it's like he's been saying it for thirty years,' complained the neviot man.

'Any sex?' asked Barzilai.

'You must be joking, Gidi. They don't even talk, let alone screw.'

All other leads to a flaw in the character of Wolfgang Gemütlich came up zero. There was no gambling, no small boys, no socializing, no night-clubbing, no mistress, no scuttling through the red-light district. On one occasion he left the house and the spirits of the trailing team rose.

Gemütlich was in a dark coat and hat, on foot, after dark and after supper, moving through the darkened suburb until he came to a private house five blocks away.

He knocked and waited. The door opened, he was admitted and it closed. Soon a ground-floor light came on, behind heavy drapes. Before the door closed, one of the Israeli watchers caught a glimpse of a grim-looking woman in a white nylon tunic.

Aesthetic baths, perhaps? Assisted showers, mixed sauna with two hefty wenches to handle the birch twigs? A check the next morning revealed the woman in the tunic was an elderly chiropodist who ran a small practice from her own home. Wolfgang Gemütlich had been having his corns trimmed.

On 1 December Gidi Barzilai received a rocket from Kobi Dror in Tel Aviv. This was not an operation without limit of time, he was warned. The United Nations had given Iraq until 16 January to get out of Kuwait. After that, there would be war.

Anything might happen. Get on with it.

'Gidi, we can follow this bastard till hell freezes over,' the two team leaders told their controller. 'There's just no dirt in his life. I don't understand the bastard. Nothing, he does nothing we can use on him.'

Barzilai was in a dilemma. They could kidnap the wife and threaten the husband that he had better co-operate or else ... Trouble was, the sleaze would trade her in rather than steal a luncheon voucher. Worse, he would call the cops.

They could kidnap Gemütlich and work him over. The trouble there was, the man would have to go back to the bank to make the transfer to close down the Jericho account. Once inside the bank, he'd yell blue murder. Kobi Dror had said, no miss and no traces.

'Let's switch to the secretary,' he said. 'Confidential secretaries often know everything their boss knows.'

So the two teams switched their attentions to the equally dull-looking Fräulein Edith Hardenberg.

She took even less time, just ten days. They tailed her to her home, a small apartment in a staid old house just off Trautenauplatz far out in the 19th District, the north-western suburb of Grinzing.

She lived alone. No lover, no boy-friend, not even a pet. A search of her private papers revealed a modest bank account, a mother in retirement in Salzburg—the apartment itself had once been rented by the mother, as the rent-book showed, but the daughter had moved in seven years earlier when the mother returned to her native Salzburg.

Edith drove a small Seat car which she parked on the street outside the flat, but mainly commuted to work by public transport, no doubt due to the parking difficulties in the city centre.

Her salary cheques revealed a stingy salary—'mean bastards' exploded the neviot searcher when he saw the sum—and her birth certificate revealed she was thirty-nine—'and looking fifty' remarked the searcher.

There were no pictures of men in the flat, just one of her mother, one of them both on holiday by some lake, and one of her apparently deceased father in the uniform of the Customs service.

If there was any man in her life it appeared to be Mozart.

'She's an opera buff, and that's all,' the neviot team leader reported back to Barzilai, after the flat had been left exactly as they found it. 'There's a big collection of LP records—she hasn't got round to compact disc yet—and they're all opera. Must spend most of her spare cash on them. Books on opera, on composers, singers and conductors. Posters of the Vienna Opera winter calendar, though she couldn't begin to afford a ticket...'

'No man in her life, eh?' mused Barzilai.

'She might fall for Pavarotti, if you can get him. Apart from that, forget it.'

But Barzilai did not forget it. He recalled a case in London, long ago; a civil servant in Defence, real spinster type; then the Sovs had produced this stunning young Yugoslav... even the judge had been sympathetic at her trial.

That evening Barzilai sent a long encrypted cable to Tel Aviv.

*　　*　　*

366

By the middle of December the build-up of the Coalition army south of the Kuwaiti border had become a great, inexorable tidal wave of men and steel.

Three hundred thousand men and women of thirty nations stretched in a series of lines across the Saudi desert from the coast and westwards for over 100 miles.

At the ports of Jubail, Dammam, Bahrain, Doha, Abu Dhabi and Dubai the cargo ships came in from the sea to disgorge guns and tanks, fuel and stores, food and bedding, ammunition and spares in endless succession.

From the docks the convoys rolled west along the Tapline Road to establish the vast logistic bases which would one day supply the invading army.

A Tornado pilot from Tabuq, flying south from a feint attack on the Iraqi border, told his squadron colleagues he had flown over the nose of a convoy of lorries and then on to the tail of the line. At 500 miles per hour, it had taken him six minutes to reach the end of the line of trucks 50 miles away, and they were rolling nose to tail.

At Logistic Base Alpha one compound had oil drums stacked three high on top of each other, on pallets 6 feet by 6 with lines between them the width of a forklift truck. The compound was 40 kilometres by 40.

And that was just the fuel. Other compounds at Log Alpha had shells, rockets, mortars, caissons of machine-gun rounds, armour-piercing anti-tank warheads and grenades. Others contained food and water, machinery and spares, tank batteries and mobile workshops.

At that time the Coalition forces were confined by

367

General Schwarzkopf to the portion of desert due south of Kuwait. What Baghdad could not know was that, before he attacked, the American general intended to send more forces across the Wadi al Batin and another hundred miles further west into the desert, to invade Iraq itself, pushing due north and then east to take the Republican Guard in flank and destroy them.

On 13 December the Rocketeers, 336th Squadron of the USAF Tactical Air Command, left their base at Thumrait in Oman and transferred to Al Kharz in Saudi Arabia. It was a decision that had been made on 1 December.

Al Kharz was a 'barebone' airfield, constructed with runways and taxi-tracks but nothing else. No control tower, no hangars, no workshops, no accommodation for anyone—just a flat sheet in the desert with strips of concrete.

But it *was* an airfield. With amazing foresight, the Saudi government had long commissioned and had built enough air bases to play home to an air power totalling more than five times the Royal Saudi Air Force.

After 1 December the American constructors moved in. In just thirty days a tented city capable of housing five thousand people and five fighter squadrons had been built.

Principal among the builders were the heavy engineers, the Red Horse teams, backed by forty huge electric generators from the Air Force. Some of the equipment came by road on low-loaders, but most by air. They built the clam-shell hangars, workshops, fuel stores, ordnance depots, flight and briefing rooms, ops., hall, control tower, store tents and garages.

For the aircrew and ground crew they erected streets of tents with roadways between, latrines, wash-houses, kitchens, mess-halls and a water tower to be replenished by convoys of trucks from the nearest water source.

Al Kharz lies 50 miles south-east of Riyadh, which turned out to be just 3 miles beyond the maximum range of the Scud missiles in Iraq's possession. It would play home for three months to five squadrons—two of F-15E Strike Eagles, the Rocketeers and the Chiefs, 335th Squadron out of Seymour Johnson who joined at this point; one of F-15C pure-fighter Eagles and two of F-16 Fighting Falcon interceptors.

There was even a special street for the 250 female personnel in the Wing; these included the lawyer, ground-crew chiefs, truck drivers, clerks, nurses and two squadron Intelligence officers.

The aircrew flew themselves up from Thumrait; the ground crew and other staff came by cargo airplanes. The entire transshipment took two days and when they arrived the engineers were still at work and would remain so until Christmas.

Don Walker had enjoyed his time in Thumrait. Living conditions were modern and excellent and, in the relaxed atmosphere of Oman, alcoholic drinks were permitted within the base.

For the first time he had met the British SAS who have a permanent training base there, and other 'contract officers' serving with the Omani forces of Sultan Qaboos. Some memorable parties were held, members of the opposite sex were eminently datable and flying the Eagles on 'feint' missions up to the Iraqi border had been great.

Of the SAS, after a trip into the desert with them in

369

light scout cars, Walker had remarked to the newly appointed squadron commander Lt.-Col. Steve Turner: 'These guys are certifiably insane.'

Al Kharz would turn out to be different. As home of the two Holy Places, Mecca and Medina, Saudi Arabia enforces strict teetotalism, apart from forbidding any exposure of the female form below the chin, excluding hands and feet.

In his General Order Number One, General Schwarzkopf had banned all alcohol for the entire Coalition forces under his command. All American units abided by that order, and it strictly applied at Al Kharz.

At the port of Dammam, however, the American off-loaders were bemused by the amount of shampoo destined for the British Royal Air Force. Crate after crate of the stuff was unloaded, put onto lorries or C-130 Hercules air-freighters and brought to the RAF squadrons.

The American port workers remained puzzled that in a largely waterless environment the British aircrew could spend so much time washing their hair. It was an enigma that would continue until the end of the war.

At the other side of the peninsula, on the desert base of Tabuq, where British Tornados shared with American Falcons, the USAF pilots were even more intrigued to see the British at sundown, seated beneath their awnings, decanting a small portion of shampoo into a glass and topping it up with bottled water.

At Al Kharz the problem did not arise. There was no shampoo. Conditions moreover were more cramped than at Thumrait. Apart from the wing commander who had a tent to himself, the others

370

from colonel downwards shared on the basis of two, four, six, eight or twelve to a tent, according to rank.

Even worse, the female personnel lines were out of bounds, a problem made even more frustrating by the fact that the American ladies, true to their culture and with no Saudi Mutawa (religious police) to see them, took to sunbathing in bikinis behind low fences they erected round their tents.

This led to a rush by the aircrew to commandeer all the hi-lux trucks on the base, vehicles with their chassis set high above the wheels. Only from the top of these, standing on tiptoe, could a real patriot proceed from his tent to the flight lines, passing through an enormous diversion to drive down the street between the female tents and check the ladies were in good shape.

Apart from these civic obligations, for most it was back to a creaking cot and the 'happy sock'.

There was also a new mood for another reason. The United Nations had issued its 16 January deadline to Saddam Hussein. The declarations out of Baghdad remained defiant. For the first time it became clear they were going to go to war. The training missions took on a new and urgent edge.

*   *   *

For some reason, 15 December in Vienna was quite warm. The sun shone and the temperature rose. At the lunch-hour Fräulein Hardenberg left the bank as usual for her modest lunch and decided on a whim to buy sandwiches and eat them in the Stadtpark a few blocks away from the Ballgasse.

It was her habit to do this through the summer and even into the autumn, and for this she always brought her sandwiches with her. On 15 December she had none.

Nevertheless, looking at the bright blue sky above Franziskanerplatz, and protected by her neat tweed coat, she decided that if Nature was going to offer, even for one day, a bit of Altweibersommer—old ladies' summer to the Viennese—she would take advantage and eat in the park.

There was a special reason she loved the small park across the Ring. At one end is the Hübner Kursalon, a glass-walled restaurant like a large conservatory, and here during the lunch-hour a small orchestra is wont to play the melodies of Strauss, that most Viennese of composers.

Without being able to afford to lunch there, others can sit outside the enclosure and enjoy the music free. Moreover, in the centre of the park, protected by his stone arch, stands the statue of the great Johann himself.

Edith Hardenberg bought her sandwiches at a local lunch-bar, found a park bench in the sun and nibbled away while she listened to the waltz tunes.

'Entschuldigung.'

She jumped, jerked out of her reverie by the low voice saying: 'Excuse me.'

If there was one thing Miss Hardenberg would have none of, it was being addressed by complete strangers. She glanced to her side.

He was young, dark haired, with soft brown eyes and his voice had a foreign accent. She was about to look firmly away again when she noticed the young man had an illustrated brochure of some kind in his hand and was pointing at a word in the text. Despite herself she glanced down. The brochure was the illustrated programme notes of the opera *The Magic*

Flute.

'Please, this word, it is not German, no?'

His forefinger was pointing at the word 'partitura'.

She should have left there and then, of course, just got up and walked away. She began to rewrap her sandwiches.

'No,' she said shortly, 'it's Italian.'

'Ah,' said the man apologetically, 'I am learning German, but I do not understand Italian. Does it mean the music, please?'

'No,' she said, 'it means the score, the music.'

'Thank you,' he said with genuine gratitude. 'It is so hard to understand your Viennese operas, but I do love them so much.'

Her fingers slowed in their flutter to wrap the remaining sandwiches and leave.

'It is set in Egypt, you know,' the young man explained. Such nonsense, to tell her that, she who knew every word of *Die Zauberflöte*.

'Indeed it is,' she said. This had gone far enough, she told herself. Whoever he was, he was a very impudent young man. Why, they were almost in conversation. The very idea.

'The same as *Aida*,' he remarked, back to studying his programme notes. 'I like Verdi, but I think I prefer Mozart more.'

Her sandwiches were rewrapped; she was ready to go. She should just stand up and go. She turned to look at him and he chose that moment to look up and smile.

It was a very shy smile, almost pleading; brown spaniel eyes topped by lashes a model would have killed for.

'There is no comparison,' she said, 'Mozart is the master of them all.'

His smile widened, even white teeth.

'He lived here once. Perhaps he sat here, right on this bench, and made his music.'

'I'm sure he did no such thing,' she said. 'The bench was not here then.'

She rose and turned. The young man rose too and gave a short Viennese bow.

'I am sorry I disturbed you, Fräulein. But thank you for your help.'

She was walking out of the park, back to her desk to finish her lunch, furious with herself. Conversations with young men in parks, whatever next? On the other hand, he was only a foreign student trying to learn about Viennese opera. No harm in that, surely. But enough is enough. She passed a poster. Of course, the Vienna Opera was staging *The Magic Flute* in three days. Perhaps it was part of the young man's study course.

Despite her passion, Edith Hardenberg had never been to an opera in the Staatsoper. She had, of course, roamed the building when it was open in the daytime, but a stalls ticket had always been beyond her.

They were almost beyond price. Season tickets for the opera were handed down from generation to generation. A season's abonnement was for the seriously rich. Other tickets could be obtained only by influence, of which she had none. Even ordinary tickets were beyond her means. She sighed and returned to her work.

That one day of warm weather was the end. The cold and the grey clouds came back. She returned to her habit of lunching at her usual café and at her usual table. She was a very neat lady, a creature of habit.

On the third day after the park she arrived at her table at the usual hour, to the minute, and half-noticed that the one next to her must be occupied. There was a pair of student books—she did not bother with the titles—and a half-drunk glass of water.

Hardly had she ordered the meal-of-the-day when the occupant of the table returned from the men's room. It was not until he sat down that he recognized her and gave a start of surprise.

'Oh, Grüss Gott—again,' he said. Her lips tightened into a disapproving line. The waitress arrived and put down her meal. She was trapped. But the young man was irrepressible.

'I finished the programme notes. I think I understand it all now.'

She nodded and began delicately to eat.

'Excellent. You are studying here?'

Now why had she asked that? What madness had got into her? But the chatter of the restaurant rose all around here. What are you worrying about, Edith? Surely a civilized conversation, even with a foreign student, could do no harm? She wondered what Herr Gemütlich would think. He would disapprove, of course.

The dark young man grinned happily.

'Yes. I study engineering. At the Technical University. When I have my degree I will go back home and help to develop my country. Please, my name is Karim.'

'Fräulein Hardenberg,' she said primly. 'And where do you come from, Herr Karim?'

'I am from Jordan.'

Oh, good gracious, an Arab. Well, she supposed, there were a lot of them at the Technical University, two blocks across the Kärntner Ring. Most of the ones she saw were street vendors, awful people selling carpets and newspapers at the pavement cafés and refusing to go away. The young man next to her looked respectable enough. Perhaps he came from a better family. But after all ... an Arab. She finished her meal and signalled for the bill. Time to leave this young man's company, even though he was remarkably polite. For an Arab.

'Still,' he said regretfully, 'I don't think I'll be able to go.'

Her bill came. She fumbled for some schilling notes.

'Go where?'

'To the Opera. To see *The Magic Flute*. Not alone, I wouldn't have the nerve. So many people. Not knowing where to go, where to applaud.'

She smiled tolerantly.

'Oh, I don't think you'll go, young man, because you won't get any tickets.'

He looked puzzled.

'Oh no, it's not that.'

He reached into his pocket and placed two pieces of paper on the table. Her table. Beside her bill. Second row of the stalls. Within feet of the singers. Centre aisle.

'I have a friend in United Nations. They get an allocation, you know. But he didn't want them, so he gave them to me.'

Gave. Not sold, gave. Beyond price and he gave them away.

'Would you,' asked the young man pleadingly, 'take me with you? Please?'

It was beautifully phrased, as if she would be taking him.

376

She thought of sitting in that great, vaulted, gilded, rococo paradise, her spirit rising with the voices of the basses, baritones, tenors and sopranos high into the painted ceiling above...

'Certainly not,' she said.

'Oh, sorry, Fräulein, I have offended you.'

He reached out and took the tickets, one half in one strong young hand, the other half in the other, and began to tear.

'No,' her hand came down on his own before more than half an inch of the priceless tickets had been torn in half. 'You mustn't do that.'

She was bright pink.

'But they are no use to me...'

'Well, I suppose...'

His face lit up.

'Then you will show me your Opera House? Yes?'

Show him the Opera. Surely that was different. Not a date. Not the sort of dates people went on who ... accepted dates. More like a tour guide, really. A Viennese courtesy, showing to a student from abroad one of the wonders of the Austrian capital. No harm in that...

They met on the steps by arrangement at seven-fifteen. She had driven in from Grinzing and parked without trouble. They joined the bustle of the moving throng alive already with anticipatory pleasure.

If Edith Hardenberg, spinster of twenty loveless summers, was ever going to have an intimation of paradise, it was that night in 1990 when she sat a few feet from the stage and allowed herself to drown in the music. If she was ever to know the sensation of being drunk, it was that evening when she permitted herself to become utterly intoxicated in the torrent of the rising and falling voices.

377

In the first half, as Papageno sang and cavorted before her, she felt a dry young hand placed on top of her own. Instinct caused her to withdraw her hand sharply. In the second half when it happened again, she did nothing, and felt, with the music, the warmth seeping into her of another person's blood-heat.

When it was over she was still intoxicated. Otherwise she would never have allowed him to walk her across the square to Freud's old haunt, the Café Landtmann, now restored to its former 1890 glory. There it was the superlative head waiter Robert himself who showed them to a table and they ate a late dinner.

Afterwards he walked her back to her car. She had calmed down. Her reserve was reasserting itself.

'I would so like you to show me the real Vienna,' said Karim quietly, 'your Vienna, the Vienna of fine museums and concerts. Otherwise, I will never understand the culture of Austria, not the way you could show it to me.'

'What are you saying, Karim?'

They stood by her car. No, she was definitely not offering him a lift to his apartment, wherever it was, and any suggestion that he come home with her would reveal exactly what sort of a wretch he really was.

'That I would like to see you again.'

'Why?'

If he tells me I am beautiful I will hit him, she thought.

'Because you are kind,' he said.

'Oh.'

She was bright pink in the darkness. Without a further word he bent forward and kissed her on the cheek. Then he was gone, striding away across the

378

square. She drove home alone.

That night Edith Hardenberg's dreams were troubled. She dreamt of long ago. Once there had been Horst who had loved her through that long hot summer of 1970 when she was nineteen and a virgin. Horst who had taken her chastity and made her love him. Horst who had walked out in the winter without a note or an explanation or a word of farewell.

At first she had thought he must have had an accident, and rang all the hospitals. Then that his employment as a travelling salesman had called him away and he would ring.

Later she learnt he had married the girl in Graz whom he had also been loving when his rounds took him there.

She had cried until the spring. Then she took all the memories of him, all the signs of his being there, and burnt them. She burnt the presents and the photos they took as they walked in the grounds and sailed on the lakes of the Schlosspark at Laxenburg, and most of all she burnt the picture of the tree under which he had loved her first, really loved her and made her his own.

She had had no more men. They just betray you and leave you, her mother had said, and Mother was right. There would be no more men, ever, she vowed.

That night a week before Christmas the dreams ebbed away before the dawn and she slept with the programme of *The Magic Flute* clutched to her thin little bosom. As she slept some of the lines seemed to ease away from the corners of her eyes and the edges of her mouth. And as she slept, she smiled. Surely there was no harm in that.

CHAPTER THIRTEEN

The big grey Mercedes was having trouble with the traffic. Hammering furiously on the horn, the driver had to force a passage through the torrent of cars, vans, market stalls and push-carts that create the tangle of life between the streets called Khulafa and Rashid.

This was old Baghdad, where traders and merchants, sellers of cloth, gold and spices, hawkers and vendors of most known commodities had plied their trades for ten centuries.

The car turned down Bank Street where both sides of the road were jammed with parked cars, and finally nosed into Shurja Street. Ahead of it the street market of spice sellers was impenetrable. The driver half-turned his head.

'This is as far as I can go.'

Leila Al-Hilla nodded and waited for the door to be opened for her. Beside the driver sat Kemal, General Kadiri's hulking personal bodyguard, a lumbering sergeant of the Tank Corps who had been attached to Kadiri's staff for years. She hated him.

After a pause, the sergeant opened his door, straightened his great frame on the sidewalk and opened the rear-passenger door. He knew she had humiliated him once again, and it showed in his eyes. She alighted from the car and gave him not a glance or word of thanks.

One reason she hated the bodyguard was that he followed her everywhere. It was his job, of course, assigned to him by Kadiri, but that did not make her dislike him less. When he was sober, Kadiri was a tough professional soldier; in matters sexual he was also insanely jealous. Hence his rule that she should never be alone in the city.

The other reason for her dislike of the bodyguard was his evident lust for her. A woman of long-degraded tastes, she could well understand that any man might lust for her body, and if the price was right she would indulge any such lust, no matter how bizarre its fulfilment. But Kemal committed the ultimate insult; as a sergeant he was poor. How dare he entertain such thoughts, yet he clearly did; a mixture of contempt for her and brutish desire. It showed when he knew General Kadiri was not looking.

For his part he knew of her revulsion and it amused him to insult her with his glances while verbally maintaining an attitude of formality.

She had complained to Kadiri about his dumb insolence, but he had merely laughed. He could suspect any man of desiring her, but Kemal was allowed many liberties because Kemal had saved his life in the marshes of Al Fao against the Iranians, and Kemal would die for him.

The bodyguard slammed the door and was at her side as they continued on foot down Shurja Street.

This zone is called Agid al Nasara, the Area of the Christians. Apart from St George's Church across the river, built by the British for themselves and their Protestant faith, there are three Christian sects in Iraq, representing between them some 7 per cent of the population.

Largest is that of the Assyrian or Syriac sect whose cathedral lies within the Area of the Christians off Shurja Street. A mile away stands the Armenian Church, close to another tangled web of small streets and alleys whose history goes back many centuries called the Camp el Arman, the old Armenian quarter.

Cheek by jowl with the Syriac Cathedral stands St Joseph's, the Church of the Chaldean Christians, the smallest sect. If the Syriac rite resembles Greek Orthodox, the Chaldeans are an offshoot of the Catholic Church.

The most notable Iraqi of the Chaldean Christians was then the Foreign Minister Tariq Aziz, though his dog-like devotion to Saddam Hussein and his policies of genocide might indicate that Mr Aziz had somehow come adrift from the teachings of the Prince of Peace. Leila Al-Hilla had also been born a Chaldean and now the link was proving useful.

The ill-assorted couple reached the wrought-iron gate giving on to the cobbled yard in front of the arched door of the Chaldean Church. Kemal stopped. As a Muslim he would not go a step further. She nodded to him and walked through the gate. Kemal watched her as she bought a small candle from a stall by the door, drew her heavy black-lace shawl over her head and entered the dark, incense-heavy interior.

The bodyguard shrugged and sauntered away a few yards to buy a can of Coke and find a place to sit and watch the doorway. He wondered why his master permitted this nonsense. The woman was a whore; the general would tire of her one day and he, Kemal, had been promised that he could have his pleasure before she was dismissed. He smiled at the prospect and a dribble of cola drink ran down his chin.

Inside the church Leila paused to light her candle from one of the hundreds that burnt adjacent to the door, then, head bowed, made her way to the confessional boxes on the far side of the nave. A black-robed priest passed but paid her no attention.

It was always the same confessional box. She entered at the precise hour, dodging ahead of a woman in black who also sought a priest to listen to her litany of sins, probably more banal than those of the younger woman who pushed her aside and took her place.

Leila closed the door behind her, turned and sat on the penitent's seat. To her right was a fretted grille. She heard a rustle behind it. He would be there; he was always there at the appointed hour.

Who was he? she wondered. Why did he pay so handsomely for the information she brought him? Not a foreigner—his Arabic was too good for that, the Arabic of one born and raised in Baghdad. And his money was good, very good.

'Leila?' The voice was a murmur, low and even. She always had to arrive after him and leave before him. He had warned her not to loiter outside in the hopes of seeing him, but how could she do that anyway, with Kemal lurking at her shoulder? The oaf would see something and report to his master. It was more than her life was worth.

'Identify yourself, please.'

'Father, I have sinned in matters of the flesh and am not worthy of your absolution.'

It was he who had invented the phrase, because no-one else would say that.

'What have you for me?'

She reached between her legs, pulled aside the crotch of her knickers and abstracted the phoney tampon he had given her weeks ago. One end unscrewed. From the hollow interior she withdrew a thin roll of paper formed into a tube no larger than a pencil. This she passed through the fret of the grille.

'Wait.'

She heard the rustle of the onion-skin paper as the man ran a skilled eye over the notes she had made, a report of the deliberations and conclusions of the previous day's planning council chaired by Saddam Hussein himself, at which General Abdullah Kadiri had been present.

'Good, Leila, very good.'

Today the money was in Swiss francs, very high-denomination notes, passed through the grille from him to her. She secreted them all in the place she had stored her information, a place she knew most Muslim men deemed unclean at a certain time. Only a doctor or the dreaded AMAM would find them there.

'How long must this go on?' she asked the grille.

'Not long now. War is coming soon. By the end of it the Rais will fall. Others will take the power. I shall be one of them. Then you will be truly rewarded, Leila. Stay calm, do your job and be patient.'

She smiled. Really rewarded. Money, lots of money, enough to go far away and be wealthy for the rest of her days.

'Go now.'

She rose and left the booth. The old woman in black had found someone else to hear her confession. Leila recrossed the nave and emerged into the sunshine. The oaf Kemal was beyond the wrought-iron gate, crumpling a tin can in one great fist, sweating in the heat. Good, let him sweat. He would sweat much more if only he knew...

Without glancing at him she turned down Shurja Street, through the teeming market, towards the

384

parked car. Kemal, furious but helpless, lumbered behind her. She took not the slightest bit of notice of a poor fellagha pushing a bicycle with an open wicker basket on the pillion, and he took not the slightest notice of her. The man was only in the market at the behest of the cook in the household where he worked, buying mace, coriander and saffron.

Alone in his confessional, the man in the black cassock of a Chaldean priest sat a while longer to ensure his agent was clear of the street. It was extremely unlikely she would recognize him, but in this game even outside chances were excessive.

He had meant what he said to her. War was coming. Even the departure of the Iron Lady from London would not change that. The Americans had the bit between their teeth and would not now back off.

So long as that fool in the palace by the river at the Tamuz Bridge did not spoil it all and pull back unilaterally from Kuwait. Fortunately he seemed hell-bent on his own destruction. The Americans would win the war, then they would come to Baghdad to finish the job. Surely they would not just win Kuwait and think that was the end of it? No people could be so powerful and so stupid.

When they came, they would need a new regime. Being Americans, they would gravitate towards someone who spoke fluent English, someone who understood their ways, their thoughts and their speech, and who would know what to say to please them and become their choice.

The very education, the very cosmopolitan urbanity that now militated against him would be in his favour. For the moment, he was exluded from the highest councils and the innermost decisions of the

Rais—because he was not of the oafish al-Tikriti tribe, or a lifetime fanatic of the Ba'ath Party or a full general or a half-brother of Saddam.

But Kadiri was Tikrit, and trusted. Only a mediocre general of tanks, and with the tastes of a rutting camel, he had once played in the dust of the alleys of Tikrit with Saddam and his clan, and that was enough. He, Kadiri, was present at every decision-making meeting, knew all the secrets; and the man in the confessional also needed to know these things, in order to make his preparations.

When he was satisfied the coast was clear the man rose and left. Instead of crossing the nave, he slipped through a side-door into the vestry, nodded at a real priest who was robing for a service, and left the church by a back door.

The man with the bicycle was only 20 feet away. He happened to glance up as the priest emerged in his black cassock into the sunlight and whirled away just in time. The man in the cassock glanced about him, noticed but thought nothing of the fellagha bent over his bicycle adjusting the chain, and walked quickly down the alley towards a small, unmarked car.

The spice-shopper had sweat running down his face and his heart pounded. Close, too damn close. He had deliberately avoided going anywhere near the Mukhabarat headquarters in Mansour just in case he ran into that face. What the hell was the man doing as a priest in the Christian quarter?

God, it had been years; years since they played together on the lawn of Mr Hartley's Tasisiya Prep School, since he had punched the boy on the jaw for insulting his kid brother, since they had recited poetry in class, always excelled by Abdelkarim Badri. It had been a long time since he had seen his old friend Hassan Rahmani, now Head of Counter-Intelligence for the Republic of Iraq.

*   *   *

It was the advent to Christmas and in the deserts of northern Saudi Arabia 300,000 Americans and Europeans turned their thoughts to home as they prepared to sit out the festival in a deeply Muslim land. But despite the approaching celebration of the birth of Christ, the build-up of the greatest invasion force since Normandy rolled on.

The portion of desert in which the Coalition forces lay was still that part due south of Kuwait. No hint had been given that eventually half those forces would sweep much further west.

At the coastal ports the new divisions were still pouring in. The British 4th Armoured Brigade had joined the Desert Rats, the 7th, to form the 1st Armoured Division. The French were boosting their contribution up to 10,000 men including the Foreign Legion.

The Americans had imported, or were about to, the 1st Cavalry Division, 2nd and 3rd Armoured Cavalry Regiments, the 1st Mechanized Infantry Division and 1st and 3rd Armoured, two divisions of Marines and the 82nd and 101st Airborne.

Right up on the border, where they wanted to be, were the Saudi Task Force and Special Forces, aided by Egyptian and Syrian divisions and other units drawn from a variety of smaller Arab nations.

The northern waters of the Arabian Gulf were almost plated with warships from the Coalition navies. Either in the Gulf or the Red Sea on the other side of Saudi Arabia, the United States had positioned five carrier groups, headed by the 'flat-tops' *Eisenhower, Independence, John F. Kennedy, Midway* and *Saratoga*, with the *America, Ranger* and *Theodore Roosevelt* still to come.

The air power of these alone, with their Tomcats, Hornets, Intruders, Prowlers, Avengers and Hawkeyes, was impressive to behold.

In the Gulf the American battleship *Wisconsin* was on station, to be joined by the *Missouri* in January.

Throughout the Gulf States and across Saudi Arabia every airfield worth the name was crammed with fighter, bomber, tanker, freighter and early-warning aircraft, all of which were already flying round the clock, though not yet invading Iraqi airspace, with the exception of the spy planes which motored overhead unseen.

In several cases the United States Air Force was sharing airfield space with squadrons of the British RAF. As the aircrew shared a common language, communication was easy, informal and friendly. Occasionally, however, misunderstandings did occur. A notable one concerned a secret British location known only as MMFD.

On an early training mission a British Tornado had been asked by the air-traffic controller whether it had reached a certain turning-point. The pilot replied that he had not: he was still over MMFD.

As time went by, many American pilots heard of this place and scoured their maps to find it. It was a puzzle for two reasons: the British apparently spent a lot of time over it and it was not located on any American air map.

The theory was floated it might be a mishearing of KKMC which stood for King Khaled Military City, a large Saudi base. This was discounted and the search went on. Finally the Americans gave up. Wherever MMFD was to be found, it was simply not on the war maps supplied to USAF squadrons by their planners in Riyadh.

Eventually the Tornado pilots admitted the secret of MMFD. It stood for 'miles and miles of fucking desert'.

On the ground, the soldiers were living in the heart of MMFD. For many, sleeping under their tanks, mobile guns and armoured cars, life was hard and, worse, boring.

There were distractions, however, and one was visiting neighbouring units and the time dragged by. The Americans were equipped with particularly good camp cots, which the British lusted for. By chance the Americans were also issued with singularly revolting pre-packed meals, probably devised by a Pentagon civil servant who would have died rather than eat them three times a day.

They were called MREs, meaning Meals-Ready-to-Eat. The US soldiery denied this quality in them, and decided MRE really stood for Meals Rejected by Ethiopians. By contrast the Brits were eating much better so, true to the capitalist ethic, a brisk trade was soon established between American beds and British rations.

Another piece of news from the British lines that bemused the Americans was the order placed by London's Ministry of Defence for half a million condoms for the soldiers in the Gulf. In the bleak deserts of Arabia such a purchase was deemed to indicate the Brits must know something the GIs did not.

The mystery was resolved the day before the Ground War started. The Americans had spent a hundred days cleaning their rifles over and over again to purge them of the all-pervasive sand, dust, grit and gravel that endlessly blew into the ends of the barrels. The Brits whipped off their condoms to reveal nice shiny barrels gleaming with gun oil.

The other principal development that occurred just before Christmas was the reintegration of the French contingency into the heart of Allied planning.

In the early days France had had a disaster of a Defence Minister called Jean-Pierre Chevènement, who appeared to enjoy a keen sympathy with Iraq and ordered the French commander to pass all Allied planning decisions on to Paris.

When this was made plain to General Schwarzkopf, he and Sir Peter de la Billière almost burst out laughing. Monsieur Chevènement was at that time also Chairman of the France–Iraq Friendship Society. Although the French contingent was commanded by a fine soldier in the form of General Michel Roquejoffre, France had to be excluded from all planning councils.

At the end of the year Pierre Joxe was appointed French Defence Minister, and at once rescinded the order. From then on General Roquejoffre could be taken into the confidence of the Americans and British.

*   *   *

Two days before Christmas Mike Martin received from Jericho the answer to a question posed a week earlier. Jericho was adamant; there had been within the previous few days a crisis cabinet meeting containing only the inner core of Saddam Hussein's cabinet, Revolutionary Command Council and top

390

generals.

At the meeting the question of Iraq leaving Kuwait voluntarily had been raised. Obviously it had not been raised as a proposal by anyone at the meeting—no-one was that stupid. All recalled too well the earlier occasion when, during the Iran–Iraq war, an Iranian suggestion that if Saddam Hussein stepped down there could be peace was broached. Saddam asked for opinions.

The Health Minister had suggested such a move might be wise, as a purely temporary ploy, of course. Saddam invited the Minister into a side-room, pulled his side-arm, shot him dead and returned to resume the cabinet meeting.

The matter of Kuwait had been raised in the form of a denunciation of the United Nations for even daring to suggest the idea. All had waited for Saddam to give a lead. He declined, sitting as so often at the head of the table like a watching cobra, eyes moving from man to man in an attempt to smoke out some hint of disloyalty.

Not unnaturally, without a lead from the Rais, the conversation had petered out. Then Saddam had begun to speak, quite quietly, which was when he was at his most dangerous.

Anyone, he said, who let the thought of admitting to such a catastrophic humiliation of Iraq in the face of the Americans cross his mind, was a man prepared to play the role of lickspittle to America for the rest of his life. For such a man there could be no place at this table.

That was the end of it. Everyone present went over the top to explain that such a thought would never, under any circumstances, occur to any of them.

Then the Iraqi dictator had added something else.

Only if Iraq could win and be seen to win would it be possible to withdraw from Iraq's nineteenth province, he said.

Everyone round the table then nodded sagely, though none could see what he was talking about.

It was a long report and Mike Martin transmitted it to the villa outside Riyadh that same night.

Chip Barber and Simon Paxman pored over it for hours. Each had decided to take a brief break from Saudi Arabia and fly home for several days, leaving the running of Mike Martin and Jericho from the Riyadh end in the hands of Julian Gray for the British and the local CIA Head of Station for the Americans. There were only twenty-four days to go until the expiry of the United Nations deadline and the start of General Chuck Horner's air war against Iraq. Both men wanted a short home-leave and Jericho's powerful report gave them the chance. They could take it with them.

'What do you think he means, "win and be seen to win"?' asked Barber.

'No idea,' said Paxman. 'We'll have to get some analysts who are better than we are to have a look at it.'

'We too. I guess nobody will be around for the next few days except the shop-minders. I'll give it the way it is to Bill Stewart and he'll probably have a few eggheads try to add an in-depth analysis before it goes on to the Director and State Department.'

'I know an egghead I'd like to have a look at it,' said Paxman, and on that note they left for the airport to catch their respective flights home.

On Christmas Eve, seated in a discreet wine bar in London's West End with Simon Paxman, Dr Terry Martin was shown the whole text of the Jericho message and asked if he would try to work out what, if anything, Saddam Hussein could mean by winning against America as a price for leaving Kuwait.

'By the way,' he asked Paxman, 'I know it breaks the rules of need-to-know, but I really am worried. I do these favours for you—give me one in return. How is my brother Mike doing in Kuwait? Is he still safe?'

Paxman stared at the doctor of Arabic studies for several seconds.

'I can only tell you that he is no longer in Kuwait,' he said. 'And that's more than my job is worth.'

Terry Martin flushed with relief.

'It's the best Christmas present I could have. Thank you, Simon.' He looked up and waved a waggish finger. 'Just one thing, don't even think of sending him into Baghdad.'

Paxman had been in the business fifteen years. He kept his face immobile, his tone light. The academic was clearly just joking.

'Really? Why not?'

Martin was finishing his glass of wine and failed to notice the flicker of alarm in the Intelligence officer's eyes.

'My dear Simon, Baghdad's the one city in the world he mustn't set foot in. You remember those tapes of Iraqi radio intercepts Sean Plummer let me have? Some of the voices had been identified. I recognized one of the names. A hell of a fluke, but I know I'm right.'

'Really?' said Paxman smoothly. 'Tell me more.'

'It's been a long time of course, but I know it was the same man. And guess what? He's now Head of Counter-Intelligence in Baghdad, Saddam's Number One spy-hunter.'

393

'Hassan Rahmani,' mumured Paxman. Terry Martin should stay off booze, even before Christmas, he can't carry it. His tongue's running away with him.

'That's the one. They were at school together, you know. We all were. Good old Mr Hartley's Prep School. Mike and Hassan were best mates. See? That's why he can never be seen around Baghdad.'

Paxman left the wine bar and stared at the dumpy figure of the Arabist heading down the street.

'Oh shit,' he said, 'oh bloody, bloody hell.'

Someone had just ruined his Christmas, and he was about to ruin Steve Laing's.

*　　　*　　　*

Edith Hardenberg had gone to Salzburg to spend the festive season with her mother, a tradition that went back many years.

Karim, the young Jordanian student, was able to visit Gidi Barzilai at his safe-house apartment, where the leader of Operation Joshua was dispensing drinks to the off-duty members of the yarid and neviot teams working under him. Only one unfortunate was up in Salzburg, keeping an eye on Miss Hardenberg in case she should return suddenly to the capital.

Karim's real name was Avi Herzog, a twenty-nine year old who had been seconded to Mossad several years earlier from Unit 504, a branch of Army Intelligence specializing in cross-border raids, which accounted for his fluent Arabic. Because of his good looks and the deceptively shy and diffident manner he could affect when he wished, Mossad had twice used him for honeytrap operations.

'So, how's it going, loverboy?' asked Gidi as he passed round the drinks.

394

'Slowly,' said Avi.

'Don't take too long. The Old Man wants a result, remember.'

'This is one very uptight lady,' replied Avi. 'Only interested in a meeting of minds—yet.'

In his cover as a student from Amman he had been set up in a small flat shared with one other Arab student, in fact a member of the neviot team, a phone-tapper by trade who also spoke Arabic. This was in case Edith Hardenberg or anyone else took it into their head to check out where and how he lived and with whom.

The shared flat would pass any inspection—it was littered with text books on engineering, and strewn with Jordanian newspapers and magazines. Both men had genuinely been enrolled in the Technical University in case a check was made there also. It was his flatmate who spoke.

'Meeting of minds? Screw that.'

'That's the point,' said Avi. 'I can't.'

When the laughter died down he added: 'By the way, I'm going to want danger money.'

'Why?' asked Gidi. 'Think she's going to bite it off when you drop your jeans?'

'Nope. It's the art galleries, concerts, operas, recitals. I could die of boredom before I get that far.'

'You just carry on the way you know how, boy-chick. You're only here because the Office says you've got something we don't.'

'Yes,' said the girl member of the yarid tracking team, 'about nine inches.'

'That's enough of that, young Yael. You can be back on traffic duty in Hayarkon Street any time you like.'

The drink, the laughter and the banter in Hebrew

flowed. Late that evening Yael discovered she was right. It was a good Christmas for the Mossad team in Vienna.

*　　*　　*

'So, what do you think, Terry?'

Steve Laing and Simon Paxman had invited Terry Martin to join them in one of the Firm's apartments in Kensington. They needed more privacy than they could get in a restaurant. It was two days before the New Year.

'Fascinating,' said Dr Martin. 'Absolutely fascinating. This is for real? Saddam really said all this?'

'Why do you ask?'

'Well, if you'll forgive my saying so, it's a strange telephone tap. The narrator seems to be reporting to someone else on a meeting he attended ... The other man on the line doesn't seem to say a thing.'

There was simply no way the Firm was going to tell Terry Martin how they had come by the report.

'The other man's interventions were perfunctory,' said Laing smoothly, 'just grunts and expressions of interest. There seemed no point in including them.'

'But this *is* the language Saddam used?'

'So we understand, yes.'

'Fascinating. The first time I've ever seen anything he said that was not destined for publication or a wider audience.'

Martin had in his hands not the handwritten report by Jericho, which had been destroyed by his own brother in Baghdad as soon as it had been read, word for word, into the tape-recorder. It was a typewritten transcript in Arabic of the text that had

396

reached Riyadh in the 'burst' transmission before Christmas. He also had the Firm's own English translation.

'That last phrase,' said Paxman, who would be heading back to Riyadh the same evening, 'where he says "win and be seen to win"—does that tell you anything?'

'Of course. But you know, you're still using the word "win" in its European or North American connotation. I would use the word "succeed" in English.'

'All right, Terry, how does he think he can succeed against America and the Coalition?' asked Laing.

'By humiliation. I told you before, he must leave America looking a complete fool.'

'But he won't pull out of Kuwait in the next twenty days? We really need to know, Terry.'

'Look, Saddam went in there because his claims would not be met,' said Martin. 'He demanded four things: take-over of Warba and Bubiyan Islands to have access to the sea; compensation for the excess oil he claims Kuwait snitched from the shared oilfield; an end to Kuwait's over-production; and a write-off of the fifteen-billion-dollar war debt. If he can get these, he can pull back with honour, leaving America hanging in the breeze. That's winning.'

'Any hint that he thinks he might get them?'

Martin shrugged.

'He thinks the United Nations peacemongers could pull the rug. He's gambling that time is on his side, that if he can keep spinning things out the resolve of the UN will ebb away. He could be right.'

'The man doesn't make sense,' snapped Laing. 'He has the deadline. January 16, not twenty days away. He's going to be crushed.'

397

'Unless,' suggested Paxman, 'one of the Permanent Members of the Security Council comes up with a last-minute peace plan to put the deadline on hold.'

Laing looked gloomy.

'Paris or Moscow, or both,' he predicted.

'If it comes to war, does he still think he could win? Beg your pardon, "succeed"?' asked Paxman.

'Yes,' said Terry Martin. 'But it's back to what I told you before—American casualties. Don't forget Saddam is a back-street gunman. His constituency is not the diplomatic corridors of Cairo and Riyadh. It's all those alleys and bazaars crammed with Palestinians and other Arabs who resent America, the backer of Israel. Any man who can leave America bleeding, whatever the damage to his own country, will be the toast of those millions.'

'But he can't do it,' insisted Laing.

'He thinks he can,' Martin countered. 'Look, he's smart enough to have worked out that in America's eyes America cannot lose, must not lose. It is simply not acceptable. Look at Vietnam. The veterans came home and they were pelted with garbage. For America, terrible casualties at the hands of a despised enemy is a form of loss. Unacceptable loss. Saddam can waste fifty thousand men any time, any place. He doesn't care. Uncle Sam does. If America takes that kind of loss she'll be shaken to the core. Heads have to roll, careers to be smashed, governments to fall. The recriminations and the self-blame would last a generation.'

'He can't do that,' said Laing.

'He thinks he can,' replied Martin.

'It's the gas weapon,' muttered Paxman.

'Maybe. By the by, did you ever find out what that

398

phrase on the phone intercept meant?'

Laing glanced across at Paxman. Jericho again. There must be no mention of Jericho.

'No. Nobody we asked had ever heard of it. No-one could work it out.'

'It could be important, Steve. Something else ... not gas.'

'Terry,' said Laing patiently, 'in less than twenty days the Americans, with us, the French, Italians, Saudis and others, are going to throw at Saddam Hussein the biggest air armada the world has ever seen. Enough firepower to exceed in a further twenty days all the tonnage dropped in the Second World War. The generals down in Riyadh are kind of busy. We really can't go down there and say: "Hold everything, guys, we have a phrase in a phone intercept we can't work out." Let's face it, it was just an excitable man on a phone suggesting that God was on their side.'

'There's nothing strange in that, Terry,' said Paxman, 'people going to war have claimed they had God's support since time began. That was all it was.'

'The other man told the speaker to shut up and get off the line,' Martin reminded them.

'So he was busy and irritable.'

'He called him the son of a whore.'

'So he didn't like him much.'

'Maybe.'

'Terry, please, leave it alone. It was just a phrase. It's the gas weapon. That's what he's counting on. All the rest of your analysis we agree with.'

Martin left first, the two Intelligence officers twenty minutes later. Shrugged into their coats, collars up, they went down the pavement looking for a taxi.

'You know,' said Laing, 'he's a clever little bugger and I quite like him. But he really is a terrible fusspot. You've heard about his private life?'

A cab went by, empty, its light off. Tea-break time. Laing swore at it.

'Yes, of course, the Box ran a check.'

The Box, or Box 500, is slang for the Security Service, M.I.5. Once, long ago, the address of M.I.5 really was PO Box 500, London.

'Well, there you are then,' said Laing.

'Steve, I really don't think that's got anything to do with it.'

Laing stopped and turned to his subordinate.

'Simon, trust me. He's got a bee in his bonnet and he's wasting our time. Take a word of advice. Just drop the professor.'

* * *

'It will be the poison gas weapon, Mr President.'

Three days after the New Year such festivities as there had been in the White House, and for most there had been no pause at all, had long died away. The whole West Wing, heart of the US Administration, was humming with activity.

In the quiet of the Oval Office George Bush sat behind the great desk, backed by the tall narrow windows, 5 inches of pale green bullet-proof glass, and beneath the seal of the United States.

Facing him was General Brent Scowcroft, the President's National Security adviser.

The President glanced down at the digest of the analyses that had just been presented to him.

'Everyone is agreed on this?' he asked.

'Yes, sir. The stuff that just came in from London

shows their people completely concur with ours. Saddam Hussein will not pull out of Iraq unless he is given an "out", a face-saver, which we will ensure he does not get.

'For the rest, he will rely on mass gas attacks on the Coalition ground forces, either before or during their invasion across the border.'

George Bush was the first American president since John F. Kennedy who had actually been in combat. He had seen American bodies killed in action. But there was something particularly hideous, especially foul, in the thought of young combat soldiers writhing through their last moments of life as the gas tore at the lung tissues and crippled the central nervous system.

'And how will he launch this gas?' he asked.

'We believe there are four options, Mr President. The obvious one is by canisters launched from fighters and strike bombers. Colin Powell has just been on the line to Chuck Horner in Riyadh. General Horner says he needs thirty-five days of unceasing air war. After day twenty no Iraqi airplane will reach the border. By day thirty no Iraqi plane will take off for more than sixty seconds. He says he guarantees it, sir. You can have his stars on it.'

'And the rest?'

'Saddam has a number of MLRS batteries. That would seem to be the second line of possibility.'

Iraq's multi-launch rocket systems were Soviet-built and based on the old Katyushkas used with devastating effect by the Soviet army in the Second World War. Now much updated, these rockets, launched in rapid sequence from a rectangular 'pack' on the back of a truck or from a fixed position, now had a range of 100 kilometres.

401

'Naturally, Mr President, because of their range they would have to be launched from within Kuwait or the Iraqi desert to the west. We believe the J-STARS will find them on their radars and they will be taken out. The Iraqis can camouflage them all they like, but the metal will show up.

'For the rest, Iraq has stockpiles of gas-tipped shells for use by tanks and artillery. Range, under 37 kilometres, 19 miles. We know the stockpiles are already on site, but at that range it's all desert—no cover. The Air boys are confident they can find them and destroy them. Then there are the Scuds. They're being taken care of even as we speak.'

'And the preventive measures?'

'They're completed, Mr President. In case of an anthrax attack, every man is being inoculated. The Brits have done it, too. We are increasing production of the anti-anthrax vaccine every hour. And every man and woman has a gas mask and a cover-all gas cape. If he tries it . . .'

The President rose, turned and stared up at the seal. The bald eagle, clutching its arrows, stared back.

Twenty years earlier he had seen those awful zip-up body bags coming back from Vietnam, and he knew that more of them were even now stored in discreet unmarked containers under the Saudi sun.

Even with all the precautions, there would be patches of exposed skin, masks that could not be reached and pulled on in time.

The following year he was going to go for re-election. But that was not the point. Win or lose, he had no intention of going down in history as the American President who had consigned tens of thousands of soldiers to die, not, as in Vietnam, over nine years but over a few weeks or even days.

'Brent...'

'Mr President.'

'James Baker is due to see Tariq Aziz shortly.'

'In six days in Geneva.'

'Ask him to come and see me, please.'

*   *   *

In the first week of January Edith Hardenberg began
to enjoy herself, really enjoy herself, for the first time
in years. There was a thrill in exploring and
explaining to her eager young friend the wonders of
culture that lay within her city.

The Winkler Bank was permitting its staff a four-
day break to include New Year's Day; after that they
would have to confine their cultural outings to the
evening, which still gave the promise of theatre,
concerts and recitals, or weekends when the
museums and galleries were still open.

They spent half a day at the Jugendstil admiring
the art nouveau, and another half-day in the
Sezession where hangs the permanent exhibition of
the works of Klimt.

The young Jordanian was delighted and excited, a
fund of questions pouring from him, and Edith
Hardenberg caught the enthusiasm, her eyes alight as
she explained that there was another wonderful
exhibition at the Künstlerhaus which was definitely a
'must' for the next weekend.

After the Klimt viewing, Karim took her to dine at
the Rotisserie Sirk. She protested at the expense, but
her new friend explained that his father was a wealthy
surgeon in Amman and that his allowance was
generous.

Amazingly, she allowed him to pour her a glass of wine and failed to notice when he topped it up. Her talk became more animated and there was a small flush on each pale cheek.

Over coffee Karim leant forward and placed his hand on hers. She looked flustered and glanced hastily around to see if anyone had noticed, but no-one bothered. She withdrew her hand, but quite slowly.

By the end of the week they had visited four of the cultural treasures she had in mind, and when they walked back through the cold darkness towards her car after an evening at the Musikverein, he took her gloved hand in his and kept it there. She did not pull it away, feeling the warmth seep through the cotton glove.

'You are very kind to do all this for me,' he said gravely, 'I am sure it must be boring for you.'

'Oh, no, it's not at all,' she said earnestly, 'I enjoy seeing and hearing all these beautiful things. I'm so glad you do, too. Quite soon you'll be an expert on European art and culture.'

When they reached her car he smiled down at her, took her wind-chilled face between both his bare but surprisingly hot hands and kissed her lightly on the lips.

'Danke, Edith.'

Then he walked away. She drove herself home as usual, but her hands were trembling and she nearly hit a tram.

*   *   *

US Secretary of State James Baker met the Iraqi Foreign Minister Tariq Aziz in Geneva on 9 January.

It was not a long meeting and it was not a friendly one. It was not intended to be. There was a single English-Arabic interpreter present, though Tariq Aziz's English was perfectly up to the task of understanding the American, who spoke slowly and with great clarity. His message was quite simple.

If, during the course of any hostilities that may occur between our countries, your government chooses to employ the internationally banned weapon of poison gas, I am authorized to inform you and President Hussein that my country will use a nuclear device. We will, in short, nuke Baghdad.

The dumpy, grey-haired Iraqi took in the sense of the message but at first could not believe it. For one thing, no man in his senses would dare convey such a bare-faced threat to the Rais. He had a habit, in the manner of former Babylonian kings, of taking out his displeasure on the message-bearer.

For another, he was not sure at first that the American was serious. The fall-out, the collateral damage of an atomic bomb, would not be confined to Baghdad, surely? It would devastate half the Middle East, would it not?

Tariq Aziz, as he headed home for Baghdad a deeply troubled man, did not know three things.

One was that the so-called 'theatre' nuclear bombs of modern science are a far cry from the Hiroshima bomb of 1945. The new, limited-damage 'clean' bombs are so called because although their heat-and-blast damage is as appalling as ever, the radioactivity left behind is of extremely short duration.

The second thing was that within the hull of the battleship *Wisconsin*, then stationed in the Gulf and joined by the *Missouri*, were three very special steel-and-concrete caissons, strong enough if the ship went down not to degrade for 10,000 years. Inside them were three Tomahawk Cruise missiles the United States hoped never to have to use.

The third was that the Secretary of State was not joking at all.

*   *   *

General Sir Peter de la Billière walked alone in the darkness of the desert night, accompanied only by the crunch of the sand beneath his feet and his troubled private thoughts.

A lifelong professional soldier and a combat veteran, his tastes were ascetic as his frame was spare. Unable to take much pleasure in the luxury offered by cities, he felt more at home and at ease in camps and bivouacs and the company of fellow soldiers. Like others before him, he appreciated the Arabian desert, its vast horizons, blazing heat and numbing cold, and many times its awesome silence.

That night, on a visit to the front lines, one of the treats he permitted himself as often as possible, he had walked away from St Patrick's Camp, leaving behind him the brooding Challenger tanks beneath their nets, crouching animals patiently waiting for their time and the hussars preparing the evening meal beneath them.

By then a close friend of General Schwarzkopf and privy to all the planning staff's innermost councils, he knew that war was coming. Less than a week before the expiry of the United Nations deadline, there was not a hint that Saddam Hussein had any intention of pulling out of Kuwait.

What worried him that night under the stars of the Saudi desert was that he could not understand what the tyrant of Baghdad thought he was up to. As a soldier, the British general liked to understand his enemy, plumb the man's intentions, his motivations, his tactics, his overall strategy.

Personally, he had nothing but contempt for the man in Baghdad. The amply documented files depicting genocide, torture and murder revolted him. Saddam was not a soldier, never had been, and what real military talent he had had in his army he had largely wasted by over-ruling his generals or having the best of them executed.

That was not the problem; the problem was that Saddam Hussein had clearly taken overall command of every aspect, political and military, and nothing he did made a fraction of sense.

He had invaded Kuwait at the wrong time and for the wrong reasons. That done, he had blown away his chances of reassuring his fellow Arabs that he was open to diplomacy, susceptible to reason and that the problem could be resolved within the ambit of inter-Arab negotiations. Had he taken that road, he could probably have counted quite rightly on the oil continuing to flow and the West gradually losing interest as the inter-Arab conferences bogged down for years.

It was his own stupidity that had brought in the West, and to cap it the Iraqi occupation of Kuwait, with its multiple rapes and brutality, its attempt to use Westerners as human shields, had guaranteed his utter isolation.

In the early days Saddam Hussein had had the rich oilfields of north-eastern Saudi Arabia at his mercy and had hung back. With his army and air force under good generalship, he could even have reached Riyadh and dictated his terms. He had failed, and

407

Desert Shield had been put in place while he masterminded one public-relations disaster after another in Baghdad.

He might be streetwise, but in all other matters he was a strategic buffoon. And yet, reasoned the British general, how could any man be so stupid?

Even in the face of the air power now ranged against him, he was making every single wrong move, politically and militarily. Had he no idea what rage from the skies was about to be visited on Iraq? Did he really not comprehend the level of the firepower that was about to set his armoury back by ten years in five weeks?

The general stopped and stared across the desert towards the north. There was no moon that night, but the stars in the desert are so bright that dim outlines can be seen by their light alone. The land was flat, running away to the labyrinth of sand-walls, fire-ditches, minefields, barbed-wire entanglements and gullies that made up the Iraqi defensive line, through which the American engineers of Big Red One would blast a path to let the Challengers roll.

And yet the tyrant of Baghdad had one single ace of which the general knew and which he feared. Saddam could simply pull out of Kuwait.

Time was not on the Allies' side; it belonged to Iraq. On 15 March the Muslim feast of Ramadan would begin. For a month no food or water should pass the lips of any Muslim between sunrise and sunset. The nights were for eating and drinking. That made going to war for a Muslim army in Ramadan almost impossible.

After 15 April, the desert would become an inferno, with temperatures rising to 130 degrees. Pressure would build up back home to bring the boys

408

out; by summer the pressure at home and the misery of the desert would become irresistible. The Allies would have to pull out, and having done so would never come back again like this. The Coalition was a once-for-all phenomenon.

So, 15 March was the limit. Working backwards, the ground war might be up to twenty days. It would have to start, if at all, by 23 February. But Chuck Horner needed his thirty-five days of air war to smash the Iraqi weapons, regiments and defences. January 17—that was the latest possible date.

Supposing Saddam pulled out? He would leave half a million Allies looking like fools, strung out in the desert, hanging in the wire, nowhere to go but back. Yet Saddam was adamant—he would not pull out.

What was that crazy man up to? he asked himself again. Was he waiting for something, some divine intervention of his own imagining, that would crush his enemies and leave him triumphant?

There was a yell out of the tank camp behind him. He turned. The Commanding Officer of the Queen's Royal Irish Hussars, Arthur Denaro, was calling him to supper. Burly, jovial Arthur Denaro, who would be in the first tank through that gap one day.

He smiled and began to walk back. It would be good to squat in the sand with the men, shovelling baked beans and bread out of a mess tin, listening to the voices in the glow of the fire, the flat twang of Lancashire, the rolling burr of Hampshire and the soft brogue of Ireland; to laugh at the leg-pulling and the jokes, the crude vocabulary of men who used blunt English to say exactly what they meant, and with good humour.

Lord rot that man in the north. What the hell was

409

he waiting for?

CHAPTER FOURTEEN

The answer to the British General's puzzlement lay on a padded trolley under the fluorescent lights of the factory 80 feet beneath the desert of Iraq where it had been built.

An engineer gave the device a large polish and stepped rapidly back to stand at attention as the door to the room opened. Only five men came in before the two armed guards from the Presidential Security Detail, the Amn-al-Khass, closed the door.

Four of the men deferred to the one in the centre. He wore as usual his combat uniform over gleaming black calf-boots, his personal side-arm at his waist, green cotton kerchief covering the triangle between jacket and throat.

One of the other four was the personal bodyguard who, even in here where everyone had been checked five times for concealed weapons, would not leave his side. Between the Rais and his bodyguard stood his son-in-law, Hussein Kamil, Head of the Ministry of Industry and Military Industrialization, the MIMI. As in so many things, it was MIMI who had taken over from the Ministry of Defence.

On the other side of the President stood the mastermind of the Iraqi programme, Dr Jaafar Al-Jaafar, the genius openly referred to as Iraq's Robert Oppenheimer. Beside him, but a bit to the rear, stood Dr Salah Siddiqui. Where Jaafar was the physicist, Siddiqui was the engineer.

The steel of their baby gleamed dully in the white
410

light. It was 14 foot long and just over 3 foot in diameter.

At the rear, 4 foot were taken up by an elaborate impact-absorbing device that would be shed as soon as the projectile had been launched. Even the remainder of the 10-foot-long casing was in fact a sabot, a sleeve in eight identical sections. Tiny explosive bolts would cause this to break away as the projectile departed on its mission, leaving the slimmer, 2-foot-diameter core to carry on alone.

The sabot was only there to fill out the 24-inch projectile to the 39 inches needed to occupy the bore of the launcher, and to protect the four rigid tail fins it concealed.

Iraq did not possess the telemetry needed to operate movable fins by radio signals from Earth, but the rigid fins would serve to stabilize the projectile in flight and prevent it from wobbling or tumbling.

At the front, the nose-cone was on ultra-tough maraging steel and needle-pointed. This, too, would eventually become dispensable.

When a rocket, having entered inner space on its flight, re-enters the earth's atmosphere, the air becoming denser on the downward flight creates a friction-heat enough to melt the nose-cone away. That is why re-entering astronauts need that heat-shield to prevent their capsule being incinerated.

The device the five Iraqis surveyed that night was similar. The steel nose-cone would ease its flight upward, but could not survive re-entry. Were it retained, the melting metal would bend and buckle, causing the falling body to sway, swerve, turn broadside on to the rushing air and burn up.

The steel nose was designed to blow apart at the apogee of flight, revealing beneath it a re-entry cone,

411

shorter, blunter and made of carbon fibre.

In the days when Dr Gerald Bull was alive he had tried to buy, on behalf of Baghdad, a British firm in Northern Ireland called Lear Fan. It was an aviation company gone bust. It had tried to build executive jets with many components made of carbon fibre. What interested Dr Bull and Baghdad was not executive airplanes, but the carbon-fibre, filament-winding machines at Lear Fan.

Carbon fibre is extremely heat-resistant but it is also very hard to work. The carbon is first reduced to a sort of 'wool' from which a thread or filament is spun. The thread is laid and cross-plaited many times over a mould, then bonded into a shell to create the desired shape.

Because carbon fibre is vital in rocket technology, and that technology is classified, great care is taken in monitoring the export of such machines. When the British Intelligence people learnt where the Lear Fan equipment was destined and consulted Washington, the deal was killed. It was then assumed Iraq would not acquire her carbon-filament technology.

The experts were wrong. Iraq tried another tack, which worked. An American supplier of air-conditioning and insulation products was persuaded to sell to an Iraqi 'front' company the machinery for spinning rock-wool. In Iraq this was modified by Iraqi engineers to spin carbon fibre.

Between the impact-absorber at the back and the nose-cone rested the work of Dr Siddiqui—a small, workaday but perfectly functioning atomic bomb, to be triggered on the gun-barrel principle, using the catalysts of lithium and polonium to create the blizzard of neutrons necessary to start the chain reaction.

412

Inside, the engineering of Dr Siddiqui was the real triumph, a spherical ball and a tubular plug, between them weighing 35 kilograms and produced under the aegis of Dr Jaafar. Both were of pure enriched Uranium 235.

A slow smile of satisfaction spread beneath the thick black moustache. The President advanced and ran a forefinger down the burnished steel.

'It will work? It will really work?' he whispered.

'Yes, sayidi Rais,' said the physicist.

The head in the black beret nodded slowly several times. 'You are to be congratulated, my brothers.'

Beneath the projectile, on a wooden stand, was a simple plaque.

It read only: QUBTH-UT-ALLAH.

*   *   *

Tariq Aziz had contemplated long and hard as to how, if at all, he could convey to his President the American threat so brutally put before him in Geneva.

Twenty years they had known each other, twenty years during which the Foreign Minister had served his master with dog-like devotion, always taking his side during those early struggles within the Ba'ath Party hierarchy when there were other claimants for power, always backing his personal judgement that the utter ruthlessness of the man from Tikrit would triumph, and always being proved right.

They had climbed the greasy pole of power in a Middle East dictatorship together, the one always in the shadow of the other. The grey-haired, stubby Aziz had managed to overcome the initial disadvantage of his higher education and grasp of

413

two European languages by sheer blind obedience.

Leaving the actual violence to others, he had watched and approved, as all must do in the court of Saddam Hussein, as purge after purge had seen columns of army officers and once-trusted Party men disgraced and taken away for execution, a sentence often preceded by agonized hours with the tormentors at Abu Ghraib.

He had seen good generals removed and shot for trying to stand up for the men under their command, and knew that real conspirators had died more horribly than he cared to imagine.

He had watched the Al-Juburi tribe, once so powerful in the Army that no-one dared to offend them, stripped and humbled, the survivors brought to heel and obedience. He had stayed silent as Saddam's half-brother Ali Hassan Majid, then Interior Minister, had masterminded the genocide of the Kurds, not simply at Halabja but at fifty other towns and villages wiped away with bombs, artillery and gas.

Tariq Aziz, like all those in the entourage of the Rais, knew that there was nowhere else for him to go. If anything happened to his master, he, too, was finished for all time.

Unlike some around the throne, he was too smart to believe that this was a popular regime. His real fear was not the foreigners, but the awful revenge of the people of Iraq if ever the veil of Saddam's protection were removed from him.

His problem that 11 January, as he waited for the personal appointment to which he had been summoned on his return from Europe, was how to phrase the American threat without attracting the inevitable rage on to himself. The Rais, he knew, could easily suspect that it was he, the Foreign Minister, who had really suggested the threat to the Americans. There is no logic to paranoia, only gut instinct, sometimes right and sometimes wrong. Many innocent men had died, and their families with them, on the basis of some inspirational suspicion by the Rais.

Two hours later, returning to his car, he was relieved, smiling and puzzled.

His relief was easy; his President had proved to be relaxed and genial. He had listened with approval to Tariq Aziz's glowing report of his mission to Geneva, of the widespread sympathy he detected in all those he spoke to with regard to Iraq's position, and of the general anti-American feeling that appeared to be growing in the West.

He had nodded understandingly as Tariq heaped blame on the American warmongers and when, finally consumed with his own sense of outrage, he mentioned what James Baker had actually said to him, the awaited explosion of rage from the Rais had not come.

While others round the table glowered and fumed, Saddam Hussein had continued to nod and to smile.

The Foreign Minister was smiling as he left because at the last meeting his Rais had actually congratulated him on his European mission. The fact that, by any normal diplomatic standards, that mission had been a disaster—rebuffed on every side, treated with freezing courtesy by his hosts, unable to dent the resolve of the coalition ranged against his country—did not seem to matter.

His puzzlement stemmed from something the Rais had said at the end of the audience. It had been an aside, a muttered remark to the Foreign Minister alone as the President had seen him to the door.

'Rafeek, dear Comrade, do not worry. Soon I shall have a surprise for the Americans. Not yet. But if the Beni el Kalb ever try to cross the border, I shall respond not with gas, but with the Fist of God.'

Tariq Aziz had nodded in agreement, even though he did not know what the Rais was talking about. With others, he found out twenty-four hours later.

*   *   *

The morning of 12 January saw the last meeting of the full Revolutionary Command Council to be held in the Presidential Palace at the corner of 14th July Street and Kindi Street. A week later it was bombed to rubble, but the bird inside was long flown.

As usual, the summons to the meeting came at the last moment. No matter how high one rose in the hierarchy, no matter how trusted one might be, no-one but a tiny handful of family, intimates and personal bodyguards ever knew exactly where the Rais would be at a given hour on any day.

If he was still alive at all after seven major and serious attempts at assassination, it was because of his obsession with personal security.

Neither the Counter-Intelligence people nor the Secret Police of Omar Khatib, and certainly not the Army; not even the Republican Guard were entrusted with that security.

The task fell to the Amn-al-Khass. Young they might be, most barely out of their teens, but their loyalty was fanatical and absolute. Their commander was the Rais' own son Kusay.

No conspirator could ever know upon which road the Rais would be travelling, when or in what vehicle.

416

His visits to army bases or industrial installations were always surprises, not only to the visited but also to those around him.

Even in Baghdad he flitted from location to location at a whim, sometimes spending a few days in the palace, at other times retiring to his bunker behind and beneath the Rashid Hotel.

Every plate set before him had to be tasted first, and the food-taster was the first-born son of the chef. Every drink came from a bottle with unbroken seal.

That morning the summons to the meeting at the palace came to each member of the RCC by special messenger one hour before the meeting. No time was thus left for preparations for an assassination.

The limousines swerved through the gate, deposited their charges and went away to a special car-park. Each member of the RCC passed through a metal-detecting arch; no personal side-arms were allowed.

When they were assembled in the large conference room, with its T-shaped table, there were thirty-three of them. Eight sat at the top of the T, flanking the empty throne at the centre. The rest faced each other down the length of the stem of the T.

Seven of those present were related to the Rais by blood and three more by marriage. These plus eight more were from Tikrit or its immediate surroundings. All were long-standing members of the Ba'ath Party.

Ten of the thirty-three were Cabinet Ministers and nine were Army or Air Force generals. Saadi Tumah Abbas, former Commander of the Republican Guard had been promoted to Defence Minister that very morning and sat beaming at the top table. He had replaced Abd al-Jabber Shenshall, the renegade

Kurd who had long thrown in his lot with the butcher of his own people.

Among the army generals were Mustafa Radi for the Infantry, Farouk Ridha of the Artillery, Ali Musuli of the Engineers and Abdullah Kadiri of the Tanks.

At the bottom of the table were the three men controlling the Intelligence apparat: Dr Ubaidi of Overseas Mukhabarat, Hassan Rahmani of Counter-Intelligence and Omar Khatib of the Secret Police.

When the Rais entered everyone rose and clapped. He smiled, took his chair, bade them be seated and began his statement. They were not here to discuss anything; they were here to be told something.

Only the son-in-law Hussein Kamil showed no surprise when the Rais reached his peroration. When, after forty minutes of speech invoking the unbroken series of triumphs that had marked his leadership, he gave them his news, the immediate reaction was of stunned silence.

That Iraq had been trying for years, they knew. That fruition in this one area of technology, that alone seemed capable of inspiring the thrill of fear throughout the world and awe even among the mighty Americans, had been achieved now on the very threshold of war seemed unbelievable. Divine intervention. But the Divinity was not in heaven above; he sat right here, with them, smiling quietly.

It was Hussein Kamil, forewarned, who rose and led the ovation. The others scrambled to follow, each fearing to be last to his feet or most subdued in his applause. Then no-one was prepared to be first to stop.

When he returned to his office two hours later,

Hassan Rahmani, the urbane and cosmopolitan Head of Counter-Intelligence, cleared his desk, ordered no interruptions and sat at his desk with a strong black coffee. He needed to think, and think deeply.

As with everyone else in that room, the news had shaken him. At a stroke the balance of power in the Middle East had changed, but no-one knew. After the Rais, with raised hands calling with admirable self-deprecation for the ovation to cease, had resumed his chairmanship, every man in the room had been sworn to silence.

This Rahmani could understand. Despite the raging euphoria that had enveloped them all as they left, and in which he had unstintingly joined, he could foresee major problems.

No device of this kind is worth a jot unless your friends and, most importantly, your enemies know that you have it. Then only did potential enemies come crawling as friends.

Some nations who had developed the weapon had simply announced the fact with a major test and let the rest of the world work out the consequences. Others, like Israel and South Africa, had simply hinted at what they possessed but never confirmed, leaving the world and particularly the neighbours to guess. Sometimes that worked better; imaginations ran riot.

But that, Rahmani became convinced, would simply not work for Iraq. If what he had been told was true, and he was not convinced the whole exercise was not another ploy, counting on an eventual leak, to gain another stay of execution, then no-one outside Iraq would believe it.

The only way for Iraq to deter would be to prove it.

419

This the Rais apparently now refused to do. There were, of course, major problems to proving any such claim.

To test on home territory was out of the question, utter madness. To send a ship deep into the south Indian Ocean, abandon it and let the test happen there, might have been possible once, but not now. All ports were firmly blockaded. But a team from the United Nations International Atomic Energy Agency in Vienna could be invited to examine, and satisfy themselves that this was no lie. After all, the IAEA had been visiting almost yearly for a decade and had always been consummately fooled as to what was going on. Given visual evidence, they would have to believe their own eyes and tests, eat humble pie over their past gullibility and confirm the truth.

Yet he, Rahmani, had just heard that route formally forbidden. Why? Because it was all a lie? Because the Rais had something else in mind? And more importantly, what was in it for him, Rahmani?

For months he had counted on Saddam Hussein blustering his way into a war he could not win; now he had done it. Rahmani had counted on the defeat culminating in the American-engineered downfall of the Rais and his own elevation in the American-sponsored successor regime. Now things had changed. He needed, he realized, time to think, to work out how best to play this amazing new card.

*   *   *

That evening, when darkness had fallen, a chalk sign appeared on a wall behind the Chaldean Church of St Joseph in the Area of the Christians. It resembled a figure of eight on its side.

The citizens of Baghdad trembled that night. Despite the ceaseless blast of propaganda on the local Iraqi radio and the blind faith of many that it was all true, there were others who quietly listened to the BBC World Service in Arabic, prepared in London but broadcast out of Cyprus, and knew that the Beni Naji were telling the truth. War was coming.

The assumption in the city was that the Americans would start with carpet-bombing of Baghdad, an assumption that went right up to the Presidential Palace itself. There would be massive civilian casualties.

The regime assumed this but did not mind. In high places the calculation was that the global effect of such massive slaughter of civilians in their homes would cause a worldwide revulsion against America, forcing her to desist and depart. That was why such a heavy foreign Press contingent was still allowed and indeed encouraged to occupy the Rashid Hotel. Guides were on stand-by to hurry the foreign TV cameras to the scenes of the genocide as soon as it started.

The subtlety of this argument somehow escaped those actually living in the homes of Baghdad. Many had already fled, the non-Iraqis heading for the Jordanian border to swell the five-month-long tide of refugees from Kuwait, the Iraqis to seek sanctuary in the countryside.

No-one suspected, including the millions of couch-potatoes glued to their screens across America and Europe, the true level of sophistication that was now within the grasp of the lugubrious Chuck Horner down in Riyadh. Nobody then could envisage that most targets would be selected from a menu prepared

421

by the cameras of satellites in space and demolished by laser-guided bombs that rarely hit what they were not aimed at.

What the citizens of Baghdad did know, as the truth gleaned from the BBC filtered through the bazaars and markets, was that four days from midnight on 12 January the deadline to quit Kuwait would expire and the American warplanes would come. So the city was quiet in expectation.

Mike Martin pedalled his bicycle slowly out of Shurja Street and round the back of the church. He saw the chalk mark on the wall as he pedalled by, and went on. At the end of the alley he paused, stepped off the bicycle and spent some time adjusting the chain while he looked back the way he had come to see if there was any movement behind him.

None. No shifting of the feet of the Secret Police in their doorways, no heads poking over the skyline of the roofs. He pedalled back, reached out with the damp cloth, erased the mark and rode away.

The figure eight meant that a message awaited him under the flagstone in the abandoned courtyard off Abu Nawas Street, down by the river, barely half a mile away.

As a boy he had played down there, running along the quay-sides with Hassan Rahmani and Abdelkarim Badri, where the vendors cooked the delicious masgouf over beds of camelthorn embers, selling the tender portions of the Tigris river carp to passers-by.

The shops were closed, the tea-houses shuttered; few people wandered along the quays as they used to. The silence served him well. At the top of Abu Nawas he saw a group of AMAM plain-clothes guards, but they took no notice of the fellagha pedalling on his master's business. He was heartened by the sight of them; the AMAM was nothing if not clumsy. If they were going to have a stake-out of a dead-letter-box, they would not put a group of men so obviously at the head of the street. Their stake-out would be an attempt at sophistication, but flawed.

The message was there. The brick went back into its place in a second, the folded paper into the crotch of his underpants. Minutes later he was crossing the Ahrar Bridge over the Tigris, back from Risafa into Karch and on to the Soviet diplomat's house in Mansour.

In nine weeks life had settled down in the walled villa. The Russian cook and her husband treated him fairly and he had picked up a smattering of their language. He shopped every day for fresh produce, which gave him good reason to service all his dead-letter-boxes. He had transmitted fourteen messages to the unseen Jericho and had received fifteen from him.

Eight times he had been stopped by the AMAM, but each time his humble demeanour, his bicycle and basket of vegetables, fruit, coffee, spices and groceries, plus his letter from the diplomatic household and his visible poverty had caused him to be sent on his way.

He could not know what war plans were shaping down in Riyadh, but he had to write all the questions and queries for Jericho in his own Arabic script after listening to them on the incoming tapes, and he had to read Jericho's answers in order to send them back in burst transmissions to Simon Paxman.

As a soldier he could only estimate that Jericho's information, political and military, had to be invaluable to a commanding general preparing to attack Iraq.

He had already acquired an oil heater for his shack and a Petromax lamp to lighten it. Hessian sacks from the market now made curtains for all the windows and the crunch of feet on the gravel warned him if anyone approached the door.

That night he returned gratefully to the warmth of his home, bolted the door, made sure all the curtains covered every square inch of the windows, lit his lamp and read Jericho's latest message. It was shorter than usual, but that did not lessen its impact. Martin read it twice to make sure that even he had not suddenly lost his grasp of Arabic, muttered, 'Jesus Christ', and removed his loose tiles to reveal the tape-recorder.

Lest there be any misunderstanding, he read the message slowly and carefully in both Arabic and English into the tape-machine before switching the controls to speed-wind and reducing his five-minute message to one and a half seconds.

He transmitted it at twenty minutes after midnight.

*   *   *

Because he knew there was a transmission window between fifteen and thirty minutes after twelve that night, Simon Paxman had not bothered to go to bed. He was playing cards with one of the radio men when the message came in. The second radio operator brought the news from the communications room.

'You'd better come and listen to this ... now, Simon,' he said.

Although the SIS operation in Riyadh involved a lot more than four men, the running of Jericho was regarded as so secret that only Paxman, the Head of

Station, Julian Gray, and two radio men were involved. Their three rooms had been virtually sealed off from the rest of the villa.

Simon Paxman listened to the voice on the big tape-machine in the 'radio shack' which was in fact a converted bedroom. Martin spoke in Arabic first, giving the literal handwritten message from Jericho twice, then his own translation twice.

As he listened Paxman felt a great cold hand moving deep in his stomach. Something had gone wrong, badly wrong. What he was hearing simply could not be. The other two men stood in silence beside him.

'Is it him?' asked Paxman urgently as soon as the message had finished. His first thought was that Martin had been taken and the voice was an impostor.

'It's him, I checked the ossy. There's no doubt it's him.'

Speech patterns have varying tones and rhythms, highs and lows, cadences that can be recorded on an oscilloscope which reduces them to a series of lines on a screen, like a heart monitor in a cardiac unit.

Every human voice is slightly different, no matter how good the mimic. Before leaving for Baghdad, Mike Martin's voice had been recorded on such a machine. Later transmissions out of Baghdad had endured the same fate, in case the slowing-down and speeding-up, together with any distortion by tape-machine or satellite transmission, might cause distortions.

The voice that came from Baghdad that night checked with the recorded voice. It was Martin speaking and no-one else.

Paxman's second fear was that Martin had been

425

caught, tortured and 'turned', that he was now broadcasting under duress. He rejected the idea as very unlikely.

There were pre-agreed words, a pause, a hesitation, a cough, that would warn the listeners in Riyadh if ever he were not transmitting as a free agent. Besides, his previous broadcast had been only three days earlier.

Brutal the Iraqi Secret Police might be, but they were not quick. And Martin was tough. A man broken and turned at such speed would be shattered, a tortured wreck, and it would show in the speech delivery.

That meant Martin was on the level—the message he had read was precisely what he had received that night from Jericho. Which left more imponderables. Either Jericho was right, mistaken or lying.

'Get Julian,' Paxman told one of the radio men.

While the man went to fetch the British Head of Station from his bed upstairs, Paxman rang the private line of his American counterpart Chip Barber.

'Chip, better get your backside over here, fast,' he said.

The CIA man came awake fast. Something in the Englishman's voice told him this was no time for sleepy banter.

'Problem, ole buddy?'

'That's the way it looks from here,' admitted Paxman.

Barber was across the city and into the SIS house in thirty minutes, sweater and trousers over his pyjamas. It was 1 a.m. By then Paxman had the tape in English and Arabic, plus a transcript in both languages. The two radio men, who had worked for years in the Middle East, were fluent and confirmed Martin's translation was quite accurate.

'He has to be joking,' breathed Barber when he heard the tape.

Paxman ran through the checks he had already made for authenticity of Martin's speaking voice.

'Look, Simon, this is just Jericho reporting what he *claims* he heard Saddam say this morning, sorry, yesterday morning. Chances are, Saddam's lying. Let's face it, he lies like he breathes.'

Lie or not, this was no matter to be dealt with in Riyadh. The local SIS and CIA stations might supply their generals with tactical and even strategic military information from Jericho, but politics went to London and Washington. Barber checked his watch. Seven p.m. in Washington.

'They'll be mixing their cocktails by now,' he said. 'Better make 'em strong, boys. I'll get this to Langley right away.'

'Cocoa and biscuits in London,' said Paxman. 'I'll have this to Century. Let them sort it out.'

Barber left to send his copy of the transmission in heavily encrypted code to Bill Stewart, with an urgency rating of 'cosmic', the highest known. That would mean that wherever he was, the cipher people would find him and tell him to go to a secure line.

Paxman did the same for Steve Laing, who would be woken in the middle of the night and told to leave his warm bed to step into a freezing night and head back to London.

There was one last thing Paxman could do, which he did. Martin had a transmission window for listening only, and it was at 4 a.m. Paxman waited up and sent his man in Baghdad a very short but very explicit message. It said Martin should make no

427

attempt until further notice to approach any of his six dead-letter-boxes. Just in case.

*　　*　　*

Karim, the Jordanian student, was making slow but steady progress in his courtship of Fräulein Edith Hardenberg. She allowed him to hold her hand when they walked through the streets of Old Vienna, the pavements crackling with frost beneath their feet. She even admitted to herself that she found the hand-holding pleasant.

In the second week of January she obtained tickets at the Burg theater—Karim paid. The performance was of a play by Grillparzer, *Gygus und sein Ring*.

She explained excitedly before they went in that it was about an old king with several sons, and the one to whom he bequeathed his ring would be the successor. Karim sat through the performance entranced and asked for several explanations in the text, to which he referred constantly during the play.

In the interval Edith was happy to answer them. Later Avi Herzog would tell Barzilai it was all as exciting as watching paint dry.

'You're a Philistine,' said the Mossad man. 'You have no culture.'

'I'm not here for my culture,' said Avi.

'Then get on with it, boy.'

On Sunday Edith, a devout Catholic, went to morning mass at the Votivkirche. Karim explained that as a Muslim he could not accompany her but would wait at a café across the square.

Afterwards, over coffee which he deliberately laced with a slug of schnapps which brought a pink flush to her cheeks, he explained the differences and similarities between Christianity and Islam—the common worship of the one true God, the line of patriarchs and prophets, the teachings of the holy books and the moral codes. Edith was fearful but fascinated. She wondered if listening to all this might imperil her immortal soul, but was amazed to learn that she had been wrong in thinking Muslims bowed down to idols.

'I would like dinner,' said Karim three days later.

'Well, yes, but you spend too much on me,' said Edith. She found she could gaze into his young face and his soft brown eyes with pleasure, while constantly warning herself that the ten-year age-gap between them made anything more than a platonic friendship quite ridiculous.

'Not in a restaurant.'

'Where then?'

'Will you cook a meal for me, Edith? You can cook? Real Viennese food?'

She went bright red at the thought. Each evening, unless she was going alone to a concert, she prepared herself a modest snack in the small alcove of her flat that served as a dining area. But, yes, she thought, she *could* cook. It had been so long.

Besides, she argued with herself, he had taken her to several expensive meals in restaurants ... and he was an extremely well brought-up and courteous young man. Surely there could be no harm in it.

* * *

To say that the Jericho report of the night of 12–13 January caused consternation in certain covert circles in London and Washington would be an understatement. Controlled panic was nearer the mark.

One of the problems was the tiny circle of people who knew of Jericho's existence, let alone the details. The need-to-know principle may sound pernickety or even obsessive, but it works for a reason.

All Agencies feel an obligation to an asset working for them in a very high-risk situation, no matter how ignoble that asset may be as a human being.

The fact that Jericho was clearly a mercenary and no high-minded ideologue was not the point. The fact that he was cynically betraying his country and its government was irrelevant. The government of Iraq was perceived to be repulsive anyway, so one rogue was playing traitor to another bunch.

The point was, apart from his obvious value and the fact that his information might well save Allied lives on the battlefield, Jericho was a high-value asset and both the Agencies running him had kept his very existence to a tiny circle of initiates. No government ministers, no politicians, no civil servants and no soldiers had been formally told that any Jericho existed.

His product therefore had been disguised in a variety of ways. A whole range of cover stories had been pleaded to explain where this torrent of information was coming from.

Military dispositions were supposed to stem from a series of defections by Iraqi soldiers from the Kuwait theatre, including a non-existent major being extensively debriefed at a secret Intelligence facility in the Middle East but outside Saudi Arabia.

Scientific and technical information regarding weapons of mass destruction was said to have been gleaned from an Iraqi science graduate who had defected to the British after studying at Imperial

430

College, London, and falling in love with an English girl, and an intensive second run-through of European technicians who had worked inside Iraq between 1985 and 1990.

Political Intelligence was attributed to a mix of refugees pouring out of Iraq, covert radio messages from occupied Kuwait and brilliant 'sigint' and 'elint'—signals Intelligence and electronic Intelligence, listening-in and aerial surveillance.

But how to explain a direct report of Saddam's own words, however bizarre their claim, conducted within a closed meeting inside his own palace, without admitting to an agent in the highest circles of Baghdad?

The dangers of making such an admission were appalling. For one thing, there are leaks. There are leaks all the time. Cabinet documents leak, civil service memoranda leak and inter-departmental messages leak.

Politicians, so far as the covert community is concerned, are the worst. To believe the nightmares of the master spooks, they talk to their wives, girl-friends, boy-friends, hairdressers, drivers and barmen. They even talk confidentially to each other with a waiter bending over the table.

Add to that the fact that Britain and America have Press and other media veterans whose investigative talents make Scotland Yard and the FBI seem slow on the uptake, and one has a problem explaining away Jericho's product without admitting to a Jericho.

Finally, London and Washington still had hundreds of Iraqi students, some certainly agents of Dr Ismail Ubaidi's Mukhabarat, prepared to report back anything they saw or heard.

431

It was not just a question of someone denouncing Jericho by name; that would be impossible. But one hint that information had come out of Baghdad that should not have come, and Rahmani's Counter-Intelligence net would go into overtime to detect and isolate the source. At best that could ensure Jericho's future silence as he clammed up to protect himself, at worst his capture.

As the countdown to the start of the air war rolled on, the two Agencies recontacted all their former experts in the matter of nuclear physics and asked for a rapid reassessment of the information already given. Was there, after all, any conceivable possibility that Iraq might have a greater and faster isotope separation facility than previously thought?

In Britain experts at Harwell and Aldermaston were consulted again; in America at Sandia, Lawrence Livermore and Los Alamos. Department Z at Livermore, the people who constantly monitor Third World proliferation, was especially pressed.

The boffins came back, rather testily, to reconfirm their advice. Even taking a worst-case scenario, they said; assuming not one but two entire gas diffusion centrifuge 'cascades' operating not for one but for two years, there was no way in Creation Iraq could have more than half the Uranium 235 she would need for a single medium-yield device.

That left the agencies with a menu of options.

Saddam was mistaken because he had been lied to himself. Conclusion: unlikely. Those responsible would pay with their lives for such an outrage against the Rais.

Saddam had said it but he was lying. Conclusion: quite feasible. To boost morale among his flagging and apprehensive supporters. But why confine the news to the innermost fanatics who were not flagging and apprehensive? Morale-boosting propaganda is for the masses, and abroad. Unanswerable.

Saddam did not say it. Conclusion: the whole report was a farrago of lies. Secondary conclusion: Jericho lied because he is greedy for money and thinks with the war coming his time will soon be over. He put a million-dollar price tag on his own information.

Jericho lied because he has been unmasked, and revealed all. Conclusion: also possible and this option poses a horrendous personal hazard to the man in Baghdad to maintain the link.

At this point the CIA moved firmly into the driving seat. Langley, being the paymaster, had a perfect right to do so.

'I'll give you the bottom line, Steve,' said Bill Stewart to Steve Laing on a secure line from the CIA to Century House on the evening of 14 January. 'Saddam's wrong or he's lying, Jericho's wrong or he's lying. Whatever, Uncle Sam is not going to pay out a million greenbacks into an account in Vienna for this kind of trash.'

'There's no way the unconsidered option might be right after all, Bill?'

'Which one's that?'

'That Saddam said it and he's right?'

'No way. It's a three-card-trick. We're not going to swallow it. Look, Jericho's been great for nine weeks, even though we're now going to have to recheck what he gave us. Half has already been proved and it's good stuff. But he's blown it with this last report. We think that's the end of the line. We don't know why, but that's the wisdom from the top of the mountain.'

'Creates problems for us, Bill.'

'I know, pal, and that's why I'm calling within minutes of the conference with the Director ending. Either Jericho has been taken and has told the goon squad everything, or he's up and running. But if he gets to know we aren't sending him any million dollars, I guess he'll turn nasty. Either way, that's bad news for your man in there. He's a good man, right?'

'The best. Hell of a nerve.'

'So get him outta there, Steve. Fast.'

'I think that's what we'll have to do, Bill. Thanks for the tip. Pity, it was a good op.'

'The best, while it lasted.'

Stewart hung up. Laing went upstaires to see Sir Colin. The decision was made within an hour.

*   *   *

By the hour of breakfast on the morning of 15 January in Saudi Arabia every member of aircrew, American, British, French, Italian, Saudi and Kuwaiti, knew that they were going to war.

The politicians and the diplomats, they believed, had failed to prevent it. Through the day all air units moved to pre-battle alert.

The nerve centres of the campaign could be located in three establishments in Riyadh.

On the outskirts of Riyadh Military Airbase was a collection of huge air-conditioned tents, known because of the green light that suffused them through the canvas as 'The Barn'. This was the first filter for the tidal wave of air-Intelligence photographs that had been flowing in for weeks and would double and treble in the weeks to come.

The product of The Barn, a synthesis of the most important photographic information pouring in

434

from so many reconnaissance sorties, went a mile up the road to the headquarters of the Royal Saudi Air Force, a great chunk of which had been made over to Central Air Force, CENTAF.

A giant building of grey mottled concrete and glass built on piles, 150 metres long, the headquarters has a basement running its full length, and it was here, one level below ground, that CENTAF was based.

Despite the size of the basement, there was still not enough space, so the car-park was crammed with an array of more green tents and Portakabins, where further interpretation took place.

In the basement was the focal point of it all, the Joint Imagery Production Centre, a warren of interconnecting rooms in which worked throughout the war 250 analysts, British and American, of all three armed forces, and of all ranks. This was the Black Hole.

Technically in charge was the overall Air Commander, General Chuck Horner, but as he was often called to the Defence Ministry a mile further up the road, the more usual presence was that of his deputy, General Buster Glosson.

The air-war planners in the Black Hole consulted on a daily, and even hourly, basis a document called the Basic Target Graphic, a list and a map of everything in Iraq that was targeted for a 'hit'. From this they derived the daily bible of every air commander, squadron Intelligence officer, planning ops. officer and aircrew in the Gulf theatre—the Air Tasking Order.

Each day's ATO was an immensely detailed document, running to over a hundred pages of typescript. It took three days to prepare.

First came Apportionment—the decision on the

percentages of the target-types in Iraq that could be struck in a single day and the types of available aircraft suitable for such a strike.

Day Two saw Allocation—the conversion of the percentage of Iraqi targets for treatment into actual numbers and locations of them. Day Three was for Distribution—the 'who gets what' decision. It was in the distribution process that it might be decided, for example, that this is for the British Tornados, this for the American Strike Eagles, this one for the Navy Tomcats, this for the Phantoms, and that one for the B-52 Stratofortresses.

Only then would each squadron and wing be sent its menu for the following day. After that it was up to them to do it—find the target, work out the route, link up with the air-refuelling tankers, plan the strike direction, calculate the secondary targets in case of a 'no-go' and work out the way home.

The squadron commander would choose his crews—many squadrons had multiple targets designated to them in a single day—pick his flight leaders and their wingmen.

The Weapons Officers, of which Don Walker was one, would select the ordnance—'iron' or 'dumb' bombs which are unguided, laser-guided bombs, laser-guided rockets, etc.

A mile further down Old Airport Road was the third building. The Saudi Defence Ministry is immense, five linked main blocks of shimmering white cement, seven storeys high with fluted columns up to the fourth.

It was on this fourth floor that General Norman Schwarzkopf had been allocated a handsome suite which he hardly ever saw, frequently bunking in a small bedsitter in the sub-basement where he could

436

be near his command post.

In all, the ministry is 400 metres long and a 100 feet high, a lavishness that paid dividends in the Gulf war when Riyadh had to play host to so many unexpected foreigners.

Below ground are two more floors of rooms running the length of the building, and of the 400 metres Coalition Command was allocated sixty.

It was here that the generals sat in conclave throughout the war, watching on a giant map as staff officers pointed out what had been done, what had been missed, what had shown up, what had moved, what the Iraqi response and dispositions had been.

Shielded from the hot sun that January day, a British squadron leader stood before the wall map showing the 700 targets listed in Iraq, 240 primaries and the rest secondary, and remarked: 'Well, that's about it.'

Alas, that was not it. Unbeknownst to the planners, for all the satellites and all the technology, sheer human ingenuity in the form of camouflage and 'maskirovka' had deceived them.

In hundreds of emplacements across Iraq and Kuwait Iraqi tanks sat and brooded under their netting, well targeted by the Allies due to the metal content picked up by overhead radars. They were in many cases made of matchboard, plywood and tinplate, the drums of scrap-iron inside giving the appropriate metallic response to the sensors.

Scores of old truck chassis now mounted replica launching tubes for Scud missiles, and these mobile 'launchers' would all be solemnly blown apart.

But more seriously, seventy primary targets concerned with weapons of mass destruction had not been spotted because they were buried deep or

437

cunningly disguised as something else.

Only later would planners puzzle over how the Iraqis had managed to reconstitute entire destroyed divisions with such unbelievable speed; only later would United Nations inspectors discover plant after plant and store after store that had escaped, and come away knowing there were yet more buried underground.

But that hot day in 1991 no-one knew these things. What the young men out on the flight lines from Tabuq in the west to Bahrain in the east and down to the ultra-secret Khamis Mushait in the south knew was that in forty hours they would go to war and some of them would not come back.

In the last full day before final briefings began most of them wrote home. Some chewed on their pencils and wondered what to say. Others thought of their wives and children and cried as they wrote; hands accustomed to controlling many tons of deadly metal sought to craft inadequate words into saying what they felt; lovers tried to express what they should have whispered before; fathers urged their sons to look after their mothers if the worst should happen.

Captain Don Walker heard the news with all the other pilots and aircrew of the Rocketeers of the 336th TFS in a terse announcement from the wing commander at Al Kharz. It was just before nine in the morning, and already the sun beat down on the desert as a sledgehammer on the waiting anvil.

There was none of the usual banter as the men filed out of the tented briefing hall, each plunged in his private thoughts. For each these were much the same; the last attempt to avoid a war had been tried and had failed; the politicians and the diplomats had shuttled from conference to conference, postured and declaimed, urged, bullied, pleaded, threatened and cajoled in order to avoid a war ... and had failed.

So at least they believed, those young men who had just learnt that the talking was over at last, failing to understand that for months past they had been destined for this day.

Walker watched his squadron commander Steve Turner stump away to his tent to write what he genuinely believed might be his last letter to Betty-Jane back in Goldsboro, North Carolina. Randy Roberts had a brief, muttered few words with Boomer Henry and they parted and walked away.

The young Oklahoman looked at the pale blue vault of sky where he had lusted to be since he was a small boy in Tulsa and where soon he might die in his thirtieth year, and turned his steps towards the perimeter. Like the others, he wanted to be alone.

There was no fence to the base at Al Kharz, just the ochre sea of sand, shale and gravel stretching away to the horizon and beyond that to the next and the next. He passed the clam-shell hangars grouped around the concrete apron where the mechanics were by then working on their charges, the crew chiefs passing among each team, conferring and checking to ensure that when each of their babies finally went to war they would be as perfect machines as the hand of man could make them.

Walker spotted his own Eagle among them, and was awed as always when he contemplated the F-15 from afar by its air of quiet menace. It crouched silently amid the teeming swarm of men and women in coveralls who crawled all over its burly frame, immune to love or lust, hate or fear, patiently waiting for the moment when it would finally do what it had been designed to do all those years ago on the

439

drawing-board—bring flame and death to the people designated by the President of America. Walker envied his Eagle; for all its myriad complexity, it could not feel anything, it could never be afraid.

He left the city of canvas behind him and walked across the plain of shale, his eyes shaded by the peak of his baseball cap and the aviator glasses, hardly feeling the heat of the sun on his shoulders.

For eight years he had flown the aircraft of his country and done so because he loved it. But never once had he really, truly, contemplated the prospect that he might die in battle. Part of every combat pilot muses with the notion of testing his skill, his nerve and the excellence of his airplane against another man in real, rather than dummy, contest. But another part always assumes that it will never happen. It will never really come to killing other mothers' sons, or being killed by them.

That morning, like all the others, he realized at last that it truly had come to this; that all those years of study and training had finally led to this day and this place; that in forty hours he would take his Eagle into the sky again, and this time he might not come back.

Like the others, he thought of home. Being an only child and a single man, he thought of his mom and dad. He remembered all the times and places of his boyhood in Tulsa, the way they had played together in the yard behind the house, the day he had been given his first catcher's glove and forced his father to pitch to him until the sun went down.

His thoughts strayed back to the vacations they had shared before he left home to go to college and the Air Force. The one he recalled best was the time his father took him, at the age of twelve, on a men-only fishing trip to Alaska in the summer recess.

Ray Walker was almost twenty years younger then, leaner and fitter, stronger than his son, before the years reversed the difference. They had taken a kayak, with a guide and other vacationers, and skimmed the icy waters of Glacier Bay, watched the black bears gathering berries on the mountain slopes, the harbour seals basking on the last remaining floes of August and the sun rise over the Mendenhall Glacier behind Juneau. Together they had hauled two 70-pound monsters out of Halibut Hole and taken the deep-running king salmon out of the channel off Sitka.

He found he was walking across a sea of baking sand in a land far from home with tears running down his face, unwiped, drying in the sun. If he died he would never marry, nor have children of his own. Twice he had almost proposed; once to a girl in college, but that was when he was very young and much infatuated, the second time to a more mature woman he had met off-base near McConnell, who let him know she could never be the wife of a jet-jockey.

Now he wanted, as he had never wanted before, to have children of his own; he wanted a woman to come home to at the end of the day, and a daughter to tuck up in her cot with a bedtime story, and a son to teach how to catch a spinning football, bat and pitch, hike and fish, the way his father had taught him. More than that he wanted to go back to Tulsa and embrace his mother again, who had worried so much for the things he had done and bravely pretended not to . . .

The young pilot finally returned to the base, sat down at a rickety table in his shared tent and sought to write a letter home. He was not a good letter-writer. Words did not come easily. He usually tended

441

to describe the things that had happened recently on the squadron, the events of the social life, the state of the weather. This was different.

He wrote two pages to his parents, like so many sons that day. He sought to explain what was going on in his head, which was not easy.

He told them about the news that had been announced that morning and what it meant, and he asked them not to worry for him. He had had the best training in the world and flew the best fighter in the world for the best air force in the world.

He wrote that he was sorry for all the times he had been a pain, and thanked them for all they had done for him over the years from the first day they had had to wipe his butt to the time they crossed the States to be present at his passing-out parade when the general pinned those coveted flier's wings on his chest.

In forty hours, he explained, he would take his Eagle off the runway again, but this time it would be different. This time, for the first time, he would seek to kill other human beings, and they would seek to kill him.

He would not see their faces nor sense their fear, as they would not know his, for that is not the way of modern war. But if they succeeded and he failed, he wanted his parents to know how much he had loved them, and hoped he had been a good son.

When he had finished he sealed his letter. Many other letters were sealed that day across the length and breadth of Saudi Arabia. Then the military postal services took them, and they were delivered to Trenton and Tulsa and London and Rouen and Rome.

*   *   *

That night Mike Martin received a burst from his controllers in Riyadh. When he played the tape back, it was Simon Paxman speaking. It was not a long message, but it was clear and to the point.

In his previous message, Jericho had been wrong, completely and utterly wrong. Every scientific check proved there was no way he could be right.

Either he had been wrong deliberately or inadvertently. In the first case he must have turned, lured by the lust for money, or been turned. In the second he would be aggrieved because the CIA absolutely refused to pay him a further dollar for this sort of product.

That being so, there was no choice but to believe either that, with Jericho's co-operation, the whole operation had been blown to Iraqi Counter-Intelligence, now in the hands of 'your friend Hassan Rahmani'; or that it soon would be if Jericho sought revenge by sending Rahmani an anonymous tip.

All six dead-letter-boxes must now be assumed to be compromised. Under no circumstances were they to be approached. Martin should make his own preparations to escape Iraq at the first safe opportunity, perhaps under the mantle of the chaos that would ensue in twenty-four hours. End of message.

Martin thought it through for the remainder of the night. He was not surprised that the West disbelieved Jericho. That the mercenary's payments were now to cease was a blow. The man had only reported the contents of a conference at which Saddam had spoken. So, Saddam had lied, nothing new in that. What else was Jericho to do—ignore it? It was the cheek of the man asking for a million dollars that had done it.

Beyond that, Paxman's logic was impeccable. Within four days, maybe five, Jericho would have checked and found no more money. He would become angry, resentful. If he was not himself blown away and in the hands of Omar Khatib the Tormentor, he might well respond by an anonymous tip-off.

Yet it would be foolish for Jericho to do that. If Martin were caught and broken, and he was uncertain how much pain he could take at the hands of Khatib and his professionals in the Gymnasium, his own information could point the finger at Jericho, whoever he was.

Still, people do foolish things. Paxman was right, the 'drops' might be under surveillance.

As for escaping Baghdad, that was easier said than done. From gossip in the markets, Martin had heard the roads out of town were thick with patrols of the AMAM and military police, looking for deserters and draft-dodgers. His own letter from the Soviet diplomat Kulikov only authorized him to serve the man as gardener in Baghdad. Hard to explain to a patrol checkpoint what he was doing heading west into the desert where his motor-cycle was buried.

On balance he decided to stay inside the Soviet compound for a while. It was probably the safest place in Baghdad.

CHAPTER FIFTEEN

The deadline for Saddam Hussein to quit Kuwait expired at midnight on 16 January. In 1,000 rooms, huts, tents and cabins across Saudi Arabia and in the

444

Red Sea and the Arabian Gulf men glanced at their watches and then at each other. There was very little to say.

Two floors beneath the Saudi Air Force Ministry, behind the steel doors that would have protected any bank vault in the world, there was almost a sense of anti-climax. After all that work, all that planning, there was nothing more to do—for a couple of hours. Now it was down to the younger men. They had their tasks, they would carry them out in the pitch blackness far above the generals' heads.

At 2.15 a.m. General Schwarzkopf entered the war room. Everyone stood. He read aloud a message to the troops, the chaplain said a prayer, and the Commander-in-Chief said: 'OK, let's get to work.'

Far out across the desert men were already at work. First across the border were not the warplanes but a flight of eight Apache helicopters belonging to the Army's 101st Airborne Division. Their task was limited but crucial.

North of the border but short of Baghdad were two powerful Iraqi radar bases, whose dishes commanded all the skies from the Gulf in the east to the western desert.

The helicopters were chosen, despite their slow speed compared to supersonic jet fighters, for two reasons. Skimming the desert, they could pass under the radar and approach the bases unseen; further, the commanders wanted human-eyeball confirmation that the bases were really wrecked, and from close range. Only the 'choppers' could give that. It would cost a lot of lives if those radars were left functioning.

The Apaches did all that was asked. They had still not been noticed when they opened fire. All their crew had night-vision helmets, which look as if they have short binoculars sticking out the front. They give the pilot complete night vision, so that in utter darkness to the naked eye he can see everything as if illuminated by a brilliant moon.

First they shattered the electrical generators that powered the radars, then the communications facilities from which their presence could be reported to missile sites further inland; finally they blew away the radar dishes.

In less than two minutes they had loosed off 27 Hellfire laser-guided missiles, 100 70mm rockets and 4,000 rounds of heavy-duty cannon. Both radar sites were left smouldering ruins.

The mission opened a huge hole in the air-defence system of Iraq, and through this hole poured the remainder of the night's attack.

Those who saw General Chuck Horner's air-war plan have suggested it was probably one of the most brilliant ever devised. It contained a surgical, step-by-step precision and enough flexibility to cope with any contingency that required a variation.

Stage One was quite clear in its objectives and led on to the other three stages. It was to destroy all Iraq's air-defence systems, to convert the Allies' air superiority, with which they started, into air supremacy. For the other three stages to succeed within the self-imposed 35-day time-limit, Allied aircraft had to have the absolute run of Iraqi airspace without let or hindrance.

In suppressing the air-defence of Iraq, the key was radar. In modern warfare radar is the single most important and most used tool, despite the brilliance of all the others in the armoury.

Radar detects the incoming warplanes; radar guides your own fighters to intercept; radar guides the anti-aircraft missiles and radar aims the guns.

Destroying the radar makes the enemy blind, like a heavyweight boxer in the ring but with no eyes. He may be big and powerful still, he may pack a fearsome punch, but his enemy can move around the sightless Samson, jabbing and slashing at the helpless giant until the foregone conclusion is reached.

With the great hole punched in the forward radar cover of Iraq, the Tornados and Eagles, F-111 Aardvarks and F-4G Wild Weasels powered through the gap, going for the radar sites further inland, heading for the missile bases guided by those radars, aiming for the command centres where the Iraqi generals sat, and blowing away the communications posts through which the generals were trying to talk to their outlying units.

From the battleships *Wisconsin* and *Missouri*, and the cruiser *San Jacinto* out in the Gulf, fifty-two Tomahawk Cruise missiles were launched that night. Guiding themselves by a combination of computerized memory-bank and television nose-camera, the Tomahawks hug the contours of the landscape, swerving on pre-ordained courses to where they have to go. When in the area, they 'see' the target, compare it with the one in their memory, identify the exact building, and home in.

The Wild Weasel is a version of the Phantom, but specializing in radar-destruction. It carries HARMs, Hi-speed Anti Radiation Missiles. When a radar dish lights up or 'illuminates' it emits electro-magnetic waves. It can't help it. The HARMs' job is to find those waves with its sensors and go straight to the heart of the radar before exploding.

Perhaps strangest of all the warplanes slipping northwards through the sky that night was the

447

F-117A, known as the 'stealth' fighter. All black and created in such a shape that its multiple angles reflect most of the radar waves directed at it, absorbing the rest into its own body, the Stealth Fighter refuses to bounce hostile radar waves back to the receiver and thus betray its existence to the enemy.

Thus invisible, the American F-117As that night simply slid unnoticed through Iraqi radar screens to drop their 2000-pound laser-guided bombs precisely onto thirty-four targets associated with the national air-defence system. Thirteen of those targets were in and around Baghdad.

When the bombs landed the Iraqis fired blindly upwards but could see nothing and missed. In Arabic the Stealths were called 'shabah'; it means 'ghost'.

They came from the secret base of Khamis Mushait deep in the south of Saudi Arabia, where they had been transferred from their equally secret home at Tonopah, Nevada. While less fortunate American airmen had to live in tents, Khamis Mushait had been built miles from anywhere but with hardened aircraft shelters and air-conditioned accommodation, which was why the prized Stealths had been put there.

Because they flew so far, theirs were among the longest missions of the war, up to six hours from take-off to landing, and all under strain. They threaded their way undetected through some of the most intense air-defence systems in the world, those of Baghdad, and not one was ever touched, on that or any other night.

When they had done what they came to do, they slipped away again, cruising like stingrays in a calm sea, and went back to Khamis Mushait.

The most dangerous jobs of the night went to the

British Tornados. Their task then and for the next week until it was discontinued was 'airfield denial', using their big and heavy JP-233 runway-busting bombs.

Their problem was twofold. The Iraqis had built their military airfields absolutely vast; Tallil was four times the size of Heathrow, with sixteen runways and taxi-tracks that could be used for take-off and landing as well. It was simply impossible to destroy it all.

The second problem was one of height and speed. The JP-233s had to be launched from a Tornado in stablized straight and level flight. Even after bomb launch, the Tornados had no choice but to overfly the target. Even if the radars were knocked out the gunners weren't; anti-aircraft artillery, known as Triple-A, came up at them in rolling waves as they approached, so that one pilot described those missions as 'flying through tubes of molten steel'.

The Americans had abandoned tests on the JP-233 bomb, judging them to be pilot-killers. They were right. But the RAF crews pressed on, losing planes and crews until they were called off and given other duties.

The bomb-droppers were not the only planes aloft that night. Behind them and with them flew an extraordinary array of back-up services.

Air superiority fighters flew 'cover' on and over the strike bombers. Iraqi ground controllers' instructions to their own pilots, the few who managed to take off that night, were jammed by the American Air Force Ravens and the Navy equivalent, the Prowler. Iraqi pilots aloft got no verbal instructions and no radar guidance. Most, wisely, went straight back home.

Circling south of the border were sixty tankers: American KC-135s and KC-10s, US Navy KA-6Ds and the British Victors and VC-10s. Their job was to receive the warplanes coming up from Saudi Arabia, refuel them for the mission, then meet them on the way back to give them more fuel to get home. This may sound routine, but actually doing it in pitch darkness was described by one flier as 'trying to shove spaghetti up a wildcat's backside'.

And out over the Gulf, where they had been for five months, the US Navy's E-2 Hawkeyes and the USAF's E-3 Sentry AWACS circled round and round, their radars picking up every friendly and every enemy aircraft in the sky, warning, advising, guiding and watching.

By dawn Iraq's radars had mainly been crushed, her missile bases blinded and her main command centres ruined. It would take four more days and nights to complete the job, but air supremacy was already in sight. Later would come the power-generating stations, telecommunications towers, telephone exchanges, relay stations, aircraft shelters, control towers and all those known facilities for the production and storage of weapons of mass destruction.

Later still would come the systematic 'degradation' to less than 50 per cent of its fighting power of the Iraqi army south and south-west of the Kuwaiti border, a condition on which General Schwarzkopf insisted before he would attack with ground troops.

Two then unknown factors would later cause changes to the course of the war. One was Iraq's decision to launch a barrage of Scud missiles at Israel; the other would be triggered by an act of sheer frustration on the part of Captain Don Walker of the 336th Tactical Fighter Squadron.

*   *   *

Dawn broke on the morning of 17 January over a Baghdad that was extremely badly shaken.

The ordinary citizens had not slept a wink through the night from 3 a.m. onwards and when daylight came some of them ventured out to peer curiously at the rubble of a score of major sites across their city. That they had survived the night seemed to many miraculous, for they were simple folk who did not realize that the twenty smoking mounds of rubble had been carefully selected and hit with such precision that the citizenry had been in no mortal danger.

But the real sense of shock was among the hierarchs. Saddam Hussein had quit the Presidential Palace and was lodged in his extraordinary multi-storey bunker behind and beneath the Rashid Hotel, which was still full of Westerners, mainly from the media.

The bunker had been built years earlier inside a vast crater dug by earth-movers, and done with mainly Swedish technology. So sophisticated were its security measures that it was in fact a box within a box, and beneath and around the inner box were springs of such strength as to protect the inhabitants from a nuclear bomb, reducing the shock waves that would flatten the city above into a minor tremor down below.

Although access was via a hydraulically operated ramp set in waste ground behind the hotel, the main structure was beneath the Rashid, which had

451

deliberately been built on the ground above as a specific repose for Westerners in Baghdad.

Any enemy wishing to attempt a deep-penetration bombing of the bunker would have to obliterate the Rashid first.

Try as they might, the sycophants surrounding the Rais were hard put to create a gloss over the night's disasters. Slowly the level of the catastrophe penetrated all their minds.

They had all counted on a blanket bombing of the city which would have left residential areas flattened and thousands of innocent civilians dead. This carnage was then to be shown to the media, who would film it all and show it to the sickened audiences back home. Thus would begin the global wave of revulsion against President Bush and America, culminating in a recall of the Security Council and the veto of China and Russia against further massacre.

By midday it was plain the Sons of Dogs from across the Atlantic were not obliging. So far as the Iraqi generals were aware bombs fell approximately where they were aimed, but that was all. With every major military installation in Baghdad deliberately sited in densely populated housing areas, it should have been impossible for massive civilian casualties to be avoided.

Yet a tour of the city revealed twenty command posts, missile sites, radar bases and communication centres blasted to rubble while those not in the targeted buildings had sustained little more than broken windows and were even now gawping at the mess.

The authorities had to be satisfied with inventing a civilian death toll and claims that American aircraft

452

had been shot out of the skies like autumn leaves.

Most Iraqis, stultified by years of propaganda, believed these first reports—for a while.

The generals in charge of air defence knew better. By midday it was clear to them they had lost almost all their radar-warning facility, their surface-to-air missiles (SAMs) were blind and communication with the outlying units was all but cut. Worse, radar operators who had survived kept insisting the damage had been done by bombers that simply had not shown up on their screens. The liars were at once put under arrest.

Some civilian casualties had indeed occurred. At least two Tomahawk Cruise missiles, their fins damaged by conventional Triple-A gunfire rather than SAM rockets, had 'gone stupid' and crashed off-target. One had demolished two houses and blown tiles off a mosque, an outrage that the Press corps was shown during the afternoon.

The other had fallen on waste ground and made a large crater. During the late afternoon the body of a woman was found at the bottom of it, badly smashed by the impact that apparently killed her.

Bombing raids continued throughout the day, so the ambulance crews were not prepared to do more than wrap the corpse hastily in a blanket, bring it to the morgue of the nearest hospital and leave it there.

The hospital happened to be close to a major Air Force command centre which had been demolished, and all beds were occupied by service personnel wounded in the attack. Several scores of bodies were taken to the same morgue, all dead from bomb-blasts. The woman's was just one of them.

With his resources at breaking point, the pathologist worked fast and cursorily. Identification and cause of death were his principal priorities, and he had no time for leisured examination. Across the city the crump of more bombs could be heard, the blast of counter-fire was unceasing and he had no doubt the evening and night would bring him more bodies.

What surprised the doctor was that all his dead bodies were service personnel, except the woman. She seemed to be about thirty, had once been comely and the concrete dust clinging to the blood of her smashed face, coupled with the place she had been found, gave cause for no other explanation than that she had been running away when the missile struck the waste ground and killed her. The body was so tagged, then wrapped for burial.

Her handbag had been found next to the body and it contained powder compact, lipstick and her identity cards. Having established that one Leila Al-Hilla was undoubtedly a civilian victim of a bomb blast, the harassed pathologist had her taken away for hasty burial.

The more elaborate post-mortem for which he did not have time that 17 January would have shown the woman had been repeatedly and savagely raped before being systematically beaten to death. The dumping in the crater came several hours later.

General Abdullah Kadiri had moved from his sumptuous office in the Defence Ministry two days earlier. There was no point in staying to be blown to bits by an American bomb, and he was sure the ministry would be hit and destroyed before the air war was many days old. He was right.

He had established himself in his villa, which he was reasonably certain was anonymous enough, albeit luxurious, not to be on any American target map. In this, too, he was right.

The villa had long since been provided with its own communications room, which staff from the ministry were now manning. All his communications to the various command headquarters of the Tank Corps around Baghdad were by buried fibre-optic cable, which was also out of reach of the bombers.

Only the further units had to be contacted by radio, with a threat of intercept, plus of course those in Kuwait.

His problem as darkness fell over Baghdad that night was not how to contact his Armoured Brigade commanders, or what orders to give them. They could take no part in the air war, being tasked to disperse their tanks as widely as possible among the rows of dummies or bury them in the subterranean bunkers and wait.

His problem was his personal security, and it was not the Americans he feared.

Two nights earlier, rising from his bed with a bursting bladder, bleary with arak as usual, he had stumbled to the bathroom. Finding the door as he thought stuck he had pushed hard. His 200 pounds of body weight had torn the inner bolt from its screws and the door flew open.

Bleary he might have been, but Abdullah Kadiri had not come from a back street outside Tikrit to command all Iraq's tanks outside the Republican Guard, not climbed the slippery ladder of Ba'ath Party internal feuding and not sustained a trusted place on the Revolutionary Command Council without ample reserves of low animal cunning.

He had stared in silence at his mistress, sitting wrapped in a robe on the lavatory seat, her paper sustained by the back of a Kleenex box, her mouth in

455

a round O of horror and surprise, her pen still poised in mid-air. Then he had hauled her to her feet and hit her on the point of the jaw.

When she came to, with a jug of water dashed in the face, he had had time to read the report she was preparing and to summon the trusty Kemal from his quarters across the yard. It was Kemal who had taken the whore down to the basement.

Kadiri had read and reread the report she had almost finished. Had it concerned his personal habits and preferences, a lever for future blackmail, he would have dismissed it and simply had her killed. In any case, no blackmail would ever have worked. The personal baseness of some of the entourage of the Rais was greater than his, he knew. He also knew that the Rais did not care.

This was worse. Apparently he had talked of things that happened within the Government and the Army. That she was spying was obvious. He needed to know for how long, what she had reported already, but most of all, for whom.

Kemal took his long-awaited pleasures first, with his master's permission. No man would lust after what remained when Kemal had finished the interrogation. It had taken several hours. Then he knew Kemal had it all; at least, all the courtesan knew.

After that, Kemal continued for his own amusement until she was dead.

Kadiri was convinced she had not known the real identity of the man who recruited and ran her to spy on him, but the picture had to fit Hassan Rahmani.

The description of the information-against-money exchanges in the confessional of St Joseph's showed the man was professional and Rahmani was certainly

456

that.

That he should be watched did not worry Kadiri. All those around the Rais were watched; indeed, they watched each other.

The rules of the Rais were simple and clear. Every figure of high rank was watched and reported on by three of his peers. A denunciation for treachery could and probably would lead to ruin. Thus few conspiracies could get very far. One of those confided in would report the matter, and it would come to the ears of the Rais.

To complicate matters, each of the entourage was occasionally provoked, to see what his reaction would be. A colleague, briefed to do so, would take his friend on one side and propose treason.

If the friend agreed, he was finished. If he failed to report the proposer, he was finished. So any approach could be a provocation—it was simply too unsafe to assume otherwise. Thus, each reported on the others.

But this was different. Rahmani was Head of Counter-Intelligence. Had he taken the initiative off his own bat, and if so, why? Was it an operation with the knowledge and approval of the Rais himself, and if so, why?

What had he said? he wondered. Things indiscreet, no doubt, but traitorous?

The body had stayed in the basement until the bombs fell, then Kemal had found a crater on a patch of waste ground to dump it. The general insisted the handbag be placed near by. Let that bastard Rahmani know what had happened to his slut.

As midnight passed, General Abdullah Kadiri sweated alone, tipping a few drops of water into his tenth tumbler of arak. If it was Rahmani alone, he would finish the bastard. But how could he know how far up the ladder he was distrusted? He would have to be careful, from henceforth, more careful than he had ever been before. Those late-night trips into the city would end. In any case, with the air war started, it was the time to cease.

*   *   *

Simon Paxman had flown back again to London. There was no point in staying in Riyadh. Jericho had been kicked firmly into touch by the CIA, although the unseen renegade in Baghdad would not know it yet, and Mike Martin was confined to quarters until he could escape to the desert and find his way to safety across the border.

Later he could swear with his hand on his heart the meeting on the evening of the 18th with Dr Terry Martin had been a true coincidence. He knew Martin lived in Bayswater, as he did himself, but it is a large borough with many shops.

With his wife away at the bedside of her sick mother, and his own return home unforeseen, Paxman had found an empty flat and an empty fridge, so he went shopping at a late-opening supermarket on Westbourne Grove.

Terry Martin's trolley nearly crashed into his own as he came round the corner of pastas and pet food. Both men were startled.

'Am I allowed to know you?' asked Martin with an embarrassed grin.

There was no-one else in that aisle at the time.

'Why not?' said Paxman. 'I'm just a humble civil servant shopping for his evening meal.'

They finished their purchases together and agreed

to adjourn to an Indian restaurant for a meal rather than cook at home alone. Hilary, it seemed, was also away.

Paxman should, of course, not have done it. He should never have felt uncomfortable that Terry Martin's elder brother was in a situation of appalling danger and that he, with others, had sent him into it. It should not have worried him that the trusting little academic should really believe that his adored sibling was safe inside Saudi Arabia. All tradecraft insists that one does not worry about that sort of thing. But he did.

There was another worry. Steve Laing was his superior at Century House, but Laing had never been to Iraq. His background was in Egypt and Jordan. Paxman knew Iraq. And Arabic. Not like Martin, of course, but Martin was exceptional. But he knew enough, from several visits before he was made Head of Iraq Desk, to have formed a sincere respect for the quality of Iraqi scientists and the ingenuity of their engineers. It was no secret that most British technical institutes reckoned their graduates from that country were the best in the Arab world.

The worry that nagged at him since he had been told by his superiors that the last Jericho report could be none other than a load of nonsense was simply the fear that, despite all the odds, Iraq might actually be further ahead than the Western scientists were prepared to credit.

He waited until the two meals had arrived, surrounded by small pots of the accessories without which no Indian meal is complete, then made up his mind.

'Terry,' he said, 'I am going to do something which, if it ever got out, means the end of my career in

459

the Service.'

Martin was startled.

'That sounds drastic. Why?'

'Because I have been officially warned off you.'

The academic was about to spoon some mango chutney on to his plate, and stopped.

'I am not thought to be reliable any more? It was Steve Laing who pulled me into all this.'

'It's not that. The view is that ... you worry too much.'

Paxman was not prepared to use Laing's word 'fusspot'.

'Perhaps I do. It's the training. Academics do not like puzzles that seem to have no answer. We have to go on worrying at it until the jumbled hieroglyphic makes sense. Was it that business of the phrase in the intercept?'

'Yes, that and other things.'

Paxman had chosen chicken khorma; Martin liked his hotter—vindaloo. Because he knew his Eastern food, he drank hot black tea, not ice-cold beer which only makes things worse. He blinked at Paxman over the edge of his mug.

'All right, so what is the great confession?'

'Will you give me your word that this goes no further?'

'Of course.'

'There's been another intercept.'

Paxman had not the slightest intention of revealing the existence of Jericho. The group who knew of that asset in Iraq was still tiny and would stay that way.

'Can I listen to it?'

'No. It's been suppressed. Don't approach Sean Plummer. He'd have to deny it, and that would reveal where you got the information.'

Martin helped himself to more raita to cool down the flaming curry.

'What does it say, this new intercept?'

Paxman told him. Martin put down his fork and wiped his face which was bright pink beneath the ginger thatch of his hair.

'Can it ... could it under any circumstances, be true?' asked Paxman.

'I don't know. I'm not a physicist. The brass has given it a no-no?'

'Absolutely. The nuclear scientists all agree it simply cannot be true. So, Saddam was lying.'

Privately, Martin thought it was a very odd radio intercept. It sounded more like information coming from inside a closed meeting.

'Saddam lies,' he said, 'all the time. But usually for public consumption. This was to his own inner core of confidants? I wonder why? Morale booster on the threshold of war?'

'That's what the powers think,' said Paxman.

'Have the generals been told?'

'No. The reasoning is, they are extremely busy right now and do not need to be bothered by something that simply has to be rubbish.'

'So, what do you want from me, Simon?'

'Saddam's mind. No-one can figure it out. Nothing he does makes sense in the West. Is he certifiably insane or crazy like a fox?'

'In his world, the latter. In his world, what he does makes sense. The terror that revolts us has no moral downside for him, and makes sense. The threats and the bluster make sense to him. Only when he tries to enter our world, with those ghastly PR exercises in Baghdad, ruffling that little English boy's hair, playing the benign uncle, that sort of thing—only

461

when he tries that does he look a complete fool. In his own world he is not a fool. He survives, he stays in power, he keeps Iraq united, his enemies fail and perish...'

'Terry, as we sit here his country is being pulverized.'

'It doesn't matter, Simon. It's all replaceable.'

'But why did he say what he is supposed to have said?'

'What do the powers think?'

'That he lied.'

'No,' said Martin, 'he lies for public consumption. To his inner core, he doesn't have to. They are his, anyway. Either the source of the information lied, and Saddam never said that; or he said it because he believed it was true.'

'Then he was himself lied to?'

'Possibly. Whoever did that will pay dearly when he finds out. But then, the intercept could be phoney. A deliberate bluff, designed to be intercepted.'

Paxman could not say what he knew: it was not an intercept. It came from Jericho. And in two years under the Israelis and three months under the Anglo-Americans, he had never been wrong.

'You've got doubts, haven't you?' said Martin.

'I suppose I have,' admitted Paxman.

Martin sighed.

'Straws in the wind, Simon. A phrase in an intercept, a man told to shut up and called a son of a whore, a phrase from Saddam about succeeding and being seen to succeed—in the hurting of America—and now this. We need a piece of string.'

'String?'

'Straws only make up a bale when you can wrap them round with string. There has to be something

462

else as to what he really has in mind. Otherwise, the powers are right and he will go for the gas weapon he already has.'

'All right. I'll look for a piece of string.'

'And I,' said Martin, 'did not meet you this evening and we have not spoken.'

'Thank you,' said Paxman.

*   *   *

Hassan Rahmani heard of the death of his agent Leila two days after it happened, on 19 January. She had not appeared for a scheduled hand-over of information from General Kadiri's bed and, fearing the worst, he had checked morgue records.

The hospital in Mansour had produced the evidence, though the corpse had been buried, with many others from the destroyed military buildings, in a mass grave.

Hassan Rahmani no more believed his agent had been hit by a stray bomb while crossing a piece of waste ground in the middle of the night than he believed in ghosts. The only ghosts in the skies above Baghdad were the invisible American bombers of which he had read in Western defence magazines, and they were not ghosts but logically contrived inventions. So was the death of Leila Al-Hilla.

His only logical conclusion was that Kadiri had discovered her extramural activities and put a stop to them. Which meant she would have talked before she died.

That meant, for him, that Kadiri had become a powerful and dangerous enemy. Worse, his principal conduit into the inner councils of the regime had been closed down.

Had he known that Kadiri was as worried as he himself, Rahmani would have been delighted. But he did not know. He only knew that from henceforward he was going to have to be extremely careful.

*   *   *

On the second day of the air war Iraq launched its first battery of missiles against Israel. The media at once announced them as being Soviet-built Scud-Bs and the title stuck throughout the rest of the war. In fact they were not Scuds at all.

The point of the onslaught was not foolish. Iraq recognized quite clearly that Israel was not a country prepared to accept large numbers of civilian casualties. As the first rocket warheads fell into the suburbs of Tel Aviv, Israel reacted by going on the warpath. This was exactly what Baghdad wanted.

Within the fifty-nation Coalition ranged against Iraq were seventeen Arab States and if there was one thing they all shared, apart from the Islamic faith, it was a hostility to Israel. Iraq calculated, probably rightly, that if Israel could be provoked into joining the war by a strike against her, the Arab nations in the Coalition would pull out. Even King Fahd, Monarch of Saudi Arabia and Keeper of the Two Holy Places, would be in an impossible position.

The first reactions to the fall of the rockets on Israel was that they might be loaded with gas or germ cultures. Had they so been, Israel could not have been restrained. It was quickly proved the warheads were of conventional explosive. But the psychological effect inside Israel was still enormous.

The United States immediately brought massive pressure on Jerusalem not to respond with a counter-strike. The Allies, Itzhak Shamir was told, would take care of it. Israel actually launched a counter-strike in the form of a wave of her own F-15 fighter-bombers but called them back while still in Israeli airspace.

The real Scud was a clumsy, obsolete Soviet missile of which Iraq had bought 900 several years earlier. It had a range of under 300 kilometres and carried a warhead of close to 1,000 pounds. It was not guided, and even in its original form would, at full range, land anywhere within half a mile of its target.

From Iraq's point of view, it was a virtually useless purchase. It could not reach Tehran in the Iran-Iraq war and it certainly could not reach Israel, even if fired from the extreme western border of Iraq.

What the Iraqis had done in the meantime, with German technical help, was bizarre. They had cut up the Scuds into chunks, and used three of them to create two new rockets. To put not too fine a point on it, the new Al-Husayn rocket was a mess.

By adding extra fuel tanks the Iraqis had increased the range to 620 kilometres so that it could (and did) reach Tehran and Israel. But its payload was cut to a pathetic 160 pounds. Its guidance, always erratic, was now chaotic. Two of them, launched at Israel, not only missed Tel Aviv, they missed the entire republic and fell in Jordan.

But as a terror weapon it almost worked. Even though the entire number of Al-Husayns that fell on Israel had less payload than one American 2000-pound bomb falling on Iraq, they sent the Israeli population into something approaching panic.

America responded in three ways. Fully 1,000 Allied airplanes were diverted from their assigned tasks over Iraq to hunt down the fixed launching sites of the rockets and the even more elusive mobile launchers.

Batteries of American Patriot missiles were sent into Israel within hours in an attempt to shoot down the incoming rockets but mainly to persuade Israel to stay out of the war.

And the SAS, and later the American Green Berets, were sent into the western deserts of Iraq to find the mobile rocket launchers and either destroy them with their own Milan missiles or call in air strikes by radio.

The Patriots, although hailed as the saviours of all creation, had limited success but that was not their fault. Raytheon had designed the Patriot to intercept airplanes, not rockets, and they were hastily adapted to a new role. The reason they hardly ever hit an incoming warhead was never disclosed.

The fact was, in extending the Scud's range by turning it into the Al-Husayn, the Iraqis had also increased its altitude. The new rocket, entering inner space on its parabolic flight, was getting red hot as it came back down, something the Scud was never designed to do. As it re-entered earth's atmosphere, it just broke up. What was descending on Israel was not an entire rocket but a falling trash-can.

The Patriot, doing its job, went up to intercept, found itself with not one piece of metal coming towards it but a dozen. So its tiny brain told it to do what it was trained to do—go for the biggest one. This was usually the spent fuel tank, tumbling downwards out of control. The warhead, much smaller and detached in the break-up, just fell free. Many failed to explode at all, and most of the battering sustained by Israeli buildings was impact-damage.

If the so-called Scud was a psychological terror, the Patriot was a psychological saviour. But the psychology worked, inasmuch as it was part of the solution.

Another part was the three-section deal covertly agreed between America and Israel. Part one was the Patriot contribution—free. Part two was the promise of the much improved Arrow rocket when it was ready—installed by 1994. Part three was the right of Israel to choose up to one hundred extra targets that the Allied air forces would obliterate. The choices were made—mainly targets in western Iraq that affected Israel: roads, bridges, airfields, anything pointing west at Israel. None of these targets, by their geographical location, had anything to do with the liberation of Kuwait on the other side of the peninsula.

The fighter-bombers of the American and British air forces assigned to Scud-hunting claimed numerous successes, claims regarded with immediate scepticism by the CIA to the rage of General Chuck Horner and General Schwarzkopf.

Two years after the war Washington officially denied that a single mobile Scud-launcher had been destroyed by air power, a suggestion capable still today of reducing any pilot involved to incandescent rage. The fact was, the pilots were largely deceived again by maskirovka.

If the southern desert of Iraq is a featureless billiard table, the western and north-west deserts are rocky, hilly and riven by a thousand wadis and gullies. This was the land over which Mike Martin had driven on his infiltration to Baghdad. Before launching its rocket attacks, Baghdad had created scores of dummy mobile Scud-launchers and these were hidden, with the real ones, across the landscape.

The habit was to produce them in the night, a tube of sheet metal mounted on an old flatbed truck, and at dawn torch a drum of oil and cotton waste inside the tube. Far away, the sensors in the AWACS picked up the heat source and logged a missile launch. The fighters vectored on to the location did the rest and claimed a kill.

The men who could not be fooled this way were the SAS. Although only a handful in numbers, they swarmed into the western deserts in their Land-Rovers and motor-bikes, lay up in the blistering days and freezing nights and watched. At 200 yards they could see what was a real mobile launcher and what was a dummy.

As the rocket launchers came out from the culverts and beneath the bridges where they were hidden from aerial observation, the silent men in the crags watched through binoculars. If there were too many Iraqis around, they quietly called in air strikes by radio. If they could get away with it, they used their own Milan anti-tank rockets which made a very nice bang when hitting the fuel tank of a real Al-Husayn.

It was soon realized there was an invisible north-south line running down the desert. West of that line, the Iraqi rockets could hit Israel; east of it, they were out of range. The job was to terrorize the Iraqi crews into not daring to venture west of that line, but to fire from east of it and lie to their superiors. It took eight days, then the rocket attacks on Israel stopped. They never started again.

Later the Baghdad to Jordan road was used as a divider. North of it was Scud-Alley North, terrain of the American Special Forces who went in by long-range helicopter. Below the road was Scud-Alley

South, bailiwick of the Special Air Service. Four good men died in those deserts, but they did the job they were sent in to do, where billions of dollars of technology had been deceived.

On Day Four of the air war, 20 January, 336th Squadron out of Al Kharz was one of the units that had not been diverted to the western deserts.

Their assignment that day included a big SAM missile site north-west of Baghdad. The SAMs were controlled by two large radar dishes.

The air attacks in General Horner's plan were now rolling northward. With just about every missile base and radar dish south of a horizontal line through southern Baghdad wiped away, the time had come to clear the airspace east, west and north of the capital.

With twenty-four Strike Eagles in the squadron, 20 January was going to be a multi-mission day. The squadron commander, Lt.-Col. Steve Turner, had allocated a twelve-plane detail for the missile base. A swarm of Eagles that large was known as a 'gorilla'.

The gorilla was led by one of the two senior flight commanders. Four of the twelve planes were packing HARMs, the radar-busting missiles that home in on infra-red signals from a radar dish. The other eight carried two long, gleaming, stainless-steel-cased laser-guided bombs known as GBU-10-I. When the radars were dead and the missiles blind, they would follow the HARMs and blow away the rocket batteries.

It did not seem as if things were going to go wrong. The twelve Eagles took off in three groups of four, established themselves in a loose echelon formation and climbed to altitude of 25,000 feet. The sky was a brilliant blue and the ochre desert below clearly visible.

The weather report over the target indicated a stronger wind than over Saudi Arabia, but no mention of a shamal, one of those rapid dust storms that can wipe out a target in seconds.

South of the border the twelve Eagles met their tankers, two KC-10s. Each tanker could suckle six hungry fighters, so one by one the Eagles drifted onto station behind the tankers and waited as the boom-operator, gazing at them through his perspex window only a few feet away, 'swam' his boom arm to lock on to their waiting fuel-nozzles.

Finally, the twelve Eagles, refuelled for their mission, turned north towards Iraq. An AWACS out over the Gulf told them there was no hostile air activity ahead of them. Had there been Iraqi fighters in the air, the Eagles carried, apart from their bombs, two kinds of air-to-air rockets: the Air-Interception-Missile 7 and the AIM-9, better known as the Sparrow and the Sidewinder.

The missile base was there all right. But its radars were not active. If the radar dishes were not operating on their arrival, they should have 'illuminated' immediately to guide the SAMs in their search for the oncoming intruders. As soon as the radars went active, the four Strike Eagles carrying the HARMs would simply take them out or, in USAF parlance, ruin their whole day.

Whether the Iraqi commander was afraid for his skin or just extremely smart the Americans never did work out. But those radars refused to come alive. The first four Eagles, led by the flight commander, dropped down and down to provoke the radars into switching on. They refused.

It would have been foolish for the bomb-carriers to go in with the radars still intact—had they suddenly illuminated without warning, the SAMs would have had the Eagles cold.

After twenty minutes over the target the attack was called off. Components of the gorilla were assigned to their secondary targets.

Don Walker had a quick word with Tim Nathanson, his wizzo sitting behind him. Secondary target for the day was a fixed Scud site south of Samarra, which was in any case being visited by other fighter-bombers because it was a known poison-gas facility.

The AWACs confirmed there was no take-off activity out of the two big Iraqi airbases at Samarra East and Balad South-east. Don Walker called up his wingman and the two-plane element headed for the Scud-site.

All communications between the American aircraft were coded by the Have-quick system, which garbles the speech to anyone trying to listen in who is not carrying the same system. The codings can be changed daily, but were common to all Allied aircraft.

Walker glanced around. The sky was clear; half a mile away his wingman Randy 'R-2' Roberts rode astern and slightly above him, with wizzo Jim 'Boomer' Henry sitting behind.

Over the Scud fixed-launcher position Walker dropped down to identify the target properly. To his rage it was obscured by swirling clouds of desert dust, a shamal that had sprung up, created by the strong desert wind down there on the floor.

His laser-guided bombs would not miss, so long as they could follow the beam projected at the target from his own aircraft. To project the guiding beam, he had to see his target.

471

Furious and running short of fuel he turned away. Two frustrations in the same morning was too much. He hated to land with a full rack of ordnance. But there was nothing for it, the road home lay south.

Three minutes later he saw an enormous industrial complex beneath him.

'What's that?' he asked Tim. The WSO checked his briefing maps.

'It's called Tarmiya.'

'Jesus, it's big.'

'Yeah.'

Although neither man knew it, the Tarmiya industrial complex contained 381 buildings and covered 10 miles by 10 miles.

'Listed?'

'Nope.'

'Going down anyway. Randy, cover my ass.'

'Got it', came over the air from his wingman.

Walker dropped his Eagle clean down to 10,000 feet. The industrial spread was huge. In the centre was one enormous building, the size of a covered sports stadium.

'Going in.'

'Don, it's non-target.'

Dropping to 8,000 feet Walker activated his laser-guidance system and lined up on the vast factory below and in front of him. His head-up display ran off the distance as it shortened and gave him a seconds-to-fire reading. As the latter hit zero he released his bombs, keeping his nose still on the approaching target.

The laser-sniffer in the nose of the two bombs was the PAVEWAY system. Under his fuselage was the guidance module, called Lantirn. The Lantirn threw an invisible infra-red beam at the target, where the beam rebounded to form a sort of funnel-shaped electronic basket pointing back towards him.

The PAVEWAY nose-cones sensed this basket, entered it and followed the funnel down and inwards until they impacted precisely where the beam was aimed.

Both bombs did their job. They blew up under the lip of the roof of the factory. Seeing them explode, Don Walker hauled back, lifted the nose of the Eagle and powered it back to 25,000 feet. An hour later he and his wingman, after another refuel in mid-air, were back at Al Kharz.

Before he lifted his nose, Walker had seen the blinding flash of the two explosions, the great column of smoke that had arisen, and caught a glimpse of the dust cloud that would follow the bombing.

What he did not see was that those two bombs tore out one end of the factory, lifting a large section of roof up into the air like the sail of a ship at sea.

Nor did he observe that the strong desert wind that morning, the same one that had created the dust storm to blot out the Scud-site, did the rest. It tore the roof off the factory, peeling it back like the lid of a sardine can, as sheets of roofing steel flew lethally in all directions.

Back at base Don Walker, like every other pilot, was extensively debriefed. It was a tiresome process for weary pilots, but it had to be done. In charge was the squadron Intelligence officer, Major Beth Kroger.

No-one pretended the gorilla had been a success, but every pilot had taken out his secondary target, except one. Their hot-shot weapons officer had flunked his secondary target and picked a tertiary one at random.

473

'What the hell you do that for?' Beth Kroger asked.

''Cos it was huge and looked important.'

'It wasn't even on the Tasking Order,' she complained. She logged the target he had chosen, its exact location and description, his own bomb-damage report, and filed it for the attention of TACC—the Tactical Air Control Centre which shared the basement of CENTAF beneath the Saudi Air Force HQ with the Black Hole analysts in Riyadh.

'If this turns out to be a water-bottling plant or a baby-food factory, they're gonna can your ass,' she warned Walker.

'You know, Beth, you're beautiful when you're angry,' he teased her.

Beth Kroger was a good career officer. If she was going to be flirted with, she preferred colonels and up. As the only three on the base were seriously married, Al Kharz was turning out to be a pain.

'You're out of line, *Captain*,' she told him and went off to file her report.

Walker sighed and went off to his cot to rest. She was right, though. If he had just totalled the world's biggest orphanage, General Horner would personally have his captain's bars for toothpicks. As it happened, they never did tell Don Walker just what he had hit that morning. But it was not an orphanage.

CHAPTER SIXTEEN

Karim came to dine with Edith Hardenberg at her flat in Grinzing that same night. He found his own way out to the suburbs by public transport and he brought with him gifts: a pair of aromatically scented candles which he placed on the small table in the eating alcove and lit; and two bottles of fine wine.

Edith let him in, pink and embarrassed as ever, then returned to fuss over the Wiener Schnitzel she was preparing in her tiny kitchen. It had been twenty years since she had prepared a meal for a man; she was finding the ordeal daunting but, to her surprise, exciting.

Karim had greeted her with a chaste peck on the cheek in the doorway, which had made her even more flustered, then found a long-player of Verdi's *Nabucco* in the library of her records and put it on the player.

Soon the aroma of the candles, musk and patchouli, joined the gentle cadences of 'The Slaves' Chorus' to drift through the apartment.

It was just as he had been told to expect it by the neviot team who had broken in weeks before; very neat, very tidy, extremely clean. The flat of a fussy lady who lived alone.

When the meal was ready Edith presented it with copious apologies. Karim tried the meat and pronounced it the best he had ever tasted, which made her even more flustered, yet immensely pleased.

They talked as they ate, of things cultural; of their projected visit to the Schönbrunn Palace and to see the fabulous Lippizaner horses at the Hofreitschule, the Spanish Riding School inside the Hofburg on Josefsplatz.

Edith ate as she did everything else, precisely, like a bird pecking at a morsel. She wore her hair scraped back as always, gripped into a severe bun behind her head.

By the light of the candles, for he had switched off

the too-bright lamp above the table, Karim was darkly handsome and courteous as ever. He topped up her wine glass all the time, so that she consumed far more than the occasional glass she permitted herself from time to time.

The effect of the food, the wine, the candles, the music and the company of her young friend slowly corroded the defences of her reserve.

Over the empty plates Karim leant forward and gazed into her eyes.

'Edith?'

'Yes.'

'May I ask you something?'

'If you wish.'

'Why do you wear your hair drawn back like that?'

It was an impertinent question, personal. She blushed more deeply.

'I . . . have always worn it like this.'

No, that was not true. There was a time, she recalled, with Horst, when it flowed about her shoulders, thick and brown, in the summer of 1970. There was a time when it had blown in the wind on the lake at the Schlosspark in Laxenburg.

Karim rose without a word and walked behind her. She felt a rising panic. This was preposterous. Skilful fingers eased the big tortoiseshell comb out of her bun. This must stop. She felt the wire pins withdrawn, her hair coming undone, falling down her back. She sat rigid at her place. The same fingers lifted her hair and drew it forward to fall on either side of her face.

Karim stood beside her and she looked up. He held out two hands and smiled.

'That's better. You look ten years younger and prettier. Let's sit on the sofa. You pick your favourite piece for the record player and I'll make coffee. Deal?'

Without permission he took her small hands and lifted her up from her seat. Letting one hand drop he led her out of the alcove into the sitting room. Then he turned into the kitchen, releasing her other hand as he did so.

Thank God he had done that. She was shaking from head to toe. Theirs was supposed to be a platonic friendship. But then, he had not touched her, not really touched her. She would, of course, never permit *that sort of thing*.

She caught sight of herself in a mirror on the wall, pink and flushed, hair about her shoulders, covering her ears, framing her face. She thought she caught half a glimpse of a girl she knew twenty years ago.

She took a grip on herself and chose a long-player. Her beloved Strauss, the waltzes every note of which she knew, 'Roses from the South', 'Vienna Woods', 'Skaters', 'Danube' ... Thank goodness he was in the kitchen, did not see her nearly drop it as she placed it on the turntable. He seemed to have great ease in finding the coffee, the water, the filters, the sugar.

She sat at one far end of the sofa when he joined her, knees together, coffee on her lap. She wanted to talk about the new concert scheduled for the Musikverein next week, but the words did not come. She sipped her coffee instead.

'Edith, please don't be frightened of me,' he murmured. 'I am your friend, no?'

'Don't be silly. Of course I'm not frightened.'

'Good. Because I will never hurt you, you know.'

Friend. Yes, they were friends, a friendship born of a mutual love of music, art, opera, culture. Nothing more, surely. Such a small gap, friend to boy-friend.

477

She knew the other secretaries at the bank had husbands and boy-friends, watched them excited before going out on a date, giggling in the hall the morning after, pitying her for being so alone.

'That's "Roses from the South", isn't it?'

'Yes, of course.'

'I think it's my favourite of all the waltzes.'

'Mine too.' That was better, back to music.

He took her coffee cup from her lap and put it beside his own on a side-table. Then he rose, took her hands and pulled her to her feet.

'What ...?'

She found her right hand taken in his left, a strong and persuasive arm around her waist, she was turning gently on the strip-pine flooring of the small space between the furniture, dancing a waltz.

Gidi Barzilai would have said, go for it boy-chick, don't waste any more time. What did he know? Nothing. First the trust, then the fall. Karim kept his right hand well up Edith's back.

As they turned, several inches of space between them, Karim brought their locked hands closer to his shoulder, with his right arm eased Edith nearer to his body. It was imperceptible.

Edith found her face against his chest, had to turn her face sideways. Her small bosom was against his body, she could sense that man-smell again. She pulled away. He let her, released her right hand and used his left to tilt her chin upwards. Then he kissed her, as they danced.

It was not a salacious kiss. He kept his lips together, made no effort to force hers apart. Her mind was a rush of thoughts and sensations, an airplane out of control, spinning, falling, protests rising to fight and failing. The Bank, Gemütlich, her

478

reputation, his youth, his foreignness, their ages, the warmth, the wine, the odour, the strength, the lips. The music stopped.

If he had done anything else, she would have thrown him out. He took his lips from hers and eased her head forward until it rested against his chest. They stayed motionless like that in the silent apartment for several seconds.

It was she who pulled away. She turned to the sofa and sat down, staring ahead of her. She found him on his knees in front of her. He took both her hands in his.

'Are you angry with me, Edith?'

'You shouldn't have done that,' she said.

'I didn't mean to. I swear it. I couldn't help it.'

'I think you should go.'

'Edith, if you are angry and you want to punish me, there is only one way you can. By not letting me see you again.'

'Well, I'm not sure.'

'Please say you'll let me see you again.'

'I suppose so.'

'If you say no, I'll abandon the study course and go home. I couldn't live in Vienna if you won't see me.'

'Don't be silly. You must study.'

'Then you will see me again?'

'All right.'

He was gone five minutes later. She put out the lights, changed into her prim cotton nightdress, scrubbed her face and brushed her teeth and went to bed.

In the darkness she lay with her knees drawn close to her chest. After two hours she did something she had not done for years. She smiled in the darkness. There was a mad thought going through her mind

479

over and over again, and she did not mind. I have a boy-friend. He is ten years younger, a student, a foreigner, an Arab and a Muslim. And I don't mind.

*   *   *

Colonel Dick Beatty of the USAF was on the graveyard shift that night, deep below Old Airport Road in Riyadh.

The Black Hole never stopped, it never slackened, and in the first days of the air war it was working harder and faster than ever.

General Chuck Horner's master-plan for the air war was experiencing the dislocation caused by the diversion of hundreds of his war planes to hunt Scud launchers instead of taking out the targets pre-assigned to them.

Any combat general will confirm the plan can be worked out to the last nut and bolt, but when the balloon goes up it is never quite like that. The crisis caused by the rockets dropping on to Israel was proving a serious problem. Tel Aviv was screaming at Washington and Washington was screaming at Riyadh. The diversion of all those warplanes to hunt the elusive mobile launchers was the price Washington had to pay to keep Israel out of retaliatory action and Washington's orders did not brook argument. Everyone could see that Israel losing patience and entering the war would prove disastrous for the frail Coalition now ranged against Iraq, but the problem was still major.

Targets originally slated for Day Three were being deferred for lack of aircraft and the knock-on effect was like dominoes. A further problem was that there could still be no reduction of BDA. It was essential

480

and it had to be done. The alternative could be appalling.

Bomb Damage Assessment was crucial because the Black Hole had to know the level of the success, or lack of it, of each day's wave of air strikes. If a major Iraqi command centre, radar emplacement or missile battery was on the Air Tasking Order, it would duly be attacked. But was it destroyed? If so, to what degree? 10 per cent, 50 per cent, or a pile of smoking rubble?

Simply to assume that the Iraqi base had been wiped out was no good. The next day unsuspecting Allied planes might be sent over that site on another mission. If the place was still functioning, pilots could die.

So each day the missions were flown and the tired pilots described exactly what they had done and what they had hit. Or thought they had hit. The next day other airplanes flew over the targets and photographed them.

Thus, each day as the Air Tasking Order began its three-day passage to preparation, the original menu of designated targets had to include the 'second visit' missions, to finish the jobs only partly done.

The fourth day of the air war, 20 January, the Allied air forces had not officially got round to wasting the industrial plants tagged as those making Weapons of Mass Destruction. They were still concentrating on SEAD—Suppression of Enemy Air Defences.

That night Colonel Beatty was preparing the list of the next day's photo-reconnaissance missions on the basis of the harvest of all those debriefing sessions with squadron intelligence officers.

By midnight he was nearly through, and the early
481

orders were already speeding their way to the various squadrons assigned to photo-recon. missions at dawn.

'Then there's this, sir.'

It was a chief petty officer, US Navy by his side. The colonel glanced at the target.

'What do you mean—Tarmiya?'

'That's what it says, sir.'

'So where the hell's Tarmiya, anyway?'

'Here, sir.'

The colonel glanced at the air map. The location meant nothing to him.

'Radar? Missiles, air base, command post?'

'No sir, industrial facility.'

The colonel was tired. It had been a long night, and it would go on until dawn.

'For Chrissake, we haven't gotten to industrials yet. Give me the list, anyway.'

He ran his eye down the list. It included every industrial facility known to the Allies that were dedicated to the production of Weapons of Mass Destruction; it had factories known to produce shells, explosives, vehicles, gun parts and tank spares.

In the first category were listed Al-Qaim, As-Sharqat, Tuwaitha, Fallujah, Hillah, Al-Atheer and Al-Furat. The colonel could not know that missing from the list was Rasha-dia where the Iraqis had installed their second gas centrifuge cascade for producing refined uranium, the problem that had eluded the experts on the Medusa Committee. That plant, discovered by the United Nations much later, was not buried but disguised as a water-bottling enterprise.

Nor could Colonel Beatty know that Al-Furat was the buried location of the first uranium cascade, the one visited by the German Dr Stemmler 'somewhere near Tuwaitha', and that its exact position had been given away by Jericho.

'I don't see any Tarmiya,' he grunted.

'No sir, it's not there,' said the CPO.

'Gimme the grid reference.'

No-one could expect the analysts to memorize hundreds of confusing Arab place names, the more so as in some cases a single name covered ten separate targets, so all targets were given a grid reference by Global Positioning System which pinned them down to twelve digits, a square 50 yards by 50.

When he had bombed the huge factory at Tarmiya, Don Walker had noted that reference, which was attached to his debriefing report.

'It's not here,' protested the colonel. 'It's not even a goddam target. Who zapped it?'

'Some pilot from the 336th at Al Kharz. Missed out on his first two assigned targets through no fault of his own. Didn't want to come home with full racks, I guess.'

'Asshole,' muttered the colonel. 'OK, give it to BDA anyway. But low priority. Don't waste film on it.'

* * *

Lieutenant-Commander Darren Cleary sat at the controls of his F-14 Tomcat, a deeply frustrated man.

Beneath him the great grey bulk of the carrier USS *Ranger* had her nose into the light breeze and was making twenty-seven knots through the water.

The sea of the northern Gulf was dead calm in the pre-dawn and the sky would soon be bright and blue. It ought to have been a day of pleasure for a young navy pilot flying one of the world's best fighter planes.

Nicknamed the Fleet Defender, the twin-finned two-man Tomcat had come to a wider audience when it starred in the film *Top Gun*. Its cockpit is probably the most sought-after chair in American combat aviation, certainly in navy flying, and to be at the controls of such an airplane on such a lovely day just a week after arriving on station in the Gulf should have made Darren Cleary very happy. The reason for his misery was that he was not assigned to a combat mission but to BDA, taking happy snapshots, as he had complained the night before. He had beseeched the Squadron Ops. Officer to let him go hunting MiGs, but to no avail.

'Someone's got to do it,' was his answer. Like all air-superiority combat pilots among the Allies in the Gulf war, he feared the Iraqi jets would quit the skies after a few days, putting an end to any chance to tangle.

So, to his chagrin, he had been 'fragged' (assigned) to a TARPS mission.

Behind him and his flight officer, two General Electric jet engines rumbled away as the deck crew hooked him up to the steam catapult on the angled flight deck, pointing his nose slightly off the centreline of the *Ranger*. Cleary waited, throttle in his left hand, control column steady and neutral in the right, as the last preparations were made. Finally the terse enquiry, the nod and that great blast of power as the throttle went forward, right through the gate into afterburn, and the catapult threw him and 68,000 pounds of warplane from zero to 150 knots in three seconds.

The grey steel of the *Ranger* vanished behind him,

the dark sea flashed below, the Tomcat felt for the rushing air around her, sensed its support and climbed smoothly away for the lightening sky.

It would be a four-hour mission with two refuels. He had twelve targets to photograph, and he would not be alone. Already up ahead of him was an A-6 Avenger with laser-guided bombs in case they should run into Triple-A, in which eventuality the Avenger would teach the Iraqi gunners to be quiet. An EA-6B Prowler was coming on the same mission, armed with HARMs in case they ran into a SAM missile site guided by radar. The Prowler would use its HARMs to blow away the radar, and the Avenger would employ its LGBs on the missiles.

In case the Iraqi Air Force showed up, two more Tomcats would be riding shotgun, above and either side of the photographer, their powerful AWG-9 in-air radars capable of discerning the Iraqi pilot's inside leg measurement before he got out of bed.

All this metal and technology was to protect what hung below and behind Darren Cleary's feet, a Tactical Air Reconnaissance Pod System.

Hanging slightly right of the Tomcat's centreline, the TARPS resembled a streamlined coffin 17 feet long and rather more complicated than a tourist's Pentax.

In its nose was a powerful frame camera with two positions: forward-and-down or straight down. Behind was the panoramic camera looking outwards, sideways and down. Behind that was the infra-red Reconnaissance Set, designed to record thermal (heat) imaging and its source. In a final twist, the pilot could see on his Head-Up Display inside his cockpit what he was photographing while still overhead.

485

Darren Cleary climbed to 15,000 feet, met up with the rest of his escorts and they proceeded to link with their assigned KC-135 tanker just south of the Iraqi border.

Without being troubled by Iraqi resistance, he photographed the eleven principal targets he had been assigned, then turned back over Tarmiya for the secondary-interest twelfth location.

As he went over Tarmiya, he glanced at his Display and muttered: 'What the fuck is that?' This was the moment the last of the 750 frames in each of his main cameras chose to run out.

After a second refuel the mission landed back on the *Ranger* without incident. Deck crew downloaded the cameras and took them off to the photolab for development to negative.

Cleary was debriefed on an uneventful mission and then went down to the light-table with the Intelligence officer. As the negatives came up on the screen with the white-light underneath, Cleary explained what each frame was and where it came from.

The Intel. officer made notes for his own report, which would be attached to Cleary's, plus the photos.

When they came to the last twenty frames, the Intel. officer asked: 'What are these?'

'Don't ask me,' said Cleary. 'They come from that target at Tarmiya; you remember, the one Riyadh tacked on at the last moment?'

'Yeah, so what are those things inside the factory?'

'Look like frisbees for giants,' suggested Cleary dubiously.

It was a phrase which stuck. The Intel. officer used it in his own report, coupled with an admission that he had not the slightest idea what they were. When

486

the package was complete a Lockheed S-3 Viking was thrown off the *Ranger*'s deck and took the whole package to Riyadh. Darren Cleary went back to air-combat missions, never tangled with the elusive MiGs and left the Gulf with the USS *Ranger* in late April 1991.

* * *

Wolfgang Gemütlich became more and more worried through that morning at the state of his private secretary.

She was polite and formal as ever, and as efficient as he could have demanded, and Herr Gemütlich demanded much. Not a man of excessive sensitivity, he saw nothing at first, but by her third visit into his private sanctum to take a letter, he observed there was something unusual about her.

Nothing light-hearted, of course, and certainly not frivolous—he would never have tolerated that. It was an air that she carried with her. On her third visit he observed her more closely as, head bent over her notepad, she took down his dictation.

True, the dowdy business suit was in place, hem below the knees. The hair was still scraped back into a bun behind her head ... It was on the fourth visit that he realized with a start of horror that Edith Hardenberg was wearing a touch of face powder. Not a lot, just a hint. He checked quickly to ensure there was no lipstick on her mouth, and was relieved to see not a trace.

Perhaps, he reasoned, he was deluding himself. It was January, the freezing weather outside might have caused chapping to her skin; no doubt the powder was to ease the soreness. But there was something

487

else.

The eyes. Not mascara, um Gotteswillen, let it not be mascara. He checked again, but there was none. He was deluded, he reassured himself. It was in the lunch-hour, as he spread his linen napkin on his blotter and ate the sandwiches dutifully prepared by Frau Gemütlich as on every day, that the solution came to him.

They sparkled. Fräulein Hardenberg's eyes sparkled. It could not be the winter weather—she had been indoors for four hours by then. The banker put down his half-eaten sandwich and realized he had seen the same syndrome among some of the younger secretaries just before going-home time on a Friday evening.

It was happiness. Edith Hardenberg was actually happy. It showed, he realized now, in the way she walked, the way she talked and the way she looked. She had been like that all morning—that and the hint of powder. It was enough to trouble Wolfgang Gemütlich deeply. He hoped she had not been spending money.

*   *   *

The snapshots taken by Lt.-Cdr. Darren Cleary came into Riyadh in the afternoon, part of a blizzard of fresh images that poured into CENTAF headquarters every day.

Some of those images were from the KH-11 and KH-12 satellites high above the earth giving the big-dimension picture, the wide angle, the whole of Iraq. If they showed no variation from the previous day, they were stacked.

Others were from the constant photo-recon.

missions at lower level by the TR-1s. Some showed Iraqi activity, military or industrial, which was new—troop movements, warplanes taxi-ing where they had not been before, missile launchers in new locations. These went to Target Analysis.

The ones from the *Ranger*'s Tomcat were of Bomb Damage Assessment. They were filtered through The Barn, the collection of green tents on the edge of the military airbase, then, duly tagged and identified, they went down the road to the Black Hole where they landed in the BDA department.

Colonel Beatty came on duty at seven that evening. He worked for two hours poring over shots of a missile site (partially destroyed, two batteries apparently still intact) and a communications centre (reduced to rubble), plus an array of hardened aircraft shelters that housed Iraqi MiGs, Mirages and Sukhois (shattered).

When he came to the dozen pictures of a factory at Tarmiya he frowned, rose and walked over to a desk manned by a British flight-sergeant of the Royal Air Force.

'Charlie, what are these?'

'Tarmiya, sir. You recall that factory hit by a Strike Eagle yesterday, the one that wasn't on the list?'

'Oh, yeah, the factory that was never even a target?'

'That's the one. A Tomcat from the *Ranger* took these just after ten this morning.'

Colonel Beatty tapped the photos in his hand.

'So what the hell's going on down here?'

'Don't know, sir. That's why I put 'em on your desk. No-one can work it out.'

'Well, that Eagle jockey certainly rattled

489

someone's cage. They're going apeshit here.'

The British NCO and the American colonel stared at the images brought back by the Tomcat from Tarmiya. They were utterly clear, the definition fantastic. Some were from the forward-and-down frame camera in the nose of the TARPS pod showing the ruined factory as the Tomcat approached at 15,000 feet, others from the panoramic camera in the mid-section of the pod. The men at The Barn had extracted the dozen best and clearest.

'How big is this factory?' asked the colonel.

'About a hundred metres by sixty, sir.'

The giant roof had been torn off, only a fragment left covering a quarter of the floor space of the Iraqi plant.

In the three-quarters that had been exposed to view the entire factory lay-out could be observed in a bird's eye view. There were subdivisions caused by party-walls, and in each division a great dark disc occupied most of the floor.

'These metal?'

'Yes, sir, according to the infra-red scanner. Steel of some kind.'

Even more intriguing, and the reason for all the attention by the BDA people, was the Iraqi reaction to Don Walker's raid. Round the roofless factory were grouped not one but five enormous cranes, their booms poised over the interior like storks pecking at a morsel. With all the damage going on in Iraq, cranes this size were at a premium.

Round the factory and inside it a swarm of labourers sweated and toiled to attach the discs to the crane-hooks for removal.

'You counted these guys, Charlie?'

'Over two hundred, sir.'

490

'And these discs'—Colonel Beatty consulted the report of the *Ranger*'s Intel. officer—'these frisbees for giants?'

'No idea, sir. Never seen anything like them.'

'Well, they're sure as hell important to Mr Saddam Hussein. Is Tarmiya really a no-target zone?'

'Well, that's the way it's been listed, colonel. But would you have a look at this?'

The flight-sergeant pulled over another photo he had retrieved from the files. The colonel peered where the NCO pointed.

'Chain-link fencing.'

'Double chain-link. And here?'

Colonel Beatty took the magnifying glass and looked again.

'Mined strip ... Triple-A batteries ... guard towers. Where did you find all these, Charlie?'

'Here. Take a big-picture look.'

Colonel Beatty stared at the fresh picture placed before him, an ultra-high-altitude shot of the whole of Tarmiya and the surrounding area. Then he breathed out in a long exhalation.

'Jesus H. Christ, we're going to have to re-evaluate the whole of Tarmiya. How the hell did we miss it?'

The fact was, the whole of the 381-building industrial complex of Tarmiya had been cleared by the first analysts as non-military and non-target for reasons that later became part of the folklore of the human moles who worked in and survived the Black Hole.

They were Americans and British, and they were all NATO men. Their training had been in assessing Soviet targets, and they looked for the Soviet way of doing things.

The clues they looked for were the standard

491

indicators. If the building or complex was military and important, it would be off-limits. It would be guarded from trespassers and protected from attack.

Were there guard towers, chain-link fencing, Triple-A batteries, missiles, mined strips, barracks? Were there signs of heavy trucks going in and out; were there heavy-duty power-lines or a designated generating station inside the enclosure? These signs meant a target. Tarmiya had none of these— apparently.

What the RAF sergeant had done, on a hunch, was to re-examine a very high-angle picture of the entire area. And there it was ... the fence, the batteries, the barracks, the reinforced gates, the missiles, the razor-wire entanglements, the mined strip. But far away.

The Iraqis had simply taken a vast tract of land 100 kilometres by 100 and fenced off the lot. No such land-grab would have been possible in Western or even Eastern Europe.

The industrial complex, of whose 381 buildings seventy later turned out to be dedicated to war production, lay at the centre of the square, widely scattered to avoid bomb damage, but still only 500 acres out of the 10,000 in the protected zone.

'Electrical power-lines? There's nothing here that would power more than a toothbrush.'

'Over here, sir. Forty-five kilometres to the west. The power-lines run in the opposite direction. Fifty quid to a pint of warm beer those power-lines are phoney. The real cable will be buried underground and run from the power station into the heart of Tarmiya. That's a 150-megawatt generating station, sir.'

'Son of a bitch,' breathed the colonel. Then he straightened up and grabbed the sheaf of photographs.

'Good job, Charlie. I'm taking all these in to Buster Glosson. Meanwhile, there's no need to wait around on that roofless factory. It's important to the Iraqis, we blow it away.'

'Yes, sir, I'll put it on the list.'

'Not for three days from now. Tomorrow. What's free?'

The flight-sergeant went to a computer console and tapped out the enquiry.

'Nothing, sir. Booked solid, every unit.'

'Can't we divert a squadron?'

'Not really. Because of the Scud-hunting we have a backlog. Oh, hold on, there's the Forty-Three Hundred down at Diego. They have capacity.'

'OK, give it to the Buffs.'

'If you'll forgive my saying so,' remarked the NCO with that elaborately courteous phrasing that masks a disagreement, 'the Buffs are not exactly precision bombers.'

'Look, Charlie, in twenty-four hours those Iraqis will have cleaned the place out. We have no choice. Give it to the Buffs.'

'Yes, sir.'

*   *   *

Mike Martin was too restless to hole up in the Soviet compound for more than a few days. The Russian steward and his wife were distraught, sleepless at night because of the endless cacophony of falling bombs and rockets, coupled with the roar of Baghdad's limitless but largely ineffective anti-aircraft fire.

They yelled imprecations out of the windows at all

493

Americans and British fliers, but they were also running out of food, and the Russian stomach is a compelling argument. The solution was to send Mahmoud the gardener to do their shopping again.

Martin had been pedalling round the city for three days when he saw the chalk mark. It was on the rear wall of one of the old Khayat houses in Karadit-Mariam and it meant that Jericho had delivered a package to the corresponding dead-letter-box.

Despite the bombing, the natural resilience of ordinary people trying to get on with their lives had begun to assert itself. Without a word being spoken, save in muttered undertones and then only to a family member who would not betray the speaker to the AMAM, the realization had dawned on the working class that the Sons of Dogs and the Sons of Naji seemed to be able to hit what they wanted to hit, and leave the rest alone.

After five days the Presidential Palace was a heap of rubble (Day Two), the Defence Ministry no longer existed, nor did the telephone exchange nor the principal generating station. Even more inconveniently, all nine bridges now decorated the bottom of the Tigris, but an array of small entrepreneurs had established ferry services across the river; some large enough to take lorries and cars, some punts carrying ten passengers and their bicycles, some mere rowing-boats.

Most major buildings remained untouched. The Rashid Hotel in Karch was still stuffed with foreign Press people, even though the Rais was assuredly in his bunker beneath it. Even worse, the headquarters of the AMAM, a collection of linked houses with old frontages and modernized interiors in a blocked-off street near Qasr-el-Abyad in Risafa, was safe.

Beneath two of those houses was the Gymnasium, never mentioned except in whispers, where Omar Khatib the Tormentor extracted his confessions.

Across the river in Mansour, the single big office block forming the headquarters of the Mukhabarat, both Foreign and Counter-Intelligence, was unmarked.

Mike Martin considered the problem of the chalk mark as he cycled back to the Soviet villa. He knew his orders were formal—no approach. Had he been a Chilean diplomat he would have obeyed that instruction and he would have been right. But Moncada had never been trained to lie immobile, if necessary for days, in a single observation post and watch the surrounding countryside until even the birds nested on his hat.

That night, on foot, he recrossed the river into Risafa as the air raids began and made his way to the vegetable market at Kasra. There were figures on the pavements here and there, scurrying towards shelter as if their humble dwellings would ward off a Tomahawk Cruise, and he was merely one of them. More importantly, his gamble regarding the AMAM patrols was paying off: they, too, had no taste for the open streets with the Americans overhead.

He found his lying-up position on the roof of a fruit warehouse, from whose edge he could see the street, the courtyard and the brick in the wall that marked the 'drop'. For eight hours, from 8 p.m. until four in the morning, he lay and watched.

If the drop was staked out, the AMAM would not have used less than twenty men. In all that time there would have been the scuffle of a boot on stone, a cough, a shifting of cramped muscles, a scrape of match, the glow of a cigarette, the guttural order to

495

stub it out; there would have been something. He simply did not believe that Khatib's or Rahmani's people could remain immobile and silent for eight hours.

Just before 4 a.m. the bombing stopped. There were no lights in the market below. He checked again for a camera mounted in a high window, but there were no high windows in the area. At ten past four he slipped off his roof, crossed the alley, a piece of blackness in a dark grey dish-dash moving through blackness, found the brick, removed the message and was gone.

He came over the wall of First Secretary Kulikov's compound just before dawn and was in his shack before anyone stirred.

The message from Jericho was simple. He had heard nothing for nine days. He had seen no chalk marks. Since his last despatch there had been no contact. No fee had arrived in his bank account. Yet his message had been retrieved; he knew this because he had checked. What was wrong?

Martin did not transmit the message to Riyadh. He knew he should not have disobeyed orders, but he believed that he, not Paxman, was the man on the spot and he had the right to make some decisions for himself. His risk that night had been a calculated one; he had been pitting his skills against men he knew to be inferior at the covert game. Had there been one hint the alley was under surveillance, he would have been gone as he had come, and no-one would have seen him.

It was possible Paxman was right and Jericho was compromised. It was also possible Jericho had simply been transmitting what he had heard Saddam Hussein say. The sticking point was the million dollars that the CIA refused to pay. Martin crafted his own reply.

He said that there had been problems caused by the start of the air war, but that nothing was wrong that a little more patience would not sort out. He told Jericho that the last despatch had indeed been collected and transmitted, but that he, Jericho, as a man of the world, would realize that a million dollars was a very large sum and that the information had to be checked out. This would take a little longer. Jericho should keep cool in these troubled times and wait for the next chalk mark to alert him to a resumption of their arrangement.

During the day Martin lodged the message behind the brick in the wall by the stagnant moat of the Old Citadel in Aadhamiya, and in the dusk made his chalk mark on the rusty red surface of the garage door in Mansour.

Twenty-four hours later the chalk mark had been expunged. Each night Martin tuned in to Riyadh, but nothing came. He knew his orders were to escape from Baghdad, and that his controllers were probably waiting for him to cross the border. He decided to wait it out a little longer.

*   *   *

Diego Garcia is not one of the world's most visited places. It happens to be a tiny island, little more than a coral atoll, at the bottom of the Chagos archipelago in the southern Indian Ocean. Once a British territory, it has for years been leased to the USA.

Despite its isolation, during the Gulf War it played host to the hastily assembled 4300th Bomb Wing of the USAF, flying B-52 Stratofortresses.

497

The B-52 was arguably the oldest veteran in the war, having been in service for over thirty years. For many of those it was the backbone of Strategic Air Command, headquartered at Omaha, Nebraska, the great flying mastodon that circled the periphery of the Soviet empire day and night packing thermo-nuclear warheads.

Old it may have been, but it remained a fearsome bomber, and in the Gulf War the updated 'G' version was used to devastating effect on the dug-in troops of Iraq's so-called élite Republican Guard in the deserts of southern Kuwait. If these cream of the Iraqi army came out of their bunkers haggard and with arms raised during the Coalition ground offensive, it was in part because their nerves had been shattered and their morale broken by round-the-clock pounding from B-52s.

There were only eighty of these bombers in the war, but so great is their carrying capacity and so enormous their bomb-load that they dropped 26,000 tons of ordnance, 40 per cent of the entire tonnage dropped in the war.

They are so big that in repose on the ground their wings, supporting eight Pratt and Whitney J-57 engines in four pods of two, droop towards the ground. On take-off with a full load, the wings become airborne first, seeming to lift above the great hull like those of a gull. Only in flight do they stick straight out the side.

One of the reasons they cast such terror into the Republican Guard in the desert was that they fly out of sight and sound, so high their bombs arrive without any warning and are the more frightening for it. But if they are good carpet bombers, pin-point accuracy is not their strong point, as the flight sergeant had tried to point out.

At dawn of 22 January three Buffs lifted off from Diego Garcia and headed towards Saudi Arabia. Each carried its maximum payload, fifty-one 750-pound 'iron' or 'dumb' bombs, prone to fall where they will from 35,000 feet. Twenty-seven bombs were housed internally, the rest on racks under each wing.

The three bombers constituted the usual 'cell' for Buff operations, and their crews had been looking forward to a day fishing, swimming and snorkelling the reef of their tropical hideaway. With resignation they plotted a course for a faraway factory they had never seen and never would.

The B-52 Stratofortress is not called the Buff because it is painted a tan or dun-brown colour, nor because it has any connection with the former regiment drawn from East Kent, England. The word is not even a derivation of the first two syllables of its number—BEE-FIFty-two. It just stands for Big Ugly Fat Fucker.

So the Buffs plodded their way northwards, found Tarmiya, picked up the 'image' of the designated factory and dropped all 153 bombs. Then they went home to the Chagos archipelago.

On the morning of the 23rd, about the time London and Washington began to yell for more pictures of these mysterious 'frisbees', a further BDA mission was assigned, but this time the photo-call was carried out by a recon. Phantom flown by the Alabama Air National Guard out of Sheikh Isa base on Bahrain, known locally as Shakey's Pizza.

In a remarkable break with tradition, the Buffs had actually hit the target. Where the frisbees factory had been was a vast gaping crater. London and Washington had to be satisfied with the dozen pictures they had from Lt.-Cdr. Darren Cleary.

The best analysts in the Black Hole had seen the pictures, shrugged their ignorance and sent them to their superiors in the two capital cities.

*   *   *

Copies went at once to JARIC, the British photo-interpretation centre, and in Washington to ENPIC.

Those passing this drab, square brick-built block on a corner in a seedy and run-down precinct of downtown Washington would be unlikely to guess what goes on inside. The only clue to the National Photographic Interpretation Centre comes from the complex exhaust flues for the air-conditioning inside, which keep at controlled temperatures an awesome battery of the most powerful computers in America.

For the rest, the dust and rain-streaked windows, the unimposing door and the trash blowing down the street outside, might suggest a not very prosperous warehouse.

But it is here that the images taken by those satellites come, it is the analysts who work here who tell the men at the National Reconnaissance Office and the Pentagon and the CIA exactly what it is that all those expensive 'birds' have seen. They are good, those analysts, up-to-the-minute in their grasp of technology, young, bright and brainy. But they had never seen any discs like those frisbees at Tarmiya. So they filed the photos and said so.

*   *   *

Experts at the Ministry of Defence in London and at the Pentagon in Washington, who knew just about

500

every conventional weapon since the crossbow, examined the pictures, shook their heads and handed them back.

In case they had anything to do with weapons of mass destruction, they were shown to scientists at Porton Down, Harwell and Aldermaston in England, and to others at Sandia, Los Alamos and Lawrence Livermore in America. The result was the same.

The best suggestion was that the discs were part of big electrical transformers destined for a new Iraqi power-generating station. That was the explanation that had to be settled for, when the request for more pictures from Riyadh was answered with the news that the Tarmiya factory had literally ceased to exist.

It was a very good explanation, but it failed to elucidate one problem: why were the Iraqi authorities in the pictures trying so desperately to cover or rescue them?

                    *   *   *

It was not until the evening of the 24th that Simon Paxman, speaking from a phone booth, rang Dr Terry Martin at his flat.

'Care for another Indian meal?' he asked.

'Can't tonight,' said Martin, 'I'm packing.'

He did not mention that Hilary was back and he also wished to spend the evening with his friend.

'Where are you going?' asked Paxman.

'America,' said Martin, 'an invitation to lecture on the Abassid Caliphate. Rather flattering actually. They seem to like my research into the law-structure of the Third Caliph. Sorry.'

'It's just that something else has come through

from the south. Another puzzle that nobody can explain. But it's not about nuances of the Arabic language, it's technical. Still . . .'

'What is it?'

'A photo. I've run off a copy.'

Martin hesitated.

'Another straw in the wind?' he asked. 'All right, same restaurant. At eight.'

'That's probably all it is,' said Paxman, 'just another straw.'

What he did not know was that what he held in his hand in that freezing phone booth was a very large piece of string.

CHAPTER SEVENTEEN

Terry Martin landed at San Francisco International just after 3 p.m. local time the following day, to be met by his host Professor Paul Maslowski, genial and welcoming in the American academic's uniform of tweed jacket and leather patches, and at once felt himself enveloped by the warm embrace of all-American hospitality.

'Betty and I figured a hotel would be kind of impersonal, wondered whether you'd prefer to stay with us?' said Maslowski as he steered his compact out of the airport complex and onto the highway.

'Thank you, that would be wonderful,' said Martin and he meant it.

'The students are really looking forward to hearing you, Terry. There aren't many of us, of course—our Arab faculty must be smaller than yours at SOAS, but they're really enthusiastic.'

'Great. I look forward to meeting them.'

The pair chatted contentedly about their shared passion, medieval Mesopotamia, until they arrived at Professor Maslowski's frame house in a suburban development at Menlo Park.

There he met Paul's wife Betty and was shown to a warm and comfortable guest room. He glanced at his watch: a quarter to five.

'Could I use the phone?' he asked as he came downstairs.

'Absolutely,' said Maslowski, 'you want to phone home?'

'No, locally, do you have a directory?'

The Professor gave him the book and left. It was under Livermore. Lawrence L. National Laboratory, out in Alameda County. He was just in time.

'Could you put me through to Department Z?' he asked when the telephonist answered. He pronounced it 'Zed'.

'Who?' asked the girl.

'Department Zee,' said Martin. 'Director's office.'

'Hold on, please.'

Another female voice came on the line.

'Director's office, can I help you?'

The British accent probably helped. Martin explained he was Dr Martin, an academic over from England on a brief visit, and would be grateful to speak with the Director. A male voice took the phone.

'Dr Martin?'

'Yes.'

'I'm Jim Jacobs, Deputy Director. How can I help you?'

'Look, I know it's terribly short notice. But I am

503

over here on a quick visit to give a lecture to the Near Eastern Studies faculty at Berkeley. Then I have to fly back. Fact is, I was wondering whether I might come out to Livermore to see you.'

The sense of puzzlement came right down the telephone wire.

'Could you give me some indication what it is about, Dr Martin?'

'Well, not easily. I am a member of the British end of the Medusa Committee. Does that ring a bell?'

'Sure does. We're about to close down right now. Would tomorrow suit you?'

'Perfectly. I have to lecture in the afternoon. Would the morning be all right?'

'Say ten o'clock?' asked Dr Jacobs.

The appointment was made. Martin had adroitly avoided mentioning that he was not a nuclear physicist at all, but an Arabist. No need to complicate matters.

*   *   *

That night, across the world in Vienna, Karim took Edith Hardenberg to bed. His seduction was neither hurried nor clumsy, but seemed to follow an evening of concert music and dinner with perfect naturalness. Even as she drove him back from the city centre to her apartment in Grinzing, Edith tried to convince herself it would just be for a coffee and a good night kiss, though deep inside she knew she was pretending.

When he took her in his arms and kissed her gently but persuasively, she just allowed him to; her earlier conviction that she would protest seemed to melt away and she could not prevent it. Nor, deep inside, did she want to any more.

When he swept her up and carried her through to her tiny bedroom, she just turned her face into his shoulder and let it happen. She hardly felt her severe little dress slipping to the floor. His fingers had a deftness that Horst had never possessed, no pushing and shoving and snagging of zips and buttons.

She was still in her slip when he joined her beneath the bettkissen, the big soft Viennese duvet, and the heat from his hard young body was like a great comfort on a bitter winter's night.

She did not know what to do so she closed her eyes tight and let it happen. Strange, awful, sinful sensations began to run through her unaccustomed nerves beneath the attentions of his lips and softly searching fingers. Horst had never been like this.

She began to panic when his lips strayed from her own and from her breasts and went to other places, bad, forbidden places, what her mother had always referred to as 'down there'.

She tried to push him away, protesting feebly, knowing the waves beginning to run through her lower body were not proper and decent, but he was eager as a spaniel puppy on a downed partridge.

He took no notice of her repeated 'nein, Karim, das sollst du nicht' and the waves became a tidal flow and she was a lost rowing boat on a crazy ocean until the last great wave crashed over her and she drowned in a sensation with which she had never once in her thirty-nine years needed to burden the ears of her father confessor at the Votivkirche.

Then she took his head in her arms and pressed his face to her thin little breasts and rocked him in silence.

Twice during the night he made love to her, once

505

just after midnight and again in the blackness before dawn, and each time he was so gentle and strong that her pent-up love came pouring to meet his in a way she had never envisaged could be possible. Only after the second time could she bring herself to run her hands over his body while he slept and wonder at the sheen of the skin and the love that she felt for every inch of it.

*   *   *

Although he had no idea his guest had any interest in the world other than Arab studies, Dr Maslowski insisted that he run Terry Martin out to Livermore in the morning rather than go to the expense of a cab.

'I guess I have a more important guy in my house than I thought I had,' he suggested on the drive. But though Martin expostulated that this was not so, the Californian scholar knew enough about the Lawrence Livermore Laboratory to know that not everyone just blew in there on a phone call. But Dr Maslowski, with masterly discretion, refrained from asking any more questions.

At the main security gate uniformed guards examined Martin's passport, made a phone call and directed them to a car-park.

'I'll wait here,' said Maslowski.

Considering the work it does, the laboratory is an odd-looking collection of buildings on Vasco Road, some modern but many dating back to the days when it was an old military base. To add to the conglomeration of styles, 'temporary' accommodation boxes that have somehow become permanent are slotted between the old barracks. Martin was led to a group of offices on the East

Avenue side of the complex.

It does not look much, but it is out of this cluster of buildings that a group of scientists monitor the spread of nuclear technology across the Third World.

Jim Jacobs turned out to be little older than Terry Martin, just under forty, a PhD and a nuclear physicist. He welcomed Martin into his paper-strewn office.

'Cold morning. Bet you thought California was going to be hot. Everyone does. Not up here, though. Coffee?'

'Love some.'

'Sugar, cream?'

'No, black please.'

Dr Jacobs pressed an intercom button.

'Sandy, could we have two coffees? Mine, you know. And one black.'

He smiled across the desk at his visitor. He did not bother to mention that he had talked with Washington to confirm the English visitor's name and that he really was a member of the Medusa Committee. Someone on the American end of the committee, whom he knew, had checked a list and confirmed the claim. Jacobs was impressed. The visitor might look young, but he must be pretty high-powered over in England. The American knew all about Medusa, because he and his colleagues had been consulted for weeks about Iraq and had handed over everything they had got, every detail of the story of foolishness and neglect on the part of the West that had damn nearly given Saddam Hussein an atomic option.

'So, how can I help?' he asked.

'I know it's a long shot,' said Martin, reaching into his attaché case, 'but I suppose you have seen this

507

already?'

He laid a copy of one of the dozen pictures of the Tarmiya factory on the desk, the one Paxman had disobediently given him. Jacobs glanced at it and nodded.

'Sure, had a dozen of them through from Washington three, four days ago. What can I say? Don't mean a thing. Can't say more to you than I said to Washington. Never seen anything like them.'

Sandy came in with a tray of coffee, a bright blonde California girl full of self-assurance.

'Hi, there,' she said to Martin.

'Oh, er, hallo. Did the Director see these?'

Jacobs frowned. The implication was that he himself might not be senior enough.

'The Director's skiing in Colorado. But I ran them past some of the best brains we have here and, believe me, they are very, very good.'

'Oh, I'm sure,' said Martin. Another blank wall. Well, it had only been a long shot.

Sandy placed the cups of coffee on the desk. Her eye fell on the photograph.

'Oh, them again,' she said.

'Yeah, them again,' said Jacobs and smiled teasingly. 'Dr Martin here thinks maybe someone ... older should have a look at them.'

'Well,' she said, 'show 'em to Daddy Lomax.'

With that she was gone.

'Who's Daddy Lomax?' asked Martin.

'Oh, take no notice. Used to work here. Retired now, lives alone up in the mountains. Pops in now and again for old times' sake. The girls adore him, he brings them mountain flowers. Funny old guy.'

They drank their coffee but there was little more to say. Jacobs had work to do. He apologized once

508

again for not being able to help. Then he showed his visitor out, returned to his sanctum and closed the door.

Martin waited in the corridor a few seconds then put his head round the door.

'Where would I find Daddy Lomax?' he asked Sandy.

'I don't know. Lives way up in the hills. Nobody's ever been there.'

'He has a phone?'

'No, no landlines go up there. I think he has a portable. The insurance company insisted. I mean, he's terribly old.'

Her face was creased with that genuine concern only California youth can show for anyone over sixty. She riffled through an index and came up with a number. Martin noted it, thanked her and left.

*　　*　　*

Ten time zones away it was evening in Baghdad. Mike Martin was on his push-bike, pedalling north-west up Port Said Street. He had just passed the old British Club at what used to be called Southgate, and because he recalled it from his boyhood he turned to stare back at it.

The lack of attention nearly caused an accident. He had reached the edge of Nafura Square and without thinking pedalled forward. There was a big limousine coming from his left and although technically it did not have right of way, its two motor-cycle outriders were clearly not going to stop.

One of them swerved violently to avoid the clumsy fellagha with the vegetable basket attached to his pillion, the motor-bike's front wheel clipping the smaller push-bike and sending it crashing to the tarmac.

Martin went down with his bicycle, sprawling on the road, his vegetables spilling out. The limousine braked, paused and swerved around him before accelerating away.

On his knees, Martin looked up as the car passed. The face of the rear-seat passenger stared out of the window at the oaf who had dared to delay him by a fraction of a second.

It was a cold face in the uniform of a Brigadier-General, thin and acerbic, channels running down either side of the nose to frame the bitter mouth. In that half-second, what Martin noticed were the eyes. Not cold or angry eyes, not blood-shot red or shrewd or even cruel. Blank eyes, utterly and completely blank, the eyes of death long gone. Then the face behind the window had passed by.

He did not need the whisperings of the two working men who pulled him to his feet and helped gather up his vegetables. He had seen the face before, but dimly, blurred, taken on a saluting base, in a photograph on a table in Riyadh weeks before. He had just seen the most feared man in Iraq after the Rais, perhaps including the Rais. It was the one they called Al Mu'azib, the Tormentor, the extractor of confessions, Head of the AMAM, Omar Khatib.

*   *   *

Terry Martin tried the number he had been given during the lunch-hour. There was no reply, just the honeyed tones of the recorded voice advising him: The party you have called is not available or is out of range. Please try your call later.

510

Paul Maslowski had taken Martin to lunch with his faculty colleagues on the campus. The conversation was lively and academic. He tried the number again after lunch on his way to Barrows Hall, guided by N.E. Studies Director Kathlene Keller, but again there was no reply.

The lecture went down well. There were twenty-seven graduates, all heading for their doctorates, and he was impressed at the level and depth of their understanding of the papers he had written on the subject of the Caliphate that ruled central Mesopotamia in what the Europeans called the Middle Ages.

When one of the students had risen to thank him for coming all that way to talk to them, and the rest had applauded, and Terry Martin had gone pink and bobbed his thanks to them, he spotted a phone on the wall in the lobby. This time there was an answer, and a gruff voice said: 'Yeah.'

'Excuse me, is that Dr Lomax?'

'There's only one, friend. That's me.'

'I know this sounds crazy, but I've come from England. I'd like to see you. My name's Terry Martin.'

'England, eh? Long ways away. What would you want with an old coot like me, Mr Martin?'

'Want to tap a long memory. Show you something. People at Livermore say you've been around longer than most, seen just about everything. I want to show you something. Difficult to explain on the phone. Could I come up and see you?'

'It ain't a tax form?'

'No.'

'Or a *Playboy* centrefold?'

''Fraid not.'

511

'Now you got me curious. Do you know the way?'

'No. I have pencil and paper. Can you describe it?'

Daddy Lomax told him how to get to where he lived. It took some time. Martin noted it all down.

'Tomorrow morning,' said the retired physicist, 'too late now, you'll get lost in the dark. And you'll need a four-wheel drive.'

*   *   *

It was one of the only two E-8A J-STARS in the Gulf war that caught the signal that morning of 27 January. The J-STARS were still experimental aircraft and were flying with largely civilian technicians on board when they were rushed in early January from their base at the Grumman Melbourne plant in Florida halfway across the world to Arabia.

That morning, one of the two flying out of Riyadh military airbase was high over the Iraqi border, still inside Saudi airspace, peering with its Norden down-and-sideways radar over a hundred miles into the western desert of Iraq.

The 'plink' was faint, but it indicated metal, moving slowly, far into Iraq, a convoy no longer than two, maybe three trucks. Still, that was what J-STAR was there for, so the mission commander told one of the AWACS circling over the northern end of the Red Sea, giving the AWACS the exact position of the small Iraqi convoy.

Inside the hull of the AWACS the mission commander logged the precise spot and looked around for an airborne element who might be available to give the convoy an unfriendly visit. All the western desert operations were still keyed towards Scud-hunting at that time, apart from the attention being given to the two huge Iraqi airbases called H2 and H3 which were situated in those deserts. The J-STAR might have picked up a mobile Scud-launcher, even though it was unusual in daylight.

The AWACS came up with an element of two F-15E Strike Eagles coming south from Scud-Alley North.

Don Walker was riding south at 20,000 feet after a mission to the outskirts of Al Qaim where he and his wingman Randy Roberts had just destroyed a fixed missile base protecting one of the poison-gas factories targeted for later destruction.

Walker took the call and checked his fuel. It was low. Worse, with his laser-guided bombs gone, his under-wing pylons contained only two Sidewinders and two Sparrows. But these were air-to-air missiles in case they ran into Iraqi jets.

Somewhere south of the border his assigned refuelling tanker was patiently waiting, and he would need every drop to get back to Al Kharz. Still, the convoy location was only 50 miles away and just 15 off his intended track. Even though he had no ordnance left, there was no harm in having a look.

His wingman had heard everything, so Walker gestured through the canopy to the flier half a mile away through the clear air and the two Eagles rolled into a dive to their right.

At 8,000 feet he could see the source of the 'plink' that had showed up on the screen of the J-STAR. It was not a Scud-launcher, but two trucks and two BRDM-2s, Soviet-made light armoured vehicles, on wheels not tracks.

From his perch he could see much more than the J-STAR. Down in a deep wadi beneath him was a single Land-Rover. At 5,000 feet he could see the four British SAS men round it, tiny ants on the brown cloth of the desert. What they could not see were the four Iraqi vehicles forming a horseshoe around them, nor the soldiers pouring down from the tailboards of the two trucks to encircle the wadi.

Don Walker had met the SAS down in Oman. He knew they were operating in the western deserts against Scud-launchers, and several of his squadron had already been in radio contact with these strange-sounding English voices from the ground when the SAS men had tagged a target they could not handle themselves.

At 3,000 feet he could see the four Britishers looking up curiously. So, half a mile away, were the Iraqis. Walker pressed his transmit button.

'Line astern, take the trucks.'

'You got it.'

Though he had neither bombs nor rockets left, tucked in the glove of his right wing, just outside the gaping air intake, was an M-61-A1 Vulcan 20mm cannon, six rotating barrels capable of spewing out its entire magazine of 450 shells with impressive speed. The 20mm cannon shell is the size of a small banana and explodes on impact. For those caught in a truck or running in the open, they can spoil everything.

Walker flicked the 'aim' and 'arm' switches and his Head-Up Display showed him the two armoured cars straight through his screen plus an aiming cross whose position had already taken account of drift and aim-off.

The first BRDM took a hundred cannon shells and blew apart. Raising his nose slightly he put the swimming cross on the plexiglass of the HUD onto the rear of the second vehicle. He saw the gas tank ignite, then he was up and over it, climbing and rolling until the brown desert appeared above his head.

Keeping the roll going, Walker brought the Eagle back down again. The horizon of blue and brown turned back to its usual position with the brown desert at the bottom and the blue sky at the top. Both BRDMs were flaming, one truck was on its side, the other shredded. Small figures ran frantically for the cover of the rocks.

Inside the wadi the four SAS men had got the message. They were aboard and rolling, down the dry water-course and away from the ambush. Just who had 'spotted' them—wandering shepherds probably—and given their position away, they would never know, but they knew who had just saved their backsides.

The Eagles lifted away, waggled their wings, and climbed towards the border and the waiting tanker.

The NCO commanding the SAS patrol was one Sergeant Peter Stephenson. He raised a hand at the departing fighters and said: 'Dunno who you are mate, but I owe you one.'

*　　　*　　　*

As it happened, Mrs Maslowski had a Suzuki jeep as a runabout, and though she had never driven it in four-wheel mode, she insisted Terry Martin borrow it. Though his flight to London was not until five that afternoon, he set off early because he did not know how long he would be. He told her he intended to be back by two at the latest.

Dr Maslowski had to return to the faculty, but

gave Martin a map so that he would not get lost.

The road to the valley of the Mocho River took him right back past Livermore, where he found Mines Road running off Tesla.

Mile by mile the last houses of the suburb of Livermore dropped away and the ground rose. He was lucky in the weather. Winter in these parts is never as cold as it can be elsewhere in the States, but the proximity of the sea gives rise to thick dense clouds and sudden banks of swirling fog. That 27 January the sky was blue and crisp, the air calm and cold.

Through the windscreen he could see the icy tip of Cedar Mountain far away. Ten miles after the turn-off he quit Mines Road and turned on to a track clinging to the side of a precipitous hill.

Down in the valley far below the Mocho glittered in the sun as it tumbled between its rocks.

The grass on either side gave way to a mix of sage-brush and she-oak; high above a pair of kites wheeled against the blue, and the track ran on, along the edge of Cedar Mountain Ridge into the wilderness.

He passed a single green farmhouse, but Lomax had told him to go to the end of the track. After another 3 miles he found the cabin, rough-hewn with raw stone chimney stack and a plume of blue woodsmoke drifting up to the sky.

He stopped in the yard and got out. From a barn a single Jersey cow surveyed him with velvet eyes. Rhythmic sounds came from the other side of the cabin, so he walked round to the front to find Daddy Lomax on a bluff looking out over the valley and the river far below.

He was seventy-five and despite Sandy's concern

516

looked as if he beat up grizzly bears for a hobby. An inch over six feet, in soiled jeans and a plaid shirt, the old scientist was splitting logs with the ease of one slicing bread.

Snow-white hair hung to his shoulders and a stubble of ivory whiskers rimmed his chin. More white curls spilled from the V on his shirt, and he seemed to feel no cold, although Terry Martin was glad of his quilted anorak.

'Found it then? Heard ya coming,' said Lomax and split one last log with a single swing. Then he laid down the axe and came over to his visitor. They shook hands; Lomax gestured to a nearby log and sat on one himself.

'Dr Martin, is it?'

'Er, yes.'

'From England?'

'Yes.'

Lomax reached into his top pocket, withdrew a pouch of tobacco and some rice paper, and began to roll a cigarette.

'Not politically correct, are you?' he asked.

'No, I don't think so.'

Lomax grunted in apparent approval.

'Had a politically correct doctor. Always yellin' at me to stop smoking.'

Martin noted the past tense.

'I suppose you left him?'

'Nope, he left me. Died last week. Fifty-six. Stress. What brings you up here?'

Martin fumbled in his attaché case.

'I ought to apologize at the outset. It's probably a waste of your time and mine. I just wondered if you'd glance at this.'

Lomax took the proffered photograph and stared

517

at it.

'You really from England?'

'Yes.'

'Helluva long way to come to show me this.'

'You recognize it?'

'Ought to. Spent five years of my life working there.'

Martin's mouth dropped open in shock.

'You've actually been there?'

'Lived there for five years.'

'At Tarmiya?'

'Where the hell's that? This is Oak Ridge.'

Martin swallowed several times.

'Dr Lomax. That photograph was taken six days ago by a US Navy fighter over-flying a bombed factory in Iraq.'

Lomax glanced up, bright blue eyes under shaggy white brows, then looked back at the photo.

'Sonofabitch,' he said at last. 'I warned the bastards. Three years ago. Wrote a paper warning that this was the sort of technology the Third World would be likely to use.'

'What happened to it?'

'Oh, they trashed it, I guess.'

'Who?'

'You know, the pointyheads.'

'Those discs, the frisbees inside the factory, you know what they are?'

'Sure. Calutrons. This is a replica of the old Oak Ridge facility.'

'Calu-what?'

Lomax glanced up again.

'You're not a doctor of science? Not a physicist?'

'No. My subject is Arabic studies.'

Lomax grunted again, as if not being a physicist

518

was a hard burden for a man to carry through life.

'Calutrons. Californian cyclotrons. Calutrons, for short.'

'What do they do?'

'EMIS. Electro-magnetic isotope separation. In your language, they refine crude Uranium 238 to filter out the bomb-grade Uranium 235. You say this place is in Iraq?'

'Yes. It was bombed by accident a week ago. This picture was taken the next day. No-one seems to know what it means.'

Lomax gazed across the valley, sucked on his butt and let a plume of azure smoke trickle away.

'Sonofabitch,' he said again. 'Mister, I live up here because I want to. Away from all that smog and traffic—had enough of that years ago. Don't have a TV, but I have a radio. This is about that man Saddam Hussein, ain't it?'

'Yes, it is. Would you tell me about calutrons?'

The old man stubbed out his butt and stared now, not just across the valley but back across many years.

'Nineteen forty-three. Long time ago, eh? Nearly fifty years. Before you were born, before most people were born nowadays. There was a bunch of us then, trying to do the impossible. We were young, eager, ingenious, and we didn't know it was impossible. So we did it.

'There was Fermi from Italy, and Pontecorvo; Fuchs from Germany, Nils Bohr from Denmark, Nunn May from England, and others. And us Yankees: Urey and Oppie and Ernest. I was very junior. Just twenty-seven.

'Most of the time we were feeling our way, doing things that had never been tried, testing out things they said couldn't be done. We had a budget that
519

nowadays wouldn't buy squat, so we worked all day and all night and took short cuts. Had to, the deadline was as tight as the money. And somehow we did it, in three years. We cracked the codes and made the bomb. Little Boy and Fat Man.

'Then the Air Force dropped them on Hiroshima and Nagasaki, and the world said we shouldn't have done it, after all. Trouble was, if we hadn't, somebody else would. Nazi Germany, Stalin's Russia...'

'Calutrons...' suggested Martin.

'Yeah. You've heard of the Manhattan Project?'

'Of course.'

'Well, we had many geniuses in Manhattan, two in particular. Robert J. Oppenheimer and Ernest O. Lawrence. Heard of them?'

'Yes.'

'Thought they were colleagues, partners, right?'

'I suppose so.'

'Wrong. They were rivals. See, we all knew the key was uranium, the world's heaviest element. And we knew by 1941 that only the lighter isotope 235 would create the chain reaction we needed. The trick was to separate the 0.7 per cent of the 235 hiding somewhere in the mass of Uranium 238.

'When America entered the war we got a big gee-up. After years of neglect, the brass wanted results yesterday. Same old story. So we tried every which way to separate those isotopes.

'Oppenheimer went for gas diffusion—reduce the uranium to a fluid and then a gas, Uranium hexafluoride, poisonous and corrosive, difficult to work. The centrifuge came later, invented by an Austrian captured by the Russians and put to work at Sukhumi. Before the centrifuge, gas diffusion was slow and hard.

'Lawrence went for the other route—electromagnetic separation by particle acceleration. Know what that means?'

'I'm afraid not.'

'Basically, you speed the atoms up to a hell of a velocity, then use giant magnets to throw them into a curve. Two racing cars enter a curve at speed, a heavy car and a light car. Which one ends up on the outside track?'

'The heavy one,' said Martin.

'Right. That's the principle. The calutrons depend on giant magnets about twenty feet across. These'—he tapped the frisbees in the photograph—'are the magnets. The lay-out is a replica of my old baby at Oak Ridge, Tennessee.'

'If they worked, why were they discontinued?' asked Martin.

'Speed,' said Lomax. 'Oppenheimer won out. His way was faster. The calutrons were extremely slow and very expensive. After 1945, and even more when that Austrian was released by the Russians and came over here to show us his centrifuge invention, the calutron technology was abandoned. Declassified. You can get all the details, and the plans, from the Library of Congress. That's probably what the Iraqis have done.'

The two men sat in silence for several minutes.

'What you are saying,' suggested Martin, 'is that Iraq decided to use Model-T Ford technology and because everyone assumed they'd go for Grand Prix racers, no-one noticed.'

'You got it, son. People forget, the old Model-T Ford may be old, *but it worked*. It got you there. It carried you from A to B. And it hardly ever broke

521

down.'

'Dr Lomax, the scientists my government and yours have been consulting know that Iraq has got one cascade of gas diffusion centrifuges working, and it has been for the past year. Another one is about to come on stream, but probably not operating yet. On that basis, they calculate Iraq cannot possibly have refined enough pure uranium, say thirty-five kilograms, to have enough for a bomb.'

'Quite right,' nodded Lomax. 'Need five years with one cascade, maybe more. Minimum three years with two cascades.'

'But supposing they've been using calutrons in tandem. If you were Head of Iraq's bomb programme, how would you play it?'

'Not that way,' said the old physicist, and began to roll another cigarette. 'Did they tell you, back in London, that you start with yellowcake, which is called 0 per cent pure, and you have to refine it to 93 per cent pure to get bomb-grade quality?'

Martin thought of Dr Hipwell, with his bonfire of a pipe, in a room under Whitehall saying just that.

'Yes, they did.'

'But they didn't bother to say that purifying the stuff from 0 to 20 takes up most of the time? They didn't say that as the stuff gets purer, the process gets faster?'

'No.'

'Well, it does. If I had calutrons and centrifuges, I wouldn't use them in tandem. I'd use them in sequence. I'd run the base uranium through the calutrons to get it from 0 to 20, maybe 25 per cent pure; then use that as the feedstock for the new cascades.'

'Why?'

'It would cut your refining time in the cascades by a factor of ten.'

Martin thought it over while Daddy Lomax puffed.

'Then when would you calculate Iraq could have those thirty-five kilograms of pure uranium?'

'Depends when they started with the calutrons.'

Martin thought. After the Israeli jets destroyed the Iraqi reactor at Osirak, Baghdad operated two policies: dispersal and duplication, scattering the laboratories all over the country so they could never all be bombed again, and using a cover-all-angles technique in purchasing and experimentation. Osirak was in 1981.

'Say they bought the components on the open market in 1982 and assembled them by 1983.'

Lomax took a stick from the ground near his feet and began to doodle in the dust.

'These guys got any problem with supplies of yellowcake, the basic feedstock?' he asked.

'No, plenty of feedstock.'

'Suppose so,' grunted Lomax, 'buy the damn stuff in K-Mart nowadays.'

After a while he tapped the photo with his stick.

'This photo shows about twenty calutrons. That all they had?'

'Maybe more. We don't know. Let's assume that's all they had working.'

'Since 1983, right?'

'Basic assumption.'

Lomax kept scratching in the dust.

'Mr Hussein got any shortage of electric power?'

Martin thought of the 150-megawatt power station across the sand from Tarmiya, and the suggestion from the Black Hole that the cable ran

523

underground into Tarmiya.

'No, no shortage of power.'

'We did,' said Lomax. 'Calcutrons take an amazing amount of electrical power to function. At Oak Ridge we built the biggest coal-fired power station ever made. Even then we had to tap into the public grid. Each time we turned 'em on, there was a brown-out right across Tennessee—soggy fries and brown light bulbs, we were using so much.'

He went on doodling with his stick, making a calculation then scratching it out and starting another in the same patch of dust.

'They got a shortage of copper wire?'

'No, they could buy that on the open market, too.'

'These giant magnets have to be wrapped in thousands of miles of copper wire,' said Lomax. 'Back in the war we couldn't get any. Needed for war production, every ounce. Know what old Lawrence did?'

'No idea.'

'Borrowed all the silver bars in Fort Knox and melted it into wire. Worked just as well. End of the war, we had to hand it all back to Fort Knox.' He chuckled. 'He was a character.'

Finally he finished and straightened up.

'If they assembled twenty calutrons in 1983 and ran the yellowcake through them till '89 ... and then took 30 per cent pure uranium and fed it into the centrifuge cascade for one year, they'd have their thirty-five keys of 93 per cent bomb-grade uranium ... November.'

'Next November?' said Martin.

Lomax rose, stretched, reached down and pulled his guest to his feet.

'No, son, last November.'

Martin drove back down the mountain and glanced at his watch. Midday. Eight p.m. in London. Paxman would have left his desk and gone home. He did not have his private number.

He could wait twelve hours in San Francisco, or fly. He decided to fly. Martin landed at Heathrow at 11 a.m. on 28 January and was with Paxman at twelve-thirty. By 2 p.m. Steve Laing was talking urgently to Harry Sinclair at the embassy in Grosvenor Square and an hour later the CIA's London Station Head was on a direct and very secure line to the Deputy Director (Operations) Bill Stewart.

*　　　*　　　*

It was not until the morning of 30 January that Bill Stewart was able to produce a full report for the DCI, William Webster.

'It checks out,' he told the former Kansas judge. 'I've had men down at that cabin near Cedar Mountain and the old man, Lomax, confirmed it all. We've traced his original paper—it was filed.

'The records from Oak Ridge confirm these discs are calutrons...'

'How on earth did it happen?' asked the DCI. 'How come we never noticed?'

'Well, the idea probably came from Jaafar Al-Jaafar, the Iraqi boss of their programme. Apart from Harwell in England, he also trained at CERN, outside Geneva. It's a giant particle accelerator.'

'So?'

'Calutrons are particle accelerators. Anyway, all

525

calutron technology was declassified in 1949. It's been available on request ever since.'

'And the calutrons—where were they bought?'

'In bits, mainly from Austria and France. The purchases raised no eyebrows because of the antiquated nature of the technology. The plant was built by Yugoslavs under contract. They said they wanted plans to build on, so the Iraqis simply gave them the plans of Oak Ridge—that's why Tarmiya is a replica.'

'When was all this?' asked the Director.

'Nineteen eighty-two.'

'So what this agent, what's his name...'

'Jericho.'

'What he said was not a lie?'

'Jericho only reported what he claims he heard Saddam Hussein say at a closed conference. I'm afraid we can no longer exclude the conclusion that this time the man was actually telling the truth.'

'And we have kicked Jericho out of play?'

'He was demanding a million dollars for his information. We have never paid that amount, and at the time...'

'For God's sake, Bill, it's cheap at the price.'

The DCI rose and went to the picture windows. The aspens were bare now, not as they had been in August, and in the valley the Potomac swept past on its way to the sea.

'Bill, I want you to get Chip Barber back into Riyadh. See if there is any way of re-establishing contact with this Jericho.'

'There is a conduit, sir. A British agent inside Baghdad. He passes for an Arab. But we suggested the Century people pull him out of there.'

'Just pray they haven't, Bill. We need Jericho back.

Never mind the funds, I'll authorize them. Wherever this device is secreted, we have to find it and bomb it into oblivion before it is too late.'

'Yes. Er ... who is going to tell the generals?'

The Director sighed.

'I'm seeing Colin Powell and Brent Scowcroft in two hours.'

Rather you than me, thought Stewart as he left.

CHAPTER EIGHTEEN

The two men from Century House arrived in Riyadh before Chip Barber from Washington. Steve Laing and Simon Paxman landed before dawn, having taken the night flight from Heathrow.

Julian Gray, the Riyadh Head of Station, met them in his usual unmarked car and brought them to the villa where he had been virtually living, with only occasional visits home to see his wife, for five months.

He was puzzled by the sudden reappearance of Paxman from London, let alone the more senior Steve Laing, to oversee an operation that had effectively been closed down.

In the villa, behind closed doors, Laing told Gray exactly why Jericho had to be traced and brought back into play without delay.

'Jesus, so the bastard's really managed to do it.'

'We have to assume so, even though we have no proof,' said Laing. 'When does Martin have a listening window?'

'Between eleven-fifteen and eleven forty-five tonight,' said Gray. 'For security, we haven't sent him anything for five days. We've been expecting him

527

to reappear over the border any time.'

'Let's hope he's still there. If not, we're in deep shit. We'll have to reinfiltrate him, and that could take for ever. The Iraqi deserts are alive with patrols.'

'How many know about this?' asked Gray.

'As few as possible, and it stays that way,' replied Laing.

A very tight need-to-know group had been established between London and Washington, but for the professionals it was still too big. In Washington there was the President and four members of his Cabinet, plus the Chairman National Security Council and Chairman Joint Chiefs of Staff. Add to that four men at Langley, of whom one, Chip Barber, was heading for Riyadh. The unfortunate Dr Lomax had an unwanted houseguest in his cabin to ensure there was no contact with the outside world.

In London, the news had gone to the new Prime Minister, John Major, the Cabinet Secretary, two members of Cabinet; at Century House three men knew.

In Riyadh there were now three at the SIS villa and Barber on his way to join them. Among the military, the information was confined to four generals, three American and one British.

Dr Terry Martin had developed a diplomatic bout of 'flu and was even then residing comfortably in an SIS safe house in the countryside, looked after by a motherly housekeeper and three not-so-motherly minders.

From henceforth, all operations against Iraq that concerned the search for, and destruction of, the device the Allies assumed to be code-named Qubth-ut-Allah, or the Fist of God, would be undertaken under the cover of active measures designed to terminate Saddam Hussein himself, or for some other plausible reason.

Two such attempts had in fact already taken place. Two targets had been identified at which the Iraqi President might be expected to reside, at least temporarily. No-one could say precisely when, for the Rais moved like a will-'o-the-wisp from hiding to hiding when he was not in the bunker in Baghdad.

Continuous overhead surveillance watched the two locations. One was a villa out in the countryside 40 miles from Baghdad, the other a big mobile home converted into a war caravan and planning centre.

On one occasion the aerial watchers had seen mobile missile batteries and light armour moving into position round the villa. A flight of Strike Eagles went in and blew the villa apart. It was a false alarm, the bird was not on the roost.

On the second occasion, two days before the end of January, the great caravan had been seen to move to a new location. Again an attack went in, again the target was not at home.

On both occasions the fliers took enormous risks in pressing their attacks, for the Iraqi gunners fought back furiously. The failure to terminate the Iraqi dictator on both occasions left the Allies in a quandary. They simply did not know Saddam Hussein's precise movements.

The fact was, no-one knew, outside of a tiny group of personal bodyguards drawn from the Amn-al-Khass commanded by his own son, Kusay.

In reality, he was moving around most of the time. Despite the assumption that Saddam was in his bunker deep underground for the whole of the air war, he was really in residence there for less than half that time.

But his safety was assured by a series of elaborate deceptions and false trails. On several occasions he was 'seen' by his own cheering troops—cynics said they were cheering because they were the ones not at the front being pounded by the Buffs. The man the Iraqi troops saw on all such occasions was one of the doubles, who could pass for Saddam among all but his closest intimates.

At other times convoys of limousines, up to a dozen, swept through the city of Baghdad with blackened windows, giving the citizenry to believe their Rais was inside one of the cars. Not so; these cavalcades were all decoys. When he moved, he sometimes went in a single unmarked car.

Even among his innermost circle, the security measures prevailed. Cabinet members were alerted for a conference with him and given just five minutes to leave their residences, get into their cars, and follow a motor-cycle outrider. Even then, the destination was not the meeting place.

They were driven to a parked coach with black windows, there to find all the other ministers sitting in the dark. There was a screen between the ministers and the driver. Even the driver had to follow a motor-cyclist from the Amn-al-Khass to the eventual destination.

Behind the driver, the ministers, generals and advisers sat in darkness like schoolboys on a mystery tour, never knowing where they were going or, afterwards, where they had been.

In most cases these meetings were held in large and secluded villas, commandeered for the day and vacated before nightfall. A special detail of the Amn-al-Khass had no other job than to find such villas when the Rais wanted a meeting, hold the villa owners incommunicado, and let them return home when the Rais was long gone.

It was small wonder the Allies could not find him. But they tried—until the first week of February. After that, all assassination attempts were called off and the military never understood why.

*   *   *

Chip Barber arrived at the British villa in Riyadh just after midday of the last day of January. After the greetings the four men sat and waited out the hours until they could contact Martin, if he was still there.

'I suppose we have a deadline on this?' asked Laing. Barber nodded.

'February 20. Stormin' Norman wants to march the troops in there on 20 February.'

Paxman whistled.

'Twenty days, hell. Is Uncle Sam going to pick up the tab for this?'

'Yep. The Director has already authorized Jericho's one million dollars to go into his account now, today. For the location of the device, assuming there's one and only one of them, we'll pay the bastard five.'

'Five million dollars?' expostulated Laing. 'Christ, no-one has ever paid anything like that for information.'

Barber shrugged.

'Jericho, whoever he is, ranks as a mercenary. He wants money, nothing else. So let him earn it. There's a catch. Arabs haggle, we don't. Five days after he gets the message, we drop the ante by half a million a day until he comes up with the precise location. He has to know that.'

The three Britishers mulled over the sums that constituted more than the salaries of all of them for a lifetime's work.

'Well,' remarked Laing, 'that should put the breeze up him.'

The message was composed during the late afternoon and evening. First, contact had to be established with Martin, who would have to confirm with pre-agreed code-words that he was still there and a free man.

Then Riyadh would tell him of the offer to Jericho, in detail, and press on him the massive urgency now involved.

The men ate sparingly, toying with food, hard pressed to cope with the tension in the room. At half-past ten Simon Paxman went into the radio shack with the others and spoke the message into the tape-machine. The spoken passage was speeded to two hundred times its real duration and came out at just under two seconds.

At ten seconds after eleven-fifteen the senior radio engineer sent a brief signal—the 'are you there?' message. Three minutes later there was a tiny burst of what sounded like static. The satellite dish caught it, and when it was slowed down the five listening men heard the voice of Mike Martin: 'Black Bear to Rocky Mountain, receiving, over.'

There was an explosion of relief in the Riyadh villa, four mature men pumping each others' backs like schoolboys who have won the inter-house football cup.

Those who have never been there can ill imagine the sensation of learning that 'one of ours' far behind the lines is still, somehow, alive and free.

'Fourteen fucking days he's sat there,' marvelled

Barber, 'why the hell didn't the bastard pull out when he was told?'

'Because he's a stubborn idiot,' muttered Laing. 'Just as well.'

The more dispassionate radio man was sending another brief interrogatory. He wanted five words to confirm, even though the oscillograph told him the voice pattern matched that of Martin, that the SAS major was not speaking under duress. Fourteen days is more than enough to break a man.

His message back to Baghdad was as short as it could be: 'Of Nelson and the North, I say again, of Nelson and the North. Out.'

Another three minutes elapsed. In Baghdad, Martin crouched on the floor of his shack at the bottom of First Secretary Kulikov's garden, caught the brief blip of sound, spoke his reply, pressed the speed-up button and transmitted a tenth-of-a-second burst back to the Saudi capital.

The listeners heard him say: 'Sing the brilliant day's renown.' The radioman grinned.

'That's him, sir. Alive and kicking and free.'

'Is that a poem?' asked Barber.

'The real second, line,' said Laing, 'is: sing the glorious day's renown. If he'd got it right, he'd have been talking with a gun to his temple. In which case . . .' He shrugged.

The radioman sent the final message, the real message, and closed down. Barber reached into his briefcase.

'I know it may not be strictly according to local custom, but diplomatic life has certain privileges.'

'I say,' murmured Gray, 'Dom Perignon. Do you think Langley can afford it?'

'Langley,' said Barber, 'has just put five million

greenbacks on the poker table. I guess it can offer you guys a bottle of fizz.'

'Jolly decent,' said Paxman.

*   *   *

A single week had brought about a transformation in Edith Hardenberg, a week, that is, and the effects of being in love.

With Karim's gentle encouragement she had been to a coiffeur in Grinzing, who had let down her hair, cut and styled it, so that it fell to her chin on both sides of her face, filling out her narrow features and giving her a hint of mature glamour.

Her lover had selected a range of make-up preparations with her shy approval; nothing garish, just a hint of eyeliner, foundation cream, a little powder and a touch of lipstick at the mouth.

At the bank, Wolfgang Gemütlich was privately aghast, secretly watching her cross the room, taller now in one-inch heels. It was not even the heels or the hair or the make-up that distressed him, though he would have flatly banned them all had Frau Gemütlich even mentioned the very idea. What perturbed him was her air, a sense of self-confidence when she presented him with his letters for signing, or took dictation.

He knew, of course, what had happened. One of those foolish girls downstairs had persuaded her to spend money. That was the key to it all, spending money. It always, in his experience, led to ruin and he feared for the worst.

Her natural shyness had not entirely evaporated, and in the bank she was as retiring as ever in speech if not quite in manner, but in Karim's presence, when they were alone, she constantly amazed herself at her boldness. For twenty years things physical had been abhorrent to her, and now she was like a traveller on a voyage of slow and wondering discovery, half-abashed and horrified, half-curious and excited. So their loving, at first wholly one-sided, became more exploratory and mutual. The first time she touched him 'down there' she thought she would die of shock and mortification, but to her surprise she had survived.

On the evening of 3 February he brought home to her flat a box wrapped in gift-paper with a ribbon.

'Karim, you mustn't do things like this. You are spending too much.'

He took her in his arms and stroked her hair. She had learned to love it when he did that.

'Look, little kitten, my father is wealthy. He makes me a generous allowance. Would you prefer me to spend it in night-clubs?'

She liked it also when he teased her. Of course, Karim would never go to one of those terrible places. So she accepted the perfumes and the toiletries that she would once, only two weeks ago, never have touched.

'Can I open it?' she asked.

'That's what it's there for.'

At first she did not understand what they were. The contents of the box seemed to be a froth of silks and lace and colours. When she understood, because she had seen adverts in magazines, not the sort she bought of course, she turned bright pink.

'Karim, I couldn't. I just couldn't.'

'Yes, you could,' he said and grinned. 'Go on, kitten, go into the bedroom and try. Close the door, I won't look.'

She laid the things out on the bed and stared at them. She, Edith Hardenberg? Never. There were stockings and girdles, panties and bras, suspenders and short nighties, in black, pink, scarlet, cream and beige. Things in filmy lace or trimmed with it, silky smooth fabrics over which the fingertips ran as over ice.

She was an hour alone in that room before she opened the door in a housecoat. Karim put down his coffee cup, rose and walked over. He stared down at her with a kind smile and began to undo the sash that held the housecoat together. She blushed red again and could not meet his gaze. She looked away. He let the housecoat fall open.

'Oh, kitten,' he said softly, 'you are sensational.'

She did not know what to say so she just put her arms round his neck, no longer frightened or horrified when her thigh touched the hardness in his jeans.

When they had made love she rose and went to the bathroom. On her return she stood and looked down at him. There was no part of him that she did not love. She sat on the edge of the bed and ran a forefinger down the faint scar along one side of his chin, the one he said he had sustained when falling through a glasshouse at his father's orchard outside Amman.

He opened his eyes, smiled and reached up for her face; she gripped his hand and nuzzled the fingers, stroking the signet ring on the smallest finger, the ring with the pale pink opal that his mother had given him.

'What shall we do tonight?' she asked.

'Let's go out,' he said, 'Sirk's at the Bristol.'

'You like steak too much.'

He reached behind her and held her small buttocks under the filmy gauze.

'That's the steak I like,' he grinned.

'Stop it, you're terrible, Karim,' she said. 'I must get changed.'

She pulled away and caught sight of herself in the mirror. How could she have changed so much? she thought. How could she ever have brought herself to wear lingerie? Then she realized why. For Karim, her Karim whom she loved and who loved her, she would do anything. Love might have come late, but it had come with the force of a mountain torrent.

*   *   *

United States Department of State
Washington, DC 20520

MEMORANDUM FOR: *James Baker, Secretary of State*
FROM: *Political Intelligence and Analysis Group*
SUBJECT: *Assassination of Saddam Hussein*
DATE: *5 February 1991*
CLASSIFICATION: Eyes only

It will certainly not have escaped your attention that since the inception of hostilities between the Coalition Air Forces flying out of Saudi Arabia and neighbouring states, and the Republic of Iraq at least two and possibly more attempts have been made to achieve the demise of the Iraqi President Saddam Hussein.

All such attempts have been by aerial bombardment and exclusively by the United States.

This group therefore considers it urgent to spell out the likely consequences of a successful attempt to assassinate Mr Hussein.

537

The ideal outcome would, of course, be for any successor regime to the present Ba'ath Party dictatorship, set up under the auspices of the victorious Coalition forces, to take the form of a humane and democratic government.

We believe such a hope to be illusory.

In the first place, Iraq is not, nor ever was, a united country. It is barely a generation away from being a patchwork quilt of rival and often warring tribes. It contains in almost equal parts two potentially hostile sects of Islam, the Sunni and Shia faiths, plus three Christian minorities. To these one should add the Kurdish nation in the north, vigorously pursuing its search for separate independence.

In second place, there has never been a shred of democratic experience in Iraq, which has passed from Turkish to Hashemite to Ba'ath *Party rule without the benefit of an intervening interlude of democracy as we understand it.*

In the event therefore of the sudden end of the present dictatorship by assassination, there are only two realistic scenarios.

The first would be an attempt to impose from outside a consensus government embracing all the principal factions along the lines of a broadly-based coalition.

In the view of this group, such a structure would survive in power for an extremely limited period. Traditional and age-old rivalries would need little time literally to pull it apart.

The Kurds would certainly use the opportunity, so long denied, to opt for secession and the establishment of their own republic in the north. A weak central government in Baghdad based upon agreement by consensus would be impotent to

538

prevent such a move.

The Turkish reaction would be predictable and furious, since their own Kurdish minority along the border areas would lose no time in joining their fellow Kurds across the border in a much-invigorated resistance to Turkish rule.

To the south-east, the Shia majority around Basra and the Shatt-al-Arab *would certainly find good reason to make overtures to* Tehran. *Iran would be sorely tempted to avenge the slaughter of its young people in the recent Iran-Iraq war by entertaining those overtures in the hope of annexing south-eastern Iraq in the face of the helplessness of Baghdad.*

The pro-Western Gulf States and Saudi Arabia would be precipitated into something approaching panic at the thought of Iran reaching to the very border of Kuwait.

Further north, the Arabs of Iranian Arabistan would find common cause with their fellow Arabs across the border in Iraq, a move which would be vigorously repressed by the Ayatollahs in Tehran.

In the rump of Iraq we would almost certainly see the outbreak of inter-tribal fighting to settle old scores and establish supremacy over what was left.

We have all observed with distress the civil war now raging between Serbs and Croats in the former Yugoslavia. So far this fighting has not yet spread to Bosnia, where a third component force in the form of the Bosnian Muslims awaits. When the fighting enters Bosnia, as one day it will, the slaughter will be even more appalling and even more intractable.

None the less, this group believes that the misery of Yugoslavia will pale into insignificance compared to the scenario now painted for an Iraq in full disintegration. In such a case, one can look forward to a major civil war in the rump of the Iraqi heartland, four border wars and the complete destabilization of the Gulf. The refugee problem alone would amount to millions.

The only other viable scenario is for Saddam Hussein to be succeeded by another general or senior member of the Ba'ath *hierarchy. But as all those in the present hierarchy are as blood-stained as their leader, it is hard to see what benefits would accrue from the replacement of one monster by another and possibly much cleverer despot.*

The ideal, though admittedly not perfect, solution must therefore be the retention of the status quo *in Iraq, except that all weapons of mass destruction will have been destroyed and the conventional power so degraded as not to present a threat to any neighbouring state for a minimum of a decade.*

It could well be argued that the continuing human rights abuses of the present Iraqi regime, if it is allowed to survive, will prove most distressing. Beyond any doubt. Yet the West has been required to witness terrible scenes in China, Russia, Vietnam, Tibet, East Timor, Cambodia and many other parts of the world. It is simply not possible for the US to impose humanity on a world-wide scale unless it is prepared to enter into permanent global war.

The least catastrophic outcome of the present war in the Gulf and the eventual invasion of Iraq is therefore the survival in power of Saddam Hussein as sole master of a unified Iraq, albeit militarily emasculated as regards foreign aggression.

For all the stated reasons, this group urges an end to all efforts to assassinate Saddam Hussein or to march to Baghdad and occupy Iraq.

Respectfully submitted,
PIAG

*   *   *

Mike Martin found the chalk mark on 7 February and retrieved the slim sylthane envelope from the dead-letter-box that same evening. Shortly after midnight he set up his satellite dish pointing out of the doorway of his shack and read the spidery Arabic script on the single page of onion-skin paper straight into the tape-machine. After the Arabic, he added his own English translation, and sent the message at 00.16, one minute into his 'window'.

When the 'burst' came through and the satellite caught it in Riyadh, the radioman on duty shouted: 'He's here, Black Bear's coming through.'

The four sleepy men in the adjoining room ran in. The big tape-machine against the wall slowed down and decrypted the message. When the technician punched the playback button the room was filled with the sound of Martin speaking Arabic. Paxman, whose Arabic was best, listened to the halfway point and hissed: 'He's found it, Jericho says he's found it.'

'Quiet, Simon.'

The Arabic stopped and the English text began. When the voice stopped and signed off, Barber smacked one bunched fist into the palm of his other hand in excitement.

'Boy, he's done it. Guys, can you get me a transcript of that, like *now*?'

The technician ran the tape back, put on earphones, addressed his word processor and began to type.

Barber went to a telephone in the living room and

541

called the underground headquarters of CENTAF. There was only one man he needed to talk to.

General Chuck Horner was a man who apparently needed very little sleep. No-one either in the Coalition Command offices beneath the Saudi Defence Ministry or the Air Force headquarters beneath the Saudi AF building on Old Airport Road was getting much sleep during those weeks, but General Horner seemed to get less than most.

Perhaps when his beloved aircrew were aloft and flying deep into enemy territory, he did not feel able to sleep. As the flying was going on twenty-four hours per day, that left little sleeping time.

He had a habit of prowling the offices of the CENTAF complex in the middle of the night, ambling from the analysts of the Black Hole along to the Tactical Air Control Centre. If a telephone rang unattended and he was near it, he would answer it. Several bemused Air Force officers out in the desert, calling up for a clarification or with a query, and expecting a duty major to come on the line, found themselves speaking to the Boss himself.

It was a very democratic habit, but occasionally brought surprises. On one occasion a squadron commander, who will have to remain nameless, called to complain that his pilots were nightly running a gauntlet of Triple-A fire on their way to their targets. Could not the Iraqi gunners be squashed by a visit from the heavy bombers, the Buffs?

General Horner told the lieutenant-colonel that this was not possible, the Buffs were fully tasked. The squadron commander out in the desert protested, but the answer was still the same.

'Well,' said the lieutenant-colonel, 'in that case you

can suck me.'

Very few officers can tell a full general to do that and get away with it. It says much for Chuck Horner's approach to his flying crews that two weeks later the feisty squadron commander got his full colonelcy.

That was where Chip Barber found him that night just before one o'clock, and they met in the general's private office inside the underground complex forty minutes later.

The general read the transcription of the English language text from Riyadh gloomily. Barber had used the word processor to annotate certain parts—it no longer looked like a radio message.

'This another of your deductions from interviewing businessmen in Europe?' he asked mordantly.

'We believe the information to be accurate, General.'

Horner grunted. Like most combat men, he had little time for the covert world, the people referred to as 'spooks'. It was ever thus. The reason is simple.

Combat is dedicated to the pursuit of optimism, cautious optimism perhaps, but nevertheless optimism or no-one would ever take part in it. The covert world is dedicated to the presumption of pessimism. The two philosophies have little in common and even by this stage of the war the US Air Force was becoming increasingly irritated by the CIA's repeated suggestion that they were destroying fewer targets than they claimed.

'And is this supposed target associated with what I think it is?' asked the general.

'We just believe it to be very important, sir.'

'Well, first thing, Mr Barber, we're going to have a

damn good look at it.'

* * *

This time it was a TR-1 out of Taif that did honours. An upgraded version of the old U-2, the TR-1 was being used as a multi-task information gatherer, able to overfly Iraq out of sight and sound, using its technology to probe deep into the defences with radar imaging and listen-in equipment. But it still had its cameras, and was occasionally used not for the broad picture, but for a single 'intimate' mission. The task of photographing a location known only as Al-Qubai was about as intimate as one can get.

There was a second reason for the TR-1; it can transmit its pictures in real-time. No waiting for the mission to come back, down-load the TARPS, develop the film, rush it across to Riyadh. As the TR-1 cruised over the designated patch of desert west of Baghdad and south of the Al-Muhammadi airbase, the images it saw came straight to a television screen in the basement of the Saudi Air Force Headquarters.

There were five men in the room, including the technician who operated the console and who could, at a word from the other four, order the computer modem to freeze-frame and run off a photographic print for study.

Chip Barber and Steve Laing were there, tolerated in their civilian dress in this mecca of military prowess; the other two were Colonel Beatty of the USAF and a Squadron Leader Peck of the RAF, both experts in target analysis.

The reason for the words 'Al-Qubai' was simply that this was the nearest village to the target; as it was too small a settlement to show up on their maps, it was the accompanying grid reference and description that mattered to the analysts.

The TR-1 found it a few miles from the grid reference sent by Jericho, but there could be no question that the description was exact, and there were no other locations remotely near that fitted the description.

The four men watched the target swim into vision, freeze on the best frame and hold. The modem punched out a print for study.

'It's under there?' breathed Laing.

'Must be,' said Colonel Beatty, 'there's nothing else like it for miles around.'

'Cunning buggers,' said Peck.

Al-Qubai was in fact the nuclear engineering plant in Dr Jaafar Al-Jaafar's entire Iraqi nuclear programme. A British nuclear engineer once remarked that his craft was '10 per cent genius and 90 per cent plumbing'. There is rather more to it than that.

The engineering plant is where the craftsmen take the product of the physicists, the calculations of the mathematicians and the computers, and the results of the chemists, and assemble the final product. It is the nuclear engineers who actually make the device into a deliverable piece of metal.

Iraq had buried their Al-Qubai plant completely beneath the desert, 80 feet down, and that was just the roof. Beneath the roof, three storeys of workshops ran further downwards. What caused Sqn. Ldr. Peck's 'cunning buggers' remark was the skill with which it had been disguised.

It is not all that difficult to build an entire factory underground, but disguising it presents major

545

problems. Once constructed in its giant crater, the sand may be bulldozed back against the ferro-concrete walls and over the roof until the building is concealed. Soakaways beneath the lowest floor may cope with drainage.

But the factory will need air-conditioning; that requires a fresh-air intake and a foul-air outlet, both stackpipes jutting out of the desert floor.

It will also need masses of electric power, implying a powerful diesel generator. That, too, needs an air intake and exhaust outlet—two more stack pipes.

There must be a down-ramp or passenger lift and cargo hoist for deliveries and departures of personnel and materials, another above-surface structure. The delivery trucks cannot roll on soft sand; they need a hard road, a spur of tarmacadam running from the nearest main road.

There will be heat emissions, concealable during the day when the outside air is hot, but not during the chill nights.

How therefore to disguise from aerial surveillance an area of virgin desert entertaining a tarmac road that seems to run to nowhere, four major stackpipes, an elevator shaft, constant arrival and departure of lorries and a frequent source of heat emissions?

It was Colonel Osman Badri, the young genius of Iraq's military engineering, who cracked it; and his solution fooled the Allies with all their spy-planes.

From the air, Al-Qubai was a 45-acre car-wrecker's yard. Though the watchers in Riyadh, even with their best magnifiers, could not see it, four of the heaps of rusting car-wrecks were welded frames, solid domes of twisted metal beneath which the pipes from below sucked in fresh air or filtered out the foul gases through the broken bodies of cars and vans.

546

The main shed, the cutting shop, with steel tanks of oxygen and acetylene ostentatiously parked outside, hid the entry to the elevator shafts. The naturalness of welding in such a place would justify a heat source.

The single-track tarred road was obvious—trucks needed to arrive with car-wrecks and leave with scrap steel.

The whole system had actually been seen, early on, by AWACS which registered a great mass of metal in the middle of the desert. A tank division? An ammunition dump? An early over-fly established it was just a wrecker's yard, and interest was abandoned.

What the four men in Riyadh could also not see was that four other mini-mountains of rusted car-bodies were also solidly welded frames, internally shaped like domes, but with hydraulic jacks beneath them. Two housed powerful anti-aircraft batteries, multi-barrelled ZSU-23-4 Russian cannon, and the other two concealed SAMs, models 6, 8 and 9, not radar-guided but the smaller heat-seeking type—a radar dish would have given the game away.

'So, it's under there,' breathed Beatty.

Even as they watched, a long truck loaded with old car bodies entered the picture. It seemed to move in little jerks, because the TR-1 flying 80,000 feet above Al-Qubai was running off 'still' frames at the rate of several a second. Fascinated, the two Intelligence officers watched until the lorry reversed into the welding shed.

'Betcha the food, water and supplies are under the car-bodies,' said Beatty. He sat back. 'Trouble is, we'll never get at the damn factory. Not even the Buffs can bomb that deep.'

'We could close them down,' said Peck. 'Crush the

lift shaft, seal 'em in. Then if they try any rescue work to unblock, we shoot them up again.'

'Sounds good,' agreed Beatty. 'How many days till the land invasion?'

'Twelve,' said Barber.

'We can do it,' said Beatty, 'high-level, laser-guided, a mass of planes, a gorilla.'

Laing shot Barber a warning glance.

'We'd prefer something a little more discreet,' said the CIA man. 'A two-ship raid, low-level, eyeball confirmation of destruction.'

There was silence.

'You guys trying to tell us something?' asked Beatty. 'Like, Baghdad is not supposed to know we're interested?'

'Could you please do it that way?' urged Laing. 'There don't seem to be any defences. The key here is disguise.'

Beatty sighed. Frigging spooks, he thought, they're trying to protect someone. None of my business.

'What do you think, Joe?' he asked the squadron leader.

'The Tornados could do it,' said Peck. 'With Buccaneers target-marking for them. Six 1,000-pound bombs right through the door of the shed. I'll bet that tin shed is ferro-concrete inside. Should contain the blast nicely.'

Beatty nodded.

'OK, you guys have it. I'll clear it with General Horner. Who do you want to use, Joe?'

'Six-oh-eight squadron at Maharraq. I know the CO, Phil Curzon. Shall I get him over here?'

Wing Commander Philip Curzon commanded twelve of the Royal Air Force's Panavia Tornados of

608th Squadron on the island of Bahrain, where they had arrived two months earlier from their base at Fallingbostel, Germany. Just after noon that day, 8 February, he received an order that brooked no denial to report immediately to the CENTAF headquarters in Riyadh. So great was the urgency that by the time he had acknowledged the message his orderly officer reported that an American Huron from Shakey's Pizza on the other side of the island had landed and was taxi-ing in to pick him up. When he boarded the UC-12B Huron after throwing on a uniform jacket and cap, he discovered the single-engined executive plane was assigned to General Horner himself.

'What the hell is going on?' the wing commander asked himself, and with justification.

At Riyadh military airbase a USAF staff car was waiting to carry him the mile down Old Airport Road to the Black Hole.

The four men who had been in conference to see the TR-1's mission pictures at ten that morning were still there. Only the technician was missing. They needed no more pictures. The ones they had were spread all over the table. Sqn. Ldr. Peck made the introductions.

Steve Laing explained what was needed and Curzon examined the photos.

Philip Curzon was no fool or he would not have been commanding a squadron of Her Majesty's very expensive blowlamps. In the early low-level missions with JP-233 bombs against Iraqi airfields he had lost two aircraft and four good men; two he knew were dead. The other two had just been paraded, battered and dazed, on Iraqi TV, another of Saddam's PR masterpieces.

549

'Why,' he asked quietly, 'not put this target on the Air Tasking Order like all the others? Why the hurry?'

'Let me be perfectly straight with you,' said Laing. 'We now believe this target to house Saddam's principal and perhaps only store of a particularly vicious poison-gas shell. There is evidence that first stocks are about to be moved to the front. Hence the urgency.'

Beatty and Peck perked up. This was the first explanation they had received to explain the spooks' interest in the factory beneath the junk yard.

'But two attack planes?' persisted Curzon. 'Just two? That makes it a very low-priority mission. What am I supposed to tell my aircrew? I'm not going to lie to them, gentlemen, please get that quite straight.'

'There's no need, and I wouldn't tolerate that either,' said Laing. 'Just tell them the truth. That aerial surveillance has indicated movement of trucks to and from the site. The analysts believe them to be military trucks, and have jumped to the conclusion this apparent scrapyard hides an ammunition dump. Principally, inside that big central shed. So that's the target. As for a low-level mission, you can see there are no missiles, no Triple-A.'

'And that's the truth?' asked the wing commander.

'I swear it.'

'Then why, gentlemen, the clear intention that if any of my crews are shot down and interrogated, Baghdad should not learn where the information really came from? You don't believe the military truck story any more than I do.'

Colonel Beatty and Sqn. Ldr. Peck sat back. This man really was squeezing the spooks hard where it hurt most. Good for him.

'Tell him, Chip,' said Laing in resignation.

'OK, Wing Commander, I'll level with you. But this is for your ears only. The rest is absolutely true. We have a defector. In the States. Came over before the war as a post-graduate. Now he's fallen for an American girl and wants to stay. During the interviews with the Immigration people, something came up. A smart interviewer passed him over to us.'

'The CIA?' asked Curzon.

'OK, yes, the CIA. We did a deal with the guy. He gets the Green Card, he helps us. When he was in Iraq, in Army Engineers, he worked on a few secret projects. Now he's spilling all. So now you know. But it's top classification. It doesn't alter the mission, and it isn't lying for you not to tell the aircrew that. Which, incidentally, you may not do.'

'One last question,' said Curzon. 'If the man is safe in the States, why the need to fool Baghdad any more?'

'There are other targets he's spilling for us. It takes time, but we may get twenty fresh targets out of him. We alert Baghdad he's singing like a canary, they move the goodies somewhere else by night. They can add two and two as well, you know.'

Philip Curzon rose and gathered the photos. Each had its exact grid reference on the map stamped down one side.

'All right. Dawn tomorrow. That shed will cease to exist.'

Then he left. On the flight back he mulled over the mission. Something inside him said it stank like an old cod. But the explanations were perfectly feasible, and he had his orders. He would not lie but he had been forbidden to disclose everything. The good side was, the target was based on deception, not protection. His men should get in and out unscathed. He already knew who would lead the attack.

Squadron Leader Lofty Williamson was happily sprawled in a chair in the evening sun when the call came. He was reading the latest edition of *World Air Power Journal*, the combat pilots' bible, and was annoyed to be torn away from a superbly authoritative article on one of the Iraqi fighters he might run into.

The squadron commander was in his office, photos spread out before him. For an hour he briefed his senior flight commander on what was wanted.

'You'll have two Bucks to mark target for you, so you should be able to loft and get the hell out of there before the ungodly know what's hit 'em.'

Williamson found his navigator, the rear-seat man the Americans call the 'wizzo', who nowadays does a lot more than navigate, being in charge of air-electronics and weapons systems. Flight Lieutenant Sid Blair was reputed to be able to find a tin can in the Sahara if it needed bombing.

Between them, with the aid of the OC Ops., they mapped out the mission. The exact location of the scrapyard was found, from its grid reference, on their air maps, which had a 1/50,000 scale, or almost an inch to the mile.

The pilot made plain he wanted to attack from the east at the very moment of the rising of the sun, so that any Iraqi gunners would have the light in their eyes and he, Williamson, would see the target with complete clarity.

Blair insisted he wanted a 'stone bonker', some unmistakable landmark along the run-in track by which he could make last-minute tiny adjustments to his course-to-steer. They found one 12 miles back from the target in an easterly direction, a radio mast exactly 1 mile from the run-in track.

Going in at dawn gave them the vital Time on Target or TOT that they needed. The reason the TOT must be kept to the second is that precision makes the difference between success and failure. If the first pilot is late even by a second, the follow-up pilot could run right into the explosion of his colleague's bombs; worse, the first pilot will have a Tornado coming up his rear end at nearly 10 miles a minute—not a pretty sight. Finally, if the first pilot is too early or the second too late, the gunners will have time to wake up and sight in. So the second fliers go in just as the shrapnel of the first explosions subside.

Williamson brought in his wingman and the second navigator, two young flight lieutenants, Peter Johns and Nicky Tyne. The precise moment the sun should rise over the low hills to the east of the target was agreed at 0708 hours, and the attack heading at 270 degrees, due west.

Two Buccaneers from Number 12 Squadron, also based at Maharraq, had been assigned. Williamson would liaise with their pilots in the morning. The armourers had been instructed to fit three 1,000-pound bombs equipped with PAVEWAY laser-guidance noses to each Tornado. At eight that night the four aircrew ate and went to bed, with a morning call set for 3 a.m.

*   *   *

It was still pitch black when an aircraftman in a truck came to the 608th Squadron sleeping quarters to take the four crew men to the Flight Hut.

If the Americans at Al Kharz were roughing it

under canvas, those based on Bahrain enjoyed the comfort of civilized living. Some were bunking two to a room at the Sheraton Hotel. Others were in brick-built bachelor accommodation nearer the airbase. Food was excellent, drink available and the worst loneliness of the combat life was assuaged by the presence of 300 trainee air hostesses at the nearby training school of Middle East Airways.

The Buccaneers had only been brought out to the Gulf a week earlier, having first been told they were not wanted. Since then they had more than proved their worth. Essentially a submarine-buster, the Bucks were more accustomed to skimming the waters of the North Sea looking for Soviet submersibles, but they did not mind the desert either.

Their speciality is low flying and although thirty-year-old veterans, they had been known, on inter-service war games with the USAF at Miramar, California, to evade the much faster American fighters simply by 'eating dirt'—flying so low as to become impossible to follow through the buttes and mesas of the desert.

The inter-Air Force rivalry will have it that the Americans do not like low-flying, and under 500 feet tend to lower their undercarriages, whereas the Royal Air Force love it and above 100 feet complain of altitude sickness. In fact both can fly low or high, but the Bucks, not supersonic but amazingly manoeuvrable, reckon they can go lower than anyone and survive.

The reason for their appearance in the Gulf was the original losses sustained by the Tornados on their first ultra-low-level missions.

Working alone, the Tornados had to launch their bombs and then follow them all the way to the target,

554

right into the heart of the Triple-A. But when they and the Buccaneers worked together the Tornados' bombs carried the laser-seeking PAVEWAY nose-cone while the Buck bore the laser transmitter, called PAVESPIKE.

Riding above and behind the Tornado, the Buck could 'mark' the target, letting the Tornado release the bomb and then get the hell out without delay.

Moreover, the Buck had the PAVESPIKE mounted in a gyroscopically-stabilized gimbal in its belly, so that it, too, could twist and weave, while keeping the laser beam right on the target until the bomb arrived and hit.

In the Flight Hut Williamson and the two Buck pilots agreed their Initial Point, the start of the bomb-run, at 12 miles east of the target shed and went to change into flying gear. As usual, they had arrived in civilian clothes; the policy on Bahrain was that too much military out on the streets might alarm the locals.

When they were all changed, Williamson as mission commander completed the briefing. It was still two hours to take-off. The thirty-second 'scramble' of Second World War pilots is a long way gone.

There was time for coffee and the next stage of preparations. Each man picked up his handgun, a small Walther PPK which they all loathed, reckoning that if attacked in the desert they might as well throw it at an Iraqi's head and hope to knock him out that way.

They also drew their £1,000 in five gold sovereigns and the 'goolie chit'. This remarkable document was introduced to the Americans in the Gulf, but the British, who have been flying combat in those parts since the 1920s, understood them well.

The 'goolie chit' is a letter in Arabic and six kinds of Bedouin dialect. It says in effect: *'Dear Mr Bedou, the presenter of this letter is a British officer. If you return him to the nearest British patrol, complete with his testicles and preferably where they ought to be and not in his mouth, you will be rewarded with £5,000 in gold.'* Sometimes it works.

The flying uniforms had reflective shoulder patches which could possibly be detected by Allied seekers if a pilot came down in the desert; but no wings above the left breast pocket, just a velcro-ed Union Jack patch.

After coffee came sterilization—not as bad as it sounds. All rings, cigarettes, lighters, letters, family photos were removed, anything that might give an interrogator a 'lever' on the personality of his prisoner. The strip search was carried out by a stunning WAAF—aircrew reckoned this was the best part of the mission, and younger pilots dropped their valuables into the most surprising places to see if Pamela could find them. Fortunately she had once been a nurse and accepted this nonsense with calm good humour.

One hour to take off. Some men ate, some couldn't, some cat-napped, some drank coffee and hoped they would not have to pee halfway through the mission, some brought up.

The bus took the eight men to their aircraft, already buzzing with riggers, fitters and armourers. Each pilot walked around his ship, checking the pre-take-off ritual. Finally they climbed aboard.

The first task was to get settled, fully strapped in and linked to the Have-quick radio so that they could talk. Then the APU—the auxiliary power unit that set all the instruments dancing.

In the rear the Inertial Nav. platform came alive, giving Sid Blair the chance to punch in his planned courses and turns. Williamson started his right engine and the Rolls-Royce RB-199 began to howl softly. Next, the left engine.

Close canopy, taxi to Number One, the holding point. Clearance from the tower, taxi to take-off point. Williamson glanced to his right. Peter Johns' Tornado was beside him and a bit back, beyond him the two Buccaneers. He raised a hand. Three white-gloved hands rose in return.

Foot-brakes on, run up to maximum 'dry' power. The Tornado was trembling gently. Through the throttle gate into afterburn, now she was shuddering against the brakes. A final thumbs-up and three acknowledgements. Brakes off, the surge, the roll, the tarmac flashing by faster and faster and then they were up, four in formation, banking over the dark sea, the lights of Manama dropping behind, setting course for the rendezvous with the tanker, the Victor of 55 Squadron waiting for them somewhere over the Saudi border with Iraq.

Williamson brought the power setting out of afterburn and settled into a climb at 300 knots to 20,000 feet. The two RB-199s are thirsty brutes, and at maximum 'dry' power will consume 140 kgs of fuel a minute—each. But with afterburn engaged, this rises to an awesome 600 kgs a minute, which is why afterburn is used sparingly—for take-off, combat and evasion.

With radar they found the Victor in the darkness, closed behind her and inserted their fuel nozzles into the drogues trailing from the tanker. Already they had used a third of their fuel. When the Tornados were topped up, they eased back for the Bucks to fill up. Then all four turned and dropped away down to the desert.

Williamson levelled his detail at 200 feet, setting a maximum cruise at 480 knots, and thus they sped into Iraq. The navigators took over, setting the first of three different courses, with two turning points, that would bring them to the Initial Point from the east. At altitude, they had glimpsed the rising sun, but back on the desert floor it was still dark.

Williamson was flying with the aid of TIALD, Thermal Imaging and Laser Designator, a device actually made in a converted biscuit factory up a back-street in Edinburgh. TIALD is a combination of a small, hyper-high-definition TV camera linked to an infra-red thermal sensor. Low over the black desert, the pilots could see everything ahead of them, the rocks, the cliffs, the outcrops, the hills, as if they glowed.

Just before the sun-rose they turned at the IP on to the bombing run. Sid Blair saw the radio mast and told his pilot to adjust course by one degree.

Williamson flicked his bomb-release catches to 'slave' mode and glanced at his Head-Up Display which was running off the miles and seconds to release point. He was down to 100 feet, over flat ground and holding steady. Somewhere behind him his wingman was doing the same. Time on Target was exact. He was easing the throttle in and out of afterburn to maintain attack speed of 540 knots.

The sun cleared the hills, the first beams sliced across the plain and there it was at 6 miles. He could see the metal glinting, the mounds of junked cars, the great grey shed in the centre, the double doors pointing towards him.

558

The Bucks were 100 feet above and 1 mile back. The talk-through from the Bucks, which had begun at the IP, continued in his ears. Six miles and closing, 5 miles, some movement in the target area, 4 miles.

'I am marking,' said the first Buck navigator. The laser beam from the Buck was right on the door of the shed. At 3 miles Williamson began his 'loft', easing the nose up, blanking out his vision of the target. No matter, the technology would do the rest. At 300 feet his HUD told him to release. He flicked the bomb switch and all three 1,000-pound bombs flew away from his underside.

Because he was 'lofting' the bombs rose slightly with him, before gravity took over and they began a graceful downward parabola towards the shed.

With his plane one and a half tons lighter, he rose fast to 1,000 feet, then threw on 135 degrees of bank and kept pulling at the control column. The Tornado was diving and turning, back to the earth and back the way it had come. His Buck flashed over him, then pulled away in its turn.

Because he had a TV camera in the belly of his aircraft, the Buccaneer navigator could see the bombs' impact right on the doors of the shed. The entire area in front of the shed dissolved in a sheet of flame and smoke, while a pillar of dust rose from the place where the shed had been. As it began to settle, Peter Johns in the second Tornado was coming in, thirty seconds behind his leader.

The Buck navigator saw more than that. The movements he had seen earlier codified into a pattern. Guns were visible.

'They've got Triple-A,' he shouted. The second Tornado was lofting. The second Buccaneer could see it all. The shed had blown to pieces under the impact of the first three bombs, revealing an inner structure twisted and bent. But there were anti-aircraft cannon blazing among the mounds of wrecked cars.

'Bombs gone,' yelled Johns and hauled his Tornado into a maximum-G turn. His own Buccaneer was also pulling away from the target, but its belly-PAVESPIKE kept the beam on the remains of the shed.

'Impact,' screamed the Buck's navigator.

There was a flicker of fire among the car wrecks. Two shoulder-borne SAMs hared off after the Tornado.

Williamson had levelled from his turning dive, back to 100 feet above the desert but heading the other way, towards the now-risen sun. He heard Peter Johns' voice shout: 'We're hit.'

Behind him Sid Blair was silent. Swearing in his anger, Williamson pulled the Tornado round again, thinking there might be a chance of holding off the Iraqi gunners with his cannon. He was too late.

He heard one of the Bucks say: 'They've got missiles down there,' then he saw Johns' Tornado, climbing, streaming smoke from a blazing engine, heard the twenty-five year old say quite clearly; 'Going down ... ejecting.'

There was nothing more any of them could do. In earlier missions the Bucks used to accompany the Tornados home. By this date it had been agreed the Bucks could go home on their own. In silence the two target markers did what they did best; they got their bellies right on the desert in the morning sun and kept them there.

Lofty Williamson was in a blind rage, convinced he had been lied to. He had not; no-one knew about the

Triple-A and the missiles hidden at Al-Qubai.

High above, a TR-1 sent real-time pictures of the destruction back to Riyadh. An E-3 Sentry had heard all the in-air talk and told Riyadh they had lost a Tornado crew.

Lofty Williamson came home alone, to debrief and vent his anger on the target selectors in Riyadh.

Beneath the CENTAF headquarters on Old Airport Road the delight of Steve Laing and Chip Barber that the Fist of God had been buried in the womb where it was created was marred by the loss of the two young men.

The Buccaneers, barrelling across the table-flat desert of south Iraq on their way to the border, came across a group of Bedouin camels grazing; this gave the pilots a tricky choice, to fly round them or under them.

CHAPTER NINETEEN

Brigadier Hassan Rahmani sat in his private office in the Mukhabarat building in Mansour and contemplated the events of the previous twenty-four hours with near despair.

That the principal military and war-production centres of his country were being systematically torn apart by bombs and rockets did not worry him. These developments, predicted by him weeks before, simply brought closer the pending American invasion and the fall from office of the man of Tikrit.

It was something he had planned for, longed for and confidently expected, unaware that midday of 11 February that it was not going to happen. Rahmani was a highly intelligent man, but he did not have a crystal ball.

What concerned him that morning was his own survival, the odds that he would ever live to see the day of Saddam Hussein's fall.

The bombing at dawn of the previous day of the nuclear engineering plant at Al-Qubai, so cunningly disguised that no-one had ever envisaged its discovery, had shaken the power élite of Baghdad to its roots.

Within minutes of the departure of the two British bombers the surviving gunners had been in contact with Baghdad to report the attack. On hearing of the event, Dr Jaafar Al-Jaafar had personally leapt into his car and driven to the spot to check on his underground staff. The academic was beside himself with rage and by noon had complained bitterly to Hussein Kamil, under whose Ministry of Industry and Military Industrialization the entire nuclear programme reposed.

Here was a programme, the diminutive scientist had reportedly screamed at Saddam's son-in-law, which, out of a total arms expenditure of 50 billion dollars in a decade, had alone consumed 8 billion, and at the very moment of its triumph it was being destroyed. Could the State offer no protection to his people, etc., etc.?

The Iraqi physicist might stand a whisker over 5 foot and be built like a mosquito, but in terms of influence he packed quite a punch, and the word was that he had gone on and on.

A chastened Hussein Kamil had reported to his father-in-law who had also been consumed by a transport of rage. When that happened, all Baghdad trembled for its life.

562

The scientists underground had not only survived but escaped, for the factory included a narrow tunnel leading half a mile under the desert and terminating in a circular shaft with handrails in the wall. The personnel had emerged this way, but it would be impossible to move heavy machinery through the same tunnel and shaft.

The main elevator and cargo hoist was a twisted wreck from the surface downwards to a depth of 20 feet, and restoring it would be a major engineering feat occupying weeks—weeks which Hassan Rahmani suspected Iraq did not have.

Had that been the end of the matter, Rahmani would simply have been relieved, for he had been a deeply worried man since that conference at the palace before the air war began when Saddam had revealed the existence of 'his' device.

What now worried Rahmani was the crazed rage of his Head of State. Deputy President Izzat Ibrahim had called him shortly after noon of the previous day, and the Head of Counter-Intelligence had never known Saddam's closest confidant to be in such a state.

Ibrahim had told him the Rais was beside himself with anger, and when that happened blood usually spilled. Only this could appease the rage of the man from Tikrit. The Deputy President had made plain that it was expected he, Rahmani, would produce results, and fast. What results, precisely, did you have in mind, he had asked Ibrahim. Find out, Ibrahim had yelled at him, how they knew.

Rahmani had been in contact with friends in the Army who had talked to their gunners, and the reports were adamant on one thing. The British raid had involved two airplanes. There had been two

563

more higher up, but it was assumed these were fighters giving cover; certainly they had not dropped any bombs.

From the Army, Rahmani had talked to Air Force Ops. Planning. Their view, and several of their officers were Western-trained, was that no target of great military significance would ever merit only a two-plane strike. No way.

So, reasoned Rahmani, if the British did not think the breaker's yard was a scrap-metal dump, what did they think it was? The answer would probably lie with the two downed British airmen. Personally, he would have loved to conduct the interrogations, convinced that with certain hallucinogenic drugs he could have had them talking within hours, and truthfully.

The Army had confirmed they had caught the pilot and navigator within three hours of the raid, out in the desert, one limping from a broken ankle. Unfortunately a detail from the AMAM had turned up with remarkable speed and taken the fliers with them. No-one argued with the AMAM. So, the two Britishers were now with Omar Khatib, and Allah have mercy on them.

Cheated of his chance to shine by producing the information supplied by the fliers, Rahmani realized he would have to contribute something. The question was—what?

The only thing that would suffice was what the Rais wanted. And what would he want? Why, a conspiracy. Then a conspiracy he would have. The key would be the transmitter.

He reached for his phone and called Major Mohsen Zayeed, the head of his unit's sigint section, the people charged with intercepting radio transmissions. It was time they talked again.

*   *   *

Twenty miles west of Baghdad lies the small town of Abu Ghraib, a most unremarkable place and yet a name known but rarely mentioned throughout Iraq. For in Ghraib stood the great prison, confined almost exclusively to use in the interrogation and confinement of political detainees. As such, it was staffed and run not by the national prison service but by the Secret Police, the AMAM.

At the time Hassan Rahmani was calling his sigint expert, a long black Mercedes approached the double timber doors of the prison. Two guards, recognizing the occupant of the car, hurled themselves at the gates and dragged them open. Just in time; the man in the car could respond with icy brutality to those causing him a momentary delay through slackness on the job.

The car went through, the gates closed. The figure in the back acknowledged the efforts of the guards with neither nod nor gesture. They were irrelevant.

At the steps to the main office building the car stopped, and another guard ran to open the rear-passenger door.

Brigadier Omar Khatib alighted, smart in tailored barathea uniform, and stalked up the steps. Doors were hastily opened for him all the way. A junior officer, an aide, brought his attaché case.

To reach his office, Khatib took the lift to the fifth and top floor, and when he was alone ordered Turkish coffee and began to study his papers, the reports of the day detailing progress in the extractions of needed information from those in the basement.

Behind his façade, Omar Khatib was as worried as his colleague across Baghdad, a man whom he loathed with the same venom as the feeling was returned.

Unlike Rahmani who, with his part-English education, grasp of languages and cosmopolitan airs, was bound to be inherently suspect, Khatib could count on the fundamental advantage of being from Tikrit. So long as he did the job with which he had been tasked by the Rais, and did it well, keeping the confessions of treachery flowing to assuage the unappeasable paranoia, he was safe.

But the last twenty-four hours had been troubling. He, too, had received a telephone call the previous day, but from the son-in-law, Hussein Kamil. Like Ibrahim to Rahmani, Kamil had brought news of the Rais' limitless rage over the bombing of Al-Qubai and was demanding results.

Unlike Rahmani, Khatib had actually got the British fliers in his hands. That was an advantage on the one hand, a snare on the other. The Rais would want to know, and fast, just how the fliers had been briefed before the mission—just how much did the Allies know about Al-Qubai and how did they learn it?

It was up to him, Khatib, to produce that information, and his men had been working on the fliers for fifteen hours, since seven the previous evening when they had arrived at Abu Ghraib. So far the fools had held out.

From the courtyard below his window came the sound of a hiss, a thwack and a low whimper. Khatib's brow furrowed in puzzlement, then cleared as he recalled.

In the inner yard below his window an Iraqi hung by his wrists from a cross-beam, pointed toes just 4 inches above the dust. Near by stood a ewer brimming with brine, once clear, now darkly pink.

Every guard and soldier crossing the yard was under standing orders to pause, take one of the two rattan canes from the jar and administer a single stroke to the back of the hanging man, between the neck and the knees. A corporal under an awning near by kept the tally.

The stupid fellow was a market trader who had been heard to refer to the President as the son of a whore, and was learning, albeit a trifle late, the true measure of respect that citizens should maintain at all times in reference to the Rais.

The intriguing thing was that he was still there. It just showed what stamina some of these working-class people had. The trader had sustained over five hundred strokes already, an impressive record. He would be dead before the thousandth—no-one had ever sustained a thousand—but it was interesting, all the same. The other interesting thing was that the man had been denounced by his ten-year-old son. Omar Khatib sipped his coffee, unscrewed his rolled-gold fountain-pen and bent over his papers.

Half an hour later there was a discreet tap at his door.

'Enter,' he called, and looked up in expectation. He needed good news and only one man could knock without being announced by the junior officer outside.

The man who entered was burly and his own mother would have been hard tested to call him handsome. The face was deeply pitted by boyhood pox and two circular scars gleamed where cysts had

567

been removed. He closed the door and stood, waiting to be addressed.

Though he was only a sergeant, his stained coveralls carried not even that rank, yet he was one of the few men with whom the brigadier felt any fellow feeling. Alone among the staff of the prison, Sergeant Ali was permitted to sit in his presence, when invited.

Khatib gestured the man to a chair and offered him a cigarette. The sergeant lit up and puffed gratefully; his work was onerous and tiring, the cigarette a welcome break. The reason Khatib would tolerate such familiarity from a man of such rank was that he harboured a genuine admiration for Ali.

Khatib held efficiency in high esteem and his trusted sergeant was one who had never failed him. Calm, methodical, a good husband and father, Ali was a true professional.

'Well?' he asked.

'The navigator is close, very close, sir. The pilot . . .' He shrugged. 'An hour or more.'

'Let me remind you, they must both be broken, Ali, nothing held back. And their stories must conform to each other. The Rais himself is counting on us.'

'Perhaps you should come, sir. I think in ten minutes you will have your answer. The navigator first, and when the pilot learns this, he will follow.'

'Very well.'

Khatib rose and the sergeant held the door open for him. Together they descended past the ground floor to the first basement level where the elevator stopped. There was a passage leading to the stairs to the sub-basement. Along the passage were steel doors and behind them, squatting amid their filth, seven American aircrew, four more British, one Italian and

568

a Kuwaiti Skyhawk pilot.

At the next level down were more cells, two occupied. Khatib peered through the judas-hole in the door of the first.

A single unshaded light bulb illuminated the cell, its walls encrusted with hardened excrement and other brown stains of old blood. In the centre, on a plastic office chair, sat a man, quite naked, down whose chest ran slicks of vomit, blood and saliva. The hands were cuffed behind him and a cloth mask with no eye-slits covered his face.

Two AMAM men in coveralls similar to those of Sergeant Ali flanked the man in the chair, their hands caressing yard-long plastic tubes packed with bitumen, which adds weight without reducing flexibility. They were standing back, taking a break. Before their interruption they had, apparently, been concentrating on the shins and kneecaps which were skinned raw and turning blue-yellow.

Khatib nodded and passed to the next door. Through the hole he could see that the second prisoner was not masked. One eye was completely closed, the pulped meat of the brow and cheek knitted together by crusted blood. When he opened his mouth there were gaps where two broken teeth had been and a froth of blood emerged from the mashed lips.

'Tyne,' he whispered, 'Nicholas Tyne. Flight Lieutenant. Five-Oh-One-Oh-Nine-Six-Eight.'

'The navigator,' whispered the sergeant. Khatib whispered back: 'Which of our men is the English-speaker?'

Ali gestured; the one on the left.

'Bring him out.'

Ali entered the cell of the navigator and emerged

with one of the interrogators. Khatib had a conference with the man in Arabic. The man nodded, re-entered the cell and masked the navigator. Only then would Khatib allow both cell doors to be opened.

The English-speaker bent towards Nicky Tyne's head and spoke through the cloth. His English was heavily accented but passable.

'All right, Flight Lieutenant, that is it. For you, it is over. No more punishment.'

The young navigator heard the words. His body seemed to slump in relief.

'But your friend, he is not so lucky. He is dying now. So, we can take him to hospital—clean white sheets, doctors, everything he needs; or we can finish the job. Your choice. When you tell us, we stop and rush him to hospital.'

Khatib nodded down the corridor to Sergeant Ali, who entered the other cell. From the open door came the sounds of the plastic quirt lashing down on a bare chest. Then the pilot began to scream.

'All right, shells,' shouted Nicky Tyne under his cowl, 'stop it, you bastards, it was an ammunition dump, for poison-gas shells...'

The beating ceased. Ali emerged breathing heavily from the pilot's cell.

'You are a genius, sayidi Brigadier.'

Khatib shrugged modestly.

'Never underestimate the sentimentality of the British and the Americans,' he told his pupil. 'Get the translators now, get all the details, every last one. When you have the transcripts, bring them to my office.'

Back in his sanctum, Brigadier Khatib made a personal phone call to Hussein Kamil. An hour later

Kamil called him back. His father-in-law was delighted; a meeting would be summoned, probably that night. Omar Khatib should hold himself available for the summons.

*　　*　　*

That evening Karim was teasing Edith again, gently and without malice, and this time about her job.

'Don't you ever get bored at the bank, darling?'

'No, it's an interesting job. Why do you ask?'

'Oh, I don't know. I just don't understand how you can think it interesting. For me it would be the most boring job in the world.'

'Well, it's not, so there.'

'All right, what's so interesting about it?'

'You know, handling accounts, placing investments, that sort of thing. It's important work.'

'Nonsense, it's about saying Good Morning, Yes sir, No sir, Of course sir, to lots of people running in and out to cash a fifty-schilling cheque. Boring.'

He was lying on his back on her bed. She walked over and lay beside him, pulling one of his arms round her shoulders so that they could cuddle. She loved to cuddle.

'You are crazy sometimes, Karim. But I love you crazy. Winkler Bank isn't an issuing bank, it's a merchant bank.'

'What's the difference?'

'We have no checking accounts, customers with cheque books running in and out. It doesn't work like that.'

'So you have no money without customers.'

'Of course we have money, but in deposit accounts.'

571

'Never had one of those,' admitted Karim. 'Just a small current account. I prefer cash anyway.'

'You can't have cash when you are talking of millions. People would steal it. So you put it in a bank and invest it.'

'You mean old Gemütlich handles millions? Of other people's money?'

'Yes, millions and millions.'

'Schillings or dollars?'

'Dollars, pounds, millions and millions.'

'Well, I wouldn't trust him with *my* money.'

She sat up, genuinely shocked.

'Herr Gemütlich is completely honest. He would never dream of doing that.'

'Maybe not, but somebody else might. Look ... say, I know a man who has an account at Winkler. His name is Schmitt. One day I go in and say: "Good morning, Herr Gemütlich, my name is Schmitt and I have an account here." He looks in his book and he says: "Yes, you do." So I say: "I'd like to withdraw it all." Then, when the real Schmitt turns up, there's nothing left. That's why cash is better for me.'

She laughed at his *naïveté* and pulled him down, nibbling his ear.

'It wouldn't work. Herr Gemütlich would probably know your precious Schmitt. Anyway, he'd have to identify himself.'

'Passports can be forged. Those damned Palestinians do it all the time.'

'And he'd need a signature, of which he would have a specimen copy.'

'So, I'd practise forging Schmitt's signature.'

'Karim, I think you might turn out to be a criminal one day. You're bad.'

They both giggled at the idea.

'Anyway, if you were a foreigner and living abroad, you'd probably have a numbered account. They are completely impregnable.'

He looked down at her from one elbow, brow furrowed.

'What's that?'

'A numbered account?'

'Mmmmmm.'

She explained how they worked.

'That's madness,' he exploded when she had finished. 'Anybody could turn up and claim ownership. If Gemütlich has never even seen the owner...'

'There are identity procedures, idiot. Very complex codes, methods of writing letters, certain ways the signatures have to be placed—all sorts of things to verify that the person is really the account owner. Unless they are all complied with, to the letter, Herr Gemütlich will not co-operate. So impersonation is impossible.'

'He must have a hell of a memory.'

'Oh, you are too stupid for words. It is all written down. Are you taking me out to dinner?'

'Do you deserve it?'

'You know I do.'

'Oh, all right. But I want an hors-d'œuvre.'

She was puzzled.

'All right, order one.'

'I mean you.'

He reached out and grabbed the waist of her skimpy panties, pulling her with a hooked finger back onto the bed. She was giggling with delight. He rolled over on top of her and began to kiss. Suddenly he stopped. She looked alarmed.

'I know what I'd do,' he breathed. 'I'd hire a

573

safe-cracker, break into old Gemütlich's safe and look at the codes. *Then* I could get away with it.'

She laughed in relief that he had not changed his mind about making love.

'Wouldn't work. Mmmmmm. Do that again.'

'Would so.'

'Aaaaaah. Wouldn't.'

'Would. Safes are broken all the time. See it in the papers every day.'

She ran her exploring hand 'down there' and her eyes opened wide.

'Ooooh, is that all for me? You're a lovely, big, strong man, Karim, and I love you. But old Gemütlich, as you call him, is a bit smarter than you...'

A minute later she no longer cared how smart Gemütlich was.

*   *   *

While the Mossad agent made love in Vienna, Mike Martin was setting up his satellite dish as midnight approached and the 11th of the month gave way to the 12th.

Iraq was then just eight days away from the scheduled invasion of 20 February. South of the border the northern slice of the desert of Saudi Arabia bristled with the biggest single concentration of men and arms, guns, tanks and stores crammed into such a relatively small piece of land since the Second World War.

The relentless pounding from the air went on, though most of the targets on General Horner's original list had been visited, sometimes twice or more. Despite the insertion of fresh targets caused by

574

the short-lived Scud-barrage on Israel, the air masterplan was back on track. Every *known* factory for the production of weapons of mass destruction had been pulverized and that included twelve new ones added by information from Jericho.

As a functioning weapon, the Iraqi Air Force had virtually ceased to exist. Rarely had her interceptor fighters, if they chose to tangle with the Eagles, Hornets, Tomcats, Falcons, Phantoms and Jaguars of the Allies, returned to their bases, and by mid-February they were not even bothering to try. Some of the cream of the fighter and fighter-bomber force had deliberately been sent to Iran, where they had at once been impounded. Others still had been destroyed inside their hardened shelters or ripped apart if caught out in the open.

At the highest level, the Allied commanders could not understand why Saddam had chosen to send the cream of his warplanes to his old enemy. The reason was, after a certain date he firmly expected every nation in the region to have no choice but to bow the knee to him; at that point he would recover his war fleet.

There was by then hardly a bridge left intact in the entire country or a functioning power-generating station.

By mid-February an increasing Allied air effort was being directed at the Iraqi army in south Kuwait and over the Kuwait border into Iraq next door.

From the east–west Saudi northern border up to the Baghdad–Basra highway, the Buffs were pounding the artillery, tank, rocket-battery and infantry positions. American A-10 Thunderbolts, nicknamed for their grace in the sky 'the flying warthog', were roaming at will doing what they did best—destroying tanks. Eagles and Tornados were also allocated the task of 'tank-plinking'.

What the Allied generals in Riyadh did not know was that forty major facilities dedicated to weapons of mass destruction still remained hidden beneath the deserts and the mountains, or that the Sixco airbases were still intact.

Since the burial of the Al-Qubai factory the mood was lighter both among the four generals who knew what it had really contained, as it was among the men of the CIA and the SIS stationed in Riyadh.

It was a mood mirrored in the brief message Mike Martin received that night. His controllers in Riyadh began by informing him of the success of the Tornado mission despite the loss of one airplane. The transmission went on to congratulate him for staying in Baghdad after being allowed to leave, and on the entire mission. Finally he was told there was little more to do. Jericho should be sent one final message, to the effect the Allies were grateful, that all his money had been paid, and that contact would be re-established after the war. Then, Martin was told, he really should escape to safety in Saudi Arabia before it became impossible.

Martin closed down his set, packed it away beneath the floor and lay on his bed before sleeping. Interesting, he thought, the armies are not coming to Baghdad. What about Saddam, wasn't that the object of the exercise? Something had changed.

*   *   *

Had he been aware of the conference then taking place in the headquarters of the Mukhabarat not half a mile away, Mike Martin's sleep would not have been so easy.

In matters of technical skill there are four levels—competent, very good, brilliant and 'a natural'. The last category goes beyond mere skill and into an area where all technical knowledge is backed by an innate 'feel', a gut instinct, a sixth sense, an empathy with the subject and the machinery that cannot appear in textbooks.

In matters of radio, Major Mohsen Zayeed was a natural. Quite young, with owlish spectacles that gave him the air of an earnest student, Zayeed lived, ate and breathed the technology of radio. His private quarters were strewn with the latest magazines from the West, and when he came across a new device that might increase the efficiency of his radio-interception department, he asked for it. Because he valued the man, Hassan Rahmani tried to get it for him.

Shortly after midnight the two men sat in Rahmani's office.

'Any progress?' asked Rahmani.

'I think so,' replied Zayeed. 'He's there, all right, no doubt about it. The trouble is, he's using burst transmissions that are almost impossible to capture. They take place so fast. Almost but not quite. With skill and patience, one can occassionally find one, even though the bursts may only be a few seconds long.'

'How close are you?' said Rahmani.

'Well, I've tracked the transmission frequencies to a fairly narrow band in the ultra-high-frequency range, which makes life easier. Several days ago I struck lucky. We were monitoring a narrow band on the off-chance, and he came on air. Listen.'

Zayeed produced a tape-recorder and ran it to 'play'. A jumbled mess of sound filled the office.

577

Rahmani looked perplexed.

'That's it?'

'It's encrypted, of course.'

'Of course,' said Rahmani. 'Can you break it?'

'Almost certainly not. The encryption is by a single silicon chip, patterned with complex microcircuitry.'

'It can't be decoded?' Rahmani was getting lost; Zayeed lived in his own private world and spoke his own private language. He was even then making a great effort to try and speak plainly to his commanding officer.

'It's not a code. To convert that jumble back to the original speech would need an identical silicon chip. The permutations are in the hundreds of millions.'

'Then what's the point?'

'The point, sir, is—I got a bearing on it.'

Hassan Rahmani leant forward in excitement.

'A bearing?'

'My second. And guess what? That message was sent in the middle of the night, thirty hours before the bombing of Al-Qubai. My guess is, the details of the nuclear plant were in it. There's more.'

'Go on.'

'He's here.'

'Here in Baghdad?'

Major Zayeed smiled and shook his head. He had saved his best piece of news till last. He wanted to be appreciated.

'No, sir, he's here in Mansour District. I think he's inside a block two kilometres by two.'

Rahmani thought furiously. This was getting close, amazingly close. The phone rang. He listened for several seconds, then put it down and rose.

'I am summoned. One last thing. How many more intercepts until you can pin it right down? To a block

578

or even a house?'

'With luck, one. I may not catch him the first time, but at the first intercept I think I can find him. I pray he will send a long message, several seconds on air. Then I can give you a square, one hundred metres by one hundred.'

Rahmani was breathing heavily as he descended to the waiting car.

They came to the meeting with the Rais in two blacked-out buses. The seven ministers came in one, the six generals and the three Intelligence chiefs in another. None saw where they were going, and beyond the screen the driver simply followed the motor-cycle.

Only when the bus drew to a halt in a walled courtyard were the nine men in the second bus allowed to emerge. It had been a forty-minute, indirect drive. Rahmani estimated they were in the country about thirty miles from Baghdad. There were no sounds of traffic noise and the stars above showed the dim outline of a large villa with black-screened windows.

Inside the principal sitting room the seven ministers were already waiting. The generals took assigned places and sat in silence. Guards showed Dr Ubaidi of Foreign Intelligence, Rahmani of Counter-Intelligence and Omar Khatib of the Secret Police to three seats facing the single large padded chair reserved for the Rais himself.

The man who had sent for them entered a few minutes later. They all rose and were gestured to sit.

For some it had been over three weeks since they had seen the President. He seemed strained, the bags under the eyes and the jowls more pronounced.

Without preamble Saddam Hussein launched into

579

the business of their meeting. There had been a bombing raid—they all knew about it, even those who before the raid had known nothing of a place called Al-Qubai.

The place was so secret that no more than a dozen men in Iraq knew exactly where it was. Yet it had been bombed. None but the highest in the land and a few dedicated technicians had ever visited the place except blindfolded or in sealed transport, yet it had been bombed.

There was silence in the room, the silence of fear. The generals, Radi of the Infantry, Kadiri of the Tanks, Ridha of the Artillery and Musuli of the Engineers, and the other two, Republican Guard and Chief of Staff, stared fixedly at the carpet ahead of them.

Our comrade, Omar Khatib, had interrogated the two British fliers, intoned the Rais. He would now explain what had happened.

No-one stared at the Rais, but now all eyes went to the rake-thin form of Omar Khatib.

The Tormentor kept his gaze on the mid-section of the Head of State, facing him across the room.

The airmen had talked, he said flatly. They had held nothing back. They had been told by their squadron commander that Allied aircraft had seen trucks, Army trucks, moving into and out of a certain car-breaking yard. From this the Sons of Dogs had gained the impression the yard disguised an ammunition dump, specifically a depository for gas-shells. It was not regarded as high priority and was not thought to have any anti-aircraft defences. So, only two planes had been assigned to the mission with two more above them to mark the target. There had been no protecting aircraft assigned to suppress the Triple-A, because it was not thought there was any. They, the pilot and the navigator, knew nothing more than that.

The Rais nodded at General Farouk Ridha.

'True or false, Rafeek?'

'It is normal, sayidi Rais,' said the man who commanded the artillery and SAM missile sites, 'for them to send in first the missile fighters to hit the defences, then the bombers for the target. They always do that. For a high-priority target, two airplanes only and no support has never happened.'

Saddam mused on the answer, his dark eyes betraying nothing of his thoughts. That was a part of the power he held over these men; they never knew which way he would react.

'Is there any chance, Rafeek Khatib, that these men have hidden things from you, that they know more than they have said?'

'No, Rais, they have been ... persuaded to co-operate completely.'

'Then that is the end of the matter?' asked the Rais quietly. 'The raid was just an unfortunate chance?'

Heads nodded round the room. The scream when it came paralysed them all.

'WRONG! You are all wrong.'

In a second the voice dropped back to a calm whisper, but the fear was instilled. They all knew that the softness of the voice could precede the most terrible of revelations, the most savage of penalties.

'There have been no trucks, no Army trucks. An excuse, given to the pilots in case they were caught. There is something more, is there not?'

Most of them were sweating despite the air-conditioning. It had always been thus, since the dawn of history, when the tyrant of the tribe called in the witch-finder and the tribe sat and trembled lest he should be the one at whom the juju-stick pointed.

'There is a conspiracy,' whispered the Rais. 'There is a traitor. Someone is a traitor, who conspires against me.'

He stayed silent for several minutes, letting them tremble. When he spoke again it was to the three men who faced him across the room.

'Find him. Find him and bring him to me. He shall learn the punishment for such crimes. He and all his family.'

Then he swept from the room followed by his personal bodyguard. The sixteen men left behind did not even look at each other, could not meet another's gaze. There would be a sacrifice. No-one knew who it would be. Each feared for himself, for some chance remark, perhaps not even that.

Fifteen of the men kept distance from the last, the witch-finder, the one they called Al Mu'azib, the Tormentor. He would produce the sacrifice.

Hassan Rahmani, too, kept silent. This was no time to mention radio intercepts. His operations were delicate, subtle, based on detection and real intelligence. The last thing he needed was to find the thumping boots of the AMAM trampling all over his investigations.

In a mood of terror the ministers and generals departed back into the night and to their duties.

*　　*　　*

'He doesn't keep them in his office safe,' said Avi Herzog, alias Karim, to his controller Gidi Barzilai over a late breakfast the next morning.

The meeting was safe, in Barzilai's own apartment.

582

Herzog had not made the phone call, from a public booth, until Edith Hardenberg was safely in the bank. Shortly after, the yarid team had arrived, bracketing their colleague in a 'box', escorting him to the rendezvous to ensure there was no chance he was being followed. Had he grown a 'tail', they would have seen it. It was their speciality.

Gidi Barzilai leant forward across the food-strewn table, eyes alight.

'Well done, boy-chick, so now I know where he doesn't keep the codes. The point is, where?'

'In his desk.'

'The desk? You're mad. Anyone can open a desk.'

'Have you seen it?'

'Gemütlich's desk? No.'

'Apparently it is very big, very ornate and very old. A real antique. Also, it has a compartment, created by the original-cabinet maker. So secret, so hard to find, Gemütlich reckons it is safer than any safe. He believes a burglar might go for the safe, but never think of the desk. Even if a burglar went through the desk, he would never find the compartment.'

'And she doesn't know where it is?'

'Nope. Never seen it opened. He always locks himself in the office when he has to refer to it.'

Barzilai thought it over.

'Cunning bastard. I wouldn't have given him credit for it. You know, he's probably right.'

'Can I break it off now, the affair?'

'No, Avi, not yet. If you're right, you've done brilliantly. But stick around, keep play-acting. If you vanish now, she will think back to your last conversation, put two and two together, have a fit of remorse, whatever. Stay with her, talk but never again about banking.'

583

Barzilai thought over his problem. Not one of his team in Vienna had ever seen the safe, but there was one man who had.

Barzilai sent a heavily coded message to Kobi Dror in Tel Aviv. The Spotter was brought in and sat in a room with an artist.

The Spotter was not multi-talented but he had one skill that was amazing; he had a photographic memory. Over five hours he sat with his eyes closed and cast his mind back to the interview he had had with Gemütlich while posing as a lawyer from New York. His principal task had been to look for alarm catches on windows and doors, for a wall-safe, wires indicating pressure pads—all the tricks for keeping a room secure. These he had noted and reported. The desk had not interested him too much. But, sitting in a room beneath King Saul Boulevard weeks later, he could close his eyes and see it all again.

Line by line he described the desk to the artist. Sometimes the Spotter would look at the drawing, make a correction and resume. The artist worked in Indian ink with a fine pen, and coloured the desk with water-colours. After five hours the artist had a sheet of finest cartridge paper on which was an exact coloured picture of the desk then sitting in the office of Herr Wolfgang Gemütlich at the Winkler Bank in the Ballgasse, Vienna.

The drawing went to Gidi Barzilai in the 'dip', the diplomatic pouch from Tel Aviv to the Israeli Embassy in Austria. He had it within two days.

Before then a check on the list of sayanim across all Europe had revealed the existence of Monsieur Michel Levy, an antiquarian of the Boulevard Raspail in Paris, noted as one of the leading experts on classical furniture on the continent.

It was not until the night of the 14th, the same day Barzilai received his painting in Vienna, that Saddam Hussein reconvened his meeting of ministers, generals and Intelligence chiefs.

Again the meeting was at the behest of AMAM chief Omar Khatib who had passed news of his success via the son-in-law Hussein Kamil, and again it was in a villa by dead of night.

The Rais simply entered the room and gestured to Khatib to report upon his findings.

'What can I say, sayidi Rais?' The Head of the Secret Police raised his hands and let them drop in a gesture of helplessness. It was a masterpiece in the acting of self-deprecation.

'The Rais was, as ever, right and we were all wrong. The bombing of Al-Qubai was indeed no accident. There *was* a traitor and he has been found.'

There was a buzz of sycophantic amazement round the room. The man in the upright padded chair with his back to the windowless wall beamed and held up his hands for such unnecessary applause to cease. It did, but not too quickly.

Was I not right, the smile said, am I not always right?

'How did you discover this, Rafeek?' asked the Rais.

'A combination of good luck and detective work,' admitted Khatib modestly. 'As for the good fortune, this as we know is the gift of Allah, who smiles upon our Rais.'

There was an assenting rumble round the room.

'Two days before the attack by the bombers of the Beni Naji, a traffic control-point was established on a road near by. It was a routine spot-check by my men on movements by possible deserters, contraband goods ... The vehicle numbers were noted.

'Two days ago I checked these and found most of the vehicles were local—vans, trucks. But one was an expensive car, registered here in Baghdad. The owner was traced, a man who might have had reason to visit Al-Qubai. But a telephone call ascertained that he had *not* visited the facility. Why, I wondered, was he in the area, then?'

Hassan Rahmani nodded. That was good detective work, if it was true. Unlike Khatib who usually relied on brute force.

'And why was he there?' asked the Rais.

Khatib paused to let the revelation sink in.

'To note a precise description of the above-ground car-wrecker's yard, to define the distance from the nearest major landmark and the exact compass bearing—everything an air force would need to find it.'

There was a universal exhalation of breath around the room.

'But that came later, sayidi Rais. First I invited the man to join me at AMAM headquarters for a little frank talk.'

Khatib's mind strayed back to the frank conversation in the basement beneath the AMAM headquarters in Saadun, Baghdad, that basement known as the Gymnasium.

Habitually Omar Khatib had his underlings conduct interrogations, contenting himself to decree the level of severity and supervise the outcome. But this had been a matter of such delicacy that he had accomplished the task himself, banning all others beyond the sound-proof door.

586

From the roof of the cell jutted two steel hooks, a yard apart, and from them hung two short chains hooked to a timber bar. The wrists of the suspect he had had lashed to the ends of the bar, so the man hung with arms a yard apart. Because the arms were not vertical, the strain was all the greater.

The feet were 4 inches off the floor, the ankles tied to another yard-long pole. The X-shaped configuration of the prisoner gave access to all parts of the body and because he hung in the centre of the room could be approached from all sides.

Omar Khatib laid the clotted rattan cane on a side table and came round to the front. The manic screaming of the man under the first fifty lashes had ceased, dying to a mumbling burble of pleas. Khatib stared him in the face.

'You are a fool, my friend. You could end all this so easily. You have betrayed the Rais, but he is merciful. All I need is your confession.'

'No, I swear ... wa-Allah-el-Adheem ... by Allah the Great, I have betrayed no-one.'

The man was weeping like a child, tears of agony pouring down his face. He was soft, Khatib noted, this will not take long.

'Yes, you have betrayed. Qubth-ut-Allah, you know what that means?'

'Of course,' whimpered the man.

'And you know where it was stored for safety?'

'Yes.'

Khatib brought his knee hard upwards into the exposed testicles. The man would have liked to double up, but could not. He vomited, the slick running down his bare body to dribble off the end of his penis.

'Yes ... what?'

'Yes, sayidi.'

'Better. And where the Fist of God was hidden, that was not known to our enemies?'

'No, sayidi, it is a secret.'

Khatib's hand flashed out and caught the hanging man across the face.

'Manyouk, filthy manyouk, then how is it that this very morning at dawn the enemy planes bombed it and destroyed our weapon?'

The prisoner opened his eyes wide, his shock overcoming his shame at the insult. Manyouk in Arabic is the man who plays the female role in a homosexual coupling.

'But that is not possible. No-one but a few know about Al-Qubai ...'

'But the enemy knew ... they have destroyed it.'

'Sayidi, I swear, this is impossible. They could never find it. The man who built it, Colonel Badri, disguised it too well ...'

The interrogation had continued for a further half-hour until its inevitable conclusion.

He was interrupted from his reverie by the Rais himself.

'And who is he, our traitor?'

'The engineer, Dr Salah Siddiqui, Rais.'

There was a gasp. The President nodded slowly, as if he had suspected the man all along.

'Might one ask,' said Hassan Rahmani, 'who the wretch was working for?'

Khatib darted a look of venom at Rahmani and took his time.

'This he did not say, sayidi Rais.'

'But he will, he will,' said the President.

'Sayidi Rais,' murmured Khatib, 'I'm afraid I have to report that at this point of his confession the traitor died.'

Rahmani was on his feet, protocol ignored.

'Mr President, I must protest. This shows the most amazing incompetence. The traitor must have had a link-line through to the enemy, some way of sending his messages. Now we may never know.'

Khatib shot him a look of such pure hate that Rahmani, who had read Kipling as a boy in Mr Hartley's school, was reminded of Krait, the dust-snake who hissed: 'Beware, for I am death.'

'What have you to say?' asked the Rais.

Khatib was contrite.

'Sayidi Rais, what can I say? The men who serve under me love you as their own father, nay more. They would die for you. When they heard this traitorous filth pouring out ... there was an excess of zeal.'

Bullshit, thought Rahmani. But the Rais was nodding slowly. It was the sort of language he liked to hear.

'It is understandable,' he said. 'These things happen. And you, Brigadier Rahmani, who criticize your colleague, have you had any success?'

It was noticeable Rahmani was not referred to as Rafeek, Comrade. He would have to be careful, very careful.

'There is a transmitter, Sayidi Rais, in Baghdad.'

He went on to reveal what Major Zayeed had told him. He thought of adding one last phrase: One more transmission, if we can catch it, and I think we will have the sender, but decided it could wait.

'Then, since the traitor is dead,' said the Rais, 'I can reveal to you what I could not say two days ago. The Fist of God is not destroyed, not even buried. Twenty-four hours before the bombing raid I ordered it to be removed to a safer place.'

It took several seconds for the applause to die down as the inner circle expressed their admiration for the sheer genius of the leader.

He told them the device had gone to the Fortress, whose whereabouts did not concern them, and from the Qa'ala it would be launched, to change all history, on the day the first combat boot of an American soldier crossed on to the holy land of Iraq.

CHAPTER TWENTY

The news that the British Tornados had missed their real target at Al-Qubai had badly shaken the man known only as Jericho. It was as much as he could do to force himself to his feet and applaud the Rais with the adoration of all the rest.

In the blacked-out bus with the other generals being transported back into central Baghdad, he had sat in silence at the back, wrapped in his own thoughts.

Inasmuch as the use of the device now hidden elsewhere at a place called Qa'ala, the Fortress, of which he had never heard and whose location he did not know, might cause many, many deaths, he cared not a jot.

It was his own position that absorbed him. For three years he had risked everything—exposure, ruin and a terrible death—to betray his country's regime. The point had not simply been to establish a huge personal fortune abroad; that he could probably have done by extortion and theft right here in Iraq, though there were risks to that as well.

590

The point had been to retire abroad with a new identity and background, provided by his foreign paymasters, secure under their mantle, safe from the vengeful assassin squads. He had seen the fate of those who simply stole and fled; they lived constantly in fear until, one day, the Iraqi avengers caught up.

He, Jericho, wanted both his fortune and security, which was why he had welcomed the transfer of his control from Israel to the Americans. They would look after him, abide by the agreement, create the new identity, allowing him to become another man with another nationality, buy his mansion by the sea in Mexico and live out a life of ease and comfort.

Now things had changed. If he kept silent and the device was used, they would think he had lied. He had not, but they would never, in their rage, believe that. Come hell or high water, the Americans would block his account and it would all have been for nothing. Somehow he had to warn that there had been a mistake. A few more risks and it would all be over— Iraq defeated, the Rais brought down, and he, Jericho, out of there and far away.

In the privacy of his office he wrote his message, as always in Arabic, on the thin paper that took up so little space. He explained the conference of that evening; that when he had sent his last message the device had indeed been at Al-Qubai as he said, but forty-eight hours later when the Tornados struck, it had gone. That this was not his fault.

He went on to say all he knew; that there was a secret place called the Fortress; that it was there, and from Qa'ala would be launched when the first American crossed the border into Iraq.

Shortly after midnight he took an unmarked car and disappeared into the backstreets of Baghdad.

591

No-one queried his right to do so; no-one would dare. He planted the message beneath a flagstone in an old courtyard off Abu Nawas Street, then made the chalk mark behind the Church of St Joseph in the area of the Christians. This time the chalk mark was slightly different. He hoped the unseen man who collected his messages would waste no time.

As it happened Mike Martin left the Soviet villa early on the morning of 15 February. The Russian cook had given him a long list of fresh produce to buy, a list that was going to prove extremely hard to fill. Food was running short. It was not the farmers in the countryside, it was the transportation problems. Most of the bridges were down, and the central Iraqi plain is a land of rivers watering the spread of crops that feed Baghdad. Forced to pay ferry charges across them all, the produce-growers were choosing to stay at home.

Luckily Martin started with the spice market in Shurja Street, then pedalled round the Church of St Joseph to the alley at the back. When he saw the chalk mark he was jolted.

The mark of that particular wall was always supposed to be a figure of eight on its side, with a single short stroke horizontally through the join of the two circles. But he had warned Jericho previously that if there were ever a real emergency, the single stroke should be replaced by two small crosses, one in each circle of the figure eight. Today the crosses were there.

Martin pedalled hard to the courtyard off Abu Nawas Street, waited till the coast was clear, stooped as always to adjust his sandal, slid a hand into the hiding-place and found the slim sylthane envelope. By midday he was back at the villa, explaining to the angry cook that he had done his best but the produce would be later than ever reaching the city. He would have to go back in the afternoon.

When he read Jericho's message it became all too plain why the man was in a panic. Martin composed a despatch of his own, explaining to Riyadh why he now felt he was forced to take matters into his own hands and make his own decision. There was no time left for conferences in Riyadh and a further interchange of messages. The worst part, for him, was Jericho's revelation that Iraqi Counter-Intelligence was aware of an illegal transmitter sending 'burst' signals. He could not know how close they were, but had to assume there could be no further extended exchange of traffic with Riyadh. Therefore he was making the decision himself.

Martin read the Jericho message in Arabic first, then his own translation, into the tape-recorder. He added his own despatch and prepared to send.

He had no transmission 'window' until late in the night—the night was always chosen so that the Kulikov household would be fast asleep. But, like Jericho, he did have an emergency procedure.

It was the transmission of a single long blast of sound, in this case a high-pitched whistle, on a completely different frequency, well outside the usual VHF band.

He checked that the Iraqi chauffeur was with First Secretary Kulikov at the embassy in the city centre, and that the Russian houseman and his wife were at lunch. Then, despite the risk of discovery, he erected the satellite dish near the open doorway and sent the whistle-blast.

In the radio shack made from a former bedroom of the SIS villa in Riyadh a single light flashed on. It was half-past one in the afternoon. The duty radio operator, handling the normal traffic between the villa and Century House in London, dropped what he was doing, yelled through the door for back-up and tuned to 'receive' on Martin's frequency-of-the-day.

The second operator put his head round the door. 'What's up?'

'Get Steve and Simon, Black Bear's coming on, and it's an emergency.'

The man left. Martin gave Riyadh fifteen minutes, then ran his main transmission.

Riyadh was not the only radio mast that caught the burst. Outside Baghdad another satellite dish, sweeping the VHF band relentlessly, caught part of it. The message was so long that, even shortened, it lasted four seconds. The Iraqi listeners caught the last two and got a 'fix'.

As soon as he had 'sent', Martin closed down and packed away his equipment beneath the tiles of his floor. Hardly had he done so than he heard footsteps on the gravel. It was the Russian houseman who, in a fit of generosity, had crossed the yard to offer him a Balkan cigarette. Martin accepted it with much bobbing and bowing, and mutterings of 'Shukran'. The Russian, proud of his good nature, walked back to the house.

Poor bastard, he thought, what a life.

When he was alone again the poor bastard began to write in closely scripted Arabic on the pad of airmail paper he kept under his pallet. While he did so, a radio genius called Major Zayeed pored over a very large-scale map of the city, and particularly of the district of Mansour. When he had finished his calculations, he double-checked them and rang

594

Brigadier Hassan Rahmani at the Mukhabarat headquarters barely five hundred yards from the diamond-shaped lozenge of Mansour that had been traced out in green ink. His appointment was fixed for four o'clock.

*　　*　　*

In Riyadh Chip Barber was stamping round the main sitting room of the villa with a processor print-out in his hand, swearing in a manner he had not done since leaving the Marines thirty years earlier.

'What the hell does he think he's doing?' he demanded of the two British Intelligence officers in the room with him.

'Easy, Chip,' said Laing, 'he's had a hell of a long run. He's under massive strain. The bad guys are closing in. All our tradecraft tells us we should get him out of there—now.'

'Yeah, I know, he's a great guy, but he has no right to do this. We're the people picking up the tab, remember?'

'We do remember,' said Paxman, 'but he's our man and he's miles out in the cold. If he chooses to stay on, it's to finish the job, as much as for you as for us.'

Barber calmed down.

'Three million dollars. How the hell am I to tell Langley he has offered Jericho a further three million greenbacks to get it right this time? That Iraqi asshole should have got it right the first time. For all we know, he could be dealing from the bottom of the deck, just to make more money.'

'Chip,' said Laing, 'we're talking about a nuke here.'

'Maybe,' growled Barber, '*maybe* we're talking about a nuke. *Maybe* Saddam got enough uranium in time, *maybe* he put it all together in time. All we really have are the calculations of some scientists and Saddam's claim, *if* indeed he ever made the claim at all. Dammit, Jericho is a mercenary, could be lying in his teeth. Scientists could be wrong, Saddam lies as he breathes. What have we actually *got* for all this money?'

'You want to take the risk?' asked Laing.

Barber slumped in a chair.

'No,' he said at length, 'no, I don't. OK, I'll clear it with Washington. Then we tell the generals. They have to know this. But I tell you guys one thing; one day I'm going to meet this Jericho, and if he's putting us on I'm going to pull his arms off and beat him to death with the soggy end.'

* * *

At four that afternoon Major Zayeed brought his maps and his calculations to Hassan Rahmani's office. Carefully he explained that he had that day secured his third triangulation and narrowed the area down to the lozenge shown on the map of Mansour. Rahmani gazed at it dubiously.

'It's a hundred yards by a hundred yards,' he said. 'I thought modern technology could get these emission-sources down to a square yard.'

'If I get a long transmission, yes I can,' explained the young major patiently. 'I can get a beam from the intercepting receiver no wider than a yard. Cross that with another intercept from a different point and you get your square yard. But these are terribly short transmissions. They're on the air and off within two

596

seconds. The best I can get is a very narrow cone, its point on the receiver, running out across country and getting wider as it goes. Maybe an angle of one second of one degree on the compass. But a couple of miles away that becomes a hundred yards. Look, it's still a small area.'

Rahmani peered at the map. The marked lozenge had four buildings in it.

'Let's get down there and look at it,' he suggested.

The two men prowled Mansour with the map until they traced the area shown. It was residential and very prosperous. The four residences were all detached, walled, standing in their own grounds. It was getting dark by the time they finished.

'Raid them in the morning,' said Rahmani. 'I'll seal the area with troops, quietly. You know what you're looking for. You go in with your specialists and take all four places apart. You find it, we have the spy.'

'One problem,' said the major. 'See that brass plaque over there? That's a Soviet Embassy residence.'

Rahmani thought it over. He would get no thanks for starting an international incident.

'Do the other three first,' he ordered. 'If you get nothing, I'll clear the Soviet building with the Foreign Ministry.'

While they talked, one of the staff of that Soviet villa was 3 miles away. The gardener Mahmoud Al-Khouri was in the old British cemetery, placing a slim sylthane envelope in a stone jar by a long-untended gravestone. Later he made a chalk mark on the wall of the Union of Journalists building. On a late-night tour of the district, he noticed just before midnight that the chalk mark had been expunged.

*   *   *

That evening there was a conference in Riyadh, a very private conference in a sealed office two floors below the Saudi Defence Ministry building. There were four generals present and two civilians, Barber and Laing. When they had finished speaking the four military men sat in gloomy silence.

'Is this for real?' asked one of the Americans.

'In terms of 100 per cent proof, we don't have that,' said Barber. 'But we think there is a very high likelihood the information is accurate.'

'What makes you so sure?' asked the USAF general.

'As you gentlemen have probably already guessed, we have for some months past had an asset working for us high in the hierarchy in Baghdad.'

There was a series of assenting grunts.

'Didn't figure all that target information was coming from Langley's crystal balls,' said the Air Force general who still resented the CIA doubting his pilots' hit record.

'The point is,' said Laing, 'so far we have never found his information to be anything but bang-on accurate. If he's lying now, it's a hell of a scam. Second point is, can we take that risk?'

There was silence for several minutes.

'There's one thing you guys are overlooking,' said the USAF man, 'delivery.'

'Delivery?' asked Barber.

'Right. Having a weapon is one thing; delivering it right on top of your enemy is another. Look, no-one can believe Saddam is into miniaturization yet. That's hyper-tech. So he can't launch this thing, if he has it, from a tank gun. Or an artillery piece—same

598

calibre. Or a Katyushka-type battery. Or a rocket.'

'Why not a rocket, General?'

'Payload,' said the flier sarcastically. 'Goddam payload. If this is a crude device, we have to be looking at half a ton. A thousand pounds, say. We now know the Al-Abeid and the Al-Tammuz rockets were still only in development when we smashed the facility at Saad-16. The Al-Abbas and the Al-Badr, same thing. Inoperative, either smashed up or a too-small payload.'

'What about the Scud?' asked Laing.

'Same thing,' said the general. 'The long-range so-called Al-Husayn keeps on breaking up on re-entry, and has a payload of 160 kilograms. Even the basic Soviet-supplied Scud has a maximum payload of 600 kilograms. Too small.'

'There's still an aircraft-launched bomb,' pointed out Barber. The Air Force general glowered.

'Gentlemen, I will give you my personal guarantee, here and now. From henceforth not one single Iraqi warplane will reach the border. Most won't even get off the tarmac. Those that do and head south will be shot down halfway to the border. I have enough AWACS, enough fighters; I can guarantee it.'

'And the Fortress?' asked Laing. 'The launch pad?'

'A top-secret hangar, probably underground, a single runway leading from the mouth; housing a Mirage, a MiG, a Sukhoi—tooled up and ready to go. But we'll get it before the border.'

The decision rested with the American general at the head of the table.

'Are you going to find the repository of this device, this so-called Fortress?' he asked quietly.

'Yes, sir. We are trying even now. We figure we may need a few more days,' answered Barber.

'Find it, and we will destroy it.'

'And the invasion in four days, sir?' asked Laing.

'I will let you know.'

*   *   *

That evening it was announced that the ground invasion of Kuwait and Iraq had been postponed and rescheduled for 24 February.

Later, historians gave two alternate reasons for this postponement. One was that the US Marines wanted to alter their main axis of attack a few miles further west and that this would require troop movements, transfer of stores and further preparations. That was true, too.

A reason later advanced in the Press was that two British computer hackers had cut into the Defence Ministry computer and badly dislocated the collation of weather reports for the attack area, causing confusion over the choice of the best day for the attack to begin from the climatic point of view.

In fact the weather was fine and clear between the 20th and the 24th, and deteriorated just as the advance began.

*   *   *

General Norman Schwarzkopf was a big and very strong man, physically, mentally and morally. But he would have been more, or perhaps less, than human if the sheer strain of those last few days had not begun to tell on him.

He had been working up to twenty hours a day for six months without a break. He had not only overseen the biggest and the fastest military build-up in history, a task that alone could have broken a lesser man, but he had coped with the complexities of relationships with the sensitivities of Saudi society, kept the peace when a dozen times internecine feuding could have wrecked the Coalition, and warded off endless well-meant but useless and exhausting interventions from Capitol Hill.

And yet it was not all this that disturbed his much-needed sleep in those last few days. It was the sheer responsibility of being in charge of all those young lives that brought the nightmare.

In the nightmare, there was the Triangle. Always the Triangle. It was a right-angled triangle of land, lying on its side. What would have been the base was the coast line from Khafji down past Jubail to the three linked cities of Dammam, Al Khoba and Dhahran.

The perpendicular line of the triangle was the border running west from the coast, first between Saudi Arabia and Kuwait, then on into the desert to become the Iraqi border.

The hypotenuse was the slanting line linking the last western outpost in the desert to the coast at Dhahran.

Within that triangle almost half a million young men and some women sat and waited for his order. Eighty per cent of them were Americans. In the east were the Saudis, other Arab contingents and the Marines. In the centre, the great American armoured and mechanized infantry units, and among them the British 1st Armoured Division. On the extreme flank, the French.

Once, the nightmare had seen tens of thousands of young men pouring into the breaches for the attack, to be soaked by a rain of poison gas and to die there between the sand walls and the razor wire. Now it was worse.

Only a week earlier, contemplating the triangle on a battle map, an Army Intelligence officer had actually suggested: 'Maybe Saddam intends to pop a nuke in there.' The man thought he was joking.

That night the commanding general tried again to sleep and failed. Always the Triangle. Too many men, too small a space.

*   *   *

At the SIS villa Laing, Paxman and the two radio technicians shared a crate of beer brought covertly from the British Embassy.

They too studied the map, they too saw the Triangle. They too felt the strain. 'One bloody bomb, one fucking small, crude, first-attempt sub-Hiroshima bomb in there, air burst or ground burst...' said Laing.

They did not need to be scientists. The first explosion would kill over 100,000 young soldiers. Within hours the radiation cloud, sucking up billions of tons of active sand from the desert, would begin to drift, covering everything in its path with death.

The ships at sea would have time to batten down, but not the ground troops or the people of the Saudi cities. Eastwards it would drift, widening as it went, over Bahrain and the Allied airfields, poisoning the sea, across to the coast of Iran, there to exterminate one of the categories Saddam Hussein had pronounced to be unworthy of life ... 'Persians, Jews and flies.'

'He can't bloody launch it,' said Paxman. 'He hasn't a rocket or plane that can do it.'

* * *

Far to the north, hidden in the Jebal at Hamreen, deep inside the breech of a gun with a barrel 180 metres long and a range of 1,000 kilometres, the Fist of God lay inert and ready to be called to fly.

* * *

The house in Qadisiyah was only half awake and quite unprepared for the visitors who came at dawn. When the owner had built it, many years before, it had been set in the midst of orchards.

It stood three miles away from the four villas in Mansour that Major Zayeed of the Counter-Intelligence Corps was even then preparing to put under surveillance.

The spread of the south-western suburbs of Baghdad had enveloped the old house and the new Qadisiyah Expressway roared through what had once been fields growing peaches and apricots.

Still, it was a fine house, owned by a prosperous man now long retired, walled within its grounds and still retaining some fruit trees at the bottom of the garden.

There were two truck loads of AMAM soldiers under the command of a major, and they did not stand on ceremony. The lock of the main gate was shot off, the gate kicked open, and the soldiers poured in, smashing the front door and beating the decrepit servant who tried to stop them.

They ran through the house, ripping open cupboards, tearing down hangings, while the terrified old man who owned the house tried to shield and protect his wife.

The soldiers stripped the place almost bare and found nothing. When the old man pleaded with them to say what it was they wanted or sought, the major roughly told him he knew perfectly well, and the search went on.

After the house the soldiers tried the garden. It was at the bottom near the wall that they found the freshly turned earth. Two of them held the old man while the soldiers dug. He protested he did not know why the earth was freshly turned; he had buried nothing. But they found it all the same.

It was in a burlap sack and all could see, when they emptied it out, that it was a radio set. The major knew nothing of radio sets, nor would he have cared, had he known, that the clapped-out Morse-sender model in the burlap bag was a world away from the ultra-modern satellite-based transmitter used by Mike Martin and still beneath the floor of his shack in Secretary Kulikov's garden. For the AMAM major, radios were the tricks of spies and that was all that mattered.

The old man began to wail that he had never seen it before, that someone must have come over the wall in the night to bury it there, but they knocked him down with their rifle butts, and his wife also when she screamed.

The major examined the trophy and even he could see that some hieroglyphics on the containing sack appeared to be characters in Hebrew.

They did not want the house servant or the old woman, just the man. He was over seventy but they carried him out face down, gripped at each ankle and wrist by four soldiers, and threw him in the back of one of the trucks like a sack of figs.

The major was happy. Acting on an anonymous

604

tip, he had done his duty. His superiors would be pleased. This was not a case for the Abu Ghraib prison. He took his prisoner to the AMAM headquarters and the Gymnasium. That, he reasoned, was the only place for Israeli spies.

*　　　*　　　*

That same day, 16 February, Gidi Barzilai was in Paris, showing his painting to Michel Levy. The old antiquarian was delighted to help. Only once had he been asked before, and that was to lend some furniture to a katsa trying to gain entry to a certain house, posing as an antique dealer.

For Michel Levy it was a pleasure, and an excitement, something to enliven the existence of an old man, to be consulted by the Mossad, to be able to help in some way.

'Boulle,' he said.

'I beg your pardon,' said Barzilai, who thought he was being rude.

'Boulle,' repeated the old man. 'Also spelled Buhl. The great French cabinet-maker. His style, you see, definitely. Mind you, this isn't by him. The period is too late for him.'

'Then who is it by?'

Monsieur Levy was over eighty with thin white hair plastered on a wrinkled scalp; but he had pink apple cheeks and bright eyes that sparkled with the pleasure of being alive. He had said kaddish for so many of his own generation.

'Well, Boulle when he died handed over his workshop to his protégé, the German Oeben. He in turn handed the tradition over to another German, Riesener. I would think this is from the Riesener
605

period. Certainly by a pupil, perhaps by the master himself. Are you going to buy it?'

He was teasing, of course. He knew the Mossad did not buy works of art. His eyes danced with merriment.

'Let's just say I am interested in it,' said Barzilai.

Levy was delighted. They were going to get up to their naughty tricks again. He would never know what, but it was fun anyway.

'Do these desks . . .'

'Bureaux,' said Levy, 'it's a bureau.'

'All right, do these bureaux ever have secret compartments in them?'

Better and better, delightful. Oh, the excitement.

'Ah, you mean a cachette. Of course. You know, young man, many years ago when a man could be called out and killed in a duel over a matter of honour, a lady having an affair had to be *very* discreet. No telephones, then, no fax, no videos. All her lover's naughty thoughts had to be put on paper. Then, where should she hide them from her husband?

'Not in a wall-safe, there weren't any. Nor an iron box—her husband would demand the key. So, the society people of those days commissioned pieces of furniture with a cachette. Not all the time, but sometimes. Had to be good workmanship, mind, or it would be too visible.'

'How would one know if a piece one was . . . thinking of buying, had such a cachette.'

Oh, this was wonderful. The man from Mossad was not going to buy a Riesener bureau, he was going to break into one.

'Would you like to see one?' asked Levy.

He made several phone calls and at length they left his shop and took a cab. It was another dealer. Levy

606

had a whispered conversation, the man nodded and left them alone. Levy had said if he could secure a sale, there'd be a small finder's fee, nothing more. The dealer was satisfied; it is often thus in the antique world.

The desk they examined was remarkably like the one in Vienna.

'Now,' said Levy, 'the cachette will not be large, or it would be detectable in the measurements, external as opposed to internal. So it will be slim, vertical or horizontal. Probably no more than two centimetres thick, hiding in a panel that appears to be solid, three centimetres thick, but is in fact two wafers of wood with the cachette between them. The clue is the release knob.'

He took out one of the top drawers.

'Feel in there,' he said.

Barzilai reached in until his fingertips touched the back.

'Feel around.'

'Nothing,' said the katsa.

'That's because there isn't anything,' said Levy. 'Not in this one. But there might be a knob, a catch or a button. A smooth button, you press it; a knob, you turn it; a catch, move it from side to side and see what happens.'

'What should happen?'

'A low click, and a small piece of marketry pops out, spring-loaded. Behind that is the cachette.'

Even the ingenuity of the cabinet-makers of the eighteenth century had its limits. Within an hour M. Levy had taught the katsa the basic ten places to look for the hidden catch that would release the spring to open the compartment.

'Never try to use force to find one,' Levy insisted.

'You won't anyway, with force, and besides it leaves traces on the woodwork.'

He nudged Barzilai and grinned. Barzilai gave the old man a good lunch at the Coupole, then took a taxi back to the airport to return to Vienna.

*   *   *

Early that morning, 16 February, Major Zayeed and his team presented themselves at the first of the three villas that were to be searched. The other two were sealed, with men posted at all the entrances and the bewildered occupants confined inside.

The major was perfectly polite, but his authority brooked no objection. Unlike the AMAM team a mile and a half away in Qadisiya, Zayeed's men were experts, caused very little permanent damage and were the more efficient for it.

Beginning at the floor level, searching for access to a hiding-place beneath the floor tiles, they worked their way steadily through the house, room by room, cupboard by cupboard and cavity by cavity.

The garden was also searched but not a trace was found. Before midday the major was satisfied at last, made his apologies to the occupants and left. Next door, he began to work through the second house.

*   *   *

In the basement beneath the AMAM headquarters in Saadun the old man was on his back, strapped at wrists and waist to a stout wooden table and surrounded by the four experts who would extract his confession. Apart from these, there was a doctor present, and Brigadier Omar Khatib consulting in a

608

corner with Sergeant Ali.

It was the Head of AMAM who decided the menu of afflictions to be undertaken. Sergeant Ali raised an eyebrow; he would, he realized, certainly need his coveralls this day. Omar Khatib nodded curtly and left. He had paperwork to attend to in his upstairs office.

The old man continued to plead that he knew nothing of any transmitter, that he had not been in the garden for days due to the inclement weather ... The interrogators were not interested. They bound both ankles to a broom handle running across the insteps. Two of the four raised the feet to the required position with the soles facing the room, while Ali and his remaining colleague took down from the walls the heavy quirts of electrical flex.

When the bastinado began, the old man screamed as they all did until the voice broke, then fainted. A bucket of icy water from the corner, where a row of them were stacked, brought him round.

Occasionally, through the morning, the men rested, easing the muscles of their arms which had become tired with their endeavours. While they rested, cups of brine were dashed against the pulpy feet. Then, refreshed, they resumed.

Between bouts of fainting the old man continued to protest that he could not even operate a radio transmitter and there must have been some mistake.

By mid-morning the skin and meat of the soles of both feet had been whipped away and the white bones glinted through the blood. Sergeant Ali sighed and nodded that this process should cease. He lit a cigarette and savoured the smoke while his assistant used a short iron bar to crack the leg bones from ankle to knees.

The old man pleaded with the doctor, as one medical practitioner to another, but the AMAM physician stared at the ceiling. He had his orders, which were to keep the prisoner alive and conscious.

*   *   *

Across the city Major Zayeed finished his search of the second villa at four o'clock, just as Gidi Barzilai and Michel Levy were rising from their table in Paris. Again, he had found nothing. Making his courteous apologies to the terrified couple who had watched their home being systematically stripped, he left and with his rummage crew moved on to the third and last villa.

*   *   *

In Saadun, the old man was fainting more frequently and the doctor protested to the interrogators that he needed time to recover. An injection was prepared and pumped into the prisoner's bloodstream. It had an almost immediate effect, bringing him back from his near-coma to wakefulness and rousing the nerves to fresh sensitivity.

When the needles in the brazier glowed red-white they were driven slowly through the shrivelled scrotum and the desiccated testicles within.

Just after six the old man went into a coma again and this time the doctor was too late. He worked furiously, the sweat of fear pouring down his face, but all his stimulants, injected directly into the heart, failed to suffice.

Ali left the room and returned after five minutes with Omar Khatib. The brigadier looked at the body

610

and years of experience told him something for which he needed no medical degree. He turned and his open palm caught the cringing doctor a fearsome crack across the side of the face.

The force of the blow as much as the reputation of the man who administered it sent the doctor crashing to the floor among his syringes and phials.

'Cretin,' hissed Khatib, 'get out of here.'

The doctor gathered his bits into his bag and left on hands and knees. The Tormentor looked at Ali's handiwork. There was the sweet smell in the air both men knew of old, an admixture of sweat, terror, urine, excrement, blood, vomit and a faint aroma of burnt meat.

'He still protested to the end,' said Ali. 'I swear, if he knew something, we'd have had it out of him.'

'Put him in a bag,' snapped Omar Khatib, 'and return him to his wife for burial.'

It was a strong white canvas sack 6 foot long and 2 foot wide, and it was dumped on the doorstep of the house in Qadisiyah at ten that evening. Slowly and with great difficulty, for both were old, the widow and the house servant lifted the bag, brought it inside and laid it on the dining table. The woman took up her station at the end of the table and began to keen her grief.

The bewildered old servant, Talat, went to the telephone, but it had been ripped from the wall and did not work. Taking his mistress's phone book, which he could not read, he went down the road to the house of the pharmacist and asked the neighbour to try to contact the young master—either of the young masters would do.

* * *

At the same hour, as the pharmacist tried to get a call through Iraq's wrecked internal telephone system, and Gidi Barzilai, back in Vienna, composed a fresh cable to Kobi Dror, Major Zayeed was reporting his day's lack of progress to Hassan Rahmani.

'It just wasn't there,' he told the Head of Counter-Intelligence. 'If it had been, we'd have found it. So, it has to be the fourth villa, the home of the diplomat.'

'You're sure you can't be wrong?' asked Rahmani. 'It couldn't be in another house?'

'No, sir. The nearest house to those four is well outside the area indicated by the crossed beams. The source of those burst transmissions was inside that diamond on the map. I'd swear to it.'

Rahmani was hesitant. Diplomats were the very devil to investigate, always prepared to rush to the Foreign Ministry with a complaint. To get inside Comrade Kulikov's residence, he would have to go high, as high as he could.

When the major was gone Rahmani phoned the Foreign Ministry. He was in luck; the Foreign Minister who had been travelling almost constantly for months was in Baghdad. More, he was still at his desk. Rahmani secured his interview for ten the next morning.

*   *   *

The pharmacist was a kindly man, and he just kept trying, all through the night. He never did reach the older son, but using a contact in the Army he managed to get a message through to the younger of his dead friend's two boys. He could not speak to the man himself, but the Army contact passed it on.

It reached the younger son at his base far away

612

from Baghdad at dawn. As soon as he heard it, the officer took his car and began to drive. Normally it would have taken him no more than two hours. That day, 17 February, it took him six. There were patrols and road-blocks. Using his rank, he could drive to the head of the queue, flash his pass and be waved on.

That did not work for the wrecked bridges. At each one he had to wait for the ferry. It was midday when he arrived at his parents' house in Qadisiyah.

His mother ran into his embrace and cried against his shoulder. He tried to extract from her details of precisely what had happened, but she was no longer young herself and was hysterical.

Finally he picked her up and carried her to her room. In the mess of medications the soldiers had left strewn all over the bathroom floor, he found a bottle of sleeping pills his father had used when winter cold brought on the arthritis. He gave his mother two and soon she slept.

In the kitchen he ordered old Talat to make them both some coffee and they sat at the table while the servant described what had happened since dawn of the previous day. When he was done, he showed his dead master's son the hole in the garden where the soldiers had found the bag. The younger man shinned up the garden wall and found the scratches where the intruder had come over in the night to bury it. Then he went back to the house.

*　　　*　　　*

Hassan Rahmani was kept waiting, which he did not like, but had his appointment with the Foreign Minister, Tariq Aziz, just before eleven.

'I don't think I quite understand you,' said the

613

grey-haired minister, peering owlishly through his glasses. 'Embassies are allowed to communicate with their capitals by radio, and their transmission are always coded.'

'Yes, Minister, and they come from the Chancery building. That is part of normal diplomatic traffic. This is different. We are talking here about a covert transmitter, as used by spies, sending burst transmissions to a receiver we are sure is not in Moscow but much closer.'

'Burst transmissions?' asked Aziz.

Rahmani explained what they were.

'I still fail to follow you. Why should some agent of the KGB, and presumably this must be a KGB operation, be sending burst messages from the residence of the First Secretary, when they have a perfect right to send them on much more powerful transmitters from the embassy?'

'I do not know.'

'Then you must offer me some kind of better explanation, Brigadier. Have you any idea what is going on outside your own office? Do you not know that late yesterday I arrived back from Moscow after intensive discussions with Mr Gorbachov, and his representative Yevgeny Primakov, who was here last week?

'Do you not know that I brought with me a peace proposal which, if the Rais accepts it—and I am presenting it to him in two hours—could cause the Soviet Union to recall the Security Council and forbid the Americans to attack us?

'And in the face of all this, at this precise moment, you expect me to humiliate the Soviet Union by ordering a raid on their First Secretary's villa? Frankly, Brigadier, you must be mad.'

614

That was the end of it. Hassan Rahmani left the ministry seething but helpless. There was one thing, however, that Tariq Aziz had not forbidden. Within the walls of his house Kulikov might be impregnable. Inside his car he might be untouchable. But the streets did not belong to Kulikov.

'I want it surrounded,' Rahmani told his best surveillance team when he returned to his office. 'Keep it quiet, discreet, low-profile. But I want total surveillance of that building. When visitors come and go, and there must be visitors, I want them tailed.'

By noon the watcher teams were in place. They sat in parked cars beneath the trees covering all four walls of the Kulikov compound and monitored both ends of the only street that led to it. Others, further away but linked by radio, would report on anyone approaching, and follow anyone who left.

*   *   *

The younger son sat in the dining room of his parents' house and looked at the long canvas bag that contained his father. He let the tears run down his face to make damp marks on the jacket of his uniform and he thought of the good days long ago. His father had been a prosperous doctor then, with a large practice, even tending to the families of some of the British community after being introduced to them by his friend Nigel Martin.

He thought of the times he and his brother had played in the Martins' garden with Mike and Terry, and he wondered what had ever happened to those two.

After an hour he noticed some stains on the canvas that seemed to be larger than they had been. He rose

615

and went to the door.

'Talat.'

'Master?'

'Bring scissors and a kitchen knife.'

Alone in the room, Colonel Osman Badri cut open the canvas bag, along the top, down one side and along the bottom. Then he pulled the top of the sack away and rolled it back. His father's body was still quite naked.

According to tradition, it was supposed to be woman's work, but this was no task for his mother. He called for water and bandages, bathed and cleaned the ravaged body, bound up the broken feet, straightened and swaddled the shattered legs and covered the blackened genitalia. As he worked he cried; and as he cried, he changed.

At dusk he called the Imam at the Alwazia Cemetery in Risafa and made arrangements for a funeral the next morning.

*　　　*　　　*

Mike Martin had in fact been into the city on his bicycle that Sunday morning, 17 February, but he had returned after buying his groceries and checking the three walls for any chalk marks, arriving back at the villa just before midday. During the afternoon he was kept busy tending the garden. Mr Kulikov, while neither Christian nor Muslim and celebrating neither the Muslim holy day on Friday nor the Christian sabbath on Sunday, was at home with a cold and complaining about the state of his roses.

While Martin worked over the flower-beds, the Mukhabarat watcher teams were quietly sliding into place beyond the wall. Jericho, he reasoned, could

616

not possibly have news in less than two days; Martin would patrol his chalk marks again the following evening.

*   *   *

The burial of Dr Badri took place at Alwazia shortly after nine o'clock. The cemeteries of Baghdad were busy in those times and the Imam had much to do. Only a few days earlier the Americans had bombed a public air-raid shelter, causing over 300 deaths. Feelings were running high. Several mourners at another funeral close by asked the silent colonel if his relative had died from American bombs. He replied shortly that death had been by natural causes.

In the Muslim custom burial takes place quickly, with no long period of waiting between death and interment. And there was no wooden coffin in the manner of Christians; the body was wrapped in cloth. The pharmacist came, supporting Mrs Badri, and they left in a group when the brief ceremony was over.

Colonel Badri was barely yards from the gate of Alwazia when he heard his name called. Standing a few yards away was a limousine with blackened windows. One at the rear was half-open. The voice called him again.

Colonel Badri asked the pharmacist to take his mother home to Qadisiya; he would join them later. When they had gone, he walked over to the car. The voice said: 'Please join me, Colonel. We need to talk.'

He opened the car door and peered inside. The sole occupant had moved to the far side to make space. Badri thought he knew the face, but vaguely. He had seen it somewhere. He climbed in and closed the door. The man in the dark grey suit pressed a button and the window rose, shutting out the sounds from outside.

'You have just buried your father.'

'Yes.' Who was the man? Why could he not place the face?

'It was foul, what was done to him. If I had learnt in time, I might have stopped it. I learnt too late.'

Osman Badri felt something like a punch in the stomach. He realized to whom he was talking, a man who had been pointed out to him at a military reception two years earlier.

'I am going to say something to you, Colonel, which, if you were to report it, would cause me to die more terribly than your father.'

There was only one such thing, thought Badri. Treason.

'Once,' said the man quietly, 'I loved the Rais.'

'So did I,' said Badri.

'But things change. He has gone mad. In his madness he piles cruelty upon cruelty. He must be stopped. You know about the Qa'ala of course.'

Badri was surprised again, this time by the sudden change of subject.

'Of course. I built it.'

'Exactly. Do you know what now resides within it?'

'No.'

The senior officer told him.

'He cannot be serious,' said Badri.

'He is completely serious. He intends to use it against the Americans. That may not be our concern. But do you know what America will do in return? It will reply in kind. Not a brick here will stand on brick, not a stone on stone. The Rais will survive

618

alone. Do you want to be part of this?'

Colonel Badri thought of the body in the cemetery, over which the sextons were even then still heaping the dry earth.

'What do you want?'

'Tell me about Qa'ala.'

'Why?'

'The Americans will destroy it.'

'You can get this information to them?'

'Trust me, there are ways. The Qa'ala . . .'

So Colonel Osman Badri, the young engineer who had once wanted to design fine buildings to last for centuries, as his ancestors had done, told the man called Jericho.

'Grid reference.'

Badri gave him that, too.

'Go back to your post, Colonel. You will be safe.'

Colonel Badri left the car and walked away. His stomach was heaving, turning and turning. Within 100 yards he began to ask himself, over and again: what have I done? Suddenly he knew he had to talk to his brother, that older brother who had always had the cooler head, the wiser counsel.

* * *

The man the Mossad team called the Spotter arrived back in Vienna that Monday, summoned from Tel Aviv. Once again he was a prestigious lawyer from New York, with all the necessary identifying paperwork to prove it.

Even though the real lawyer was no longer on vacation, the chance that Gemütlich, who hated telephones and fax machines, would telephone New York to check was regarded as minimal. It was a risk

619

the Mossad was prepared to take.

Once again the Spotter installed himself at the Sheraton and wrote a personal letter to Herr Gemütlich. He again apologized for his unannounced arrival in the Austrian capital, but explained he was accompanied by his firm's accountant, and that the pair of them wished to make a first substantial deposit on behalf of their client.

The letter was delivered by hand in the late afternoon, and the following morning Gemütlich's reply arrived at the hotel, offering a meeting at ten in the morning.

The Spotter was indeed accompanied. The man with him was known simply as the Cracksman, for that was his speciality.

If the Mossad possesses at its Tel Aviv headquarters a virtually unrivalled collection of dummy companies, false passports, headed notepapers and all the other paraphernalia for deception, pride of place must still go to its safe-crackers and locksmiths. The Mossad's ability to break into locked places has its own niche in the covert world. At the science of burglary, the Mossad has long been regarded simply as the best. Had a neviot team been in charge at Watergate, no-one would ever have known.

So high is the reputation of Israeli lock-pickers that when British manufacturers sent a new product to the SIS for their comments, Century House would pass it on to Tel Aviv. The Mossad, devious to a fault, would study it, find how to pick it, then return it to London as 'impregnable'. The SIS found out about this.

The next time a British lock company came up with a particularly brilliant new lock, Century House asked them to take it back, keep it, but provide a slightly 'easier' one for analysis. It was the easier one that was sent to Tel Aviv. There it was studied and finally picked, then returned to London as 'unbreakable'. But it was the original lock the SIS advised the manufacturer to market.

This led to an embarrassing incident a year later when a Mossad locksmith spent three sweaty and infuriating hours working at such a lock in the corridor of an office block in a European capital before emerging livid with rage. Since then the British have tested their own locks and left the Mossad to work it out for themselves.

The lock-picker brought from Tel Aviv was not the best in Israel but the second-best. There was a reason for this; he had something the best lock-picker did not have.

The young man underwent a six-hour briefing from Gidi Barzilai during the night on the subject of the eighteenth-century work of the German-French cabinet-maker Riesener, and a full description by the Spotter on the internal lay-out of the Winkler building. The yarid surveillance team completed his education with a run-down of the movements of the night-watch, as observed by the times and places of lights going on and off inside the bank during the night.

*   *   *

That same Monday Mike Martin waited until five in the afternoon before he wheeled his bone-shaker bicycle across the gravelled yard to the rear gate of the Kulikov garden, opened the gate and let himself out.

He mounted and began to ride down the road in the direction of the nearest ferry crossing of the river, at the place where the Jumhuriya Bridge used to be before the Tornados offered it their personal attention.

He turned the corner, out of sight of the villa, and saw the first parked car. Then the second, further on. When the two men emerged from the second car and took up station in the centre of the road, his stomach began to tighten. He risked a glance behind him; two men from the other car had blocked any retreat. Knowing it was all over, he pedalled on. There was nothing else to do. One of the men ahead of him pointed to the side of the road.

'Hey you,' he shouted, 'over here.'

He came to a stop under the trees by the side of the road. Three more men emerged, soldiers. Their guns pointed straight at him. Slowly he raised his hands.

CHAPTER TWENTY-ONE

That afternoon in Riyadh, the British and American ambassadors met, apparently informally, for the purpose of indulging in the peculiarly English habit of taking tea and cakes.

Also present on the lawn of the British Embassy were Chip Barber, supposedly on the US embassy staff, and Steve Laing who would tell any casual enquirer that he was with his country's cultural section. A third guest, in a rare break from his duties below ground, was General Norman Schwarzkopf.

Within a short time all five men found themselves together in a corner of the lawn, nursing their cups of tea. It made life easier when everyone knew what everyone else really did for a living.

Among all the guests the sole topic of talk was the imminent war, but these five men had information denied to all the rest. Among it was the news of the details of the peace plan presented that day by Tariq Aziz to Saddam Hussein, the plan brought back from Moscow and the talks with Mikhail Gorbachov. It was a subject of worry, but for different reasons.

General Schwarzkopf had already that day headed off a suggestion out of Washington that he might attack earlier than planned. The Soviet peace plan called for a declared ceasefire, and an Iraqi pull-out from Kuwait on the following day.

Washington knew these details not from Baghdad, but from Moscow. The immediate reply from the White House was that the plan had merits, but failed to address key issues. It made no mention of Iraq's annulment for ever of its claim on Kuwait; it did not bear in mind the unimaginable damage done to Kuwait—the 500 oil fires, the millions of tons of crude oil gushing into the Gulf to poison its waters, the 200 executed Kuwaitis, the sacking of Kuwait City.

'Colin Powell tells me,' said the general, 'that State Department is pushing for an even harder line. They want to demand unconditional surrender.'

'So they do, to be sure,' murmured the American envoy.

'So I told 'em,' said the general, 'I told 'em, you need an Arabist to look at this.'

'Indeed,' replied the British Ambassador, 'and why should that be?'

Both the ambassadors were consummate diplomats who had worked for years in the Middle

623

East. Both *were* Arabists.

'Well,' said the Commander-in-Chief, 'that kind of ultimatum does not work with Arabs. They'll die first.'

There was silence in the group. The ambassadors searched the general's guileless face for a hint of irony.

The two Intelligence officers stayed quiet, but both men had the same thought in their minds: that is precisely the point, my dear general.

*　　*　　*

'You have come from the house of the Russian.'

It was a statement, not a question. The Counter-Intelligence man was in plain clothes, but clearly an officer.

'Yes, bey.'

'Papers.'

Martin rummaged through the pockets of his dish-dash and produced his ID card and the soiled and crumpled letter originally issued to him by First Secretary Kulikov. The officer studied the card, glanced up to compare the faces, and looked at the letter.

The Israeli forgers had done their work well. The simple, stubbled face of Mahmoud Al-Khouri stared through the grubby plastic.

'Search him,' said the officer.

The other plain clothesman ran his hands over the body under the dish-dash, then shook his head. No weapons.

'Pockets.'

The pockets revealed some dinar notes, some coins, a penknife, different coloured pieces of chalk

624

and a sylthane bag. The officer held up the last piece.

'What is this?'

'The infidel threw it away. I use it for my tobacco.'

'There is no tobacco in it.'

'No, bey, I have run out. I was hoping to buy some in the market.'

'And don't call me "bey". That went out with the Turks. Where do you come from, anyway?'

Martin described the small village far in the north.

'It is well known thereabouts for its melons,' he added helpfully.

'Be quiet about your thrice-damned melons,' snapped the officer, who had the impression his soldiers were trying not to smile.

A large limousine cruised into the far end of the street and stopped, 200 yards away. The junior officer nudged his superior and nodded. The senior man turned, looked and told Martin: 'Wait here.'

He walked back to the large car and stooped to address someone through the rear window.

'Who have you got?' asked Hassan Rahmani.

'Gardener/handyman, sir. Works there. Does the roses and the gravel, shops for the cook.'

'Smart?'

'No, sir, practically simple-minded. A peasant from up-country, comes from some melon-patch in the north.'

Rahmani thought it over. If he detained the fool, the Russians would wonder why their man had not come back. That would alert them. He hoped that if the Russian peace initiative failed, he would get his permission to raid the place. If he let the man complete his errands and return, he might alert his employers. In Rahmani's experience there was one language every poor Iraqi spoke and spoke well. He

625

produced a wallet and peeled out 100 dinars.

'Give him this. Tell him to complete his shopping and return. Then he is to keep his eyes open for someone with a big, silver umbrella. If he keeps silent about us and reports tomorrow on what he has seen, he will be well rewarded. If he tells the Russians, I will hand him over to the AMAM.'

'Yes, Brigadier.'

The officer took the money, walked back and instructed the gardener as to what he had to do. The man looked puzzled.

'An umbrella, sayidi?'

'Yes, a big silver one, maybe black, pointing at the sky. Have you ever seen one?'

'No, sayidi,' said the man sadly, 'whenever it rains they all run inside.'

'By Allah the Great,' murmured the officer, 'it's not for the rain, oaf, it's for sending messages.'

'An umbrella that sends messages,' repeated the gardener slowly, 'I will look for one, sayidi.'

'Get on your way,' said the officer in despair. 'And stay silent about what you have seen here.'

Martin pedalled down the road, past the limousine. As he approached, Rahmani lowered his head into the rear seat. No need to let the peasant see the Head of Counter-Intelligence for the Republic of Iraq.

Martin found the chalk mark at seven and recovered the message at nine. He read it by the light from the window of a café, not electric light for there was none any more, but a petrol lamp. When he saw the text he let out a low whistle, folded the paper small and stuffed it inside his underpants.

There was no question of going back to the villa. The transmitter was 'blown' and a further message

626

would spell disaster. He contemplated the bus station, but there were Army and AMAM patrols all over it, looking for deserters.

Instead he went to the fruit market at Kasra and found a truck driver heading west. The man was only going a few miles beyond Habbaniyah, and 20 dinars persuaded him to take a passenger. Many trucks preferred to drive by night, believing that the Sons of Dogs, up there in their airplanes, could not see them in the dark, unaware that by night or day battered fruit trucks were not General Chuck Horner's top priority.

So they drove through the night, by headlamps generating at least one candlepower, and at dawn Martin found himself deposited on the highway just west of Lake Habbaniyah, where the driver turned off for the rich farms of the upper Euphrates Valley.

They had been stopped twice by patrols, but on each occasion Martin had produced his papers, and the Russian letter, explaining that he had worked as gardener for the infidel, but they were going home and had dismissed him. He whined about the way they had treated him, until the impatient soldiers told him to be quiet and get on his way.

*   *   *

That night Osman Badri was not far from Mike Martin, but ahead of him and heading in the same direction. His destination was the fighter base where his elder brother Abdelkarim was the squadron commander.

During the 1980s a Belgian construction company called Sixco had been contracted to build eight super-protected airbases to house the cream of Iraq's best

627

fighters.

The key to them was that almost everything was buried underground—barracks, hangars, fuel stores, ammunition magazines, workshops, briefing rooms, crew quarters and the big diesel generators to power the bases.

The only things visible above ground were the actual runways, 3,000 metres long. But as these appeared to have no buildings or hangars associated with them, the Allies thought they were 'barebones' airfields like Al Kharz in Saudi Arabia before the Americans moved in.

A closer inspection on the ground would have revealed 1-metre-thick concrete blast doors set into downward-leading ramps at the ends of the runways. Each base was in a square 5 kilometres by 5, the perimeter surrounded by barbed-wire fencing. But as with Tarmiya, the Sixco bases appeared inactive and were left alone.

To operate out of them, the pilots would be briefed underground, get into their cockpits and start their engines there. Only when they were fully run-up, with blast walls protecting the rest of the base from their jet exhaust and diverting the gases upwards to mingle with the hot desert air outside, would the doors to the ramps be opened.

The fighters could race up the ramps, emerge at full power, afterburners on, scream down the runway and be airborne in seconds. Even when the AWACS spotted them, they appeared to have come from nowhere and were assumed to be on a low-level mission originating somewhere else.

Colonel Abdelkarim Badri was stationed at one of these Sixco bases, known only as KM 160 because it was off the Baghdad-Ar Rutba road, 160 kilometres west of Baghdad. His younger brother presented himself at the guard post in the wire just after sundown.

Because of his rank, a phone call was at once made from the guard hut to the squadron commander's private quarters and soon a jeep appeared, trundling across the empty desert, apparently having come from nowhere.

A young Air Force lieutenant escorted the visitor into the base, the jeep rolling down another hidden but small ramp into the below-ground complex.

Leaving the jeep in a car-park, the lieutenant led the way down long concrete corridors, past caverns where mechanics worked on MiG 29s. The air was clean and filtered, and everywhere was the hum of generators.

Eventually they entered the senior officers' area and the lieutenant knocked at a door. At a command from inside, he showed Osman Badri into the CO's apartment.

Abdelkarim rose and the brothers embraced. The older man was thirty-seven, also a colonel and darkly handsome with a slim Ronald Colman moustache. He was unmarried, but never lacked for female attention. His looks, his sardonic manner, his dashing uniform and pilot's wings had ensured it. Nor was his appearance a sham; Air Force generals admitted he was the best fighter pilot in the country and the Russians who had trained him on the ace of the Soviet fighter fleet, the MiG 29 'Fulcrum' supersonic fighter, agreed with that.

'Well, my brother, what brings you out here?' he asked.

Osman, when he had sat down and taken a coffee from a freshly perked brew, had time to study his older sibling. There were lines of strain round the mouth that had not been there before, and weariness in the eyes.

Abdelkarim was neither a fool nor a coward. He had flown eight missions against the Americans and the British. He had returned from them all—just. He had seen his best colleagues shot down or blown apart by Sparrow and Sidewinder missiles, and he had dodged four himself.

The odds, he recognized after his first attempt to intercept the American strike bombers, were impossible. On his own side, he had neither information nor guidance as to where the enemy was, how many, of what type, at what height or on which heading. The Iraqi radars were down, the control and command centres in pieces, the pilots simply on their own.

Worse, the Americans with their AWACS could pick up the Iraqi warplanes before they had reached 1,000 feet, telling their own pilots where to go and what to do to secure the best attacking position. For the Iraqis, Abdelkarim Badri knew, every combat mission was a suicide quest.

Of all this he said nothing, forcing a smile and a request for his brother's news. That news killed the smile.

Osman related the events of the past sixty hours; the arrival of the AMAM troops at dawn, the search, the discovery in the garden, the beating of their mother and Talat and the arrest of their father. He told how he had been summoned when the neighbouring pharmacist finally got a message to him, and how he had driven home to find their father's body on the dining-room table.

Abdelkarim's mouth tightened to an angry line

630

when Osman revealed what he had discovered when he cut open the body bag, and the way their father had been buried that morning.

The older man leant forward sharply when Osman told how he had been intercepted as he left the cemetery and of the conversation that had taken place.

'You told him all that?' he asked, when his brother had finished.

'Yes.'

'Is it true, all true? You really built this Fortress, this Qa'ala?'

'Yes.'

'And you told him where it is, so that he can tell the Americans?'

'Yes. Did I do wrong?'

Abdelkarim thought for some while.

'How many men, in all Iraq, knew these things, my brother?'

'Six,' said Osman.

'Name them.'

'The Rais himself, Hussein Kamil who provided the finance and the manpower; Amer Saadi who provided the technology. Then General Ridha who supplied the artillerymen and General Musuli of the Engineers—he proposed me for the job. And me, I built it.'

'The helicopter pilots who bring in the visitors?'

'They have to know the directions in order to navigate. But not what is inside. And they are kept quarantined in a base somewhere, I don't know where.'

'Visitors, how many could know?'

'None. They are blindfolded before take-off and until they have arrived.'

631

'If the Americans destroy this Qubth-ut-Allah, who do you think the AMAM will suspect? The Rais, the ministers, the generals—or you?'

Osman put his head in his hands.

'What have I done?' he moaned.

'I'm afraid, little brother, you have destroyed us all.'

Both men knew the rules. For treason the Rais does not demand a single sacrifice, but the extirpation of three generations; father and uncles so there will be no more of the tainted seed; brothers for the same reason; and sons and nephews so that none may grow up to carry on the vendetta against him. Osman Badri began quietly to weep.

Abdelkarim rose, pulled Osman to his feet and embraced him.

'You did right, brother, you did the right thing. Now we must see how to get out of here.'

He checked his watch: eight o'clock.

'There are no telephone lines for the public from here to Baghdad,' he said. 'Only underground lines to the Defence people in their various bunkers. But this message is not for them. How long would it take you to drive to our mother's house?'

'Three, maybe four hours,' said Osman.

'You have eight, to get there and back. Tell our mother to pack all she values into our father's car. She can drive it, not well but enough. She should take Talat, and go to Talat's village. She should seek shelter with his tribe until one of us contacts her. Understood?'

'Yes. I can be back by dawn. Why?'

'Before dawn. Tomorrow I am leading a flight of MiGs across to Iran. Others have gone before. It is a crazy scheme by the Rais to save his best fighter planes. Nonsense, of course, but it may save our lives. You will come with me.'

'I thought the MiG 29 was a single-seater?'

'I have one trainer version with two seats. The UB model. You will be dressed as an Air Force officer. With luck we can get away with it. Go now.'

*   *   *

Mike Martin was walking west that night along the Ar Rutba road when the car of Osman Badri flashed past him, heading towards Baghdad. Neither took any notice of the other. Martin's destination was the next river crossing 15 miles ahead. There, with the bridge down, trucks would have to wait for the ferry and he would have a better chance of paying another driver to take him further west.

In the small hours of the morning he found exactly such a truck, but it could only take him to a point just beyond Muhammadi. There he began to wait again. At three o'clock the car of Col. Badri sped back again. He did not hail it and it did not stop. The driver was clearly in a hurry. Just before dawn a third lorry came along, pulling out of a side-road onto the main highway, and paused to take him aboard. Again he paid the driver from his dwindling stock of dinar notes, grateful to whoever had thought to give him the wad of money back in Mansour. By dawn, he assumed, the Kulikov household would complain that they had lost their gardener.

A search of his shack would reveal the writing pad beneath the mattress, an odd possession for an illiterate, and a further search would reveal the transmitter beneath the tiles. By midday the hunt would be well up, starting in Baghdad but spreading across the country. By nightfall he needed to be far away in the desert, heading for the border.

The truck in which he rode was beyond KM 160 when the flight of MiG 29s took off.

*   *   *

Osman Badri was terrified, being one of those people with a deep loathing of flying. In the underground caverns that made up the base, he had stood to one side as his brother briefed the four young pilots who would form the rest of the flight. Most of Abdelkarim's contemporaries were dead, and these were youngsters, more than a decade his junior, not long out of training school. They listened with rapt attention to their squadron commander and nodded their assent.

Inside the MiG, even with the canopy closed, Osman thought he had never heard a roar like it as, in the enclosed space, the two RD 33 Soviet turbo-fans ran up to maximum dry power. Crouching in the rear cockpit behind his brother, Osman saw the great blast doors open on their hydraulic pistons, a square of pale blue sky appearing at the end of the cavern. The noise increased as the pilot ran his throttle through the gate and into afterburn, and the twin-finned Soviet interceptor shuddered against her brakes.

When the brakes came off, Osman thought he had been kicked in the small of the back by a mule. The MiG leapt forward, the concrete walls flashed past, the jet took the ramp and emerged into the dawn light.

Osman shut his eyes and prayed. The rumbling of the wheels ceased, he seemed to be drifting, and

634

opened his eyes. They were airborne, the lead MiG circling low over KM 160 as the other four jets screamed out of the tunnel below. Then the doors closed and the airbase ceased to exist.

All around him, because the UB version is a trainer, were dials and clocks, buttons, switches, screens, knobs and levers. Between his legs was a duplicate control column. His brother had told him to leave everything alone, which he was glad to.

At 1,000 feet the flight of five MiGs formed into a staggered line, the four youngsters behind the squadron commander. His brother set course just south of due east, keeping low, hoping to avoid detection and to cross the southern outskirts of Baghdad, losing his MiGs from prying American eyes in the clutter of industrial estates and other radar images.

It was a high-risk gamble, trying to avoid the radars of the AWACS out over the Gulf, but he had no choice. His orders were formal, and now Abdelkarim Badri had an extra reason for wishing to reach Iran.

Luck was with him that morning, through one of those flukes in warfare that are not supposed to occur, but do. At the end of every long 'shift' on station over the Gulf, the AWACS had to return to base, being replaced by another. It was called 'changing the cab rank'. During the cab-rank changes, there was sometimes a brief window when radar cover was suspended. The MiG flight's low passage across South Baghdad and Salman Pak coincided with just such a lucky break.

The Iraqi pilot hoped that by keeping to 1,000 feet he could slip under any American flights, which tended to operate at 20,000 feet and upwards. He wanted to skirt the Iraqi town of Al Kut to its north, then head straight for the safety of the Iranian border at its nearest point.

That morning, at that hour, Captain Don Walker of the 336th Tactical Fighter Squadron out of Al Kharz was leading a flight of four Strike Eagles north towards Al Kut, his mission to bomb a major river bridge over the Tigris across which Republican Guard tanks had been caught by a J-STAR heading south for Kuwait.

The 336th had spent much of its war on night missions, but the bridge north of Al Kut was a 'quick fix', meaning there was no time to lose if Iraqi tanks were using it to head south. So the bombing raid that morning had the coding 'Jeremiah directs'; General Chuck Horner wanted it done, and now.

The Eagles were loaded with 2,000-pound laser-guided bombs and air-to-air missiles. Because of the positioning of the bomb-attachment pylons beneath the wings of the Eagle, the load was asymmetric, the bombs on one side being heavier than the Sparrow missiles on the other. It was called 'the bastard load'. Automatic trim control compensated for this, but it was still not the load most pilots would choose to have hanging underneath them in a dog-fight.

As the MiGs, now down to 500 feet and skimming the landscape, approached from the west, the Eagles were coming up from the south, 80 miles away.

The first indication Abdelkarim Badri had of their presence was a low warbling in his ears. His brother behind him did not know what it was, but the fighter pilots knew. The trainer MiG was in the lead, the four juniors strung out behind him in a loose V formation. They all heard it, too.

The warbling came from their RWR—Radar

636

Warning Receiver. It meant there were other radars up there somewhere, sweeping the sky.

The four Eagles had their radars in the 'search' mode, the beams running out ahead of them to see what was there. The Soviet Radar Warning Receivers had picked up these beams and were telling their pilots.

There was nothing the MiGs could do but keep going. At 500 feet they were well below the Eagles and heading across the Eagles' projected track.

At 60 miles the warbling in the Iraqi pilots' ears rose to a shrill bleep. That meant the RWRs were telling them: someone out there has gone out of search mode and locked on to you.

Behind Don Walker his wizzo Tim saw the change in his radar's attitude. From a gentle side-to-side scan, the American radars had gone to lock-on, narrowing their beams and concentrating on what they had found.

'We have five unidentifieds, ten o'clock low,' the wizzo muttered, and engaged IFF. The other three wizzos in the flight did the same.

Identification Friend or Foe is a sort of transponder carried by all combat airplanes. It sends out a pulse on certain frequencies, which are changed daily. Warplanes on the same side will receive this pulse and reply: 'I am a friend.' Enemy aircraft cannot do so. The five blips on the radar screen crossing the track of the Eagles miles ahead and close to the ground might have been five 'friendlies' coming back from a mission. More than likely— there were far more Allied aircraft in the skies than Iraqis.

Tim questioned the unidentifieds on Modes One, Two and Four. No response.

637

'Hostiles,' he reported. Don Walker flicked his missile switches to radar, muttered 'Engage' to his other three pilots, dropped the nose and headed down.

Abdelkarim Badri was at a disadvantage and he knew it. He knew it from the moment the Americans locked on to him. He knew without any IFF to tell him that these other aircraft could not possibly be fellow Iraqis. He knew he had been spotted by hostiles and he knew his young colleagues would be no match for them.

His disadvantage lay in the MiG he flew. Because it was the trainer version, the only type with two seats, it was never destined for combat. Where the single-seater MiGs had look-around radars to service their missiles, the trainer version had a simple ranging radar, of no operational use at all and giving Colonel Badri only a 60-degree sweep out of the nose. He knew someone had locked onto him, but he could not see them.

'What do you have?' he barked at his wingman. The reply was breathless and frightened.

'Four hostiles, three o'clock high, diving fast.'

So, the gamble had failed. The Americans were bucketing down the sky from the south, intent on blowing them all out of the air.

'Scatter, dive, go to afterburner, head for Iran,' he shouted.

The young pilots needed no second bidding. From the jet-pipes of each MiG a blast of flame leapt backwards as the four throttles went through the gate, punching the fighters through the sound barrier and almost doubling their speed.

Despite the huge increase in fuel consumption, the single-seaters could keep their afterburners going long enough to evade the Americans and still reach Iran. Their headstart on the Eagles meant the Americans would never catch them, even though they too would now be in afterburn.

Abdelkarim Badri had no such option. In making their trainer version, the Soviet engineers had not only fitted a simpler radar, but to accommodate the extra weight of the student and his cockpit, they had considerably reduced the internal fuel capacity.

The fighter colonel was carrying under-wing long-range fuel tanks, but these would not be enough. He had four choices. It took him no more than two seconds to work them out.

He could go to afterburner, escape the Americans and return to an Iraqi base, there to be arrested and handed over sooner or later to the AMAM for torture and death.

He could engage afterburner and continue for Iran, evading the Americans but running out of fuel soon after crossing the border. Even if he and his brother ejected safely, they would fall among the Persian tribesmen who had suffered so horribly in the Iran-Iraq war from the cargoes dropped on them by Iraqi aviators.

He could use the afterburner to avoid the Eagles, then fly south to eject over Saudi Arabia and become a prisoner. It never occurred to him that he would be treated humanely.

There were some lines that came into his head from long ago, lines from a poem he had learnt at Mr Hartley's school in that Baghdad of his boyhood. Tennyson? Wordsworth? No, Macaulay, that was it, Macaulay, something about a man in his last moments, something he had read out in class.

639

*To every man upon this earth
Death cometh soon or late.
And how can man die better
Than facing fearful odds,
For the ashes of his fathers
And the temples of his Gods?*

Colonel Abdelkarim Badri pushed his throttle through the gate into afterburner, hauled the MiG Fulcrum into a climbing turn and went up to meet the oncoming Americans.

As soon as he turned, the four Eagles came into his radar range. Two had scattered, racing down after the fleeing single-seaters, all of them with afterburner engaged, all beyond the sound barrier.

But the leader of the Americans was coming straight down and at him. Badri felt the shudder as the Fulcrum went supersonic, adjusted the control column a fraction and went for the diving Eagle ahead of him.

'Christ, he's coming straight at us,' said Tim from the rear seat. Walker did not need to be told. His own radar screen showed him the four vanishing blips of the Iraqi aircraft fleeing for Iran, and the single glow of the enemy fighter climbing towards him to engage. The range-finder was unwinding like an alarm clock out of control. At 30 miles, they were hurtling towards each other at a closing speed of 2,200 m.p.h. He still could not see the Fulcrum visually, but it would not be long.

In the MiG, Col. Osman Badri was totally bewildered. He had understood nothing of what had happened. The sudden thump of the afterburner engaging had hit him in the small of the back again, and the seven-G turn had caused him to black out for

640

several seconds.

'What is happening?' he shouted into his mask, unaware that the mute button was engaged so his brother could not hear him.

Don Walker's thumb was poised over his missile controls.

He had two choices: the longer-range AIM-7 Sparrow which was radar-guided from the Eagle itself, or the shorter-range AIM-9 Sidewinder, which was a heat-seeker.

At 15 miles he could see it, the small black dot racing up towards him. The twin fins showed it was a MiG 29 Fulcrum, arguably one of the best interceptor fighters in the world, in the right hands. Walker did not know he faced the unarmed trainer UB version. What he did know was that it might carry the AA-10 Soviet missile with a range as long as his own AIM-7s. That was why he chose the Sparrows.

At 12 miles he launched two Sparrows dead ahead. The missiles flashed away, picking up the radar energy reflected from the MiG and obediently heading straight towards it.

Abdelkarim Badri saw the flashes as the Sparrows left the Eagle, giving him a few more seconds of life unless he could force the American to break off. He reached down to his left and pulled a single lever.

Don Walker had often wondered what it would be like and now he knew. From the underside of the MiG's wings came an answering flicker of light. It was like a cold hand gripping the entrails, the icy, freezing sensation of pure fear. Another man had launched two missiles at him, he was staring certain death straight in the face.

Two seconds after he had launched the Sparrows,

Walker wished he had chosen the Sidewinders. The reason was simple; the Sidewinders were fire-and-forget missiles, they would find the target no matter where the Eagle was. The Sparrows needed the Eagle to guide them; if he broke away now the missiles, without guidance, would 'gimbal' or 'go stupid', wandering off across the sky to fall harmlessly to earth.

He was within a fraction of a second of breaking off when he saw the 'missiles' launched by the MiG tumbling away towards the ground. In disbelief he realized they were not rockets at all; the Iraqi had tricked him by releasing his under-wing fuel tanks. The aluminium canisters had caught the morning sun as they fell, glittering like the ignited fuel of launching missiles. It was a trick and he, Don Walker, of Tulsa, Oklahoma, had damn nearly fallen for it.

In the MiG Abdelkarim Badri realized the American was not going to break off. He had tested the man's nerve and he had lost. In the rear seat Osman had found the transmit button. He could see by looking over his shoulder that they were climbing, already miles above the ground.

'Where are we going?' he screamed. The last thing he heard was the voice of Abdelkarim, quite calm.

'Peace, my brother. To greet our father. Allah-o-Akhbar.'

Walker watched the two Sparrows explode at that moment, great peonies of red flame 3 miles away, then the broken fragments of the Soviet fighter tumbling down to the landscape below. He felt the sweat trickling down his chest in rivulets.

His wingman, Randy Roberts, who had held station above and behind him, appeared off his right wingtip, the white-gloved hand raised with the thumb erect. He replied in kind, and the other two Eagles, having abandoned their fruitless chase of the remaining MiGs, swam up from below to re-form. Thus the formation went on to the bridge above Al Kut.

Such is the speed of events in fighter combat that the entire action, from the first radar lock-on to the destruction of the Fulcrum, had taken just 38 seconds.

*   *   *

The Spotter was at the Winkler Bank on the dot of ten that morning, accompanied by his 'accountant'. The younger man bore a deep attaché case containing US $100,000 in cash.

The money was actually a temporary loan arranged by the banking sayan, who was much relieved to be told it would simply be deposited with the Winkler Bank for a while, then retrieved and returned to him.

When he saw the money, Herr Gemütlich was delighted. He would have been less enthusiastic had he noticed that the dollars occupied only half the thickness of the attaché case, and he would have been horrified to see what lay beneath the false bottom.

For the sake of discretion, the accountant was banished to Fräulein Hardenberg's room while the lawyer and the banker arranged the confidential operating codes for the new account. He returned to take charge of the receipt for the money and by eleven the matter was concluded. Herr Gemütlich summoned the commissionaire to escort the visitors back to the lobby and the front door.

On the way down the accountant whispered

something into the American lawyer's ear, and the lawyer translated it to the porter. With a curt nod the porter stopped the old grille-fronted lift at the mezzanine floor and the three got out.

The lawyer pointed out the door of the men's room to his colleague and the accountant went in. The lawyer and the porter remained on the landing outside.

At this point there came to their ears the sounds of a fracas in the lobby, clearly audible because the lobby was 20 feet along the corridor and down fifteen marble steps.

With a muttered excuse the commissionaire strode along the corridor until he could see from the top of the stairs down to the hallway. What he saw caused him to run down the marble steps to sort the matter out.

It was an outrageous scene. Somehow three rowdies, clearly drunk, had entered the lobby and were harassing the receptionist for money for more liquid refreshment. She would later say they had tricked her into opening the front door by claiming they were the postman.

Full of indignation, the commissionaire sought to bustle the hooligans outside. No-one noticed that one of the rowdies, on entering, had dropped a cigarette packet against the door jamb so that, although normally self-closing, the door would not quite shut.

Nor did anyone notice, in the jostling and pushing, a fourth man enter the lobby on hands and knees. When he stood up, he was at once joined by the lawyer of New York, who had followed the commissionaire down the stairs to the lobby.

They stood to one side as the commissionaire

hustled the three rowdies back where they belonged—in the street. When he turned round, the bank servant saw that the lawyer and the accountant had descended from the mezzanine of their own accord. With profuse apologies for the unseemly mêlée, he ushered them out.

Once on the pavement, the accountant let out a huge sigh of relief.

'I hope I never have to do that again,' he said.

'Don't worry,' said the lawyer, 'you did pretty well.'

They spoke in Hebrew, because the 'accountant' knew no other language. He was in fact a bank teller from Beershe'eva and the only reason he was in Vienna, on his first and last covert assignment, was because he also happened to be the identical twin of the Cracksman, then standing immobile in the darkness of the cleaning closet on the mezzanine floor. There he would remain motionless for twelve hours.

*   *   *

Mike Martin arrived in Ar Rutba in the middle of the afternoon. It had taken him twenty hours to cover a distance that normally would take no more than six in a car.

On the outskirts of the town he found a herdsman with a flock of goats, and left him somewhat mystified but quite happy by buying four of them for his remaining handful of dinars at a price almost twice what the herdsman would have secured in the market.

The goats seemed happy to be led off into the desert, even though they now wore halters of cord.

They could hardly be expected to know that they were only there to explain why Mike Martin was wandering around the desert south of the road in the afternoon sun.

His problem was that he had no compass; it was with the rest of his gear beneath the tiles of a shack in Mansour. Using the sun and his cheap watch, he worked out as best he could the bearing from the radio mast in the town to the wadi where his motor-cycle was buried.

It was a 5-mile hike, slowed by the goats, but they were worth having because twice he saw soldiers staring at him from the road until he was out of sight. But the soldiers took no action.

He found the right wadi just before sundown, identifying the marks scored into the nearby rocks, and rested until the light was gone before starting to dig. The happy goats wandered off.

It was still there, wrapped in its plastic bag, a rangy 125cc Yamaha cross-country motor-cycle, all in black, with panniers for the extra fuel tanks. The burried compass was there, plus the handgun and ammunition.

For many years the SAS favoured the Browning 13-shot, but about that time had changed to the Swiss Sig Sauer 9mm. It was the heftier Swiss automatic that he strapped in its holster to his right hip. From then on, there would be no more question of pretence; no Iraqi peasant would be riding that machine in those parts. If he was intercepted he would have to shoot and escape.

He rode through the night, making far better time than the Land-Rovers had been able to do. With the motor-cross bike he could speed across the flat patches and drive the machine over the rocky ridges of the wadis, using engine and feet.

At midnight he refuelled and drank water, with some K-rations from the packs left in the cache. Then he rode on due south for the Saudi border.

He never knew when he crossed the border. It was all a featureless wasteland of rocks and sand, gravel and scree, and given the zigzag course he had to cover, there was no way of knowing how many miles he had covered.

He expected to know he was in Saudi Arabia when he came to the Tapline Road, the only highway in those parts. The land became easier, and he was riding at 20 m.p.h. when he saw the vehicle. Had he not been so tired he would have reacted faster; but he was half-drugged with exhaustion and his reflexes were slow.

The front wheel of the bike hit the trip-wire and he was off, tumbling over and over until he came to rest on his back. When he opened his eyes and looked up, there was a figure standing over him and the glint of starlight on metal.

'Bouge pas, mec.'

Not Arabic. He racked his tired mind. Something a long time ago. Yes, Haileybury, some unfortunate schoolmaster trying to teach him the intricacies of the language of Corneille, Racine and Molière.

'Ne tirez pas,' he said slowly. 'Je suis Anglais.'

There are only three British sergeants in the French Foreign Legion, and one of them is called McCullin.

'Are you now?' he said in English. 'Well, you'd better get your arse over to the half-track. And I'll have that pistol if you don't mind.'

The Legion patrol was well west of its assigned position in the Allied line, running a check on the Tapline Road for possible Iraqi deserters. With Sgt.

McCullin as interpreter, Martin explained to the French lieutenant that he had been on a mission inside Iraq.

That was quite acceptable to the Legion; working behind the lines was one of their specialities. The good news was that they had a radio.

*   *   *

The Cracksman waited patiently in the darkness of the broom cupboard through the Tuesday and into the night. He heard various male staff enter the washroom, do what they came for and leave. Through the wall he could hear the lift occasionally whine its way up and down to the top floor. He sat on his briefcase with his back to the wall and an occasional glance at his luminous watch told him of the passing hours.

Between half-past five and six he heard the staff walking past on their way to the lobby and home. At six, he knew, the nightwatchman would arrive, to be admitted by the commissionaire, who by then would have checked every one of the staff past his desk according to the daily list.

When the commissionaire left just after six, the night-watch would lock the front door and set the alarms. Then he would settle down with the portable TV he brought every evening, and watch the game shows until it was time for his first round.

According to the yarid team, even the cleaners were supervised. They did the common parts—halls and stairways and washrooms—during the nights of Monday, Wednesday and Friday, but on a Tuesday night the Cracksman should remain undisturbed. On Saturday they came back to clean the private offices

648

under the eye of the commissionaire, who remained with them at all times.

The routine of the night-watch was apparently always the same. He made three tours of the building, testing all doors, at 10 p.m., two in the morning and at five.

Between coming on duty and his first tour, he watched his TV and ate his packed supper. In the longest gap, between ten and two, he dozed, setting a small alarm to tell him when it was two in the morning. The Cracksman intended to make his burglary during that gap.

He had already seen Gemütlich's office, and its all-important door. The latter was of solid timber but happily not alarmed. The window was alarmed and he had noted the faint outline of two pressure pads between the parquet and the carpet.

At ten precisely he heard the lift rumbling upwards, bearing the night-watch to begin his tour of the office doors, starting at the top and coming downwards floor by floor on foot.

Half an hour later the elderly man had finished, put his head round the door of the men's room, flashed on the light to check the wired and alarmed window, closed the door and returned to his desk in the lobby. There he chose to watch a late game show.

At 10.45 the Cracksman, in complete darkness, left the men's room and stole up the stairs to the fourth floor.

The door of Herr Gemütlich's office took him fifteen minutes. The last tumbler of the four-lever mortice deadlock tumbled back and he stepped inside.

Although he wore a band round his head holding a small penlight, he took another and larger torch to

649

scan the room. By its light he could avoid the two pressure pads and approach the desk from its unguarded side. Then he switched it off and resumed by the light only of the pen-torch.

The locks on the three top drawers were no problem, small brass affairs over a hundred years old. When the three drawers were removed, he inserted his hand and began to feel for a knob, button or lever. Nothing. It was an hour later, at the rear of the third drawer down on the right-hand side, that he found it. A small lever, in brass, no more than an inch long. When he pushed it, there was a low click and a strip of inlay at the base of the pillar jumped open a centimetre.

The tray inside was quite shallow, less than an inch, but it was enough to contain twenty-two sheets of thin paper. Each was a replica of the letter of authority that alone would suffice to operate the accounts under Gemütlich's charge.

The Cracksman produced his camera and a clamper, a device of four fold-back aluminium legs which kept the pre-focused camera at exactly the right distance from the paper beneath it to get a high-definition exposure.

The top of the pile of sheets was the one describing the operating method of the account opened the previous morning by the Spotter, on behalf of the fictitious client in America. The one he wanted was the seventh down. The number he already knew—the Mossad had been paying money into Jericho's account for two years before the Americans took over.

To be on the safe side, he photographed them all anyway. After returning the cachette to its original state, he replaced and relocked all the drawers and withdrew, sealing the office door behind him. He was back in the broom closet by ten past one.

When the bank opened for morning business, the Cracksman let the lift run up and down for half an hour, knowing the commissionaire never needed to escort the staff to their offices. The first visitor appeared at ten to ten. When the lift had gone past him, the Cracksman stole out of the men's room, tiptoed to the end of the corridor and looked down into the lobby. The desk of the commissionaire was empty; he was upstairs escorting a client.

The Cracksman produced a bleeper and pressed twice. Within three seconds the front doorbell rang. The receptionist activated her speaker system and asked: 'Ja?'

'Lieferung,' said a tinny voice. She pressed the door-release catch and a big cheerful delivery-man entered the lobby. He bore a large oil painting wrapped in brown paper and string.

'Here you are, lady, all cleaned and ready to rehang,' he said.

Behind him the door slid to its close. As it did so a hand came round the edge at floor level and inserted a wad of paper. The door appeared to close but the catch did not engage.

The deliveryman stood the oil painting on the edge of the receptionist's desk. It was big, 5 foot wide and 4 foot tall. It blocked her whole view of the lobby.

'But I know nothing about . . .' she protested. The head of the deliveryman came round the edge of the painting.

'Just sign for its safe receipt, please,' he said, and put in front of her a clipboard with a receipt form. As she studied it, the Cracksman came down the marble steps and slipped out of the door.

'But this says Harzmann Galerie,' she pointed out.

'That's right. Ballgasse, Number Fourteen.'

'But we're Number Eight. This is the Winkler Bank. The gallery is further up.'

The puzzled deliveryman made his apologies and left. The commissionaire came back down the marble steps. She explained what had happened. He snorted, resumed his seat across the lobby from the reception desk and returned to the morning paper.

* * *

When the Blackhawk helicopter brought Mike Martin into the Riyadh Military Air Base at midday there was a small and expectant committee to meet him. Steve Laing was there, with Chip Barber. The man he had not expected to see was his commanding officer, Colonel Bruce Craig. While he had been in Baghdad the deployment of the SAS in the western deserts of Iraq had grown to involve two full squadrons out of Hereford's four. One had remained at Hereford as the stand-by squadron, the other was in smaller units on training missions around the world.

'You got it, Mike?' asked Laing.

'Yes. Jericho's last message, couldn't get it out by radio.'

He explained briefly why, and handed over the single grubby sheet of paper with Jericho's report.

'Man, we were worried when we couldn't get you these past forty-eight hours,' said Barber. 'You've done a great job, Major.'

'Just one thing, gentlemen,' said Col. Craig. 'If you have finished with him, can I have my officer back?'

Laing was studying the paper, deciphering the

Arabic as best he could. He looked up.

'Why yes, I suppose so. With our sincere thanks.'

'Wait a minute,' said Barber. 'What are you going to do with him now, Colonel?'

'Oh, a bunk in our base across the airfield, some food . . .'

'Got a better idea,' said Barber. 'Major, how does a Kansas steak and fries, an hour in a marble bathtub and a big soft bed grab you?'

'By the balls,' laughed Martin.

'Right. Colonel, your man gets a suite at the Hyatt down the road for twenty-four hours, courtesy of my people. Agreed?'

'OK. See you this time tomorrow, Mike,' said Craig.

On the short drive to the hotel opposite the CENTAF headquarters Martin gave Laing and Barber a translation of the Jericho message. Laing took a verbatim note.

'That's it,' said Barber, 'the air boys will go in there and blow it away.'

It needed Chip Barber to check the soiled Iraqi peasant into the best suite in the Hyatt, and when he was settled the CIA man left to cross the road to the Black Hole.

Martin had his hour in the deep, steaming bath, used the complimentary tackle on the wash-stand to shave and shampoo, and when he came out the steak and fries were on a tray in the sitting room.

He was halfway through the meal when sleep overtook him. He just managed to make the wide soft bed next door, then he was asleep.

While he slept a number of things happened. Freshly pressed shorts, trousers, socks, shoes and shirt were delivered to the sitting room.

In Vienna Gidi Barzilai sent the operational details of the Jericho numbered account to Tel Aviv where an identical replica was prepared with the appropriate wording.

Karim met Edith Hardenberg when she left the bank after work, took her for a coffee and explained that he had to return to Jordan for a week to visit his mother who was sick. She accepted his reason, held his hand and told him to hurry back to her as soon as he could.

Orders went out from the Black Hole to the airbase at Taif where a TR-1 spy plane was preparing to take off for a mission to the far north of Iraq to take further pictures of a major weapons complex at As-Sharqat.

The mission was given a new task, with fresh map co-ordinates, specifically to visit and photograph an area of a range of hills in the northern sector of the Jebal al Hamreen. When the squadron commander protested at the sudden change, he was told the orders were classified as 'Jeremiah directs'. The protest ended.

The TR-1 took off just after two and by four its images were appearing on the screens inside the designated conference room down the corridor from the Black Hole.

There was cloud and rain over the Jebal that day, but with its infra-red and thermal-imaging radar, the ASARS-2 device that defies cloud, rain, hail, sleet, snow and darkness, the spyplane got its pictures anyway.

They were studied as they arrived by Colonel Beatty of the USAF and Squadron Leader Peck of the Royal Air Force, the two top photo-recon. analysts in the Black Hole.

654

The planning conference began at six. There were only eight men present. In the chair was General Horner's deputy, the equally decisive but more jovial General Buster Glosson. The two Intelligence officers Steve Laing and Chip Barber were there because it was they who had brought the target and knew the background to its revelation. The two analysts, Beatty and Peck, were required to explain their interpretation of the pictures of the area. And there were three staff officers, two American and one British, who would note what had to be done and ensure that it was.

Colonel Beatty opened with what was to become the leitmotif of the conference.

'We have a problem here,' he said.

'Then explain it,' said the general.

'Sir, the information provided gives us a grid reference. Twelve figures, six of longitude and six of latitude. But it is not a SATNAV reference, pinning the area down to a few square yards. We are talking about one square kilometre. To be on the safe side, we enlarged the area to one square mile.'

'So?'

'And there it is.'

Colonel Beatty gestured to the wall. Almost the entire space was covered by a blown-up photograph, high-definition, computer-enhanced and covering 6 feet by 6 feet. Everyone stared at it.

'I don't see anything,' said the general. 'Just mountains.'

'That, sir, is the problem. It isn't there.'

The attention switched to the spooks. It was, after all, *their* Intelligence.

'What,' said the general slowly, 'is supposed to be there?'

'A gun,' said Laing.

'A gun?'

'The so-called Babylon gun.'

'I thought you guys had intercepted all of them at the manufacturing stage.'

'So did we. Apparently, one got through.'

'We've been through this before. It's supposed to be a rocket, or a secret fight-bomber base. No gun can fire a payload that big.'

'This one can, sir. I've checked with London. A barrel over 180 metres long, a bore of one metre. A payload of over half a ton. A range of up to 1,000 kilometres, according to the propellant used.'

'And the range from here to the Triangle?'

'470 miles, or 750 kilometres. General, can your fighters intercept a shell?'

'No.'

'Patriot missiles?'

'Possibly, if they're in the right place at the right time and can spot it in time. Probably not.'

'The point is,' interjected Col. Beatty, 'gun or missile, it isn't there.'

'Buried underground, like the Al-Qubai assembly factory?' suggested Barber.

'That was disguised with a car-wrecker's yard on top,' said Sqn. Ldr. Peck. 'Here there's nothing. No road, no tracks, no power lines, no defences, no helipad, no razor wire, no guard barracks, just a wilderness of hills and low mountains with valleys between.'

'Supposing,' said Laing defensively, 'they used the same trick as at Tarmiya—putting the defence perimeter so far out it's way off the frame?'

'We tried that,' said Beatty, 'we looked 50 miles out in all directions. Nothing, no defences.'

656

'Just a pure deception operation?' proposed Barber.

'No way, the Iraqis *always* defend their prize assets, even from their own people. Look, see here.'

Col. Beatty advanced to the picture and pointed out a group of huts.

'A peasant village, right next door. Wood-smoke, goat pens, goats here out foraging in the valley. There are two others off the frame.'

'Maybe they hollowed out the whole mountain,' said Laing. 'You did, at Cheyenne Mountain.'

'That's a series of caverns, tunnels, a warren of rooms behind reinforced doors,' said Beatty. 'You are talking of a barrel 180 metres long. Try to get that inside a mountain, you'd bring the whole damn thing down on top. Look, gentlemen, I can see the breech, the magazine, all the living quarters being underground, but a chunk of that barrel has to stick out. It doesn't.'

They all stared at the picture again. Within the square were three hills and a portion of a fourth. The largest of the three was unmarked by any blast-proof doors, or access road.

'If it's in there somewhere,' proposed Peck, 'why not saturate-bomb the square mile? That would bring down any mountain on top of the weapon.'

'Good idea,' said Beatty. 'General, we could use the Buffs. Paste the whole square mile.'

'May I make a suggestion?' asked Barber.

'Please do,' said General Glosson.

'If I were Saddam Hussein, with his paranoia, and I had one single weapon of this value, I'd have a man in command I could trust. And I'd give him orders that if ever the fortress came under bombing attack, he was to fire. In short, if the first couple of bombs fell wide, and a square mile is quite a big area, the rest might be a fraction of a second too late.'

General Glosson leant forward.

'What is your precise point, Mr Barber?'

'General, if the Fist of God is inside these hills, it is hidden by a deception operation of extreme skill. The only way to be 100 per cent certain of destroying it is by a similar operation. A single plane, coming out of nowhere, delivering one attack and hitting the target on the button first and only time.'

'I don't know how many times I have to say this,' said the exasperated Col. Beatty, 'but we don't know where the button is ... precisely.'

'I think my colleague is talking about target-marking,' said Laing.

'But that means another airplane,' objected Peck. 'Like the Buccaneers marking for the Tornados. Even the target-marker must see the target first.'

'It worked with the Scuds,' said Laing.

'Sure, the SAS men marked the missile launchers and we blew them away. But they were right there, on the ground, 1,000 yards from the missiles with binoculars,' said Peck.

'Precisely.'

There was silence for several seconds.

'You are talking,' said General Glosson, 'of putting men into the mountains to give us a 10-square-yard target.'

The debate went on for two more hours. But it always came back to Laing's argument.

First find it, then mark it, then destroy it—and all without the Iraqis noticing until it is too late.

At midnight a corporal of the Royal Air Force went to the Hyatt Hotel. He could get no reply from the sitting-room door, so the night manager let him

658

in. He went into the bedroom and shook by the shoulder the man sleeping in a towelling robe on top of the bed.

'Sir, wake up, sir. You're wanted across the road, Major.'

CHAPTER TWENTY-TWO

'It's there,' said Mike Martin two hours later.

'Where?' asked Col. Beatty with genuine curiosity.

'In there somewhere.'

In the conference room down the corridor from the Black Hole Martin was leaning over the table studying a photograph of a larger section of the Jebal al Hamreen range. It showed a square 5 miles by 5 miles. He pointed with his forefinger.

'The villages, the three villages, here, here and here.'

'What about them?'

'They're phoney. They're beautifully done, they're perfect replicas of the villages of mountain peasants, but they're full of guards.'

Col. Beatty stared at the three villages. One was in a valley only half a mile from the middle of the three mountains at the centre of the frame. The other two occupied terraces on the mountain slopes further out.

None was big enough to support a mosque, indeed they were little more than hamlets. Each had its main and central barn for the storage of winter hay and feed, and smaller barns for the sheep and goats. A dozen humble shacks made up the rest of the settlements, mud-brick dwellings with thatch or tinplate roofs of the kind that can be seen anywhere in the mountains of the Middle East. In summer there might be small patches of tilled crops near by, but not in winter.

Life in the mountains of Iraq is harsh in winter, with slanting bitter rain and scudding clouds. The notion that all parts of the Middle East are warm is a popular fallacy.

'OK, Major, you know Iraq, I don't. Why are they phoney?'

'Life-support system,' said Martin. 'Too many villages, too many peasants, too many goats and sheep. Not enough forage. They'd starve.'

'Shit,' said Beatty with feeling, 'so damn simple.'

'That may be, but it proves Jericho wasn't lying, or mistaken again. If they've done that, they're hiding something.'

Colonel Craig, commanding officer of the 22nd SAS, had joined them in the basement. He had been talking quietly to Steve Laing. Now he came over.

'What do you reckon, Mike?'

'It's there, Bruce. One could probably see it—at 1,000 yards with good binoculars.'

'The brass wants to put a team in to mark it. You're out.'

'Bullshit, sir. These hills are probably alive with foot patrols. You can see there are no roads.'

'So? Patrols can be avoided.'

'And if you run into any? There's no-one speaks Arabic like me, and you know it. Besides, it's a HALO drop. Helicopters won't work either.'

'You've had all the action you need, so far as I can gather.'

'That's crap, too. I haven't seen any action at all. I'm fed up with spooking. Let me have this one. The others have had the desert for weeks while I've been tending a garden.'

Colonel Craig raised an eyebrow. He had not asked Laing exactly what Martin had been up to—he would not have been told anyway—but he was surprised one of his best officers had been posing as a gardener.

'Come back to the base. We can plan better there. If I like your idea, you can have it.'

Before dawn General Schwarzkopf had agreed there was no alternative and gave his consent. In that cordoned-off corner of the Riyadh military airbase that was the private preserve of the SAS Martin had outlined his ideas to Col. Craig and had been given the go-ahead.

Co-ordination of planning would reside with Col. Craig for the men on the ground and with General Glosson for the eventual fighter-strike.

Buster Glosson took morning coffee with his friend and superior Chuck Horner.

'Any ideas for the unit we'd like to use on this one?' he asked.

General Horner thought back to a certain officer who two weeks earlier had advised him to do something extremely rude.

'Yeah,' he said, 'give it to the 336th.'

*   *   *

Mike Martin had won his argument with Colonel Craig by pointing out—logically—that with most of the SAS soldiers in the Gulf theatre already deployed inside Iraq he was the senior officer available, that he was Commander of B Squadron which was then on operations in the desert under the command of his Number Two, and that he alone spoke fluent Arabic.

661

But the clinching argument was his experience of free-fall parachuting. While serving with 3rd Battalion Parachute Regiment he had attended the Number One Para Training School at RAF Brize Norton and had jumped with the trials team. Later he did the free-fall course at Netheravon and jumped with the Paras' display team, the Red Devils, better known in those circles as the Red Freds.

The only way into the Iraqi mountains without raising the alarm was going to be a HALO drop—High Altitude, Low Opening—meaning coming out of the aircraft at 25,000 feet and falling free to open the chutes at 3,500 feet. It was not a job for newcomers.

The planning of the entire mission ought to have taken a week, but there was no time for that. The only solution was for the various aspects of the drop, the cross-country march and the selection of the Lying-Up Position to be planned simultaneously. For that he needed men he could trust with his life, which was precisely what he was going to do anyway.

Back at the SAS corner of the military airbase of Riyadh, his first question to Colonel Craig was: 'Who can I have?'

The list was short; there were so many away on operations in the desert.

When the adjutant showed him the list, one name sprang out at him.

'Peter Stephenson, definite.'

'You're lucky,' said Craig, 'he came back over the border a week ago. Been resting ever since. He's fit.'

Martin had known Sergeant Stephenson when the sergeant had been a corporal and he a captain on his first tour with the Regiment as a troop commander. Like himself, Stephenson was a free-faller and a member of the Air Troop of his own squadron.

'He's good,' said Craig, pointing at another name. 'A mountain man. I suggest you'll need two of them.'

The name he pointed at was Corporal Ben Eastman.

'I know him. You're right. I'll take him any time. Who else?'

Last selection was Corporal Kevin North, from another squadron. Martin had never operated with him, but North was a mountain specialist and highly recommended by his troop commander.

There were five areas of planning that had to be accomplished simultaneously. He divided up the tasks between them with himself in overall charge.

First came the selection of the aircraft to drop them. Without hesitation Martin went for the C-130 Hercules, the habitual launch-pad of the SAS, and there were then nine of them serving in the Gulf. They were all based at nearby King Khaled International Airport. Even better news came with breakfast; three of them were from No. 47 Squadron, based at Lyneham in Wiltshire, the same squadron that had years of experience liaising with the SAS free-fallers.

Among the crew of one of the three was a certain Flight Lieutenant Glyn Morris.

Throughout the Gulf war the Hercules transports had been part of the hub-and-spoke operation, shifting cargo arriving at Riyadh to the outlying bases of the Royal Air Force at Tabuk, Muharraq, Dhahran and even Seeb in Oman. Morris had been serving as loadmaster or cargo supervisor, but his real function on this planet was as a PJI, Parachute Jump Instructor, and Martin had jumped under his supervision before.

Contrary to the notion that the Paras and the SAS

663

look after their own parachuting, all combat dropping in the British Armed Forces comes under the RAF, and the relationship is based on the mutual trust that each party knows exactly what it is doing.

Air Commodore Ian Macfadyen, commanding the RAF in the Gulf, at once seconded the desired Hercules to the SAS mission the moment it arrived back from stores-dumping at Tabuk, and riggers began to convert it for the HALO mission scheduled for the same night.

Chief among the conversion tasks was the construction of an oxygen console on the floor of the cargo bay. Flying mainly at low level, the Hercules, till that point, had never needed oxygen in the rear to keep troops alive at high altitude. Flt. Lt. Morris needed no training in what he was doing, and brought in a second PJI from another Hercules, Flt. Sgt. Sammy Dawlish. They worked throughout the day on the Hercules and had it ready by sundown.

The second priority was that of the parachutes themselves. At that point the SAS had not dropped into Iraq from the skies—they had gone into the Iraqi deserts on wheels, but in the run-up to the actual war training missions had been constant.

At the military airbase there was a sealed and temperature-controlled Safety Equipment Section, where the SAS had stored its parachutes. Martin asked for and got an allocation of eight main chutes and eight reserves, although he and his men would only need four of each. Sgt. Stephenson was allocated the task of checking and packing all eight throughout the day.

The chutes were no longer the circular aeroconical type associated with the Parachute Regiment, but the newer design called 'squares'. They are not really square but oblong, and have two layers of fabric. In flight, air is conducted between the layers, forming a semi-rigid 'wing' with an aerofoil cross-section, enabling the free-faller to 'fly' the chute downwards with greater mobility to turn and to manoeuvre. These are the type normally seen at free-falling displays.

The two corporals got the task of obtaining and checking all the remaining stores that would be needed. These included four sets of clothing, four big Bergen rucksacks, water bottles, helmets, belts, weapons, HVCs—the high-value concentrates which would be all there was to eat—ammunition, first-aid kits ... the list went on and on. Each man would be carrying 80 pounds in those Bergens, and might need every ounce of them.

Fitters and mechanics worked on the Hercules itself in a designated hangar, overhauling the engines and servicing every other moving part.

The Squadron CO nominated his best aircrew, whose navigator accompanied Colonel Craig back to the Black Hole to select a suitable dropping zone, the all-important DZ.

Martin himself was taken in hand by six technicians, four American and two British, and introduced to the 'toys' he would have to operate to find the target, locate it to a few square yards and relay the information back to Riyadh.

When he had finished, his various devices were security-packed against accidental breakage and taken across to the hangar where the mountain of gear for the four men grew and grew. For extra safety, there were two of each of the scientific devices, adding again to the weight the men would carry.

Martin himself went to join the planners in the

Black Hole. They were bent over a large table strewn with fresh pictures taken by another TR-1 that morning just after dawn. The weather had been clear and the photos showed every nook and crevice of the Jebal al Hamreen.

'We assume,' said Col. Craig, 'that this damn gun must be pointing south to south-east. The best observation point would therefore seem to be here.'

He indicated a series of crevices in the side of a mountain to the south of the presumed Fortress, the hill in the centre of the group within the square kilometre that had been designated by the dead Colonel Osman Badri.

'As for a DZ, there's a small valley here, about forty kilometres south ... you can see the water glinting in a wee stream running down the valley.'

Martin looked. It was a tiny depression in the hills, 500 yards long and about 100 wide, with grassy banks strewn with rocks, and the rill trickling its winter water along the bottom of the dip.

'It's the best?' asked Martin. Col. Craig shrugged.

'Frankly, it's about all you've got. The next is seventy clicks away from the target; get any closer and they could see you land.'

On the map, in daylight, it would be a cinch; in pitch darkness, plunging through freezing air at 120 m.p.h., it would be easy to miss. There would be no lights to guide, no flares on the ground. From blackness into blackness.

'I'll take it,' he said. The RAF navigator straightened up.

'Right, I'll get weaving.'

He would have a busy afternoon. It would be his job to find his way without lights and across a moonless sky, not to the dropping zone, but to a

666

point in space from which, bearing in mind wind drift, four falling bodies would have to leave his aircraft to find that tiny valley. Even falling bodies drift downwind; his job would be to estimate how much.

It was not until the hour of dusk that all the men met again in the hangar that was banned to everyone else on the base. The Hercules stood ready, fuelled. Beneath one wing was the mound of gear the four men would need. Dawlish, the RAF Jump Instructor, had repacked every one of the eight 48-pound chutes as if he would be using them himself. Stephenson was satisfied. In one corner was a large briefing table. Martin, who had brought enlarged photographs from the Black Hole with him, took Stephenson, Eastman and North over to the table to work out the route march from the DZ to those crevices where they intended to lie up and study the Fortress for however long it took. It looked like two nights of hard march, with a lie-up in the intervening day. There could be no question of marching in daylight, and the route could not be direct.

Finally each man packed his Bergen from the bottom up, the last item being the Belt Order, a heavy webbing belt with numerous pockets, which would be unpacked after landing and worn round the waist.

American hamburgers and sodas were brought from the commissary at sundown and the four men rested until take-off. This was scheduled for 9.45 p.m., aiming for a drop at 11.30 p.m.

Martin always reckoned the waiting was worst; after the frantic activity of the day it was like a long anti-climax. There was nothing to concentrate on but the tension, the constant nagging thought that, despite all the checks and double-checks, something

667

vital had been forgotten. It was the period when some men ate, or read, or wrote home, or dozed, or just went to the lavatory and emptied themselves.

At nine a tractor towed the Hercules out onto the apron and the crew of pilot, co-pilot, navigator and flight engineer began their engine run-up checks. Twenty minutes later a black-windowed bus entered the hangar to take the men and their gear to the drop-plane, waiting with rear doors open and ramp down.

The two PJIs were ready for them, with the loadmaster and chute rigger. Only seven walked up the ramp on foot and into the vast cavern of the Herc. The ramp came up and the doors closed. The rigger had gone back to the bus; he would not fly with them.

With the PJIs and the loadmaster, the four soldiers strapped themselves to the seats along the wall, and waited. At 9.44 p.m. the Hercules lifted off from Riyadh and turned her blunt nose to the north.

While the RAF plane rose into the night sky on 21 February, an American helicopter was asked to stay to one side before coming in to settle close to the American sector of the base.

It had been sent to Al Kharz to pick up two men. Steve Turner, the squadron commander of the 336th Tactical Fighter Squadron, had been summoned to Riyadh on the orders of General Buster Glosson. With him, as ordered, he brought the man he considered his best pilot for low-level ground-attack sorties.

Neither the CO of the Rocketeers nor Captain Don Walker had the faintest idea why they were wanted. In a small briefing room below CENTAF headquarters an hour later they were told why, and what was needed. They were also told that no-one

668

else, with the sole exception of Walker's weapons systems officer, the man flying in the seat behind him, was allowed to know the full details.

Then they were helicoptered back to their base.

*   *   *

After take-off the four soldiers could unbuckle and move around the hull of the aircraft, by the dim red lights overhead. Martin went forward, up the ladder to the flight deck and sat for a while with the crew.

They flew at 10,000 feet towards the Iraqi border, then began to climb. At 25,000 feet the Hercules levelled off and crossed into Iraq, seemingly alone in the starlit sky.

In fact they were not alone. Over the Gulf an AWACS had orders to keep a constant eye on the sky around and below them. If any Iraqi radar screen, for some unknown reason not already 'totalled' by the Allied air forces, chose to 'illuminate', it was to be immediately attacked. To this end two flights of Wild Weasels with anti-radar HARM missiles were below them.

In case some Iraqi fighter pilot chose to take to the sky that night, a flight of RAF Jaguars was above and to the left of them, a flight of F-15C Eagles to the right. The Hercules was flying in a protective box of lethal technology. No other pilot in the sky that night knew why. They just had their orders.

In fact, if anyone in Iraq saw any blip on the radar that night, it was assumed the freighter was just heading north to Turkey.

The loadmaster did his all to make his guests comfortable with tea, coffee, soft drinks and biscuits.

Forty minutes before Release Point the navigator

669

flashed a warning light indicating P-minus-forty and the last preparations began.

The four soldiers put on their main and reserve parachutes, the former across the breadth of the shoulders, the latter lower down the back. Then came the Bergens, hung upside down at the back beneath the chutes with the point between the legs. Weapons, the silenced Heckler and Koch MP5 SD sub-machine-gun, were clipped down the left side and the personal oxygen tank hooked across the belly.

Finally they put on their helmets and oxygen masks before connecting the latter to the centre console, a frame structure the size of a large dining table, crammed with bottles of oxygen. When everyone was breathing and comfortable, the pilot was informed and began to bleed the air and pressure level inside the hull out into the night until both had equalized.

It took almost twenty minutes. Then they sat again, waiting. Fifteen minutes before Release Point a further message came from the flight deck, into the ears of the loadmaster. He told the PJIs to gesture to the soldiers to switch from main console oxygen to their own personal mini-bottles. These had thirty minutes supply, and they would need three to four minutes of that for the drop itself.

At that point only the navigator on the flight deck knew exactly where he was; the SAS team had total confidence they would be dropped in the right place.

By now the loadmaster was in contact with the soldiers by a constant stream of hand signals, which ended when he pointed both hands at the lights above the console. Into the loadmaster's ears came a stream of instructions from the navigator.

The men rose and started to move, slowly, like

spacemen weighed down by their gear, towards the ramp. The PJIs, also on mobile oxygen bottles, went with them.

The SAS men stood in a line in front of the still-closed tailgate door, each checking the equipment in front of him.

At P-minus-four the tailgate came down and they stared out into 25,000 feet of rushing black air. Another hand signal, two fingers raised by the PJI, told them they were at P-minus-two. The men shuffled to the very edge of the ramp and looked at the lights (unilluminated) on each side of the gaping aperture. The lights went red, goggles were drawn down. The lights went green.

All four men turned on one heel, facing into the cavern, and jumped backwards, arms apart, faces down. The sill of the ramp flashed beneath their masks and the Hercules was gone.

Sergeant Stephenson led the way.

Stabilizing their fall position, the four men dropped through the night sky for 5 miles without a sound. At 3,500 feet automatic pressure-operated releases jerked open the parachute packs and the fabric exploded out. In second position, Mike Martin saw the shadow 50 foot beneath him appear to stop moving. In the same second he felt the vibration of his own main chute opening, then the 'square' took the strain and he slowed from 120 m.p.h. to 14, with hesitators taking up some of the shock.

At 1,000 feet, each man undid the snap-locks that held his Bergen to his backside and cinched the load down his legs, there to hook on to his feet. The Bergens would remain there all the way down, being released only 100 feet above the ground to hang at the full extent of the 14-foot nylon retaining-line.

671

The sergeant's parachute was moving away to his right so Mike Martin followed. The sky was clear, the stars visible, black shapes of mountains rushed upwards on all sides. Then he saw what the sergeant had seen, the glitter of water in the stream running through the valley.

Peter Stephenson went down right in the centre of the zone, a few yards from the edge of the stream, on soft grass and moss. Martin dropped his Bergen on its line, swerved, stopped in the air, felt the Bergen hit the ground beneath him and settled gently on to both feet.

Cpl. Eastman swept past and above him, turned, glided back in and dropped 50 yards way. Martin was unbuckling his chute harness and did not see Kevin North land at all.

In fact the mountaineer was the fourth and last in the line, descending 100 yards away, but onto the slope of the hill rather than the grassland. He was trying to close up to his colleagues, hauling down on his guidance 'stats' when the Bergen beneath him hit the hill. As it touched the ground, the Bergen was dragged sideways by the drifting man above, to whose waist it was attached. It bumped along the hillside for 5 yards, then snagged between two rocks.

The sudden yank on the lanyard pulled North down and sideways so that he landed not on his feet but on his side. There were not many rocks on that hillside but one of them smashed his left femur in eight places.

The corporal felt the bone shatter with complete clarity, but the jar was so severe it numbed the pain. For a few seconds. Then it came in waves. He rolled over and clutched his thigh with two hands, whispering over and over: 'No, no, please God, no.'

672

Though he did not realize it, because it happened inside the leg, he began to bleed. One of the shards of bone in the multiple fracture had sliced clean through the femoral artery which began to pump out his life-blood into the mess of his thigh.

The other three found him a minute later. They had all unhitched their billowing chutes and Bergens, convinced he would be doing the same. When they realized he was not with them, they came to look. Stephenson brought out his pen-light and shone it on the leg.

'Oh, shit,' he whispered. They had first-aid kits, even shell-dressings, but nothing to cope with this.

The corporal needed trauma therapy, plasma, major surgery, and fast. Stephenson ran back to North's Bergen, ripped out a first-aid kit and began to prepare a jab of morphine. There was no need. With the blood, the pain was fading.

North opened his eyes, focused on the face of Mike Martin above him, whispered, 'I'm sorry, Boss,' and closed his eyes again. Two minutes later he was gone.

At another time, and in another place, Martin might have been able to vent some sign of the pain that he felt at losing a man like North, operating under his command. There was no time; this was not the place. The two remaining NCOs recognized this and went about what they had to do in grim silence. Grief could come later.

Martin had hoped to bundle up the spilled parachutes and clear the valley before finding a rocky crevasse to bury the surplus gear. Now that was impossible. He had North's body to cope with.

'Pete, start getting together everything we bury. Find a hollow scrape somewhere, or make one. Ben, start collecting rocks.'

Martin bent over the body, removed the dog tags and machine-pistol, then went to help Eastman. Together, with knives and hands, the three men scraped a hollow in the springy turf and laid the body in it. There was more to pile on top; four opened main parachutes, four still-packed reserves, four oxygen bottles, lanyards, webbing.

Then they began to pile rocks on top, not in a neat shape like a cairn which would be spotted, but in a random way as if the rocks had tumbled from the mountainside. Water was brought from the brook to sluice the rock and the grass of its red stains. Bare patches where the rocks they were using had stood were scuffed with feet and fragments of moss from the water's edge stamped into them. The valley had to be made to look as much as possible as it had an hour before midnight.

They had hoped to put in five hours of marching before dawn, but the job took them over three. Some of the contents of North's Bergen stayed inside and were buried with him; his clothes, food and water. Other items they had to divide between them, making their own loads even heavier.

An hour before dawn they left the valley and went into SOP—standing operating procedure. Sgt. Stephenson took the role of lead scout, moving up ahead of the other two, dropping to the ground before cresting a ridge to peer over the top in case there was a nasty surprise on the other side.

The route lay upwards, and he set a gruelling pace. Although a small and wiry man, and five years older than Martin, he could march most men clean off their feet and carry an 80-pound load while he did it.

Clouds came over the mountains just when Martin needed them, delaying the dawn and giving him an extra hour. In ninety minutes of hard march they covered 8 miles, putting several ridges and two hills between them and the valley. Finally the advance of the grey light forced them to look for a lying-up position.

Martin chose a horizontal crack in the rocks under an overhang, screened by sere grass and just above a dry wadi. In the last of the darkness they ate some rations, sipped water, covered themselves with scrim netting and lay down to sleep. There were three duty watches and Martin took the first.

He nudged Stephenson awake at 11 a.m. and slept while the sergeant stood guard. It was at 4 p.m. that Ben Eastman poked Martin in the ribs with a rigid finger. As the major's eyes opened he saw Eastman with his forefinger to his lips. Martin listened. From the wadi 10 feet beneath their ledge came the guttural sounds of voices in Arabic.

Sgt. Stephenson came awake and raised an eyebrow. What do we do now? Martin listened for a while. There were four of them, on patrol, bored with their task of endlessly marching through the mountains, and tired. Within ten minutes he knew they intended to camp there for the night.

He had lost enough time already. He needed to move by six when darkness would fall over the hills, and he needed every hour to cover the miles to those crevices in the hill across the valley from the Fortress. He might need more time to search for those crevices and find them.

The conversation from the wadi below indicated the Iraqis were going to search for wood for a camp-fire. They would be certain to cast an eye on the bushes behind which the SAS men lay. Even if they did not, it might be hours before they would sleep

675

deeply enough for Martin's patrol to slip past them and get away. There was nothing for it.

At a signal from Martin the other two eased out their flat, double-edged knives and the three men slid over the scree into the wadi below.

When the job was over, Martin flickered through the dead Iraqis' pay-books. All, he noticed, had the patronymic Al-Ubaidi. They were all of the Ubaidi tribe, mountain men who came from these parts. All wore the insignia of the Republican Guard. Clearly the Guard had been culled of these mountains—fighters to form the patrols whose job was to keep the Fortress safe from intruders. He noted they were lean, spare men, without an ounce of fat on them, and probably tireless in hill country like this.

It still cost an hour to drag the four bodies into the crevice, cut apart their camouflaged tent to form a tarpaulin and to decorate the tarp with bushes, weeds and grass. But when they were finished it would have taken an extremely sharp eye to spot the hiding-place beneath the overhang. Fortunately the Iraqi patrol had had no radio, so they would probably not check in with their base until they arrived back, whenever that might be. Now, they would never get back, but with luck it would be two days before they were missed.

As darkness set in, the SAS men marched on, trying by the starlight to recall the shapes of the mountains in the photographs, following the compass heading towards the mountain they sought.

The map Martin carried was a brilliant confection, drawn by a computer on the basis of the aerial photos by the TR-1 and showing the route between the DZ and the intended Lying-Up Position. Pausing at intervals to consult his hand-held SATNAV

676

positioner and study the map by pen-light, Martin could check their direction and progress. By midnight both were good. He estimated a further 10 miles to march.

In the Brecons in Wales, Martin and his men could have kept up 4 m.p.h. over this kind of terrain, a brisk walk on a flat surface for those taking their dogs for an evening stroll without an 80-pound rucksack. Tabbing at that rate was quite normal.

But in these hostile hills, with the possibility of patrols all around them, progress had to be slower. They had had one brush with the Iraqis and a second would be too many.

An advantage they had over the Iraqis was their NVGs, the night-vision goggles they wore like frogs' eyes on stalks. With the new wide-angle version they could see the countryside ahead of them in a pale green glow, for the job of the image-intensifiers was to gather every scrap of natural light in the environment and concentrate it into the viewer's retina.

Two hours before dawn they saw the bulk of the Fortress in front of them and began to climb the slope to their left. The mountain they had chosen was on the southern fringe of the square kilometre provided by Jericho and from the crevices near the summit they should be able to look across at the southern face of the Fortress—if indeed it *was* the Fortress—at an almost equal height to its peak.

They climbed hard for an hour, the breath coming in rasping gasps. Sgt. Stephenson in the lead cut into a tiny goat-track which led upwards and round the curve of the mountain. Just short of the summit they found the crevice the TR-1 had seen on its down-and-sideways camera. It was better than Martin could have hoped, a natural crack in the rock 8 foot long, 4 foot deep and 2 foot high. Outside the crack was a ledge 2 foot across, on which Martin's torso could lie with his lower body and feet inside the rocks.

The men brought out their scrim netting and began to make their niche invisible from watching eyes.

Food and water were stuffed into the pouches of the Belt Orders, Martin's pieces of technical equipment laid ready to hand, weapons checked and set close by. Just before the sun rose, Martin used one of his devices.

It was a transmitter, much smaller than the one he had had in Baghdad, barely the size of two cigarette packets. It linked to a cadmium-nickel battery with enough power to give him more talking time than he would ever need.

The frequency was fixed and at the other end there was a listening watch for twenty-fours hours a day. To attract attention he only had to press the 'transmit' button in an agreed sequence of blips and pauses, then wait for the speaker to respond with the answering sequence.

The third component of the set was a dish aerial, foldaway like the one in Baghdad, but smaller. Though he was now further north than the Iraqi capital, he was also much higher.

Martin set up the dish, pointing towards the south, linked the battery to the set and the set to the aerial, then pressed the transmit button. One-two-three-four-five; pause; one-two-three; pause, one, pause, one.

Five seconds later the radio in his hands squawked softly. Four blips, four blips, two.

He pressed transmit, kept the thumb down and said into the speaker: 'Come Nineveh, come Tyre. I say again, Come Nineveh, come Tyre.'

He released the transmit button and waited. The set gave an excited one-two-three; pause; one, pause, four. Received and acknowledged.

Martin put the set away in its water-proof cover, took his powerful field glasses and eased his torso on to the ledge. Behind him Sgt. Stephenson and Cpl. Eastman were sandwiched like embryos into the crevice under the rock, but apparently quite comfortable. Two twigs held up the netting in front of him, giving a slit through which he slid the binoculars for which a bird-watcher would have given his right arm.

As the sun seeped into the mountains of Hamreen on the morning of 23 February, Major Martin began to study the masterpiece of his old school friend Osman Badri, the Qa'ala that no machine could see.

* * *

In Riyadh Steve Laing and Simon Paxman stared at the sheet handed them by the engineer who had come running out of the radio shack.

'Bloody hell,' said Laing with feeling, 'he's there, he's on the frigging mountain.'

Twenty minutes later the news reached Al Kharz from General Glosson's office.

* * *

Captain Don Walker had returned to his base in the small hours of the 22nd, grabbed some sleep in what was left of the night and began work just after sunrise when the pilots who had flown missions during the night were completing their debrief and shuffling off to bed.

By midday he had a plan to present to his superior officers. It was sent at once to Riyadh and approved. During the afternoon the appropriate aircraft, crew and support services were allocated.

What was planned was a four-ship raid on an Iraqi airbase well north of Baghdad called Tikrit East, not far from the birthplace of Saddam Hussein. It would be a night raid with 2,000-pound laser-guided bombs. Don Walker would lead it, with his usual wingman and another element of two Eagles.

Miraculously the mission appeared on the Air Tasking Order from Riyadh, although it had only been devised twelve hours and not three days earlier.

The other three needed crews were at once taken off any other tasking and assigned to the Tikrit East mission, slated for the night of the 22nd (maybe) or any other night they were ordered. Until then they were on permanent one-hour stand-by.

The four Strike Eagles were prepared by sundown of the 22nd and at 10 p.m. the mission was cancelled. No other mission was substituted. The eight air crew were told to rest, while the remainder of the squadron went tank 'plinking' among the Republican Guard units north of Kuwait.

When they returned in the dawn of the 23rd, the four idle air crew came in for their turn of ribbing.

With the mission planning staff, a route was worked out for Tikrit East which would take the four Eagles up the corridor between Baghdad and the Iranian border to the east, with a turn of course through 45 degrees over Lake As Sa'diyah and then straight on, north-west to Tikrit.

As he sipped his breakfast coffee in the mess hall, Don Walker was summoned outside by his squadron commander.

'Your target-marker is in place,' he was told. 'Get some rest. It could be a rough night.'

*   *   *

By the rising sun Mike Martin began to study the mountain across the steep valley. On full magnification his glasses could pick out individual bushes; pulling the focus back, he could see an area any size he wanted.

For the first hour it looked like just a mountain. The grass grew as on all the others. There were stunted shrubs and bushes as on all the rest. Here and there a patch of bare rock, occasionally a small boulder clung to the slopes. Like all the other hills within his vision, it was of an irregular shape. There seemed nothing out of place.

From time to time he squeezed his eyes tight to rest them, pillowed his head on his forearms for a while and started again.

By mid-morning a pattern began to emerge. On certain parts of the mountain the grass appeared to grow in a manner different from that on other parts. There were areas where the vegetation seemed too regular, as if in lines. But there was no door, unless it was on the other side, no road, no track with tyre marks, no standpipe venting foul air from inside, no mark of present or previous excavation. It was the moving sun that gave the first clue.

Shortly after eleven he thought he caught a glint of something in the grass. He brought the glasses back to that patch and went to full magnification. The sun went behind a cloud. When it came out, the glint flashed again. Then he saw the source; a fragment of

681

wire in the grass.

He blinked and tried again. Slantwise, a length of wire a foot long in the grass. It was part of a longer strand, green plastic-covered wire, of which a small part had been abraded to reveal the metal beneath.

The wire was one of several, all buried in the grass, occasionally revealed as the wind blew the stems from side to side. Diagonals in the opposite direction, a patch of chain-link wire, underneath the grass.

By midday he could see it better. A section of mountainside where green wire mesh held the soil to a surface below the earth; the grass and shrubs planted in every diamond-shaped gap between the fencing, growing through the gaps, covering the wire beneath.

Then he saw the terracing. One part of the mountainside was made up of concrete blocks, presumably concrete, each set back 3 inches from the one below it. Along the horizontal terraces thus created were runnels of earth out of which the shrubs grew. Where they sprouted they were in horizontal lines. At first it did not look so, because they were of different heights, but when he studied their stems only, it became clear they were indeed in lines. Nature does not grow in lines.

He tried other parts of the mountain, but the pattern ended, then began again further to his left. It was in the early afternoon that he solved it.

The analysts in Riyadh had been right—up to a point. Had anyone attempted to gouge out the whole centre of the hill, it would have fallen in. Whoever had done this must have taken three existing hills, cut away the inner faces and built up the gaps between the peaks to create a gigantic crater.

In filling the gaps, the builder had followed the

contours of the real hills, stepping his rows of concrete blocks backwards and upwards, creating the mini-terraces, pouring tens of thousands of tons of topsoil down from the top.

The cladding must have come later; sheets of green vinyl-coated chain-link wire probably stapled to the concrete beneath, holding the earth to the slopes. Then the grass seed, sprayed on to the earth, there to root and spread, with bushes and shrubs sown into deeper bowls left in the concrete terraces.

The grass through the previous summer had matted, creating its own bonding network of roots, and the shrubs had sprouted upwards through the wire and the grass to match the undergrowth on the original hills.

Above the crater, the roof of the fortress was surely a geodesic dome, so cast that it, too, contained thousands of pockets where grass could grow. There were even artificial boulders, painted the grey of real rocks, with streaks where the rain had run off.

Martin began to concentrate on the area near the point where the rim of the crater would have been before the construction of the rotunda.

It was about fifty feet below the summit of the dome that he found what he sought. He had already swept his glasses across the slight protruberance fifty times and not noticed.

It was a rocky outcrop, faded grey, but two black lines ran across it from side to side. The more he studied the lines the more he wondered why anyone would have clambered so high to draw two lines across a boulder.

A squall of wind came from the north-east, ruffling the scrim netting round his face. The same wind caused one of the lines to move. When the wind

683

dropped, the line ceased to move. Then Martin realized they were not drawn lines, but steel wires, running across the rock and away into the grass.

Smaller boulders stood round the perimeter of the large one, like sentries in a ring. Why so circular, why steel wires? Supposing someone, down below, jerked hard on those wires ... would the boulder move?

At half-past three he realized it was not a boulder. It was a grey tarpaulin, weighted down by a circle of rocks, to be twitched to one side when the wires were jerked downwards into the cavern beneath.

Under the tarp he gradually made out a shape, circular, 5 foot in diameter. He was staring at a canvas sheet beneath which, invisible to him, the last three foot of the Babylon gun projected, from its breech 200 yards inside the crater, up into the sky. It was pointing south-south-east towards Dhahran, 750 kilometres away.

'Range-finder,' he muttered to the men behind him. He passed back the binoculars and took the implement offered to him. It was like a telescope.

When he held it to his eye, as they had shown him in Riyadh, he saw the mountain and the tarp that hid the gun, but not with any magnification.

On the prism were four V-shaped chevrons, the points all directed inwards. Slowly he rotated the knurled knob on the side of the scope, until all four points touched each other to form a cross. The cross rested on the tarpaulin.

Taking the scope from his eye he consulted the numbers on the rotating band. 1,080 yards.

'Compass,' he said. He pushed the range-finder behind him and took the electronic compass. This was no device dependent on a dish swimming in a bowl of alcohol, nor even a pointer balanced on a gimbal. He held it to his eye, sighted the tarpaulin across the valley and pressed the button. The compass did the rest, giving him a bearing from his own position to the tarpaulin of 348 degrees, 10 minutes and 18 seconds.

The SATNAV positioner gave him the last thing he needed—his own exact location on the planet's surface to the nearest square 15 yards by 15 yards.

It was a clumsy business trying to erect the satellite dish in the confined space and took ten minutes. When he called Riyadh the response was immediate. Slowly Martin read to the listeners in the Saudi capital three sets of figures; his own exact position, the compass direction from himself to the target, and the range. Riyadh could work out the rest and give the pilot his co-ordinates.

Martin crawled back into the crevice, to be replaced by Stephenson who would keep an eye open for Iraqi patrols, and tried to sleep.

At half-past eight, in complete darkness, he tested the infra-red target marker. In shape it was like a large flash-lamp with a pistol-grip, but it had an eye-piece at the back.

He linked it to its battery, aimed it at the Fortress and looked. The whole mountain was as clearly lit as if bathed in a great green moon. He swung the barrel of the image intensifier up to the tarpaulin that masked the barrel of Babylon and squeezed the pistol-trigger.

A single, invisible beam of infra-red light raced across the valley and he saw a small red dot appear on the mountainside. Moving the night-sight, he settled the red dot on the tarpaulin and kept it there for half a minute. Satisfied, he switched it off and crawled back beneath the netting.

*   *   *

The four Strike Eagles took off from Al Kharz at
10.45 p.m. and climbed to 20,000 feet. For three of
the crews it was a routine mission to hit an Iraqi
airbase. Each Eagle carried two 2,000-pound laser-
guided bombs, apart from their self-defence air-to-
air missiles.

Refuelling from their designated KC-10 tanker
just south of the Iraqi border was normal and
uneventful. When they were topped up, they turned
away in loose formation and the flight, coded
Bluejay, set course almost due north, passing over the
Iraqi town of As-Samawah at 11.14 p.m.

They flew in radio silence as always and without
lights, each wizzo clearly able to see the other three
aircraft on his radar. The night was clear and the
AWACS over the Gulf had given them a 'picture
clear' advice, meaning no Iraqi fighters were up.

At 11.39 p.m. Don Walker's wizzo muttered:
'Turning point in five.'

They all heard it and understood they would be
turning over Lake As Sa'diyah in five minutes.

Just as they went into the 45-degree turn to port, to
set the new heading for Tikrit East, the other three
aircrew heard Don Walker say quite clearly: 'Bluejay
flight ... leader has engine problems. I'm going to
RTB. Bluejay Three, take over.'

Bluejay Three was Bull Baker that night, leader of
the other two-plane element. From that transmission
onwards, things began to go wrong and in a very
weird manner.

Walker's wingman Randy 'R-2' Roberts closed up
with his leader but could see no apparent trouble
from Walker's engines, yet the Bluejay Leader was

losing power and height. If he was going to RTB—return to base—it would be normal for his wingman to stay with him, unless the problem was minimal. Engine trouble far over enemy territory is not minimal.

'Roger that,' acknowledged Baker.

Then they heard Walker say: 'Bluejay Two, rejoin Bluejay Three, I say again, rejoin. That is an order. Proceed to Tikrit East.'

The wingman, now baffled, did as he was ordered and climbed back to rejoin the remainder of Bluejay. Their commander continued to lose height over the lake; they could see him on their radars.

At the same moment they realized he had done the unthinkable. For some reason, confusion caused by the engine problem perhaps, he had spoken not on the Have-quick coded radio, but 'in clear'. More amazingly, he had actually mentioned their destination.

Out over the Gulf a young USAF sergeant manning part of the battery of consoles in the hull of the AWACS plane summoned his mission commander in perplexity.

'We have a problem, sir. Bluejay Leader has engine trouble. He wants to RTB.'

'Right, noted,' said the mission commander. In most airplanes the pilot is the captain and in complete charge. In an AWACS the pilot has that charge for the safety of the airplane, but the mission commander calls the shots when it comes to giving orders across the air.

'But sir,' protested the sergeant, 'Bluejay Leader spoke in clear. Gave the mission target. Shall I RTB them all?'

'Negative, mission continues,' said the

687

commander. 'Carry on.'

The sergeant returned to his console completely bewildered. This was madness; if the Iraqis had heard that transmission, their air defences at Tikrit East would be on full alert.

Then he heard Walker again.

'Bluejay Leader, Mayday, Mayday. Both engines out. Ejecting.'

He was still speaking 'in clear'. The Iraqis, if they were listening, could hear it all.

In fact he was right. The messages had been heard. At Tikrit East the gunners were hauling their tarpaulins off their Triple-A and the heat-seeking missiles were waiting for the sound of incoming engines. Other units were being alerted to go at once to the area of the lake to search for two downed aircrew.

'Sir, Bluejay Leader is down. We have to RTB the rest of them.'

'Noted. Negative,' said the mission commander. He glanced at his watch. He had his orders. He did not know why, but he would obey them.

Bluejay Flight was by then nine minutes from target, heading into a reception committee. The three pilots rode their Eagles in stony silence.

In the AWACS the sergeant could still see the blip of Bluejay Leader, way down over the surface of the lake. Clearly the Eagle had been abandoned and would crash at any moment.

Four minutes later the mission commander appeared to change his mind.

'Bluejay Flight, AWACS to Bluejay Flight, RTB, I say again RTB.'

The three Strike Eagles, depressed and despondent at the night's events, peeled away from their course and set heading for home. The Iraqi gunners at Tikrit East, deprived of radar, waited in vain for another hour.

In the southern fringes of the Jebal al Hamreen another Iraqi listening post had heard the interchange. The signals colonel in charge was not tasked with alerting Tikrit East or any other air base to approaching enemy aircraft. His sole job was to ensure none entered the Jebal.

As the Bluejay Flight had turned over the lake he had gone to amber alert; the track from the lake to the airbase would have taken the Eagles along the southern fringe of the range. When one of them crashed he was delighted; when the other three peeled away to the south, he was relieved. He stood his alert down.

Don Walker had spiralled down to the surface of the lake until he levelled at 100 feet and made his 'Mayday' call. As he skimmed the waters of As Sa'diyah he punched in his new co-ordinates and turned north into the Jebal. At the same time he went to LANTIRN.

Low-Altitude Navigation and Targeting, Infra-Red for Night is the American equivalent of the British TIALD system. Switching to LANTIRN, Walker could look through his canopy and see the landscape ahead of him clearly lit by the infra-red beam being emitted from beneath his wing.

Columns of information on his Head-Up Display were now giving him course and speed, height, time to Launch Point.

He could have gone to automatic pilot, allowing the computer to fly the Eagle, throwing it down the canyons and the valleys, past the cliffs and hillsides, while the pilot kept his hands on his thighs. But he preferred to stay on 'manual' and fly it himself.

With the aid of recon. photos supplied by the Black Hole, he had plotted a course up through the range that never let him come above the skyline. He stayed low, hugging the valley floors, swerving from gap to gap, a roller-coaster zigzag course that carried him upwards into the range towards the Fortress.

When Walker had made his Mayday call, Mike Martin's radio had squawked out a series of pre-agreed blips. Martin had crawled forward to the ledge above the valley, aimed the infra-red target-marker at the tarpaulin 1,000 yards away, settled the red dot on to the dead centre of the target, and now kept it there.

The blips on the radio had meant 'seven minutes to bomb-launch' and from then on Martin was not to move the red spot by an inch.

'About time,' muttered Eastman, 'I'm bloody freezing in here.'

'Not long,' said Stephenson, cramming the last bits and pieces into his Bergen, 'then you'll have all the running you want, Benny.'

Only the radio remained unpacked, ready for its next transmission.

In the rear seat of the Eagle Tim the wizzo could see the same information as his pilot. Four minutes to launch, three-thirty, three . . . the figures on the HUD counted downwards as the Eagle screamed through the mountains to its target. It flashed over the small dip where Martin and his men had landed, and took seconds to cover the terrain across which they had laboured beneath their packs.

'Ninety seconds to launch . . .'

The SAS men heard the sound of the engines coming from the south as the Eagle began its 'loft'.

690

The fighter-bomber came over the last ridge 3 miles south of the target just as the countdown hit zero. In the darkness the two torpedo-shaped bombs left their pylons beneath the wings and climbed for a few seconds, driven by their own inertia.

In the three dummy villages the Republican Guards were drowned in the roar of the jet engines erupting from nowhere over their heads, jumped from their bunks and ran to their weapons. In a few seconds the roofs of the forage barns were lifting away on their hydraulic jacks to expose the missiles beneath.

The two bombs felt the tug of gravity and began to fall. In their noses, infra-red seekers sniffed for the guiding beam, the upturned bucket of invisible rays bouncing back from the red spot on their target, the bucket which, once entered, they could never leave.

Mike Martin lay prone, waiting, buffeted by engine noise as the mountains trembled, and held the red dot steady on the Babylon gun.

He never saw the bombs. One second he was gazing at a pale green mountain in the light of the image-intensifier, the next he had to pull his eyes away and shield them as night turned into blood-red day.

The two bombs impacted simultaneously, three seconds before the Guard colonel deep below the hollow mountain reached for his 'launch' lever. He never made it.

Looking across the valley without the night-sight, Martin saw the entire top of the Fortress erupt in flame. By its glare he caught the fleeting image of a massive barrel, rearing like a stricken beast, twisting and turning in the blast, breaking, crashing back with the fragments of the dome into the crater beneath.

'Bloody hell fire,' whispered Sergeant Stephenson at his elbow. It was not a bad analogy. Orange fire began to glow down in the crater as the first explosion flashes died away and a dim half-light returned to the mountains. Martin began keying in his 'alert' codes for the listeners in Riyadh.

Don Walker had rolled the Eagle after the bomb launch, pulling 135 degrees of bank, hauling down and through to find and pursue a reciprocal heading back to the south. But because he was not over flat land, and mountains rose all around him, he had to gain more altitude than normal or risk clipping one of the peaks.

It was the village furthest away from the Fortress that got the best shot. For a fraction of a second he was above them, on one wing-tip, pulling round to the south, when the two missiles were launched. These were not Russian SAMs but the best Iraq had got, Franco-German Rolands.

The first was low, racing after the Eagle as it dropped out of sight across the mountains. The Roland failed to clear the ridge. The second skimmed the rocks of the peak and caught up with the fighter in the next valley. Walker felt the tremendous shock as the missile impacted into the body of his aircraft, destroying and almost ripping out the starboard engine.

The Eagle was thrown across the sky, its delicate systems in disarray, flaming fuel forming a comet's tail behind it. Walker tested the controls, a soggy pudding where once there had been firm response. It was over, his airplane was dying underneath him, all his fire-warning lights on, thirty tons of burning metal about to fall out of the sky.

'Eject, eject...'

The canopy automatically shattered a micro-second before the two ejector seats came through, shooting upwards into the night, turning, stabilizing. Their sensors knew at once they were too low and blew apart the straps retaining the pilot into his seat, throwing him clear of the falling metal so that his parachute could open.

Walker had never bailed out before. The sense of shock numbed him for a while, robbed him of the power of decision. Fortunately the manufacturers had thought of that. As the heavy metal seat fell away the parachute snapped itself open and unfurled. Dazed, Walker found himself in pitch darkness, swinging in his harness over a valley he could not see.

It was not a long drop, he had been far too low for that. In seconds the ground came up and hit him, he was knocked over, tumbling, rolling, hands frantically scrabbling for the harness-release catch. Then the parachute was gone, blowing away down the valley, and he was on his back on wiry turf. He got up.

'Tim,' he called. 'Tim, you OK?'

He began to run up the valley floor, looking for another chute, certain they had both landed in the same area.

He was right in that. Both airmen had fallen two valleys to the south of their target. In the sky to the north he could make out a dim reddish glow.

After three minutes he crashed into something and banged his knee. He thought it was a rock, but in the dim light saw it was one of the ejector seats. His perhaps. Tim's? He went on looking.

Walker found his wizzo. The young man had ejected perfectly, but part of the missile blast had wrecked the seat-separation unit on his ejector. He

693

had landed on the mountainside locked into the seat, parachute still tucked beneath him. The impact of the crash had torn the body from the seat at last, but no man survives a shock like that.

Tim Nathanson lay on his back in the valley, a tangle of broken limbs, face masked by his helmet and visor. Walker tore away the mask, removed the dog tags, turned away from the glow in the mountains and began to run, tears streaming down his face.

He ran until he could run no more, then found a crevice in the mountain and crawled in to rest.

Two minutes after the explosions in the Fortress Martin had his contact with Riyadh. He sent his series of blips and then his message. It was: 'Now Barabbas, I say again, Now Barabbas.'

The three SAS men closed down the radio, packed it, hitched their Bergens on to their backs and began to get off that mountain—fast. There would be patrols now as never before, not looking for them for it was unlikely the Iraqis would work out for some time how the bombing raid had been so accurate, but looking for the downed American aircrew.

Sgt. Stephenson had taken a bearing on the flaming jet as it passed over their heads, and the direction it had fallen. Assuming it had careered on for a while after the ejections, the aircrew, had they survived, ought to be somewhere along that heading. They moved fast, just ahead of the Ubaidi tribesmen of the Guard then pouring out of their villages and heading upwards into the range.

Twenty minutes later Mike Martin and the two SAS men found the body of the dead Weapons Systems Officer. There was nothing they could do, so they moved on.

Ten minutes afterwards they heard, behind them, the continuous rattle of small arms fire. It continued for some time. The Al-Ubaidi had found the body too, and in their rage had emptied their magazines into it. The gesture also gave their position away. The SAS men pressed on.

Don Walker hardly felt the blade of Sergeant Stephenson's knife against his throat. It was light as a thread of silk on the gullet. But he looked up and saw the figure of a man standing over him. He was dark and lean; there was a gun in his right hand pointing at Walker's chest, and the man wore the uniform of a captain in the Iraqi Republican Guard, Mountain Division. Then the man spoke.

'Bloody silly time to drop in for tea. Shall we just get the hell out of here?'

*   *   *

That night General Norman Schwarzkopf was sitting alone in his suite on the fourth floor of the Saudi Defence Ministry building.

It was not where he had spent much of the past seven months, for most of that time he had been out visiting as many combat units as he could, or down in the sub-basement with his staff and planners. But the large and comfortable office was where he went when he wanted to be alone.

That night he sat at his desk, adorned by the red telephone that linked him in a top-security net to Washington, and waited.

At ten minutes before one in the morning of 24 February, the other phone rang.

'General Schwarzkopf?' It was a British accent.

'Yes. This is he.'

'I have a message for you, sir.'

'Shoot.'

'It is: Now Barabbas, sir. Now Barabbas.'

'Thank you,' said the C.-in-C. and replaced the receiver. At 0400 hours that day the ground invasion went in.

CHAPTER TWENTY-THREE

The three SAS men marched hard through the rest of the night. They set a pace onwards and upwards that left Don Walker, who carried no rucksack and thought he was in good physical shape, exhausted and gasping for breath.

Sometimes he would drop to his knees, aware that he could go no further, that even death would be preferable to the endless pain in every muscle.

When that happened he would feel two steely hands, one under each armpit, and hear the cockney voice of Sgt. Stephenson in his ear.

'Come on, mate, only a little further. See that ridge, we'll probably rest on the other side of it.'

But they never did. Instead of heading south to the foothills of the Jebal Hamreen, where he reckoned they would meet a screen of Republican Guards with vehicles, Mike Martin headed east into the high hills running to the Iranian border. It was a tack that forced the patrols of the Al-Ubaidi mountain men to come after them.

Just after dawn, looking back and down, Martin saw a group of six of them, fitter than the rest, still climbing and closing. When the Republican Guards reached the next crest they found one of their quarry sitting slumped on the ground, facing away from them.

Dropping behind the rocks the tribesmen opened up, riddling the foreigner through the back. The corpse toppled over. The six men in the Guards patrol broke cover and ran forward.

Too late they saw that the body was a Bergen rucksack, draped with a camouflaged smock, topped by Walker's flying helmet. The three silenced Heckler and Koch MP5s cut them down as they stood round the 'body'.

Above the town of Khanaqin Martin finally called a halt and made a transmission to Riyadh. Stephenson and Eastman kept watch, facing down to the west from where any pursuing patrols must come.

Martin simply told Riyadh that there were three SAS men left, and they had a single American flier with them. In case the message was intercepted, he did not give their position. Then they pressed on.

High in the mountains, close to the border, they found shelter in a stone bothy, used by the local shepherds in summer when the flocks came to the upper pastures. There, with guards posted in rota, they waited out the four days of the ground war, as far to the south the Allied tanks and air power crushed the Iraqi army in a ninety-hour blitzkrieg and rolled into Kuwait.

*   *   *

On that same day, the first of the ground war, a lone soldier entered Iraq from the west. He was an Israeli of the Sayeret Matkal commandos, picked for his excellent Arabic.

An Israeli helicopter, fitted with long-range tanks

and in the livery of the Jordanian army, came out of the Negev and skimmed across the Jordanian desert to deposit the man just inside Iraq, south of the Ruweishid crossing point.

When it had left him, it turned and flew back across Jordan and into Israel, unspotted.

Like Martin, the soldier had a light-weight, rugged motor-cycle with heavy-duty 'desert' tyres. Although disguised to look old, battered, dirty, rusted and dented, its engine was in superb condition and it carried extra fuel in two panniers astride the back wheel.

The soldier followed the main road eastwards and by sundown entered Baghdad.

The concerns of his superiors for his security had been over-cautious. By that amazing bush telegraph that seems able to outstrip even electronics, the people of Baghdad already knew their army was being crushed in the deserts of south Iraq and Kuwait. By the evening of the first day, the AMAM had taken to its barracks and stayed there.

Now that the bombing had stopped, for all the Allied airplanes were needed over the battlefield, the people of Baghdad circulated freely, talking openly of the imminent arrival of the Americans and British to sweep away Saddam Hussein.

It was a euphoria that would last a week, until it became plain the Allies were not coming and the rule of the AMAM closed over them again.

The central bus station was a seething mass of soldiers, most stripped down to singlets and shorts, having thrown away their uniforms in the desert. These were the deserters who had evaded the execution squads waiting behind the front line. They were selling their Kalashnikovs for the price of a

698

ticket home to their villages. At the start of the week these rifles were fetching 35 dinars each; four days later the price was down to 17.

The Israeli infiltrator had one job, which he accomplished during the night. The Mossad only knew of the three dead-letter-boxes for getting a message to Jericho that had been left behind by Alfonso Benz Moncada in August. As it happened, Martin had discontinued two of them for security reasons, but the third still operated.

The Israeli deposited identical messages in all three 'drops', made the three appropriate chalk marks, took his motor-bike and rode west again, joining the throng of refugees heading that way.

It took him another day to reach the border. Here he cut south of the main road into empty desert, crossed into Jordan, recovered his hidden directional beacon and used it. The bleep-bleep beam was picked up at once by an Israeli aircraft circling over the Negev, and the helicopter returned to the rendezvous to recover the infiltrator.

He did not sleep for those fifty hours and ate little, but he fulfilled his mission and returned home safely.

* * *

On the third day of the ground war, Edith Hardenberg returned to her desk at the Winkler Bank both puzzled and angry. On the previous morning, just as she was about to leave for work, she had received a telephone call.

The speaker, in faultless German with a Salzburg accent, introduced himself as the neighbour of her mother. He told her that Frau Hardenberg had had a bad fall down the stairs after slipping on an icy patch,

699

and was in a bad way.

She at once tried to call her mother, but repeatedly heard the engaged tone. Finally frantic, she called the Salzburg exchange, who informed her the phone must be out of order.

Telephoning the bank that she would not be in for work, she had driven to Salzburg through the snow and slush, arriving in the late morning. Her mother, perfectly fit and well, was surprised to see her. There had been no fall, no injury. Worse, some vandal had cut her telephone line outside the flat.

By the time she returned to Vienna, it was too late to go in for work.

When she appeared at her desk she found Wolfgang Gemütlich in an even worse mood than she. He reproached her bitterly for her absence the previous day, and listened to her explanation in bad humour.

The reason for his own misery was not long in coming. In the mid-morning of the previous day a young man had appeared at the bank and insisted on seeing him.

The visitor explained that his name was Aziz and that he was the son of the owner of a substantial numbered account. His father, explained the Arab, was indisposed but wished his son to act in his place.

At this, Aziz Junior had produced documentation that fully and perfectly authenticated him as his father's ambassador, with complete authority to operate the numbered account. Herr Gemütlich had examined the documents of authority for the slightest flaw, but there was none. He had been left with no alternative but to concede.

The young wretch had insisted his father's wishes were to close down the entire account and transfer the contents elsewhere. This, mind you, Fräulein Hardenberg, just two days after the arrival in the account of a further three million dollar credit, bringing the aggregate total to over ten million dollars.

Edith Hardenberg listened to Gemütlich's tale of woe very quietly, then asked about the visitor. Yes, she was told, his first name had been Karim. Now she mentioned it, there had been a signet ring with a pink opal on the small finger of one hand and, indeed, a scar along the chin. Had he been less consumed by his own sense of outrage, the banker might have wondered at such precise questioning by his secretary about a man she could not have seen.

He had known, of course, Gemütlich admitted, that the account-holder must be some sort of Arab, but had no idea the man was from Iraq, or had a son.

After work, Edith Hardenberg went home and began to clean her little flat. She scrubbed and scoured it for hours. There were two cardboard boxes that she took to the large rubbish skip a few hundred yards away and dumped. One contained a number of items of make-up, perfumes, lotions and bath salts, the other a variety of pieces of ladies' underwear. Then she returned to her cleaning.

Neighbours said later she played music through the evening and late into the night, not her usual Mozart and Strauss, but Verdi and especially something from *Nabucco*. A particularly keen-eared neighbour identified the piece as 'The Slaves' Chorus', which she played over and over again.

In the small hours of the morning the music stopped, and she left in her car with two items from her kitchen.

It was a retired accountant, walking his dog in the

701

Prater Park at seven the next morning who found her. He had left the Hauptallee to allow his dog to do its business in the forest away from the road.

She was in her neat grey tweed coat, with her hair in a bun behind her head, thick lisle stockings on her legs and sensible flat-heeled shoes on her feet. The clothes line looped over the branch of the oak had not betrayed her, and the kitchen steps were a metre away.

She was quite still and stiff in death, her hands by her side and her toes pointed neatly downwards. Always a very neat lady, was Edith Hardenberg.

* * *

February 28 was the last day of the ground war. In the Iraqi deserts west of Kuwait the Iraqi army had been outflanked and annihilated. South of the city, the Republican Guard divisions that had rolled into Kuwait on 2 August had ceased to exist. On that day the forces occupying the city, having set fire to everything that would burn and sought to destroy what would not, left for the north in a snaking column of half-tracks, lorries, vans, cars and carts.

The column was caught in the place where the highway north cuts through the Mutla Ridge. The Eagles and Jaguars, Tomcats and Hornets, Tornados and Thunderbolts, Phantoms and Apaches hurtled down on to the column and reduced it to charred wreckage. With the head of the column destroyed and blocking the road, the remainder could escape neither forwards nor backwards, and because of the cut in the Ridge could not leave the road. Many died in that column and the rest surrendered. By sundown the first Arab forces were entering Kuwait to liberate it.

* * *

That evening Mike Martin made contact again with Riyadh and heard the news. He gave his position, and that of a reasonably flat meadow near by.

The SAS men and Walker were out of food, melting snow to drink, and bitterly cold, not daring to light a fire in case it gave away their position. The war was over, but the patrols of mountain guards might well not know that, or care.

Just after dawn two long-range Blackhawk helos loaned by the American 101st Airborne Division came for them. So great was the distance from the Saudi border that they had come from the firebase camp set up by the 101st 50 miles inside Iraq after the biggest helicopter assault in history. Even from the firebase on the Euphrates River, it was a long haul to the border mountains near Khanaqin.

That was why there were two of them; the second had even more fuel for the journey home.

To be on the safe side, eight Eagles circled above, giving protective cover as the refuelling in the meadow was carried out. Don Walker squinted upwards.

'Hey, they're my guys,' he shouted. As the two Blackhawks clattered the way back again, the Strike Eagles rode shotgun until they were south of the border.

They said farewell to each other on a wind-blasted strip of sand, surrounded by the detritus of a defeated army near the Saudi-Iraqi border. The whirling blades of a Blackhawk whipped up the dust and gravel before taking Don Walker to Dhahran and a flight back to Al Kharz. A British Puma stood further away, to take the SAS men to their own secret and cordoned base.

*   *   *

That evening, at a comfortable country house in the rolling downs of Sussex, Dr Terry Martin was told where his brother had actually been since October and that he was now out of Iraq and safe in Saudi Arabia.

The academic was almost ill with relief, and the SIS gave him a lift back to London, where he resumed his life as a lecturer at the School of Oriental and African Studies.

*   *   *

Two days later, on 3 March, the commanders of the Coalition forces met in a tent on a small and bare Iraqi airstrip called Safwan with two generals from Baghdad to negotiate the surrender.

The only spokesmen for the Allied side were Generals Norman Schwarzkopf and Prince Khalid bin Sultan. At the American general's side sat the commander of the British forces, General Sir Peter de la Billière.

Both the Western officers to this day believe that only two Iraqi generals came to Safwan. In fact there were three.

The American security net was extremely tight, to exclude the possibility of any assassin reaching the tent in which the opposing generals met. An entire American division encircled the airfield, facing outwards.

Unlike the Allied commanders who had arrived from the south by a series of helicopters, the Iraqi party had been ordered to drive to a road junction north of the airstrip. There they left their cars to transfer to a number of American armoured personnel vehicles called humvees and be driven by US drivers the last 2 miles to the airstrip and the cluster of tents where they were awaited.

Ten minutes after the party of generals entered the negotiation tent with their interpreters, another black Mercedes limousine was seen coming down the Basra road towards the junction. The road-block there was commanded by that time by a captain of the US 7th Armoured Brigade, all more senior officers having proceeded to the airstrip. The unexpected limousine was at once stopped.

In the back of the car was a third Iraqi general, albeit only a brigadier-general, bearing a black attaché case. Neither he nor his driver spoke English, and the captain spoke no Arabic. He was about to radio the airstrip for orders when a jeep driven by one American colonel and bearing another in the passenger seat drove up. The driver was in the uniform of the Green Beret Special Forces, the passenger had the insignia of G2, the Military Intelligence.

Both men flashed their ID at the captain, who examined the cards, recognized their authenticity and threw up a salute.

'It's OK, Captain, we've been expecting this bastard,' said the Green Beret colonel. 'Seems he was delayed by a flat tyre.'

'That case,' said the G2 officer pointing at the attaché case of the Iraqi brigadier who now stood uncomprehending by the side of his car, 'contains the names of all our POWs, including the missing aircrew. Stormin' Norman wants it, and now.'

There were no humvees left. The Green Beret colonel gave the Iraqi a rough shove towards the jeep. The captain was perplexed. He knew nothing of any third Iraqi general. He also knew his unit had recently got into the Bear's bad books by having claimed to occupy Safwan when it had not achieved that objective. The last thing he needed was to call down more of General Schwarzkopf's wrath on the 7th Armoured by detaining the list of missing American aircrew. The jeep drove away in the direction of Safwan. The captain shrugged and gestured the Iraqi driver to park with all the others.

On the road to the airstrip the jeep passed between rows of parked American armoured vehicles for up to a mile. Then there was an empty section of road before the cordon of Apache helicopters surrounding the actual negotiation area.

Clear of the tanks, the G2 colonel turned to the Iraqi and spoke in good Arabic.

'Under your seat,' he said, 'don't get out the jeep, but get them on, fast.'

The Iraqi wore the dark green uniform of his country. The rolled clothes beneath his seat were in the light tan of a colonel of the Saudi Special Forces. He quickly exchanged trousers, jacket and beret.

Just before the ring of Apaches on the tarmac, the jeep peeled away into the desert, skirted the airstrip and drove on south. On the far side of Safwan, the vehicle regained the main road to Kuwait, 20 miles away.

The US tanks were on every side, facing outwards. Their job was to forbid the penetration of any infiltrators. Their commanders, atop their turrets, watched one of their own jeeps bearing two of their own colonels and a Saudi officer drive out of the perimeter and away from the protected zone, so it did not concern them.

It took the jeep almost an hour to reach Kuwait airport, then a devastated wreck, gutted by the Iraqis and covered by a black pall of smoke from the oilfield fires blazing all over the emirate. The journey took so long because, to avoid the carnage of the Mutla Ridge road, it had diverted in a big sweep through the desert west of the city.

Five miles short of the airport the G2 colonel took a hand communicator from the glove compartment and keyed in a series of bleeps. Over the airport a single airplane began its approach.

The makeshift airport control-tower was a trailer manned by Americans. The incoming aircraft was a British Aerospace HS 125. Not only that, it was the personal airplane of the British commander, General de la Billière. It must have been; it had all the right markings and the right call-sign. The air traffic controller cleared it to land.

The HS 125 did not taxi to the wreckage of the airport building but to a distant dispersal point where it made rendezvous with an American jeep. The door opened, the ladder came down and three men boarded the twin-jet.

'Granby one, clearance for take-off,' the traffic controller heard. He was handling an incoming Canadian Hercules with medicines for the hospital on board.

'Hold, Granby One ... what is your flight plan?'

He meant, that was damn fast, where the hell do you think you're going?

'Sorry, Kuwait Tower.' The voice was clipped and

707

precise, pure Royal Air Force. The controller had heard the RAF before, and they all sounded the same. Preppy.

'Kuwait Tower, we've just taken on board a colonel of the Saudi Special Forces. Feeling very sick. One of the staff of Prince Khalid. General Schwarzkopf asked for his immediate evacuation, so Sir Peter offered his own plane. Clearance take-off please, old boy.'

In two breaths the British pilot had mentioned one general, one prince and one knight of the realm. The controller was a master sergeant, and good at his job. He had a fine career in the United States Air Force. Refusing to evacuate a sick Saudi colonel on the staff of a prince at the request of a general in the plane of the British commander might just not do that career any good.

'Granby One, clear take-off,' he said.

The HS 125 lifted away from Kuwait but instead of heading for Riyadh which has one of the finest hospitals in the Middle East, it set course due west along the kingdom's northern border.

The ever-alert AWACS saw it and called up, asking for its destination. This time the pukka British voice came back explaining that they were flying to the British base at Akrotiri in Cyprus to evacuate back home a close friend and fellow officer of General de la Billière who had been badly wounded by a landmine. The mission commander in the AWACS knew nothing of this, but wondered how exactly he should object. Have it shot down?

Fifteen minutes later the HS 125 left Saudi airspace and crossed the border of Jordan.

The Iraqi sitting in the back of the executive jet knew nothing of all this, but was impressed by the

708

efficiency of the British and Americans. He had been dubious on receiving the last message from his paymasters in the West, but on reflection agreed it would be wise to quit now rather than wait for later and have to do it on his own and without help. The plan outlined to him in that message had worked like a dream.

One of the two pilots in RAF tropical uniform came back from the flight deck and muttered in English to the American G2 colonel, who grinned.

'Welcome to freedom, Brigadier,' he said in Arabic to his guest, 'we are out of Saudi airspace. Soon we'll have you in an airliner to America. By the way, I have something for you.'

He withdrew a slip of paper from his breast pocket and showed it to the Iraqi, who read it with great pleasure. It was a simple total, the sum lodged in his bank account in Vienna, now over ten million US dollars.

The Green Beret reached into a locker and produced several glasses and a collection of miniatures of Scotch. He poured one bottle into each glass and handed them around.

'Well, my friend, to retirement and prosperity.'

He drank, the other American drank. The Iraqi smiled and drank.

'Have a rest,' said the G2 colonel in Arabic. 'We'll be there in less than an hour.'

After that they left him alone. He leant his head back onto the cushion of his seat and let his mind drift over the past twenty weeks that had made his fortune.

He had taken great risks, but they had paid off. He recalled the day he had sat in that conference room in the Presidential Palace and heard the Rais announce that at last Iraq possessed, in the nick of time, her own atomic bomb. That had come as a genuine shock, as had the sudden cut-off of all communications after he had told the Americans.

Then they had suddenly come back, more insistent than ever, demanding to know where the device was stored.

He had not had the faintest idea, but for the offered bounty of five million dollars it was clearly the time to stake everything. Then it had been easier than he could have imagined.

The wretched nuclear engineer, Dr Salah Siddiqi, had been picked up on the streets of Baghdad and accused, amid the sea of his own pain, of having betrayed the location of the device. Protesting his innocence he had given away the site of Al-Qubai and the camouflage of the car-wreckers' yard. How could the scientist know that he was being interrogated three days before the bombing, not two days after it?

Jericho's next shock had been to learn of the shooting down of the two British fliers. That had not been foreseen. He desperately needed to know whether, in their briefing, they had been given any indication as to how the information arrived in the hands of the Allies.

Relief when it became plain they knew nothing beyond their brief, that the place might be a store of artillery ammunition, had been short-lived, when the Rais insisted there must have been a traitor. From then on Dr Siddiqi, chained in a cell beneath the Gymnasium, had to be despatched, which he was with a massive injection of air into the heart, causing a coronary embolism.

The records of the time of his interrogation, from three days before the bombing to two days after it, had been duly changed.

But the greatest of all the shocks had been to learn that the Allies had missed, that the bomb had been removed to some hidden place called Qa'ala, the Fortress. What fortress? Where?

A chance remark by the nuclear engineer before he died had revealed the ace of camouflage was a certain Colonel Osman Badri of the Engineers, but a check of records showed the young officer was a passionate fan of the President. How to change that view?

The answer lay in the arrest on trumped-up charges and messy murder of his much-loved father. After that the disullusionned Badri had been putty in Jericho's hands during the meeting in the back of the car following the funeral.

The man called Jericho, also nicknamed Mu'azib the Tormentor, felt at peace with the world. A drowsy numbness crept over him, the effect perhaps of the strain of the past few days. He tried to move, but found his limbs would not function. The two American colonels were looking down at him, talking in a language he could not understand but knew was not English. He tried to respond but his mouth would not frame any words.

The HS 125 had turned south-west, dropping across the Jordanian coast and down to 10,000 feet. Over the Gulf of Aqaba the Green Beret pulled back the passenger door and a rushing torrent of air filled the cabin, even though the twin-jet had slowed almost to the point of stall.

The two colonels eased him up, unprotesting, limp and helpless, trying to say something but unable. Over the blue water south of Aqaba Brigadier Omar Khatib left the airplane and plunged to the water, there to break apart on impact. The sharks did the

711

rest.

The HS 125 turned north, passed over Eilat after re-entering Israeli airspace, finally landing at Sde Dov, the military airfield north of Tel Aviv. There the two pilots stripped off their British uniforms and the colonels their American dress. All four returned to their habitual Israeli ranks. The executive jet was stripped of its Royal Air Force livery, repainted as it used to be and returned to the air charter sayan in Cyprus who had loaned it.

The money from Vienna was transferred first to the Kanoo Bank in Bahrain, then on to another in America. Part was retransferred to the Hapoalim Bank in Tel Aviv and returned to the Israeli government; it was what Israel had paid Jericho until the transfer to the CIA. The balance, over eight million dollars, went into what the Mossad calls 'The Fun Fund'.

*   *   *

Five days after the war ended two more long-range American helicopters returned to the valleys of the Hamreen. They asked no permission and sought no approval.

The body of the Strike Eagle's Weapons Systems Officer, Lieutenant Tim Nathanson, was never found. The Guards had torn it apart with their machine-gun bursts, and the jackals, fennecs, crows and kites had done the rest.

To this day his bones must lie somewhere in those cold valleys, not a hundred miles from where his forefathers once toiled and wept by the waters of Babylon.

His father received the news in Washington, sat

shiva for him and said kaddish, and grieved alone in the mansion of Georgetown.

The body of Corporal Kevin North *was* recovered. As the Blackhawks stood by, British hands tore apart the cairn and recovered the corporal, who was put in a body-bag and flown first to Riyadh and thence home to England in a Hercules transport.

In the middle of April a brief ceremony was held at the SAS headquarters camp, a collection of low-built redbrick barracks on the outskirts of Hereford.

There is no graveyard for the SAS; no cemetery collects their dead. Many of them lie in fifty foreign battlefields whose very names are unknown to most.

Some are under the sands of the Libyan desert where they fell fighting Rommel in 1941 and 1942. Others are among the Greek islands, the Abruzzi mountains, the Jura and the Vosges. They lie scattered in Malaysia and Borneo, Yemen, Muscat and Oman, in jungles and freezing wastes and beneath the cold waters of the Atlantic off the Falklands.

Where the bodies were recovered, they came home to Britain, but always to be handed to the families for burial. Even then, no headstone ever mentions the SAS, for the Regiment accredited is the original unit from which the soldier came to the SAS—Fusiliers, Paras, Guards, whatever.

There is only one monument. In the heart of the Lines at Hereford stands a short and stocky tower, clad in timber board and painted a dull chocolate brown. At its peak a clock keeps the hours, so the edifice is known simply as the Clocktower.

Round its base are sheets of dull bronze on which are etched all the names and the places where they died.

That April there were five new names to be unveiled. One was shot by the Iraqis in captivity, two killed in a firefight as they tried to slip back over the Saudi border. A fourth died of hypothermia after days in soaking clothes and freezing weather. The fifth was Corporal North.

There were several former commanders of the Regiment there, that day in the rain. John Simpson came, and Earl Johnny Slim and Sir Peter. The Director of Special Forces, J.P. Lovat, was there, and Colonel Bruce Craig, then the CO. And Major Mike Martin and a few others.

Because they were at home, those still serving could wear the rarely-seen sand-coloured beret with its emblem of the winged dagger and the motto 'Who Dares Wins'.

It was not a long ceremony. The officers and men saw the fabric pulled aside, the newly etched names stood out bold and white against the bronze. They saluted and left to walk back to the various mess buildings.

Shortly after, Mike Martin went to his small hatchback car in the park, drove out through the guarded gates and turned towards the cottage he still kept in a village in the hills of Herefordshire.

He thought as he drove of all the things that had happened in the streets and sands of Kuwait; and in the skies above; in the alleys and bazaars of Baghdad and in the hills of the Hamreen. Because he was a secretive man, he was glad at least of one thing; that no-one would ever know.

A Final Note
All wars must teach lessons. If they do not do so they were fought in vain and those who died in them did so

for naught.

The Gulf War taught two clear lessons, if the Powers have the wit to learn them.

The first is that it is madness for the thirty most industrially developed nations of the world, who dispose between them of 95 per cent of high-tech weaponry and the means for its production, to sell these artefacts to the crazed, the aggressive and the dangerous for short-term financial profit.

For a decade the regime of the Republic of Iraq was allowed to arm itself to a frightening level by a combination of political foolishness, bureaucratic blindness and corporate greed. The eventual destruction, in part, of that war machine cost vastly more than its provision.

A recurrence could easily be prevented by the establishment of a central register of all exports to certain regimes, with draconian penalties for non-disclosure. Analysts able to examine the broad picture would soon see, by type and quantity of materials ordered or delivered, whether weapons of mass destruction were in preparation.

The alternative will be a proliferation of high-tech weaponry to make the years of the Cold War seem like an age of peace and tranquillity.

The second lesson concerns the gathering of information. At the end of the Cold War many hoped this could safely be curbed. The reality shows the opposite.

During the Seventies and Eighties technical advances in the gathering of electronic and signals Intelligence were so impressive that governments of the Free World were led to believe, as the scientists produced their expensive miracles, that machines alone could do the job. The role of 'humint', the

715

gathering of information by people, was down-graded.

In the Gulf war the full panoply of Western technical wizardry was brought to bear and, partly because of its impressive cost, presumed to be virtually infallible.

It was not. With a combination of skill, ingenuity, guile and hard work, large parts of Iraq's arsenal and the means of its production had already been hidden or so disguised that the machines could not see them.

The pilots flew with great courage and skill, but often they, too, were deceived by the cunning of those who devised the replicas and the camouflage.

The fact that germ warfare, poison gas or the nuclear possibility were never employed was, like the outcome of the Battle of Waterloo, 'a damn close-run thing'.

What became plain by the end was that for certain tasks in certain places there is still no substitute for the oldest information-gathering device on earth: the Human Eyeball, Mark One.